THE WEHRMACHT
RETREATS

THE WEHRMACHT

RETREATS

Fighting a Lost

War, 1943

Robert M. Citino

UNIVERSITY PRESS OF KANSAS

Published by the University Press of Kansas (Lawrence, Kansas 66045), which was
organized by the Kansas Board of Regents and is operated and funded by Emporia
State University, Fort Hays State University, Kansas State University, Pittsburg
State University, the University of Kansas, and Wichita State University

Library of Congress Cataloging-in-Publication Data

Citino, Robert Michael, 1958–
  The Wehrmacht retreats : fighting a lost war, 1943 / Robert M. Citino.
    p. cm. — (Modern war studies)
  Includes bibliographical references and index.
  ISBN 978-0-7006-1826-2 (cloth : alk. paper)
  1. Germany—Armed Forces—History—World War, 1939–1945. 2. World War,
1939–1945—Campaigns—Eastern Front. 3. World War, 1939–1945—Campaigns—
Italy. 4. World War, 1939–1945—Campaigns—Tunisia. 5. Germany—History,
Military—20th century. I. Title.
  D757.C59 2012
  940.54'1343—dc23   2011040436

British Library Cataloguing-in-Publication Data is available.

Printed in the United States of America

10 9 8 7 6 5 4 3 2 1

To our best friends,

Jeff and Pam

Contents

Illustrations

Maps

Photographs

Acknowledgments

All books are collaborations, a form of synergy between an author and those who lend inspiration and support. As with all my books, I begin by thanking my mentors when I was a graduate student at Indiana University: Barbara and Charles Jelavich. Even today, I marvel at how fortunate I was, and how wonderful they were to a young man who wasn't quite sure just what he wanted to do. Since then, my colleagues at Lake Erie College and Eastern Michigan University—Kim McQuaid, Mark Higbee, and Ronald Delph, to name a few—have been an unerring source of ideas and insight. No one could work at my current school, the University of North Texas, and especially its excellent Military History Center, without feeling the muse. My colleagues Geoff Wawro and Mike Leggiere never seem to stop researching and writing, and they always make me want to do likewise.

The current work benefited from the sharp eye of my friends Dennis Showalter, Evan Mawdsley, and especially Gerhard Weinberg. All of them—and too many others to mention—kept me from embarrassing errors, but more importantly helped me to sharpen the argument. I might say the same about my current group of graduate students at UNT: Adam Rinkleff, Luke Truxal, Charlotte Decoster, Simone De Santiago Ramos, and Jesse Pyles, along with my two US Army officers who are currently teaching at West Point, William Nance and David Musick. Thanks to one and all.

As always, I send out a special word of thanks to all the good folks at the United States Army Heritage and Education Center (USAHEC) in Carlisle, PA. A world-class facility; amazing holdings in military history and some of the most helpful staff possible: USAHEC has it all. In particular, I would like to thank Louise Arnold-Friend for archival service and document delivery above and beyond the call of duty.

The photographs in this book came from two sources. Paul Sadler had been a G.I. during the war and brought back a photo album from the European theater. It is a marvelous visual source from the era, with an abundance of high quality, glossy images. His son, Bruce, was gracious enough to allow me to reproduce some of the photographs. The others came from Christian Ankjersterne, an "old friend" of mine from Denmark whom I have never, in fact, met in the flesh. The wonders of the Internet!

Finally, to my wonderful family—my wife Roberta and my three brilliant daughters, Allison, Laura, and Emily—a simple word of thanks: for the help, for the love, and for allowing me to live in the present and the past simultaneously.

Preface

Introduction: The German Way of War

Consider this scene from a well-known episode in German military history. It is November 1942. A great war is raging, and all the indicators have suddenly gone negative:

The general sat down at his desk, preparing to set pen to paper. It had been a bad day, and frankly, he was having a hard time concentrating. He was under a great deal of strain lately, and he knew it was beginning to tell on him. He had even developed a facial tic that he did his damnedest to hide and that his staff officers tried not to notice.

"A rough day," he thought. He wasn't sure *rough* quite covered it. Once again, there was bad news from the front: the final breakdown of Operation Hubertus, the last assault in the city's northern sector, and his last throw of the dice—and not much of a throw at that. He had spent the week before the attack trying, and failing, to scrounge up enough infantry to launch it. In the end, he'd relied mainly on combat engineers. They'd done all right, he supposed. They could blow things up. They were good at that. Fire and movement? Not so good. They'd gotten close to the riverbank—within a few hundred yards, in fact.

But not close enough. The general tried to concentrate. The failure of Hubertus was the least of his problems. That news from the front he could handle. It was what was happening in his rear. He wasn't sure what to say about that. Had something like this ever even happened to a German army before?

He glanced at the situation map, hoping that it had somehow changed. But no. It was the same ugly story: huge red arrows north and south of the city, immense Soviet offensives, spearheaded by what his intelligence officers had sworn to him just a week ago were impossible numbers of tanks. The last few days, they had been driving deep into his flank and rear. Who was there to stop them? The general knew the answer to that one, and it wasn't good.

He had just now gotten the confirmation. The Soviet pincers had linked up far behind Stalingrad, at the town of Kalach, on the Don.

Kesselschlacht. Every German commander recognized the term: the battle of encirclement, the "cauldron." He knew his history as well as anyone in the officer corps. It was a way of war that German armies had perfected over the centuries, at Leipzig, Königgrätz, Tannenberg, the Flanders offensive of 1940, the opening of Barbarossa. When it worked, you encircled entire enemy armies, and took hundreds of thousands of prisoners.

But now who was trapped? He was a thousand miles deep inside hostile territory, his army literally embedded in the city, having fought to a standstill. His tanks had been practically useless in a street fight. He had even sent away his horse transport—too many mouths to feed. What did he need transport for? He thought of another term: *Bewegungskrieg,* the "war of movement," with rapid maneuver and bold attacks, always seeking the enemy's flanks and rear. He shook his head. So much for that; his own army had barely moved an inch in the last month.

Anger welled up, as it had on and off for the past few days. For weeks he'd been telling anyone who would listen that his situation was growing impossible, with huge dangling flanks north and south of the city held by the Romanian armies. He didn't have much use for his allies—undertrained, underarmed, underenthusiastic, sitting out there in an open plain, with no terrain protection at all. Well, he thought, at least no one needed to worry about the Romanians any more. That problem had been solved. They'd been obliterated in the opening moments of the Soviet offensive.

So it had all gone wrong. He could already hear them talking back at headquarters. Not everyone had been happy with his appointment to a field command—"No experience," they'd said. "No drive." And, some of them had added, "No family." If von Reichenau were still alive, the general thought bitterly, then he'd be the one sitting here, staring at the same unforgiving map, facing the same hopeless situation. "I wonder if his family connections would be helping him now," he muttered to himself.

He glanced down to the surface of his writing desk. Buried underneath today's grim news was a telegram from the man who had put them all here. He had gotten it five days ago, but it seemed like five years. He pulled it out and read it once more. Its empty words exhorted the 6th Army to one more great effort in Stalingrad, calling on their energy, their "guts" (*Schneid*). What nonsense. He had had orders to read it to all the German commanders down to the regimental level.

He'd seen the reaction of some of them, the doubt. Others had swallowed it whole. "Even I did," he recalled. The general closed his eyes momentarily, trying to concentrate. Sometimes Hitler seemed . . . crazy. Unbalanced.

It was November 22, 1942, and General Friedrich Paulus was not a happy man. There was a dispatch to be written, however, and he was nothing if not a dutiful officer.

He drew a breath, and finally set pen to paper: "Armee eingeschlossen," he began. "The army is surrounded. . . ."[1]

For the German army, the Wehrmacht, the debacle at Stalingrad represented more than a simple defeat. It was the precise moment in which a traditional, centuries-old military culture, a "way of war," we might say, crashed into the realities of the industrialized warfare of the twentieth century.[2] This way of war had originated in the kingdom of Prussia nearly 300 years ago and was responsible for creating and sustaining the so-called Second Reich in the wars of unification and beyond. It had collapsed during World War I, only to be reborn better and more effective than ever in the interwar era and the early years of World War II. By the time General Paulus sat down to write his dispatch at Stalingrad, however, it had proven itself obsolete. Indeed, in the context of this great world war that Germany had first risked and then ignited, it had the faint whiff of nostalgia about it. It had almost become quaint.

German officers described their method of making war as *Bewegungskrieg*, the war of movement on the operational level. Originating in the duchy of Brandenburg during the reign of Frederick William II, the Great Elector, brought to its first flowering during the reign of the Prussian king Frederick the Great (1740–1786), given a broad philosophical underpinning by Karl Gottlieb von Clausewitz, and brought to its second flowering by Field Marshal Helmuth von Moltke during the wars of unification, *Bewegungskrieg* evolved as a way for a small, relatively impoverished kingdom to make its weight felt in international and military affairs. With their state crammed into a tight spot on the north German plain, lacking much in the way of defensible boundaries, ringed by enemies and potential enemies, it became an article of faith for Prussian–German planners and field commanders alike that they could not win a long, drawn-out war of attrition. The balance in numbers, resources, and factories would always tilt in favor of their enemies in such a contest. Fighting a war of attrition, therefore, was simply another name for "losing slowly." What Germany had to do was to fight brief, sharp wars—*kurtz und vives,* Frederick the Great called them, "short and lively"—featuring rapid and decisive campaigns that identified, fixed in place, and then smashed the enemy's main body within weeks of the outbreak of the fighting.[3]

Bewegungskrieg was the solution to this strategic problem. Though styled the "war of movement" or "mobile war," it had little to do with simple mobility or a faster march rate. Indeed, Prusso-German armies were often armed and equipped in markedly similar ways to the enemies they faced, so having any advantage in pure mobility would be difficult. Rather than mere tactical maneuverability, this was a way of war that stressed the maneuver of large (what we would today call "operational level") formations: divisions, corps, and armies. The aim was to maneuver these large formations in such a way that they would strike the mass of the enemy army a powerful blow, perhaps even an annihilating one, early on in the fighting, perhaps within a few weeks.

The way to do that was not to gather them in a central location and launch a frontal assault to steamroll the enemy. Indeed, *Bewegungskrieg* was based on the notion that Germany could never afford such an expensive type of war. Instead, German commanders were expected to shape the campaign in such a way that they landed a heavy blow on the enemy's flank, or both of them, or even, if possible, into the enemy's rear. The aim of these maneuvers was not merely to surround the hostile army and then starve it into submission, but to allow German formations to subject it to "concentric operations"—simultaneous attacks from all points of the compass. The German term for such a scenario was *Kesselschlacht,* literally "cauldron battle," but we might translate it more expansively as the battle of "encirclement and destruction."

All this was easier said than done. Enemy armies rarely sit around and allow themselves to be encircled. The Germans had found over the centuries that prosecuting *Bewegungskrieg* brought with it certain corollary demands. The first was a flexible form of command that left a great deal of initiative in the hands of lower-ranking commanders. It has become customary in the west to speak of *Auftragstaktik* (mission tactics). The higher commander gave his subordinate commanders a general mission (*Auftrag*). It was to be brief, clear, and, if possible, delivered verbally rather than in writing. It might be something as simple as pointing at a terrain formation in the distance. That done, it was up to the subordinates themselves to devise the means and method of achieving the mission. As we study the historical record more carefully, however, we note that *Auftragstaktik* is a term that the Germans themselves seem to have used only rarely. Rather it is more correct to speak, as they did, of the *Selbständigkeit der Unterführer*, the "independence of the subordinate commander," in which the officer in the field was a virtual free agent in terms of his maneuver scheme and operational approach.[4]

The obvious objection that a modern analyst might make to such a scheme—that it could easily degenerate into an every-man-for-himself series of private wars rather than an integrated war-fighting plan—is a valid one, as far as it goes. The annals of Prussian–German military history feature some of the most skilled and successful commanders of all time, certainly—names like Georg von Derfflinger and Frederick the Great, Friedrich Wilhelm von Seydlitz and Gebhard Leberecht von Blücher, Moltke and Schlieffen, and Guderian and Manstein. But we must also be honest: they also include lesser lights like Eduard von Flies, who unwisely attacked a Hanoverian army twice his own size at the battle of Langensalza and essentially had his own command destroyed in the process, three days before the circumstances would have forced the Hanoverians to surrender anyway[5]; Karl von Steinmetz, whose rash moves in the opening days of the Franco-Prussian war nearly ruined Moltke's carefully designed maneuver scheme altogether[6]; and, perhaps the classic example, Hermann von François, commander of the I Corps in the East Prussian campaign in 1914, who not only marched his corps directly into the path of the oncoming Russian 1st Army, but tipped off the Russians to a carefully laid army-strength ambush, and incidentally caused his commanding officer, General Max von Prittwitz of the 8th Army, to suffer something resembling a nervous breakdown.[7]

Thus there was no special inoculation against bad generalship in the Prussian–German tradition. There were, however, two factors that helped to prevent *Auftragstaktik* from breaking down into a free-for-all. The first was a shared tradition of aggressive behavior under any and all circumstances. It did not matter whether an officer was especially gifted or not; he was expected to march to the sound of the guns, and he usually did. In virtually all of Prussia's and Germany's wars, the operational approach was not all that complex: it involved locating the enemy, particularly his vulnerable flank or rear, and then launching a highly aggressive attack on him. Field commanders in the Prussian tradition took a great deal of pride in getting in their blow first, thus showing up not only the enemy but often their fellow officers. "The Prussian army always attacks," Frederick the Great once said. As a general rule of military operations, it certainly has its shortcomings; it did add up to a reasonable synergy in what was otherwise a loose system of command, however.

The second factor mitigating the chaotic implications of *Auf-tragstaktik* was a carefully articulated staff system, in which each oper-ational level commander in the field (division on up) had a chief of the General Staff at his side as his principal military advisor. These were the intellectual elite of the army, its brain trust. They had come up through the same schools (especially the *Kriegsakademie*), they possessed the same outlook, and they tended to give remarkably similar advice when analyzing the same battlefield situation. The commander still bore ultimate responsibility for what transpired, but the better ones listened carefully to their chief of staff.

Aggression (the commander) tempered by intellect (the staff offi-cer): it was the German formula for military success. Although we mod-erns tend to view the latter with a more positive eye, German officers themselves did not necessarily share our prejudices. The man who dared, who launched attacks no matter what the situation, who chafed at the leash of higher authority—far from being condemned, these com-manders tended to win the approbation of their fellows. Military his-torians since 1914 have filled their books on Tannenberg with condemnations of General François's impetuosity; his contemporaries in the army did not. The same might be said for Steinmetz and Flies and all the others mentioned above. Launching frontal attacks at 1–2 odds is generally not a good idea. But Friedrich Karl, the Red Prince and commander of the Prussian 1st Army in July 1866, had done just that to kick off the battle of Königgrätz.[8] He had become a hero in the process, not by adding up the odds and doing the rational thing, but by ignoring the abacus and doing what his gut told him to do. The elder Moltke may have been the brains of that army—who can doubt it?—but the Red Prince was its heart, and in the eyes of many of his fellows, he was the true victor of Königgrätz. "You've never lost a battle if you don't have the feeling you're beaten," he once wrote about a later bat-tle in which he had gotten himself into a sticky situation. "And I didn't have that feeling."[9] For the Red Prince, and for so many of his fellow Prussian officers over the centuries, it was all a matter of will. When it came to a more rational calculus, reconciling ends and means, for exam-ple—that was someone else's business.

The Problem: The Death of the Wehrmacht?

It should be apparent to us—at a distance of so many years—that the defeat at Stalingrad (and the nearly simultaneous crushing defeat of

Field Marshal Erwin Rommel's German–Italian *Panzerarmee* at El Alamein) had taken an ax to every one of these bedrock German beliefs about the nature of war.[10] The war of movement? It had come to a screeching halt, in virtually simultaneous fashion, at three widely separated locations on the map. At Alamein, in the Caucasus, and at Stalingrad, *Bewegungskrieg* had given way to the static war of position (*Stellungskrieg*). It was a grinding attritional struggle, highly expensive in men and matériel, and just the sort of thing the Germans had historically tried to avoid. The virtue of aggressive field command? In the Alamein bottleneck, Rommel had fought himself down, quite literally, to the last man and tank, leaving him practically helpless against the offensive launched by General Bernard Law Montgomery's better-supplied 8th Army. General Paulus, too, had spent the entire fall of 1942 feeding one infantry division after another into the mill of urban combat at Stalingrad. By the end, he had no reserve left, no troops to spare for flank protection or liaison with neighboring armies, and no ability at all to respond to Operation Uranus, the well-planned Soviet counteroffensive north and south of the city. In the Caucasus, the Germans had made a last lunge in November for Ordzhonikidze, the gateway city to the Georgian Military Road and thus to the vast Soviet oil fields further south. They had come close—a single mile or so from the city itself, but in the process they too had fought themselves out. A Soviet counterattack drove them back, and the lead German units barely managed to break out of an encirclement.[11] Elsewhere in the Caucasus, two German armies, 1st Panzer in the east and 17th in the west, were stuck fast in the mountain, the victim of logistical difficulties, rough terrain, and a solidified Soviet defensive line, but above all the victim of an overly ambitious and aggressive operational plan.

Finally, the twin disasters had not been kind to that last hallmark of Prussian–German war making, whether we call it *Auftragstaktik* or "the independence of the subordinate commander." Certainly, Nazi Germany would seem to be a highly unlikely place to generate freedom of thought or action on the part of the field commander. In the course of the 1942 campaign, Adolf Hitler took his share of scalps from the officer corps, micromanaging, harassing, and firing his commanders wholesale—the chief of staff since the outbreak of the war, General Franz Halder; the commander of Army Group A, Field Marshal Wilhelm List; the commander of the unfortunate XXXXVIII Panzer Corps, General Ferdinand Heim; and others.[12] The Führer had even taken over command of Army Group A himself at one point, with a predictable impact on its battlefield performance.

We need to be cautious in our evaluation here, however. Blaming Hitler for everything that went wrong in the east in 1942 is one of the war's most enduring myths, and we rarely stop to consider what a convenient excuse he became for the officer corps after the war. The size and sprawl of the various fronts, as well as their distance from Germany, still allowed the field commander a great deal of freedom in the day-to-day conduct of operations. Hitler could and did intervene where he chose, however, and his interventions became all the more disturbing by their very unpredictability and capriciousness. He might have once had a certain beginner's luck earlier in the war, in the planning and conduct of the 1940 campaign, for example. At some point in 1942, however, the German official history is surely correct in asserting that his decision making passed from the realm of the fresh and the unconventional into that of the "unprofessional and defective."[13] The "dual campaign"—the decision to go for Stalingrad and the Caucasus at same time rather than sequentially—was the unfortunate result.[14]

In the end, 1942 had shown up the weaknesses in the traditional German way of war. Methods of war making that were born in a tiny duchy and matured in a small kingdom, that dealt with rapid campaigns over distances of 100–200 miles, that depended on a good road network and a relatively prosperous infrastructure had fallen apart when tasked with the conquest of the Suez Canal, the Volga, and the oil fields of Baku. It is not easy to determine the precise moment at which Germany lost World War II; the arguments over the turning point of the war have been going on for decades and will never stop. But certainly we can say that as a matter of objective reality, the German army had no real hope of winning the war through *Bewegungskrieg*—that is, through rapid and decisive offensive action—as the year 1943 dawned. In that sense, 1942 really did represent the death of the Wehrmacht.

Yes, we might say, but so what? War—and particularly the twentieth-century industrial version of it—is a contest of nations, political systems, and economic structures. It is not a mere abstract duel between military cultures. It is too complex a phenomenon to be treated in such a reductionist fashion, too chance ridden, too contingent on a thousand different factors that can change its course from moment to moment. With Germany's traditional military culture having come up short, a decisive victory for the Wehrmacht was no longer in the cards, if it ever had been. But in the short term, that abstract fact changed little. There was still a war to be fought.

Let us be even more specific. The introduction of "culture" as an arena for the military historian has opened up many questions and penetrated many mysteries over the past decade. It can include discussions of separate national ways of war, military cultures that are said to determine how individual armies fight.[15] It can include institutional military culture, the way that a given military establishment sees itself, its history, and its relationship to the broader society. Finally, it can include analysis of national culture, the matrix out of which military institutions spring. In all of these cases, culture serves as the water in which the human actors swim, filled with unstated assumptions and default settings of which they may be only dimly aware. It is the envelope of possibilities and expectations in which they live. It is "the box," and thinking outside of it is a great deal harder than it sounds.

For all the importance of these cultural preconditions, however, they do not add up to anything approaching historical inevitability. The historical actors may feel and assume certain attitudes, often unconsciously, but they still have lives to live, choices to make, and actions to undertake. To borrow several terms from the rich historiography of the Holocaust, military historians need to take into account both "intentionalism" (the role that humans themselves play in making their own history) and "structuralism" or "functionalism" (the degree to which preconditions, long-term causes, and systemic factors determine human history).[16]

We must keep this in mind as we look at the situation facing the Reich at the end of its horrible year. Those of us who study the war may find it difficult, even impossible, to conceive of a way that Nazi Germany could have staved off defeat after 1942. The strength of the Grand Alliance was only beginning to wax; the massive matériel and industrial resources of the United States, in particular, had barely begun to arrive in the theater of war. Potentially, the Allies could swat Germany like a fly. But "potential victory" and "actual victory" are very different things. Despite all that had gone awry, and despite the smashing of Germany's last hope for decisive battlefield success and the irretrievable loss of the 6th Army at Stalingrad, no one in the high command was suggesting surrender. Germany would fight on. "We shall create the 6th Army anew," Hitler confidently told his chief of staff, General Kurt Zeitzler, and 1943 would see action raging on virtually all fronts.[17]

There is a famous, although apparently apocryphal, tale from the start of the war. On that fateful day back in September 1939, when the news first broke that Great Britain was about to declare war on Germany, Hitler had supposedly turned to his foreign minister, Joachim von Ribbentrop, and posed a simple question. The query facing the

German army as the year 1943 dawned was the same one Hitler allegedly asked back then: "What now"?[18]

The Work: Fighting a Lost War

The Wehrmacht Retreats will offer a detailed operational analysis of the great land campaigns of the German Wehrmacht—actually the *Heer*, or army—in the year 1943. Like two of my earlier works, *The German Way of War: From the Thirty Years' War to the Third Reich* (2005) and *Death of the Wehrmacht: The German Campaigns of 1942* (2007), it will attempt to place these modern events in the context of certain long-standing traditions of German military history and culture. Those works sought to analyze German military operations through the lens of what Fernand Braudel called the *longue durée*. Such a long-term view—involving centuries—is useful in clarifying seemingly inexplicable historical events by uncovering an often overlooked factor: just what it was that the historical actors thought they were doing. Without going into the detail of those earlier books—and the reader is encouraged to consult them for the long-term argument—the present work will continue to do the same for the German campaigns of 1943. It will lay special stress on the officer corps and its assumptions about military operations, its view of Prussia–Germany's military history, and its professional evaluation of the enemy armies it was facing. In other words, we will attempt to describe the *mentalités* of the German military caste in a period when the fortunes of war had definitely turned against the Wehrmacht.

By definition, a book discussing the campaigns of 1943 must open in medias res. As the year dawned, campaigns were ongoing, German armies were in hectic retreat in Egypt, along the Don, and in the Caucasus, and the Allies were doing their best to pursue them. We will begin in the Mediterranean, with the arrival of the new gun in town, the U.S. Army. In tandem with its veteran partner, the British, the Americans landed on the shores of French North Africa in November 1942 in Operation Torch. Once ashore, the invaders found themselves racing for Tunis to cut off the retreat of Field Marshal Erwin Rommel's *Panzerarmee* as it streamed away from El Alamein. In reality, it was never much of a race because the Germans arrived there the day after the Allied landing. Nevertheless, it was a fascinating campaign, with pocket-sized armies and a great deal of gritty fighting of the battlegroup (*Kampfgruppen*) variety in difficult terrain, and the inherent fascination of watching the U.S. Army try to sort itself out into fighting trim. It wouldn't be easy. The Allies failed to seize Tunis before the end of 1942, and the New Year would see both sides strongly reinforced for a proper campaign.

While the Germans could count the first phase of the Tunisian fighting as a small victory, Soviet armies were trampling all over them in the east. With Soviet armored spearheads poised hundreds of miles closer to Rostov than the German Caucasus armies were, the situation was ripe for yet another Stalingrad-scale disaster. It was during this Soviet "Donbas campaign" that Field Marshal Manstein would, once again, rewrite the book on large-scale mechanized defensive operations. During later decades, when NATO was planning for war with the Warsaw Pact, Manstein's achievement—holding off much larger hostile forces, launching repeated and well-timed counterblows against them, and eventually smashing them—would become a matter of high interest to planners in the U.S. Army.[19]

From the Donbas, we will shift back to the great campaign in Tunisia. Rommel's ability to outpace his pursuers after Alamein allowed him to link up with the German force defending Tunisia, the 5th Panzer Army under General Hans-Jürgen von Arnim, giving the Axis a definite, though temporary, superiority in numbers. Rommel and Arnim used it to launch twin offensives (Operations *Morgenluft* and *Frühlingswind*) against U.S. forces in Tunisia (the II Corps under General Lloyd R. Fredendall). The twin offensives would smash through one U.S. defensive position after another, including the Kasserine Pass, but would ultimately fail, the victim of rushed planning, a confused set of command relationships, and insufficient logistical support. Despite the outcome, however, Kasserine Pass had a major impact on the psyche and behavior of the U.S., British, and German armies for the rest of the war.

The end of the Tunisian campaign in May 1943 saw the Wehrmacht deep in the planning cycle for yet another offensive in the East. Operation Citadel (*Zitadelle*) was a straightforward, two-pronged drive aiming to destroy Soviet forces deployed inside the Kursk salient, a vast bulge in the lines in the northern Ukraine. Citadel became the subject of a great deal of interest in the postwar era, and indeed, the literature of the Eastern Front continues to describe it as "the greatest tank battle of all time."[20] This was particularly so for the climax of the battle, the clash between the II (S.S.) Panzer Corps and the 5th Guards Tank Army near the town of Prokhorovka. Recently, however, historians have been cutting Kursk down to size, reducing it from an all-out

attempt at a strategic breakthrough on the 1941–1942 model to an operation with more limited goals: maintenance of the initiative in the east
and a spoiling attack to destroy a Soviet buildup on the central front.

From Kursk, the narrative will shift back to Europe, following the
Allies from Tunisia to Sicily. Here a massive and complex invasion plan
(Operation Husky) showed just how formidable a strategic power the
Western Alliance could be: no coastline in Europe could be safe against
such a massive huge array of naval, air, and land power. Hitler himself
claimed to have halted the Kursk offensive in midstream in order to
respond to the Allied invasion. Most historians have scoffed at the
notion, but as we shall see, the Führer was telling the truth. Husky was
a small campaign with strategic results: the overthrow of Benito Mussolini and the shaking of the Axis alliance to its foundations. On the
operational level, however, the campaign in many ways proved frus-
trating. A force of some 500,000 men, enjoying clear superiority in the
air and absolute supremacy at sea, failed to trap or destroy a much
smaller Axis garrison, essentially comprising three German divisions.
The Axis managed to evacuate the entire force back to safety across the
Strait of Messina to the Italian mainland—a "bitter victory" for the
Allies indeed.[21]

From Sicily, we will head east once more. Later German officers
would often label the German failure at Kursk as a victory forsaken,
claiming that the Wehrmacht had been on the verge of a breakthrough
when Hitler pulled the plug. Those claims fail to take into account what
happened immediately afterward: massive Soviet counterstrokes north
and south of the salient. Operation Kutuzov against the Orel salient
and Operation Rumiantsev toward Belgorod and Kharkov displayed a
newly mature Soviet "operational art" in action, combining brute force,
mass, and doctrinal sophistication into a nearly irresistible package. In
1943, the Wehrmacht learned there was no position it could defend if
the Soviets wanted to take it badly enough and were willing to suffer
the casualties—and they almost always were. The autumn would see
the Germans retreating in some disarray all along the southern sector
of the front, with four massive Soviet army groups chasing them back
across the Dnepr. The failure of the Germans to defend even the line
of this great river demonstrated how badly blooded they had been by
the events of the year.

Finally, we will make one last trip to the Mediterranean. The Anglo-
Americans would follow up Sicily with one of the most controversial
campaigns of the war, and one that American historians in particular
continue to debate. The Allies timed the invasion of Italy (three sepa-

rate operations code named Baytown, Slapstick, and Avalanche) to coincide with Italian surrender, hoping to use to altered political conditions to effect a quick seizure of southern Italy, at least. What they got was something very different: a lightning German campaign to disarm their erstwhile ally and occupy virtually all of Italy (Operation Axis); a dogfight on the beaches of Salerno, where U.S. 5th Army (General Mark W. Clark commanding) came close to disaster; and a hard slog up a narrow, mountainous peninsula that the Almighty had apparently designed for defense. First there was hardening of the front along what the Germans called their Winter Line (*Winterstellung*), then absolute deadlock on the Gustav Line south of Monte Cassino. Accounts of the campaign often describe the Germans as masters of defensive warfare in this campaign, although such a claim requires some nuance. At any rate, the Germans defended themselves quite competently, even in the face of massive matériel superiority on the part of the Allies. The end of 1943 would see the Allied armies stuck in the mud some distance from Rome and wondering just how they might break out of their predicament. The answer would come in January 1944 at a place called Anzio.

What will emerge from this narrative is the absolute interconnectedness of the various fronts in this multifront war.[22] Parochialism continues to be an occupational hazard of writing the history of World War II: European theater of operation versus the Pacific, and within the ETO, Western Front versus Eastern Front. In fact, the history of the war should integrate the fronts whenever possible, and that is particularly so in attempting to analyze the behavior of the *Macht in der Mitte*, the "power in the middle": Germany.[23] On any given day, as we shall see, German planners might be dealing with Panzer operations deep inside the Soviet Union, trying to vector the destination of an Allied invasion fleet, and deciding where to send increasingly scarce resources and reinforcements, all at once. They handled it better on some days than others, and there were some days it must have seemed like a bad idea to get out of bed.

As in all of my books, *The Wehrmacht Retreats* will try to refrain from lecturing the historical actors on what they ought to have done. It will eschew the "good general–bad general" approach to military history,[24] one that assumes there are clear solutions to every battlefield problem and awards victory points to the commander who gets the right answer. Modern warfare is far too complex for us to grade like a true-or-false exam, and at any rate, it is puzzling enough merely to explain why the historical actors did what they did, let alone grade them. Likewise, this book will not attempt to describe how the Germans might have won the war if only they had made this or that clever operational maneuver or avoided this or that mistake—an interesting intellectual exercise, perhaps, and one that can be quite entertaining, but not something that I undertake here.

Instead, I will attempt to answer more fundamental questions. How, for example, does a military establishment historically configured for *Bewegungskrieg*—violent aggression, relentless assault, and mobile offensive operations—react when it suddenly and unexpectedly finds itself thrown onto the defensive? How did German commanders view their newest enemy, the U.S. Army? They had been fighting the British for over three years now and the Soviets for a year and a half, and they had a pretty good idea of how those opponents tended to react. The Americans, with their nearly limitless base of resources, a firepower-drenched war-fighting doctrine, and a level of mechanization that the Wehrmacht could not begin to match, were something new to the equation. How did the Germans cope with this fresh battlefield challenge? Finally, since the Allies held the initiative (*das Gesetz des Handelns*) for most of 1943, choosing when and where to launch their offensives, *The Wehrmacht Retreats* will analyze their operations in detail as well. This emphasis will be especially noticeable in the early chapters detailing the debut of Germany's new enemy, the U.S. Army. The arrival of the U.S. Army, clumsy and not yet fully battleworthy but bristling with weapons and equipment, was in many ways *the* story of 1943, and it deserves careful treatment and analysis. With the entire Grand Alliance now in the European theater in force, the Germans had lost the war. Why, despite what was already a sizable matériel and manpower superiority, were the Allies unable to turn 1943 into something more decisive?

THE WEHRMACHT
RETREATS

1

The Last Victory?
The Race to Tunis

Introduction: One Month that Shook the World
(October 23–November 23, 1942)

How much folk wisdom has the human race developed over the millennia to discuss the way bad things all seem to happen at once? "When it rains, it pours," we say. We often claim to be "having a bad day" when too many problems arise, or we blame it on our biorhythms. We even have a target number: "Bad things," we say, "happen in threes."

With that in mind, let us take a historical snapshot, a close-up of a brief period in a long and highly destructive war. It is a tense period for the German Wehrmacht, with battles raging in Stalingrad, the Caucasus, and in Egypt's western desert.

Friday, October 23: Commander of the British 8th Army, General Bernard Law Montgomery, puts the finishing touches on Operation Lightfoot, his grand offensive at El Alamein against the German–Italian force arrayed in front of him, Field Marshal Erwin Rommel's *Panzerarmee Afrika*.

Sunday, October 25: A German attack by the German 79th Infantry Division into Stalingrad's northern industrial zone, targeting the "Red October" and "Barrikady" factories, breaks down with heavy German casualties. Losses among the infantry have risen to catastrophic levels, and the 79th Division joins a long list of others that are now considered to be "no longer capable of attack" (*angriffsunfähig*).[1]

That same Sunday: Deep in the Caucasus, the German III Panzer Corps (General Eberhard von Mackensen) launches an offensive toward the key city of Ordzhonikidze. With winter coming on, it is the Wehrmacht's last chance to win something decisive in this theater.

That same Sunday: Rommel returns to Africa. Realizing that the main weight of Montgomery's attack is striking the left flank of the *Panzerarmee*, he orders his veteran 21st Panzer Division up from the south. It is his only operational reserve.

Thursday, October 29: After six days of defending against 8th Army's massive assault, Rommel's force is crumbling, but Montgomery is also feeling the heat to speed things up. He reaches the obvious conclusion that "it is becoming essential to break through somewhere."[2]

That same Thursday: Mackensen's Panzer corps reaches Ardon, at the head of the Ossetian Military Road. The path seems open to Ordzhonikidze.

Monday, November 2: Montgomery regroups his tank forces, throws in another fresh formation, the 7th Armoured Division, and begins Operation Supercharge, a concentrated assault against Rommel's left (northern) flank. It breaks through almost immediately.

Tuesday, November 3. Realizing that the entire *Panzerarmee* stands on the brink of destruction, Rommel decides to retreat. He wires Hitler to inform him.[3]

That same Tuesday: Mackensen's lead units drive to within a single mile of Ordzhonikidze. This would be an important victory for the Wehrmacht after a season of disappointment. Soviet resistance is stiffening, but is it already too late?

Wednesday, November 4: Hitler wires Rommel, denying him permission to retreat. It is time, the Führer says, "to stand fast, to take not one step backwards, and to throw every gun and every man who you can free up into the battle." Rommel is shocked: "It was like we had all been hit over the head," he later wrote.[4]

Friday, November 6: Stalemate in Stalingrad. General Alfred Jodl of the high command of the Wehrmacht (*Oberkommando der Wehrmacht*, or OKW) is perplexed. We have "practically conquered Stalingrad," he notes, but apparently the Soviet defenders do not agree.[5]

That same Friday: A Soviet counterattack outside of Ordzhonikidze strikes Mackensen's overextended spearhead. The drive on Ordzhonikidze is over, and for the Wehrmacht, so is the Caucasus campaign.

Sunday, November 8: A massive Anglo-American force lands on the northern shores of French North Africa, in Morocco, at Oran, and at Algiers. The ultimate goal of Operation Torch is the key Mediterranean port of Tunis.

Monday, November 9: In a conversation with Italian foreign minister Count Galeazzo Ciano, Hitler declares that "the Axis must establish itself in Tunis" before the Americans do.[6] He tells Ciano that he has already decided to send units of the Luftwaffe to Tunisia.

That same Monday: Hitler decides to hold a "Tunisian bridgehead." German airborne units are airlifted to Tunis that night and take possession of the airport.

Wednesday, November 11: The Wehrmacht launches Operation Hubertus, its last attempt to take Stalingrad before the onset of winter.

That same Wednesday: The Wehrmacht begins Operation Anton, the occupation of Vichy France and Corsica.

Thursday, November 12: Tunis occupied by German paratroopers.

Sunday, November 15: Local Soviet counterattacks retake all the meager gains of Operation Hubertus.

Monday, November 16: The first snows fall in Stalingrad.

Tuesday, November 17: Hitler sends Paulus a *Führerbefehl* to be read to all the troops of 6th Army. He calls on their energy and spirit (*Schneid*) and urges them on to even greater exertion.[7]

Thursday, November 19: Soviet armies open Operation Uranus, a massive counteroffensive north and south of Stalingrad.

Monday, November 23: Soviet mechanized columns link up at Kalach on the Don, far behind Stalingrad, encircling the German 6th Army in the city. It is the largest field army in the entire German battle array—a catastrophic loss that will never be made good.

It had been quite a month for the Wehrmacht, no doubt. In the course of this brief period, the Wehrmacht's condition had gone from stable to critical. To German officials and officers involved in operational planning, it must have seemed as if every single day brought a new hope, a new crisis, or a new disaster. By the end, what some of the officer corps might have suspected or felt in their bones as early as December 1941 now suddenly became manifest with awful clarity to virtually all of them. There was no longer any doubt: Germany was fighting a losing war.

Operation Supercharge. Operation Torch. Operation Uranus. Perhaps the folk wisdom is right: trouble really does come in threes.

The Newest Enemy

Hitler's comment about "reaching Tunis before the Americans" is revealing. Apparently he thought they had come alone and was unaware that U.S. forces were sailing as part of a coalition expeditionary force along with the British. He had been waiting for this moment for a long time. As far back as his so-called Second Book, written in 1928 before he came to power, he had foreseen a showdown between the Reich and the United States (or the "American union," as he called it). Far from the degenerate "mongrel" state in thrall to the "half-Jew Rosenfelt" that Hitler would later conjure up in his wartime table talk, America appeared then in a much more positive—and more dangerous—light. It was, he wrote, a power already setting new standards of strength and prosperity, one that had benefited from emigration of the best and the brightest "Nordic" elements from all over Europe, a "young, racially select people" destined for a "hegemonic position" in world affairs.[8] It would be the task of a National Socialist government, the future Führer wrote, to prepare Germany for war with America.

Wars generate their own strange narratives. Despite the commonly held American view of World War II as a holy war to crush fascism and bring freedom to the oppressed masses of the world, an anti-Hitler "crusade in Europe," the United States certainly took its time getting involved.[9] Let us consider a few time frames: the war lasted almost precisely six years, if we date it from the invasion of Poland (September 1, 1939) to the Japanese surrender on board the U.S.S. *Missouri* (September 2, 1945). American participation spanned less than four years of that total, a little over half the war. Another way of looking at it: of seven campaigning seasons, the United States missed the first three and was active only in the final four. Full-scale war had already been raging in Europe for two years and in Asia for four before the United States got involved, and by that time, Japan had overrun much of China while the German Wehrmacht had done much the same to Europe.

When the United States finally did enter the war, it was not by choice. The warlords in Tokyo brought the United States into the conflict on December 7, 1941, and a few days later, Hitler joined in by declaring war on the United States. Nearly a year later, however, a veritable lifetime in the age of modern societies and mass media, the U.S. Army still had not fired a shot at its German adversary. When the armies finally did meet in battle, late in 1942, the encounter took place not in Europe, the logical place for these two armies to fight. Rather, it happened in Tunisia, a French colony in Africa that had not—to put it mildly—figured prominently in either German or American planning just a few short months before. An urgent crusade in Europe, in other words, began late and started in a most unlikely spot.

Normally, the scenario outlined above would be good news for the late-arriving power. The warring states have clinched, traded blows, and spent themselves. The intervening power is at maximum strength, is fresh and eager to have a go, and can therefore represent a kind of decisive weight in the struggle. It can enter the war, decide the issue, and then dictate to the exhausted combatants, friend and foe alike. In the case of World War II, the United States had had years to prepare and bring itself to a peak of readiness. Even with all that lead time, however, and after two years of an increasingly aggressive foreign policy that telegraphed to all concerned that the United States was not going to sit passively and allow Germany and Japan to conquer the world, no one can say that the U.S. Army was in any way ready to fight World War II. There is a clear tone of bewilderment in the dispatch sent to London by Field Marshal Sir John Dill, chief British military representative in the United States, just after Pearl Harbor, in which he opined that Britain's new partners were not only unprepared, but "more unready for war than it is possible to imagine."[10]

If Dill had a longer memory, he might have thought back to 1917. In that year, the United States had entered World War I, and it had been grossly unprepared for that one as well. The U.S. Army's experience of war at the time was chasing Pancho Villa around the United States' border regions with Mexico. In April 1917, the nation had to gear up not only for a major war, but for a major war overseas, something completely new in American history. It would take a year for the United States to assemble, train, and transport an army to Europe. Even when it arrived, the American Expeditionary Force (AEF) under General John Pershing would have to use French weapons. The Renault FT-17 tank, the SPAD XIII fighter plane, both 75mm and 155mm artillery—all of it came from France. The paradox, then, was that U.S. industry, the largest and most productive heavy industrial base in the world, would play a relatively small role in arming U.S. forces for the great clash overseas.

The post-1917 period saw the United States army in a typical postwar drawdown. At least three lines intersected on the graph: the interests of budget-minded politicians eager to get the state back into the black; a war-weary citizenry yearning to return to normalcy after the recent unpleasantness; and hundreds of thousands of soldiers thankful to have survived the ordeal and mentally packing their barracks bags the moment they heard the good news. It was a perfect storm in a democratic society, and post–World War I U.S. administrations were no more able to resist it than any of the others before or since. The army shrank to a fraction of its wartime size, and with U.S. public opinion strongly isolationist, interest in military affairs had never been lower. By one measure, the United States in 1939 was the seventeenth largest military power in the world, just behind the sixteenth largest, Romania. The U.S. Army contained only three fully manned infantry divisions, plus a single cavalry division. By spring 1940, there were five infantry divisions, at a time when the Wehrmacht was fielding 136 divisions and the Japanese already had over a million troops active in China. There is a fascinating image from an issue of *Life* magazine in 1938 captioned, "This is Half of the U.S. Army's Only Mechanized Cavalry Brigade," which displays a handful of "combat cars" and trucks drawn up for a photo op.[11] Part of a conscious saber-rattling campaign on the part of *Life*, it didn't look like much, and it wasn't.

The army's problems ran deeper than mere numbers, however. It was also floundering in a great deal of confusion over its doctrine—its ideas, policies, and procedures for war fighting. The interwar era was a particularly vibrant time in military affairs, the era of a great international debate over the issue of mechanization—that is to say, the role the tank and airplane would play in the war of the future. To most observers, the tank was the key to breaking the stalemate of trench warfare in the last year of World War I and thus seemed to be the weapon of the future. In Great Britain, Colonel J. F. C. Fuller and a retired captain, B. H. Liddell Hart, described modern armies based around tanks and aircraft, using their superior mobility to outflank and destroy the fixed enemy defenses that had proven so difficult in World War I.[12]

In Germany, reformers like General Hans von Seeckt and Colonel Heinz Guderian likewise envisioned future mechanized armies, and both the pre-Hitler *Reichswehr* and the Nazi-era Wehrmacht carried out large-scale exercises to field test motorized and mechanized formations. These maneuvers resulted in the creation of the Panzer division, a unit with tanks as its principal strike force, but containing a full complement of supporting arms: mechanized infantry, self-propelled artillery, supply columns, bridging trains, and more. The Panzer division, in other words, was a combined arms formation "in which the other arms were brought up to the standards of mobility of the tank," in Guderian's classic formulation.[13]

By comparison to the European powers, the United States missed out on the mechanization debate altogether. This is not to say that no one in the U.S. military cared about the issues or did not understand the utility of armor. The AEF had used tanks and aircraft in World War I, and the army had even established a Tank Corps, an independent formation consisting of tanks alone. It had taken part in some heavy fighting, and by the end of the war, it contained some 5,000 vehicles and 20,000 personnel.[14] The war had been a short one for the United States, however, and the postwar army remained wedded to some conservative views. In 1920, the National Defense Act authorized a strength of just 17,000 officers and 280,000 men for the regular army.[15] To provide some sense of proportion, this was about one-third the size of the French army, while France had a population about one-third the size of the United States. The act also abolished the Tank Corps and reassigned all its tanks to the infantry branch, in effect subordinating armor to the foot soldier. Two of its leading commanders, Colonel George Patton and Lieutenant Colonel Dwight D. Eisenhower, reverted back to their old branches, cavalry and infantry, respectively. Typical for this pocket-sized army, both returned to their prewar rank of captain. Official doctrine reflected this conservative era. The army's field service regulations of 1923 saw one purpose only for both air power and armor: to support the infantry. The 1939 revision would hedge a bit ("as a rule," it stated, tanks were "to assist the advance of infantry foot troops").[16]

Isolated individuals would continue to call for reform, with Patton arguing for a greater role for armor and Brigadier General William ("Billy") Mitchell preaching the air power gospel so loudly that he was court-martialed for insubordination in 1925. Mitchell felt he had proven his point in the July 1921 test bombing of the captured German battleship *Ostfriesland*, but not everyone agreed with him.[17] By and large, the reform clique remained without influence. Because Patton was in the cavalry—and one of the greatest equestrians in the history of the U.S. Army—he was forbidden by law to have contact with the tanks. At any rate, the army was so small and so widely dispersed, and the budget for weaponry so tiny, that there never was much hope for designing and producing new weapons or testing them under anything approaching realistic conditions.

Beyond the failure to mechanize lay more deeply rooted problems, however. Like all military forces, the U.S. Army had to operate within the matrix of its own culture and history. In 1939, the army was 163 years old. During that time, it had fought one great force-on-force conflict: the Civil War. It had also fought a number of smaller wars against European or European-style armies (the Revolutionary War, the War of 1812, the Mexican War of 1846–1847, and the Spanish–American War of 1898). Finally, as the AEF, it had seen a few months of intense combat in World War I in 1918. Subtract these 13 years or so, and it had spent 150 of its 163 years on the frontier defending against or hunting down elusive Native American tribes, with uneven success. In other words, it had spent far more time as a border constabulary than it had fighting large-scale European-style warfare. As a result, it had over the years developed a preference for certain attributes: high mobility, small formations, light weapons, tough, self-reliant soldiers, and a deemphasis on the supporting arms.[18]

At its best, an army's military culture can act as an interpretive key to help soldiers understand recent events. At its worst, it may act as a self-reinforcing prejudice. The fighting in World War I is an example of the latter. It hardly changed the U.S. Army at all. The AEF had entered the fighting determined not to get bogged down in the trench warfare that was bleeding Europe to death. It arrived with a doctrine it called "open warfare," essentially dispensing with long preparatory artillery fires and sending the infantry forward supported only by its own small arms.[19] Open warfare was a hypothesis, unfortunately. It had not been tested, nor had it been worked out in all its particulars. Applied to the 1918 battlefield, it almost proved disastrous. U.S. troops suffered enormous casualties in the early fighting, and continued to do so until American field commanders began to listen to the well-meaning admonitions of their French and British counterparts. The Allies saw such U.S. tactics as suicidal, and frankly, they knew what they were talking about, having gone through the same learning curve just a few years earlier. By the war's end, the AEF was laying on the heavy metal, launching huge barrages before sending the infantry forward, just like all the other armies had been doing since 1915. It had been a tough lesson, and like all wartime lessons, it had been learned in blood.

It was also soon forgotten. In 1919, the army convened a superior board to evaluate the lessons of the recent war. The board's findings maintained that trench warfare had arisen due "to the lack of aggressiveness of both sides" and warned that in the future, "infantry had to be self-reliant," rather than relying too much on "the auxiliary arms," which tended to "destroy the initiative." All these points are arguably correct, even if they seem dubiously applied here. What was less defensible was the board's claim that the results of the fighting had validated the U.S. concept of open warfare.[20] In fact, it had done anything but.

Given its history, then, it should not surprise us that when the army was first developing armor and other mechanized weapons in the 1930s, lightness and maneuverability, not armor or the ability to take a pounding, were on the top of the list of attributes. The tanks that resulted would be consistently lighter than the German tanks they had to fight in North Africa and Europe. At a time when the Germans were already mounting 75mm guns in the turrets of their main battle tank, the *Panzerkampfwagen* (armored fighting vehicle) Mark IV, for example, the standard U.S. tank, the M2 medium, had only a 37mm gun. And as the Germans were upgrading to a longer, higher-velocity 75mm gun (in both a new version of the Mark IV and in the Mark V "Panther"), and then upgrading even further to an 88mm gun (in the Mark VI "Tiger"), the standard U.S. main battle tank, the M4 Sherman, was still using a short-barreled, lower-velocity 75mm gun. Tank comparisons can use various criteria, and one can make a strong case for the qualities of the Sherman—its gyrostabilized gun, for example, enabled it to fire on the move without losing target acquisition. Nevertheless, for the duration of World War II, U.S. tanks were unable to stand up to German armor in a one-on-one fight.[21]

To most people, that inferiority would seem like a problem. To the one man who mattered, however, the chief of the U.S. Army Ground Forces (AGF), General Lesley McNair, it was no problem at all. He did not believe that tanks should be fighting other tanks. Tank-on-tank duels, he wrote, were "unsound and unnecessary."[22] Armor's mission was not to fight enemy armor, but to wait in reserve until the infantry and artillery had broken through enemy defenses, then come up and rapidly exploit into the enemy's rear, like the horse cavalry of old. The task of defeating enemy tanks, in McNair's view, fell to a different class of vehicle altogether, a new conception known as the tank destroyer. The TD was a lightly armored vehicle, sometimes even open topped, highly mobile and mounting an antitank gun. In McNair's vision, the tank destroyer would hunt down and kill German tanks, which would in turn free up U.S. armor for the cavalry role of exploitation and pursuit.

McNair's views became U.S. doctrine without a great deal of devil's advocacy or field testing, the same way that open warfare had become doctrine in 1917 and the same way that "daylight precision bombing" was becoming doctrine in the U.S. Army air forces.[23] Although analysts have been pretty hard on McNair ever since, one can make a case for the tank destroyer. Raw U.S. infantry was going to need all the fire support it could get early on, and tank destroyers—cheaper and much easier to produce than a full-blown tank—provided it. On the downside, the tank destroyer's light armor made it easy prey for the German tanks it was supposed to be stalking, and it was especially unsuited for the role of infantry support, a role into which the ground troops pressed it repeatedly.

The year 1940 would change the U.S. Army forever. In May, the Wehrmacht launched its great offensive in the west, attacking France and the Low Countries. With the Panzers in the lead and the dive-bombing Stukas screaming overhead, the Germans obliterated the mass of the French army in two weeks, then overran the rest of the country in June. If there was one event that "solved" the problem of mechanization, one that proved that the future of warfare belonged to concentrated masses of armor, this seemed to be it. In July, after that dramatic German victory, U.S. Army chief of staff General George Marshall signed orders creating a new organization called the Armored Force, under the command of General Adna R. Chaffee Jr.[24] The first two U.S. armored divisions made their appearance, the 1st (nicknamed "Old Ironsides") under Major General Bruce Magruder and the 2nd ("Hell on Wheels") under Major General Charles L. Scott. In November, Scott moved up to command I Armored Corps, and his divisional command went to George Patton, now a brigadier general. The army had not completely shed its old ways. Chaffee was an old cavalryman and still saw the tank primarily as a means to carry out "offensive operations against hostile rear areas"—that it, the traditional exploitation role.[25] Nevertheless, tanks had now become an integral part of the U.S. Army.

As it modernized its force, the United States was also mobilizing its considerable reserves of manpower. In September 1940, President Franklin D. Roosevelt signed the Selective Service Act into law, the first peacetime draft in U.S. history. Some 16 million men registered for the draft that fall, and by the end of 1940, there were 630,000 men in the force, which now numbered 13 divisions; by June 1941, those numbers had risen to 1,400,000 men and 36 divisions. The military budget for 1940 was $9,000,000,000—more than all the U.S. military budgets combined dating back to 1920.[26]

As force levels exploded and new equipment came online, large-scale maneuvers became possible for the first time. The fall of 1941 would see three great exercises: Arkansas in August, Louisiana in September, and the Carolinas in November.[27] Counting all three, over 750,000 men had taken part, and tanks and mobile infantry featured prominently in the latter two. These maneuvers not only provided U.S. officers and enlisted men with realistic experience of life in the field, as all maneuvers do, but they also introduced the U.S. Army to large-scale, high-speed mechanized operations. In the second phase of the Louisiana maneuvers, for example, General Patton showed his flair for maneuver by launching 2nd Armored Division (part of the Blue force) on a 400-mile end sweep into the rear of the Red force.[28] He actually took his division outside of the maneuver area and supplied the drive through purchases from local gas stations along the route, rather than from the five-gallon "jerry cans" then in official use—hundreds of which were necessary to fuel an armored unit. When the Blue commanders protested his actions as a violation of the maneuver regulations, Patton retorted that he was "unaware of the existence of any rules in war."[29] In the Carolina maneuvers, Patton's tanks actually captured the commander of the enemy side, Lieutenant General Hugh Drum. The maneuver umpires ordered Drum released so that the exercises could continue.[30] Patton would emerge from the maneuvers as one of the army's rising stars, a folk hero to many Americans before the army had fired a shot.

Beyond hardening the troops and field-testing the armor, the maneuvers had also put the officer corps to the test. Their outcome, or at least the way that General Marshall and his aides parsed the outcome, would determine the cohort of field commanders who would fight the war in Europe. Of the 42 divisional, corps, and army commanders who took part in the exercises, Marshall relieved or pushed aside no fewer than 31 to make way for younger officers. In 1942, 20 of the army's 27 divisional commanders would get the ax. It had taken a while, and it was just in time, but the U.S. Army was putting its game face on.[31]

Getting Started: The First Year

So the U.S. Army was ready, but ready to do what? In 1973, U.S. military historian Russell Weigley wrote his seminal book, *The American Way of War*.[32] In it he noted the U.S. tendency in its wars to gather overwhelming force, attack the enemy's main field army, and flatten it, a "strategy of annihilation." It had not always been thus. The early republic, he noted, facing war with England and fielding tiny armies across a vast continent, had to be content with a "strategy of attrition" or "strategy of exhaustion."[33] The desire to win big had developed as the country had grown, with America's wealth, resources, and power eventually leading to a preference for total victory—what Weigley characterized as the destruction of the enemy's armed force, along with the complete overthrow of the foe himself, ending in his unconditional surrender.

At the heart of Weigley's thesis was the Civil War, as close to a total war as the United States had ever seen before 1940, and especially the figure of General Ulysses S. Grant. Grant was a commander noted not for his operational subtlety, but more for his recognition of what had to be done and his imperviousness to casualties. His calculus was simple: he could afford the losses, and his chief opponent, General Robert E. Lee, could not. Lee was a master of subtle maneuver, the art of war that risked all on a single throw of the dice, and he had to be. Commanding an army that would probably lose a prolonged war of attrition, he needed a rapid and dramatic victory in a single campaign. Grant could maneuver when he had to, and he did it con brio in the course of his career—for example, in the Vicksburg campaign. In the course of that operational sequence, still considered by many analysts to be one of the classics of the art, he actually managed to do the seemingly impossible: outmaneuver a fixed fortress. Once he came east in 1864, however, he had the men and matériel to spare, and he felt no need to dance around. During the Wilderness campaign during the war's final year, Grant grabbed Lee, attacked him, and kept attacking, refusing to allow him to maneuver and eventually bleeding him to death.[34]

His rejection of anything too clever or overly precious was his legacy to later generations of U.S. war fighters. At a time when the rest of the world's modern armies were drinking the seductive elixir of Moltkean-style warfare—risky and independent movements by "separated portions of the army" (*getrennte Heeresteile*),[35] maneuver on "exterior lines"[36] to hem in the enemy and destroy him in a single battle of encirclement (a "cauldron battle," the Prussians called it, or *Kesselschlacht*)—Grant begged to differ. As he saw it, success in warfare was largely a matter of marshaling superior resources, not surprising or beguiling anyone, then moving forward on all fronts. It was an unvarnished, plebeian path to victory, one that offered no real glamour and bestowed no particular reputation for genius on the general. It was entirely of a piece with this plain-spoken man. Indeed, it was an ideally republican form of war for the modern age.

It is interesting to note how strongly Grant's legacy dominated U.S. strategy in World War II. It is almost a test case for the prevalence of military culture and how ingrained historical patterns can become. Each country and each military establishment believes it is following principles of war. What each one is following, however, is often its own history and its own way of war.

General Marshall, for example, saw strategy in basic terms: the United States was at war with Germany and Japan, but of the two, Germany was by far the more dangerous. The United States had to concentrate on defeating Germany, therefore, even if it meant accepting a string of embarrassing defeats in the Pacific. Marshall envisioned a massive buildup of forces in Great Britain (Operation Bolero) followed by a cross–English Channel invasion of western Europe (Operation Sledgehammer, later Operation Roundup).[37] This was the only route by which the Allies could get at the mass of the Wehrmacht and destroy it. He considered other potential operational scenarios, some quite fanciful, but remained unimpressed. "Through France passes our shortest route to the heart of Germany," Marshall stated in his plain-spoken way.[38] He wasn't presenting an argument as much as he was stating a fact, and it was unlikely he could have seen things any other way. Marshall intended to go for the jugular, a "Germany first" war of overwhelming strength along the direct route.

We can see the imprint of his vision in the so-called Victory Plan drawn up by Major Albert C. Wedemeyer in the summer of 1941.[39] Wedemeyer, working quickly, came up with some startling numbers for what the United States would need to win a war with the Axis: an army (and army air force) of nearly 9,000,000 men, a total of no fewer than 215 divisions, and a tank force of 61 armored divisions and 61 mechanized divisions.[40] As an example of military prophecy, the "Victory Plan" had its problems. Although the total number of men proved remarkably prescient, Wedemeyer's other numbers were inflated. The army would field only 16 armored divisions in World War II, not 61, and zero mechanized divisions. The total number of divisions was nowhere near 215; the United States would fight the war with just 90. To quibble about the numbers is to miss the point. As an example of the culture of U.S. strategic thought, a plan for the gathering of overwhelming force, there is no better example.

Devising the strategy was one thing. Implementing it would be far harder than anyone could have imagined. For the next two and a half years, as the planners prepared for the cross-Channel invasion, the U.S. Army saw a great deal of fighting. Unfortunately, it took place everywhere but Marshall's chosen battlefield. First, not everyone in the U.S. military was excited about "Germany first." For all the notions of a unitary American way of war, one of the most salient characteristics of U.S. military history has been service independence and interservice rivalry. The various major services, two in World War II and three today, really do argue their briefs to the president as if their interests were identical with the interests of the nation as a whole, and to be honest, it hasn't worked out all that badly over the years. In 1942, while the army was gearing up to fight the Germans, the U.S. Navy had a war of its own against the Japanese. Although nothing much was happening in Europe, there was action all over the map in the Pacific: a decisive victory over the Imperial Japanese Navy at Midway in June 1942, which smashed the power of the Japanese carrier fleet[41]; and the first U.S. counterpunch of the war, the amphibious landing on the island of Guadalcanal in the Solomon Islands in August.[42] To Admiral Ernest J. King, commander in chief of the U.S. fleet and the chief of naval operations, a Germany-first strategy made no sense. He thought—and it is hard to argue—that Midway had knocked Japan off balance and that U.S. forces needed to keep up the pressure if they wanted to avoid harder fighting later on.[43] The result was that more and more resources began to flow into the Pacific, far more than the 25 percent of combined resources that the British and American governments had envisioned at the Arcadia Conference in late 1941.

Second, there was another dissenting voice that demanded a hearing: the partner in the anti-Hitler coalition. Great Britain also had a traditional "way in warfare": avoiding direct confrontation and expensive frontal assaults and using naval power to harass the strategic periphery, keeping the enemy off balance with hit-and-run raids, and forcing him into a long, destabilizing war of attrition.[44] It had abandoned this highly successful strategy during World War I, had sent a huge British expeditionary force to the continent, and had suffered massive losses doing so—around one million dead. There was no enthusiasm at all in London for Sledgehammer or Roundup. They seemed likely to generate massive casualties even if they succeeded, and they might well fail. Indeed, a landing on the French coast in August 1942, an attempt by a British–Canadian force to seize the port of Dieppe (Operation Jubilee), had ended in disaster, with the invading force smashed and much of it taken prisoner. As a result, Churchill and his advisors had a different suggestion altogether for how to proceed in 1942, a plan originally called Operation Gymnast, then Super-Gymnast, and finally Operation Torch.[45] It would be an amphibious landing in French North Africa, specifically in Morocco and Algeria, French colonies then under the control of the puppet Vichy regime.

Torch was attractive to the British for a number of reasons. First, it would solve a pressing operational problem. In the summer of 1942, German and Italian forces under Field Marshal Erwin Rommel (*Panzerarmee Afrika*) were launching an invasion of Egypt, driving a confused British 8th Army back in some disarray, and lunging toward the Suez Canal. If Torch worked, it would place a huge force in Rommel's strategic rear, probably requiring an Axis evacuation of Africa altogether. For once, there might be a German Dunkirk. Moreover, victory in North Africa would give the Allies complete control of the Mediterranean, reopening Suez to Allied shipping, which now was having to steam all the way around the Cape of Good Hope. Finally—and the British had to tread lightly here—Torch would give the rookie U.S. Army a gentle introduction to the World War II battlefield and a chance to sharpen its skills in a smaller, less decisive theater before it tried to do anything too drastic. It is a point of view that still rankles Americans who read about it, but if anyone knew just how hard it was to come up to speed against a veteran German Panzer force, it was the British. In fact, they were still having trouble at the moment, almost three years into the war.

Apart from interservice and coalition rivalries, there were also insurmountable problems inherent in Marshall's quick cross-Channel invasion. First, staff studies for Sledgehammer and Roundup were demonstrating that a direct invasion of western Europe was going to be a tough and complex undertaking, especially for an inexperienced U.S. Army. It required many skills and much information: precise timing of far-flung landings; intricate cooperation of land, sea, and air forces; and detailed knowledge of such arcane items as the weather and tides on various regions of the French coast. In addition, a landing would require immense amounts of shipping—a finite resource that all the involved parties were having to juggle against the demands of a global war, plus a great deal of specialized equipment that hadn't even been invented yet, let alone produced: the "landing ship—infantry" (LSI) and "landing ship—tank" (LST), for example.[46] When all was said and done, it was clear to Marshall that his forces were going to be nowhere near ready for any landing in 1942, or even 1943.

Although no one on the U.S. side seemed enthusiastic about Gymnast, and most were actively opposed, President Roosevelt eventually agreed to it. He did so over the objections of Marshall, who objected to any diversion away from plans for Bolero and Roundup, and over those of King, who wanted to concentrate against Japan. The chief of staff and the COMINCH-CNO actually sent the president a note in

July arguing against any North African adventure. Rather than carrying out this peripheral operation, the United States "should turn to the Pacific for decisive action against Japan."[47] Marshall later claimed it was a bluff, but trying to bluff one of the wiliest politicians in American history was a loser's game. Roosevelt used the note to stage one of the war's great political set pieces, an object lesson in American civics and the tradition of civilian control of the military. He didn't mind disagreements among the Allies, but there was no room for "taking up your dishes and going away," he growled.[48] There was also no room for commanders in uniform to give their commander in chief anything that seemed like an ultimatum. He placed a quick telephone call to Marshall and King, demanding that they send him detailed plans for their "Pacific Ocean alternative." When would you like it, they asked him? This afternoon, the president said.

Once over the shock, they had to admit to him that the United States was no more prepared to send a mass army to the Pacific than it was to North Africa or Europe. Roosevelt's reasoning in all of this was remarkably simple: the United States was at war, it was a political necessity to fight the Germans somewhere in 1942, and there was no chance of fighting them anywhere else. He was growing impatient. The country had spent a great deal of money building an immense military establishment, which as yet hadn't done a thing. "It is of the highest importance," he said at the time, "that U.S. ground troops be brought into action against the enemy in 1942."[49] There was also the matter of the Soviet Union, then tied in a life-or-death struggle with the vast majority of the Wehrmacht. In the summer of 1942, the Germans were just then launching Operation Blue, their offensive towards the Don, Stalingrad, and the oil fields of the Caucasus, and a hard-pressed Stalin was calling for the opening of an immediate second front against Germany.[50] Given the realities, that could only mean one thing. On July 30, 1942, the president summoned his commanders to the White House and announced his final decision on the matter. Torch was a go.

And that was that. Roosevelt's decision to invade Africa has generated a great deal of heat over the years, first in the postwar memoirs, then later in the scholarly histories. By and large, the fault line has been one of nationality, with American commanders (and later American historians) crying foul, describing Torch as a senseless diversion of effort, and criticizing the way that Torch harnessed U.S. power to the "British empire machine."[51] As this brief survey has indicated, however, inter-Allied tension may well be a distorting lens through which to view the war today. Systemic constraints were at work in 1942. The gap between what Marshall wanted to do (launch direct blows against the enemy's heartland), and what he was able to do in reality (commanding a half-trained army whose weapons were still being designed) was so vast that the U.S. Army might well have wound up in North Africa even without British prodding.

Torch: The Plan

Roosevelt's decision, as much as it forced his officers into a common-sense reappraisal of their actual situation, certainly brought problems of its own.[52] It came so late that Allied planners had a mere six weeks to work up Torch—a blink of an eye given the immensity of the operation. The staffs certainly had enough to think about: two slow, heavily laden transport fleets, closely escorted by warships, would have to cross the Atlantic to North Africa from the United States and Great Britain, departing from Hampton Roads in Virginia and the Clyde River estuary in Scotland, respectively. The crossing from America involved a distance of more than 3,000 miles and thus would be the longest amphibious operation of all time by a considerable margin. After a hazardous two-week voyage, the two fleets would have to carry out a tricky rendezvous at sea in an assembly area off Gibraltar. They would then split up for their objectives, carrying out simultaneous landings over 900 miles of coastline fronting on two separate seas (the Atlantic and the Mediterranean). A lot of things could go wrong in an operation of this size, especially with a green U.S. Army, an untried staff, and a commander, Lieutenant General Dwight D. Eisenhower, who had never before commanded troops in combat.

Besides its sheer size, the operational scheme itself was a highly complex one. There would not be a single landing but three simultaneous ones. The Western Task Force would be an all-U.S. effort, sailing from American ports under the command of Major General George S. Patton. He would land 35,000 men near the port of Casablanca on the Atlantic coast of Africa with three divisions (2nd Armored, 3rd and 9th Infantry Divisions). The Central Task Force (Major General Lloyd R. Fredendall) would come down from Great Britain, landing 39,000 men (1st Armored Division, 1st Infantry Division, and the 509th Parachute Infantry Regiment) in and around the port of Oran. Finally, the Eastern Task Force would be a half-U.S., half-British affair under Major General Charles W. Ryder. Also sailing down from Britain, Ryder would put U.S. 34th Infantry Division and British 78th Infantry Division ashore in and around Algiers.[53] Each landing group had its own powerful Naval Task Force in support. When gathered off Gibraltar, they would amount to 340 vessels of all types—the greatest military armada of modern times. Air assets, likewise, were so large and spread over such a vast expanse that they had to be split into two, an Eastern Air Command under British air marshal Sir William Welsh and a Western Air Command under U.S. major general James Doolittle, with Cape Tenez in Algeria, roughly midway between Oran and Algiers, being the dividing line between them.

Torch's size and complexity added up to a number of uncertainties. First, there were the thousand and one things that could go wrong at sea. During their long approach voyage, the fleets faced a serious threat from enemy U-boats if German intelligence managed to get wind of Torch in advance. Even if the U-boat threat did not materialize, there was always the possibility of storms or mechanical failure at sea. The convoys would have to be merciless. Any ship that could not keep up would simply have to be left to its fate.

The problem of the operational objective was also troubling. Torch could have only one strategic aim: the port of Tunis. If the Allies got there first, they could choke off Rommel's *Panzerarmee* and trap it in Africa. If the Germans did, they could rush reinforcements to Africa by the relatively safe means of air transport and build up their forces far faster than the Allies could by sea. It was therefore imperative to land as close to Tunis as possible. Getting too close to Tunis, however, would put the convoys within the range of German aircraft based at airbases in Sicily and Sardinia. In the end, the Allies chose a relatively conservative solution, landing only as far east as Algiers and depositing one entire landing force outside the Mediterranean altogether. Morocco was the safest landing, but it put a major portion of the Allied force over 1,000 miles away from the main objective of Tunis. Even Eisenhower recognized that the chances of capturing Tunis had now shrunk "from the realm of the probable to the remotely possible," but there really was no ideal solution to this problem.[54]

Without doubt, the largest of the imponderables was the attitude of the defenders. Vichy France was officially a part of the Axis, and so French North Africa was technically enemy territory. Defending it was an army of some 120,000 men, lightly armed colonial troops useful for patrolling and handling the occasional band of desert raiders, but hardly configured for firepower-intensive modern operations. Intelligence suggested that there was support for the Allied cause within the colony, that much of the population would greet U.S. troops as liberators, and that many French soldiers would lay down their arms rather than fire on them. Admiral Jean Francois Darlan, commander in chief of the French armed forces, had been hinting since 1941 that he could bring the Vichy regime over to the Allied side in return for a sufficient amount of U.S. military aid. American agents had been hearing similar things from General Pierre Juin, French commander in chief for North Africa.[55]

To sort this all out, on October 21, just a few weeks before the start of Torch, Eisenhower's top aide, Major General Mark W. Clark, carried out a secret mission into North Africa. Landing by submarine at Cherchel west of Algiers, he met with the chief of staff for French forces in Algiers, General Charles Mast. It was a guarded conversation. Mast was loyal to neither Darlan nor Juin. Instead, he recommended that the Allies put their faith in General Henri Giraud, who had recently escaped from German captivity and had become a French hero in the process. Giraud was then in hiding in southern France. If the Allies backed Giraud, Mast promised, then all of French Africa would rise up in revolt and cooperate with U.S. forces. He demanded weapons, which Clark agreed to provide. He also demanded that General Giraud be brought to North Africa, which sounded reasonable enough. He then went on to demand that Giraud be put in command of the entire Allied campaign in North Africa. Clark wasn't having that, and the two men hemmed and hawed for hours, until word came that the police had gotten wind of the meeting and were on their way to arrest everybody.[56]

Clark barely got out of North Africa alive, but despite that near fiasco, he was able to report that there seemed to be a great deal of pro-American sympathy among French officers in North Africa. It was equally clear they did not hold the same affection for the British. There was still a great deal of bad blood over Dunkirk, where the British had understandably prioritized their own troops for the evacuation (even while taking over 100,000 French troops off the beaches). In June 1940, when France had signed an armistice with the Germans, the Royal Navy launched an attack on the French fleet stationed at Mers el Kebir in Algeria. They sank one battleship, heavily damaged others, and killed over 1,300 French sailors. So it was almost certain that the French would fight the British. As a result, Torch would have U.S. troops spearheading the landings at all three sites. Only at Algiers would their be a significant British presence on day one, the plan here being to form a British 1st Army under General Kenneth Anderson, assemble it rapidly, and send it hurtling at top speed toward Tunis.

Time constraints, vast distances, inexperienced commanders, rookie troops, untested equipment and doctrine, uneasy Allies, the uncertainties of dealing with the French, a question mark as supreme commander—Torch promised to be quite a ride.

Torch: The Operation

Even the simplest operation sees things go wrong. The complexity of the Torch landings on November 8, 1942, was bound to generate some glitches, and it did. Let us start with Oran, the geographical center of the operation.[57] Here elements of the 1st Infantry Division and the 1st Armored Division landed at two beaches to the west of the port (labeled X and Y) and a third one some 30 miles to the east (Z Beach). Students of World War II who are versed in the Normandy landings of 1944 need to discard their notions of sophisticated technology and dedicated landing craft. These were primitive landings, with the troops arriving in a variety of assault boats, many of simple plywood construction in which the men jumped over the side. The landings at all three lettered beaches went well enough. Unfortunately, at Oran itself, a detailed plan to run troops directly into the port and seize it by a surprise coup de main (Operation Reservist), was a catastrophe. The force detailed to Reservist (3rd Battalion of the 6th Armored Regiment, 1st Armored Division) ran into a blizzard of French fire and was essentially destroyed, with 346 of 393 men involved winding up as casualties, a figure of over 90 percent. Likewise, a parachute drop by the 2nd Battalion of the 509th Parachute Infantry Regiment (Operation Villain) went badly wrong. Heading for two airfields south of Oran, and La Sénia and Tafaraoui, the transports veered far off course and dropped the men into a dry lake bed, the Sebkra D'Oran, about 30 miles away from their intended drop zones. Some of the planes actually landed in the bed itself, and a few of the men managed to hitch a ride with a U.S. armored column that had landed at X Beach and was now driving inland.

Reservist and Villain had been disasters, and even worse, unnecessary operations. Enough men got ashore, and once commanders and men sorted out their initial confusion, U.S. forces encircled Oran and drove on the city against uneven French opposition. The commander of the 1st Infantry Division, Major General ("Terrible") Terry Allen and his assistant divisional commander, Brigadier General Theodore Roosevelt Jr., both distinguished themselves in the fighting with aggressive leadership from the front. Finally, one last special operation deserves mention: a landing by the U.S. 1st Ranger Battalion (Lieutenant Colonel William O. Darby) succeeded in capturing two forts north of Arzew (Ft. de la Pointe and Ft. du Nord), whose guns might well have caused real problems to the main landings. Oran surrendered on November 10.

At Algiers, we see more of the same.[58] Here, no fewer than six landings took place, two each at Apple and Bear beaches west of the city, and two at Charlie Beach to the east. They went smoothly enough, but once again, Allied reach exceeded its grasp when a frontal attempt to sail directly into Algiers harbor and seize the port (Operation Terminal) ran into strong French fire. Casualties were massive: virtually all of the 3rd Battalion of the 135th Infantry Regiment. At Bear Beach, the 168th Infantry Regiment (34th Infantry Division) drifted a full eight miles away from its intended landing zone and actually landed at Apple. Still, enough of the force managed to land and press inland to surround Algiers, forcing its surrender on November 9.

The toughest fighting took place in the west.[59] Here, Patton's Western Task Force landed at Safi, south of Casablanca, as well as at Fedala and Mehdia to the north. At Safi, a frontal assault (Operation Blackstone) actually worked for once, with elements of 47th Infantry Regiment sailing directly into the port on board two old destroyers, U.S.S. *Cole* and U.S.S. *Bernadou*. When the French opened fire, this time there was a response as the battleship U.S.S. *New York* and cruiser U.S.S. *Philadelphia* opened fire from nine miles away. With *New York*'s 14-inch shells pulverizing Safi's defenders, U.S. troops seized the town while suffering only four dead (out of a total of 29 casualties).

In contrast to the happy news out of Safi, the Fedala landing nearly turned into disaster. This was in essence the main Casablanca landing, the centerpiece of the Moroccan campaign. It got off to a bad start. There was a great deal of confusion in the landing, with troops strewn all over the coast, often miles from their designated beaches. Making matters worse was the presence of the French battleship *Jean Bart*, then under construction in Casablanca harbor; it opened fire on the vulnerable U.S. transport fleet with its own massive 380mm- (15-inch) guns. Joining in were the heavy 200mm- (8-inch) guns of the coastal fortress at El Hank, just northwest of Casablanca. Answering them were the 16-inch guns of the U.S.S. *Massachusetts*, making this the only battleship-on-battleship battle the U.S. Navy would fight in the Atlantic. The American vessel got the better of things, scoring five hits on *Jean Bart* and silencing its fire. While the big ships were busy with one another, a French destroyer squadron slipped out of Casablanca harbor, heading straight for the U.S. transport fleet. The French ships were just four miles from their target when aircraft from the carriers U.S.S. *Ranger* and U.S.S. *Suwanee* intercepted them and gave them a serious pummeling. Although it ended well for the Americans, it had also been far too close for comfort.

The landing at Mehdia, 80 miles north of Casablanca, also turned into a very tough fight. Once again, U.S. troops (60th Infantry Regiment and the 66th Armored Regiment, under the command of Brigadier General Lucian Truscott) landed all over the map, badly off course. One of Truscott's three battalions landed a full five miles to the north, and so was out of action on day one. As the landing force pressed inland, it had the misfortune of running into the toughest French resistance in all of the Torch landings, centered around an old fortress overlooking the beach, inevitably nicknamed by U.S. troops the Kasbah. A small French counterattack near the Kasbah by a handful of old tanks saw some U.S. soldiers panic, throw down their weapons, and try to flee. This was probably the closest that any American troops came to being thrown back into the sea. Truscott kept a cool head, however; he got his units sorted out and managed to defeat a second French tank attack coming up from Rabat in the south, supported by a small number of light tanks of his own. He then managed to take the Kasbah and the airfield inland from Mehdia at Port Lyautey. Helping seize the latter objective were 75 commandos transported up the Sebou River on board the destroyer U.S.S. *Dallas*.

Casablanca still held out, however, with the French defenders behind a tough perimeter that was as well supported by artillery as any position in the French colonial empire. On November 10, an increasingly frustrated General Patton received a cable from his friend Eisenhower: "Dear Georgie," it read, "the only tough nut is in your hands. Crack it open quickly and ask for what you want."[60] Patton interpreted this note in characteristic fashion, giving orders that night to destroy the city through a massive bombardment from land, sea, and air the next day. He notified the French commanders in Casablanca of his intention, and they promptly surrendered the city. U.S. forces had conquered Morocco, but the cost had been high in the context of Operation Torch: 1,100 U.S. casualties, of whom 337 were dead.

The Allies had won their beachhead, but the experience had been more bewildering than exhilarating. If there was a common thread at all the landing sites, it was the immense confusion. It could manifest itself in various forms: commanders almost always lost contact with their assault formations; troops landed in a disoriented state and tended to mill about or even take a nap; transports carrying vital equipment failed to land, or landed in the wrong place; supplies were simply dumped on the beach, often in unlabeled crates, and the troops themselves spent a fair amount of time rummaging through them to see what was there. At Fedala, for example, U.S. troops were supposed to occupy a small bridgehead four miles wide. They actually landed up and down no less than 42 miles of coastline. Of the 78 light tanks that were supposed to land, only five arrived.[61] That was day one. On day two, bad weather and rough seas threw U.S. landing craft and transports all over the place. Shaking things out into any sort of order was a nightmare.

Once in action, U.S. troops proved to be raw indeed. They tended to go to ground at the first sign of enemy fire—light by later standards of this war, but real enough to them. They failed to coordinate the various arms, and thus they had difficulty overcoming even limited French resistance. Finally, prelanding intelligence on the French attitude had been simplistic and naive. In fact, the Allied landings triggered a sort of French civil war in North Africa, a highly complex situation, and it was hard to say which French units would resist and which might surrender. The only thing to do was to start shooting and see what happened.

The U.S. had a fairly extensive intelligence network in North Africa, a group of U.S. vice consuls whom Roosevelt dubbed his "12 Apostles."[62] Technically serving as "food control officers" monitoring the trade agreement between Vichy France and the United States, they had been as busy as bees in the run-up to Operation Torch: handing out bags of cash, stealing Italian, French, and Spanish diplomatic codes, and organizing anti-Vichy insurrections in all three Allied landing zones, at Algiers, Oran, and Rabat. All three began simultaneously with the Allied landings, and all failed miserably. It was, as Rick Atkinson describes in *An Army at Dawn*, a classic *opéra bouffe*, replete with struggles for precedence between the Vichy officers, uncertainty among their American patrons, and a higher-than-normal level of snafu and dissonance.[63] There would come a time in the post-1945 era when U.S. agents would become expert at sponsoring coups across the globe, but that time was not yet. As things collapsed around him, the American spymaster in Algiers, diplomat Robert Murphy, actually wondered whether he'd gotten the date of the landings wrong—a bad sign for all concerned. He spent that first night in prison, as did his colleague Kenneth Pendar. Murphy would note in his memoirs that their Senegalese guard offered the two men a Gitane cigarette—the customary last smoke offered to a condemned man. Thankfully, it never came to that.

In evaluating the landings, Patton probably said it best: "The men were poor," he wrote afterward, "the officers worse. . . . Had the landings been opposed by Germans, we would never have gotten ashore."[64] Of course, what Patton didn't say was that the dismal performance of the U.S. Army just might have been the best justification of all for Operation Torch.

The Race for Tunis (November–December 1942)

As planned, the aftermath of Torch had General Anderson taking command of British 1st Army and launching a drive east into Tunisia, aiming ultimately for the ports of Bizerte and Tunis.[65] The stakes were high. At the end of October, the British 8th Army under General Bernard Law Montgomery had decisively defeated Rommel's *Panzerarmee Afrika* at El Alamein deep inside Egypt, and the Axis force was in full retreat toward Tunisia under its new designation as the German–Italian Panzer Army (*Deutsch–Italienische Panzerarmee*). If Anderson could reach Tunis before Rommel did, the entire Axis army would be cut off and stranded in Africa. It was as juicy an operational target as the North African war had ever offered. And so began what the western newspapers immediately dubbed the "race for Tunis."

The Torch landings had caught the Wehrmacht in a moment of intersecting crises. El Alamein had just hit, and by November 4, Rommel was in full flight. At the same moment, German forces deep in the Caucasus along the Terek River had just made their last throw of the dice, with III Panzer Corps (General Eberhard von Mackensen) driving on the city of Ordzhonikidze, the gateway city to the Georgian Military Road and thus to the great oil fields of the southern Caucasus region. Spearheading the drive had been two Panzer divisions, the 13th and 23rd. He had come close to the city—absurdly close, in fact: a single mile—but a Soviet counteroffensive out of the city on November 6 hit the 13th Panzer Division hard, smashing it frontally, driving around its flanks, and encircling the division's main body. Relief forces would break into the pocket and relieve the division in the next few days, but Mackensen's drive on Ordzhonikidze had failed.

Two campaigns had thus ended in defeat, and another one was about to end in catastrophe. In Stalingrad, General Friedrich Paulus and the German 6th Army were on the verge of a final attempt to take the city before winter. Operation Hubertus was an attempt to smash the last Soviet resistance in the northern industrial districts. It featured no fewer than eight battalions of combat engineers—every last battalion of these irreplaceable specialist troops in Army Group B, Paulus's parent formation. While the Germans were planning Hubertus, the Soviets were amassing huge forces of the Southwestern and Stalingrad fronts north and south of the city for Operation Uranus, the planned encirclement of the 6th Army. Hubertus would begin on November 11, and after making some initial gains, fail. Uranus would open on November 19 and succeed, quickly smashing through the threadbare Romanian armies protecting the flanks of German forces fighting in Stalingrad. On November 23, hard-driving Soviet tank columns linked up at Kalach on the Don, far behind Stalingrad, dooming the German 6th Army still fighting inside the city.

For all these reasons, then, Torch was probably the last thing the Germans needed at the moment. Both Hitler and the OKW had known a landing was coming, but no one had known where. Recently, Hitler had been leaning toward Norway, the result of clever British disinformation.[66] His high commander for the south (*Oberbefehlshaber-Süd*, or *OB-Süd*), Field Marshal Albert Kesselring, had envisioned an Allied landing to reinforce Malta.[67] Benito Mussolini had not been surprised—he'd been telling anyone who would listen that the Allies were going to land in North Africa.[68] Indeed, if the Allies reached Tunis and cut off the *Panzerarmee* in Africa, fascist Italy would be under the gun. Torch had shaken the Axis alliance to its foundations.

As surprised as they had all been, German reaction time was typically swift. The danger facing Rommel was grave, and the situation at Stalingrad was about to turn ugly, but these places were far away. Now that the Western Allies had landed in the Mediterranean, the threat of them slashing their way to Tunis and landing in southern Europe was real enough. The Red Army might fight its way into Germany in two or three years. Once ensconced in Italy, the Allies would be a lot closer than that.

The day after the landings, November 9, was a hectic day for the high command and the army. Hitler told Italian foreign minister Galeazzo Ciano that he had decided to create a "Tunisian bridgehead" (*Brückenkopf Tunisien*).[69] He called in Kesselring and told the marshal that he could have a "free hand" to organize the defenses in Tunisia as he saw fit. The marshal jumped at the opportunity, and Luftwaffe units would arrive in Tunis that very day, one fighter and two Stuka groups organized into a generic "Battle Unit Tunis" (*Gefechtsverband Tunis*), under the command of the Luftwaffe's Colonel Harlinghausen. Following them were German airborne units, small elements of the 5th

Fallschirmjäger Regiment, and elements of Kesselring's headquarters battalion, fighting as *Kampfgruppe Schirmer*. They were airlifted to Tunisia, landing at El Aouina airfield just northeast of Tunis in the evening. By November 12, they had taken possession of the city itself.[70] In the meantime, German troops occupied all of Vichy France and Corsica. This was Operation Anton, a move they had been planning since late 1940 in case of an Allied landing in Africa.[71] Wisely or unwisely, Hitler had decided to fight in Tunisia, which he now called "the cornerstone of our conduct of the war on the southern flank in Europe."[72] The moniker "race for Tunis," therefore, was already obsolete the day it was coined. While the Allies were just getting themselves off the beaches, the Germans had already arrived.

Although this was officially an Italian theater, placed under the authority of the Italian Supreme Command (the *Commando Supremo*), German field marshal Albert Kesselring received command of all Axis air and ground forces in the Mediterranean. Kesselring was one of the war's most fascinating characters, a man appropriately nicknamed "Smiling Albert." His easy smile and bonhomie, to be sure, marked him as unusual in the ranks of the German officer corps, who were not typically a fun-loving bunch. But in most ways, he was a typical German general. One of the characteristics of Prussian–German field commanders over the centuries had been their notion that they were capable of mastering even the most difficult strategic situation, the worst imbalance of men and matériel, and they could do it through sheer force of will. Rommel himself had thought the same thing just a few short weeks earlier, before El Alamein, and Kesselring, as yet essentially untested in theater command, thought so too. Indeed, one of the reasons that the Wehrmacht stayed in the field so long against a world of enemies was that there was always another officer, raised in what we might call the Prussian school, who was ready and eager to replace an older and wiser colleague, one who had just been overwhelmed by Allied superiority in matériel, or who had just survived a carpet bombing, for example, or who had managed to live through a barrage of Allied naval gunfire used in a tactical role on land, or had gotten through a massive Soviet offensive on the eastern front with all his limbs intact. Kesselring was not the first, and he would not be the last.

His first act was to hand over the field command in Tunisia to General Walther K. Nehring, a tough veteran of the desert war and the commander of the *Afrika Korps* under Rommel from May to September 1942.[73] Nehring, too, possessed all the standard long-term attributes of the Prussian–German officer corps. He was a hard driver who led from the front and liked to laugh at danger. Unfortunately, as an incredible number of Wehrmacht generals would find out in this war, sometimes danger laughed back. At the time of Kesselring's call, Nehring was in Europe convalescing from serious injuries that he had received at the battle of Alam Halfa back in September. The Wehrmacht couldn't spare talent, however, able-bodied or not, and so the new field commander would report to Tunisia with an arm wound that was still festering. As we shall see, he would not be the only walking wounded among the Wehrmacht's field commanders by this point in the war.

His first mission was to set up a temporary Nehring Staff (*Stab Nehring*), form a bridgehead in the area of Tunis and Bizerte, and "broaden it as far as possible to the west" (*soweit als möglich nach Westen zu erweitern*).[74] An inspection tour of Tunisia, planned as a quick one-night in-and-out, turned into a hair-raiser for Nehring when his plane crashed on the El Aouina runway and he and his party were nearly killed. The situation on the ground wasn't much better. Conditions were chaotic, the attitude of the Vichy French authorities was unclear, and German strength was still minuscule. Along with the paratroopers, other small units had arrived: an infantry battalion, a Panzer company, one artillery and two antiaircraft battalions, assembled into Battle Unit Lederer (*Gefechtsverband Lederer*), but it hardly seemed enough when Nehring's intelligence officers were reporting that 70,000 Allied troops had already landed to the west.[75] He noted other problems in defending Tunis: no real headquarters, no chain of command, no communications equipment. It was a dispirited Nehring who arrived at El Aouina airfield that evening, ready to board a replacement aircraft promised him by Kesselring. Its failure to appear set the seal on a long, rough day, and Nehring wound up hitching a ride on a plane bound for Trapani in Sicily. He had been "deeply impressed" by his experience that day, he would later write, "although hardly cheered."[76]

As a few days passed and the Allies still hadn't arrived, Nehring's anxieties eased. More flights were arriving daily to fill out his formations, and, helped by OKW's decision to pull transport aircraft out of the campaign to supply the doomed pocket in Stalingrad, German troops began to arrive. The high command had already promised him three German divisions: the 10th Panzer Division (General Wolfgang Fischer) and 1st Parachute Panzer Division "Hermann Göring" (General Paul Conrath) from France, plus a new formation, the 334th Infantry Division (Colonel, later General, Friedrich Weber), then being formed in Germany.[77] The Italian *Superga* Mountain Infantry Division (General Dante Lorenzelli) was also on the way.[78] None of these divi-

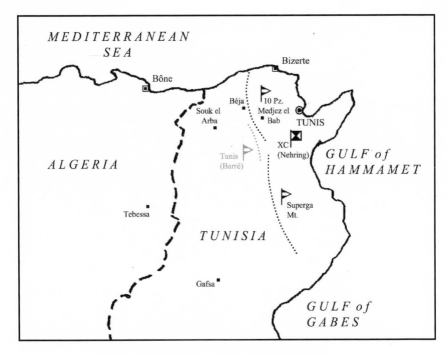

Tunisia: Initial Axis Deployment (mid-November 1942)

sions would be arriving overnight, and indeed they never did arrive fully. All suffered losses at sea during the trip to North Africa or left crucial support formations behind in Europe.[79] Nevertheless, by mid-November, Nehring had established a formal headquarters (XC Corps), and he had formed two small bridgeheads: one around Tunis under Colonel Harlinghausen, and a second one at Bizerte under Colonel Stolz (who had replaced Colonel Lederer).[80]

We should be careful about conjuring up an image of a solid two-formation corps, however. Each of these bridgeheads contained a few thousand men at most, along with a handful of tanks, and even after a solid month of sea- and airlift, Nehring had fewer than 25,000 German and Italian troops under his command. Despite the divisional designations, the early battles in the race to Tunis would involve a bewildering array of tiny German *Gefechtsverbanden* and *Kampfgruppen*. Consider the order of battle for November 26, for example. It contains not a single division: *Kampfgruppe Koch* (elements of the 5th *Fallschirmjäger* Regiment under Colonel Walther Koch); the *Barenthin* Regiment (an ad hoc unit of *Fallschirmjäger* reinforced by flak and *Nebelwerfer* multiple rocket launchers, under Colonel Walther Barenthin, commander of engineers for the XI *Fliegerkorps*); the 17th, 18th, 20th, and 21st replacement battalions (*Marschbataillonen*), the 21st *Fallschirmjäger* Engineer Battalion under Major Rudolf Witzig; the 190th Panzer Battalion (69 tanks) from Fischer's 10th Panzer Division, as well as other advance elements of the division; and finally, a miscellany of antitank, assault artillery, and *Nebelwerfer* formations.[81]

Throughout this phase of the campaign, Nehring would assemble or disassemble his formations as the need arose, or as commanders took up new duties. *Gefechtsverband* Lederer became *Gefechtsverband Stolz* on November 16, for example, and two days later morphed into *Gefechtsverband Broich*. That same day, Colonel Koch, commanding the 5th *Fallschirmjäger* Regiment, relieved Colonel Harlinghausen, freeing up the latter to concentrate on his Luftwaffe command, and Koch's ground forces began to appear on the situation maps as *Kampfgruppe Koch*. It has all been enough to keep buffs of the campaign busy beyond words, and indeed, these constant changes of name and designation are significant: they indicate how much of the campaign in Tunisia would be a colossal improvisation, a "come as you are" war for the Wehrmacht.

While Axis forces were arriving in Tunisia, if slowly, the Allies were having trouble getting started. It is 560 miles from Algiers to Tunis, and while there was no real opposition, the Allies were finding it difficult to shift from the confusion of landing mode into a posture of high-speed forward maneuver. Like the grandly named "divisions" and "corps" under Nehring, General Anderson's "British 1st Army" contained but a single division, the British 78th Infantry (General Vyvyan Evelegh).[82] There are many reasons for this, and most of the historiography blames Anderson's own lack of drive, but the real culprit was the geography and extreme dispersion of Allied troops. Patton's formations, for example, were still 500 miles to the west of Algiers. Allied lines of communication, the distance from the ports to the forward units, were immensely long, and they got longer with each bound forward. As a result, a huge number of Allied troops had to stay behind to help feed supply, fuel, and ammunition to the forward fighting units.[83] Guarding the mountain of supplies the Allies had brought along took thousands of men, and theft by the local Arab population was a serious problem from the start. It all added up to a serious drain on the amount of combat power that could go forward. By December, by one count, there were 180,000 U.S. troops in North Africa, but fewer than 12,000 of them were actually far forward enough to claim to be "at the front."[84]

The sane solution to the administrative problem was to seek the cooperation of the French. After all, France had been ruling this region for decades. French officials knew the local culture, and French police knew all the local criminals. In Morocco, for example, Patton estimated that it would take 60,000 troops just to keep order among the local tribes, and those were troops he simply did not have. This was the context for Eisenhower's decision, in mid-November, to strike a deal with Admiral Darlan. The admiral agreed to bring French troops over to the Allied side and promised French assistance in keeping the rear areas quiet, in return for Allied recognition of his status as "High Commissioner of French North Africa." The arrangement made perfect sense on many levels, but unfortunately, it ignited a firestorm of controversy in both the United States and the United Kingdom. Both the print media and the radio raked Eisenhower over the coals for collaborating with a Nazi sympathizer. Darlan had been a key member of the Vichy government, after all, and recognizing him meant recognizing the legitimacy of Vichy law in North Africa, including anti-Semitic restrictions barring Jews from public office, the civil service, and the army. To editorial writers back home, this wasn't exactly what this war was supposed to be about. "Are we fighting Nazis or sleeping with them?" asked the well-known CBS radio commentator Edward R. Murrow.[85] At any rate, the "Darlan deal" became a moot point on December 24, 1942, when the "Little Fellow," as U.S. officers called him, was the target of an assassin's bullet in Algiers.[86] Frankly, no one on the U.S. side was very sad to see him go. General Clark called the killing, in his typically delicate way, "the lancing of a troublesome boil," and that just about summed up Allied opinion.[87]

The impact of all this on the race for Tunis was highly negative. The complexity of the political struggle within French North Africa took up far too much of General Eisenhower's time and energy in this period. It is probably fair to say that for a few crucial weeks, the general lost his focus on the urgency of the operational situation. On December 22, in fact, Marshall felt it necessary to send Eisenhower a testy message: "Delegate your international problems to your subordinates," Marshall's telegram ran, "and give your complete attention to the battle in Tunisia."[88] The chief of staff's message politely begged the question of just what Eisenhower had been doing up to now, and Eisenhower himself was too skilled in the politics of the military profession to read the note as anything but what it was: a strong reproach.

What emerged from this curious military matrix of distracted command, rough terrain, vast distances, and a tiny force commitment was a series of meeting engagements in northern Tunisia. Anderson was rolling east with a single division; Nehring was probing out from Tunis and Bizerte to fulfill his mission of enlarging the bridgehead to the west. The campaign opened with an early, and brief, phase of mobile operations. On November 11, the 6th Battalion, Royal West Kent Regiment, landed at Bougie, 100 miles east of Algiers, and took control of Djidjelli airfield there. The next day, the British 6th Commando landed at Bône, 125 miles to the east of Bougie, in concert with a small air drop by 3rd Battalion, 1st Parachute Regiment. On November 14, Anderson launched 1st Army into Tunisia. All told, his little army mustered barely 12,000 men, but it continued to hurtle forward. He ordered another air drop at the town of Souk el Arba, on the Algeria–Tunisia border, this one by the British 1st Parachute Battalion. Commandeering local buses, the battalion motored on to Béja, 40 miles to the northeast. Far to the south, the U.S. 2nd Battalion (509th Parachute Infantry Regiment) dropped successfully onto Tébessa and, also by bus, drove on to Gafsa on the edge of the desert.[89]

All of these operations were successful and threw Anderson's front forward hundreds of miles. In the iron logic of the desert war, however, the Allies were already outrunning their air cover. German Stuka raids against Bougie and Bône on November 12 and 13 did serious damage to both ports.[90] Casualties were light, but losses in ships and matériel were high, and as Anderson would later note, "the infantry were, for some time to come, operating only with what they could carry and in the clothes they wore when they left their ships."[91] Rommel and Montgomery, generals with more experience fighting in North Africa, would no doubt have nodded their heads wisely and commiserated with Anderson. If there was one lesson they had learned over and over again, it was that moving too far, too fast could be dangerous in the desert.

As the Allies were heading in, Nehring was probing out. From the two small disconnected bridgeheads guarding Bizerte and Tunis, small mixed German columns were heading west. Their objective was indefinite—perhaps the Algerian border if they could get there before the Allies. Beyond his immediate mission, Nehring also had to secure a number of locations far to the south, the ports of Sousse, Gabès, and Sfax along the coastal road, in order to hold open a line of retreat for Rommel's *Panzerarmee*.[92] Having to detach units from an already microscopic force and disperse over hundreds of miles of wilderness had very little to do with a traditional German way of war, which emphasized concentration, shock, and striking power, attributes summed up in the German term *Kampfkraft* ("fighting power"), but there was nothing to be done about that.[93]

Starting on November 17, day 10 of Allied operations in French North Africa, the principal adversaries finally met on the ground, on the Djebel Abiod–Jefna road and Sidi Nsir in the north, at Tebourba in the center, and at Bou Arada to the south. Often described as "battles" today, and certainly intense enough in their own way, all these were in fact skirmishes that rarely rose above battalion level. Both sides had carried out an "advance to contact"[94] and now had to react, sort things out on the fly, and decide how to proceed. In such a freewheeling operational environment, it was by and large the Germans who got the better of things. They enjoyed a number of advantages: they were much more experienced, first of all, used to traveling light, but they also had a tradition of independent command that left a great deal of initiative in the hands of the officer on the spot. All these encounter battles were essentially the same. Reconnaissance patrols led the way. Initial contact was a surprise. The side with greater strength on the spot quickly gained the upper hand and pushed back the enemy advance guard. With both sides at roughly equal strength, however, neither main body was capable of landing a knockout blow on the other. Thus, the record was mixed. In the north, the Germans pulled off a successful ambush on Highway 7, the road to Jefna, with Major Witzig's airborne engineers and tank columns breaking through elements of the British 36th Brigade and nearly destroying the 6th Royal West Kents.[95] In the center, the two sides fought to a rough stalemate around Sidi Nsir. In the south, German Panzers managed to push the British back to Medjez el Bab. The final verdict: advantage Wehrmacht. The hectic eastward rush of British 1st Army had come to a halt.

General Anderson attempted to restart it on November 25. Although he was still commanding only a single infantry division, Evelegh's trusty 78th, his operational scheme called for three thrusts to the east: 36th Brigade on the left (in the north), 11th Brigade about 25 miles to the south (on the right), and in the broken ground between them, seeking some operational space or target of opportunity, "Blade Force," a small ad hoc formation of 2,600 men and a typical British "jock column" of mixed mobile units.[96] Analysts have often accused Anderson of dispersing his force, and certainly three thrusts were probably two too many for a single division. Concentrating into a single thrust was no guarantee of success either, however. It would simply have allowed the Germans to maximize their own scarce resources in the defense. The lesson here: short of some unexpected event or miracle, any offensive undertaken at rough numerical parity will probably fail to produce anything decisive.

Although it was clear that the Allies were losing whatever small amount of initiative they had held in this campaign, there was one bright spot in the Allied offensive. On November 25, the 1st Battalion of the U.S. 1st Armored Regiment, commanded by Lieutenant Colonel John Waters, was probing aggressively to the east. Part of Blade Force, it managed to split the seam between the German forces defending against the 36th and 11th British Brigades. At about midday, Waters's lead units came up over a small rise near Djedeida to discover a tanker's dream: an enemy airfield packed wingtip to wingtip with aircraft. Before the stunned German ground crews could react, a company of light tanks, little M-3 Stuarts, rushed onto the runway, blasting away with 37mm cannon and machine guns. They destroyed two dozen German planes and a mountain of fuel and ammunition before retiring.[97]

The Djedeida raid was the high-water mark of the Allied drive, the first great exploit for U.S. tanks in this war, and perhaps the greatest moment in the entire operational career of the M-3 Stuart. It also took place just 15 miles from Tunis. General Nehring—whose entire career had shown that he was not one to panic—was shaken enough by this raid, and by a mistaken dispatch that reported U.S. armor only nine miles away from his headquarters, that he decided to abandon Medjez el Bab and to tighten his perimeter around Tunis. His sudden decision, in turn, was the signal for a change in the German command. Believing that Nehring had lost his nerve, Kesselring decided to name a new ground commander in early December.[98] General Hans-Jürgen von Arnim would soon arrive to take over the command, now upgraded to 5th Panzer Army. As the Germans pulled back, the Allied drive to the east continued, with elements of the British 11th Brigade and Blade Force driving smartly up the road from Medjez el Bab to Tebourba. There they launched a vigorous attack but failed to do much beyond creating a sharp salient in the line.

This was the moment that Nehring had been waiting for. Elements of the 10th Panzer Division had been arriving daily, and Nehring had deployed them in the relatively open space between Bizerte and Tunis, where they could occupy a kind of central position against either of the British brigades moving in from the west, and attack the first one to come within reach. As it turned out, it was 11th Brigade, with Blade Force attached, around Tebourba. Nehring's solution to the operational problem facing him was the same one that any German commander of his generation would have devised. Indeed, it had been the Prussian art of war for many centuries, and Nehring was the latest in a long line of commanders to study a map under varied circumstances and come up

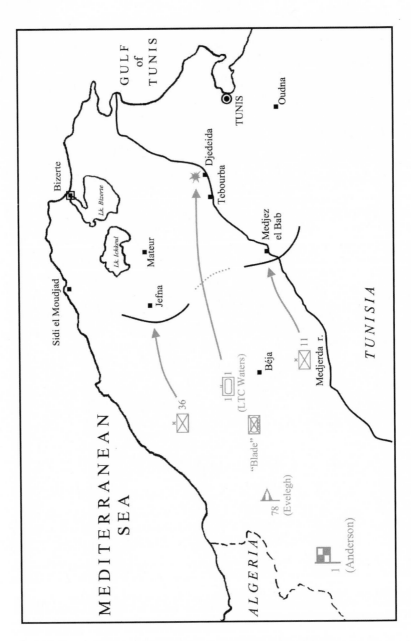

The Allied High-water Mark: 1/1's Raid on Djedeida (November 25, 1942)

with the same stratagem. For the German officer, there was only one path to victory: the concentric (*konzentrisch*) attack by independent columns.

It was a small-scale affair. Nehring had only about 4,000 men and 60 tanks from 10th Panzer Division, attacking in three *Kampfgruppen* (*Gruppe Lueder, Gruppe Hudel,* and *Gruppe Djedeida*), along with 5,000 paratroopers from *Gruppe Schirmer* and *Gruppe Koch,* two march battalions, and a Tiger tank company (six tanks, although breakdowns reduced it to four). The plan was to make the force seem a lot larger than it was and hit the Allies from multiple directions. The armored *Kampfgruppen* from 10th Panzer Division would attack the Allied grouping at Tebourba from the north and northeast, the paratroopers of *Gruppe Koch* from the south, and the Tiger tanks and march battalions—perhaps one of the oddest operational couplings of the entire war—would drive in from the east.[99]

The orders went out on November 30, and the unnamed operation opened on December 1 with General Fischer in personal command. While the force from Djedeida pinned the defenders frontally, a flanking force of armor drove down on them from the north through Chouigui Pass, and the paratroopers came up from El Rathan. Hit from multiple directions, the Allies did what a lot of other forces had done over the years against the Wehrmacht. They defended stubbornly for a day or two, wavered on December 3, then fell apart on December 4, routing back towards Medjez el Bab, surrendering over 1,000 prisoners, and losing the proverbial mountain of equipment. When a hastily arriving U.S. armor brigade (Combat Command B of the 1st Armored Division) arrived, trying to restore the situation, it attacked impetuously across hundreds of yards of open ground and was largely destroyed in two days of fierce fighting.

Nehring's miniature *Kesselschlacht* at Tebourba had turned the tide of the campaign. After a brief pause for regrouping, his victorious little force would restart the offensive on December 9, driving toward Medjez el Bab. Allied defenses stiffened there, however, and Nehring could not lever the defenders out of the town. His own force was far too brittle for a sustained advance—undersupplied and undersupported. He was also smarting from every casualty. He possessed nowhere near the normal complement of medical troops, and he had to arrange to drive the badly wounded back to Tunis for treatment. Tebourba had been a victory, Nehring would later write, but one that took place "under the most difficult circumstances and with emergency equipment"—not to mention an overall commander who had already been fired.[100]

Conclusions: Failure at Tunis

The historian can find many reasons for the German success in holding their bridgehead around Tunis. One, for example, was their clear air superiority at this stage of the fighting. Allied airpower was flying from a single dirt strip at Bône. It could accommodate only a handful of fighters and had to shut down altogether in bad weather. The Axis, meanwhile, had 850 aircraft operating out of all-weather airfields around Tunis and Bizerte.[101] Not only were Allied forces exhausted and undersupplied after their high-speed run to the east, but they now had to contend with nearly constant bombardment, and the combination was simply too much. In a more general sense, however, early December was the moment that Clausewitz had called the *Kulminationspunkt*, the "culmination point" of a campaign, when the attacker's initial strength has carried him as far as he could go and he is now ripe for the counterstroke.[102]

For the Allies, December would see one disaster following another. A final attempt at an amphibious assault, a landing by British and U.S. commandos at Sidi el Moudjad on December 1, was another fiasco, with a quick German counterattack smashing the landing force and taking a number of prisoners. A last airborne landing by British 2nd Parachute Battalion on the extreme right of the line, at Oudna airfield south of even Tunis, was even worse, with German Panzers overrunning much of the battalion in the first 24 hours.[103]

Without a doubt, however, the low point of the Allies' campaign in Tunisia was their attack on "Longstop Hill," their attempt to push out northeast of Medjez el Bab on December 22–26.[104] Everything that could go wrong, did. Faulty British reconnaissance, apparently performed by a telescope at a distance of seven miles, had failed to note that Longstop was actually two hills, not one, with the nearer hill (Djebel el Ahmera) hiding the existence of the farther (Djebel el Rhar), and with a deep ravine separating the two. British intelligence reckoned German troop strength on the hill to be a company; it was actually closer to a full battalion. A British regiment (the storied Coldstream Guards) attacked and seized its initial objectives on the hill. As planned, U.S. troops of the 1st Battalion of the 18th Infantry Regiment now arrived to relieve the guards. The relief in place—always one of the trickiest of tactical actions—went badly, and 1/18 promptly lost the hill to a German counterattack. With the Americans reeling, the British had to turn around and reenter the battle. They did so, not without a fair share of grumbling, and together the Allies managed to grind their way forward up the first hill. They could make no progress toward the second one, however, whose existence had come as a complete surprise to them. The entire fight took place in a driving rain, and soldiers on both sides spent most of the five-day battle slipping and sliding in the mud. A final German counterattack on Christmas Day swept both Allies off the hill altogether, with much of 1/18 destroyed in the fighting, and the Germans would henceforth designate Longstop Hill on their maps as the *Weihnachtshügel*, or "Christmas Hill."

The aftermath of the battle for Longstop degenerated into an orgy of Anglo-U.S. finger-pointing. The British complained that "Alice" (their denigrating internal code name for the U.S. soldier) was a hopeless amateur. The Americans claimed that Anderson was using them as cannon fodder and assigning them to the bloodiest fighting. In fact, both sides were probably right. At any rate, as 1942 drew to a close, the weather had turned nasty, no one was going anywhere, and it was clear that the campaigning season was over.

On December 24, Eisenhower came forward from Algiers to see for himself and was appalled at the conditions he witnessed on the front. He met with General Anderson, slogged his way thru ankle-deep mud and driving rain, and actually looked on as four of his GIs tried—and failed—to extricate a motorcycle out of the muck. He now called a halt to all further offensive operations. It was, he later wrote, "a bitter decision."[105] Having lost his first skirmish against the Axis forces in Africa, Eisenhower would have to fight a full-scale campaign to evict them from Tunisia in 1943.

Although it is clear that Allied forces only had a slim chance to win the race, the campaign had also revealed some serious problems in U.S. doctrine, personnel, and equipment. U.S. infantrymen continued to be timid in the advance, though it is hard to blame them. They had no real defense against German tanks. The main antitank weapon, a 2.36-inch tube-launched antitank rocket launcher nicknamed the bazooka, had proven worthless, and there would be not a single documented bazooka kill of a German tank in the entire campaign. U.S. armor, in contrast, was usually far too bold, coming up recklessly against German tanks with bigger guns and heavier armor, and paying the price. American commanders understood that they had a problem. The prewar U.S. medium tank, the M2, only had a 37mm gun and was now obsolete. Its replacement, the M4 Sherman (75mm) was still in development, however, so there was need for a stopgap. The result was the M3 Grant. Although it had the same 37mm peashooter in the turret as the M2, it also had a 75mm short-barreled gun mounted in a semifixed mounting (a "sponson") on the right front of the hull. Because the gun barely moved, the only way to aim it was to aim the tank—hardly an ideal situation. The Grant was heavily armored, however, and that was a good thing, because it was as tall as a house (10 feet, actually) and thus presented a massive target profile to German fire. Finally, U.S. tank destroyers were finding it difficult to play their assigned role and were already acting as surrogate tanks, also with predictably bad results.[106] McNair's vision for the tank destroyer was already bumping into reality, and U.S. crews were finding it difficult to use a lightly armored vehicle aggressively without getting themselves killed. Only in the most purely technical arm, artillery, was the U.S. Army able to claim a degree of satisfaction. Time and again in the early fighting, it was the arrival of the guns that had saved the day for the infantry, and artillery was the one American weapon that the German Panzers were already learning to fear. All in all, however, the army had a long way to go in the exercise of combined arms, putting infantry, armor, and artillery into battle in a coordinated way.

Perhaps the most serious failing was in the area of command and control, or C2. As U.S. formations came up to the front, they received often contradictory orders that sent them hither and yon, wherever there happened to be a hole or an emergency. U.S. divisions rarely fought as full units, but rather as a battalion here and a battalion there. The result was a loss of cohesion and a great deal of confusion. The fact that all of them were under the operational command of a foreign officer corps who did not entirely trust their fighting qualities did not help. Nevertheless, it was clear that the U.S. Army's biggest problem was not the British, but itself. To their credit, most U.S. officers seemed to realize it, however much they might grind their teeth about British arrogance.

Despite the negatives, and there were enough to fill a book, there had been that one shining moment. Company A of the 1st Armored Battalion, commanded by Major Rudolf Barlow, had spent a rough day on November 25 battling against German armor in the Chouigui Pass. His light Stuart tanks were hardly battle worthy as reconnaissance vehicles, let alone as main battle tanks. As his little machines crested that low ridge outside of Djedeida, however, he must have felt like the luckiest man on the face of the earth: German aircraft parked wingtip to wingtip. A stupefied Barlow radioed his battalion commander, Lieutenant Colonel John Waters: "Look," he said, "right in front of me is an airport full of German airplanes, sitting there, the men all sitting out on the gasoline barrels, shooting the breeze in the sunlight." Then the kicker: "What should I do?" Waters nearly shouted back, "For God's sake, attack them. Go at them."

After a laconic "Okay, fine," to his commander, Barlow gave the order. As 17 Stuarts came down from the ridge and approached the field, the Germans waved their hellos. "They thought we were Italian armor coming in." A few minutes later, the Djedeida airfield was an inferno, a mass of twisted, smoking ruins and dead German pilots and ground crews.[107]

A small episode in a larger drama? Certainly. There can be no doubt about the U.S. Army's troubles in Tunisia. It was having trouble getting organized. Coordination of the arms was a problem. The higher officers were of uneven quality; the men were often confused. There was one thing this army could do, however, and the raid on Djedeida demonstrated it: it could move like lightning. If you took your eyes off it for a moment and gave it some operational space, you had better prepare to be surprised.

Perhaps the most interesting feature of the first campaign for Tunis was how utterly unprepared both sides were to fight it. The Wehrmacht currently had over 150 divisions engaged in the Soviet Union, and was bleeding to death there on a daily basis. The very day that the encounter battles began at Medjez el Bab and Jefna, the Red Army was encircling the German 6th Army at Stalingrad. For the campaign in Tunisia, however, one that threatened to tear the Axis apart, the Wehrmacht could barely scrape together a single division. By mid-December, when Arnim arrived to take over 5th Panzer Army, he still had something less than the "A-team" deployed in the field: an ad hoc Division *Broich* in the north, elements of the 10th Panzer Division in the center, and the Italian *Superga* Division in the south.[108] There were reasons for the Axis to contest Tunisia, in other words, but a gaggle of *Kampfgruppen* were probably not going to get the job done in the long run.

The Anglo-American alliance did little better. The Allies had chosen the time and place of this fight, after all. They had decided on a landing in Morocco and Algeria with plans to drive on Tunis, seal off North Africa, and trap Rommel's *Panzerarmee* to the east. Historians have been waxing poetic about Operation Torch ever since: the size of the armada, the complexity, the vast distances involved, the uncertainty and risk, the moment when "an army at dawn made for the open sea in a cause none could yet comprehend," preparing to "wash ashore in Africa, ready to right a world gone wrong."[109]

All true, certainly, and perhaps even worthy of the poetry! Yet in the end, all that this vast military force—hundreds of thousands of men equipped with thousands of tanks and supported by hundreds of warships—could assemble for the drive on its objective was a single understrength, underequipped division. The British had fought with their customary caution, something to which their years of warfare with the Wehrmacht had conditioned them. The Americans had fought boldly but for the most part ineptly. They had a great deal of spirit and enthusiasm, to be sure. Although it might bode well for the future, it didn't offer all that much at present.

The final results were mixed. The Allies had fallen short of their objective and faced more hard fighting in Tunisia. The Wehrmacht had stood fast and held out, and had apparently won this first preliminary round. All that this "victory" meant, however, was the requirement to fight a great *Stellungskrieg*—a static war of position—in the upcoming spring. It would be a bruising, matériel-intensive campaign, just the sort that generations of German officers and had tried to avoid. The race for Tunis raises an interesting question for military historians to ponder: is it possible for both sides to lose a campaign?

2

Manstein, the Battle of Kharkov, and the Limits of Command

"Against the Grain": Manstein Goes to Rastenburg

Looking back later in his life, Field Marshal Erich von Manstein would remember vividly that winter day early in 1943. He had just been summoned to headquarters for a conference with the Führer and supreme commander of the German armed forces, Adolf Hitler. As the flight carried him to the *Wolfsschanze* in Rastenburg, East Prussia, he had a chance to think about the upcoming conversation. The topic of discussion was no mystery: it would be the disaster that had struck German arms on the Eastern Front. The situation map was a nightmare. The encirclement and destruction of the German 6th Army at Stalingrad; immense offensives by the Red Army that had destroyed the satellite Romanian, Italian, and Hungarian armies; an apparently unstoppable Soviet drive on Rostov that was threatening to cut off not just an individual army, but all of Army Group A, then slowly wending its way out of the Caucasus—one hole after another in the dike. Even someone of Manstein's undeniable operational talent was finding it difficult to plug them. It had been that way ever since he had received command of the newly formed Army Group Don in the wake of the Stalingrad encirclement, and it would, he suspected, remain that way for a long time to come.

The objective state of the battlefront was not, however, what troubled Manstein the most. As he looked back on that meeting years later, he remembered being more troubled by something particular that he had to say to the Führer. And certainly, he had a lot to say. Hitler's erratic leadership had now become a serious hindrance to military operations. His habit of sitting on difficult requests was beginning to assume bizarre forms, especially as the emergency increasingly called for quick decisions. They were all talking about it: the increasing tendency for everything in this campaign to come too late (described ruefully by one commander as "das tragische 'Zu Spät'").[1] Hitler's drift into wishful thinking, ignoring the realities of the situation (a strategy *als ob*, "as if" things were different), was just now coming into flower, even if it had not yet reached the pathological forms it would in 1945. Exhibit A was the decision to cram nearly a half million men into the so-called Taman bridgehead in the Kuban, rather than bring them out of the Caucasus altogether. Apparently Hitler hoped for a renewed offensive into the Caucasus next year, but that was something that Manstein was fairly certain would never happen. Likewise, they were all noticing an increasing tendency to obsess over minutiae rather than focusing on the operational matter at hand. Zeitzler, the chief of the general staff, complained of it repeatedly. Manstein could predict with certainty that he was about to hear a long monologue on the economic importance of holding the Donbas, the eastern bend of the Donets basin, with its rich coalfields. No matter that the coal of the region was entirely unsuitable for German locomotives and industry. Hitler had a set list of responses: it was equally important to deny the enemy those same coalfields, and without them, Soviet industry would soon begin experiencing serious, even crippling, shortages. It seemed to be a fair argument, Manstein supposed, although it was pretty clear that the loss of the Donbas for the past year hadn't done much to hurt Soviet productions: guns, tanks, and equipment of all sorts seemed to be pouring to Soviet front-line formations in unprecedented numbers.

Manstein had a solution to this *Führungskrise* ("leadership crisis"), however. He intended to advise Hitler that the time had come to appoint a chief of staff who would exercise day-to-day command responsibility for the entire Eastern Front. Such a solution would protect Hitler's prestige from the damaging political consequences of battlefield defeat, and it would also place the conduct of operations in safe, sober, and professional hands. It would have to be someone who could work with the Führer, someone whom Hitler trusted implicitly. It also had to be someone with a brilliant operational touch.

That someone, in fact, could only be Manstein himself.

Again, however, none of this was foremost on Manstein's mind. He wasn't flying all the way from Stalino to complain about Hitler's debating style, and he knew that Hitler would reject out of hand any suggestion Manstein made that he step aside. Instead, the field marshal was thinking of the operational recommendations he had sent to Hitler a week ago by teleprinter message. They had called for an immediate retreat of Army Group Don's right wing from Rostov back to the Mius River. Only by shortening the absurdly long *Balkon* ("balcony") of German troops projecting far out toward the Don River could Manstein scrounge up enough formations to launch any sort of counterstroke. Even now, Soviet offensives were churning forward all across the southern portions of the front, reaching out ever farther to the north and west, seeking the German flank over the middle Donets River, and indeed, threatening the crucial crossing points over the mighty Dnepr itself at Kremenchug, Dnepropetrovsk, and Zaporozhye. For the first time, the Soviets were going deep on the Wehrmacht. Even as Manstein flew to Rastenburg, Soviet armored formations were motoring in the clear, hundreds of miles to the west of major German formations, and thus already in their rear. Until that situation was mastered, "standing fast" or "bitter resistance," already two of Hitler's pet phrases, were empty words. There could be only one operational response for the time being.

And that was what was bothering Manstein the most. He was flying to Rastenburg to argue for a retreat. Convincing Hitler would not be easy, he knew. Convincing himself, perhaps, would be just as hard. The Wehrmacht had not done a great deal of retreating in this war—quite the contrary. Just a few short months ago, in September 1942, the glossy magazine *Die Wehrmacht* had run an article entitled "Drei Jahre Krieg—Drei Jahre Sieg": "Three Years of War—Three Years of Victory."[2] Even allowing for its obvious propaganda excesses, it was a fair description of how things had gone up till then. Outside of the check in front of Moscow, the war had featured a "series of impeccable victories" (*ein Reihe makelloser Siege*) for the Wehrmacht—and Manstein had had a lot to do with that.

Events of the last few months had changed all that and were forcing some hard choices on all of them. For the time being, there was no choice but to retreat or perish, but that did not make it any more palatable to the field marshal. "In my own case," Manstein would later write, "it went right against the grain" (*es ist gerade für mich meiner Wesenart nach besonders schwer gewesen*). Perhaps a better translation is, "It shook me to the core." Having to goad Hitler into "voluntarily surrendering territory that the Wehrmacht had conquered at the coast of such heavy sacrifices" (*mit schweren Opfern erobertes Gebiet freiwillig aufzugeben*) was completely foreign to his nature, as it would have been to virtually all German staff and field commanders of his generation. "I should have very much preferred to be able to submit plans for successful offensives (*ergfolgreiche Offensivpläne*) to him," he remembered, rather than have to recommend "the now inevitable withdrawals" (*unabwendbar gewordener Rückzüge*).[3]

Indeed, here was the authentic voice of the German military tradition speaking, the voice of a long and well-established military culture dating back to famous captains like Frederick the Great, Gebhard Leberecht von Blücher, and Helmuth von Moltke the Elder. That voice had been the lodestar for entire generations of Prussian–German officers, guiding the great ones like Friedrich Karl, the Red Prince of the Wars of Unification and the hero of Königgrätz, as well as less successful ones like Karl von Steinmetz and Hermann von François. It meant disregarding the numerical or material odds and pulling through on will alone. It meant risking all on a gamble, having faith in the apparently illogical notion that to win a battle, one first had to "dare to lose it," in the words of the great military historian Hans Delbrück, a man who was no friend of the Prussian military caste.[4] When Manstein spoke of going "against the grain" by recommending a retreat from the Donets to the Mius—and he recognized that it was quite unavoidable given the present ragged state of the Eastern Front—he was channeling the oldest and most basic of the Prussian military qualities. He was speaking the voice of aggression.

The Role of Military Genius in War

For all the complex subjects it has to tackle in attempting to analyze modern military operations, military history sooner or later boils down to a few simple questions: Do human beings make history? Is the individual personality sovereign in wartime? Or is the conduct of warfare more dependent on impersonal phenomena like time, space, weather, and chance, factors that are largely independent of human agency?

Military historians are, by and large, a fairly conservative group. Patterns of training in peacetime, the evolution of technology, debates over doctrine, ways of war, competing socioeconomic systems, the impact of political ideologies—all scholars admit that they have a role to play, often an important one, in the way that wars unfold. As a collective, however, military historians prefer to look to the individual when they are analyzing military operations. They emphasize the "great man"—the general who at some crucial moment managed to bend an unruly battlefield situation to his will. It might involve shifting a reserve division to a decisive spot on the battlefield; or identifying a critical enemy weakness that he is then able to exploit; or devising a bold stratagem that transforms a seemingly hopeless situation; or being aggressive enough to take advantage of a fleeting opportunity when it offers itself. Add those four items together—clever planning, skillful maneuver, the ability to take things in at a single glance and see what must be done (Napoleon's famous *coup d'oeil*), and an innate sense of aggression, and you have a good taxonomy of the term "military genius," or at least what historians usually mean when they use the term.

Any attempt to discuss genius in wartime has to begin with Carl von Clausewitz. In his monumental work *On War* (*Vom Kriege*), the Prussian sage laid down some conceptual ground rules that have dominated military history ever since. In the section "On the Theory of War" (book 2, chapter 2), Clausewitz registers his objection to so many attempts in his day to explain the conduct of war through "principles, rules, or even systems," which, in his view, "failed to take adequate account of the endless complexities involved." Above all, these "one-sided (*einseitig*) points of view" failed to account for the role of genius, "which rises above all rules." Here is Clausewitz, a thinker often reputed to be opaque and difficult to understand, in direct fire mode: "Pity the soldier who is supposed to crawl among these scraps of rules, not good enough for genius, which genius can ignore, or laugh at! No; what genius does is the best rule, and theory can do no better than show how and why this should be the case."[5]

In general, later generations of military historians have taken Clausewitz to heart. No matter how sophisticated their modes of analysis or how varied their influences, they still tend to look to the man. They can take into account the differences in military systems between the Prussians and the Franco-Imperial Army in 1757, for example, parsing matters of soldierly motivation, variances in training, and the different societies out of which they sprung, but they still tend to say that Frederick the Great won the Battle of Rossbach. There is some truth to this claim. The steady calm he exhibited when he realized that the French were trying to sip around his left flank, the rapidity with which he had his army break camp and head to the east, the ease with which his well-drilled cavalry outpaced their adversary, and then finally the culminating maneuver down onto the point of the Franco-Imperial column, literally "crossing their T" and riding over them before they were fully deployed—let us just say that there were good reasons why his contemporaries decided to dub Frederick "the Great."

We can quibble around the edges of this particular *Rossbach-Bild*, of course. It was General Friedrich von Seydlitz who commanded the

Prussian cavalry, not Frederick, and the brio of both the top-speed ride and the great charge itself may belong as much to the general as it did to the king. The Franco-Imperial army, with a dual-hatted leadership and a polyglot rank and file, was a command-and-control implosion waiting to happen. The French were tied to a logistics train a hundred miles long, burdened not just with the traditional military impedimenta, but also with wigs and perfumes and cognac and silk stockings and every manner of creature comforts, and as a result, any maneuver they tried to make was probably going to be too slow for their own good.[6] All these things are true. Yet Rossbach seems destined forevermore to be one of the battles trotted out when historians want to discuss Frederick's greatness.

It is much the same with other alleged examples of battlefield genius: Robert E. Lee at Chancellorsville; Moltke at Königgrätz; Napoleon at Arcola or Ulm or Austerlitz or Friedland or any number of his other battles. Certainly we can say that there were systemic factors at work in all these decisive victories. Lee had a gifted subordinate commander, General Thomas "Stonewall" Jackson, whose intuition and aggressiveness matched his own, and he also had an army full of soldiers who had as yet no real reason to fear their Union adversaries.[7] Moltke possessed an imposing list of systemic advantages: a blizzard of firepower generated by the first production model breech-loading rifle, the Dreyse needle gun; hardy infantry drilled to fight in nimble company-sized columns; a flexible system of command, usually called *Auftragstaktik* (mission tactics), in which subordinate commanders received general directives but could choose the means and methods of achieving the mission themselves; and a group of highly aggressive attack dogs masquerading as an officer corps.[8] Napoleon had something even better: the French Revolution and its attendant social transformation; an aroused populace fighting for its newly won liberties; and the reformed army of the late Royal period, equally adept at fighting in line, column, or *ordre mixte*.[9]

However, the same military historical dynamic persists in all these cases. History recalls Lee, Moltke, and Napoleon as geniuses, and their victories, we instinctively feel, are theirs alone. In the theater of our imagination, they are able to operate with impunity, to shape reality to suit their will, to ignore the rules or to laugh at them, in the famous formulation of Clausewitz. They appear to make the rules rather than follow them. The battles of Chancellorsville and Fredericksburg are inconceivable without Lee's presence, and military historians will always link Moltke with the great Prussian victory at Königgrätz. The battle serves as the main item we enter into evidence to prove the genius of the former. As for the great Napoleon, it is not just military historians who have canonized him. So, too, did many of those who knew him best: his adversaries on the field of battle. The Duke of Wellington once commented famously that "Napoleon's hat is worth 40,000 men." Even more vivid was the basic principle of the so-called Trachenberg Plan, the Allied operational directive for the 1813 campaign. It actually stipulated that any Allied commander encountering a force led by Napoleon in person should do the sensible thing and retreat as soon as possible.[10]

This stress on the role of the individual, what scholarly historians refer to as "personalism," is almost unique to military history. Social and economic historians have always, by definition, concentrated more on the great impersonal forces that they believe move history. Diplomatic historians have emerged from the archives to focus more on the interplay between domestic and foreign policies, between public opinion at home and what happens in the international diplomatic sphere. The historical profession at large today is obsessed with either more profound or more nebulous issues of culture and memory. Yet military historians continue to debate very traditional issues of generalship and genius. This conservative methodological approach is one of the reasons that the broader profession mistrusts military history, insofar as that mistrust is not ideologically driven.

Military history soldiers on, however, especially operational military history, in a determined personalist quest to praise this commander and to criticize that one. Those who stray from that path, seeking to go beyond generalship as the primary criterion of success or failure to more sophisticated categories of analysis—historians like Dennis Showalter, for example—are all the more conspicuous by their rarity.

This is not to suggest a complete abandonment of the individual or a complete reordering of military history's priorities, merely to mollify the rest of the profession. When the great scorer comes to write against all our names, military historians may well find themselves rewarded by sticking to the basics and refusing to chase the scholarly flavor of the week. Modern military operations, however, are highly complex phenomena, influenced not only by a variety of interrelated factors like time, space, supply, weather, and terrain, but also by a number of imponderables. They are not merely "contingent"—that is, with one thing leading to another; they are sometimes utterly unpredictable in their course, with chance occurrences that can sometimes leave the historian wide-eyed. As a result, they are among the most complex of all subjects for historical inquiry, and the individual general, however convenient he may be as a symbol for all that goes right or wrong, often has only a limited ability to influence the course of battle. It is precisely this factor—the limits on generalship in the modern era of mass armies and high technology—that requires operational military historians to do more than cry "Ecce homo!"[11]

Manstein and the Relief of Stalingrad

Field Marshal Erich von Manstein certainly was a genius, and he was always happy to tell you so. He spent much of the war doing just that, and the memoirs he wrote afterward featured his genius as the principal theme, along with denigrating judgments of just about every other officer in the army.[12] His personality could be acerbic and his tongue sharp. One of his operations officers, Colonel Theodor Busse, would later look back on meeting him and recall, "During the first few weeks I hated his guts; I never left his presence without smarting."[13]

There is truth in the old saying, however, that it isn't bragging if you can back it up. Manstein could. He understood both modern mobile operations and the traditional German way of war in which he had to formulate and execute them. He could take in a highly complex situation with a single glance at the map, and once he had made a decision, he saw it through ruthlessly and single-mindedly. His fellow officers recognized him as a highly skilled operator. General Wilhelm Keitel, chief of the wartime *Oberkommando der Wehrmacht* (OKW), a man with whom he had his share of professional scrapes, praised his "outstanding talents,"[14] Busse his "superior art of command, his bold power of decision, and his way of moving to the assigned goal despite interference from above or any local setbacks,"[15] and General Friedrich Wilhelm von Mellenthin his "studied discretion and recognizable shrewdness, his quick and sure grasp of the most complex situations," as well as the "absolute trust" he inspired in his subordinates.[16] Despite some muttering on their parts, they continued to support his memory well into the postwar era. His eightieth birthday, in 1967, was the occasion for a volume of encomia by his fellow officers, *Nie ausser Dienst*, in which the general inspector of the Bundeswehr, General Ulrich de Maizière, labeled Manstein "the most capable German general of the Second World War" (*der fähigste deutsche General des Zweiten Weltkriegs*), although he did qualify his praise by adding "in the realm of operational command" (*auf dem Felde der operativen Führung*).[17]

Postwar historians have generally agreed with those assessments. In his enormously influential book, *The Other Side of the Hill* (1948), later published in the United States as *The German Generals Talk*, B. H. Liddell Hart christened him "the ablest of the German generals," one "who combined modern ideas of mobility with a classical sense of manoeuvre, a mastery of technical detail, and great driving power."[18] Such phrases soon became the received wisdom after the war. Another early tribute from a British source is typical:

> In his person he epitomized all the virtues of the great German General Staff at its zenith: high intellect, untiring industry, personal courage, great driving power, receptivity to new ideas, imagination, great technical skill and originality. Time and time again on the Eastern Front, without air dominance or command of the Black Sea, he gained victory after victory often at the odds of seven to one. It was fortunate for the Allies that at the time of Stalingrad and afterwards Hitler never really allowed him a free hand. . . .
>
> Manstein may well have been the most versatile commander of World War II. To him, war was an art demanding clarity of thought, bold decision and great technical skill. . . . He shone not only as a higher commander and staff officer of genius but also as a commander of armoured forces in the same class as Guderian. He excelled both as a tactician and a strategist both in victory and defeat.[19]

Closer to our own day, the leading operational historian of the 1942–1943 winter campaign, Dana V. Sadarananda, praised Manstein's "firm, decisive, inspiring, energetic, and . . . farsighted guidance to Army Group Don" in that most difficult time.[20] It would take the advent of a new, more critical historiography—one that tends to emphasize the crimes of the Wehrmacht more than its operational victories and defeats—to tarnish the field marshal, and both the primary documents and the secondary literature have now established beyond any reasonable doubt his deep involvement in the German *Vernichtungskrieg* (war of annihilation) in the east, his eager cooperation with the murderous *Einsatzgruppen* working in 11th Army's zone of operations in the Crimea, for example.[21] Even a magisterial recent biography, one that paints the broadest possible portrait and includes a fair amount of criticism of its subject, however, still grants him the title of "Hitler's greatest general."[22]

Perhaps it is time to carry the demythologizing of the field marshal even farther. It should now be possible to view Manstein's career as emblematic of deep-seated problems within the German officer corps. Like virtually all his colleagues, he was relentlessly focused on the operational level of war, he was hopelessly naive about the nature of the enemies that Germany was facing, and he still had fantasies—even after the declaration by the Allies that the war would go on until the "unconditional surrender" of the Axis powers—that he might win some battlefield victory so dramatic that it would lead to a *Remis-Frieden*, a "stalemate peace," borrowing a term from chess.[23] We might say that Manstein saw modern war as a kind of bloody chess game, one that he could win simply by out-thinking his opponent, planning several operational steps ahead, and devising a combination that would rescue Germany from even the most hopeless position on the board.

In the 1942–1943 winter campaign, he was going to need all of those skills and more. The past few months had been strange ones for him. A show of virtuosity as commander of 11th Army in the Crimea in the spring and early summer of 1942 had earned him a field marshal's baton, and his operations in the great encirclement battle of Kerch and the reduction of the Soviet fortress of Sevastopol are still worthy of study.[24] The start of Operation Blue, the make-or-break offensive in the southern sector of the Soviet Union, however, saw him far removed from the action. Originally tasked to cross over from the Crimea to the Taman peninsula to support the drive into the Caucasus, he and his army were instead transferred far to the north to prepare an assault on Leningrad once conditions were ripe. They never were. The Soviets were by now deep in a cycle of relentless counterattacks to break the German ring around the great city, and Manstein found his command mired in tough positional fighting, which he handled no better or worse than any other German general in this war.[25] Engaging in a *Stellungskrieg* against well-equipped adversaries made them all look very ordinary. As a result, he and the 11th Army missed out entirely on Blue.

Perhaps that was just as well. Prussian–German armies had experienced the thrill of victory and the agony of defeat over the centuries, of course. Absolute debacles, however, had been pretty rare, and that was especially true of operational-level debacles, the level of war in which the German officer corps felt itself most at home. One would need to go back to Jena and Auerstädt in 1806 to find a disaster equivalent to what had just taken place at Stalingrad. Blue had been a classic German operation in the style of *Bewegungskrieg*, the war of movement, with large formations (divisions, corps, and armies) maneuvering concentrically to encircle and smash their adversaries in a *Kesselschlacht*, a "cauldron battle," but more correctly a "battle of encirclement." The operational plan itself called for a carefully phased and sequenced set of army-level maneuvers, designed to trap and destroy Soviet forces in the great bend of the Don River somewhere around Millerovo.

The plan briefed well, but unfortunately, the German assault formations had moved a bit too slowly, and the Soviets had managed to slip the noose with a helter-skelter retreat to the East. A second attempt to encircle them, at Rostov, had failed as well. The Wehrmacht had gone through its entire repertoire of maneuver and eaten through much of its limited store of supplies; all it could show for it were two "blows into the air" (*Luftstossen*). The end of the operation saw its best formations embedded in Stalingrad and in the Caucasus, just short of their strategic objectives, shorn of their ability to maneuver, and, frankly, not long for this world.[26]

On November 19, the Soviets launched Operation Uranus, a breakthrough attempt north and south of Stalingrad. Targeting the weak Romanians armies holding the flanks, they easily overran them and linked up a few days later at Kalach on the Don. The 6th Army, Germany's principal and best-equipped fighting formation in 1942, was now encircled inside Stalingrad. The Wehrmacht, in other words, had not simply been outnumbered and outproduced, two conditions that had obtained on the Eastern Front since the beginning of the German invasion; it had been outmaneuvered. The opening words of the situation report from 6th Army commander, General Friedrich Paulus, are chilling enough in any context, but seen through the historical lens of traditional German military operations, they take on an even greater weight: "Armee eingeschlossen," he wrote in desperation: "The army is surrounded."[27]

The long-term implications are more obvious in retrospect, however, and there was still a war to be fought. On November 20, supreme commander Adolf Hitler and his chief of the General Staff, General Kurt Zeitzler, responded to the emergency by activating a new formation called Army Group Don and appointing Manstein to command it. The news reached the field marshal in Vitebsk, and he now set out by train for Novocherkassk. Given the urgency of the situation, he has received criticism for his relatively leisurely travel schedule. The weather had been too bad for flying, he would later claim, although he may well have preferred the longer travel time to study the map and to prepare himself for what was clearly a horrible, perhaps even hopeless, situation.

The principal formation tasked with carrying out the 1942 offensive had been Army Group South. In the course of the fighting, however, it had been split into two: Army Group A (commanded by Field Marshal Wilhelm List until his dismissal in September 1942, then by Hitler himself for a time, and finally by Field Marshal Ewald von Kleist) carried out the drive into the Caucasus, while Army Group B (General Maximilian von Weichs) had to take Stalingrad and guard the long operational flank along the Don River. The end of Operation Blue saw the Wehrmacht strung out into one of the most bizarre situation maps of the war: Army Group A was deep in the Caucasus facing more or less due south, its right wing anchored on the Black Sea and its left strung out along the Terek River just north of Grozny; Army Group B faced roughly northeast, following the course of the Don. Its extreme right wing consisted of the 6th Army, jammed into Stalingrad. Much of Army Group B consisted of non-German elements: the 3rd and 4th Romanian armies, the 2nd Hungarian Army, and the 8th Italian Army, holding an immensely long front along the Don. Liaison between the two army groups was virtually nil, with a single German division, the 16th Motorized, sitting on a lonely perch at Elista on the Kalmyk steppe.

It was an absurd arrangement, and the Soviet counteroffensive had exploited it in style. After smashing the Romanian armies on either flank of Stalingrad and encircling German 6th Army in the city, it had driven over the Don River to the Chir, the smaller river that flows into the Don at Nizhne Chirskaya. With Army Group B now fighting for its life and Army Group A sitting deep in the Caucasus chain to the south, a yawning void had opened between them. This was the operational space to be occupied by Army Group Don. Inserted between Army Groups A and B, it had the dual task of reopening a supply path to Stalingrad and of reconquering the territory lost to Operation Uranus.

Most of the operational analysis of Manstein's generalship emphasizes the first point: relieving 6th Army in Stalingrad. In fact, that was probably an impossible task. Besides encircling the German 6th Army, and perhaps even more important from the standpoint of further operations, the Soviets had also destroyed two of the Wehrmacht's four satellite armies on the Eastern Front, prying open great operational-level gaps in the defensive position where 3rd and 4th Romanian armies used to be.[28] As a result, the prospects of relieving the 6th Army were dim from the start. The Germans had exhausted themselves just getting to Stalingrad, and there were precious few reserves available to

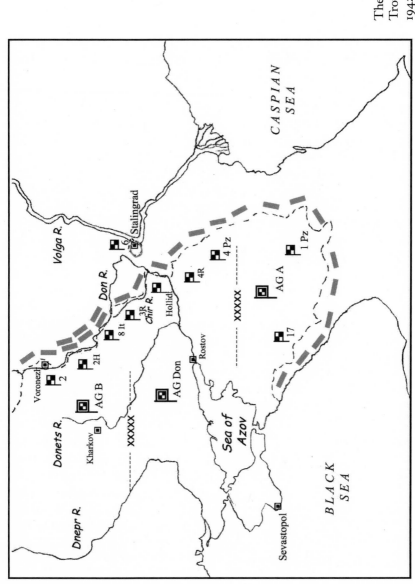

The Wehrmacht in Trouble (December 1942)

break the Soviet ring. While there was discussion of an immediate breakout, 6th Army was so deeply embedded in the city, and the army had shed so much of its operational mobility, that it would have been a great deal harder than most historians have been willing to admit. For Paulus, that left a strategy of sitting it out, being resupplied (sporadically) from the air, and waiting for a relief offensive from outside the pocket. The fact that Hitler had decided to devote precious air transport to the newly formed "Tunisian bridgehead" made it even more difficult to keep supplying the pocket, and 6th Army was starving by mid-December. Every Ju-52 flying to Tunis meant one less flying to Stalingrad.

German hopes for a relief offensive receded on an almost daily basis that December. Continued Soviet attacks on the northern wing pushed the Germans back across the Don to the Chir, then across the Chir to the almost featureless plain leading to the Donets. All the Germans could throw in the path of these armor-heavy attacks were a series of ad hoc *Gruppen*—groups of various size thrown together hastily from the flotsam and jetsam of the defeated forces along the Don. Rather than divisions and corps, the situation maps from the period offer us *Gruppe Stumpffeld, Gruppe Stahel, Gruppe Abraham, Gruppe Spang, Gruppe Pfeiffer*, and others.[29] While it is easy to romanticize them as a symbol of the Wehrmacht's supposedly miraculous improvisatory genius, the reality was something very different. All of them were formations of minimal fighting value, what the Germans called *Alarmeinheiten* (emergency units). They consisted of rear area troops, remnants of destroyed formations, and the new Luftwaffe field divisions (a phenomenon that even now has not received the careful scholarly examination it deserves). One German officer and eyewitness describes the *Alarmeinheiten* as "construction battalions, railroad troops, rear echelons, Cossack bands, Luftwaffe ground personnel, all more or less thrown together."[30] Headquarters on all levels wound up randomly commanding troops in their vicinity, whether they were suited to command them or not. Thus, *Gruppe Stumpffeld*, while under the commander of the 108th Artillery Regiment, consisted almost entirely of infantry; *Gruppe Stahel* was under the staff of the VIII *Fliegerkorps*; and *Gruppe Abraham* actually went into combat under the "IIa" (the chief personnel officer) of the 6th Army—an officer, needless to say, with little recent combat experience.[31] These diverse *Gruppen* would eventually coalesce into *"Armee-Abteilungen"* ("provisional armies"), multicorps formations commanded by (and named for) whomever happened to be available, short of administrative personnel, heavy weapons, transport, and engineers. The current dire situation along the Chir saw virtually all of them handed rifles, ordered to comport themselves as infantry, and sent out to face the Soviet enemy.

The results were predictable. Some broke and ran on first contact. A few acquitted themselves respectably. At the very least, we can say that each got in the way of their Soviet attackers, and that was usually enough to slow up the momentum of a Soviet drive. We are also now aware today of something that no one on the German side could have known at the time: all of those *Alarmeinheiten* benefited from a momentary ebb in the momentum of the Soviet offensives, as the Red Army command realized that the Stalingrad *Kessel* was far larger than they had suspected, and therefore required more and more formations to man the perimeter along the encirclement.

While the Soviets managed to grind their way across the Chir during the first two weeks of December, heading south, they never did manage a clean breakthrough. What they did succeed in doing was keeping the Germans on the defensive, gradually pushing them back from Stalingrad, and thus reducing the chances of a relief effort into the pocket. One by one, German formations slated for the relief found themselves sucked into the fighting along the Chir, the best example here being *Armee-Abteilung Hollidt*, another improvised group hastily assembled from the reserve formations of Army Group B (essentially the XVII Corps, consisting of two regular German infantry divisions, along with the defeated remnants of the 3rd Romanian Army's I and II Corps). Tasked originally for the drive on Stalingrad, it found itself instead fighting along the upper Chir all through December.[32]

When the relief attempt finally came, it was something of an anticlimax. Operation Winter Storm (*Wintergewitter*) may well have been the most important operation of the war, but all that the Wehrmacht could spare for it was a solitary formation, the LVII Panzer Corps under General Friedrich Kirchner. He had a brace of Panzer divisions under him: the 23rd, detached from Army Group A and badly under strength after tough fighting in the Caucasus; and the 6th, under the command of the redoubtable General Erhard Raus, one of the Wehrmacht's greatest armor commanders of the war. Raus and his men had just spent several months in France, resting, refitting, and receiving replacements of armor. His division would by necessity have to do most of the heavy lifting in Winter Storm; 23rd Panzer Division had no more than 30 tanks to its name.

While Winter Storm was originally intended as a multicorps offensive, the dynamic of this phase of the fighting robbed it of one promised division after another: the 15th Luftwaffe Field Division was still assembling; 3rd Mountain Division had to remain with Army Group Center to deal with various local emergencies; and the high command eventually decided to deploy the 17th Panzer Division (also from Army Group Center) behind the right wing of the Italian 8th Army along the Don, as it was increasingly clear that the Soviets were massing forces for an attack in this sector. Finally, the reconstituted XXXXVIII Panzer Corps, slated to drive in from the west once LVII Panzer Corps got going, was having all the trouble it could handle simply holding its own front along the lower Chir.[33]

As a result, Winter Storm was probably a forlorn hope from the beginning. Two mismatched divisions would have to travel more than 90 miles from their assembly point at Kotelnikovo to Stalingrad. The penetration would by definition be needle-thin. While a pair of Romanian corps would guard their flanks—VI Corps on the left (2nd and 18th Infantry Divisions) and VII Corps on the right (1st and 4th Infantry Divisions, along with Cavalry Group Popescu)—no one was expecting them to keep up with the advance of LVII Corps's Panzers, or to do much of anything save defend themselves. Altogether, we may characterize Winter Storm as too much mission and too little force. "A wretched balance," one German officer would later call it, and it is difficult to argue with that description.[34]

The relief operation began on December 12th, and things went well enough at first. Lacking either surprise or any real possibility of maneuver, the two divisions drove northeast, almost straight up the rail line out of Kotelnikovo on a nearly featureless plain, with 6th Panzer to the left of the line and 23rd to the right. The assault penetrated the initial Soviet defenses (302nd Rifle Division on the right and 126th on the left) and managed to breech the first river line (the Aksai) that evening. Soon, however, the Soviets peeled off a couple of mechanized corps from the Stalingrad encirclement (4th in the right and 13th on the left) and deployed them astride the German line of approach. High-speed maneuver gave way to tough positional fighting, and finally to a locking of the front some 35 miles south of Stalingrad. That may seem like a pretty close shave, and most of the histories of the campaign speak of how close the Germans came, but with large Soviet mechanized probes lapping around both flanks of the narrow German penetration, LVII Panzer Corps was a lot farther away than it looked on the map, and the German high command called off the offensive on December 23.

Winter Storm had failed. 6th Army was probably doomed before it, but it was definitely doomed now. Inside Stalingrad, Paulus was supposed to have been preparing for a breakout to meet Winter Storm and to initiate it upon receipt of the code word "Thunder Clap" (*Donnerschlag*). Although there is dispute over this point, it appears that he never received it, and even if he had, it is unlikely that he could have done much to affect the operational situation. He had very little maneuver capability by this point.[35]

Army Group Don, in other words, had failed in its first assignment. Yet it is difficult to see what Manstein could have done one way or the other. He had an Army Group, yes, but it was filled with the wreckage of units smashed in the initial Soviet offensive at Stalingrad. Whatever he could bring to the table as a planner and commander, no matter how brilliant his operational genius, there wasn't much he could do about that. Hitler was already promising him a new armored corps made from freshly equipped S.S. divisions, but it was still a long way off in time and space, and Manstein knew it. A rabble of ad hoc formations like *Gruppe Spang* wasn't going to reopen a path to Stalingrad, nor were those clueless Luftwaffe divisions. He attempted to dignify all this in his memoirs, titling the pertinent chapter the "Tragedy (*Tragödie*) of Stalingrad," and going so far as to liken the 6th Army's sacrifice to that of the Spartans at Thermopylae by leading off with the famous epitaph of Simonides (*Wanderer, kommst Du nach Sparta . . .*). The opening of the chapter continues the theme:

> These verses tell us of the heroism of the defenders of Thermopylae. They have been known ever since as a hymn of praise to bravery, loyalty, and obedience. But no one will ever carve them in stone in honor of the martyrdom of German 6th Army in Stalingrad, in this city on the Volga. Nor will anyone ever raise a cross or memorial over the vanished traces of the German soldiers who died there, hungry and frozen.[36]

More prosaically, Manstein defended the sacrifice of 6th Army as a way of diverting so much Soviet strength away from Army Group Don while he scrambled to rebuild the shattered front.

In fact, both sides of his argument—the poetic and the operational— are difficult to take seriously. To use the language of chess for which the field marshal had such affection, a modern field army is not a pawn, a minor piece to be sacrificed for position. As one German source put it, "an army of 300,000 men is not a machine gun nest or a bunker (*kein MG-Nest oder Bunker*) whose defenders may under certain circumstances have to be sacrificed for the whole."[37] Losing a field army is a catastrophe, not a triumph to be celebrated or a tragedy to be memorialized in epic or song.

In the end, Manstein had little effect on the failed Stalingrad relief. The Red Army was responsible for Stalingrad. It is always useful to remember the old nugget that "the enemy gets a vote," and in December 1942, the Red Army was definitely exercising its right. Fresh from smashing the Romanians in Uranus, the Soviets would launch a second great offensive in December. They now decided to reach further up the Don with a massive assault against the Italian 8th Army. It is possible to see the new Soviet doctrine of "consecutive operations" at work here, one that had emerged from the theoretical work of the interwar era. Its departure point was the idea that modern armies had grown so large, and their recuperative powers so great, that it would rarely be possible to destroy them with one grand offensive. Rather, it was necessary to subject them to blow after blow, to smash them and to keep smashing them, never letting up the pressure or allowing the defenders to recover their equilibrium. It is also possible to see a much older and much simpler notion here, one that is probably as old as warfare itself: the ruthless identification and exploitation of an adversary's weak spot.

The original Soviet conception, Operation Saturn, aimed big. It included a concentric drive by the three armies of the Southwestern Front (right to left, 1st Guards Army, 3rd Guards Army, and 5th Tank Army) against the 8th Italian Army along the Don, as well as against *Armee-Abteilung Hollidt*. Once the assault formations had pierced the Axis front and reached the Donets River crossing at Kamensk, Saturn would insert a second echelon (2nd Guards Army) for a drive to the south, seizing Rostov on the Don and choking off Army Group A, still at this point far down in the Caucasus. The entire German southern wing would thus be endangered, not simply the 6th Army in Stalingrad.

Unfortunately for that bold operational prospectus, the Soviets had to downsize. The incredible scale of the pocket in Stalingrad, estimated first at 90,000 men and then rapidly revised upward to over 200,000, forced the Soviet command into some hard choices. The second echelon now fell away, with the 2nd Army committed to the reduction of the Stalingrad pocket, and Saturn became "Little Saturn," a much shallower envelopment of the Italian 8th Army and *Armee-Abteilung Hollidt*, with the assault formations concentrating on the destruction of their immediate operational targets, rather than preparing for a deeper drive south toward Rostov.[38]

The foreshortened operation opened on December 16 and remains one of the great operational-level successes of the war. No student of the conflict should be surprised that the Italian army failed to withstand a great armored onslaught. The same dynamic that had led to the demise of the Romanians was at work here: a largely nonmotorized force attempting to hold an unfortified position along a meandering riverbank against a highly mobile, heavily armored enemy. One of the army's four corps, in fact, consisted of *Alpini*, good mountain infantry now tasked to defend a battle space as flat as a pancake.

All that being said, the speed and totality of the Italian collapse along the Don is still shocking and speaks of something different: a complete breakdown in morale and cohesion in the weeks leading up to the offensive. There was a general panic, and many units simply gave up without any fighting at all. The Soviet assault penetrated at will, linked up behind the lines, and surrounded and destroyed major portions of the Italian line one by one. The German XXIX Corps, holding the right flank of the army but consisting of Italian divisions, also found itself thrown into headlong flight, and would spend the next two weeks as a kind of "movable pocket," constantly threatened with encirclement by Soviet armored columns but heading steadily south. It would finally reach the safety of friendly lines on December 28, after what one German officer called "a true Odyssey," along with 5,000 of its original complement of nearly 40,000 men.[39]

Most worrisome to the Germans had been a series of deep penetrations by individual Soviet mobile formations. General V. M. Badanov's 24th Tank Corps, for example, had broken into the open, lunged 150 miles south to Tatsinskaya by Christmas Eve, and actually overran a Luftwaffe airfield there—always a signal achievement in this war. For hours, Badanov's T-34s drove back and forth across the runways, shooting up grounded aircraft, lightly armed Luftwaffe security formations, and supplies at will. Some sources describe over 300 German aircraft destroyed, an incredible and probably inflated figure, but with Tatsinskaya serving as one of the principal fields for the Stalingrad airlift, German losses were certainly high. Unfortunately, Badanov's great lunge had left him out of contact with supporting formations. He wound up surrounded by various German reserves and *Alarmeinheiten*, and the subsequent fighting would see most of his command destroyed.[40] Nevertheless, the episode had terrified the German command at all levels, raising the specter of waking up one morning to find Soviet tanks in Rostov.

Despite Badanov's misadventure, Little Saturn had been another disaster for the Germans. The destruction of the Italians had torn a huge gap in the German defensive position, Army Groups B and Don were

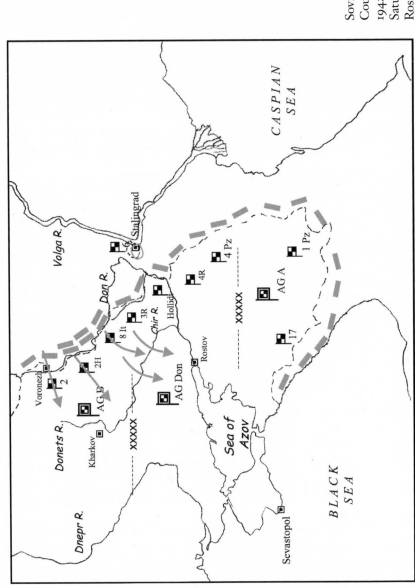

Soviet Winter
Counteroffensives,
1942–43: Little
Saturn, Ostrogozhk-
Rossosh, Gallop, Star

no longer in contact with one another, and Soviet tank corps roamed in open space between them. Moreover, by forcing Manstein to redeploy 6th Panzer Division to the west, Little Saturn meant the end of Winter Storm. The year ended much as the last one had, with German forces on the run in the east. Manstein's operational skills notwithstanding, perhaps in some situations, there is simply nothing to be done.

The Backhand Blow

Nor did the New Year bring much relief. The same operational dynamic was at work through what was a dark January for the Wehrmacht.[41] The Soviets clearly held the initiative, what the Germans call the "Gesetz der Handelns." On January 13, the Red Army struck a third time, further still up the Don, as Voronezh Front (General F. I. Golikov) launched the Ostrogozhsk–Rossosh operation. Targeting the Hungarian 2nd Army (General Gusztáv Jány), it managed to do the same thing to the undergunned Hungarians that Uranus had done to the Romanians and Little Saturn to the Italians: erase it from the order of battle. Once again, there is no reason to see why it should have been otherwise. Jány's army consisted of nine light divisions, each containing only two regiments; they were holding impossibly long frontages, and they were poorly equipped, especially with antitank weapons. One Hungarian historian describes 2nd Army's line on the Don as "merely a reinforced observation post on the river, not a sturdy defense at all."[42] Individual units here or there made a stand, but there were also mass surrenders and panic-stricken columns steaming westward in temperatures of −45°C. Just two weeks later, on January 29, the Southwestern Front (General N. F. Vatutin) launched a fourth major blow across the Donets River and into the Donets basin (the *Donbas*) itself, code named Operation Gallop.[43] Finally, on February 2, the Voronezh Front launched Operation Star on the extreme right wing of the Southern Front. It smashed into the German 2nd Army (General Hans von Salmuth), by now utterly threadbare as a result of the number of formations it had surrendered to the emergency to the south, with great force. Exceeding all expectations, Star drove back the defenders, not Italians or Romanians or Hungarians this time, but a core formation of the *Ostheer*, threatening 2nd Army with a Stalingrad-style encirclement and reconquering the major cities of Kursk, Belgorod, and Kharkov.[44] Red Army expert David Glantz counts no fewer than "eight separate operations conducted simultaneously or consecutively by the Red Amy's Bryansk, Voronezh, Southwestern, and Southern Fronts" from January to early March 1943. Soviet historians have labeled all of these operations collectively as a "strategic offensive,"[45] with the Red Army lunging forward some 350 miles and opening up a 300-mile-wide gap between Army Group Center and the tattered remnants of Army Group B to its immediate south.[46]

Manstein's impact on all this had essentially been nil. He had successfully managed chaos, shifting units hither and yon as emergencies arose, integrating the meager reinforcements coming up to the front, and attempting to talk some operational sense into the high command— that is, Hitler—regarding the need to restore a degree of maneuver to the front. In this quest, however, he was aided immeasurably by the chief of the General Staff, General Kurt Zeitzler, a true believer in educating the army along National Socialist lines, but also a man of undeniable operational acumen.[47]

Zeitzler had his first success at the end of 1942 when Hitler finally consented to a withdrawal of Army Group A from the Caucasus.[48] This was good news. The two constituent formations, the 17th Army in the west (General Richard Ruoff) and the 1st Panzer in the east (General Eberhard von Mackensen) would now be available for mobile operations against the onrushing Soviets. Zeitzler's sense of accomplishment diminished the next day when he received new orders: rather than evacuate the Caucasus altogether, Army Group A would withdraw to a so-called Kuban bridgehead, perhaps with an eye to renewing the offensive into the Caucasus in 1943. In the course of the retreat, those orders would be changed again. Now only one of the armies, the 17th, would hold the Kuban, while the 1st Panzer would leave the Caucasus to rejoin its sister formations in the Ukraine.

The retreat of Army Group A from a potential tomb was an epic of sorts, and it deserves more attention that it usually receives in the histories. For the 1st Panzer Army especially, the drama was intense. Deployed deep along the Terek River, it was over 350 miles from the Rostov gateway, and safety. It had to negotiate a long, hard road, bitter cold temperatures, an enemy nipping at its heels the entire way, and the desperation that comes in situations where failure is not an option. Behind the gripping narrative, however, lay a great deal of care and planning. Kleist and his army commanders had been planning for a retreat in secret even as Hitler was remaining obstinate and refusing his permission. The early lead time allowed the army group to construct four great intermediate positions (*grosse Zwischenlinien*) for the retreat even before it started: along the Kuma River, along the Kalaus, on both sides of Armavir, and at Maikop. Timing was also crucial, with the 1st Panzer Army having to move before the 17th Army and swing back in a great arc to the northwest. Needless to say, liaison and contact between the two armies was crucial, and if the Soviets managed to drive a wedge between them, both were probably doomed.

Things started out well enough, and at least one account has German infantry singing to the tune of a well-known marching song,

> Es geht alles vorüber
> Es geht alles vorbei.
> Zurück gehts im Winter
> Und vorwärts im Mai.
>
> (Everything comes to an end,
> Everything passes away.
> We're moving back in the winter
> But we'll come back strong in May.)[49]

By the time the 1st Panzer Army reached the Kuma line by January 10, however, the singing had stopped. Losses were rising, with frostbite being deadlier than enemy attacks. The 50th Infantry Division (part of LII Corps, one of the army's three constituent formations) was soon down to about a quarter of its allotted strength. Supply was a constant worry; the 1st Panzer Army was theoretically falling back on its base, but the base itself was receding under the weight of Soviet attacks. The artillery had a bare fraction of its normal supply of shells, and the situation only got worse after Soviet air attacks destroyed the last great munitions depot at Mineralny Wody. The retreat continued, however. The Soviets were having just as many problems with maneuver and supply, and the mud, snowstorms, and ice probably served to hinder their attacks more than the German retreat. By January 22, the 1st Panzer Army had reached the Armavir position and the 17th Army stood along the Kuban on both sides of Krasnodar, the retreat had come to an end, and General Kleist received an entirely deserved field marshal's baton.[50]

With the retreat of the 1st Panzer Army from the Caucasus at the end of January, what had been a swirling, even chaotic, campaign was beginning to sort itself out into more recognizable patterns. From our perspective today, it is possible to see signs that all these Soviet offensives were reaching what Clausewitz had called the "culmination point," the moment at which offensive power begins to wear down, friction reasserts itself, and the machine eventually stops.[51] Supplies of all sorts were running low, the tanks corps were losing their cutting edge, and machines and men were nearing exhaustion. It had been an amazing ride for the Red Army, one that had started on the Volga, reconquered the immense bend of the Don River, and was now hurtling across the Donets toward the Dnepr. It had been one of the most successful military campaigns in modern history. What David Glantz calls "the ravages of time and distance" were beginning to show, however, and actual fighting strength was probably half of what it had been at the start of the winter offensives.[52]

While the Soviets were wearing down, the German line was finally starting to solidify. The various *Armee-Abteilungen* may still have been short of manpower, heavy artillery and equipment, and administrative personnel, but they had at least been working together for months now, and familiarity had bred a sense of confidence. With *Armee-Abteilung Hollidt* in place of 6th Army, *Armee-Abteilung Fretter-Pico* where the Italian 8th Army used to be, and *Armee-Abteilung Lanz* forming a new mobile command in the Kharkov region, the Germans had at least restored a semblance of a line. Adding to the fresh sense of well-being was the long-awaited arrival of the new II S.S. Panzer Corps under General Paul Hausser. Its three Panzer divisions, 1st S.S. (*Leibstandarte Adolf Hitler*), 2nd S.S. (*Das Reich*), and 3rd S.S. (*Totenkopf*), were bursting with manpower, new equipment, and self-confidence.

That sense of swagger took a hit early on; the corps arrived piecemeal and was thrown into the path of Operation Star, the lunge westward by Voronezh Front. Fighting under *Armee-Abteilung Lanz* and ordered to hold Kharkov till the last man, S.S. commander General Paul Hausser took one look at the situation maps, with Soviet tank corps about to bypass him north and south of the city, and decided to skedaddle. His disobedience went unpunished. Someone had to pay for the loss of Kharkov, however, and Hitler decided to dismiss the regular army commander on the scene, General Hubert Lanz, on the grounds that he had sanctioned Hausser's withdrawal. The *Armee-Abteilung* now came under the command of General Werner Kempf (and thus became *Armee-Abteilung Kempf*).[53]

This combination of Soviet overstretch and a barely perceptible German revival led Manstein to devise a new operational conception. He was nothing if not operationally minded. First, because there were no more reinforcements coming out from the homeland, something would have to be done to free up troops within the theater itself. Manstein looked to the immense "balcony" occupied by *Armee-Abteilung Hollidt*,

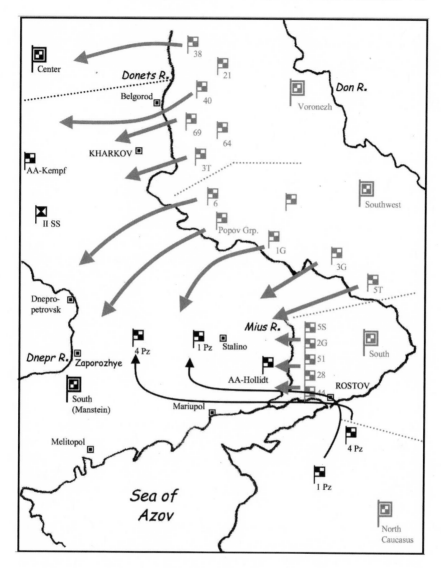

The "Rochade": Manstein's Operational Art (February 1943)

Armee-Abteilung Fretter-Pico, and the 1st and 4th Panzer Armies, all currently deployed far into the eastern bend of the Donets and lower Don rivers. This entire position, including the eastern half of the "Donbas" itself, would have to be abandoned in favor of a much straighter, and thus shorter, line to the east, along the Mius River. It was not unfamiliar. In fact, it was same line the Wehrmacht had held during the winter of 1941–1942. Holding a shorter line would free up troops for more mobile operations.

But where would those operations take place? Here, Manstein opted for a typically bold solution. He had always been a gambler, and he took a gambler's delight in a risky bet that paid off big. His plan for the 1940 campaign had been filled with dangerous gambits: the feint from the north by Army Group B, the risky drive by almost all of the Panzer formations through the Ardennes forest by Rundstedt's Army Group A, the bold lunge clear across the rear of the Allied armies further north in Belgium. That plan could have fallen apart on a multitude of occasions. His operational solution this time was no less daring. Borrowing again from the vocabulary of chess, Manstein envisioned a *Rochade*, a "castling maneuver," with the formations on the extreme right wing of the German position—the 1st and 4th Panzer Armies—now being shifted to the extreme left. Once they had arrived, they would launch a counteroffensive into the spent Soviet assault formations whose commanders were still driving them relentlessly to the west. It would be what Manstein liked to call a *Schlag aus der Nachhand*, a "backhand blow" that was most effective once the enemy had committed himself, had driven far forward of his base, and had exhausted his energy and supplies.[54]

After sending these proposals to Hitler and the high command of the army (OKH), Manstein received a summons to meet with the Führer on February 6 at the East Prussian headquarters in Rastenburg. Although Manstein painted the conference in epic terms in *Verlorene Siege*,[55] a battle of wills between two men dedicated to radically different visions of war fighting, there was a synergy between the two by this point in the war, between the operator and the advocate of a *Halte-Strategie*.[56] Hitler, for all his irrationality in other areas, had probably been right to demand a no-retreat policy up till now. A retreat by immobile forces in the midst of winter made no sense and would almost certainly have resulted in higher German losses than the catastrophic ones already suffered. But Manstein was also right: the time had come to maneuver, to restore "operational mobility" (*bewegliche Operationsführung*), and to fight *Bewegungskrieg*, the kind of war in which German superiority in both leadership and troops could reassert itself.[57] Hitler knew it. Less than a week after the 6th Army's final surrender at Stalingrad, the Führer was in the midst of what we might call a teachable moment.

There was no real struggle here. Although Hitler did put up a fight to Manstein's suggestions, especially the need to abandon the eastern Donbas, it was essentially half-hearted. There was the by now typical haggling over minutiae and statistics, and a desultory argument over the quality of the coal from the region. Hitler wanted to use the II S.S. Panzer Corps in a direct counterattack on Kharkov; Manstein preferred to let the Soviets come and strike them when they were spent. Anyone who has read the stenographic minutes of the Führer's conferences from this period will not see any of this as particularly obstructionist. Compared to what General Zeitzler and the rest had to endure on a daily basis, it was fairly small potatoes.[58] Even Manstein's incredible suggestion that he elbow Hitler aside and take over the day-to-day command of the war in the east failed to get much of a rise.

We must also recognize that Manstein himself was not particularly pleased with what he had to say. He was not happy about having to retreat either. He really did consider his Soviet adversary to be hopelessly inept, especially in terms of generalship, and there is a certain note of wounded pride in his memoirs about having to surrender territory voluntarily.[59] There really was no choice, however, and both men agreed. Manstein came away from the Rastenburg meeting with what he wanted: Hitler's approval for the new operation. A *Rochade* it would be, although Manstein was concerned that by this point the decision had come too late.

The principal threat now was Operation Gallop, the great Soviet operation in the Donbas. The Southwestern Front—6th Army (General F. M. Kharitonov), 1st Guards Army (General D. D. Lelyushenko), and Mobile Group Popov, a prototype tank army under the command of General M. M. Popov and consisting of four tank corps and supporting formations—had leaped over the Donets and was now driving west and south at top speed. Juicy operational targets abounded. Reaching the coast of the Sea of Azov at Mariupol or Taganrog, for example, would cut off all German forces still deployed to the east, the 1st and 4th Panzer Armies and *Armee-Abteilung Hollidt*. Even worse would result from Soviet forces crossing the Dnepr River. Seizing the crossings over the great river at Dnepropetrovsk, Zaporozhye, or Kremenchug would cut off supply to the entire German southern wing, potentially turning an operational-level victory into a strategic triumph—a "Super-Stalingrad" of sorts.[60] The two Panzer armies had to hurry, a problem made even worse by weather: they were moving along the coast, areas where the thaw had already set in and the mud had arrived with a vengeance. Soviet forces far to the north were still driving smoothly along frozen, hard roads.

There was therefore a certain frantic quality to German preparations, and so hurried was the planning that the operation never really received a name. There was, however, unity of command, with Manstein's Army Group Don renamed Army Group South and Army Groups A and B dissolved. Manstein now had something he had wanted since November: theater command. By mid-February, the pullback from the Don–Donets "balcony" had succeeded, and *Armee-Abteilung Hollidt* had retreated into the *Maulwurfstellung*, the "mole position" behind the Mius. *Armee-Abteilung Fretter-Pico*, now reduced in status to XXX Corps, deployed to its left, defending along the middle Donets up to Slavyansk. Using this position as an operational shield, Mackensen's 1st Panzer Army, still weary from its long trek out of the Caucasus, came up into the line on the left. Unfortunately, with Soviet forces still hurtling southward, it had to go into battle almost immediately, with predictable results. The III Panzer Corps, whose 3rd and 7th Panzer Divisions had probably 40 tanks between them, drove north from Stalino, ran into heavy opposition, and soon bogged down. The same happened to its left, where XXXX Panzer Corps (11th Panzer Division, 333rd Infantry Division, and elements of S.S. Division *Wiking*) went into the attack without a great deal of preparation and ran into hard-driving Soviet armored columns coming down from Lissichansk and Slavyansk. Once again, there was a certain amount of panic within German command circles as Mobile Group Popov made a clean breakthrough into the operational depth of the German position.[61] Much like Badanov's experience in Little Saturn, however, Popov eventually found himself isolated at Krasnoarmeiskoe and under concentric attack by virtually all of the XXXX Panzer Corps.

By February 21, the 4th Panzer Army had arrived in the theater and fallen in on the 1st Panzer Army's left, the final step in Manstein's *Rochade*. The entire array was facing almost due north, with the line along the Mius then falling off and forming a right angle to it. General Hermann Hoth's men had moved hundreds of miles in four days (February 16–19), and they too were exhausted. Nevertheless, both German Panzer armies were in hand and concentrated for action, and the problem of supply had become much easier to solve now that the formations were not lying 400 miles to the east over two major rivers. Moreover, by this time, the operation had taken on an amazing shape, as strange in its way as Operation Blue in the previous fall. As Soviet forces faced more and more opposition on the road south, they had begun to slide to their right. Mobile Group Popov was already surrounded, but the rest of the Southwestern Front was motoring in open space in the 100-mile gap between Slavyansk and Kharkov, driving west and southwest and heading for the Dnepr: the 6th Army on the right and the 1st Guards Army on the left. Two more tank corps, the 25th and 1st Guards, were driving on Zaporozhye, the headquarters of both Army Group Don and the 4th Air Fleet. With no major German formations between them and their targets, it must have seemed like a done deal. Meanwhile, sliding alongside the Soviets to the south, the Germans were desperately trying to extend their line to the left, or west. There was a race on, and the winner was open to question.

In the end, the Germans would win the race, and it makes a certain sense: they were falling back on their supply bases while the Soviets were running away from theirs. Beyond that general notion, however, or the Clausewitzian idea of an inevitable "culmination point" to all offensive operations, there was another aspect of this campaign that was peculiar to the Soviet military experience. "Deep battle" held as many dangers as opportunities for the Red Army. "Deep" had become a buzzword to this generation of Soviet officers, and buzzwords can be deadly. Far from achieving some new breakthrough into a scientifically calculated operational art, Soviet formations in this period tended to advance until they collapsed from losses, from lack of supply and replacements, and perhaps from a simple sense of exhaustion.[62]

Deep battle, in other words, implied a tendency to overreach, to underestimate enemy strength, and to overestimate the degree to which deep strikes would "paralyze the foe"—whatever that was supposed to mean. Joseph Stalin, General G. K. Zhukov, and the Stavka alike had overreached badly in 1941, they had reprised that mistake in the disaster in front of Kharkov in May 1942, and they were about to do it one more time. This would be the second winter in a row that the Soviet high command managed to conjure up a German enemy who was ripe for the picking, and the second year in a row that they would be shocked. Now that military history has finally begun to dispense with enthusiasm for any special German genius for war and to view the Wehrmacht's operations in a colder and more rational light, it would be a tragedy to substitute any special respect for Soviet war making. It was extraordinarily clumsy, wasteful of lives and manpower, and dangerous to its own men, as its huge casualty statistics would bear out for the rest of the war.[63]

As a result, there was never really a moment in this operation that can legitimately be named a "turning point," one in which the momentum shifted and the Soviets suddenly realized that they were beaten. One moment the 6th and 1st Guards Armies were driving west, riding high, and aiming for the Dnepr. On February 19, Soviet armored columns seized the town of Sinelnikovo, cutting the main east–west railroad from Dnepropetrovsk to Stalino, halting all railroad traffic and placing the entire German southern wing out of supply. Hitler himself was visiting Manstein's headquarters in Zaporozhye on the east, unprotected side of the Dnepr at the time. The news that T-34s were only 50 kilometers away led to a hurried evacuation, with the Führer being trundled onto a plane and flown off for his own safety. The Soviets didn't know how close they had come to bagging the enemy *supremo*, of course, but they did know a number of other things. Intelligence was flowing into front and army headquarters alike of massive German troop movements to the west, which all levels of Soviet command from Vatutin on down interpreted as another sign of a wild and desperate German flight for the Dnepr crossings.[64] Army commanders urged their men on with redoubled urgency. The enemy was on the run, and on the ropes.

As it drove toward the Dnepr, the Red Army was riding high. Then suddenly it was crushed. On February 21, Hoth's 4th Panzer Army launched its counterattack. Two convergent thrusts—one from the south spearheaded by the LVII Corps on the left and the XXXXVIII Panzer Corps on the right, and one from the region of Poltava in the northwest by II S.S. Panzer Corps—caught the spearheads of the Soviet 6th and 1st Guards Armies completely by surprise, took them in front, flanks, and rear, and scattered them. Friendly casualties, at least for these few days, were minimal; Soviet casualties were nearly total in terms of matériel and high enough in men. And no wonder: formation after formation was, quite literally, running out of fuel just at the moment that the German counterattack struck. Although in many ways a classic expression of the German way of war, *Bewegungskrieg* and "concentric operations," there was no real *Kesselschlacht*, no huge haul of prisoners. The Soviet front simply exploded, and there were nowhere near enough German formations to draw a ring around most of them.

Over the course of the next few weeks, the Germans kept up the momentum of their drive to the north. Mackensen's 1st Panzer Army ground forward to the line of the Donets, although the Soviets managed to hold a few sturdy bridgeheads south of the river. To Mackensen's left, armored spearheads of the II S.S. and XXXXVIII Panzer Corps had the Soviets on the run, and there seemed for a brief moment to have been a breakdown in enemy command and control. Suddenly it seemed as if it were 1941 again, or perhaps even 1940. There was even a recrudescence of the oldest Prussian–German tradition of all, the

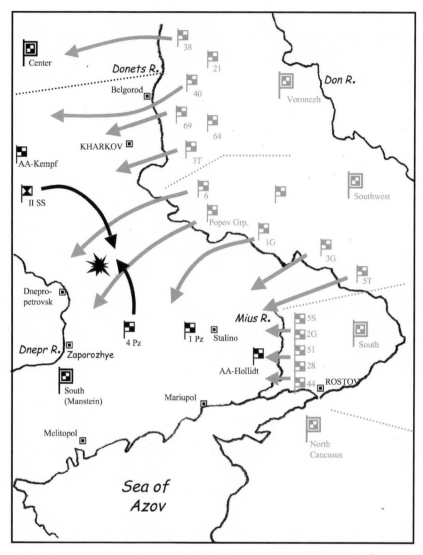

Schlag aus der Nachhand: Manstein's Backhand Blow (February 1943)

"independence of the subordinate commander." As S.S. General Paul Hausser drove his corps on Kharkov, he received explicit orders from Manstein to avoid anything that smacked of positional or street fighting in the city. Kharkov could be taken by a quick coup (*Handstreich*) if the opportunity presented itself, but it was not to become a trap.[65] The ugly memory of Stalingrad was still too fresh, the wounds still open.

Looping around to the north in an elegant little maneuver, II S.S. Panzer fought its way into Kharkov from the northeast and cleared the city after three days of gritty fighting (March 12–14). It was not a trap, but it certainly wasn't a coup.

From there, it was another short hop north to Belgorod, which the Germans took on March 23. By this point, the thaw had come, the mud had arrived, and no one was going anywhere. A planned coordinating strike by the neighboring 2nd Army (part of Army Group Center) never materialized, a sign of how badly that formation had suffered from Soviet attacks in Operation Star. The proposed target of the 2nd Army, the industrial city of Kursk and the attendant salient in the line around it, remained firmly in Soviet hands.

Conclusion: Manstein and the Limits of Genius

We began this account with a discussion of the role that personality plays, not only in modern military operations, but in our historical analysis of them. The Donets–Kharkov campaign of early 1943 would seem to be a testament to Manstein's genius, and that is almost always how it has appeared in the literature. The field marshal had shown a deft touch, first in remaining calm when it looked like the entire front was about to collapse around him, then in keeping his ends and means clearly aligned, and finally in remembering that the campaign had to end with a maneuver-based counterattack and that it was senseless to slug it out toe to toe with an enemy who could vastly outproduce him. Above all, his timing had been perfect—rare on the operational level.

Yet Manstein's genius is ultimately an unsatisfying explanation for what happened along the banks of the Donets in early 1943. He was not a completely free agent but the product of a long-standing military tradition. In a brief analysis of the Kharkov campaign by two soldier-scholars of the German *Bundeswehr*, Friedhelm Klein and Karl-Heinz Frieser, the authors argue in conventional fashion for the importance of the commander: "The transformation of an apparently unavoidable catastrophe on the Donets in the winter of 1943 into a victory is due not least to the personality of the military commander: Field Marshall von Manstein." They go on to add an important proviso, however: "Like few others," they argue, "he embodied the traditional thought of the German General Staff."[66] Notions of the "war of movement," or of war as a "free creative activity,"[67] or of the "independence of the subordinate commander"—these were concepts that were decades, perhaps even centuries, old. In their text, Frieser and Klein reproduce the entire operational plan for Manstein's February 21 counterattack, and it is a model of traditional Prussian–German brevity. It consists of a single sentence, which the officers on the spot would have to interpret, internalize, and apply as best they saw fit:

> Army Group South defends the *Maulwurfstellung* along the Mius and northwards to Slavyansk, strikes the enemy in the gap between 1st Panzer Army and *Armee-Abteilung Lanz* (*Kempf*) with 4th Panzer Army, and covers the deep flank and the attack of 4th Panzer Army in the Poltava–Achtyrka region with *Armee-Abteilung Lanz* (*Kempf*).[68]

It was a simple order, but one that set into motion three field armies containing no fewer than one million men.

Frieser and Klein are correct to set Manstein's achievement into context and perspective. As they point out, even the mechanics of the operation itself were hardly new. Since the 1880s, German staff officers had been practicing the rapid shifting of armies to ward off threats that might arise suddenly or surprisingly. Germany's strategic situation in the heart of Europe, ringed by enemies or potential ones, demanded it. The *Kaiserreich* even had its own exposed "balcony" against the Russians, East Prussia, a sector where a mere passive defense would never suffice, and where a vigorous counterblow was the only means of protecting the province. They had already been practicing the *Rochade* and the "backhand blow" for decades, when Erich von Manstein was but a boy. In 1914, two of them, Field Marshal Paul von Hindenburg and his chief of staff, General Erich Ludendorff, had carried out a highly successful operation near Tannenberg that bore more than a passing similarity to Manstein's successful *retour offensive* on the Donets.[69]

Should we not go deeper here, however? If Manstein's strengths were actually those of the officer corps to which he belonged and the operational school that trained him, can we not say the same thing about his weaknesses? The simplistic equating of war with mobile operations, the absence of any sense of politics, the naive belief that somehow these extraordinarily expensive and bloody military campaigns might add up to a strategic victory—these too were the legacy of the German General Staff.

Finally, is it possible to see Manstein, like all the commanders on both sides in this campaign, as being caught up in webs that he could not perceive? As the victorious general in the final phase of the fighting, he had fought his traditional way of war to perfection, and in the process he managed to do what had seemed to be impossible: he had reformed his front, torn open by the destruction of an entire field army at Stalingrad. No account of this campaign, no matter how brief it might be, omits the trope that Manstein had restored the front "to approximately where it had stood at the start of the 1942 campaign."[70] There was something approaching stupefaction even within the hard-boiled ranks of the General Staff. "One hesitates even now to believe it," one of them wrote at the time.[71] "We're in Kharkov again!" exulted a headline in the glossy magazine, *Die Wehrmacht*,[72] and the same issue of the journal crowed that Manstein's blow represented a "turning point in the winter war."[73]

Give him his due. Mastering one crisis after another, and finally with Soviet tanks knocking on the very door of the Dnepr River crossings, Manstein had engineered a dramatic revival, smashing the enemy in front of him and thrusting forward all the way back to the Donets. In the process, however, he had driven his army up to a long, meandering river line that it would not be able to hold in the coming year. Despite all the hyperbole heaped upon Manstein and the soldiers of the Wehrmacht for the victory at Kharkov, it was not a victory at all; at best, it was more like a "brief glimpse of victory."[74] Manstein knew it, the high command knew it, and together they would attempt the expedient of the Kursk offensive in the summer of 1943—just four months hence—in order to do something about it. *Bewegungskrieg*, in other words, led the Wehrmacht not to triumph in early 1943, but to the abyss.

As for the Soviet commanders, they too had remained in character throughout the winter campaign. After their initial, dramatic successes against the 6th Army and the armies of the Axis allies, they doggedly adhered to their new doctrine. Even as their momentum began to lag, they had driven on until they imploded. These were commanders who recognized no limits, and who certainly didn't seem bothered by Clausewitzian notions of a "culmination point." Their faith in "deep battle" made them dangerous at the start of their offensives, but it had eventually proven disastrous. The casualties included Badanov's 24th Tank Corps, Mobile Group Popov, and eventually most of the 1st Guards Army and 6th Army alike.

The winter campaign of 1943, far from serving as a display of individual or collective genius, offers us instead the fascinating spectacle of two armies trapped, like helpless prey, in the talons of their own doctrine.

3

The Limits of Fighting Power:
Triumph and Disaster in Tunisia, 1943

Introduction

How easy is decision making in wartime? Historians can make it sound easy, and the essence of military history over the years has involved critiquing command decisions. We like to label this decision mistaken and that one correct, point out how the errors of this commander determined the outcome of the battle, and how the genius of that one changed the course of the war. Although it is an easy handle for grasping complex events, it is also a vast oversimplification of the nearly intractable problems of modern warfare. Military professionals—the better ones, at least—are more likely to think in terms of the "operational problem," a battlefield conundrum in which there are two or more logical alternatives but no tidy or perfect solution.

With that in mind, let us transport ourselves back to the dawn of 1943. The Allies have lost the race to Tunis and are gearing up for a major campaign in 1943 to clear their Axis adversary out of the Tunisian bridgehead. Before they can do that, however, their commander, General Dwight D. Eisenhower, has to make a decision. Were we able to listen to his thoughts, they might well have gone something like this.[1]

What a rotten time. He normally loved the holidays. Then again, he'd never had to spend them in Tunisia before. Sunny Africa? Where do people come up with this stuff? It hadn't stopped raining for weeks, and it wasn't going to end anytime soon. That last trip up to the front . . . he thought he'd never get the mud off. It was time to face facts. This campaign was over. No one was going anywhere. He was stuck.

No use blaming the weather, though. He'd been studying war for a long time, and the first thing you learn: both sides have the same weather.

This was worse than the weather. The men didn't fight, the tanks were worthless—and don't even get him started on those tank destroyers. Georgie was right. The men were bad and the officers worse. And the British—insufferable.

Then there was the delicate matter of the supreme commander, the "untested" commander. If he read that phrase one more time in the press, he was going to scream. Well, they should be happy now. He was no longer "untested." He'd been tested all right. The trouble was, no one was all that happy with the results. That thunderbolt he'd gotten from Marshall, telling him to "give your complete attention to the battle in Tunisia." What did he think he'd been doing? Did they think he'd been happy with the way things had turned out? It had gotten so every time there was a knock on his door, he thought it might be his successor. He wouldn't be surprised; neither would a lot of other people.

He turned to the map on the table. He felt bone tired. Whether this was his last week as commander or not, he had work to do. The first call of the next campaign, he thought to himself: where to deploy for the winter. There was a fairly simple calculus at work here, with two obvious choices, two major mountain ranges that defined the Tunisian theater. The first was a western mountain range—the Western (or "Grand") Dorsal—from the northeast to the southwest. The second was an eastern one (the Eastern Dorsal) from the north–south, meeting together in the north to form an inverted Y.

Ike thought about it. It was a simple problem: A or B. But there was so much to think about. Perhaps he should deploy on the Western Dorsal, the "textbook solution," as they liked to call it, with the steepest mountains and thus the most easily defended. The trouble was, the drive on Tunis had petered out just short of its objective. His boys were already deep inside eastern Tunisia. Choosing the Western Dorsal meant going back and giving up his hard-won forward positions, sacrificing ground that would have to be fought for again. It would be secure, but Ike knew that they hadn't all come to Tunisia for security; they had come to seize the place and destroy the enemy forces holding it. He looked more carefully at the mountain line of the Eastern Dorsal. Staying here meant keeping as close as possible to Tunis. It would also hem in the Germans, reducing their maneuver room and guarding against a hook around the southern Allied flank. What a nightmare, Ike thought. The Allies held only a shallow series of coastal enclaves in Africa, so if the Germans broke into the rear—well, that would be that.

He rubbed his chin thoughtfully. Forward deployment sounded good. It would brief well to Marshall and to FDR, show them Ike hadn't lost his nerve. There were risks. He measured the front: a 250-mile line. Units would be thinned out beyond reasonable limits, with no real theater reserve to back them up. Huge stretches of the line would have to be held by the French XIX Corps. He liked their commanders personally—respect for the French was part of the West Point experience. But this was a colonial force, poorly equipped, undersupplied, and liable to come apart in intense fighting. There was nothing to be done about that. Perhaps he could spare a unit or two to backstop them.

One more thing suddenly occurred to him: holding on the Eastern Dorsal also meant bringing forward the U.S. II Corps and inserting it into the line on the right. Green troops—but, he hoped, a bit less green than in the previous season. He still had faith in the corps commander, Fredendall. He'd heard some complaints about him lately, but then again, he was hearing complaints about everybody nowadays. Lloyd was tough, a cowboy.[2] He'd whip 'em into shape.

When all was said and done, of course, Eisenhower chose the Eastern Dorsal. It was a gutsy move, it has not gone uncriticized, and it nearly proved disastrous, but this was a problem without a perfect solution. The armchair generals among us can spend the rest of our lives chewing over the whys and wherefores of this one before finally making our decision. Eisenhower had about a week to make his.

The Tunisian Campaign: Opening Moves and the Great Retreat

By January 1943, the Tunisian front had stabilized. For all his skills at managing an often fractious coalition, Eisenhower has typically drawn fire from historians for his caution and lack of drive as an operational commander. To say that he was a careful, conservative battle manager rather than a cut-and-thrust operational swordsman is to state the obvious. This time he made the bold choice by opting to hold the forward position in Tunisia, a 250-mile front along the Eastern Dorsal. The British 1st Army, under General Anderson, held the portion opposite Tunis in the north. By now, Anderson had the V Corps (General Charles Allfrey) under his command. The corps contained two complete divisions, the 78th Infantry and the 6th Armoured. To the right of

V Corps, opposite Kairouan, lay the French XIX Corps. General Alphonse Juin was in overall command of French troops in Tunisia, and General Louis-Marie Koeltz was in operational command of the corps itself. It too contained two divisions by now, the Tunis and the Morocco.[3] The only major change that Eisenhower had to implement that winter was to bring U.S. II Corps (Lieutenant General Lloyd Fredendall) up to the front and insert it into the line. Fredendall's two divisions, 1st Infantry Division (Major General Terry Allen) and 1st Armoured Division (Major General Orlando Ward), would stand guard in the south—that is, on the extreme right of the Allied line in Tunisia. It was a logical decision, firmly grounded in the terrain, the overall strategic situation, and above all in Eisenhower's refusal to relinquish hard-won gains during the previous campaign.[4]

There was logic aplenty to the new deployment, if no particular spark of creativity or daring. It divided the front into three sectors, each correlating to one of the three Allies, and placed two divisions apiece in each sector. It recalls Napoleon's perhaps apocryphal comment that such an even, linear deployment was fine if the goal was to prevent smuggling rather than fight and win a campaign of maneuver. To be fair, however, Eisenhower had dressed his line in classic style, and that was a welcome change from the operational chaos of the race to Tunis, which saw battalions of varying nationalities plugged in as interchangeable parts in the course of the fighting.

Despite that advantage, the forward deployment led to a tough operational situation for the Allies. The winter of 1942–1943 would see nearly constant sparring along the Eastern Dorsal, and the Germans got the better of it. In the north, the British kept pounding away at their enemy to no good effect, with yet another drive by the 36th Brigade bogging down in front of Jefna, and with the 6th Armoured Division meeting the same fate at Bou Arada. To the right of the British, the French surprised no one on the Allied side by proving far too light to endure the pounding inherent in modern operations against an enemy equipped with heavy weapons. The French colonial army had its virtues—minimal supply requirements, for example, and the ability to negotiate even the most broken terrain—but not for this type of fight. Arnim was as competent a general as the Germans produced in World War II, and he quickly sized up the situation. All through January, he kept up the pressure on the French because it was apparent to him that even limited attacks threatened to rupture their front altogether.

On January 18, for example, he assembled a mixed assault force from elements of the 10th Panzer Division, 334th Infantry Division, and Ital-

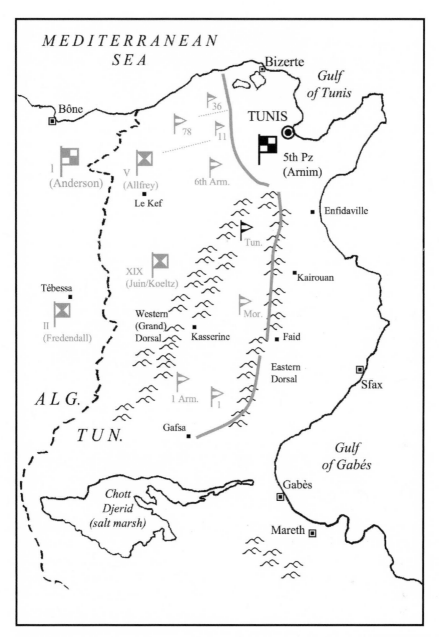

Ike's Winter Line: Tunisia, 1942–1943

ian *Superga* Division, placed them under the leadership of Colonel Friedrich Weber (*Kampfgruppe Weber*) and launched Operation Messenger (*Eilbote*).[5] Phase one of the operation smashed French defenses along the reservoir and dam on the Kebir River (the "Barrage de l'Oued Kebir"), which served as the principal water source for Tunis. The second phase (*Eilbote* II) began on January 30 and saw the 21st Panzer Division blasting the French out of the Faid pass, driving them off the Eastern Dorsal in this sector. With the French hanging on by a thread, Eisenhower's neat and tidy line had already begun to crumble. As more U.S. and British troops came up to the front, both he and Anderson had to divert them to plug yet more holes in the French line. The line held, although the Allies never did succeed in retaking the Faid. The bigger issue was this: against the will of the Allied command, but inexorably, the line along the Eastern Dorsal soon became yet another a jumble of disconnected battalions, and even basic questions of who commanded whom at any given moment came to be hopelessly confused.

In the southern sector, Fredendall and his II Corps had arrived in force by the New Year. Neither he nor his supreme commander had any intention of sitting passively and engaging in positional defense. Eager to prove their mettle—both to their British ally and perhaps to themselves as well—they began to plan for an offensive of their own.[6] Operation Satin was the result. From its base near Gafsa, II Corps would drive on Gabès and from there swing left, up the Mediterranean coast to the port of Sfax. Satin promised big rewards—if it worked. A drive into the vulnerable German rear would give U.S. forces complete freedom of maneuver, as well as a commanding central position between Arnim's 5th Army in Tunisia and Rommel's *Panzerarmee* scurrying back out of Libya. It could win the Tunisian campaign in a stroke, and enthusiasm was high in the U.S. camp. The British took one look at the plan for Satin, however, and nearly fainted. It was far too ambitious, they complained, well beyond Allied logistical capabilities, and would probably result in the entire U.S. force being trapped on the coast when Rommel finally arrived. Their arguments convinced Eisenhower to abandon a plan on which he had already invested a great deal of time and energy. Privately, the British were shaking their heads: one more sign of U.S. amateurism.

Fredendall eventually pieced together a scaled-down version of Satin, a sharp raid by the 1st Armored Division from Gafsa to Sened Station. Launched on January 24, it hit a mainly Italian garrison and took hundreds of prisoners before retiring. A follow-up drive through Sened toward Maknassy by the 168th Infantry Regiment precisely a week later misfired completely, however, when German Stukas caught the advancing U.S. columns out in the open and inflicted heavy casualties on them.[7] There was some panic in the ranks—there were still a lot of men in the regiment under fire for the first time—and Fredendall now decided to pull the corps all the way back to his original start line at Gafsa.

Only adding to all these worries was the arrival of Rommel's German–Italian *Panzerarmee* in the south. It had been a true epic, a nearly three-month retreat of some 1,500 miles along a single line of communication, pursued by superior forces, under nearly constant air attack.[8] Military historians are rarely eager to spend much time singing the praises of great retreats, and this amazing modern-day *Anabasis* has largely vanished from the modern historiography.[9] Most accounts have Rommel retreating from El Alamein in early November 1942 and then disappearing until his magical reappearance in Tunisia in late January 1943. The Great Retreat deserves better treatment than it has received, at least as much as his earlier drives across the desert in 1941 and 1942. Some on his staff who saw Rommel in these days describe him as dispirited or even despairing.[10] They may be true, but the retreat showed that he still had more than enough situational awareness, and perhaps even simple professional pride, to give a good account of himself. On more than one occasion he was able to slip the noose that Montgomery's 8th Army was just about to tie off, and that was especially true of the opening days of the retreat.

We may date the start of the Great Retreat to noon on November 2, at the height of the battle of El Alamein—the Third Battle of Alamein. Rommel had finally realized that he was beaten and had begun to pull his still intact formations out of the line in order to begin a retreat. No sooner had he done so than he had received an order from Hitler via telegram, a bombshell, probably the hardest blow Rommel had ever suffered in a lifetime of campaigning. In it, the Führer ordered Rommel "to stand fast, to take not one step backwards, and to throw every gun and every man who you can free up into the battle." The order ended with what Rommel must have considered the emptiest of exhortations: "Despite his superiority, your enemy must also be at the end of his strength. It would not be the first time in history that a strong will has triumphed over the bigger battalions of the enemy." With regard to Rommel's troops, Hitler urged, "you can show them no other road than the one that leads to victory or death."[11]

Rommel's near disbelief at this senseless *Haltbefehl* (stand-fast order) is well attested to in the literature.[12] More was at work here than Hitler's false conception of military operations. On a deeper, more personal level, this was the moment that Rommel realized that the man he had worshiped up to now was actually an amateur and perhaps even a charlatan. The field marshal spent the day in a fog and would never fully recover from the shock. Nevertheless, there was still the matter at hand: the survival or destruction of his entire army. Hitler's order had arrived at the worst possible time, and the final British attack at El Alamein had caught the *Panzerarmee* completely off balance—not retreating, but certainly not prepared to defend itself either. An afternoon British attack at Tel el Mansfra, spearheaded by the British 1st Armoured Division, smashed the *Afrika Korps*, overrunning the right wing of the 15th Panzer Division and simply steamrolling what was left of the 21st Panzer Division. Simultaneously, the British 7th Armoured Division, the famous Desert Rats, drove over the Italian XX (Motorized) Corps, already in an advanced state of dissolution. Individual soldiers and formations here and there across the battlefield made a stand, but their battle was lost.[13]

At El Alamein, Montgomery finally beat Rommel. He was not able to destroy him, however, and has been answering questions at the bar of history ever since.[14] An almost perfect confluence of circumstances had arisen, including Hitler's order blocking any retreat. As this war would show many times, however, there were orders issued from headquarters, and there was what actually happened on the battlefield, and they were not always the same thing. As devastating as the *Haltbefehl* might have been to Rommel personally, it had very little staying power on his men. Events soon overtook it altogether, as soldiers who felt as if they'd already gone beyond the call of duty simply fled in any direction that seemed to offer momentary safety, usually, but not always, to the west.[15] As Rommel had found out many times in the past 18 months, no matter how powerful a blow you landed, actually destroying an enemy force in the desert almost always failed.[16] On the European continent, sealing off an enemy's retreat routes was a fairly simple matter of interdicting or blocking three or four principal roads. In the desert, 360-degree coverage was necessary, and achieving it was usually impossible.

So while the British were able to smash Rommel's forward position and break into his rear, they never really were in a position to round up their adversary in the classic style. Montgomery has received a great deal of criticism for the leisurely nature of his follow-up. A vigorous pursuit had been part of his original vision: two complete armored divisions grouped into X Corps, pouring through the gaps in Rommel's shredded defenses and functioning as a *corps de chasse* to complete the destruction of the beaten foe, Murat style.[17] The fight for the El Alamein position had been so difficult, however, and the breakthrough achieved so slowly, that the X Corps was already mired in the fighting. It wasn't ready to pursue anyone. As the Germans well knew, once mobile conditions had degenerated into a *Stellungskrieg* (a war of position), battle almost never ended decisively or with much of a pursuit for the victor.

By the time Rommel had recovered his own personal equilibrium, his army had managed to break contact with Montgomery. The retreat began with nightfall on November 4, and by morning, the *Panzerarmee*, savaged but still intact and in hand, was heading west. What happened now was an unfolding in reverse of Rommel's original invasion of Egypt back in the summer, the giddy time when he had been riding that post-Gazala, post-Tobruk high. The place names were familiar: from El Alamein roughly 50 miles back to Fuka and thence 50 miles more back to Mersa Matruh. The 33rd and 580th Reconnaissance Battalions, the same ones that formed the advance guard of the drive into Egypt, now provided the covering force for the retreat.[18] Combined into *Gruppe Voss* (for their commander), they played a particularly crucial role on the Fuka–Mersa Matruh road on the night of November 6–7, when Rommel's command was still shaky and when several of his army's constituent formations, the 1st Fallschirmjäger Brigade (often "Brigade Ramcke" in the literature) and the Italian X Corps, for example, were off his situation maps altogether.

Rommel intended to stay at Mersa Matruh for several days, regather the flock, and attempt to put the army back into fighting shape. That was impossible, however. With Montgomery still nipping at his heels, and with his intelligence reports telling him that strong British armored forces were 20 miles south of Mersa Matruh and lapping around his flank, Rommel once again gave the order to retreat. Some good news had also arrived: a report from General Ramcke. He and the 600 survivors of his brigade had managed to elude the British after a three-day march through the deep desert and had now rejoined the main column.[19] Rommel had already given up the brigade as lost. By the night of November 8, the *Panzerarmee* had reached the Sidi Barrani–Buq Buq sector. It got no rest here either.[20] With British armor still roaming free on the flank, the retreat continued, back to Sollum, Halfaya, and Sidi Omar on the border with Libya by the night of November 9. The invasion of Egypt was over. Rommel had retreated some 200 miles in six days.

Anyone at all familiar with the course of the desert war knew what was about to happen next. Rommel lacked the materiél to base on defense on Tobruk, and there was no hope of holding out in the great bulge of Cyrenaica, where the terrain broadened out hundreds of miles. All the advantages were with the attacker. The British had cut across the bulge to trap the retreating Italians at Beda Fomm in early 1941.[21] Rommel had returned the favor in the spring; the British had done it again after Operation Crusader,[22] and Rommel had done it one last time in January 1942, exploding out of the box and lunging to Gazala.[23] The only thing to do was to hightail it along the one good hard-surfaced road, the Via Balbia, and get out of the bulge altogether, abandon Tobruk and Benghazi, and try to form a defense in the narrow and unflankable Mersa el Brega–El Agheila position, where it had all started for the Desert Fox in 1941.

For the next two weeks, the *Panzerarmee* launched itself into a high-speed drive across Cyrenaica. The redoubtable 90th Light Division provided the rear guard along the main road, while the reconnaissance battalions ranged deep to the south, protecting the main column from British flanking attempts.[24] There were minor disasters along the way. A British attack against Halfaya pass on November 11 combined a frontal blow with a drive into the deep flank and booted the *Panzerarmee* out of it ignominiously, overrunning a regiment of the Italian *Pistoia* Division in the process and capturing three batteries of precious German artillery. The supply situation was wretched. That same day, as the army was reeling back from the Halfaya, a supply column arrived. It brought no gasoline, which Rommel needed desperately, and 1,300 men as replacements, which he definitely did not, and who were soon caught up in the retreat and taking up precious space on the trucks.[25] This was the context for his November 14 decision to make the "largest possible bound" to the west, to leave Montgomery in the dust and buy himself some time.[26] He displayed a skillful touch, ruthlessly rationing gasoline and providing it to whichever formation seemed to need it at the most at any given moment. Honesty demands that we also observe that Rommel's increase of speed was largely due to having shed a great deal of slow, straight-leg Italian infantry along the way. Montgomery's own supply lines were beginning to creak, and he had to draw in the reins at crucial moments. By November 26, the entire *Panzerarmee* had retreated to the Mersa el Brega position.[27]

Here Rommel was able to rest and take stock. His army was a mess. The once formidable *Afrika Korps*, the heart of his force, now barely registered the strength of a reinforced regiment. The 90th Light Division mustered about a battalion and a half. The 164th Light Division nominally possessed nine battalions and six batteries; it now had two and two.[28]

Still, the army was intact, the cadre holding firm, and morale, despite some understandable fatigue, still high, at least among the Germans. The Italian infantry were by now mainly replacements from the rear, but they would be fighting in fixed fortifications at the Mersa position and would probably give a relatively good accounting of themselves; they almost always had in the desert. There was even something rare by this point in the war, a more or less full-strength Italian armored division, the *Centauro*. Often the object of mockery by historians, Italian armor represented a major accretion of strength at this point.[29]

This was an all-too-familiar story in the desert war. The attacker landed a great blow and lunged 1,000 miles across the desert. In so doing, he exhausted himself. The defenders survived the initial blow and fell back on their supply bases, and in so doing, gained strength by the day.[30] The British seemed to realize this, and the drive on Mersa now reverted to classic Montgomery form: no flanking attempt, but rather a deliberate advance by phase lines with his corps abreast. Not until December 12, seventeen full days since Rommel had arrived at Mersa, did the British open their assault.[31] By now, Rommel had already pulled his infantry out of the line and had them retreating down the road to the west. The Mersa assault struck air,[32] or at least a delaying resistance (*hinhaltender Widerstand*) by Rommel's motorized formations.[33] While the British slowly chewed through the Mersa *Stellung*, he had already ordered work to begin on the next defensive position to the rear, this one at Buerat, 130 miles east of Tripoli. Even as that work was ongoing, resulting eventually in a 36-mile-wide line of fortifications at Buerat, Italian infantry was also digging a third line even farther back between Tarhuna and Homs, hard up against Tripoli and thus forming the principal position for the defense of the city. Rommel, however, was actually talking about a withdrawal all the way to the Tunisian–Libyan border, where the French had dug a prewar line of fortifications at Mareth.

That was all in the future. By now, what had been a mobile campaign had slowed to a crawl. Distance, human exhaustion, wear and tear on the machines, lack of fuel, incessant rain (a factor rarely considered in analysis of the Desert War)—it all added up. Both sides were swimming against the current of obstacles. Mussolini sent a missive to his troops to "resist to the last ditch in the Buerat position,"[34] but his own theater commander, General Ettore Bastico (supreme commander in Libya), was already preparing plans for a retreat further to the west. The Italian army in Africa was treating Mussolini with the same respect that the Germans were offering Hitler. Montgomery, for his part, was still moving forward step by step toward Buerat. The German official history describes the advance as "systematic, and in view of the ruinous state of the Panzerarmee perhaps too systematic," which seems unfair.[35] We know a great deal more today about the actual state of the *Panzerarmee* than Montgomery did, even with the benefit of Ultra intercepts. As always, Ultra was a real advantage, but not an absolute one. Once one subtracted the fear that the Germans were feeding it disinformation, and then further subtracted the Allied unwillingness to act on Ultra intelligence too vigorously, for fear of giving the game away, one was left with an advantage, but nothing more than that.

At any rate, the 8th Army did not come up against the Buerat position until January 15. It was a classic Montgomery set piece, and no one did it better by this point in the war. He certainly did not have the preponderance of force he usually required. This was a XXX Corps operation only. Montgomery was now launching a major attack between Benghazi and Tripoli, a stretch of 675 miles lacking even a single minor port to land supply from the sea.[36] Nevertheless, given Rommel's own weakness, a single British corps should have been more than enough. Two divisions—the 50th and 51st Highland—would advance along the main road near the coast, while the 7th Armoured and 2nd New Zealand would advance toward Beni Ulid and Tarhuna, well inland. Linking the two wings was the 22nd Armoured Brigade. The corps also had 23rd Armoured Brigade, but the British already considered its Valentine tanks obsolescent, "fit for one major action and no more," in the words of the British official history.[37] Montgomery's headquarters were at Benghazi, far to the rear, and the eve of the offensive saw yet another major storm. With both visibility and travel down to near zero, Montgomery decided not to bring forward his X Corps.

The Buerat attack went in with major air support, Bostons and Baltimores and U.S. B-25 Mitchells.[38] The attack along the coast ran into Italian infantry in their fortifications, as well as 90th Light Division, and soon came to a halt. The inland drive, however, was nearly irresistible given the balance of forces. The 2nd New Zealand Division, with strong support from 80 armored cars, pushed back the 33rd Reconnaissance Battalion. The arrival of the reinforcing 3rd Reconnaissance Battalion slowed down the kiwis but could not completely retrieve the situation. The Germans soon recognized the enemy *Schwerpunkt*: the 7th Armoured Division with over 100 armored cars and 150 tanks. Driving hard toward Fortino in the desert, on Rommel's far right flank, it crashed into what was left of the 15th Panzer Division.[39] There were two days of hard fighting, in the course of which a large gap opened between the 90th Light Division and the 15th Panzer. Late on January 16, Rommel ordered a retirement—this recognized master of the offensive also had no lack of the famous "fingertip feel" (*Fingerspitzengefühl*) for the defensive battle—and now ordered his army to withdraw to a temporary line stretching from Beni Ulid to Bir Durfan and from there to Tauorga. By January 18, the *Panzerarmee* had withdrawn to the Tarhuna–Homs line. Tripoli, more than any other city the heart of the Italian colonial empire, had now come into the Allied crosshairs.

The British launched the attack on the Tarhuna–Homs position the next day, January 19. Rommel had no hope of holding out here any more than he had at Buerat, and he had already ordered his Italian infantry formations to the west. The British attack—as deliberate as always—met heavy resistance. Rommel was now in one of the most highly complex situations of the war. The tactical situation, relayed to him by the daily casualty reports, demanded an immediate retreat; the strategic situation, reinforced by an incessant stream of dispatches from Mussolini and the Italian high command, demanded that he stand fast. Nothing less than the integrity of the Italian empire and the Axis alliance demanded it. Rommel and the German way of war he represented so well excelled on the intermediate, or operational, level—division versus division, we might say. Every one of his higher formations fought "cleverly," in the words of the British official history, but that meant little once his divisions had shrunk to the size of battalions.[40] By one German intelligence count, the British had something like 650 battle tanks in Libya by mid-January; the *Panzerarmee* had 93, of which 57 were lighter Italian models. Already Rommel was ordering the destruction of matériel and facilities in Tripoli and plotting out his retreat route to the west. His 21st Panzer Division was not even involved in the fighting for Tripoli. Rommel had already sent it back to Sfax in Tunisia to ensure the safety of his retreat route. The *Panzerarmee* evacuated the port on the night of January 22–23, and British troops entered Tripoli on January 23, with Montgomery taking the official surrender of the city at noon.[41]

Although the Great Retreat did not end here, the imminent danger to the *Panzerarmee* had passed. Montgomery had now just taken a major city—by North African standards at least. It was a lot to digest, and doing it right, as the Allies would find time and time again in this war, was a large and time-consuming administrative task. The *Panzerarmee* continued west until it reached the Mareth line across the border in Tunisia. As any number of sources indicate, the fortifications there were in bad repair. "Bad repair," however, is better than nothing, which is what Rommel had been working with up to now. The El Alamein pursuit was over, and Montgomery had failed in his objective of destroying his adversary.

Does Montgomery deserve the criticism he has gotten? Some of it, no doubt. He had an absolute numerical and material superiority. He had the benefit of Ultra intelligence the entire way. He was able to read Rommel's dispatches not too long after the German commander wrote them. The list goes on, and a reasonable person might argue that it should have been enough. In fact, he barely came close to his quarry. There was hardly any fighting in the course of the pursuit. The British official history has it about right: "Since the battle of El Alamein the purely fighting side of the 8th Army had traveled far rather than fought much."[42] Once again, a reasonable argument might conclude that Rommel had bested Montgomery in a game of wits.

There was more at work here than the interplay of personality, however—more than a simplistic good general/bad general dichotomy. As it would for the entire war, Ultra proved to be less than the sum of its parts. It generated enormous reams of paper that someone had to type, sort, file, and resend to the appropriate Allied commander. It was an enormous bureaucracy, and as the German official history concludes, "great logistical and bureaucratic apparatuses, the kind that were typical in the command structures of the western allies, had many advantages, but encouraging rapid decision-making was not among them."[43] Ultra also tended to report what Rommel was telling his superiors, as opposed to what he actually intended to do on the battlefield. The latter was usually closely held among the field marshal and a few select staff officers. Most importantly, Ultra failed to take into account the German tradition of independent field command. Whether labeled "mission command" (*Auftragstaktik*) or the "independence of the subordinate commander" (*Selbständigkeit der Unterführer*), it meant that Ultra was giving the Allies only the barest possible information as to the overall mission, without a great deal of detail as to how the lower level commanders intended to carry it out. Finally, *Auftragstaktik* itself was a major advantage for the Germans. If there was a "British way of war" in World War II, it dealt much more with battle management— the systematic buildup of resources, phase lines, and strict schedules— than it did with maneuver warfare. By contrast, the war of movement on the operational level, or *Bewegungskrieg*, had been the preferred German way of war for three centuries. Handing off initiative to the lower commanders was a basic aspect of this German way, and it worked to Rommel's advantage as the ever-shrinking *Panzerarmee* made its way across the vast expanses of Libya.

It flies in the face of the common wisdom, but systemic factors determined the outcome of the Great Retreat far more than did the qualities of the generalship involved. It was more than Rommel versus Montgomery. Certainly, if Montgomery had more of Rommel's cutthroat recklessness, he probably would have smashed the *Panzerarmee* somewhere just west of El Alamein. Then again, if Rommel had more of Montgomery's "infinite capacity for taking pains,"[44] patience, and love of detail, he might have been sitting comfortably in Alexandria by now, drawing up regulations for German civil government in Egypt. Asking either of them to be something he was not hardly seems to be a suitable task for the historian.

Battle of the Kasserine Pass

Rommel's arrival in Tunisia in early February meant that the Axis had now reclaimed the initiative in North Africa.[45] Leaving a token force to guard the Mareth line, where a line of inland mountains formed a natural chokepoint, Rommel was now free to turn the mass of his strength against the allied forces to the west. The united strength of two armies, Rommel's *Panzerarmee* and Arnim's 5th Panzer Army, could now turn on the Allied force of their choice with a reasonable chance of smashing it. Although we should not exaggerate Rommel's strength, we should also recognize that his soldiers, both Germans and Italians, were wily veterans of a dozen battles, and for all the attrition they had suffered en route, they were still a force to be reckoned with. Altogether, the two Axis armies numbered over 100,000 men. The Axis actually had numerical superiority in Tunisia. What they did not have was a great deal of time. Every day that they tarried brought Montgomery one day closer to Tunisia, and the clock was ticking. It was a tough operational situation, but to any German officer trained in the traditional art, it could mean only one thing. It was go time—time to launch a great offensive.

The question was, where? As the combined staffs of the two Axis armies surveyed the operational situation, it was clear that they had about two weeks until the 8th Army arrived in Tunisia in strength. Studying the situation map, their eyes fell not on the French—they had

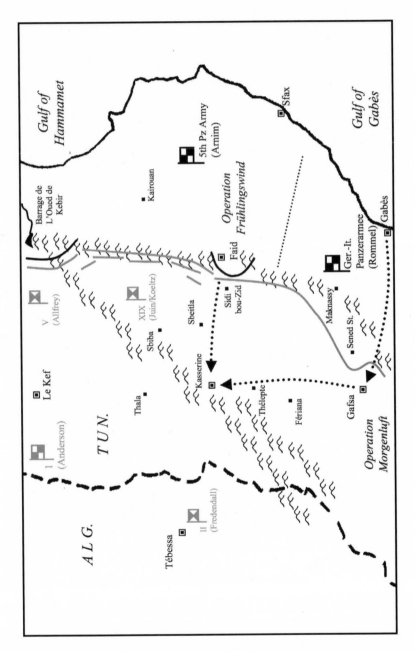

Weak Spot: Targeting the U.S. II Corps (February 1943)

already played that card more than once, and the Allies were learning to parry it—but on another force that had repeatedly failed in combat and whose problems seemed endemic rather than temporary: the U.S. Army's II Corps on the extreme southern portion of the front.

By the end of January, a two-part plan had emerged. Arnim's 5th Panzer Army would lead off with Operation *Frühlingswind* ("Spring Breeze"). Two Panzer Divisions (the 10th and the 21st) would take advantage of the dominant position on the Eastern Dorsal at the Faid pass and smash the vulnerable U.S. forward position at Sidi bou Zid. It would be a Panzer attack in the grand style, spearheaded by over 200 tanks, including a dozen of the new Mark VI Tiger giants. Once that attack had fixed U.S. attention to that sector, Rommel's *Panzerarmee* would launch Operation *Morgenluft* ("Morning Air"). Once again, the spearhead would be the mobile units, a brace of armored divisions, the 15th Panzer Division and the Italian armored division *Centauro* formed into the German Africa Corps (*Deutsches Afrika Korps*, or DAK). They would come up from Gabès in the south, overrun Gafsa, and smash U.S. defenses in the Kasserine pass along the Western Dorsal.[46] From here, the commanders would reassess the situation and make a decision on the direction of the next bound forward. All things considered, it was a reasonable plan, with a good chance of success. If there was a flaw, it was that it relied on the cooperation of two strong-willed and competent commanders, neither of whom intended to defer to the other. In fact, Marshal Kesselring, commander in chief of the south, had to intervene repeatedly in the planning process to soothe wounded feelings and to protect threatened prerogatives, and haggling about who would control which armored units was still taking place on the eve of the offensive—hardly an auspicious omen for the start of a complex and risky operational scheme.[47]

The Axis offensive in Tunisia opened on Valentine's Day, February 14, 1943. "Spring Breeze" came first and opened with a bang. Two Panzer divisions, an enormous concentration of force by Wehrmacht standards, combined for the initial thrust. The 10th Panzer Division erupted out of the Faid pass east of Sidi bou Zid, enveloping U.S. defenses to the north. On its left, the 21st Panzer Division emerged from Maïzila pass, looping around to the south. They caught U.S. troops badly positioned at two hills flanking the town, Djebel Lessouda to the north and Djebel Ksaïra to the south. The hills were miles apart, far too distant for mutual support. The two pincers closed fast, and it took only 12 hours for the Germans to encircle the entire U.S. position. The speed of the German advance swallowed the central U.S.

armored reserve at Sidi bou Zid (Combat Command A of the 1st Armored Division) before it could react, and a hasty counterattack from the north by the 2nd Battalion/1st Armored Regiment (Lieutenant Colonel James D. Alger) was a fiasco, with the tanks disappearing into an onrushing sea of German Panzers.[48] The 168th Infantry Regiment was holding the Sidi bou Zid position, and its commander, Colonel Thomas Drake, radioed General Fredendall, sensibly, for permission to retreat. He was told to hold on until help arrived. Fredendall was 100 miles away from the battlefield at the time, safe in a newly constructed underground bunker, so perhaps he did not have quite the urgency that Drake was feeling at the time.[49] The promised help never arrived, and much of the 168th—about 1,400 men in all—were taken prisoner or cut down as they tried to clamber down off the hills under German fire. One of the prisoners was Colonel John Waters, Patton's son-in-law and one of the heroes of the Djedeida airfield raid.[50] Once he had secured the Sidi bou Zid position and seen to it that U.S. prisoners were streaming to the rear under escort, Arnim continued his drive to the west, heading toward Sbeitla. It fell on February 17 to a well-coordinated attack of German Panzers and Stuka dive-bombers, and once again there were signs of panic as the U.S. defenses dissolved under an onslaught that the green American defenders only dimly understood.

While this drama unfolded, "Morning Air" had also gotten underway.[51] As the DAK came up to Gafsa, Rommel found it evacuated by U.S. troops and occupied it on February 15. Aware by now that something big was underway, General Anderson had ordered the entire U.S. line to swing back to the Western Dorsal, thus abandoning the winter line that Eisenhower had ordered held at such cost. The Panzers continued north, overrunning newly constructed U.S. airfields at Fériana and Thélepte on February 17.[52] Disaster ensued here when C Company of the 805th Tank Destroyer Battalion failed to get the retreat order and instead launched a senseless counterattack into the teeth of the onrushing Germans.[53] It was magnificent, but it was hardly war. Main gunfire from the Panzers soon destroyed all 12 tank destroyers in the melee that followed. Equipment variances aside, it was an all too typical result when veteran crews faced rookies.

It is not unfair to say that at this precise moment, the U.S. Army on the Tunisian front was in free fall. Even the Germans seemed caught off guard by the speed and totality of their success, and their surprise was the background for a new dispute that suddenly arose between Rommel and Arnim about how to exploit the rapidly developing situation. Arnim wanted a quick right turn to the north to lever the British off the entire Eastern Dorsal. Rommel, who up to now had seemed dubious about the prospects of the offensive, had a bolder plan. Success had apparently reinvigorated him. He now demanded personal command over all the German Panzer divisions. Once concentrated in his own hands, they would stage a breakthrough at the Kasserine Pass and launch a thrust against Tébessa, the principal U.S. supply depot in Tunisia, and then against Fredendall's headquarters nine miles to the southeast. Once in control of what wags in the U.S. Army were already calling "Speedy Valley," as a result of Fredendall's combat jitters, Rommel would have his choice of operational targets.[54] He was now mulling over a 140-mile drive north to Bône on the Mediterranean coast to encircle the entire Allied force in Africa. Arnim had his doubts about the feasibility of such a bold scheme and wanted to keep the 15th and 21st Panzer Divisions under his own control for what he saw as a smaller but more realistic solution. Kesselring was back in Europe conferring with Hitler at the time, and once again, he had to step in, this time by telegram, to adjudicate between his two warring commanders. He came up with a compromise. Rommel would get his Panzer divisions, but he would have to forego the drive on Bône in favor of a shorter northern hook toward the key British supply base of Le Kef, 70 miles to the north. It was a less dramatic, safer scheme, but one that still promised to cripple Allied operations in Tunisia for some time.

As a result of this back and forth, it was not until February 19 that Rommel was able to get moving again. His plans now called for two simultaneous strikes, one through the Kasserine Pass by the *Afrika Korps*, another against the so-called Sbiba Gap to the north by 21st Panzer Division. It was an *exzentrisch* move, in other words, with his principal maneuver units driving away from one another (as opposed to a *konzentrisch* maneuver, where the arrows converged). In traditional German war making, it was a clear sign that he did not think that he had much to fear from the Americans.[55] Meanwhile, the 10th Panzer Division would remain at Sbeitla to reinforce whichever blow happened to succeed.

As it turned out, that was the one at Kasserine. On February 19–20, the *Afrika Korps* attacked and smashed a motley collection of U.S. defenders under the designation of Task Force Stark. It included a handful of infantry, a few engineer units that had been rushed to the front and had only rudimentary tactical training, and a couple of batteries of French artillery.[56] The traditional U.S. narrative of the war has weaker allies relying on American backstops and air strikes for survival, but this was a point in the war when the U.S. Army could apparently still not fight on its own without French assistance. General Fredendall had given the commander of the task force, Colonel Alexander Stark, the bombastic order "to go to Kasserine right away and pull a Stonewall Jackson," but it did not quite work out that way.[57] Over the course of the next two days, German and Italian armor of the *Afrika Korps* launched a frontal drive against the pass. It did not break through, but it did fix the defenders in place while Axis infantry methodically worked its way up the heights overlooking the pass, Djebel Chambi in the southwest and Djebel Semamma in the northeast. Counterattacks by U.S. tanks ran into a buzz saw of fire of German 88mm antitank guns, and by the evening of February 20, the U.S. defenses in the Kasserine Pass had collapsed, the survivors were streaming away in confusion, and the battlefield was littered with the wrecks of some 200 U.S. tanks.[58] As planned, the 10th Panzer Division now came up to the breakthrough point, and Rommel, sensing blood, launched his exploitation. Once again, it consisted of two simultaneous *exzentrisch* drives toward Thala and Le Kef in the north and Tébessa in the west. As far as Rommel was concerned, he was still driving free.

What happened over the next few days still strikes the analyst as surprising. With U.S. forces hounded from position to position, their final position on the Western Dorsal pierced, and no major terrain obstruction between Rommel and Tébessa or the sea, U.S. defenses finally began to coalesce. It is certainly hard to say that it had anything to do with Fredendall, who was still a long way away, and who appears in the memoirs acting like a broken man. "They have broken through and you can't stop them," he told one of his officers at the time.[59] He was clearly on the verge of abandoning his headquarters in Speedy Valley. Indeed, he had already ordered demolitions prepared in his vast underground bunker complex, one that had taken innumerable man-hours and an untold amount of resources to construct.

Nor was it Eisenhower who drew a line in the sand after Kasserine and declared "not a step back." The opening of the offensives had caught him by surprise as much as anyone. Indeed, he had apparently been out visiting old Roman ruins when the German offensive opened. Since then, he had contributed little if anything to the course of the battle. Lately, he had been trying a more hands-off approach to his command, his response to flack from Marshall about taking "too many trips to the front."[60] It is only fair to point out that this was the exact opposite of the chief of staff's earlier advice, telling Eisenhower to pay more attention to the battle in Tunisia.

The high command may have been in disarray, but something was clearly happening at the front. Accounts of the battle make it seem almost miraculous. The fever suddenly passed, the panic faded as quickly as it had appeared, and U.S. defenses suddenly stiffened. In fact, there were operational dynamics at work here. Believing that he had II Corps on the run, Rommel had now committed himself to three simultaneous thrusts. Even a commander usually dubbed a genius suddenly looks much more mortal when moving in three directions at once. Moving from right to left, the drive on Sbiba by the 21st Panzer Division failed completely, with the attack coming to a screeching halt on February 20 against four full U.S. and British infantry regiments, backed by accurate U.S. artillery fire provided by the 151st Field Artillery Battalion. The thrust on Thala ran into a similar wall of high explosive; here, it was the British 26th Armoured Brigade holding the front, backed by the newly arrived artillery of the U.S. 9th Infantry Division, under Brigadier General Stafford LeRoy Irwin. It was only four days ago that Irwin and his guns had been stationed west of Oran back in Algeria. They had driven 800 miles in that short time before coming into the line at Thala.[61] Finally, Rommel had launched a third drive, this one on Tébessa. It too came to grief against a tough defensive stand of the 16th Infantry Regiment (commanded in person by the 1st Infantry Division commander, General Allen) blocking the way along the Djebel el Hamra and the Bou Chebka Pass. Supporting the 16th were strong armored counterattacks courtesy of Combat Command B (1st Armored Division) under its commander, Brigadier General Paul Robinett. Once again, highly accurate U.S. artillery played a key role, with the 1st Infantry Division artillery command, Brigadier General Clift Andrus, laying down a wall of fire on the Germans unlike anything they had ever seen before in Africa. Just for the record, veteran German troops from the Eastern Front said they had never seen anything like it there either.[62]

Three divergent attacks, and three failures. All of Rommel's assault formations had by now taken heavy losses, and his supplies were dwindling. According to his logistics staff, he had just four days of rations and only about 250 kilometers' worth of fuel. That was barely enough to motor back to the Mareth position, let alone fight there. Meanwhile, his men could see that the situation had changed. Rather than using superior skill at maneuver warfare to administer a quick smackdown to an amateur, they were now in battle against a steady foe with an apparently limitless supply of ammunition, and the force of their own attacks was ebbing. It was an old story in the history of German war making: *Bewegungskrieg* had, almost overnight, given way to *Stellungskrieg*. Kesselring was back in Africa, and on February 22, he came forward to

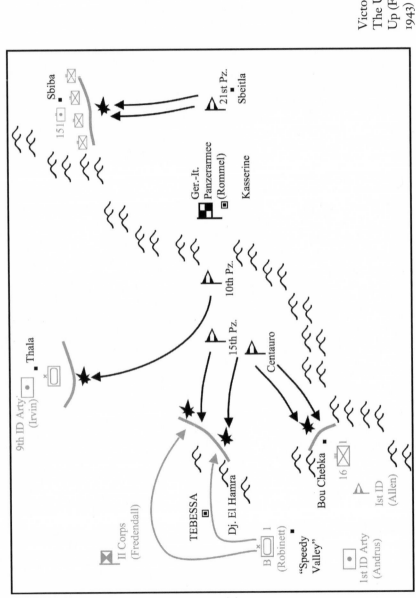

Victory at Kasserine:
The U.S. Army Steps
Up (February 21–23,
1943)

meet with Rommel. The two men agreed that it was time to get Rommel's army back to the Mareth line to meet Montgomery, whose advance guards were just beginning to arrive. The Panzers retreated out of the Kasserine Pass on February 23 and headed back to their original start lines. The last German offensive in North Africa had failed.

Some of it was due to their own mistakes. Rommel's tendency to attack in all directions at once was questionable. Then again, that tendency had been a questionable part of Rommel's generalship from the start of his career. There were numerous colleagues in the Wehrmacht's officer corps who knew that someday, Rommel's inability to distinguish between the command of a mechanized army and the leadership of a raiding party would bring him to grief.[63] Likewise, the command muddle had been inexcusable. In the course of the brief campaign, Arnim had withheld about half of the 10th Panzer Division from Rommel's control, saving those units for an intended offensive in the north, despite explicit orders from Kesselring. That, too, had been seen before in German military history: the commander who was expected to think and act independently of his superior was certainly not about to bow meekly to the wishes of one of his equals, and that is what Arnim and Rommel were.

Neither Rommel's *exzentrisch* offensive blows nor command friction lost the battle of Kasserine Pass, however. Rather, the encounter showed more than anything else a U.S. Army finally pulling itself together, assembling a package that included solid field-grade leadership (majors, lieutenant colonels, and colonels), vast material resources, and an immense level of firepower. It was a combination the Germans were going to find more and more difficult to counter as the war dragged on. Perhaps it is best to give Rommel the last word. At Kasserine, he would later write, "Die Amerikaner hatten sich vorzüglich geschlagen"[64]—"they had fought brilliantly." On this point, at least, we should recognize his authority as absolute.

The U.S. interpretation of Kasserine, oddly enough, tends to focus on the early near disaster rather than the later recovery. Fredendall lost his job in the midst of the fighting and has appeared in most of the histories as a buffoon. Although "blaming the general" is the most simplistic form of military history, it is occasionally hard to avoid. The evidence against him is overwhelming. Fredendall really was obsessed with security to the exclusion of all other missions. Certain that he was a target for German spying, he really did issue bizarre orders like, "Have your boss report to the French gentleman whose name begins with J at a place which begins with D which is five grid squares to the left of M," which had his own officers scratching their heads.[65] He really did spend the Battle of Kasserine Pass holed up in that vast underground bunker complex at "Speedy Valley," 100 miles from where his men were fighting and dying at Sidi bou Zid on the first day. He really did seem to go to pieces as one piece of bad news from the front followed another. Witnesses speak of him chain smoking, perhaps even drinking, and muttering dark words to his subordinates. As the Panzer spearheads approached Tébessa, the principal U.S. supply base in Africa, Fredendall really did begin preparing to bug out, which would have represented an operational disaster of the first magnitude. Only a timely defensive stand—as in just in time—by the men and the field grades under his command had saved him from that ignominy. After the battle, Eisenhower would kick him upstairs and back to the states for a training command. His replacements, General George S. Patton and then General Omar S. Bradley, would show that there was not all that much wrong with II Corps that solid leadership could not fix.

Surely this or that point of the "Fredendall indictment" might need qualification. Chain smoking? This was the 1940s. Just about everyone in the army from ordinary privates on up smoked in this era. Despairing words? Every general utters a few from time to time. But in the end, it is difficult to find much good to say about a general described by one of his own armor commanders, General Ernest Harmon, as a "physical and moral coward."[66]

Still, even Fredendall deserves his day in court. The animus toward him, ranging from his own officers to historians writing many decades later, is so sharp that it is apparent he has become more than a mere bad general. He has become a symbol of everything that was wrong with the infant U.S. Army in Tunisia. For those U.S. officers like Eisenhower, Bradley, and Patton, the commanders who went on to win the war, Fredendall was an embarrassing reminder of a time that they had done everything possible to forget. Without approving his generalship or attempting to argue that it was not so bad, can we not historicize Fredendall? Surely he was neither the first nor the last officer to shine brightly in a peacetime army, only to be found wanting in war.

The End in Tunisia (March–May 1943)

The German failure at Kasserine was the beginning of the end in Tunisia. With a rapid and decisive solution no longer available through the employment of *Bewegungskrieg*, the fight here had become one of attrition, and that was a battle that the Axis was destined to lose. It was, wrote a later German authority, "the end in a real sense of operational warfare in North Africa."[67] As one sign that the Germans knew it, OKW now changed the name of the famed *Panzerarmee* to 1st Italian Army under the command of General Giovanni Messe. If the end really was near, at least it would not be the *Panzerarmee* going down to defeat. Messe's command and Arnim's 5th Panzer Army now made up a generically named *Heeresgruppe Afrika* (Army Group Africa) under Rommel. For his own part, the field marshal was not long for Africa: he had disobeyed too many orders and ruffled too many feathers, and he had little to show for it by this point in the war, no matter how exciting his exploits might have been. He left Africa for the last time on March 9, Arnim moved upstairs to lead Army Group Africa, and 5th Panzer Army came under the command of the experienced armor commander General Gustav von Värst.

All of this was merely rearranging the deck chairs. Axis offensive strength was displaying its last flickers. Arnim launched a general offensive by the 5th Panzer Army in the northern sector of the front, Operation *Ochsenkopf* (literally "Ox Head," more colloquially "Blockhead"), on February 26, but it went nowhere. Its main significance to the narrative is that it was the reason that Arnim had refused to hand over his armor to Rommel at Kasserine. Rommel's last throw, a blow against 8th Army along the Mareth line in the south by what was left of his Panzer formations, was much worse and qualifies as the one genuine fiasco of Rommel's career. The field marshal did not intend Operation Capri to be a breakthrough operation, but rather a spoiling attack designed to smash as much of Montgomery's strength as possible, thus throwing off the Allied timetable and delaying what Rommel now viewed as the inevitable fall of Tunisia. Launched on March 6, the assault aimed at Montgomery's forward positions near the village of Medenine.[68]

For the Wehrmacht, Capri was a perfect storm of failure. The problems began with a lack of resources. Rommel's three Panzer divisions (the 10th, 15th, and 21st) had 160 tanks between them, just about what one full-strength Panzer Division was supposed to have. Montgomery, by contrast, had four divisions in the line, 400 tanks, and over 800 artillery and antitank guns. Axis strength in the air was plummeting toward zero, while Montgomery could call upon three fighter wings based at forward airfields. All of that "infinite capacity for taking pains" that Montgomery liked to brag about was now bearing fruit. For once, he and Ultra were even on the same page, and Montgomery was able to place the tanks, men, and guns where they were supposed to be—one of the few times in the entire war that Ultra actually worked in the way most historians claim. The Panzers spearheaded the attack at 6:00 A.M., although it is problematic to call this an attack. Better to say that the tanks served as target practice for British artillery and air strikes, and we might say the same for the follow-on infantry assault at 2:30 P.M. German losses were heavy, amounting to 52 tanks, a third of Rommel's total armored strength, and he called off the attack later that day. Every modern battle generates reams of documentation dedicated to parsing and analyzing it, but Montgomery's pithy remark, "The Marshal has made a balls of it," should suffice to analyze the final assault at Medenine.[69] Rommel drew the appropriate conclusion from the disaster and decided to take that long-deferred offer from the Führer of a period of rest and recuperation in Europe. Although it would be unfair to say that Rommel abandoned his men—indeed, no one in the force had been warning longer about the impending disaster—it is fair to say that he realized that there was nothing more to be done in this theater.

As indicated by Medenine, the Allies had by now clearly won the battle in the air, with some 3,000 Allied aircraft ranging over the battle space and confronting just 300 Axis planes. During the course of the fighting, the Allies would build 100 all-weather airfields in Tunisia—an incredible commitment of resources, time, and concrete. After the Battle of Kasserine Pass, U.S. engineers built five new airfields near Sbeitla. Impressive enough perhaps, but what was even more impressive was that they managed to do it in just 72 hours. Likewise, the Allies had long ago won the battle of supply; that particular issue was never in doubt at any point in this war. Kasserine had landed a hard blow on the Americans, but it had also worsened the Axis supply situation by eating through a major portion of the Axis stockpile of ammunition and fuel. Now, in the wake of the failed offensive, Axis logistics essentially collapsed. The dominance of Allied air and naval strength was taking a heavy toll on Axis transport shipping. Axis planners estimated a requirement of some 140,000 tons of supply per month. In March 1943, only 29,000 tons made it to Africa. By comparison—and the years have done nothing to dull the shock of these numbers—that same month saw the U.S. alone bring 400,000 tons of supply into the theater.[70] Resources don't win wars all by themselves, and the history of the past centuries proves it, from the American Revolution to Vietnam. But it might be safe to say that it goes a long way toward winning conventional high-intensity wars of the sort being fought in Tunisia.

Beyond merely marshaling their resources, the Allies were learning to transform those resources into dominant strength on the ground, which had been the problem all along. With two complete Allied armies in the theater, Anderson's 1st and Montgomery's 8th, Eisenhower created a higher command in February, the 18th Army Group under British General Harold Alexander.[71] As more divisions flooded into Tunisia, 250,000 Allied soldiers were facing some 120,000 Axis. The U.S. II Corps had now doubled in size to four divisions, with its original components (1st Infantry Division, 1st Armored Division) now standing alongside the 9th and 34th Infantry Divisions. It also had a new commander; Eisenhower had sacked Fredendall in the midst of the Kasserine Pass fight and replaced him with General Patton. Giving Patton orders to "kick II Corps in the butt" may well rank among the most unnecessary words in the long history of war.[72] Patton did just that, restoring a sense of discipline to what had been a pretty lax command. Some of it was doubtless what World War II GIs learned to call "chickenshit": uniforms had to be regulation, boots polished, and chin straps fastened. On balance, however, it was a good thing. He also promised the men of his new command that they would "kick the bastards out of Africa,"[73] and he began to deliver on that too.

The new, improved II Corps made its debut by launching what was essentially a replay of Fredendall's scaled-down Operation Satin. On March 17, U.S. forces began driving east, retaking Gafsa and driving out its Italian garrison in an undertaking known in that less sensitive era as Operation Wop.[74] From Gafsa, they pushed beyond to take Sened Station. When the tanks of the 10th Panzer Division launched a counterattack on Patton at El Guettar, 10 miles southeast of Gafsa, 1st Infantry Division coolly held them off with steady infantry and, once again, with world-class artillery. The drive now restarted, and on the 25th, 1st Armored Division took Maknassy. Although II Corps probably outnumbered its adversaries in this sector by 4 to 1, there had been no real breakthrough. There had been steady, sustained progress, however, and considering past performance, that was something on which to build.

As II Corps was heading east, 8th Army was launching its last great North African set-piece battle against the Mareth line in the south. As with all of Montgomery's operations, this one was characterized by deliberation and careful planning rather than speed or daring. Analysts usually portray them as a combined frontal offensive with a simultaneous flanking maneuver, but that makes them seem more dynamic than they were. They amounted to a placing of a force on the flank rather than an attempt to catch the enemy between two converging fires. The point was merely to stretch the enemy force as thinly as possible across a longer front, and given the endemic material inferiority of the Axis force Montgomery faced, the tactic worked more often than not. Such was the case at Mareth. Rommel was gone by now, but he had studied the Mareth problem for months, and his successors—Arnim and Värst—were able to make the same basic calculations. Montgomery's original plan, code-named Pugilist Gallop, called for a frontal assault by the three divisions of XXX Corps (5th Northumberland Division, 51st Highland Division, 4th Indian Division, 201st Guards Brigade) against the Axis position along the Wadi Zigzaou in front of Mareth. Once they made a penetration, X Corps (1st and 7th Armoured divisions and 4th Light Armoured Brigade) were in reserve, ready for the exploitation. At the same time, a provisional New Zealand Corps (2nd New Zealand Division, 8th Armoured Brigade, the French regimental-sized formation known as "L Force," consisting of Senegalese infantry and French officers) embarked on a wide sweep against the inland flank of the Mareth line.[75]

The Axis position at Mareth stretched from the coast some 22 miles and terminated in the Matmata Hills. Defending it were nine divisions, five German and four Italian—an impressive force on paper. The infantry divisions manned the main defensive line. Moving inland from the sea, they included the Young Fascist Division, the *Trieste* Division, the 90th Light Division (more or less in the center of the Mareth position), the *Spezia* Division, the *Pistoia* Motorized Division, and the 164th Light Division. Although the battle array might appear to be sufficient for such a short line, all these units were in fact grossly understrength. *Trieste* and *Spezia* were binary divisions, containing only two regiments of three battalions apiece, while the Young Fascists weren't even up to that minimal strength, putting just five battalions into the line. The 164th Division had only four battalions of its regular allotment of nine, and in fact amounted to little more than a reinforced regiment. Behind the main line were three Panzer Divisions—15th, 21st, and 10th—but anyone following the campaign by now will not be surprised to find them a shadow of their authorized strength. The 10th Panzer Division, for example, contained only 32 tanks.[76]

Like all Montgomery's battles, this one was more difficult than analysts think it should have been. Even when outnumbering the enemy 610 tanks to 150, he still tended toward caution. Opening on March 20, the frontal attack by XXX Corps failed, as did virtually all frontal attacks in World War II. An attempt to get across the Wadi Zigzaou by placing heavy bundles of straw and sticks (known as fascines) failed completely, with many of the bundles being set on fire by defensive fire. There were heavy casualties among the attackers and some scenes of panic. Montgomery, as always, stayed cool when he received the news—so cool that some have accused him of being unfeeling. He already had a force on the Axis flank: the New Zealand Corps. He now changed plans, ordering X Corps to get round the flank of the Mareth line and reinforce the New Zealanders. Operation Pugilist Gallop became Supercharge II, a conscious reference to a similar change of plans in the midst of the El Alamein offensive. The move was deliberate enough to permit a German response, with the Panzer divisions redeploying to the western flank and ensuring the cohesion of the flank. The fighting here was tough, but over two days, British superiority in tanks, incessant artillery fire, and uncontested control of the air rendered the Axis situation untenable. By March 26, General Messe issued orders to abandon the Mareth line and retreat back to the next defensive bottleneck, the Wadi Akarit position 35 miles to the north, where the impassable Chott el Fedjadj salt marsh provided protection on the inland flank. Montgomery had failed to destroy the 1st Italian Army at Mareth, but he had taken 5,000 Italian prisoners, mainly soldiers of the infantry divisions who were almost always sacrificed in such positional battles.

It was not evident at the time, but this was the last straw for the Italians. On the night of April 5, when Montgomery began his assault on the Wadi Akarit (or "Chott position"), his forward elements of the 4th Indian Division began to report mass surrenders among the Italians, some 4,000 that first night. With the defensive position shattered within hours, he soon had X Corps racing north in exploitation. Joining him were elements of Patton's II Corps, coming in from the west. On April 7th, the two forces made contact, and the Allies had finally established a unified front in Tunisia. By this time, Messe's 1st Italian Army was long gone. It had made a great retreat of its own, lunging all the way back up the coast to Enfidaville, more than 200 miles to the north. The "Tunisian bridgehead" was now a bare lodgement around Tunis. From Enfidaville, the line headed due west, then turned 90 degrees to the right, heading north through Medjez el Bab and thence to the sea— a front just 100 miles long, compared to the previous 400 miles.

While Italian forces were by now utterly threadbare, the Germans were not in much better shape. The Allies had closed the ring around the enemy in Tunisia, and the endgame had clearly begun. The biggest problem they faced now was a technical one. The junction of the two Allied armies had the effect of "pinching out" the U.S. II Corps. Eisenhower and Alexander now decided to pull it out of the line and redeploy it to the north under its new commander, General Bradley. It was a complex move as these things go, with II Corps having to cut across the rear area of 1st Army, but an increasingly competent U.S. command managed to pull it off with minimal disruption.[77]

As the Allies prepared for their final drive, opposition across the front was collapsing. Axis supply was drying up, and morale was plummeting. Even the humblest foot soldier had to have been aware of the hopelessness of the cause. Neither Eisenhower nor his field commanders could know that in detail, of course, although they were beginning to read the signs. On April 19, the 8th Army opened the drive on Tunis, battering the Enfidaville position with XXX Corps, followed three days later by 1st Army moving in from the west. Today it has become customary in the literature to emphasize the difficulties of that final drive, and indeed, the first attacks met determined resistance. Montgomery's first attempt to crack the Enfidaville position failed so badly that Alexander decided to strip him of a handful of divisions and transfer them to Anderson's 1st Army, which, presumably, could make better use of them. By the end of April, the 4th Indian Division and the 7th Armoured Division were fighting as part of the British V Corps. They spearheaded the great drive to the east that cracked open the Axis line on May 1, driving through Massicault on the direct route to Tunis. Axis resistance gave way everywhere, and soon the Allies were motoring in the clear. Tunis and Bizerte both fell on May 7, the former to the British and the latter to the Americans, and the last Axis resistance in the Cape Bon peninsula ceased a few days later.[78]

Conclusion

And so this attenuated campaign had finally come to an end. Some 250,000 Axis prisoners of war fell into Allied hands, including Generals Messe and Arnim and a host of other high-ranking officers. The three divisions of Rommel's old *Afrika Korps*—15th and 21st Panzer and the 90th Light Division, formations that had written an epic in the annals of German military history—went into captivity wholesale. Already there were some in the ranks who were speaking of a "Tunisgrad" in North Africa, a catastrophe equivalent to Stalingrad, and the term appears commonly in the literature even today.[79] Equating the two requires a certain amount of nuance, however. At Stalingrad, the Wehrmacht lost the principal field formation in its 1942 battle array, the 6th Army: 330,000 men at the start of the campaign, along with almost all the heavy weapons and combat engineers in Army Group South. It was an operational defeat, but also a strategic catastrophe. Tunis, by comparison, was merely a disaster. Perhaps one-third of the quarter million total were fighting troops; indeed, a short time before the end, Rommel had estimated the total Axis fighting strength in Africa as 120,000 men,[80] and there had been serious losses and only meager replacements since then. Of those fighters, let us estimate that about half had been German. A great deal of the manpower scooped up at "Tunisgrad" belonged to the detritus of the Italian administration in the African colonies, possessions that Italy had now lost forever.[81]

It may seem churlish to end on such a negative note, however. The Tunisian campaign had been complete victory for the Allies after all— a bit later than anyone would have liked, but a satisfying end to a tough fight. The drive on Tunis would become a model for all later Allied campaigns, including the great drive across western Europe in 1944. It did not rely on surprise, complex maneuver, or brilliant generalship, all components of the German way of war. Rather, battle management became the key to turning resources into fighting power. It combined overwhelming preponderance of strength on the ground, absolute dominance in the air, a logistics pipeline with enough bandwidth to support continuous operations across the front without letup or pause, and commanders who did their job and minded their Ps and Qs. Patton was an anomaly, but then again, he would have been an anomaly in just about any walk of life he had chosen.

The U.S. Army exemplified this development. Bradley proved to be a highly competent corps commander. He didn't display much flash, but his even steadiness sat well with the officers and men under his command. By the end of the fight, his "corps" was the size of some World War II–era armies. His field-grade officers had always been decent, and the rank and file now had enough experience under their belts to qualify as veterans. Moving with four divisions abreast (from left to right, the 9th, 34th, and 1st Infantry Divisions, and the 1st Armored Division), with the Germans in front of him flattened by U.S. artillery, and with incessant air attacks bringing the entire depth of the defensive position under attack in classic style, Bradley made steady if unspectacular progress in that final drive. His corps took Mateur on May 3 and then Bizerte on May 7, the latter having been almost completely destroyed by Allied bombing.

It is a good time to pause and reflect. Bradley's drive on Bizerte took place only two and a half months after the disasters at Sidi bou Zid and Kasserine and the destruction of entire U.S. infantry regiments with one blow. In that brief time, the U.S. Army had managed to find its footing and develop an operational skill set. It was not a fine rapier, and it never would be. It preferred to batter. It liked its high explosive, and it used more of it than any military force in history. Its operations were rarely pretty. Its infantry were loath to do anything too daring or aggressive, and why should they? Why stick out one's neck when artillery or air strikes could do the killing much more efficiently? All these attributes are well known. What sometimes receives less attention is its extremely high level of mobility. It had a higher degree of mechanization than any other army in the world, and once it forced or found a seam in the enemy's line, it had an ability to eat up the miles that was truly rare for the day. It really did combine what we might call classically American attributes: a preference for industrial-age warfare and mass production on the one hand, and a long, storied tradition of high-speed cavalry chases on the Great Plains on the other. In that sense, the U.S. Army in Tunisia was an almost perfect manifestation of a way of war—a military culture deeply embedded in history, culture, and tradition.[82]

As for the Wehrmacht, it fought this campaign much as it had all the others of this war, and as German armies had fought the previous ones, stretching back hundreds of years. All the familiar characteristics were present: a series of discrete operations aimed at a carefully chosen point in the enemy's defenses (the *Schwerpunkt*, often translated as "center of gravity" but meaning here "point of main effort"); rapid and violent initial blows by multiple columns seeking a breakthrough into the enemy's operational depth; concentric (*konzentrisch*) operations to smash the enemy's main body, or as much of it as possible, in a *Kesselschlacht*. There were the same aggressive army commanders (Kesselring, Arnim, and Rommel), the independent-minded field- and company-grade officers. They shared a notion, to the very end, that German will, energy, and *Schneid* could compensate for inferiority in the purely material realm. The German army in Tunisia went down doing what it had always done: launching offensive operations—*Morgenluft, Frühlingswind, Ochsenkopf,* Rommel's last, unnamed abortive assault at Medenine. Of course, none of them had worked, and after the disasters the army had suffered in 1942, at Stalingrad and at El Alamein, the classic German way of war would never succeed again. However, the pattern was so ingrained in this officer corps that it kept trying. It is perhaps tempting to quote the well-known definition of insanity: doing the same thing over and over again and expecting a different result.

Was it insane? Perhaps. It would be interesting to ask the Allies that question, however. Beating the Wehrmacht had not been easy. This clash of ways of war in Tunisia—one of them characterized by a high level of aggression and a preference for maneuver warfare, the other seeking to turn every encounter with the enemy into a grinding *Materialschlacht*—was by definition going to generate high casualties. The Allies suffered 70,000 casualties in Tunisia: 36,000 for the British, 16,000 for the French, and 18,000 for the United States. In its first campaign of the war, the U.S. Army had lost 2,715 men killed in action, 8,978 wounded, and 6,528 missing, many of whom were later added to the rolls of the dead.

For the Allies, these numbers pointed to the real significance of the Tunisian campaign: what it portended for the future. The cost of conquering this small French colony pointed to a future calculus that was anything but comforting to the Allies. It took seven months of tough fighting and 70,000 casualties to subdue a handful of German divisions. If Eisenhower or any of the Allied commanders had any illusions about how difficult it was going to be to make a forced entry into Europe, smash the Wehrmacht, and occupy Germany, Tunisia should have dispelled them altogether.

For the Germans, both the losses and the portents were even worse. It is easy to miss the fact that Tunisia had been the first great campaign fought entirely in a so-called OKW theater. Back in 1938, Hitler had taken over leadership of the armed forces and created a small personal staff for himself, the high command of the armed forces (*Oberkommando der Wehrmacht*, or OKW). He intended not only to coordinate planning between the services—army, navy, and air force—but also to serve as a counterweight to the historically dominant bodies in German war making: the high command of the army (*Oberkommando des Heeres*, OKH) and the General Staff. Hitler distrusted them: they were traditional groupings with strong institutional identification and loyalties, and thus potential threats to his own power. They were also bastions of the old Junker social elite that he despised.

In the course of the war, he had used the OKW to cut the General Staff out of the planning loop whenever it suited him. He had also greatly expanded it, until by the end of 1943 it contained 44 agencies and commands.[83] He had also placed an increasing number of theaters under OKW jurisdiction: Norway, occupied France, Finland, the Balkans, Crete, North Africa, and others. The exception was the Eastern Front, which remained an OKH theater—a sensible decision because virtually all of the army was fighting there. The result was a nightmare of parallel and competing bureaucracies. Even something as simple as the transfer of a division from Russia (OKH front) to France (OKW) and back again (OKH) was guaranteed to generate a blizzard of paperwork and expend more institutional energy than it was worth.

Tunisia had not been the army's show, in other words. Zeitzler, the General Staff, and the OKH had nothing to do with planning or conducting operations there. It was entirely in the hands of Hitler and his small OKW staff, especially his chief of operations, General Alfred Jodl. Hitler had spent the entire war railing against the "fine gentlemen" on the General Staff and blaming them for the debacles of 1941–1942. Now, in Tunisia, he and his handpicked assistants had a chance to run a campaign as he saw fit. The result had been a minor-league Stalingrad.[84]

It is easy to say that they had all botched this campaign: Hitler and Jodl and Keitel, Kesselring, even Rommel and Arnim. Perhaps, however, it was a campaign that they had no real business fighting. North Africa was something unique in Prussian–German military history: an overseas operation involving an expeditionary force, a years-long, logistics-intensive affair, a venture requiring control of the seas and the delicate touch required by littoral warfare. All of these were entirely alien to the German tradition, and the Wehrmacht as currently constituted was unsuited to fight and win in such an environment. One has to dig pretty deeply to find anything even remotely similar in the past: the punitive expedition against the Boxers, perhaps, or the suppression of the Hereros in Namibia, but even these anomalous examples offered no lessons applicable to North Africa. Although many things had gone wrong, Hitler and the OKW had been particularly inept at judging the timing: when to reinforce, when to drive on, when to hold back, and especially, in the early spring of 1943, when to cut and run altogether. Whether the campaign was winnable can still generate debate. Surely, however, defeat could have come without the loss of all hands.

Now, as they pored grimly over the unending roll of prisoners taken in the big roundup at Tunis and Cape Bon, where no fewer than 3,600 German officers had just fallen into Allied hands, they might have done well to recall the words of Frederick the Great. He had never spent a great deal of time worrying about the Mediterranean or Africa or dreaming of a far-flung Prussian empire. The king wasn't much of a navy man. His idea of going deep on his adversary was marching into neighboring provinces like Silesia or Bohemia or Moravia. He once got as far west as Rossbach in Thuringia. He had met a French army there in late 1757 and had enjoyed a pretty good day. He was a wise man, all in all, one of the most highly aggressive battlefield commanders of all time, but also a ruler who knew his limitations and those of the state that he guided.

Once, late in his reign, the English ambassador to Berlin had asked him for his opinion of a war that was then raging in an obscure corner of the globe, in far-off North America. The British army was desperately trying to suppress a rebellion among its unruly subjects, and the ambassador wanted a second opinion. Old Fritz chewed over the question a bit before answering. "Believe me," he answered "it's tough enough to wage a war when it is happening close by. Fighting one on another continent altogether? That's about as much as the human mind can take."[85]

4

The Battle of Kursk:
A Reassessment

Introduction

Is there such a thing as history, or are there only various points of view that we more properly call "histories"? Consider these three vignettes of the Wehrmacht at war, all dating from the midpoint of 1943.[1]

If he heard one more of his generals whining about the upcoming offensive. . . . He could feel the anger rising again.[2] As long as everything ran well, they were fine. When things turned tough, they melted. Always the same talk: operations, tactics, supply . . . as if that was all that mattered in war! Hadn't these fine gentlemen ever read Clausewitz? They certainly quoted him often enough. But none of them ever seemed to think about the political side. . . . No. That was apparently his job.

Things had taken a bad turn. Anyone could see that. Stalingrad, Tunis, problems with the U-boats . . . he could feel it. The whole damn thing was in danger of crashing down, but all they could do was complain.

Cancel the Kursk offensive? That's what they were all telling him now. He had to laugh. Of course! How simple! Why hadn't *he* thought of it? Cancel the offensive! Hand over the initiative to his enemies. Let the anti-Mussolini gang come to power in Italy. Let Antonescu go down in Romania—the king was just waiting for a chance to strike. Damn! Why hadn't Antonescu listened to him? "Build a popular movement," he told the Romanian dictator. "Don't rely on the army." Antonescu didn't listen. No one ever listened. In Hungary, that fox Horthy was just waiting for an opportunity. If we looked away for a minute, he would be signing a treaty with the English.

No . . . he wasn't going to cancel Citadel. They knew that. So now they had come up with a new argument: wait until the Russians had attacked, give up ground, lead them on, and then hit them with a backhand. He felt the anger again: going back, giving up ground, freeing up troops for mobile operations. "Operieren"—he was starting to hate that word. "Operating." One thing he had learned in the Great War: you took ground, you held it. You didn't give it up so that you could "operate."

Idiots. Why couldn't they see? Every war had its ups and downs. Why should this one be different? Maybe all those early victories had been too easy for them. The first setback sent them all to pieces. They might have been more educated than he was, but he'd read more history than all of them put together. Frederick the Great didn't despair after Kunersdorf, and he had nothing left at all by then.[3] He was a fugitive without an army.

No, old Fritz didn't give in.

And neither would he.

➤•◄

Had Hitler gone mad?[4]

The Army Group commanders had been in a feisty mood tonight, exchanging some frank talk—too frank at times. It made the chief of the operations department nervous. You couldn't be too careful. But there were times you just couldn't help it. First Stalingrad, then Tunis. And now this.

Had he gone mad?

They had gathered together in Mauerwald before tomorrow morning's meeting with the Führer. It wasn't a happy group at the moment. Stalingrad had been bad enough . . . then Tunis. Hitler wasn't thinking things through. Half-measures—always half-measures![5] They should have gotten out of Africa the moment the Allies landed in the west, or taken Gibraltar or Malta. They should have done something, for God's sake! Not just . . . sit there.

Now the same thing was happening in the east. Anyone looking at a map could see it, the chief thought to himself. It was time to pull back, straighten out the front, free up troops currently wasted holding all those twists and turns. They'd already proven they could do it successfully. Army Group Center and its *Büffelbewegung*.[6] Now that, he thought, had been an elegant little operation, what they'd all been trained to do. Yet Hitler didn't want to hear about it. *Operieren* meant "pull back," "retreat," and that meant an early retirement for any officer stupid enough to suggest it. Then Hitler would just get someone more pliable. They'd all seen it before.

No retreat. Hitler wanted that attack. *Der Kursker Bogen*—the "Kursk bulge," the most obvious spot on the map. How stupid did he think the Russian was? Any trained staff officer could see it. No possibility of surprise here, outside of the timing. . . . Maybe last March, right after Kharkov, it would have worked. Or early spring. But it was already mid-June.[7]

What was he waiting for?

Had he gone mad?

➤·◄

July 4, 1943. Nighttime.[8]

The major wasn't happy.

He spat on the ground. The sergeant had just reported in with a message from the Führer, the "order of the day" before the big offensive. It was four pages long.

Four pages! The longer the war went on, the longer the speeches.[9] He didn't know much history, but he wondered whether Frederick the Great or Napoleon had talked this much.

The battalion had been together for a long time and had gone through a lot. They didn't need a lot of words. Give them some chow, enough ammunition, a good night's sleep every now and then. That was about it.

New tanks were coming in, brand-new, hardly driven Panthers. Had their main guns even fired a shot? He spat again. He knew something about tanks. You had to break them in—gently. Anyway, he'd heard that those bastards in the S.S. were getting all the new stuff anyway. He'd stick with his Mark IVs for now.

New tanks? What they all needed was more infantry. Any idiot could see that, but infantry didn't seem to be on anyone's priority list.

He was holding something else in his hand, some pamphlets the Reds had dropped earlier. He flipped through them: photos from Stalingrad, German prisoners, proclamations from Seydlitz urging them all to surrender. He'd met Seydlitz once. The man was tough as nails. God only knew what the Russians did to him.[10]

Now this! A pioneer company just coming in. According to the sergeant, intelligence had just discovered some newly built Russian defensive position to their front. They were going to need engineering support to break through.

Six hours before the attack? A bit late, in his opinion.[11] This wasn't going right. He'd been around a while, and he could feel it in his bones.

The major wasn't happy.

⇒⋅⇐

Indeed. It was the eve of the big German offensive of 1943, aiming for the great bulge in the Soviet lines in front of the industrial city of Kursk. The Wehrmacht stood on the verge of catastrophe, and no one seemed particularly happy.

The Incredible Shrinking Battle of Kursk

The greatest tank battle of all time?[12] Well, maybe. The phrase should be instantly familiar to every scholar, student, or aficionado of World War II. For decades, we have applied it to describe the battle of Kursk, Operation Citadel (*Zitadelle*), the monstrous armored clash between the German and Soviet armies in the summer of 1943.[13] Neither side held back: the Germans were making their last throw of the dice in the east, desperately trying to chew through a tough Soviet defensive position into open ground, where, they believed, their superior training and initiative could equalize superior enemy numbers; an increasingly confident Soviet army parried the blow, but they also counterattacked from day one, first in isolated spots and later inserting their operational and strategic reserves all over the map.

In the traditional narrative, the climax of the battle came near a nondescript village named Prokhorovka on July 12. In one corner was the Soviet 5th Guards Tank Army under General P. A. Rotmistrov; in the other, the II (S.S.) Panzer Corps, under the one-eyed S.S. general Paul Hausser. Once again, the Germans were on the prowl, seeking a crossing over the Psel River, the last natural obstacle in front of Kursk. Once again, the Soviets alternated between holding on grimly and launching vicious counterstrokes.

What a day! Prokhorovka would become a watchword for the destructiveness of modern warfare, a struggle of fiendish intensity, with each side aware that he was in a kind of last-ditch situation, and that there was no substitute for victory. The violence and confusion knew no bounds: intermingled columns, point-blank main gunfire, and yes— every student of the war has heard it—tanks actually ramming one another in the scorching July heat. Rotmistrov would later describe the battlefield in apocalyptic terms: "Dead bodies, destroyed tanks, crushed guns, and numerous shell craters dotted the battlefield. There was not a single blade of grass to be seen: only burnt, black, and smoldering earth throughout the entire depth of our attack—up to eight miles."[14]

Another source described the Prokhorovka battlefield as "an immense knotted mass of tanks," and the phrase has entered the literature and popular consciousness alike. In the end, the Soviets held, inflicting monstrous loses on their S.S. counterparts. The Germans failed to break through, and Operation Citadel was effectively over.

It is a compelling, even irresistible, narrative. Kursk has it all: the elite mechanized formations of the German *Waffen* S.S. (the "armed S.S.," the parallel army designed to serve as the German army's mechanized elite), desperate Soviet heroism in defense of the homeland, and tanks—lots of tanks, and new ones to boot.[15] For the Germans, the new Panthers and Tigers made an appearance, not to mention a gigantic tank destroyer they named Ferdinand. For the Soviets, the trusty T-34 proved once again to be the margin between victory and defeat. The significance of the battle, like its size, has always appeared to be massive. For all those historians who point to the German defeat in front of Moscow (1941) as the turning point of the war, or the encirclement of German 6th Army at Stalingrad (1942), there have always been a sizable number who see that turning point in Kursk. It was the "swan song of the German panzers,"[16] their collective death ride, the moment when it became clear just who was dictating to whom in this war.

More recently, however, scholars have been cutting Kursk down to size. Adding a welcome new voice to the discussion have been Soviet researchers who finally managed to gain access to the archival sources only after the fall of communism. To this group one should add the name of the formidable American scholar, David Glantz.[17] A retired U.S. Army colonel, he reads Russian, has cultivated his sources inside Russia, and has churned out book after book revising our view of the German–Soviet war. All of these scholars have told us a lot of things that the German records also confirm. Kursk was never a "last-ditch" anything. The Wehrmacht was not seeking some dramatic breakthrough into operational space here. Its attack was fairly localized, consisting of just two regular armies (the 9th Army in the north and the 4th Panzer in the south) plus a "provisional" one guarding 4th Panzer Army's right flank (*Armee-Abteilung Kempf*). Compare this to Operation Barbarossa in 1941. Then, the Wehrmacht had attacked the Soviets on an immense front from the Baltic to the Black seas. Its losses in that campaign meant that by 1942, it had to choose a single sector for its offensive, and it went south with multiple armies in Operation Blue. Its losses in that campaign—the complete destruction, at Stalingrad, of its largest field army in the east—meant that by 1943, it had been reduced to launching a kind of spoiling operation: trying to destroy those Soviet forces conveniently deployed in the Kursk salient. Success here would ease some of the pressure on the creaking Eastern Front, dislocate Soviet plans for a new Soviet offensive out of Kursk, and result in a shortening of the line (*Frontverkürzung*), freeing up urgently needed German forces for use elsewhere.[18]

Certainly, the combat was terrible and the losses were high. Modern mechanized mass armies have a way of mauling each other when engaging in this type of close-range positional warfare. But that apocalyptic battle at Prokhorovka? Apparently it didn't happen. At least it doesn't appear in any of the German-language sources, and in only a handful of Soviet ones. There was fighting there, but in its traditionally accepted form—the "immense knotted mass of tanks," the furious melee, the wildest single day in the history of armored warfare—Prokhorovka doesn't really exist.[19]

The Germans were nothing in World War II if not meticulous record keepers, even of their worst atrocities, and so one would expect to find a big red number in the German armor listings for July 12, the day the tanks battled at Prokhorovka. Perhaps, if you discovered documents in the archives, you might even expect to see marginalia scrawled alongside the table of figures or multiple exclamation marks, for example. Instead, one finds hardly anything at all. No great tank apocalypse, no death ride, no swan song of the German Panzers. Ask most of the German tank crews who were there, and they probably would have told a tale of a hard defensive struggle against a massive Soviet counterstroke. They had taken moderate losses, but they had dished out some serious pain to the attackers. A good day's work, all in all.[20]

For the myth of Prokhorovka, it is clear today that we have to look to the writings of General Rotmistrov, commander of the Soviet 5th Guards Tank Army.[21] Tasked to launch a counterstroke to halt the drive of Army Group South (and its spearhead, II S.S. Panzer Corps), he did so with gusto, launching a massive frontal assault into the teeth of the advancing Germans. Mixing it up close range with Panthers and Tigers almost always had deleterious consequences. His losses were stupendous, and only recently have researchers mining post-Soviet archives been telling the tale. His spearhead, the 29th Tank Corps, for example, lost 95 of its 122 T-34 tanks, 36 of 70 light T-70s, and 19 of 20 assault guns.[22] It did not have to be this way. Soviet formations fighting alongside Rotmistrov fought with less boldness but more wisdom, and they brought the Germans to a halt without such mind-boggling losses.[23]

In Stalinist Russia, these facts meant that Rotmistrov had some explaining to do, and explain it he did. In his memoirs, he painted what became the received version of Prokhorovka, owning up to his own losses, yes, but claiming to have destroyed 400 tanks and broken the back of the II S.S. Panzer Corps that day. Destroying 400 tanks really would have been an achievement because the S.S. only had 267 tanks in the entire corps at Prokhorovka.[24] Indeed, German losses for all of Army Group South in the entire 12 days of the Kursk offensive amounted to just 161 tanks. Rotmistrov also claimed to have destroyed no fewer than 70 Tigers. Again, that would have been a signal achievement. The actual number of Tigers lost at Prokhorovka? Zero.[25]

And from there? Well, let us just say that ever since, historians and authors have been off and running. "The greatest tank battle of all time." "The battle of 6,000 tanks."[26] Descriptions of a vast meeting engagement of 1,500 tanks on a battlefield "500 meters wide and 1,000 meters deep at most." Mind-boggling, even ridiculous numbers, when you stop to think about it.[27] The problem has been that until recently, few people have stopped to think about it.

The numbers are literally impossible. Was Prokhorovka a big battle? Absolutely. The turning point of the war? Maybe yes, maybe no. We'll be arguing about that one forever; that is the nature of "turning point" debates. The greatest tank battle in history? Almost certainly not.

Troubled Plan, Troubled Origins

Writing after the war, veteran German armor officer General F. W. von Mellenthin had little good to say about the operational plan for the Kursk offensive. "Broadly speaking," he sniffed, "the plan was very simple."[28] As part of a General Staff that defined war fighting largely in terms of the elegance of its maneuver scheme, Mellenthin couldn't help but feel a sense of professional embarrassment over the design of Citadel. War was an art, they all believed, one "based on scientific principles,"[29] but still an art. The Eastern Front in 1943 was immense, with open rolling plains stretching to infinity in all directions. What an operational palette this was, and what possibilities existed for *Bewegungskrieg*, the war of movement! A feint here, a surprise attack there, a sudden withdrawal, a surprise assault—the potential number of attack scenarios was unlimited. It was particularly true of the wide-open southern sector, with its relative absence of covering or channeling terrain. In the Ukraine, it was relatively easy to set the front in motion because no army could guard every position and strengthen every flank. Once that had happened, they all knew—and this was another article of faith—that German superiority in planning, training, and mobility could truly come to the fore and win victories no matter how dispiriting the odds.[30]

If ever an army truly needed a victory, it was the Wehrmacht in 1943. It was now in its third campaigning season in the Soviet Union. The catastrophe in front of Moscow had essentially destroyed it. Rebuilt in 1942 with youthful conscripts, it had marched off to disaster at Stalingrad. The flow of the war had definitely turned against Germany on all fronts. It was time to make a dramatic statement. Instead of calling on every one of the refinements in its military art, however, all that the heirs of this long and storied military tradition could come up with in 1943 was a lumbering strike against the most obvious spot on the map. "Instead of seeking to create conditions in which maneuver would be possible," Mellenthin complained, "the German Supreme Command could think of nothing better than to fling our magnificent Panzer Divisions against Kursk."[31]

Anyone who studies this history of Prussian–German operations will find it easy to sympathize with Mellenthin. Of all of the great German campaigns, Citadel remains one of the easiest to narrate, which might be one of its problems. The Kursk salient was a bulge in the lines in the northern Ukraine, an annoying interruption in a front that ran relatively straight across the rest of the front from the Sea of Azov to the Arctic. As such, it was an obvious target. It was also a convenient operational boundary between Army Groups Center and South. As the plan eventually developed, one army from each Army Group—the 9th Army (General Walther Model) from Army Group Center and the 4th Panzer Army (General Hermann Hoth) from Army Group South—would attack the bases of the salient, penetrate the Soviet defenses in front of them, and advance concentrically until they had linked up and trapped Soviet forces in an immense *Kessel*. Protecting the open southern flank of the 4th Panzer Army as it advanced to the north was a third army-sized unit, *Armee-Abteilung Kempf* (Army Detachment Kempf, named for its commander). Although it was auxiliary to Citadel rather than central, it would come to play a key role in the way the offensive unfolded.

Two armies. An obvious bulge. A concentric advance. The plan for Citadel envisioned no prebattle maneuver, no attempt to get the foe off-balance, no feint in favor of the main assault, no surprise. Moreover, the defenders had had four months to fortify their positions around this obvious target. For a force as skilled in the techniques of field fortification as the Red Army, it might as well have been four

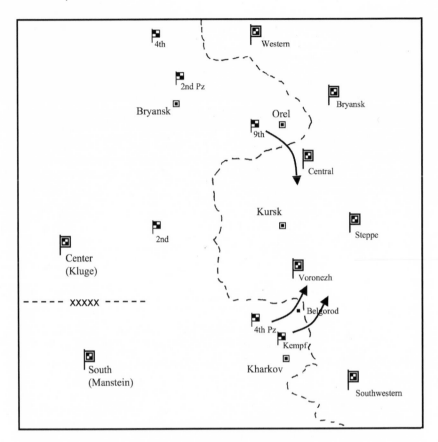

Failed Breakthrough: Operation Citadel (July 5–8, 1943)

years. As a result, the Kursk salient was as well prepared to receive an attack as any spot along this 2,000-mile front. It fairly bristled with mutually supporting strongpoints, artillery emplacements, nests of anti-tank guns, one of the densest concentrations of mines ever laid down in war, and no fewer than eight defensive belts, the result of the labor of some 300,000 civilians put to work by the Soviet authorities.[32]

No position is impregnable in and of itself. The ground troops on both sides, as always, have to decide that. Even here, however, the Soviets were looking good at Kursk. Those two German armies mentioned above, Model's 9th and Hoth's 4th Panzer, were going to be trying their luck against three Soviet *fronts* (the Russian word for army groups). Model would have to break through the Central Front (General K. K. Rokossovsky) in the northern half of the bulge, while Hoth had to do the same to the Voronezh Front (General N. F. Vatutin) in the south. Even if one or both of these German drives succeeded, standing behind these two Soviet fronts in reserve lay the Steppe Front (General I. S. Konev), its mission to feed troops into the fighting to the west or to act as a last-ditch backstop in case things went badly wrong inside the salient. The Steppe Front was one of the largest strategic reserves ever assembled. It says a great deal about the Red Army by this point in the war that it could afford to keep five infantry armies, one tank army, one air army, and six reserve corps (two of which were tank corps) out of the main action altogether, ready to be called upon as needed.

Looking back from the present day, Citadel's chances of success appear slim. Indeed, we are tempted to label it doomed from the start. Reading any of the numerous histories of the battle leads to that conclusion. At the same time, however, we should recognize that historical actors almost never decide to do anything that they think to be impossible. Clearly, the Germans felt they had some prospects for success at Kursk. The question thus remains: how did the plan for Citadel form? From whence did it come, and from whom?

For decades after the war, the answer to all of these questions was simple. It came from Hitler. This point of view, enshrined first in the memoirs of General Kurt Zeitzler, the chief of the Army General Staff, passed through a number of iterations and variants, including the most influential of all the official German memoirs, Erich von Manstein's *Lost Victories*. As a narrative, it seemed to make sense: an amateur Führer ordering a senseless attack against a nearly unassailable position, overriding the objections of his more sober professional officers, and getting his way in the end, as he always did. It fit neatly into so many postwar assumptions about Hitler, which had not only judged him morally (quite rightly, to be sure) but had also felt the need to call every single one of his military judgments into question as well, perhaps to dispel any lingering notions of his "genius."

Over the years, however, it became more and more difficult to blame Hitler alone for the offensive against Kursk. In fact, it is clear today that they all owned it—Hitler, the staff, and the field commanders alike. The historical record is clear that the initial inspiration for a strike at Kursk came not from Hitler but from Manstein himself. Back in March 1943, at the conclusion of his successful winter counteroffensive, even as Hitler was declaring that 1943 would see no grand offensives, Manstein was already calling for further aggressive action in the east.[33] His successful drive north to Kharkov had caught Soviet forces by surprise, destroying one army altogether and mauling a couple of others. The great city of Kharkov itself had fallen, the Soviet defenses in the entire sector appeared to be in disarray, and Manstein thought that the time had come for a follow-up offensive to the north, perhaps in cooperation with the forces of Army Group Center, to retake Kursk. Hitler also wanted to maintain the momentum of the German offensive, although he was looking in a different direction altogether: toward the city of Izyum and the Donets.

After a great deal of back and forth, Hitler's opinion prevailed. On March 13, Hitler issued Operational Order (*Operationsbefehl*) No. 5.[34] It called for the formation of "a strong panzer army" on the northern flank of Army Group South, ready to attack "to the north out of the Kharkov area"[35]; at the same time, Army Group Center was to form an "attack group," it mission "to attack in conjunction with the northern flank of Army Group South."[36] The order mentioned neither the city of Kursk nor the operational name Citadel, but the conception was clearly there: a two army group/two army assault from north and south against the Kursk salient. Operational Order No. 5 looked to a start date "no later than mid-April"[37] because it would be necessary for both of the involved army groups to strip their respective fronts to provide divisions for the assault. Adding impetus would be the nine divisions freed up by the *Büffelbewegung*,[38] the successful evacuation of the Rzhev salient by General Model's 9th Army, along with several divisions from France and two from a long-overdue shortening of the Kuban bridgehead in the far south.

In the end, this initial offensive failed to meet Hitler's original timeline, and the reasons still look pretty solid even after all these years. The rainy season (the *Tauwetter*, the Germans called it) was approaching, leading inexorably to the season of mud (the *Schlammperiod*), and even the most basic administrative movement was already becoming more and more difficult. Beyond the weather, the waning of German strength was also a problem. Kharkov had been an impressive victory, but it could not hide the strategic defeat that the Wehrmacht had suffered at Stalingrad. Army Group South was short an entire army in its order of battle, and Army Group Center was no better off. It had handed over much of its strength and most of its mobile formations to Army Group South earlier in 1942 to make the summer offensive, Operation Blue, possible in the first place. Expecting these two Army Groups to suddenly launch themselves into a mobile campaign was delusional.[39]

In reading through the staff meetings that Hitler had held with Manstein and the other field commanders in February and March, one can also perceive a certain sense of bewilderment after the wild ride of the past few months and a refusal to test the patience of the war gods any more than they already had. The commander of the 4th Panzer Army, General Hoth, a man with a certain reputation for dourness but also one of the most aggressive Panzer commanders of all time, put it this way on March 21 in response to an inquiry from Manstein regarding the possibility of further offensive action:

> The troops, who for months have been fighting day and night without rest, have been under severe stress. The previous orders of the Führer have led them to believe that they had earned a certain period of rest. There will be some disappointment now if they receive orders to leave their present, quite makeshift, positions. A series of reports from commanders, even ones with reputations as "daredevils," have made it clear that the troops at least partly have become apathetic and have only reached their current operational goal, the Donets, under the strongest urgings of their leaders.[40]

Difficulties in assembling and refreshing the assault formations soon became evident, and a new operational order appeared on April 5, this one envisioning a May 3 start date.

During this entire period, Manstein was continuing to press his case for early action. He soon had an ally in the cause: General Zeitzler, the chief of the General Staff. Often treated in the literature as a strong supporter of Hitler and a lukewarm ally of the traditional army, he was in fact a man of some operational acumen. He was no opponent of the regime.[41] He wanted to strengthen it, we might say, by ridding it of its more obvious deficiencies in the area of military leadership. In the spring of 1943, that desire meant backing the man usually recognized as the most operationally gifted of the German commanders, Manstein, in his various disputes with the Führer. Zeitzler soon set pen to paper with yet another iteration of the Kursk offensive, this one dubbed "Operation Citadel."

The new directive appeared on April 15, 1943. This was Operational Order No. 6, penned by Zeitzler and sent out over Hitler's signature.[42] "I have decided to launch Operation 'Citadel,'" it began, "as the first of this year's offensives as soon as the weather permits."[43] Although sometimes criticized for its characteristic "Führer style" (*Führerstil*) of proclamation,[44] it is more accurate to describe the tone of the document as pleading. Oddly enough for a German operational order, a genre historically known for its sobriety and terseness of expression, this one opened with a pep talk:

> This assault is of the utmost importance. It must succeed rapidly and totally. It must give us the initiative for this spring and summer.
>
> For this reason, all preparations must be carried out with utmost care and energy. The best formations, the best weapons, the best commanders must be present with great stocks of ammunition placed at each *Schwerpunkt*. Every commander, every man must be indoctrinated with the decisive significance of this offensive. The victory of Kursk must be a signal to the world.[45]

"Der Sieg von Kursk muss für die Welt wie en Fanal wirken." At least one participant in the deliberations claims that Hitler interjected this line into the typescript in his own hand.[46] It is always a revealing thing when a commander feels the need to explain to his troops how important a battle is, and one cannot help but note a sense of whistling past the graveyard here, of a military command that realizes how slim the odds have become. It is an aspect that historians have noted in other German operations of the war, and that is not surprising, given that the entire conflict had constituted a colossal gamble against the odds.[47]

In describing the operation, however, the order was firmly rooted in classic German military traditions, concepts, and phrases. Here, surely, we see the hand of Zeitzler, the trained General Staff officer. "The goal of the offensive is to launch a concentrated, ruthless, and rapid blow by one assault army each from the vicinity of Belgorod and one from south of Orel in order to surround (*einzukesseln*) the hostile formations in the vicinity of Kursk and to destroy them through concentric attack (*durch konzentrischen Angriff zu vernichten*)."[48] Such phrases had appeared many times before in German military history and discourse; as the foundational concept of the *Kesselschlacht*, they had formed the essence of the German way of war for centuries and would have been instantly familiar to past generations of German commanders.

Operational Order No. 6 specified May 3 as the earliest possible start date. It also added a six-day window for the armies to take up their assault positions and launch their attack. The attack orders from OKH for Citadel, therefore, would have to arrive no later than April 28. That deadline came and went. A mélange of factors were at work here: uncertainty about Soviet defensive deployments brought a two-day delay, heavy rains another four-day delay. The most important factor, however, was the attitude of General Model, commander of the 9th Army. Unhappy with the situation on his front, both the state of his own army as well as the Soviet buildup he could spot in front of him, he went to Hitler to tell him so in late April. The offensive was still possible, Model argued, but only if his army received strong reinforcements, especially the new tank designs just then beginning to arrive at the front, the Mark V Panthers and the Mark VI Tigers, as well as the tank destroyer nicknamed Ferdinand. Integrating them into the assault, Model believed, would provide the offensive punch that he required.[49]

So far, the narrative has been a simple one: Manstein had proposed a Kursk offensive and Zeitzler had agreed, drawing up the preliminary sketches in March and then more definite operational orders in April. Anyone who gave a careful read to the oft-maligned military memoirs would have taken note of it. Likewise, virtually all the memoirs discuss the crucial two-day staff meeting in Munich on May 3–4, in which Hitler and his army group commanders, General Heinz Guderian, the recently appointed general inspector of the Panzer Troops, economics and war production czar Albert Speer, and the Luftwaffe chief of staff, General Hans Jeschonnek, gathered to discuss the Kursk option.

The Munich meeting offers us a classic example of command dissonance.[50] It has become a trope of the historical scholarship on the Third Reich to argue that the regime, far from being "totalitarian," was actually "polycratic," with contending centers of power vying for influence at any one time, with "influence" usually being defined as proximity to Hitler.[51] This seems to be an applicable concept in the military sphere as well. The Munich meeting was not one of those classic, one-sided Führer monologues of legend; rather, it seems to have been an honest exchange of opinions among those present.

One modern historian has called it a "war among the generals,"[52] however, and that, too, seems appropriate. This was, after all, a most difficult time for the army. Germany had sustained a series of blows: the disaster at Stalingrad, the imminent fall of Tunis and the end of Axis resistance in Africa, the first real problems with the U-boat campaign, and the start of the combined Allied bombing offensive over Germany. The army had won a reprieve from the executioner at Kharkov in early 1943, but it had been by the slimmest of margins, won with the last reserves of strength, and most of them seemed to have few illusions about that. They were all in the midst of a teachable moment, and there were legitimate differences of opinion over how to proceed. It is clear from the record of the meeting that even Hitler had not yet decided what to do. He did not attempt to impose any solution, nor did he speak against the ideas of his subordinates. Contrary to another commonly held model of decision making in National Socialist Germany, no one at this conference tried to "lead towards the Führer" by cleverly anticipating what Hitler wanted to hear and then suggesting it.[53] It is obvious that the Führer himself had no idea what he wanted to hear.

Hitler opened the meeting with a sober discussion (Guderian describes his tone as *sachlich*) of Zeitzler's plan for an offensive at Kursk.[54] Without either endorsing or rejecting it, he then went on to outline the opinions that he had already heard against it. These had originated mainly from Model, whose army would command the northern thrust. Recent 9th Army photo reconnaissance had shown that the salient had become a beehive of Soviet activity, and that it was well on its way to becoming "a deep, carefully organized defensive system."[55] The Soviet command had withdrawn its mobile formations from their advanced positions along the front line and had made Zeitzler's intended breakthrough zones "unusually strong in artillery and anti-tank guns."[56] Model feared that he wasn't going to be strong enough to punch through the Soviet defenses in front of him. For all these reasons, they should either cancel the attack or subject it to radical revision. His arguments had evidently impressed Hitler. Model was an optimist, a hard charger, and loyal to the core. If he saw problems, that was a good indication that there were problems. Perhaps, Hitler mused aloud, there should be a month-long postponement. He had already heard Model's arguments in favor of waiting until the Panthers and Tigers had arrived, and he was more and more inclined to agree.

Hitler then turned to Manstein. There is dispute in the literature of his exact response. Guderian has him "as usual in Hitler's presence, not having his best day." His response was equivocal. An offensive from the south would have worked in April, he claimed, but its success was now doubtful unless he received two new full-strength infantry divisions. Hitler responded, again per Guderian, that those divisions simply did not exist and that Manstein would have to do without them. The Führer then repeated the question but received "no clear answer" (*keine eindeutige Antwort*) from the field marshal.[57]

Manstein's own lengthy account in *Verlorene Siege* paints his performance in better and wiser colors, but he still admits a certain degree of ambiguity. The Kursk offensive had been his idea in the first place, so simply rejecting it was out of the question. Nevertheless, he did speak up against any plan to postpone it further. Waiting for more and newer tanks was a losing proposition, he said. The Soviets would use the extra time to match, then overmatch, German numbers at the front, which would be no problem for them because they were producing far more tanks per month than Germany was. The postponement would also allow Soviet troops, their morale shot after the shock of Kharkov last March, to renew themselves and recover their battleworthiness. Soviet strength was growing all across the front of Army Group South. The Red Army was not in a position to launch attacks along the Donets or Mius at the moment, but in another month it would be. Above all, Manstein noted, the fall of Tunis might soon result in an Allied landing on the European mainland, and Citadel could therefore be taking place during a war on two fronts. For all these reasons, "as tempting as it was to wait for a further strengthening of our Panzer forces,"[58] he remained firm in his support of an immediate assault. In case there was a postponement, he would require—besides more tanks—two new infantry divisions "in order to overcome the enemy's positional defenses" (feindlichen Stellungssystems).

He closed this "on the one hand–on the other hand" presentation by declaring that Citadel was not going to be easy. He wanted Hitler to know that he was ready, however. Like any rider preparing for a difficult jump, he knew that he "first had to throw his heart over the hurdle." There was apparently some puzzlement in the room, as even Manstein would later admit in his memoirs: "It soon became clear to me that it was a comparison that Hitler, knowing nothing of riders or horses, did not find at all pleasing."[59]

From here, the discussion moved round the table. Field Marshal Günther von Kluge, Army Group Center commander, was either firm in his support (according to Guderian) or firm in his support as long as there was no postponement (according to Manstein). Other sources place Kluge and his chief of the General Staff (Ia), Colonel Henning von Tresckow, at the center of support for the Zeitzler plan. It is easy to speculate why this should be so: Citadel promised to restore Army Group Center to a more central role in the fighting, after over a year in which it had been very much a subsidiary front.[60] It had surrendered most of its Panzers to Army Group South, and its principal operational achievement had been a cleverly conceived and well-executed retreat (the withdrawal from the Rzhev salient in the Büffelbewegung). We might also mention in this context that Kluge could not have been happy about Model going directly to Hitler, violating the chain of command, rather than bringing his objections first to Kluge.[61] At any rate, he disputed the reports of Model's aerial reconnaissance, claiming that many of the works in this newly dug defensive Stellung were remnants of previous trench systems from earlier fighting.[62]

Others spoke, with varying points of emphasis and degrees of intensity. Guderian, who was not involved in operational planning but was trying to solidify the influence of his new position as general inspector of the Panzer Troops, was opposed to any offensive, postponed or otherwise. An offensive at Kursk was "pointless" (*zwecklos*), he said.[63] Now was the time to be preparing the mobile reserves for battle against the Western powers, who were going to be landing in Europe any day now. Nor should anyone be expecting any miracles from the Panther or Tiger—every new tank, Guderian argued, had "teething troubles" (*Kinderkrankheiten*),[64] and these new models were not going to be any exception. Speer also spoke up against the attack. He was just now getting the problems of industrial production sorted out, and the losses sure to be sustained in a renewed offensive were not going to help. Jeschonnek supported the offensive, but he also pointed out that the Luftwaffe saw no real advantage in any sort of postponement.[65]

When all was said and done, the final count was Zeitzler and Kluge for the offensive, Model against it as presently constituted, Guderian and Speer against it in any form, Manstein both for and against it, depending on how one read his response, Jeschonnek for it without postponement, and Hitler uncommitted. A no doubt perplexed Führer decided, quite reasonably, given the divided nature of the counsels within his high command, to postpone Citadel until June 12. That would solve many problems, but in particular it would bring Model on board, and Model's enthusiasm for the attack was crucial.

The following weeks saw German preparations for the Kursk offensive intensify. But matching the increased activity to the front was a growing level of doubt within all levels of the command. All the options looked bad, as they sometimes do in war. The Wehrmacht could not sit in the east and simply wait to get hammered. Retreat was also out of the question, at least as long as Hitler was at the helm. The Kursk offensive was going to be expensive, even if it worked. No one knew what to do, Hitler least of all. The Munich discussions had settled nothing. Although he seemingly derived no greater joy in life than screaming at his rear-echelon staff officers, at Munich he had heard from the war fighters—his army and army group commanders—and that had always been more difficult for him. Their lack of unanimity at Munich had to have been unsettling.

Consider this famous scene, just a few days after that Munich meeting. On May 10, Hitler and Guderian had a brief meeting to discuss ways and means to increase tank production. Guderian urged him, once again, to cancel the Kursk offensive altogether. "Why do you want to attack in the East at all?" he asked. As Guderian tells it, Keitel, the OKW chief, was present and now broke in. "We have to attack, for political reasons," he said. Guderian responded to Keitel, dismissively, "Do you think anyone even knows where Kursk is? It is all the same to the world whether we hold Kursk or not." Turning again to Hitler, he repeated the question: Why are we attacking in the east at all this year? Hitler answered, "You're right. Whenever I think about this attack, I get a queasy feeling in my stomach." Guderian had heard all he needed to hear. "Then you have the right attitude towards this situation," he responded. "Leave it alone!"[66]

Hitler didn't leave it alone, of course. More postponements followed as spring turned into summer. The focus now shifted to another front: North Africa. The fall of Tunis and the loss of Africa raised serious questions about the future of Italy. It had been a catastrophic defeat for the Axis partner, the loss not only of a field army, but of its Italian empire. Would Italy stay in the war? Was this the end of the Axis? Hitler now had to consider the notion of abandoning Citadel and dispatching some of the Panzer divisions to southern Europe, to prepare for the extreme eventuality of Italy leaving the war. Zeitzler, for his part, was growing impatient with the repeated postponements, and Hitler's chief operations officer on the OKW, General Alfred Jodl, was playing on Zeitzler's uncertainty and arguing against Citadel.

Hitler spent June moving simultaneously on two tracks. He was monitoring the situation in Italy carefully, and thus considering canceling Citadel altogether. He was also starting to toy with new approaches to Citadel. There are staff studies from the period that radically redrew the operation, redeploying the principal assault formations to the west of the Kursk bulge, attacking it more or less frontally from that direction, and heading straight for Kursk itself.[67] It was a direct approach, but one that might still restore some measure of surprise and bypass the sectors with the most formidable Soviet defenses. The new approach proved to be a nonstarter, with both army commanders, Model and Hoth, warning that such a massive redeployment was impossible by this late date. Not until June 16 did the situation in Italy appear stable enough to give Citadel the go-ahead, this time with a start date of early July.

There was one other possibility for an offensive at Kursk besides the "launch–don't launch" option, however, and as the weeks dragged by, it received more and more consideration. Manstein's victory at Kharkov ending the 1942–1943 winter campaign had been a classic example of the up-tempo war of movement (*Bewegungskrieg*). Once the rains had come, however, the front line had solidified almost exactly where the armies had stopped in March 1943. Both sides had dug in since then, as they had in the previous campaigning season, improving their defenses and creating favorable start positions for a renewed offensive. What this meant for Citadel as currently construed was that it would have to begin under conditions of *Stellungskrieg*, the grinding form of positional warfare that German armies had historically tried to avoid. The assault formations would first have to chew their way through a heavily fortified line, prepared defenses, and a wall of Soviet fire before they could even begin their all-important concentric maneuver on Kursk.

Manstein thought he saw an answer to the Kursk problem. Rather than a "blow from the forehand" (*Schlag aus der Vorhand*), an offensive directly against the salient, he would do what he had done earlier in the year. Let the Soviets launch their offensive first. Cede as much territory in the opening phases of the operation to absorb the blow. Then, when Soviet momentum began to flag, when the logistics were beginning to creak, and when the attack reached its culmination point, strike a blow as deeply as possible into the enemy flank. Rather than a forehand, then, it would be a "blow from the backhand" (*Schlag aus der Nachhand*).[68] It had succeeded for him before, in the Crimea and at Kharkov, and he was confident it would work again. Lay some bait in front of the Soviets, he felt, lure them on, hit them at the moment of his choosing, and they would come apart.

As Manstein surveyed the situation maps, he envisioned a number of potential backhand scenarios in play for the summer of 1943. Perhaps the most likely one was a Soviet offensive against the extreme right wing of Army Group South, currently holding a thin defensive line along the Mius River.[69] Here, the lure for the Soviets would be the Donbas with its rich mines and heavy industry, as well as the Dnepr River crossings at Dnepropetrovsk and Zaporozhye. Manstein proposed allowing the attackers to crash through the Mius barrier and head west. The distances involved were prodigious, and at some point the momentum would ebb. Having carefully husbanded his mobile reserves, Manstein would then be in a position to launch a counteroffensive. It would erupt from the north, drive south and southeast deep into the Soviet flank, and eventually reach the coast at the Sea of Azov. If it worked, it would trap all the Soviet forces in a gigantic *Kessel*, perhaps on the same order of magnitude as the great encirclement at Kiev in September 1941.

If the Soviet attack came out of the Kursk salient instead of across the Mius, Manstein would apply the same dynamic. Once again, the Soviet target would be the Dnepr crossings, perhaps a drive to the southwest toward Cherkassy and Kremenchug. Again, these were vast distances, quite unlike anything in Western Europe. Once again, having retreated back onto his lines of communication, Manstein would be sitting in a highly favorable position. In this case, his counterblow would originate in the south and drive to the north. In cooperation with Army Group Center on his left, the possibilities for a *Kesselschlacht* would be enormous.

All during the spring arguments over how to schedule Citadel, Manstein peppered Hitler with plans for a radical backhand revision of it. Manstein's notions of opening up the front for mobile operations, perhaps involving large-scale withdrawals, smacked to Hitler of lack of resolve, however. He complained during this period that he was getting increasingly weary of hearing the word *operieren*. He didn't want his officers to "operate"; he wanted them to stand and fight. German officers took up Manstein's argument in their postwar writings, and historians continue to echo the idea today.[70] It is a seductive image, particularly when contrasted to Hitler's crude notion of holding every position, no matter how insignificant, to the last man. At any rate, the Führer had the last word, and he rejected Manstein's call for a backhand operation.

All this back and forth between the commanders, not to mention the repeated postponements of Operation Citadel, had two results. First, by giving the Soviets more time to prepare, they made the attack more dangerous, and perhaps ruined its chances of succeeding. At the same time, however, as the months passed and the Wehrmacht went deeper and deeper into its planning and preparation cycle, deploying thousands of tanks and guns and hundreds of thousands of men around the salient, a cancellation of the attack became increasingly unlikely. By now, Citadel had consumed the greater part of the army's planning time and psychic energy for over three months, and throwing it overboard was in no one's interest. The operation had taken on a life and a momentum all its own. Attacking the Kursk salient had perhaps made sense in March, when the planners were still arguing over whether to do it. It made much less sense in June, when launching it was really no longer in doubt. Hitler had played a role, certainly, and has to bear responsibility.

So, too, do they all. Hurtling toward defeat, the Wehrmacht's perilous strategic situation had bred something akin to command paralysis.

The Battle of Kursk

PREPARATION AND DEPLOYMENT

For all the troubles in the planning process, the Wehrmacht managed to assemble an imposing array of force for the offensive. It included virtually all of the Panzer divisions left in the Wehrmacht. While the Panzers were gathering at Kursk, Army Group A in the south had but a single Panzer division remaining in its order of battle, and Army Group North had none.[71] This great concentration of force was due entirely to Hitler, a function of his long series of operational postponements. An attack carried out in March would have possessed only a fraction of the German striking power, and incidentally, it would have struck only the barest fraction of the Red Army's strength. Contrary to the common analysis, that would not necessarily have been a good thing. Although an early offensive might well have taken Kursk, it would have done nothing at all to injure the Soviets materially on a level that would have affected their attack plans for 1943.

Moving around the salient from north to south, we would first encounter General Model's 9th Army, facing to the south.[72] From west to east, it included the following:

XX Corps (General Rudolf Freiherr von Roman), containing four widely stretched and understrength infantry divisions, the 45th, 72nd, 137th, and 251st.

XXXXVI Panzer Corps (General Hans Zorn), consisting of four infantry divisions, the 7th, 31st, 102nd, and 258th, plus *Gruppe Manteuffel*—a brigade-sized mobile formation of three light Jäger battalions—and an assault gun battalion.

XXXXVII Panzer Corps (General Joachim Lemelsen), containing the 2nd, 9th, and 20th Panzer Divisions, the full-strength (that is, nine battalion) 6th Infantry Division, Tiger Tank Battalion 505, and two assault gun battalions.

XXXXI Panzer Corps (General Josef Harpe), consisting of 18th Panzer Division, flanked on the left and right by the 86th and 292nd Infantry Divisions, respectively, and supported by the 656th *Panzerjäger* Regiment, containing two battalions of 45 Ferdinands apiece.

XXIII Corps (General Johannes Friessner), containing two infantry divisions, the 216th and 385th, along with the 78th *Sturmdivision*, an assault division reinforced by self-propelled artillery, as well as an assault battalion.

Model's army was one of the strongest ever assembled in the course of the war in the east and included a major portion of the Wehrmacht's available strength: a five-corps formation containing 19 divisions, four of them mechanized. The army's mission was to penetrate the Soviet defenses to the front, with the operational *Schwerpunkt* belonging to XXXXVII Panzer Corps, with its three Panzer divisions and a Tiger battalion. The corps would push due south between the rail line and road from Orel through Olkhovatka to Kursk, with its ultimate objective the high ground north of the city. Here the Panzers would meet the onrushing formations of 4th Panzer Army coming up from the south, effect a linkup, and effectively *Kessel* all Soviet forces in the salient. The commander of Army Group Center, Field Marshal von Kluge, also had a relatively large mobile reserve in hand, including 4th and 12th Panzer Divisions, assembled into an ad hoc corps-sized formation under General Hans-Karl Freiherr von Esebeck (and thus dubbed *Gruppe Esebeck*), along with 10th *Panzergrenadier* Division. All told, the Germans deployed no fewer than seven mechanized divisions along the northern face of the salient.

There was a matching force in the south, consisting of Hoth's 4th Panzer Army. It was also a noteworthy array.[73] Again moving from west to east, it consisted of the following:

LII Corps (General Eugen Ott), containing three understrength infantry divisions, the 57th, 255th, and 332nd.

XXXXVIII Panzer Corps (General Otto von Knobelsdorff), consisting of the 3rd and 11th Panzer Divisions, the *Grossdeutschland Panzergrenadier* Division, along with the full-strength 167th Infantry Division and extensive corps troops such as the 10th Panzer Brigade containing the 51st Panzer Battalion (45 Tigers) and 52nd Panzer Battalion (200 Panthers).

II (S.S.) Panzer Corps (S.S. *Obergruppenführer* Paul Hausser), containing the three newly formed and highly touted divisions of the *Waffen-S.S.*, elite formations largely by virtue of their first call on recruits, replacements, and new equipment. It contained three full-strength S.S. *Panzergrenadier* divisions (1st S.S. *Leibstandarte* Adolf Hitler, 2nd S.S. *Das Reich*, and 3rd S.S. *Totenkopf*). With four battalions per regiment (as opposed to the normal three) and with each division containing its own heavy company of Tigers, Hausser's corps was by a considerable margin the strongest in the German order of battle at Kursk.

Both Knobelsdorff and Hausser had crucial tasks. The XXXXVIII Panzer Corps would launch its assault on both sides of Butovo, push north through Oboyan to Kursk, and there link up with Model. The II S.S. Panzer Corps would accompany it on the right, but also had to be concerned with Soviet armored reserves entering the salient from the southeast via Prokhorovka. As a result, Hausser had his corps echeloned to the right, ready to face a threat from that direction.

Finally, protecting the right flank of 4th Panzer Army was General Werner Kempf's *Armee-Abteilung Kempf*. Although his task was essentially a defensive one, Kempf was to approach it as aggressively as possible. Indeed, one German source spoke of Kempf's mission as an "offensive screen" (*offensive Abdeckung*).[74] For that purpose, he had III Panzer Corps on his left wing, maintaining contact with II S.S. Panzer Corps on Hoth's right (6th, 7th, and 19th Panzer Divisions, the 168th Infantry Division, and the 503rd Tiger Tank Battalion, under the command of General Hermann Breith); the XI Corps (106th and 320th Infantry Divisions, a scratch force that Manstein had cobbled together back in March and that was still serving under the redoubtable Panzer commander General Erhard Raus, and thus designated Corps Raus); and, finally, rounding out the Kursk deployment on the extreme right, and largely tasked with holding the line along the Donets opposite Volchansk, XXXXII Corps (three thinly stretched infantry divisions, the 39th, 161st, and 282nd, under the command of General Franz Mattenklott).

As in all German offensives, airpower was also present in abundance. The lessons of 1942 were still fresh in the minds of the high command. At Kerch and Sevastopol, at Kharkov and Kalach, the Wehrmacht had repeatedly proven in the previous year that it could still break into the open and force a battle of maneuver on the Soviets, but only if it could deploy virtually the entirely Luftwaffe over a relatively small battle space. The same lesson had also repeatedly obtained in North Africa, at Gazala and Tobruk.[75] At Kursk, both the 4th Air Force (*Luftflotte* 4, under General Otto Dessloch) and 6th Air Force (*Luftflotte* 6, under General Robert Ritter von Greim) would take part, with the former providing direct air support for 4th Panzer Army and *Armee-Abteilung Kempf*, and the latter doing the same for the 9th Army. No less than the army, the Luftwaffe had suffered a mauling at Stalingrad and in the winter battles to follow. Replacement craft and crews had arrived, however, serviceability rates were good (75% for the VIII *Flieger Korps*, the formation of *Luftflotte* 4 tasked with ground support for the battle), and morale was still high.[76]

All told, then, the Germans were able to deploy 650,000 men in three armies, supported by some 2,600 tanks and assault guns and 1,800 planes, directed against a salient that was just about 160 miles from north to south.[77] As one modern authority has pointed out, the numbers of tanks and aircraft involved here were just about the same that the Wehrmacht had deployed for all of Operation Barbarossa back in 1941 (3,500 tanks and 1,800 aircraft), and the front then had been 10 times larger, about 1,800 miles in length.

These are impressive numbers, but we need to mention two problems. First, the Germans managed to achieve these force levels only by stripping the rest of the massive front to both north and south, as well as by throwing in new formations and new machines that one day might have constituted a stout reserve force on the Eastern Front, but that were hardly ready for combat at the moment. Building up a force for a one-shot throw by borrowing troops from other fronts and by stealing them from the future was no way to run a war.

The second problem was that the Soviets had more than matched the German buildup. Facing Model in the north were defending forces of Central Front (General Rokossovksy), five complete rifle armies in the line, from left to right the 60th, 65th, 70th, 13th, and 48th; the latter three manned the first two defensive belts in front of the German assault, while the 60th and 65th monitored the western face of the salient; 13th Army (General N. P. Pukhov) held the shoulder of the salient—that is, the sector facing the main German assault. Standing in reserve in the north was the 2nd Tank Army (General A. G. Rodin), along with the 9th and 19th Tank Corps. Rokossovsky commanded a powerful combined arms force: six armies, over 700,000 men, nearly 1,800 tanks, and over 10,000 guns and mortars.

Facing Manstein's army group in the south was General Vatutin's Voronezh Front. He had four rifle armies in the line, from left to right the 38th, 40th, 6th Guards, and 7th Guards. Standing in reserve was the 1st Tank Army (General M. E. Katukov), the 69th Rifle Army, along with the 35th Guards Rifle Corps, the 2nd Guards Tanks Corp, and the 5th Guards Tank Corps, along with what Glantz and House call "an imposing array of artillery and other support troops."[78] Vatutin, too, commanded an imposing force: 625,000 men, 1,700 tanks, and 8,718 guns and mortars.

Finally, although not committed to the fighting at the outset, another entire army group, the Steppe Front (General Konev), deployed in the eastern mouth of the salient in case all else failed and the Germans broke through. Konev had an immense force under his command: five rifle armies (4th and 5th Guards, 27th, 47th, and 53rd), the 5th Guards Tank Army, the 3rd, 5th, and 7th Guards Cavalry Corps, the 4th Guards Tank Corps, and the 1st and 3rd Guards Mechanized Corps, another 575,000 men and 1,500 tanks.[79]

Reaching a final calculation about numbers at Kursk continues to exercise the faithful among both scholars and aficionados of the battle. A prudent estimate for the three Soviet fronts (Voronezh, Central, and Steppe) would be 1,800,000 men, about double the German force commitment, and about 5,000 tanks—again, about double the German total. In guns and mortars, the Soviets vastly outstripped their adversary, about 20,000 to 9,000.[80] Four air armies were also available for duty: the 2nd, 16th, and 5th in immediate support of Voronezh, Central, Steppe, and Voronezh fronts, and 15th attached to the neighboring Bryansk Front north of Orel, but available for deployment in the fighting around Kursk. The first three air armies alone amounted to some 3,000 aircraft. One could argue about the quality of this or that Soviet model of aircraft or whether their pilots had yet reached the training standard of the Luftwaffe. Nevertheless, the weeks before the offensive saw repeated Soviet air attacks on German installations and airfields, and the Luftwaffe was never able to win air superiority over the battlefield, let alone the air supremacy it had enjoyed in earlier campaigns.[81]

FAILURE

After all the debate, discussion, and controversy, after all the planning and replanning, postponements, and reschedulings, Citadel turned out to be something rare on this level of war making: a complete and utter misfire. The sheer amount of matériel present could not mask the paucity of the Wehrmacht's operational conception. In the end, it was what it was: a simplistic frontal assault.[82]

The offensive opened on July 5, with massive tank assaults from both north and south, and with *Luftflotten* 4 and 6 thundering overhead, but both pincers soon ground to a halt. With the Soviets hunkered down behind eight concentric lines of prepared defense in the salient, with over 3,000 miles of trench dug and 400,000 mines sown, with every village and hill fortified, and with the Soviet high command having guessed right as to the main German sectors of attack—this was a simple operational problem to solve—it is hard to see how it could have been otherwise. Although a tactical analysis might show this or that company or battalion managing to get forward, on the operational level, it was something akin to a dead stop.

It was *Stellungskrieg* with a vengeance. The Germans did not so much attack the Soviet fortified zone as become enmeshed in it. On 4th Panzer Army's front, Hoth's Panzers never really did manage to get any momentum. The tale of the attack on XXXXVIII Panzer Corps's front is a case in point. The attack got stuck almost immediately, a combination of Soviet defensive prowess, rains that flooded the many dry gullies south and southeast of Butowo, and a sea of mines. Knobelsdorff had three mobile divisions abreast, from left to right 3rd Panzer, *Grossdeutschland*, and 11th Panzer. Rather than slash directly to the north, on two occasions (July 10–11 and July 14), he had to detour *Grossdeutschland* to the west to try and outflank tough defenses in front of the 3rd Panzer. It was a fight of tiny villages and anonymous heights like Hills 243, 247, and 260.8, incessant Soviet counterattacks, first by the local reserves, than by whole units coming out of the Voronezh Front reserve, and deadly artillery strikes by both sides. Both dealt out and suffered a great deal of damage. Static warfare of this sort is always matériel-intensive and casualties are always high—one of the reasons that Prussians and Germans armies had always tried to avoid it. At their best in open field combat, they could look quite mortal in this environment. Even if a division such as *Grossdeutschland* managed to find a weak spot or a seam in the defenses and bound forward a few miles, all it had done was make a needlelike penetration with long, vulnerable flanks. It had achieved nothing lasting, and it often found itself riding to the salvation of neighboring units that had not been so fortunate. After 10 days, XXXXVIII Panzer Corps had penetrated a grand total of 12 miles, and the murderous intensity of the combat had greatly thinned its ranks, especially those of the hardy *Grossdeutschland* Division. The corps was nowhere near a linkup with Model, and it was clear, in the words of its chief of staff, that "the back of the German attack had been broken and its momentum had gone."[83]

Indeed, Model was having even more serious problems by this time. His drive to the south had cracked through the initial defensive line on a 35-mile front and advanced some eight miles on the first day. It then almost immediately screeched to a halt, gripped even more firmly by Soviet defenses than Hoth had been. Here the principal position was a heavily fortified ridge southwest of Olkhovatka. Central Front commander Rokossovsky skillfully fed his reserves into the battle, combining direct assaults on German penetrations with threats to their flanks. He could afford to. Model tried to storm the ridge on July 10 and then again on July 11, and had failed both times.[84] Losses were staggering on both sides. The new German tanks like the Panther and the Tiger proved themselves as killing machines, but breakdowns, lack of sufficient secondary armament, and crew unfamiliarity with the equipment prevented them from spearheading any sort of operational breakthrough. A frustrated Model had to admit that, on his front at least, the Wehrmacht was now facing a "rolling battle of attrition."[85]

Accounts of the German assault at Kursk usually focus on the II S.S. Panzer Corps, the formation on Hoth's right wing. It is true that Hausser's corps, containing the three beefiest divisions in the German order of battle, managed the deepest penetration at all—about 25 miles in 10 days. Even here, however, we should exercise caution. Facing the same tough defenses as it neighboring formations, it managed an aggressive break-in (*Einbruch*). It certainly did not achieve any sort of clean breakthrough (*Durchbruch*). It had Soviet formations clinging to it the entire way, frontally and on its flanks. Those threats to the flank were a particular problem. The attack by *Armee-Abteilung Kempf* was the least successful of all. Because Kempf was stuck from day one, every mile that II S.S. Panzer drove forward was another mile of vulnerable flank that it had to protect; it did so by inclining more and more toward its right, as opposed to a straight drive to the north. On July 9, Hoth received reconnaissance reports indicating the movement of heavy armored forces from the east, heading out of Prokhorovka. He had envisioned just this sort of thing during the planning phase and had worked out preliminary orders to counter it. With the *Armee-Abteilung* still nowhere near protecting the flank of 4th Panzer Army, Hoth ordered the II S.S. Panzer to wheel to the right and head for the threat.[86]

These developments set the stage for the climax of the battle of Kursk. Hausser's corps wheeled right with three divisions abreast, *Totenkopf* on the left, the *Leibstandarte* in the center, and *Das Reich* on the right. On July 12, they ran into a counterattack by the entire 5th Guards Tank Army under General Rotmistrov. Heading out of Prokhorovka just as II S.S. Panzer was heading toward it, the two great armored formations slammed into one another at around 8:30 A.M. "It turned out," Rotmistrov would later write, "that both we and the Germans went over to the offensive simultaneously." What resulted from this happenstance may or may not have been the greatest tank battle of all time, but it certainly was big enough to satisfy even the most diehard devotee of armor.

On the tactical level, Prokhorovka was a tank melee at short, often point-blank range. With the Germans having the bigger, more powerful machines, especially their Tigers, the Soviet T-34s had little choice but to charge in and thereby reduce the German advantage in range.

On the eve of the battle, Rotmistrov and his commander Vatutin (Voronezh Front), had discussed how to deal with the enemy behemoths and the necessity of getting in close. "In other words, engage in hand-to-hand and board them," Vatutin had recommended, his gallows humor serving to impress on Rotmistrov the urgency of the situation.[87] The chaos in such a situation beggars the imagination even today, and two leading authorities on the battle describe the result as "a confused and confusing series of meeting engagements and hasty attacks, with each side committing its forces piecemeal."[88]

On the operational level, however, things are a bit easier to sort out. The Soviets managed to extend the battlefield enough to threaten II S.S. Panzer's flanks and to bring the German drive to a halt. On the German left, attacks by the Soviet 5th Guards Army (General A. S. Zhadov) forced the *Totenkopf* Division to detach units for flank security. On the right (*Das Reich*), attacks by the independent Soviet II Guards Tank Corps represented an even graver threat. The right wing of the II S.S. Panzer Corps was almost completely open. The left wing of *Armee-Abteilung Kempf*, III Panzer Corps, was making good progress by now, but a gap still existed between the two corps. As a result, *Das Reich* spent most of the day trying to fight its way forward while at the same time dropping off infantry to protect its vulnerable right. "Russian attacks on our flanks are tying down half of our effectives," complained one S.S. regimental commander.[89]

By the end of the day, the two behemoths had fought themselves to a draw. Tactically, the Germans had dealt out enormous punishment to the 5th Guards Tank Army, but they too had lost something: their momentum, along with a full day that they could not afford.

In *Verlorene Siege*, Manstein argues that Army Group South was on the verge of a complete operational breakthrough at this point, and that in refusing to follow up, the high command "threw away the victory" (*den Sieg verschenkte*).[90] Manstein was correct in noting that his assault formations had inflicted far heavier losses than they had suffered, and Soviet pressure to his front was slackening. The brawl at Prokhorokva had virtually destroyed the strongest Soviet tank army, Rotmistrov's 5th, its losses probably topping 400 tanks. There were more Soviet reserve formations as yet unengaged, however—plenty more. Even if II S.S. Panzer could have broken through them, the question must still arise: break through to where? In the absence of any pressure from a northern pincer, and thus any possibility of a *Kesselschlacht*, a Panzer thrust to the east of Kursk was a drive to nowhere. The Germans had neither the manpower nor the logistical network to support it. In some perfect operational world, the II S.S. Panzer might have driven on to Moscow and beyond, but such thoughts are fantasy, not reality.

The end of this ill-fated offensive is well known. On Saturday, July 10, as Model was launching his first unsuccessful drive against Olkhovatka and II S.S. Panzer Corps was making its turn toward Prokhorovka, the long-awaited Allied landing on the European continent had finally taken place. This was Operation Husky, the invasion of Sicily, and the early reports seemed to confirm Hitler's worst fears. Italian soldiers were surrendering in droves or quietly disappearing from the front, the island was almost certainly going to be lost, mainland Italy was in an uproar, and Mussolini's hold on power suddenly looked tenuous. The Axis, which for all of Italy's weakness was nevertheless crucial to Germany's position in Europe, was teetering. That Monday, July 12, is most famous as the day of fire at Prokhorovka, but it was a signal moment on the Eastern Front for another reason, the launch of the first great Soviet summer offensive of the war: a massive drive into the German-held Orel salient north of Kursk. Manstein's backhand blow had come into play after all, only for the wrong side.

On Tuesday, July 13, Hitler summoned his army group commanders in Operation Citadel to his headquarters in East Prussia. It was time for a talk.

Kursk and the German Way of War

Hitler's decision to call off Operation Citadel was a sensible one, given the overall situation on the Eastern Front and in Western Europe. It also makes sense if we view it through the prism of traditional German military culture. What had just transpired at Kursk should have come as a surprise to no one in the command. Every German officer knew that an offensive undertaken under conditions of a *Stellungskrieg* would burn enormous amounts of time and energy, destroy a mountain of equipment, and generate an unacceptably highly number of friendly casualties. The staff officers had learned all these lessons as young men at the *Kriegsakademie*, and a lifetime of exercises, maneuvers, and war games had pounded it into the heads of the field commanders. The roots ran deep, back to the Prussian army and Frederick the Great's notion that all of Prussia's wars had to be *kurtz und vives* ("short and lively"), using high mobility, aggression, and surprise to overcome the armies of his larger and more prosperous adversaries. It also looked back to Blücher in the Napoleonic wars, Prince Frederick Charles (the Red Prince) at

Königgrätz in 1866, General Constantin von Alvensleben, commander of the III Corps at Mars-la-Tour in 1870[91]—all men who had defied the odds and who relied on will, wits, and a sense of moral superiority when the material factors were lacking.

The revolutionary developments of the late nineteenth century had shaken that well-entrenched military culture. The rise of the mass army, the introduction of the rifled musket, the increasing inability of modern armies to win decisive battles—all of these developments seemed to mark an end to the kind of up-tempo, front-loaded military campaigns that were a Prusso-German stock in trade. The Boer War of 1899–1902, for example, had sent a ripple through German military planners, as an irregular force of semiliterate farmers with high-powered rifles had fought the British army to a standstill at the Modder River, Magersfontein, and Spion Kop.[92] A few years after that, the machine gun arrived in the arsenal, and the Russo-Japanese War (1904–1905) demonstrated how modern armies fighting out of entrenchments could use it to slaughter one another in unprecedented numbers.[93] Trench warfare made a reappearance during the First Balkan War of 1912, at Kirk Kilisse and Adrianople and especially in the last-ditch Turkish defense in front of Constantinople, in the bottleneck at the Chatalja narrows.[94]

The classic expression of *Stellungskrieg* had been the trench deadlock of World War I.[95] By 1915, the Western Front had hardened, and for the next two years, repeated attacks on both sides cost millions of casualties but barely moved the front an inch in either direction. The apparent collapse of its traditional way of war, *Bewegungskrieg*, the war of movement, had led the German army into a fundamental reappraisal of its prewar training. The wartime high command withdrew a number of its most experienced company- and field-grade officers from the front line and consulted them about their experiences. The most celebrated example, Captain Willy Martin Rohr, received the command of a new *Sturmabteilung*, a storm detachment, given the task of devising new means and methods of cracking an enemy trench line and restoring mobile conditions to the front.[96]

The result was an entirely new doctrine of infantry assault, Germany's famous *Stosstrupp* tactics. Independent squads spearheaded the attack, identifying weak spots in the defense, bypassing all obstacles, and leaving them for the follow-up waves of regular infantry, moving constantly forward. This new tactical system, often mislabeled as "infiltration tactics," had debuted in 1917 at the battles of Caporetto and Riga, smashing the Italian and Russian armies they faced, and then captured the attention of the world in the great German offensives of 1918. Three successive operations—Michael, Georgette, and Blücher—had smashed through the prepared Allied defenses, inflicting hundreds of thousands of casualties and lunging forward 50 miles at a bound, a shocking thing in the context of the trench deadlock of 1915–1917. However, the pain they inflicted had not come cheap. Any tactical system— even one as carefully crafted as this—that forced men to charge forward against *Maschinenwaffen* ("machine weapons") was going to be costly. The offensives wound up killing nearly as many of the attackers as the defenders. Even worse, they failed to lead to any sort of strategic breakthrough. The Allies fell back, often in confusion, but with enough cohesion left to reform their lines and to prevent the Germans from reaching any truly strategic targets. In other words, the 1918 offensives had been operational-level victories—impressive, to be sure, but not impressive enough.

That failure had been the backdrop for the German achievement in the interwar era: the development of the Panzer division, close cooperation with the ground attack arm of the Luftwaffe, and command and control improved immeasurably thanks to radio communication. Contrary to received wisdom, the Germans did not invent blitzkrieg in this era. They were not trying to devise something new but rather to find a way to break the deadlock of *Stellungskrieg* and to resuscitate *Bewegungskrieg*. The Panzer–Stuka combination was merely a means to this end, and it had succeeded beyond their wildest dreams, resulting in the dramatic victories of the war's first two years: Case White in Poland, *Weserübung* in Denmark and Norway, and Case Yellow in the west.

Even in the midst of this era, which until 1941 had been characterized by a series of relatively cheap German victories, there had been moments in which the operational posture had reverted to *Stellungskrieg*. In every one of them, usually ignored by historians of the blitzkrieg, German losses had been heavy. The assault on the Mlawa and Modlin positions in the Polish campaign in 1939, the hasty attempts to rush the Dutch fortifications in 1940, the drive against the Metaxas line in Greece in 1941, certain portions of the campaign on Crete—all of them had taught the still-young Wehrmacht an old lesson. Maneuver was the key to rapid victory and to reduced losses.

The initial invasion of the Soviet Union in 1941, Operation Barbarossa, had been in many ways the pinnacle of German *Bewegungskrieg*, as the Wehrmacht turned encirclement after encirclement, one *Kesselschlacht* after another. Even here, however, there had been numerous occasions in which German assault troops, even those including

Panzer columns, had come up against prepared Soviet defenses. The Luga line in the north, Brest Litovsk in the center, and the Pripet marshes in the south were all tough fights that cost time and lives. If the Germans had learned anything in that first campaign in the east, it was that if they let Ivan dig in, then they had better get ready for a difficult time in digging him out. It is no exaggeration to say that a few tough Soviet defensive stands had been the margin of survival for the Red Army during Operation Typhoon, the final German lunge for Moscow as winter was coming on. The defense of Tula, which for weeks withstood the attacks of General Heinz Guderian's 2nd Panzer Army, deserves particular attention in this context.

We see the same thing in 1942. In Operation Blue, the Wehrmacht had once again lunged forward hundreds of miles, encircling huge Soviet forces at Kerch, Kharkov, and Kalach. It had also come up against prepared Soviet defenses at Sevastopol, in the Caucasus, and especially at Stalingrad. In the first case, it had battered its way to victory, although the cost was high in men and matériel. In the latter two, it had come within a hair's breadth of victory. At Ordzhonikidze in the Caucasus, it fought its way to within a mile of the gateway city to the high mountain range. In the final drive for the Volga during the Stalingrad fight, Operation Hubertus, a combined force of German infantry and combat engineers had driven to within a few hundred yards of the riverbank, the final strip of the city still in Soviet hands.

Let us fast-forward to spring 1943. As the German command echelon sat enmeshed in the difficult question of how to proceed, the oldest German operational imperative of all began to reassert itself. This was an army that wanted to fight *Bewegungskrieg* and had an aversion to *Stellungskrieg*. The idea for an offensive began as part of a mobile operation. At the end of the triumph at Kharkov, Manstein had suggested a continuation of the offensive to the north, in cooperation with an attack by Army Group Center to the south, roughly the operational précis that would eventually guide planning for the summer offensive. At that point, however, there were no prepared defenses around Kursk. The Soviets had only just retaken the city as part of their winter offensive, and they were still shaky from their prodigious losses in men and matériel during the winter fighting. Manstein's skillful *Rochade*, or castling maneuver, and his well-timed blow into the flank of their advancing armies had dealt them a grievous blow. He felt the time was ripe to follow up, and he wasn't the only one.

As we have seen, the proposed offensive never took place. Postponement followed postponement. The more time that passed, the more enthusiasm diminished within the officer corps. Manstein might well have retaken Kursk by a coup de main in March, but he knew the possibilities were increasingly unlikely as the Soviets bulked up their forces inside the salient and fortified their defensive positions. A direct blow at Kursk was now going to be a tough fight. The staff experimented with various approaches—directly from the west, deep into the shoulders of the bulge in order to engage the Soviet reserves of the Steppe Front from the outset, directly north and south of the city of Kursk itself—but none of them eased the difficulty. No matter how many points of the compass from which it originated, it was clear that the opening of the German offensive would be akin to the trench warfare of World War I. Despite all the tanks and mechanized formations, any direct attack in this sector was going to be a *Stellungskrieg*.

Manstein had also come up with various suggestions for some sort of backhand blow. But just how realistic were these plans? Had the Soviets learned nothing from previous campaigns? Were they really going to be so obliging a second time? How exactly was Manstein going to get them to repeat their past mistakes? It is easy to forget the exact conditions that had led to the field marshal's last triumph at Kharkov. The Red Army had just made a great lunge westward in the winter of 1942–1943. It had been a five-month epic: thousands of miles, subzero temperatures, ice and snow. Of course Soviet logistics had broken down in the course of their bound forward. It was highly unlikely, however, that a much stronger Red Army, campaigning on good, hard ground in the summer months, was going to wear itself down as much as it had done in that previous campaign. It was just as likely, given the imbalance of forces, that a massive Soviet offensive would bind up Germany's mechanized formations in positional defense. Concentrating enough of them to launch a counterstroke was not going to be easy. One modern authority on German operations states that Manstein had come to see the backhand blow as a "recipe for success" (*Erfolgsrezept*), and that may be part of the problem: there is no recipe.[97]

What still fascinates about this entire Kursk episode is the degree to which the German command, despite all that had happened in the past year, remained wedded to an old prescription for war. *Einzukesseln. Konzentrischen Angriff. Vernichten.* Such words had been part of German military discourse for centuries. The degree to which an operation was "concentric" or not had long been the chief Prusso-German criterion for evaluating it, because only a concentric attack on a previously surrounded enemy could bring the decisive success of the *Kesselschlacht*. Leipzig in 1813, Königgrätz in 1866, Sedan in 1870, Tannenberg in 1914, and the great battle of Flanders (*Flandernschlacht*) in 1940 had all followed a similar script, endeavoring to surround (*einzukesseln*) and destroy through concentric operations. They were the classic operations, their memory passed down from one generation to the next in the nearly hereditary caste of the German officer corps. They were the operations to emulate.

Now, in 1943, they had all become so intent on the *Kesselschlacht*, on surrounding their enemy and then destroying him through a series of aggressive concentric operations, that they had become blind to the absurdities of trying to achieve one under these circumstances. They could literally see no other way of proceeding beyond a rote devotion to the historical German way of war, even when it no longer had a chance of success. In 1942, they had discovered the problem of operating concentrically in such a vast environment as the Eastern Front, especially in the wide open spaces of its southern wing. Concentrating forces against a single point left you open to flank assault from multiple positions. The maneuvers at some point had to become *exzentrisch*, with formations moving away from one another. Even in the extremely simple operational moment that was Citadel, threats to the flanks of the formations maneuvering concentrically had been crucial to the breakdown. The failure of XXXXVIII Panzer Corps to get moving; the problems on the right flank of II S.S. Panzer Corps as *Armee-Abteilung Kempf* got mired in the fortified zone to its front; Hoth's decision to wheel right towards Prokhorovka—the concentric scheme for Citadel had broken down within a matter of days.

Whether taking advantage of the Kursk bulge right in front of their noses (as in Hitler's case), or conducting a more complex, wider-ranging search (Manstein's scheme for an encirclement on the shores of the Sea of Azov), the German high command was seeking a battle of encirclement for which a badly wounded Wehrmacht no longer had the strength.

There is much that separates Manstein from Hitler, of course: the trained professional from the amateur, the war fighter from the politician, the refined Junker from the crude agitator from the street. In this case, however, both of them seem far more alike than different, and both were following a script that had been written a long time before they were born. For the Führer and his greatest field marshal, Kursk was indeed a drama. Call it "two characters in search of a *Kesselschlacht*."

Finally, it is time to question the principal underlying assumption of *Bewegungskrieg*. Manstein believed, as did they all, that it was in mobile battle that the top-to-bottom superiority of the Wehrmacht would once again become manifest. By liberating the officer and his men from the tyranny of matériel, the war of movement allowed the human factor to have full play. Manstein and company were certain that they had better-trained soldiers than the Red Army, a more refined officer corps, quicker decision making, higher levels of initiative at all ranks, and much more. By 1943, however, every one of these points had become debatable. Was the average Soviet soldier really inferior to his German counterpart? Was the Soviet officer corps actually less capable than the German?

The most meaningless way to analyze Citadel—and indeed the entire war—is to argue which army was better. In 1943, the Wehrmacht still had a great number of strengths: a highly trained, devoted, and aggressive officer corps; manpower ready to die in great numbers for the cause, for ideological reasons, or for loyalty to the group; and, for the first time in the eastern campaign, matériel and equipment that enjoyed a clear qualitative edge, teething problems and all. The Soviets, however, were also holding some high cards: a highly competent high command, its confidence rising after the victories in Stalingrad and the Caucasus; field-grade officers and men who had learned to trust one another's abilities to handle German offensive tactics; their traditional strength in the often-neglected art of field fortification.

We may also identify one last, crucial advantage for the Red Army: its size. There were many reasons for the Red Army's victory at Kursk, but we would be foolish to ignore its numbers. The Soviets had parried the German blow at Kursk—although not without some anxious moments—all the while preparing massive blows at numerous other points along the front. The Wehrmacht, by contrast, literally had to strip the rest of the Eastern Front of its Panzer divisions in order to launch Citadel. Within the discourse of military history, attributing victory to an army's size often seems tantamount to criticizing its quality, but there is no shame in outnumbering your opponent. Size really does matter, and quantity really does have a quality all its own. The Germans found that out at Kursk, and they might well have found it out had they followed Manstein's advice, waited, then attempted to launch some sort of backhand blow.

A *Ritterkreuz* (Knight's Cross) ceremony in the ruins of Stalingrad, October 1942. Courtesy of Christian Ankerstjerne.

Armored reconnaissance patrol at a well in Tunisia, January 1943. Although the desert war took place in a relatively empty quarter, civilians were a constant presence in the Tunisian campaign. The vehicle is an Sd Kfz 233. Courtesy of Christian Ankerstjerne.

Self-propelled 88mm antitank gun (the *Nashorn*, or "rhinoceros"), entering a river. Courtesy of Christian Ankerstjerne.

An up-armored Pzkw IV in Italy, 1943. Courtesy of Christian Ankerstjerne.

Eastern Front, self-propelled rocket artillery (15cm Panzerwerfer 42) being loaded before firing. Courtesy of Christian Ankerstjerne.

Eastern Front, early 1943, antiaircraft halftrack (Sd Kfz 7/1). Note the kill marks. Courtesy of Christian Ankerstjerne.

Rendezvous with fate. Panzer III headed for Stalingrad, late 1942. Courtesy of Christian Ankerstjerne.

North Africa, March 1943, armored halftrack (Sd Kfz 251), with a field-added 50mm antitank gun (5cm Pak 38). Courtesy of Christian Ankerstjerne.

North Africa, March 1943, armored reconnaissance vehicle (Sd Kfz 233) in Tunisia. Courtesy of Christian Ankerstjerne.

A motley German mechanized column on the Eastern Front in late 1943. Note the armored half-tracks (Sd Kfz 250 and Sd Kfz 251), the trucks, and the *panje* wagon. Courtesy of Christian Ankerstjerne.

Self-propelled antiaircraft guns deployed in Southern France, fall 1943. Courtesy of Christian Ankerstjerne.

Panzer III crossing a stream in Tunisia. Courtesy of Christian Ankerstjerne.

Self-propelled 150mm artillery (the *Hummel*, or "Bumblebee"). Courtesy of Christian Ankerstjerne.

Eastern Front, August 1943, Tiger tank in action near Mga. Courtesy of
Christian Ankerstjerne.

Panzer IV crews being evaluated after a drill in the Balkans, July 1943.
Courtesy of Christian Ankerstjerne.

A brief moment of rest in
January 1943: leaning against
a Panzer IV, reading the
newspaper. Courtesy of
Christian Ankerstjerne.

Italy: U.S. soldiers looking at the destruction left behind by an air strike against a German armored column. Courtesy of Christian Ankerstjerne.

Panzergrenadiers dismounting from an armored personal carrier (Sd Kfz 251), July 1943. Courtesy of Christian Ankerstjerne.

Panzer III. Note the oil barrel on the rear of the vehicle. Courtesy of Christian Ankerstjerne.

Final resting place for a Panzer III crew. Courtesy of Christian Ankerstjerne.

Mud. Captured Soviet Stalinez heavy tractor pulling German trucks.
Courtesy of Christian Ankerstjerne.

Half-track (Sd Kfz 2
Kettenkraftrad) delivering
supplies to a German
garrison in the Bosnian
mountains. Courtesy of
Christian Ankerstjerne.

Knocked out Mark V Panther tank. Courtesy of Christian Ankerstjerne.

Column of Mark V Panther tanks. Courtesy of Christian Ankerstjerne.

Armored reconnaissance vehicle (Sd Kfz 233) in Tunisia, January 1943. Courtesy of Christian Ankerstjerne.

Panzer III fording a river in the Soviet Union, August 1943. Courtesy of Christian Ankerstjerne.

Assault gun (Sturmgeschütz III, or StuG) driving past a pair of weary and wounded Panzergrenadiers. Eastern Front, September 1943. Courtesy of Christian Ankerstjerne.

Assault gun commander, May 1943. Courtesy of Christian Ankerstjerne.

Yet another city fight 1943, a regular feature of the 1943 action. Paul G. Sadler Collection.

Even as the military situation collapsed, propaganda photos presented images of poise and confidence. Paul G. Sadler Collection.

Mark IV Panzer outfitted for winter conditions, something all too rare in the Wehrmacht. Paul G. Sadler Collection.

An iconic shot of the Wehrmacht on the move: young troops marching off to their own destruction. Paul G. Sadler Collection.

5

Smashing the Axis: Operation Husky and the Sicilian Campaign

Introduction

It is axiomatic in military history that things looks different on the other side of the hill. The enemy has different concerns, different views, a different mission. Even ideas of victory and defeat may be radically different. One key task for every commander is trying to bridge that gap, trying to put yourself into the enemy's shoes, get into his "decision cycle."[1]

It's different on the other side of the hill.

So they say.

⟫•⟪

Sicily, July 12, 1943.[2]

The American commander: Even years later, the memory of it still took his breath away. He had finally gotten out of his headquarters at Malta and sailed to the front in a British destroyer, bringing along a couple of reporters. John Gunther got some good local color. They landed near Pozzallo in the southeast and met the Canadians—fine troops, good boys. They saw the rest of the beaches, too. Things were going . . . well. Well enough, anyway. They'd had typical landing problems; this battalion was out of place; that supply ship had failed to arrive. But it had been nothing like North Africa. They'd all learned a lot since then.

He remembered how he'd felt as they rounded the shore into the sweeping Bay of Gela, heading toward the U.S. beaches, and suddenly catching sight of hundreds of ships, both large and small, with heavy battleships and Higgins boats and tiny lighters and everything in between. Overhead, he could hear the artificial thunder of aircraft, hundreds of fighters hovering like mother hawks protecting their young. The roar was deafening.

As they floated off Licata, he squinted at the shore. Even at this distance, without binoculars, the general could see them: thousands, tens of thousands of troops, organizing, forming up, advancing inland.

This was power—more power than he had ever seen in his life. For a moment, it took his breath away.[3]

He remembered that sudden feeling of certainty, after all the worries, the missteps, that botched job at Kasserine, all the debates over what to do next.

At that moment, Eisenhower realized one thing: they were going to win this war.

The German commander[4]: Even years later, the memory was still vivid. He'd known an invasion was coming. They all did. They had been planning for it for months, working out deployments and maneuver schemes. What to do if the Italians folded. If? He meant when. He wiped his forehead with his handkerchief.

And now it was here. He had decided to do a personal reconnaissance, the oldest Prussian military tradition of all. General Frido von Senger und Etterlin had been born in Baden, and he'd been in the army long enough to know his duty. As he ascended the low rise north of Licata, he looked out to sea. It couldn't be. He wiped his eyes. But it was. An incredible sight. Ships! Hundreds of them, perhaps thousands—more ships that he'd ever seen in his life. It might as well have been every ship in the world. The beach in front of him was already crawling with U.S. soldiers. He wasn't sure about them yet. He'd heard they'd given a decent accounting of themselves in Tunisia, at least at the end. He wouldn't know. He'd been in Russia at the time. And in the air—he had never seen so many aircraft. Some of them had strange shapes, but they looked fast enough. There were times in Russia when seeing even a single Luftwaffe plane overhead was a cause to celebrate.

The feeling of being in the presence of so much power was overwhelming.[5] In that one moment, a thought formed with certainty in Senger's mind: this island was lost.

And so was the war.

War is asymmetric. Today, the word is on everyone's lips. As military buzzwords go, it is not the worst, and it offers the commander a sage piece of advice: never assume that your enemy is thinking the same thing that you are.

There are places and times, however—and Sicily 1943 appears to be one of them—when you might travel to the other side of the hill and find out that things look exactly the same as they look on your side.

Husky: Origins and Planning

From January 14 to 24, 1943, the Tunisian campaign came to a screeching halt. The brass had arrived in North Africa: President Roosevelt, Prime Minister Churchill, their service chiefs (now grouped together into the Combined Chiefs of Staff, or CCS), and a horde of aides, assistants, flunkies, and reporters. Despite the crowd, they were actually light a man. Soviet dictator and generalissimo Joseph Stalin had received an invitation, but he had declined. He had every reason to do so, what with the Red Army's winter counteroffensive versus the Wehrmacht coming to a climax just then. If any one man had reason to be in the Soviet Union at that moment, he was that man.[6]

The destination of this high-level delegation was Casablanca.[7] It was time to make some basic decisions about the way this war was going. One key area of discussion was the air campaign against Germany, and already there were fissures in the so-called Grand Alliance. The U.S. Army Air Forces (USAAF) preferred a policy of daylight precision bombing, designed to smash crucial areas of the German war economy. The Royal Air Force (RAF) by contrast, had already been at it for three full years and had found that daylight bombing meant extremely high losses of friendly aircraft. It had long ago switched to a policy of nighttime area bombing—that is, dropping its bombs more or less at random on enemy cities to break German civilian morale. The conference solved this thorny contradiction through what historians usually label a compromise, but what was actually a punt—a decision not to make a decision. In Directive Point Blank, the conferees essentially agreed that both sides were right. The two air forces stationed in the United Kingdom (the U.S. 8th Air Force under General Ira C. Eaker and the RAF Bomber Command under General Arthur "Bomber" Harris) would each get the chance to pursue their respective visions. "Round-the-clock bombing," they called it. It was inspired wordplay, but it could not obscure what was a strange form of strategy. A strategy that could not decide between two diametrically opposed courses of action and that split the available forces to follow both at the same time is no strategy at all.[8]

There were equally tough disagreements regarding land strategy. Strategy for the near term was already set. The Allies had to finish the campaign in North Africa, smash the Axis forces there, and occupy Tunis. After that, however, the uncertainties multiplied. There was an irreconcilable split between U.S. and British planners over where to head after Tunisia. General George C. Marshall, the U.S. Army chief of staff, remained as single-minded as ever. He wanted to return the focus to the main event: an invasion of Western Europe, now known as Operation Roundup. In other words, he called for a return to direct action versus Germany after what he clearly saw as the Torch–Tunisia detour. Sharing his preference were most of the top-ranking American planners, such as Major General Thomas T. Handy of the U.S. Army's Operations Division (OPD).[9] The British, by contrast, wanted to continue what was starting to shape up as a successful peripheral strategy.[10] They were looking to exploit the success of Torch by a thrust into the Mediterranean Sea, either by invading Sardinia (Operation Brimstone) or Sicily (Husky). Seizing either one of these big Italian islands, they thought, might bring about the collapse of Italy and thus the end of the Axis. Intensive discussions within and between the two camps narrowed the choice to Husky. A landing on Sicily would secure Allied sea lanes through the entire Mediterranean, while even a successful landing on Sardinia seemed more of a dead end. Roosevelt described the results of taking Sardinia in characteristic cut-to-the-chase terms. They'd all be standing in the same box they were in now, he pointed out, shouting "Hooray! Where do we go from here?"[11]

Marshall finally agreed to Husky, but not because he liked it. He had to bow to the same logic and dynamic of war that had led to Torch in the first place. There were immense Allied forces available in North Africa, but with Roundup still in the planning stages, there was nowhere else they were going to be fighting the Wehrmacht in 1943. In essence, the Casablanca conference came up with a workable compromise on land strategy. The United States traded its support for an invasion of Sicily in 1943 in return for a British promise to back a great cross-Channel invasion in 1944.

The spirit of compromise also guided the choice of command team. The conference chose General Dwight D. Eisenhower as overall commander of Operation Husky. Although it seems inevitable today, it was not a sure thing at the time. The Tunisian campaign was badly bogged down, and things were about to get a great deal worse. Reflecting British suspicion of U.S. fighting qualities, the planners also named a team of three commanders to assist him: General Harold Alexander as his deputy in command of the ground forces, Admiral Sir Andrew Cunningham in command of the naval forces, and Air Chief Marshal Sir Arthur Tedder commanding the air forces. They were there to watch Eisenhower, to steady his hand, and to wean the Americans away from the "unprofessional and slap-dash" methods that were on display in Tunisia.[12]

There was one final result of the Casablanca conference, and one that is still controversial. At the closing press conference, President Roosevelt made an apparently offhand comment that the war would go on until Germany's "unconditional surrender."[13] It was, in other words, war to the bitter end, at least for Germany. Churchill later claimed to have been surprised by Roosevelt's words, but it seems clear today that the two of them had discussed the issue before the announcement. Even today it remains controversial, and all shades of opinion are present in the literature. Most scholars agree with the wisdom of the declaration. It served to bind together the Western allies more closely than ever before, and it also eased Soviet fears of a separate peace between the Western allies and Germany. Set against that positive outlook is a huge body of contemporary testimony that it was a mistake, giving the Axis no reason to negotiate, tying their populations more closely than ever to their governments, striking a grave blow to the German resistance, and giving the Wehrmacht no choice but to fight to the bitter end.[14]

What is generally missing from a discussion of the unconditional surrender policy is how inevitable it was. Whatever the elected officials and the military planners might have come up with in the realm of high strategy, it is unlikely that the American people, to name just one of the actors in this wartime drama, were ever going to tolerate a peace treaty that left Hitler or the Nazis in power in Germany, or the Japanese militarists in Tokyo. If there really is an American way of war, a tendency to fight until the total overthrow the nation's adversaries and the occupation of his homeland, it was in full force in the continental United States in 1943. A month ago, both print media and radio had been up in arms about Eisenhower's seeming dalliance with the Vichyite Admiral Darlan. How much hotter would things get if word ever leaked that the Roosevelt administration was planning a deal with Hitler?

Historians have often pointed out how, with the Tunisian campaign still raging, planning for Husky had to be both rushed and ad hoc.[15] The combined Anglo-American staffs held their planning sessions in the St. George's Hotel in Algiers and became known as Force 141, for their room number. Here they went through one iteration of the plan after another, eight in all (usually identified as Husky One through Husky

Eight), plus a ninth that a dissatisfied Montgomery had his staff work out over the Easter holiday (and thus known as the Easter Plan).[16] Such quick sequencing is hardly unusual in terms of the modern planning cycle, however. The next operation almost always follows hard on the heels of the preceding one. It is probably fair to say that for a neophyte U.S. command and an alliance still feeling its way forward, Husky came a few weeks earlier than it might have.

What they all found inside that crowded room in the hotel was an operation of nearly mind-boggling complexity. A number of contentious issues arose almost immediately. The first had to do with the shape of the landing itself. There are two basic strategies for an amphibious operation. Against weak opposition, the invaders typically land at widely separated beaches. One might call to mind here the example of Operation Torch, with its landings at a dozen separate beaches many hundreds of miles apart. If the invaders expect tough resistance, however, they have to land much closer together for mutual support. The problem was that Force 141 really didn't know what to expect. The Italians might fold once the invaders landed; indeed, the majority opinion within the Allied camp was that they would. Allied intelligence had reported that German divisions were also present on the island, however, and opinion was unanimous that they would fight, and fight hard.[17] Making the decision even tougher was the third dimension: the demand of Marshal Tedder and the Allied air force commanders that the amphibious forces land widely separated so that they could overrun many of the Sicilian airfields in the first hours of the operation.[18] The original operational scheme was a highly complex series of landings by echelon, one in the southeast, one in the south a few days later, and then a third near Palermo in the northwest.[19]

Faced with these contradictory expectations, Allied planners, as they would for the rest of the war, came down squarely in the middle. Massive forces would land in southeastern Sicily, the 15th Army Group under General Alexander. Alexander's command included two armies, the British 8th, under the command of Field Marshal Montgomery, and the U.S. 7th, under General George S. Patton. The operational plan called for seven full divisions to be landing on day one, making Husky the largest amphibious operation of the war—even larger than the landings in Operation Overlord. Although the force was massive, the landing scheme had them dispersed along a full 105 miles of coastline, and the landings would take place at no fewer than 26 separate sites. The aim was to handle both of the potential scenarios regarding the strength of the defenders: the landings would take maximum advantage of Italian weakness (dispersion) and offer maximum protection against German strength (concentration) at the same time. It was, perhaps, an attempt to square an impossible circle.

A second difficult issue was the timing of the operation. According to the British idea of best practice, the landing should take place at night. They realized that a night landing increased the level of friendly confusion, but it was the only way to avoid having to face fully alerted defenders. Eisenhower, however, also envisioned a series of preliminary airborne drops on the island, and they required bright moonlight. The naval planners on both sides, by contrast, had a preference for total darkness during the approach to the island, and they complained that Eisenhower's airborne schemes were putting them all at risk. He was, they warned, jeopardizing the entire operation because of the desire to use paratroops. To complicate matters further, Eisenhower managed to win the backing of the air officers on both sides. They needed moon-light for the preliminary aerial bombardment. Once again, the end result was—no surprise here—a compromise. The landing would take place during a second quarter moon, an interval that was dark enough for the navy but also light enough for the airmen. When they consulted the charts, that could only mean the interval of July 10–14.[20]

Finally, there was the issue of inter-Allied distrust. The final plan for Husky gave the British army the starring role. Early forms of the plan called for a two-army landing, with each army landing near its own big port: Syracuse in the southeastern corner of the island for the British 8th Army, and Palermo in the northwest for the U.S. 7th Army. That scheme lasted all through the plan's first eight iterations. Mont-gomery was not happy with it, however, because it left each army hang-ing on its own limb and risked defeat in detail if strong German forces were present. He wanted the Americans moved to protect his left flank. Landing the whole invasion on the south shore of the island, with the two armies side by side, would be more prudent, he thought, and if there was one quality on which Montgomery had based his career, it was prudence. His arguments, advanced in the Easter Plan prepared by his staff in Cairo, seemed convincing enough to Eisenhower, and in essence they became the new plan.[21]

In its final form, Operation Husky would have Montgomery's 8th Army landing near Syracuse, advance north over the eastern coastal plain to Catania, and then drive further north toward the last major city on the island, Messina. Its fall would trap all the Axis forces on Sicily. Patton's 7th Army would land to the west between Gela and Licata, and its principal mission would be to protect Montgomery's flank. The Americans would not even have their own major port, having to rely instead on the much smaller facilities of the two tiny ports, as well as on "beach maintenance"—the difficult landing of supplies directly onto the shore. Assisting them in that tricky endeavor would be a new and untested piece of technology: an amphibious six-wheel, 2.5-ton truck code named the DUKW, colloquially known as the duck.[22]

Needless to say, there were many in the U.S. Army—officers and men alike, from Patton on down—who were not particularly happy with the plan. "A British plot," Patton fumed. It appeared not only needlessly insulting in reducing the U.S. Army to a bit part. It also seemed dangerous, even reckless: open beaches, no cover, no port. Moreover, it is almost certainly true that reducing the American role in Husky was a major concern of Montgomery's Easter Plan. No one in the higher planning echelons of the British Army in the Mediterranean trusted the U.S. Army. No one said it out loud, but then again, no one had to. U.S. officers groused, but they had their orders. In the end, even Patton, about to command his first army in combat, voiced his support. He might not like the plan, he said, but he would do his "goddamndest to carry it out."[23]

In the first week of July, great flotillas left their ports in North Africa. The British 8th Army would come from the east, from ports in Libya and Egypt, the U.S. 7th Army from the west, from six ports in Algeria. All told, the invasion armada included some 2,590 ships—"the most gigantic fleet in world history," according to its commander, Vice Admiral Henry Kent Hewitt.[24] It was carrying 180,000 men, 600 tanks, 1,800 guns, and 14,000 motorized vehicles. Air support was massive, involving some 3,600 aircraft, and they had already spent the last month hammering away at targets on Sicily and the Italian boot. It was, and still is, an amazing display of force, but it was perhaps an even more amazing display of planning, procurement, and administration. It was the Allies at their best.

German Planning in the Mediterranean

The scholarship on Husky tends to concentrate on the difficulties the British and Americans were having being civil to one another. However much the Anglo-American alliance might have been creaking by this point, however, at least the two sides were not planning to betray and/or attack one another. Such was the state of the Axis by this point in the war that things had come to that sorry pass. The high command of the Wehrmacht (OKW) had already drawn up a "Survey of the Situation Should Italy Withdraw from the War."[25] The discourse between Field Marshal Albert Kesselring, the German high commander for the south and chief of the Italian *commando supremo*, General Vittorio Ambrosio, was turning acrid, and the same might be said for the relationship between Hitler and Mussolini. The two high commands were haggling daily over how many German divisions to introduce into Italy itself, with the Italians clearly disinclined to allow too much German power into the country.[26] Rather than German troops and formations, Mussolini wanted ever more equipment and matériel. A note in early May spoke of 300 tanks, 50 antiaircraft batteries, and enough aircraft to outfit 50 squadrons.[27] The demands were unrealistic, given Germany's own matériel deficiencies by this point, and the Italians almost certainly made them so the Germans would turn them down.

Popular opinion in Italy was turning sour, even more so after the collapse in Tunis—the majority of the prisoners there were Italian. Allied bombing was beginning in earnest; Italian cities had almost no antiaircraft installations or fighter cover, and the dead would eventually rise into the tens of thousands. German soldiers in Italy and Sicily were increasingly the targets of popular anger, catcalls, and the occasional act of violence. It was no wonder, one Italian official had told Baron Konstantin von Neurath at the time: "You haven't made yourself popular. You've requisitioned here and eaten up all their chickens there."[28]

The Germans were secretly returning the disfavor, and planning for Operation Alarich was already well underway by spring, specifying the harsh measures to be taken if Italy defected.[29] By the summer, the operation would have a new name: ironically enough, Operation *Achse* ("Axis"). It would be a signal moment in the history of warfare: a premeditated and murderous assault by one ally on another who was trying to surrender, and Italian casualties would, again, run into the tens of thousands. Being an enemy to the Wehrmacht may have been dangerous, but apparently, so was befriending it. Compared to this ugly situation, professional disagreements between the Anglo-American planning staffs over the precise operational scheme for Husky, the timing, or the allocation of port facilities in Sicily seem positively quaint.

Viewed as a high-level strategic problem, it is probably true that Germany's position in the Mediterranean was hopeless. The ally was faltering. The enemy had dominance in the air and absolute control of the sea. The vast preponderance of its own army was tied down 1,000 miles to the east in a war of attrition in the Soviet Union. The ground forces that Germany could spare for the Mediterranean theater were by definition going to be inadequate. That they were heavy mechanized and Panzer formations, and thus not at all configured to fight island or littoral warfare, should go without saying.

Before they could worry about the fight, however, they had to figure out where it might take place. The Mediterranean was a large theater, and the Allies had their pick of juicy operational targets. Would it be the big islands of Sardinia or Corsica in the western Mediterranean? They would be natural landing sites should the Allies be planning a large-scale landing in southern France at some point. Sardinia alone had enough airfields to bring much of western Italy within the range of Allied tactical air—a useful thing should the Allies be planning a follow-up descent somewhere on the Italian boot. The eastern Mediterranean held the Balkans, a site that had been the obsession of European statesmen and soldiers for centuries as the gateway to the Middle East. An Allied landing here, working in concert with the already active resistance groups in Greece and Yugoslavia, would insert a large enemy force on the deep flank and rear of German forces fighting in the Soviet Union—a potential strategic disaster for the Wehrmacht. Between those two options on the flank, there was Sicily in the middle, staring the Allies directly in the face and a mere hop from their current strategic base in Tunis.

It was all a matter of guesswork. Hitler was leaning toward the Balkans; he had already fought a campaign there in 1941 to protect his southern flank, so his focus was perhaps understandable. His Luftwaffe commander in the theater, Field Marshal Wolfram von Richtofen, disagreed: Sardinia seemed to him to be the logical choice, and he had already moved most of his air defenses assets there.[30] Mussolini, often maligned as a strategist (and for good reason), was certain this time that the target would be Sicily, the direct line to mainland Italy and the most serious threat to the survival of his regime, and Kesselring seemed to agree with him.[31]

Opinion also differed on whether the Wehrmacht could defend any of these places with the meager forces at hand. The recently appointed German liaison to the Italian forces on Sicily, General Frido von Senger und Etterlin, paints a vivid portrait of the strategic confusion.[32] He met with Hitler, who voiced confidence about holding Sicily. So did most of the OKW staff, at least while in Hitler's presence; Senger mentions OKW chief Field Marshal Wilhelm Keitel and the deputy chief of operations, General Walter Warlimont, by name. Once he had them in private, however, they sang a different tune. Warlimont thought it might be best "to transfer the mass of the troops from Sicily to the mainland" in the event of an Allied attack.[33] Keitel "was as skeptical as Warlimont over the prospect of defending the island."[34] He then met with Kesselring, who was as optimistic as ever—too optimistic, thought Senger: "Commanders of German land forces were usually prone to underestimate the chances of a landing by an opponent possessing naval and air superiority."[35] Kesselring was apparently still stuck in 1942, thinking of the past German success in repelling a landing at Dieppe and not realizing that the Allies had graduated onto a completely new level of amphibious operations. Finally, Senger met with Field Marshal Wolfram von Richtofen, commander of *Luftflotte* 2, tasked with support for Mediterranean operations. Richtofen wasn't interested in Sicily at all; instead, he had focused all his attention on Sardinia, which was the logical place, he thought, for an Allied landing. All in all, Senger wrote, it was "a regrettable divergence of views."[36]

Historians of military intelligence often claim that a clever and fully realized Allied deception known as Operation Mincemeat—floating a dead body with false operational papers in the Mediterranean where the Germans could pick it up, the famous episode of "the man who never was"—was the key to weakening the defense of Sicily.[37] The faux documents pointed to a landing in the Peloponnesus, with a follow-up operation planned for Sardinia.[38] The Allies also ran a simultaneous campaign against German communications in northern Greece at the time, Operation Animals, to confirm Hitler's suspicions.[39] It is hard to quantify the impact of all this. All of these sectors were going to require defending troops, and the final German deployment in the Mediterranean seems a prudent one given the circumstances, providing coverage to the western islands, Sicily, and Greece as equally as possible, with force levels favoring the Balkans. That made perfect sense, Mincemeat or no, because the Balkans were on the mainland. Even if Hitler and the staff had guessed right about Sicily, they had to ask themselves how many divisions they could deploy there, as well as how many divisions they wanted to risk sending to an island sitting in enemy-controlled waters.

In the end, the answer to both of those questions was "not many." The mass surrender at Tunis had swallowed up whole units and their cadres, and the well was running dry. A number of German replacement battalions (*Marschbataillonen*) were already in southern France or Italy, part of the now-defunct buildup for Tunisia (*Tunis-Stau*).[40] Along with personnel on leave or wounded who had recovered sufficiently from their injuries, this small manpower pool became the basis for a number of hastily reconstituted divisions: the 1st Paratroop Panzer Division Her-

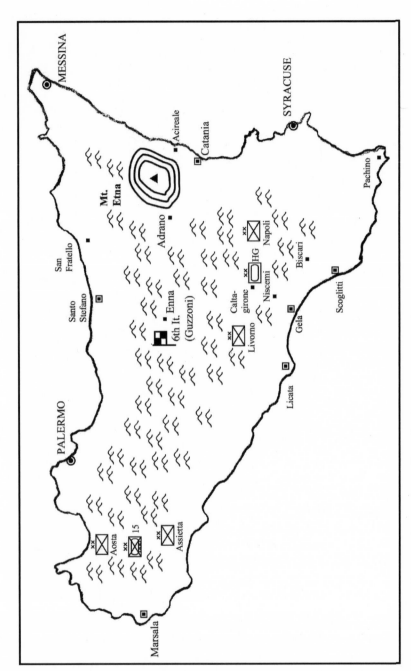

Operation Husky: Axis Dispositions (Day One)

mann Göring (*Fallschirmjäger-Panzer-Division 1. Hermann Göring*), the 29th *Panzergrenadier* Division, the Sicily Division (later the 15th *Panzergrenadier* Division), the Sardinia Division (later the 90th *Panzergrenadier* Division), and others. The Hermann Göring and 15th *Panzergrenadier* Divisions would form the backbone of the German defense of Sicily.[41]

However, the OKW was attempting to cover too much with too little. Haste led to confusion, and virtually all of the new formations would display understandable cohesion problems in battle. The Hermann Göring Parachute Panzer Division might have had a forbidding name, but the commander, General Paul Conrath, described the men disparagingly as a gathering of "supply troops, drivers, and rear-area personnel."[42] Moreover, with his manpower assembled from Germany, the Netherlands, France, and Italy, he found it impossible to exert the "intensive influence on training" that was a divisional commander's primary task.[43] He did not meet the officers and men who would be serving under him until he arrived in Sicily. What he found there were regimental commanders who were not up to snuff, and a mass of inexperienced manpower, mostly air force personnel about to go into land battle and understandably bewildered by it. On the eve of Husky, he complained, the division "was not fully ready to fight."[44]

There was nothing to be done about it. It was June 1943. With the eyes of its supreme command fixed firmly on the Kursk bulge by this point, a wobbly Wehrmacht would have to defend Sicily with the meager forces at hand.

Husky: The Landing

For all of its dramatic gravitas as the return of Allied armies to the European continent, Husky opened badly. The airborne landings about which so much controversy had swirled back in Algiers led off the operation on the night of July 9 and turned out to be a disaster. The British 1st Airlanding Brigade was to come by glider and land near the crucial Ponte Grande (the "big bridge") south of Syracuse.[45] The planes departed on schedule, rendezvoused over Malta using the beacon there to guide them, and then moved on to Sicily. Then things began to go wrong, and the gliders scattered badly en route. Usually attributed in the literature to heavy winds, green U.S. crews on the tow planes, and planning and pilot error of every description, it is probably more accurate to blame the abnormally high friction level of any big airborne drop at night. Things were practically guaranteed to go wrong at some point. Nevertheless, this was as bad as it could be. Most of the gliders dropped into the sea with the loss of all their men. Only 54 of 144 landed in Sicily at all, and of those, just two got anywhere near the bridge. The result on the ground was that rather than an intended 1,700 men, fewer than 100 managed to reach Ponte Grande.[46] Brought under fire almost immediately by local Italian reserves, their situation went from bad to critical that first day, and they were eventually overrun—a highly trained elite sacrificed to no good purpose.[47]

In contrast to this utter disaster, the U.S. landings were merely bad.[48] It was the debut of the newly formed 82nd Airborne Division. Its 505th Parachute Infantry Regiment as well as a battalion of the 504th, some 400 men in all designated Wolf Force, were to drop on the Piano Lupo, a hill mass seven miles northeast of Gela behind the U.S. beaches. Here, they would be in an ideal spot to block any enemy forces trying to counterattack the bridgehead. They too scattered, for all of the reasons listed above, and instead of landing within a five-mile radius of one another, they wound up sprawled over 65 miles of southeastern Sicily. Fewer than 200 men actually reached the Piano Lupo. The commander of the 505th Parachute Infantry Regiment, Colonel James Gavin, was 25 miles from his drop zone. It apparently took him a while to ascertain that he had, in fact, landed on Sicily.[49] Most of the troopers spent the first day or so roaming the countryside in small bands and opening fire on any Italian or German patrols they happened to encounter. They did cause a bit of a ruckus, but they came nowhere near having any sort of operational impact. They "did not interfere with the conduct of the battle," was the terse evaluation of one German staff officer.[50] Again, it was a case of an elite force squandered.

By contrast, the seaborne landings went as smoothly as any landing in the war. The men and their units got ashore when and where they were supposed to—something that came as a great relief to everyone involved after the slapdash amateurism of Operation Torch. One major improvement had come in the crucial area of landing craft. It had been only eight months since Torch, but in that short time, five new variations of the larger landing ship and no fewer than nine new variants of the smaller landing craft had come into service. Accompanying them came a barrage of new acronyms: the LSI (landing ship infantry) and the LST (landing ship tank), the LCI (landing craft infantry) and the LCT (landing craft tank), as well as the all-purpose LCVP (landing craft, vehicle, personnel, also known as the Higgins boat for its designer).[51] There is a stereotype of the U.S. soldier in World War II as being a tinkerer—playing around with his equipment until he got just the right mix of performance, simplicity, and ease of repair. Perhaps it isn't a stereotype at all.[52]

The landings commenced at 2:45 A.M. on July 10. The British 8th Army came with two corps. The XXX Corps (General Oliver Leese) came ashore around Cape Passero and the Pachino peninsula on the southeastern corner of the island, with 1st Canadian Infantry Division, British 51st Infantry Division, and British 231st Infantry Brigade landing from left to right. By the end of the day, the corps held a line from Ispica in the southwest to Noto in the northeast, running roughly parallel to Highway 115. Higher up on the eastern coast, the XIII Corps (General Miles Dempsey) landed two more infantry divisions, the 50th near Avola and the 5th near Cassibile. Resistance in front of both corps was spotty, with Italian coastal batteries firing sporadically or not at all and with virtually no opposition on land. By early afternoon, XIII Corps had seized Syracuse, the island's major port, and had already begun pushing to the north.

Although things were a bit more difficult on the U.S. beaches as a result of the wind and weather, the landings succeeded here as well. The II Corps (General Omar Bradley) came ashore with 1st Infantry Division at Gela and 45th Infantry Division at Scoglitti, while 3rd Infantry Division (subordinated directly to the 7th Army commander, Patton) secured the left flank, landing on both sides of Licata. Typically for the U.S. Army in this war, as well as later ones in the century, it enjoyed dispensing with regular formations in combat in favor of task forces and regimental combat teams, which it formed and shaped to the particular mission. In this case, the operational maps offer us Joss Force (3rd Infantry Division, Combat Command A of the 2nd Armored Division, and a ranger battalion); Shark Force (Bradley's II Corps, further subdivided into Dime, Wolf, and Cent forces), and Kool Force, the reserve formations, these being further subdivided into a floating reserve (Kool Force) and the forces still in Africa, which received no more precise designation.[53] No military establishment's operations have been more difficult to analyze, criticize, or even follow.

The landing forces ran into a massive force on Sicily—a massive Italian force, that is. Defending the island were over 300,000 men of the Italian 6th Army, under the command of General Alfredo Guzzoni, with its headquarters at the centrally located town of Enna. Guzzoni had two regular army corps under him: the XII Corps in the western tip of the island, at Salemi (containing the *Aosta* and *Assietta* Divisions, the 202nd, 207th, and 208th Coastal Divisions, and the independent

136th Infantry Regiment); and the XVI Corps in the east, at Vizzini (containing the *Napoli* Division, the 206th and 213th Coastal Divisions, and the 18th and 19th Coastal Brigades). A fourth regular division, *Livorno*, stood in reserve. The coastal divisions were an interesting case. They were mainly local boys, poorly armed and indifferently trained. No one expected them to give much of an accounting of themselves, and they didn't. Also dotting the island, technically part of Guzzoni's reserve, were a number of battalion-sized groups: eight Tactical Groups designed for positional defense, and eight more Mobile Groups to carry out local counterattacks.[54] There were also two German divisions present, part of the minisurge of German forces into the Mediterranean in the spring: the 15th *Panzergrenadier* Division and the Hermann Göring Parachute Panzer Division, the latter reinforced by a company of Tiger tanks. All told, the Allied invasion met 28,000 German and 175,000 front-line Italian troops on Sicily. Counting some 57,000 supply and support personnel, the number of Axis personnel on the island stood at about 260,000 men.

Of course, that number shrank calamitously for Guzzoni in the first few hours of the invasion. Trying to identify the turning point in a campaign is usually a senseless exercise, but in this case, it occurred on the first day. Faced with the Allied onslaught, the vast majority of those Italian coastal troops (and not a few of the regulars) greeted the invasion by deserting their posts, throwing down their weapons and surrendering, or trading their uniforms for civilian garb and making off into the rugged Sicilian interior. The standard narrative of the Sicilian campaign mocks them as cowards, or as yet further proof of the comic results when modern Italy tries to make war. The Germans thought they were all these things and something else besides: traitors. In his postwar memoirs, Kesselring puts it this way:

> One disappointment followed another. The Italian coastal divisions were an utter failure, not one of their counterattack divisions reaching the enemy in time or even at all—the *Napoli* Division in the southwest corner of the island had melted into thin air. The commandant of the fortress of Augusta meanwhile surrendered without even waiting to be attacked. Cowardice or treachery? Whether or not the court-martial promised me by Mussolini was ever held I never discovered.[55]

It is understandable why the Germans were upset. They had come to a dangerous island to help their allies defend it; now those same allies had left them in the lurch—and potentially trapped on the island. Once again, however, the German memoirs were crucial in fixing a narrative of this campaign. Later U.S. and British historians essentially echoed it, but why they should have done so is hard to understand. There was no cold war pressure here, no need to learn lessons from the Germans. The Italian soldiers who deserted on Sicily were the first fighters in an anti-Mussolini revolution in Italy, voting with their feet every bit as much as Russian soldiers had in 1917. They did the Allies a great service by contributing materially to German defeat on Sicily, and they transformed what could have been a tough fight into a minor footnote in the history books. They risked being shot if they were caught. Although it may require too much redefinition of the term to call them heroes, what they did took a courage all its own. Considering the state of their training and equipment, they would have been fools to stay, fight, and almost certainly die for Mussolini.

The German Assault on Day One: Niscemi and Biscari

As a result of the defection of the Italians, the burden of defending Sicily would fall heavily on the two German divisions. The landings had caught them at a bad time, just after a major redeployment. The 15th *Panzergrenadier* Division, originating out of the old Sicily Division, had been all alone on the island since late May. The main weight of its deployment had been in the center and southeastern corner of the island; on June 29, one of its regiments (Regimental Group *Fullriede*, later the 129th *Panzergrenadier* Regiment) had even conducted a war game (*Kriegsspiel*) testing various responses to an enemy landing at Gela. With the arrival of the Hermann Göring Division in late June, however, orders had come down from Field Marshal Kesselring to General Eberhard Rodt, the commander of the 15th *Panzergrenadier*, to redeploy his division to Salemi, in the island's western tip.[56] The Göring Division would now take its place in the east. Rodt argued, unsuccessfully, that it made more sense to send the new division west and allow his own division to stay where it was, rather than have two divisions settling into new environs at a dangerous moment. He later speculated that Field Marshal Göring himself—the man, not the division—may have been behind the orders; his namesake division had already been trapped once on faraway shores in Tunisia, and perhaps he wanted to keep it safely in eastern Sicily so that it would be closer to Messina if it had to evacuate again. Given what we know of wartime decision making in the Third Reich, it is a plausible tale. "The fact is that things were being arranged behind the scenes," General Senger later wrote. It was "a classic example of the predominance of personal over professional motives," a complaint voiced by other Wehrmacht officers throughout the war.[57] Balancing these accusations, in this case at least, is the fact that the Hermann Göring Division was a full-blown Panzer division, and thus more suited to the kind of aggressive counterattacks against an Allied landing that Field Marshal Kesselring had in mind.

As a result of the flipping of their two divisions, which only began on July 6, the Allied invasion caught the 15th *Panzergrenadier* Division in western Sicily and threatened to isolate it altogether. The Hermann Göring Division, however, was almost directly behind the U.S. beaches at Caltagirone. A glance at the situation map reveals a dicey situation for the Americans, and one seemingly made to order for a Panzer division. U.S forces, elements of the 1st and 45th Infantry Divisions, were just now shaking themselves out into battle array, as every recently landed amphibious force has to. They were on unfamiliar ground, and they knew their own reputation for unsteadiness under enemy fire. The headquarters of the Hermann Göring Division was at Caltagirone, just 15 miles from the beach, half an hour away, and the divisional commander, General Paul Conrath, knew exactly what that meant: it was time to attack.[58]

Conrath was a trained German officer, and his plan of attack showed all the appropriate characteristics. He began by breaking up the division into two regimental-sized battle groups (*Kampfgruppen*). One contained most of his infantry assets (a two-battalion motorized infantry regiment, a self-propelled artillery battalion, and a Tiger tank company). The other contained the concentrated mass of his armor: a two-battalion tank regiment (90 Mark III and Mark IV tanks), two self-propelled artillery battalions, and the division's reconnaissance and engineer battalions. Conrath envisioned a two-pronged attack through Niscemi (the armored *Kampfgruppe*) and Biscari (the infantry), which would then converge concentrically (*konzentrisch*) on the beaches east of Gela.[59] Whatever the tactical or operational problem, the Wehrmacht almost always came up with the same solution: the concentric attack. A German way of war was still at work here: quick response time, concentric operations, independence of the subordinate commander, and a level of aggression the would have made old Blücher proud. Guzzoni had ordered the attack, but it is pretty clear today that Conrath was going to launch one anyway, whether Guzzoni wanted it or not. In fact, he seems to have lost radio contact with Guzzoni at some point that morning, although he was able to reach General Frido von Senger und Etterlin, the German liaison officer to 6th Army headquarters, and inform him of the attack. For this one brief day, Conrath was as much a free agent as any divisional commander in the war.[60]

Despite its almost classic lines, Conrath's great Panzer drive fizzled completely. All the characteristics of an inexperienced division were on full display. The earlier the attack went in, the better the chances of catching the enemy unprepared and disorganized. He had his troops on alert at 2:20 A.M., almost a half hour before the Allies set foot on the beaches. His attack orders went out around 3:00 A.M., both columns were on the road by 4:00 A.M. from their divisional assembly area at Caltagirone, and he intended to begin the attack around 9:00 A.M. As they moved to their starting positions north of Niscemi and Biscari, however, Conrath and his men had some unpleasant surprises. Their comrades in arms, General Rodt and his 15th *Panzergrenadier* Division, knew this terrain well from their earlier studies and tactical exercises, especially the trails, paths, and folds that are so important in a relatively road-poor country. Unfortunately, they were far to the west in Salemi. Conrath and his officers hardly knew the district at all—not surprising because they had all just arrived. The tertiary roads they were using were far worse than they had expected, and the terrain was unbelievably rough.[61] As the sun came up, Allied fighter bombers began to arrive, forcing them off the road again and again. The divisional officer cadre was inexperienced, and Conrath was particularly distressed by the quality of his regimental officers, men whom he was just now getting to know. The manpower consisted largely of young draftees seeing action for the first time, and they showed it. They were enthusiastic enough, but march discipline was sloppy, and everything seemed to take just a bit longer than it should have. Both the air attacks and a few minor skirmishes with detached pockets of U.S. paratroopers had them on the verge of panic, and Conrath had to intervene to stem it.[62] The result: not until 2:00 P.M., nearly 11 hours after Conrath's first orders went out, were his columns in place for the assault.

By the time of the German attack, the U.S. commanders—General Terry Allen of the 1st Infantry Division and Major General Troy H. Middleton of the 45th—were able to build up just enough of a defensive front to halt it. Conrath's armored *Kampfgruppe* on the right hit the U.S. 2nd Battalion of the 16th Infantry Regiment (1st Division), but soon screeched to a halt south of Niscemi near the village of Priolo.[63] Although they were nowhere near the bridgehead at the moment, they were within easy range of U.S. naval vessels just offshore. It was at Priolo that Wehrmacht ground elements first made contact with shellfire from 5- and 6-inch naval guns—hardly a fair fight. U.S. small arms fire also managed to pin the reconnaissance and pioneer battalions, the only contingents of German infantry accompanying the armor column. Conrath intervened personally at 3:00 P.M. to get the attack moving again, but to no avail. By 5:00 P.M., hearing no news of the infantry column and unsure whether it was making progress, he had to admit defeat and halted the attack.

The infantry column, led by Colonel Hellmut Bergengruen, the divisional operations officer, was having its own problems by this point.[64] It launched its attack at 2:00 P.M. just south of Biscari, immediately lost radio contact with divisional headquarters, and then ran into the U.S. 1st Battalion, 180th Infantry regiment (45th Division), moving to the north. By 3:30, this *Kampfgruppe* had also gotten stuck despite Bergengruen's repeated calls for further action.[65] Most disappointing here was the failure of the Tiger tank company.[66] Of all the terrain on which a Mark VI might choose to fight, the mountains and olive groves of Sicily were probably at the bottom of the list. Even on good ground, this heavy tank had transmission problems and a defective steering mechanism, and several of them broke down, blocking the way for the rest of the column. Once the radio was back in action, an angry Conrath ordered them all to get moving again. This time the Tigers led off, broke though the thin U.S. line of the 1/180th, and took the battalion commander, Lieutenant Colonel William Schaefer, prisoner.[67] But before the *Kampfgruppe* could exploit the situation, another U.S. battalion—the 3/180—came trundling up the road into defensive positions. Again, the Germans halted. This time, a brief firefight sent some of the German infantry running off in a panic; Bergengruen had to calm them and get them back in the line, and as night fell, the fighting drew to a close.

The counterattack toward the beaches on day one was a complete misfire for the Germans, with a Panzer Division stopped dead in its tracks by two vastly understrength infantry battalions. Conrath had not been happy with what he had seen:

> The failure of both *Kampfgruppen* lay in the inexperience of the troops, in the unsatisfactory training, in the faulty cooperation of the combined arms, and in the deficient ability of the commanders of both the Panzer and the Grenadier Regiment.

"The young soldiers of the division fought bravely," he wrote, but it hadn't been enough.[68] He had a point. We can easily forget that the

Hermann Göring Division was filled with raw recruits who were just as green, and considerably less well equipped, than the Americans they were facing. Middelton's 45th was a National Guard division that had never been in combat before.[69] It had come straight from the continental United States. Although that meant it was inexperienced, it also meant that it hadn't been in Tunisia during Kasserine Pass, and apparently it was not steeped in any sort of Wehrmacht mystique.[70]

Not everyone blamed the inexperience of the manpower, however, and Conrath himself has come in for his share of blame in postwar analysis. Kesselring, for example, criticized the separation of the infantry and armor into two *Kampfgruppen*, rather than the creation of two more evenly balanced columns. "General Conrath had too little experience in combat with modern combined arms," the marshal would later claim. "It is incorrect armor tactics for the tank units to march separate from the armored infantry as occurred here."[71] As is typical in such disputes, both Conrath and Kesselring are probably right.

Almost lost in the discussion of that first day has been the real threat to the U.S. bridgehead, and it hadn't been from the Germans. At Gela, the Italians launched a sizable and rapid assault with elements of the *Livorno* Division (General Domenico Chirieleison) and Mobile Group E. Backed by armor—World War I–era Renault FT-17s, it should be noted—the attackers actually penetrated into the center of the town. They were nearly at the water's edge before encountering elements of the 26th Infantry Regiment (1st Infantry Division), a battalion of U.S. Army rangers, and yet another lost group of U.S. paratroopers. Here, too, naval gunfire played a role. At Gela, the Italians were literally under the guns of the destroyer U.S.S. *Shubrick*, which systematically destroyed one tank after another.[72]

The German Counterattack on Day Two: To the Beach

The Americans had dodged a bullet at Biscari and Niscemi, but the next day would prove to be even more difficult. From General Patton on down, everyone in the U.S. command realized that another German blow was about to fall. The Germans had a Panzer division within throwing distance of the sea, and the beachhead itself was the mass of administrative confusion typical of a recently landed force. The U.S. Army's official history describes the 45th Division beaches as presenting a "most deplorable picture":

Backed by soft sand dunes and with few usable exits, the five assault beaches were cluttered with masses of stranded landing craft and milling groups of men and vehicles soon after the initial landing. Many landing craft were hung up on offshore sand bars, unable to retract. Others broached on the beaches, the sea breaking completely over some, eddying into others over lowered ramps. Scattered and disorganized shore parties were still not functioning properly as late as 0800.[73]

Plenty of men had landed, but almost no heavy weapons, artillery, or armor. Patton had ordered that 10 M-4 Sherman tanks to be brought ashore, but once landed, they almost immediately bogged down in the soft sand. They would spend much of the day desperately trying to get free while the sound of gunfire roared around them. He also took the expedient of landing units from his floating reserve during the night. It was rather early in the game for that, but it is a sign of how dire the situation must have appeared. During the night of July 10–11, elements of the 2nd Armored Division and the 18th Infantry Regiment (1st Infantry Division) came ashore. Patton's decision did manage to cram more soldiers into the bridgehead—about four infantry battalions' worth—but once again, most of them arrived bearing small arms only.

The Axis defenders spent a busy night as well. They knew that they would have to attack the next morning, that it would be their last chance to crush the landing, and that with no reserves or reinforcements forthcoming, it was something of a last gasp. Conrath would later state his belief that "The Allies had already won the battle for Sicily on July 10th."[74] The uncertainties of the command situation were doing nothing to lighten his mood. In the course of the night, Conrath had learned through General Senger that his division was subordinate to the Italian XVI Corps for the coming fight. He also had received a series of contradictory directives. One, from General Guzzoni of the 6th Army, was ordering him to attack toward Gela as part of a concerted, two-division drive, teaming him with the Italian *Livorno* Division, currently sitting a few miles to his right.[75] The two divisions would make for the beach, *Livorno* driving on Gela from the northwest and Hermann Göring from the northeast. Conrath had agreed to the general outline of the plan, but he received no further details in the course of the day. At 3:50 A.M., he received a second order, this one from his Supreme Commander South, Kesselring. The marshal was out of communications with Guzzoni and was having to follow the action indirectly through a linkup with Luftwaffe headquarters in Catania and

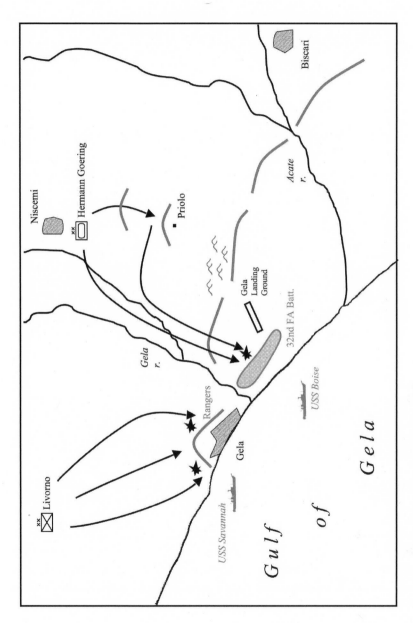

Trouble on the Beachhead: Gela (July 11, 1943)

Taormina.[76] Already disgruntled at the failure of the Italians to oppose the landing, he ordered Conrath to launch a counterattack toward Gela as early as possible that morning. A third order now came in, this one again from Guzzoni.[77] News had just come in of the rapid fall of Syracuse to the British on day one. With the southeastern flank now compromised, Guzzoni wanted Conrath to drive for the beaches and then wheel southeast—that is, toward the U.S. 45th and 3rd Infantry Division beaches. Conrath had to be more than a bit befuddled.

At dawn on July 11, the Axis defenders of Sicily threw most of two complete divisions, the *Livorno* Division on the right and Hermann Göring on the left, against the U.S. 1st Infantry Division in the Gela bridgehead, supported by Luftwaffe airstrikes.[78] The target for both divisions was Gela, although given the confusing welter of orders, it is hard to say that they cooperated in any real way. Once again, Conrath would divide his division into separate *Kampfgruppen*, two west of the Acate River and one east of it, in order to launch a concentric attack on his target. On his right, most of the 2nd Panzer Battalion would come down from the Ponte Olivo airfield, driving along Highway 117; the center *Kampfgruppe*, formed around the 1st Panzer Battalion, would originate at Casa Priolo, drive down Highway 115, and link up with the 2nd near the Gela–Farello landing ground on the coastal highway. Finally, at Biscari, far to the left, an infantry *Kampfgruppe*, consisting mainly of the 2nd *Panzergrenadier* Regiment and the Tigers, would wheel right, cross the Acate River at the Ponte Dirillo Bridge, and link up with the other two. General Chirieleison's *Livorno* Division would likewise head for the beach in three columns, mixed battle groups of the 33rd and 34th Infantry Regiments.

This assault started a great deal closer to the beaches and had much less rugged terrain to negotiate. As a result, both the Italians and the Germans broke through the U.S. front almost immediately, heading for Gela, the landing ground just to the east of the town, and the sea. The *Livorno* Division got close to Gela. It was a tough fight, but it was essentially a replay of the previous day. Once again, the attackers came to a halt under the fire of a few companies of U.S. rangers who were defending the town, supported by their own 4.2-inch mortars and some captured 77mm Italian artillery. Once again, the American defenders were able to call on naval gunfire from a cruiser offshore, the U.S.S. *Savannah*, firing nearly 500 5-inch shells at impossible-to-miss ranges. One thing that was different this day at Gela was the arrival of General Patton himself, wading ashore, screaming at loitering soldiers to "get your asses off this beach," pointing to the Italian enemy and telling the Ranger commander to "kill every one of the goddam bastards."[79] That didn't happen, but casualties in the *Livorno* Division (a *divisione binaria*, or binary division containing only two regiments) were high enough to break the back of the attack, and *Livorno* recoiled in some confusion. Binary or not, an Italian division in World War II was far too light to take this kind of pounding.

Things got much more serious to the east. West of the Acate, the two armored *Kampfgruppen*—a great force of 60 German Panzers— drove forward relentlessly in two columns. It was an impressive display of maneuver and shock, bypassing U.S. defenses when possible and overrunning them when necessary. By noon, the two Panzer columns had converged near the coastal highway just west of Santa Spina. They were a mere 2,000 yards from the sea and were raking the beaches, U.S. supply dumps, and even landing craft with direct fire, with both main gun and machine gun. U.S. shore personnel were burning papers and destroying radar equipment lest it should fall into enemy hands, and Conrath received at least one report from the field that "pressure from the Hermann Göring division (has) forced the enemy to re-embark temporarily,"[80] a missive that he dutifully sent on to Guzzoni, who dispatched it to Kesselring.

There is no doubt that the Gela bridgehead itself was now at stake. Even at this moment of seeming German triumph, however, the balance of forces was shifting. In the midst of the confusion, a group of DUKWs landed, carrying the U.S. 32nd Field Artillery Battery. Meeting the gunners was the 1st Infantry Division's artillery commander, Brigadier General Clift Andrus, who calmly hustled them into position along the edge of the sand dunes along the beach, pointing in the general direction of the melee and telling them, "There's plenty of good hunting up there."[81] Within minutes, they were pouring rounds into the Panzer columns, once again at point-blank range, and Panzer IIIs and IVs were exploding into flames. Soon joining the fight were four of the 10 stranded Sherman tanks, who had finally managed to extricate themselves from the beach. Finally, naval guns put the exclamation point on this vivid demonstration of American firepower, with the cruiser U.S.S. *Boise* edging to within 3,000 yards of the waterline and pouring on the 6 inch. Nothing could stand against so much firepower, and certainly not a couple of Panzer battalions on a naked beach. Conrath called a retreat at 2:00 P.M., and soon the surviving tanks were scurrying for the hills.

It was just enough to bring the attack to a halt. The defenses had held, the bridgehead was safe, and U.S. firepower had laid a big hurt on the German attackers, with some 40 German tanks left burning on the plain at Gela, including 10 of the 17 Tigers that had taken part. The victory had been more than a case of massing fires, however. That third German *Kampfgruppe* coming down from Biscari never came into play at all. As it drove for the Ponte Dirillo over the Acate River, it suddenly came under flanking fire on the Biazzo Ridge from an unknown enemy. It turned out to be none other than Colonel Gavin, with a by now sizable force of paratroopers he had assembled along the way. It was a classic case of marching to the sound of the guns—rare in this war. In the course of a gritty daylong fight, during which his mortar men even disabled a few Tigers, Gavin Force brought the third *Kampfgruppe* to a halt and materially upset the German plans for a truly concentric attack.[82]

Although it had been a bit too close for comfort, the Gela fight is open to multiple narratives and interpretations. First, on the strategic level, even if the beachhead had been compromised, it is arguable whether or not it would have wrecked the Sicilian campaign. The British were already ashore in force, the major port of Syracuse was already in their hands, and the Germans had just used up their one and only Panzer division. There would have been some humiliation on the part of the Americans and some schadenfreude on the part of the British, with incalculable effects for the rest of the war, but the Sicilian campaign would have gone on. General Terry Allen, commander of the 1st Infantry Division, got it just right: "The situation could have been critical," he said. "As it was, it was merely embarrassing."[83]

On the operational and tactical levels, however, Gela offers an intriguing glimpse of two contrasting ways of war. The Germans had stayed faithful to their traditional recipe: aggressive assault, *konzentrisch* attack, a *Kesselschlacht*, even if only in miniature. As always, they dominated the proceedings early on. Eight hours later, however, they wound up milling around in confusion, unable to hide on an open beach, getting pulverized by multiple sources of superior U.S. firepower. It is unclear what they were trying to surround at Gela, if indeed they were not merely acting according to military doctrine that was in some sense centuries old and perhaps by now merely assumed rather than consciously designed. As for the American conduct of the Gela fight, it has been all too common in the literature to view the use of naval gunfire in negative terms, as if it were a blot on the honor of the land force. Alternatively, it appears suddenly, as a kind of deus ex machina, swooping out of nowhere to rescue the ground troops and save the day.

It was neither. The use of naval gunfire in the tactical role had been the subject of intensive discussion and negotiation between the army and navy long before Husky brought them all to Sicily. It was not a desperate expedient. Certainly one can identify problems with it. The *Boise* had to hold its fire repeatedly in the course of the day because the troops on both sides were too closely intermingled and no one in either U.S. service wanted a big-gun fratricide. Naval gunfire is a blunt instrument, not the most delicate or flexible tactical weapon for use in ground combat. It was highly effective at these ranges, however, and from the beginning, it was part of the operational plan. Those helpless German tanks brewing up one by one had no answer to naval gunfire, as in some sense a resource- and manpower-poor Wehrmacht had no answer to a U.S. Army that could afford to be this profligate with its supplies and ammunition, or to an enemy who enjoyed absolute control of the seas. The fact that one of these armies was waning and the other was just beginning to wax only made the disparity in their ways of war more obvious.

Why did the Americans resort to naval gunfire at Gela? Because they could.

The Campaign for Sicily

The further course of operations demonstrated what could happen if the U.S. Army attempted anything too fancy in the operational sphere. The night of the successful defense of Gela, General Patton ordered an airborne operation by 2,300 men of the 504th Parachute Infantry Regiment. The purpose of the landing was not to discomfit the enemy, but to reinforce what was by now a fairly jittery bridgehead. Unfortunately, when the C-47 transports arrived overhead, nervous U.S. antiaircraft gunners mistook them for enemy—easy enough to do at night—and opened up on them with every gun in sight. One plane after another went down in flames (23 out of a total of 144), and the slaughter didn't end there.[84] Hundreds of men were riddled with bullets as they floated down helplessly, and even those who did land safely often found themselves in vicious firefights in the dead of night with their own U.S. comrades, not all of whom had the same sign and countersign, "Ulysses" and "Grant" for the airborne and "Think" and "Quickly" for the ground troops.[85] It was the latest, but by no means the last, botched airborne landing of this war, and perhaps a warning to U.S. planners against overly complex operations.

With the landings complete, however, the campaign for Sicily proper now began. No understanding of what happened can be complete without an analysis of the three operational dynamics that were at work. The British commanders, for example, General Alexander of the 15th Army Group and General Bernard Law Montgomery of the 8th Army, had no confidence whatsoever in the fighting qualities of their U.S. allies. Rather than attempt either to defend or refute their point of view, historians should simply accept it as part of their analytical toolbox for the Sicilian campaign. Likewise, the U.S. Army leadership—Eisenhower as supreme commander, Patton of the 7th Army, General Omar N. Bradley of the II Corps—were well aware of their partner's contempt, and they saw Husky not merely as a chance to destroy the German armies facing them and perhaps break up the Axis altogether. Rather, they saw it as a way to prove their worth and outdo the British. Once again, rather than attempt to defend or challenge that attitude, historians should simply accept it as an integral part of the operational dynamic on Sicily.

Finally, as in all the Mediterranean campaigns, the Axis chain of command in Sicily was overly complex, and decision making was often convoluted. Marshal Kesselring was the German Supreme Commander South. As always, he began the campaign confident that he could drive the Allied armies into the sea before they could establish themselves firmly on the island.[86] The Axis ground force commander on Sicily, General Guzzoni of the Italian 6th Army, thought that was a ridiculous notion, given Allied superiority in the air and absolute supremacy at sea. His German liaison officer, General Senger und Etterlin, agreed with him. Both thought that the best they could hope for was to fight a delaying action and retreat back to the Etna position based on the great volcano in the northeast corner of Sicily. Here, they could draw up in a defensive arc around the port of Messina so that Axis troops could eventually evacuate the island. Senger felt that some of Kesselring's motivation came from a need to restore his reputation, badly damaged after the debacle in Tunisia. He needed, Senger later wrote, an "eye-catching defensive success."[87] That may well be true. Whatever the cause, the early days of the fighting saw Kesselring summoning German reinforcements to Sicily to fight a battle that most of his commanders on the ground already viewed as lost.[88] They included the 29th *Panzergrenadier* Division and much of the 1st Paratroop (*Fallschirmjäger*) Division, joining the two divisions already there (the 15th *Panzergrenadier* and the Hermann Göring Panzer Division). He also recalled the 15th *Panzergrenadiers* back to the east to rejoin their sister division, essentially abandoning western Sicily. The battles of days one and two, however, which wrecked the Italian 6th Army and severely mauled the Hermann Göring Division, soon brought Kesselring back down to earth. He now agreed on a fighting retreat to Etna, thereby declaring a battle lost that he had just reinforced a mere 24 hours earlier. After the first two days, the Germans were thinking mainly of evacuating Sicily with the fewest possible friendly casualties.

These were the systemic factors in the Sicilian campaign: British mistrust, a U.S. desire to prove itself, and a Wehrmacht that didn't intend to stick around any longer than was absolutely necessary. They determined the course and outcome of the fighting far more than this or that individual command decision, as indeed they determine the outcome of most campaigns. We have to view the Allied "failure" to trap the Axis forces on Sicily—an indictment contained in virtually every analysis of this campaign—in this light. In theory, it seemed to be easy enough. In reality, the odds were small, precisely because of the operational dynamics listed above.

Looking back, there might well have been a chance for the Allies to bag most of the defenders of Sicily, but it came early and vanished quickly. In the first week, there was a yawning gap between the two Wehrmacht formations on the island. The 15th *Panzergrenadier* Division was still at Salemi in the west. It had orders to return, but that was going to take time given the omnipresence of Allied airpower and a lack of quality roads. With the Hermann Göring Division committed in the east, there was for a time no contact at all between the two divisions. On the Allied side, Montgomery's 8th Army was starting its drive up the eastern coast toward Catania, and typically was moving in a highly deliberate fashion. A mechanized German battle group under General Colonel Wilhelm Schmalz (*Kampfgruppe Schmalz*), built around one of the regiments of the Hermann Göring Panzer Division and now reinforced by recently dropped airborne forces, was contesting the British drive every step of the way.[89] The U.S. 7th Army, by contrast, had almost no enemy troops in front of it, once Conrath had drawn back the Hermann Göring Division. Patton's army was in an ideal position to drive straight across Sicily from its bridgehead between Licata and Gela, which would have cut the island, and the Wehrmacht forces defending it, in two. At the very least, it might have trapped significant portions of the 15th *Panzergrenadier* Division in the west.

The Americans didn't get that chance, however. Contrary to the original operational scheme, the 8th Army was soon claiming virtually the entire highway network in eastern Sicily. Montgomery had in mind a repeat of his Mareth maneuver, a frontal assault up the Catania road toward Mt. Etna by XXX Corps, supported by some sort of wide flanking maneuver inland by XIII Corps. The original plan had Patton act-

ing as a shield to Montgomery's sword, preventing any German interference with a British thrust to the north. Montgomery had no intention of launching a simple frontal assault against the tallest mountain
in Sicily, however. He needed a flanking force to the west of Etna. Distrusting U.S. fighting abilities, he wanted it to be a British force. He
got the backing of General Alexander, and on July 13, orders went out
placing Highway 124 at the disposal of the British and moving the operational boundary between 7th and 8th Armies far to the west, running
roughly through Enna.

The impact of the "stolen highway" on the U.S. Army, which
seemed about to be shut out of the action on Sicily altogether, was
intense. The officers, in particular, went ballistic. "What fools we are,"
said Patton. "Tell Montgomery to stay out of my way or I'll drive those
Krauts right up his ass."[90] General Bradley called it "the most arrogant,
egotistical, selfish and dangerous move" of the war and warned that
"this will raise hell with us." Patton's deputy, Major General Geoffrey
Keyes, warned that the British were going "to sell us down the river."[91]

Some of the language might have verged into hyperbole, but the out-
rage—perhaps even the insecurity—was real enough. It was the emotional matrix out of which Patton devised what became the signature
event of the campaign: getting permission to launch his entire army on
a high-speed dash across Sicily to the west and north. Alexander didn't
mind. Why not have the Americans doing something rather than sitting there stewing? The western sweep opened on July 18 and soon
shifted into high gear.[92] Once it got moving, no force in the world could
move faster than the U.S. Army. Patton had Bradley's II Corps on his
right (containing the 1st and 45th Infantry Divisions) heading north
and northwest, a Provisional Corps under Keyes (3rd Infantry Division,
82nd Airborne Division) following the coastline to the west, and the
2nd Armored Division in army reserve. It was a powerful force, and a
highly mobile one. These may have been infantry divisions, but they
were U.S. infantry divisions, and that meant an immense number of
vehicles and a rapid pace. Towns fell in a rush: Ribera on the 19th, Ler-
cara Friddi on the 20th, Corleone, Castelvetrano, and Salemi on the
21st. Over 50,000 prisoners of war fell into U.S. hands. Patton was in
his element, his element being top-speed maneuver rather than actual
fighting. "Mount up and continue," he told his men. "Don't stop except
for gas!"[93] The climax of the sweep was the fall of Palermo on July 22,
the first city to be conquered by the U.S. Army in World War II. That
left only the ports of Marsala and Trapani in the far western tip of the
island. They fell the next day.

Patton and his men had overrun all of western Sicily in a week with minimal casualties. He would later call the great ride "a glorious chapter in the history of war" and tell the men of the 7th Army, "Your fame shall never die!"[94] It is easy to chuckle at the exaggeration. There had been no opposition; there had been more running around than fighting; and virtually all the prisoners he had taken were Italians eager to surrender. The U.S. 7th Army, meanwhile, was exhausted and badly in need of resupply—something that Bradley, for one, would moan about for the rest of the campaign. On the plus side, it made for good copy in the papers back home, and that was no small thing by this point in the war. As a way of establishing the bona fides of the U.S. Army, proving its ability to carry out large-scale and rapid maneuver, and perhaps even establishing a sense of self-worth in a force too often defined by its behavior at the Kasserine Pass, the western sweep served an important purpose. Patton knew that it made him a hero to the American public. He was too savvy not to know that. There are times, however, when self-interest and the interest of the institution are perfectly aligned, and this was one of them.

We need to remember our third operational dynamic, however: the disappearing Wehrmacht. To the Germans—Kesselring, Senger, and the divisional commanders—Patton's ride was utterly insignificant in a military sense. The Wehrmacht had spent that time scurrying away to the north and east. By the time Patton had gotten to where he wanted to be—Palermo—the Germans, too, were exactly where they wanted to be: sitting in a nice compact arc around Messina, first from Catania in the east, curving around Etna to San Stefano in the north, and then a tighter one from Acireale in the east to San Fratello in the north. They were now under a single, unified German command, the XIV Panzer Corps, under General Hans Hube, a one-armed officer with a fearsome reputation and a number of hair-raising adventures on the Eastern Front. His soldiers there called him *der Mann*—not the common designation of the commander as "the old man," but in this case simply, "the Man."[95]

What the Wehrmacht needed now was a cool head, and Hube provided it. Less than a year ago, he had spearheaded the drive of his division from the Don to the Volga in a single bound, then had to hold open a narrow corridor against repeated tank-heavy Soviet attacks from two separate directions. Holding a nice solid line in front of Messina must have seemed like a walk in the park. He had three divisions abreast: the Hermann Göring on his left, the 29th *Panzergrenadier* on his right, and the 15th *Panzergrenadier* in the center, with surviving elements of the Italian divisions, *Livorno, Assietta,* and *Aosta* interspersed among them.

Using the same metaphor it had trotted out in Tunisia, the U.S. and British press would describe the rest of the campaign as a "race for Messina," this one between Patton and Montgomery. Once again, however, it was not much of a race. With two Allied armies abreast (the 7th on the left and the 8th on the right) facing three German divisions ensconced in some of the most forbidding mountain terrain in Europe, it was by definition going to be a slow grind. Here the Germans were content to fight *Stellungskrieg*, bleeding their enemies in a delaying action (*hinhaltender Widerstand*). The Germans would seize a position on high ground, wait for the Allies to attack, inflict heavy casualties, and then retreat back to the next position. The point was not to defend Sicily but to buy enough time to evacuate troops across the Strait of Messina back to the mainland.

Given the situation, this phase of the campaign would see some hard fighting. On August 1, for example, the U.S. 1st Infantry Division launched an assault against the fortified town of Troina. For the next six days, it struggled forward against fierce German resistance. The mountains limited the effectiveness of U.S. artillery and air strikes, attempts to flank the town both north and south came to naught, and in the end the Germans were able to break contact and withdraw. Heavy losses in the division, as well as what seemed to be a breakdown of discipline in the ranks, led Bradley and Patton to dismiss the division commander, Major General Terry Allen, as well as his assistant division commander, Brigadier General Theodore Roosevelt.[96] The same day that Troina fell, Montgomery finally managed to outflank the German defenders on Etna. It had worked out much as he had envisioned it early on, even if it was a bit late. Elements of the Canadian 1st Division and the British 78th Division worked their way round the base of the mountain, driving on Adrano and stretching the defense until it could not hold. On August 13, the 7th and 8th Armies linked up once again at Randazzo, reestablishing a cohesive Allied front north of Etna.[97]

The end was now clearly in sight. Patton tried to restart his momentum in the north, launching frontal assaults in concert with a series of amphibious end runs, small-scale landings behind the German lines to compromise their defenses. The first, on August 8, was an attempt to bypass the German position at San Fratello. It went smoothly, but mainly because the Germans were already pulling out. A second, at Brolo on August 11, went badly, with the defenders nearly driving the small force back into the sea. A third, at Falcone on August 15, hit air; once again, the Germans were already gone. In fact, the landing force was met by patrols of the U.S. 3rd Infantry Division, who had already reached Falcone by land.

Hube, for his part, was slowly and systematically backpedaling. When the Messina triangle became too narrow for him to deploy three divisions abreast, he pulled 15th *Panzergrenadier* out of the line and held the position with just two divisions: 29th *Panzergrenadier* on his right and Hermann Göring on his left. With the Messina peninsula tapering to a narrow tip, the Allies couldn't deploy many more troops than he could. It was a source of unending frustration to them, but it provided a lesson at least as old as Thermopylae, and perhaps as old as warfare itself. Meanwhile, his rear echelon troops were turning the Strait of Messina into a fortress, deploying over 500 antiaircraft guns on the Sicilian and Calabrian shores on both sides of it. For a few short weeks, it may well have been one of the most dangerous little pieces of airspace anywhere in the world. Operation *Lehrgang* ("course of study" or "curriculum"), the evacuation of Sicily, was about to begin.[98] All Hube had to do was to mark out his intermediate lines and retire to them one by one. It was a process requiring a good eye and some steady troops, and Hube had both.

Operation *Lehrgang* began on August 11 and lasted for five days. It is only a two-mile run across the strait at its narrowest, and the Germans put anything that could float into action: transports, ferries, launches of every description. Only now, with the Germans abandoning their last defensive lines, did the Allies finally race for Messina. Montgomery encountered a last-second hang-up in the German minefields north of Taormina, which slowed him up just enough to allow Patton to win the race. U.S. forces entered Messina on the morning of August 17, and Patton soon joined them to take the formal surrender of the city. Montgomery's spearheads were at Tremestieri, just a mile or so down the coast, and he would get to Messina the next day. Of course, the town was nearly empty. The Germans had left the building.

Conclusions

It has not been easy to evaluate Husky in an objective manner. Let us start with a few definite points. In 38 days of battle, the Allies had overrun Sicily and driven its defenders from the island at a cost of 20,000 friendly casualties (12,000 British and 8,000 American). Considering all the things that can go wrong in even the simplest operational scheme, the roles of fog and uncertainty and contingency that are so much a part of military historical discourse today, Husky was a marvel. Having the operation go as smoothly as it did should have gladdened the hearts of everyone on the Allied side.

Likewise, on the strategic level, Husky marked a crucial stepping-stone on the path to Allied victory. It was the first direct assault on an Axis homeland. The invasion led to the downfall of Benito Mussolini even as the fighting was still raging; surrender negotiations were already underway between the Allies and the new government of Marshal Pietro Badoglio. One down, we might say, and two to go.

Finally, from the distinct perspective of the U.S. Army, Husky was a satisfying operation. The army had taken part in a plan that had clearly reduced it to second-class status. It had performed loyally and well even when smarting under the perceived insults of its ally. It had bravely defended its beachhead, it had beaten back a direct assault from the vaunted German Panzers, and it had made them pay dearly. In the course of the fighting, it had finally cut loose and carried out its first large-scale, independent operation of the war: Patton's sweep to Palermo. Any army that could drive this fast and shoot this well was going to be trouble at some point. Although it remained to be seen whether the U.S. Army would ever be the equal of the Wehrmacht in a tactical sense, and a "Kasserine complex" was still noticeable among many, it had certainly proven that it was the equal of the British, an important milestone in its own development.

Thus—a signal victory! Or was it? Even today, Husky continues to generate controversy. The best-known work in the current literature, by the inestimable author and scholar Carlo D'Este, is entitled *Bitter Victory*. After all, Allied might hadn't driven the Germans off of Sicily at all. They had decided to leave, then fought a skillful delaying action, with just three divisions holding off an Allied force that eventually numbered nearly 500,000 men. The evacuation itself went flawlessly, rescuing 55,000 German and 70,000 Italian soldiers, and was completely unhindered by Allied air or naval power, the areas in which the Allies held the most decisive advantages of all. Operation *Lehrgang* wouldn't have been easy to stop, but as dangerous as it might have been, the Allies never even tried. The combined air forces were concerned about antiaircraft over Messina, certainly, but the real reason they weren't available to stop the evacuation was that they were ranging wide and deep into Italy, carrying out strategic bombing against targets like Naples, Bologna, and Rome. Likewise, both the U.S. and British navies have traditions of aggressive command and derring-do, but neither one wanted to risk the Messina narrows, waters in which they would be ridiculously easy targets and where their principal advantage, long-range gunnery, would hardly come into play at all.

Even Patton himself, the victor of Messina, admitted to feeling let down by the way the campaign had ended. His reward for victory, one of the best-known narratives of the war, was a dressing-down from Eisenhower, the result of two demented incidents in which he slapped shell-shocked soldiers in the 15th and 93rd evacuation hospitals. Despite all his playacting and the folderol with which he surrounded himself, Patton was in many ways a typical man of his time. In an age in which knowledge of human psychology was still in its infancy, many people didn't have much use for newfangled concepts like combat fatigue. These men must be shirkers, Patton felt, maybe even cowards. Whatever his personal views, however, U.S. officers do not lay hands on their men. Eisenhower only made him apologize to the soldiers involved and to the divisions under his command. Unfortunately, in November, U.S. radio personality Drew Pearson got hold of the story and broadcast it, and soon much of the American public was debating whether or not their conquering hero of a few months ago should be fired altogether. It was in some ways a fitting end to Husky.

Perhaps individual campaigns aren't always as asymmetric as we like to claim. We should always question our own buzzwords. Perhaps there are military situations, particularly in the midst of vast, complex wars, in which victory is so nebulous as to seem virtually indistinguishable from defeat—campaigns from which both sides can emerge equally puzzled about the significance of what has just taken place.

6

Manstein's War: *Bewegungskrieg* in the East, July–December 1943

Introduction

The American novelist F. Scott Fitzgerald famously wrote that despite all our attempts to live our lives free of encumbrances or limitations, we often find it impossible. "So we beat on," he wrote in his greatest novel, "boats against the current, borne back ceaselessly into the past."[1]

With that in mind, let us travel backward in time to a vanished world, one that we moderns can scarcely imagine. The place is Europe, the year is 1757, and two hostile armies are about to clash near the Bohemian town of Kolin.[2]

"Damn!" the king shouted.

He could hear the sound of firing off to his right, on his flank. What in the hell was happening over there? He had told his generals over and over again that the maneuver had to be done quickly and quietly. He had told them to drum it into their men: no loud talking, no smoking, no pauses. Keep marching. Get around the Austrian flank and hit them from the right. Smash them before they had a chance to react.

It was a risk, as always. The enemy army was so much larger than his. He did his sums. The Austrians had twice the number of men he had. They were in good position on the high ground in front of Kolin, and he was marching right across their front. But their men were contemptible, he knew, and their officers were even worse. He had beaten them before, and he could do so again. All he had to do was to surprise them and hit them in their flank. They would crumble.

The sound of gunfire on his right told him that he had failed. Someone had broken cover, or failed to keep march discipline, or—god forbid—had decided to attack prematurely. His officers were all good men from the finest families in the kingdom, old Junker stock, hard on themselves and even harder on their troops. Sometimes, he thought, they were a bit too aggressive in combat, too eager to prove themselves. He understood that, however. He too had lost his mind enough times in the heat of battle.

That was apparently what had happened now. He called his aides to him. A quick *Kriegsrat*—a war council. He hadn't spared his words, nor had he wasted his time being polite. He wanted answers. What had happened? Who was at fault? It didn't take long. They all seemed terrified of him. "One of the division commanders," they stammered. Apparently a few of his men had taken fire from an Austrian light infantry detachment holding Kolin village. He could feel the anger rising as he heard the reports. Those goddamn Croats! Barbarians! They were always causing trouble.

One thing that Frederick the Great did know, however, was how to respond to an officer who had fouled up one of his plans, general or no general, Junker or not. He turned to one of his aides. In his best, most royal and enraged howl, he shouted, "Get me General Manstein!"[3] When they hesitated, he added, "Immediately!"

They knew that tone. General Manstein was in trouble.

Military historians should read more literature. For all the specialized terminology we like to use—"turning maneuvers" and "holding operations," references to "economy of force" and "strategic withdrawals," dissections of *Bewegungskrieg* and "operational art," or "methodical battle" and the "American way of war"—perhaps it takes a novelist to nail it. Historians usually judge a commander against criteria that assume he is a free agent, able to choose freely from among a range of logical options. Having done that, they then assign points for good decisions and demerits for bad ones.

What if the actors are not completely free, however? What if context and experience, even history itself, all work to limit the range of choices? What if field commanders are nothing more than "boats against the current, borne back ceaselessly into the past," unable to escape the dead weight of their own experience?

The Death of Operation Citadel:
Nine Days that Shook the World

On July 13, 1943, Adolf Hitler summoned the Army Group commanders currently involved in Operation Citadel to his headquarters, the
Wolfsschanze in Rastenburg, East Prussia. There he gave Field Marshal
Erich von Manstein (Army Group South) and Field Marshal Günther
von Kluge (Army Group Center) the bad news: Citadel was finished,
and it was time to revert to a defensive posture on the Eastern Front.[4]
Manstein argued with him, as always. Things were looking up in the
southern sector, the field marshal claimed. His assault had destroyed
the Soviet strategic reserve at Prokhorovka, and a breakthrough was
imminent—he could feel it. Kluge held a different view. The assault
from the north by the 9th Army had failed to make anything more than
a local dent in the defenses, he noted, and the Soviets were clearly massing for some sort of counterattack. Both officers soon realized that their
arguments were moot, however. Hitler had made his decision, and he
now presented his reasons. The Allies had invaded Sicily three days
before, and the sizable Italian forces on the island had apparently
already collapsed.[5] It was going to be necessary to transfer major forces
from the Eastern Front to the west in order to shore Germany's collapsing strategic position.

From our later perspective, his reasoning can appear flimsy, if not
altogether specious. Was this really possible? Could a landing by a mere
seven Allied divisions on a faraway island achieve what hundreds of
Soviet divisions and nearly two million soldiers of the Red Army had
been unable to do: halt the German summer offensive at Kursk?

In fact, the Führer's position was entirely plausible, once we study
a more precise timeline. World War II was a long war, embracing nearly
six calendar years and seven campaigning seasons, and it covered the
earth like a Sherwin Williams advertisement. Occasionally, however,
analyzing the course of the conflict requires an analysis on the micro
level.

Let us travel back to the summer of 1943. Call it "nine days that
shook the world."[6]

⤞⤝

Monday, July 5. The Germans launch their assault against the Kursk
bulge, with the 9th Army attacking from the north and 4th Panzer
Army from the south. The aim is a concentric maneuver on the city of
Kursk, a linkup there, and a signature *Kesselschlacht* against all Soviet

forces inside the salient. Instead, over the next three days, the operation locks itself into a matériel-intensive *Stellungskrieg*, just the sort of battle the *Wehrmacht* cannot afford. It is a shattering disappointment to Hitler and the staff, given that this will be the major German offensive effort—indeed, the only offensive effort—of this campaigning season. They have been slaving and arguing and wrangling over Citadel for months. It had been continually scheduled, canceled, and rescheduled, mostly because it was clear that the Allies were about to land an amphibious blow somewhere in the West. No one wanted to be embroiled too deeply at Kursk when the Allies came ashore. They finally take the plunge—and run into a wall. Kursk is more than a lost battle; it is a year wasted.[7]

Friday, July 9. General Hermann Hoth, 4th Panzer Army commander, receives reports of large Soviet armored reserves heading into the salient and toward the front. They turn out to be the Soviet 5th Guards Tank Army (General P. A. Rotmistrov). Using the traditional German prerogatives of independent command, Hoth decides to move his army away from its northward orientation and wheel it to the northeast, intending to intercept the Soviet reserves near the small town of Prokhorovka.[8]

Friday, July 9, near midnight. The first report comes into German headquarters of U.S. and British airborne landings on the island of Sicily.

Saturday, July 10, early morning. The long-awaited Allied invasion of the European continent begins two Allied armies land on the southern coast of Sicily. Operation Husky answers thorny questions that have been the subject of intense debate within the German high command for months: the timing, place, and size of the initial Allied blow against Europe. Hitler is surprised because he has been expecting a landing in the Balkans, but he is optimistic that the island can be held, and so is his Supreme Commander South (*Oberbefehlshaber-Süd*), Field Marshal Albert Kesselring.[9]

Saturday, July 10, noon. Initial reports have thousands, and then tens of thousands, of Italian soldiers abandoning their posts, fading away into the interior, or surrendering to the Allies. The first attempt to drive the Allies into the sea, carried out by the Hermann Göring Parachute Panzer Division, fails.

Saturday, July 10, night. The largest port in Sicily, Syracuse, falls to elements of the British 8th Army without a fight.

Sunday, July 11. A second, and better prepared, assault against the U.S. beachhead in Sicily, near the tiny port of Gela, also fails. Virtually the entire Italian 6th Army in Sicily—over 200,000 men—has ceased fighting, leaving the defense in the hands of a mere two German formations, the Hermann Göring and 15th *Panzergrenadier* Divisions.

Sunday, July 11. The southern pincer at Kursk—the 4th Panzer Army and its flank guard to the right, *Armee-Abteilung* Kempf—begins making progress to its front. It isn't much, but it is something. Army Group Center's contribution to Citadel, the northern pincer under General Walther Model's 9th Army, has come to a complete standstill after a tiny penetration of just 12 miles. The northern face of the salient is now relatively quiet.

Monday, July 12. A great clash of armor takes place at Prokhorovka, with Hoth's spearhead, the II S.S. Panzer Corps, running headlong into the 5th Guards Tank Army. There is carnage. On the flanks, XXXXVIII Panzer corps (on the left) and III Panzer Corps (on the right) engage in equally intense fighting with Soviet forces to their respective fronts. Although the first reports speak of heavy Soviet losses, it is clear that there is going to be no quick breakthrough at Kursk.

The same day. The first reports come into Rastenburg of a Soviet counteroffensive north of Kursk, where the Germans hold a salient of their own around the city of Orel. The target is the German 2nd Panzer Army, which, despite its name, hardly possesses a single tank. Its mission has been essentially static, protecting the deep flank and rear of Model's 9th Army. The Soviet operation code-named Kutuzov thus represents a clear and present danger to 9th Army, and indeed to all German forces around Orel. Kluge orders Model, the 9th Army commander, to remove two Panzer Divisions from the attack toward Kursk and devote them to warding off this new danger.[10]

The same day. Kesselring flies to Sicily to view the situation for himself. Reversing the optimism he has held just 24 hours before, he quickly decides that the situation is hopeless.[11] The defenders cannot hold the island, and planning must start for an evacuation across the Strait of Messina. To avoid a complete breakdown in the defense while preparations get underway, he contacts OKW to demand the immediate transfer of another German division, the 29th *Panzergrenadier*, to Sicily. Hitler agrees, and also decides to call off Citadel, summoning Manstein and Kluge to a meeting the next day, July 13.

Two points emerge from this chronology. The first is the immense burden of command in World War II, with reports coming in nonstop from the four corners of creation, bearing sketchy first impressions of vast operations—reports that often prove to be wildly inaccurate. Intelligence gathering and evaluation required the service of thousands of highly trained personnel. Hitler and his tiny staff (and the equally tiny staffs of all the other high command echelons of the Wehrmacht) would have been entirely inadequate to the purpose even if Hitler himself had been a much more gifted strategist and commander. In 1943, for example, the Operations section of the German General Staff contained precisely 17 officers. Thinking back on it later, one of its members, General Johann Adolf Graf von Kielmansegg, exclaimed, "People today don't believe this number!"[12] He would later go on to serve as the postwar supreme commander of NATO forces in Central Europe. He remembered counting the number of officers on his staff one day, and was astonished again: "You would have to hang a zero on that 17, and it still wouldn't be enough."[13]

Second, clear strategic and operational links exist, far stronger than generally assumed, between Citadel and Husky, the massive clash of armor deep inside the Soviet Union and the great amphibious operation coming up out of the Mediterranean.[14] The two worked synergistically, rather than in isolation. Launching the battle of Kursk was the immediate problem, a great battle staring the Wehrmacht in the face in early 1943. The high command could see it and take comfort in the fact that it was preparing, arming, and planning for it. Citadel was essentially an operational question—a tough one, but comfortable conceptual ground for an army used to this sort of thing.

Husky was the more mysterious terror. Where? When? How large? That tiny cadre of staff officers we have just mentioned could stay awake deep into the night debating such questions, and they often did just that. Moreover, Husky touched on issues of international politics, coalition warfare, and perhaps even ideology. In that sense, it might have kept Hitler awake at nights too. These were areas in which his officers had remarkably little interest, but which he viewed, quite rightly, as central to the war. Today, history reduces the question of Italian participation in the war to a series of anecdotes of military incompetence and political stupidity. That is certainly not how it looked to Hitler in 1943. Italy was Germany's only major ally in Europe, like it or not, and whether it stood strong or fell apart was a matter of real import.

Not to call forth any sympathy for the devil, but running this war was a bear. Back in late 1942, Hitler had dismissed General Franz Halder as the chief of the General Staff, over what appears today to be a sequence of trivial disagreements over the operation in the Caucasus.

On that occasion, he had spoken to the chief of the Operations Department (*Operationsabteilung*), General Adolf Heusinger. In the course of their conversation, Heusinger had requested a field command, something he had been desiring since 1937, when he first joined the staff. Hitler refused, and Heusinger responded by offering his resignation. Hitler refused to consider it. "Your refusal troubles me," Heusinger had replied. Hitler's retort was pithy and direct, a rare thing in such a voluble and unstable individual. It was a moment of insight, and one that still held true a year later, in the summer of 1943: "A lot of things trouble me," he told Heusinger. "Believe it" ("Auch mir fällt vieles schwer, das können Sie mir glauben . . . ").[15]

Indeed, in the summer of 1943, a lot of things were bothering Hitler, the staff, and the entire Wehrmacht. The ongoing debate among historians over the question, "Who killed Citadel?" needs to take the broadest possible view, rather than rely on *einseitig* (one-sided) argumentation.[16] Operation Kutuzov, the Soviet blow against the Orel salient, was certainly a massive blow, but reports about it had just started to come in, and the high command was only starting to sift through them. Did it play a major role in the cancellation of Citadel? Of course. On the basis of the conformation of the front, with one salient curling around another, it had to. So, too, did the collapse of the Axis alliance, a grave blow to Germany's strategic position.

What killed Citadel? Given the chronology we have just examined and the requirements of a multifront war, the only possible answer is: a lot of things.

The Red Army: Operational Art in 1943

Of all the revisions to the standard narrative of World War II, the transformation of our view of the Red Army has been the most fundamental and the most significant. For decades, the German narrative held sway in the English-speaking world. It was a classic case of a meme—a point of view generated in one culture that migrates to another, becomes part of the new host's worldview, and soon forms an unquestioned assumption. The German meme described the Soviet army as a faceless and mindless horde, with the officers terrorizing their men into obedience and dictator Josef Stalin terrorizing the officers. It had no finesse. Its idea of the military art was to smash everything in its path through numbers, brute force, and sheer size.[17] As the former chief of staff for the XXXX Panzer Corps General Carl Wagener put it in his typically succinct "military German" (*Militärdeutsch*): on the Eastern Front, "quantity had triumphed over quality."[18] The better army lost, in other words, and the elite force vanished beneath the superior numbers of the herd.

General F. W. von Mellenthin served as chief of staff for the well-traveled XXXXVIII Panzer Corps and had fought against the Soviet army on the Chir in 1942 and at Kursk in 1943. In his highly influential book *Panzer Battles*, he went even farther than Wagener. Consider these passages from the section of his book entitled "Psychology of the Russian Soldier":

> No one belonging to the cultural circle of the West is ever likely to fathom the character and soul of these Asiatics, born and bred on the other side of the European frontiers. . . . There is no way of telling what the Russian will do next; he will tumble from one extreme to the other. With experience it is quite easy to foretell what a soldier from any other country will do, but never with a Russian. His qualities are as unusual and as many-sided as those of his vast and rambling country. He is patient and enduring beyond imagination, incredibly brave and courageous—yet at times he can be a contemptible coward. . . . The Russian is quite unpredictable; today he does not care whether his flanks are threatened or not, tomorrow he trembles at the idea of having his flanks exposed. He disregards accepted tactical principles but sticks to the letter of his field manuals. Perhaps the key to this attitude lies in the fact the Russian is not a conscious soldier, thinking on independent lines, but is the victim of moods which a Westerner cannot analyze. He is essentially a primitive being, innately courageous, and dominated by certain emotions and instincts. His individuality is easily swallowed up in the mass, while his powers of endurance are derived from long centuries of suffering and privation. Thanks to the innate strength of these qualities, the Russian is superior in many ways to the more conscious soldier of the West, who can only make good his deficiencies by superior mental and moral training.[19]

Indeed, "the cultural circle of the west" adopted this point of view wholesale in the postwar era. Mellenthin's "Russian" soldier—actually a Russian or a Ukrainian or a Georgian or a Tatar—appears here as "Ivan the Primitive," an archetype who is instinctive, emotional, prone to panic, unpredictable. The author implicitly places him in opposition to the normative figure of "Fritz," the archetypical German *Landser*, who is civilized, rational, steady, and motivated by the higher ideals as opposed to his base instincts. "Ivan" becomes a figure who is immediately recognizable to modern cultural historians: he is "the Other," a negative mirror image of our own beliefs, expectations, and norms.[20]

Today, it is easy to see how this happened. Contrary to the received wisdom on the subject, the losers often write the history. Consider the pantheon of great captains from Hannibal to Napoleon to Robert E. Lee. They are all considered to be the most gifted commanders of their respective eras, even though each of them captained the losing squad. Never has this paradox been more evident than in the post-1945 era. What we think of as "the history of World War II" is, like all histories, actually a construct: take a few early impressions, mix in a few post-1945 biases—some minor and some major—and then reinforce over and over again until "truth" forms. The principal ingredient in this historiographical cocktail has been the memoir, and the master source for these memoirs has been the German officer corps. The list of books to be consulted is an imposing one. It includes Mellenthin's *Panzer Battles*, Heinz Guderian's *Panzer Leader*,[21] Hans von Luck's *Panzer Commander*,[22] Erich von Manstein's *Lost Battles*, Heinz Werner Schmidt's *With Rommel in the Desert* (a memoir written by Rommel's aide-de-camp in North Africa),[23] Frido von Senger und Etterlin's *Neither Fear nor Hope* (dealing mainly with the Sicilian and Italian campaigns, but also containing important sections on the early years of the war),[24] and many, many more. In addition, we have the Foreign Military Studies series, published by the U.S. Department of the Army and based on interviews with captive German generals, most of which remain unpublished but can be consulted at various archives, especially the U.S. Army Heritage and Education Center in Carlisle, Pennsylvania.[25]

These sources are problematic in many ways. The generals being interviewed usually did not have access to their personal papers or office files. Many of their records had been destroyed in Allied bombing raids. Their testimony was not always completely reliable.[26] Much of the testimony was of necessity highly general, lacking detailed references to corps, divisions, and precise terrain features. For this reason alone, no researcher should ever rely on the Foreign Military Studies reports without finding corroborating evidence.

The problems run even deeper than lack of documentation, however. In dealing with the delicate events of their recent past, not to mention the crimes in which they may have participated, the German generals were evasive. They left many things out altogether—their loyalty to Hitler and their enthusiasm in carrying out his racial policies, for example. They also put many things in. The number of times that the generals claimed in their memoirs to have "stood up to Hitler" is legion. Would that it were true! Above all, however, their real reason for writing these memoirs was professional exculpation: denying responsibility for the disastrous war and shifting all blame for it onto Hitler's shoulders.[27] In a way, Hitler was the ideal alibi. He was dead, of course, and so could not speak for himself. He was also Hitler, the worst mass murderer of all time and thus unlikely to have many defenders eager to argue his brief. The generals could have at him as they liked, and they usually went unchallenged.

One final factor deserves mention. The generals were now more or less permanent guests of the U.S. or British governments, institutions that had a new security problem in the 1950s. There was a new conflict raging, a cold war that might go hot at any moment. Statesmen and officers in the West wanted to know how to fight and beat the Soviet Union in any upcoming conflict, already nicknamed "World War III" even before it had broken out. But who had recent experience in fighting the Russians? Men like Guderian, Manstein, and Mellenthin, that's who. At a time when the U.S. Army, especially, was eager to learn as much as it could about the Soviet Union, its military establishment, and its operational techniques, memoirs like *Panzer Leader* or *Lost Victories* must have appeared like holy writ. Reputable publishing houses published these memoirs, all soon appeared in English translation, and the corporate view of the German officer corps became part and parcel of the Western interpretation of the war, even down to a not-so-subtle identification with the Wehrmacht, at least when it was fighting in the East against the Red Army.

Timing is everything. The cold war made it easy for even highly educated men to read the above comments by Mellenthin—or those where he claims that "a feature of the Russian soldier is his utter contempt for life or death,"[28] or where he describes Russian tactics as "the employment of masses of men and material, often thrown in unintelligently and without variations,"[29] or even where he actually claims that the Russian soldier was able to ignore "cold and heat" and "hunger and thirst"—and nod their head in agreement.[30] We should be fair, however, and admit that however absurd these rhetorical flourishes may appear to us, they would have appeared in a different light to a U.S. Army officer reading them in 1956 (the year the book first appeared in English translation).

Today, historians working in the archives, and freed from the now-

obsolete prejudices of the cold war, have shattered this image.[31] They
have proven many times over that the German memoirs are at best
unreliable and at worst deliberately misleading, and that the images they
have bequeathed to us run the gamut from debatable to utterly specious. Thanks to modern research, the Red Army now occupies a different position in the history of World War II. Today it is known as a
highly skilled and brilliantly led force that absorbed the best the
Wehrmacht had to offer in 1941, then turned the tables and eventually
smashed it. From a primitive horde, it has now become the seedbed of
modern military operations and the progenitor of something that even
the U.S. Army calls "operational art."[32] In the eyes of modern military
analysts, Ivan is no longer the Other, standing in opposition to the
archetype. He has become the archetype. In histories of World War II
written since 1990, he has become the new normal.

This new and improved view of Soviet operations looks carefully at
the military reforms of the later imperial and early Soviet periods. The-
oreticians like G. S. Isserson, V. K. Triandafillov, and M. N. Tukhachevsky worked within a distinctive matrix of military culture, a blend
of much that was new with a solid and traditional foundation.[33] The
Soviet army drew much of its first wave of commanders from the ranks
of the old tsarist army. It had also inherited two separate operational
traditions, both of which stemmed from the enormous size of the country. One featured massed infantry formations carrying out broad-front
offensives, in the style of 1916's Brusilov offensive, on discrete operational sectors, or fronts. At the same time there was a more mobile heritage of deep strikes, utilizing long-range cavalry as a *corps volant*.[34] Their
experience in the Russian civil war as well as the Russo-Polish war had
given the young new officer corps a shared heritage. They had come
to realize the operational advantages and disadvantages of the region's
vast open spaces. They had come to see the possibilities of fighting a
new kind of deep battle using deeply echeloned forces on the same
operational axis to penetrate the enemy's front line and to move hundreds of miles at a bound into the strategic depth of his position.
Finally, they had come to see the absolute necessity to launch consecutive operations.[35] Modern mass armies were simply too large and too
durable to destroy in a single climactic battle, in the style of Napoleon
or the great Helmuth von Moltke. Rather, one had to pound them
repeatedly in a series of nonstop, large-scale offensive operations, one
after the other, until they broke. Although interested in the developments that they saw taking place in Germany and the West, they were
also critical where necessary. Above all, Soviet commanders never fell

into the trap—then prevalent in the writings of British armored prophets J. F. C. Fuller and B. H. Liddell Hart—of seeing smaller mechanized armies as a cure for the problems of mass industrialized war. Mass armies were here to stay, and indeed were a prerequisite for both deep and consecutive operations. Here is Tukhachevsky writing in 1931:

> Let's imagine a war between Great Britain and the USA, a war, for example, which breaks out along the Canadian border. Both armies are mechanized, but the English have, let's say, Fuller's cadre of 18 divisions, and the U.S. Army had 180 divisions. The first has 5,000 tanks and 3,000 aircraft, but the second has 50,000 tanks and 30,000 planes. The small English Army would be simply crushed. Is it not already clear that talk about small, but mobile, mechanized armies in major wars is a cock-and-bull story? Only frivolous people can take them seriously.[36]

Tukhachevsky's art of war blended finesse with mass. He envisioned using powerful shock groups, mixed groups of infantry, tanks, and artillery, to make the breakthrough on extremely narrow frontages.[37] Behind the breakthrough forces would be a second wave (or echelon) of highly mobile armor and cavalry groups, and behind them a third. They would move on the same operational axis, driving deep into the enemy's rear areas and constantly feeding in fresh new units. Codified in the field regulations of 1936, it was one of the freshest military doc- trines of its day. German observers were present at the 1936 Soviet fall maneuvers, and they came away impressed with the commitment to mechanization. They saw tanks perform in meeting engagements, in breakthrough operations, in an assault on an enemy's advanced posi- tion, in a counterattack, in pursuit, even in a massive river-crossing assault. "We see," wrote one them, "a grand breadth of vision, a radi- cal exhaustion of all possibilities, an almost boundless trust in the strength of armor."[38]

Since then, deep battle had had its ups and downs. We might speak of a Soviet military schizophrenia. With Stalin's approval, Tukhachevsky was able to implement his vision. Massive mechanized corps made their appearance in the Soviet order of battle, and the new factories created by Stalin's five-year plans churned out thousands of tanks and armored vehicles. In the late 1930s, however, Tukhachevsky ran afoul of Stalin and disappeared in the purges, and so did a sizable percentage of the Red Army's higher officer corps. Moreover, the performance of

armor—both Soviet and German—in the Spanish civil war did not seem
to herald the coming of any new age. More often than not, the tanks
fell victim to well-placed antitank guns. The result was a new direction
in Soviet doctrine, one that deemphasized large formations of armor.
The mechanized corps disappeared, and tank formations were down-
sized into much smaller brigades, used primarily for old-school infantry
support. Then came the great German victory in France in 1940. Soviet
planners shifted gears one more time, junking the brigades and revert-
ing to mechanized corps.[39]

   War came to the Soviet Union at the worst possible time, in the
midst of that last shift. The army did fight deep battle of a sort in 1941.
Unfortunately, it was on the receiving end of it, and it was the
Wehrmacht that was going deep. The Red Army managed to survive
that ordeal, but only by sacrificing the richest portions of the country
and losing four million casualties—hardly a strategy that anyone should
want to emulate. Although it launched a successful winter counteroffensive in front of Moscow, the next campaigning season would see similar problems. At Kerch and Kharkov in May 1942, than again along the
Donets River during the German summer offensive, Operation Blue,
the Soviets were on the run again, carrying out a helter-skelter retreat
from their initial positions along the Donets, scurrying back to the
Don, and thence back to the Volga. The retreat, whose size, scale, and
rapidity caught even the Germans by surprise, probably began on orders
from Stalin and his chief military advisor and troubleshooter, General
G. K. Zhukov. There is little that is more traditional in Russian military history than the great retreat that trades space for time and lures
the invader into the vastness of the country, where he outruns his own
supply lines and becomes vulnerable to the counterstroke. Whatever
its strategic basis, however, the great retreat of 1942 was a mess on the
tactical level, with heavily fortified defenses abandoned without a fight
and a mountain of equipment lost to the onrushing Wehrmacht. Stalin
was alarmed enough that he had to issue his famous Order 227, "Not a
Step Back!" (*Ni Shagu Nazad!*).[40] It promised summary execution for
cowards, set up penal battalions for those caught shirking their duty,
and established blocking units whose task it was to keep shaky units in
the line, with gunfire and bayonet if necessary.

   Soviet defenses did not stiffen until Stalingrad and the Caucasus, the
first a heavily fortified urban zone and the latter one of the world's most
rugged mountain ranges. These were places that benefited the defenders and placed clear limitations on German skill in mobile, open field

campaigning. Now, with the Germans embedded in two widely separated positional battles from which they could not easily extricate themselves, Zhukov and the staff were able to hit them with the greatest counterpunch of the war: Operation Uranus, a carefully prepared encirclement of the German 6th Army in Stalingrad. Further operations that winter—Little Saturn, Gallop, and Star—had hounded the Germans mercilessly, driven them to the west, and smashed their Romanian, Hungarian, and Italian allies altogether. The operational sequence had ended badly for the Soviets, with their logistics strained past the breaking point and Manstein launching his counterstroke around Kharkov. They suffered enormous casualties, but the Soviet high command had to have been satisfied with the results of the winter battles.

At Kursk, the Red Army showed how far it had come. Blunting a massive German offensive before it ever got rolling, it showed that it could stand toe to toe with its formerly irresistible nemesis. It was a different Soviet Army—version 2.0, we might say. Its officers had learned how to maximize their strengths (mass, power, the depth of the country) and minimize their weaknesses (lack of flexibility, low initiative among many of the field grades, and the generally poor quality of the noncommissioned officers). Confidence was high. Even Stalin was learning. He now tended to remain out of the operational details. However cruel his day-to-day treatment of his officer corps, and the accounts of this are legion, the Boss (*Vozhd*) had come to see the wisdom of leaving the planning to the professionals—exactly the opposite of Hitler.[41] Stalingrad may or may not have been the turning point of the war, but it was certainly the turning point for the Red Army. They had all learned some hard lessons since the German invasion, and the results had been highly satisfying of late.

Perhaps its only remaining limitation was its dependence on the weather: the Soviet army was clearly at its best, and the Germans at their worst, in the winter. After two years in the Soviet Union, General Wagener wrote, "It had already become a rule that the German side sought a decision in the summer, the Russians in the winter."[42] At Moscow in 1941 and at Stalingrad in 1942, the Soviets had made a definite ally of the cold and the snow. Weather had acted as a kind of great equalizer, especially by reducing German skill in operational-level maneuver. The Red Army had still not been able to launch any sort of grand offensive in the summer.

Not until now, that is.

Operation Kutuzov

Soviet operations in this middle period of the war present a dual face. On the one hand, their geographical scale was unbelievably vast, from the Volga over the Donets to the Dnepr, and from the Kuban to the Crimea. The forces involved were immense and the sheer number of campaigns mind-numbing. On the other hand, the individual operations themselves shine forth with a kind of simple clarity that makes them relatively simple to describe, analyze, and understand. So, too, it was with Operation Kutuzov.[43]

Think of Kutuzov as Citadel in reverse. Just as the Germans had tried to run a concentric attack around the Kursk salient, so did the Soviets against the Orel salient, standing just opposite and to the north of Kursk. Of course, the Red Army could spare far heavier forces for the purpose, echeloned in depth, than could the Wehrmacht. Their high command did not have to agonize over it, as did the Germans. They did not have to postpone it repeatedly in order to gather sufficient force, nor did they have to strip formations from the rest of the front. The Soviets had been planning an offensive of this sort as early as April 1943, just about the time the Germans were first conceiving Citadel. Like the Germans, the Soviets were planning to use armies from two army groups, in this case the Western Front (to the north of the Orel salient) and the Bryansk Front (to the east of it). The Western Front (General V. D. Sokolovsky) would contribute two armies. From right to left, they were the 50th Army (General I. V. Boldin) and the 11th Guards Army (General I. K. Bagramian). Bagramian's army would be the *Schwerpunkt*, with support lent by the 1st Tank Corps (General V. V. Butkov) and the 5th Tank Corps (General M. S. Sakhno). The most reliable authority places the number of Soviet forces on the northern wing of Operation Kutuzov at 211,458 men, 745 tanks and self-propelled guns, and 4,285 guns and mortars.[44] Such was the imbalance of forces by this point in the war that two complete armies could start the offensive in reserve on this front: 11th Army (General I. I. Fediuninsky) and the newly formed 4th Tank Army (General V. M. Badanov). Both stood ready to support Bagramian's drive south to Orel.

Deployed on the left of the Western Front were the three armies of the Bryansk Front (General M. M. Popov), given the mission of driving on Orel from the northeast and east. It was almost as powerful as its neighbor, containing three armies committed to two separate attacks. Moving from left to right, the 63rd Army (V. I. Kolpakchi) and 3rd Army (General A. V. Gorbatov) would move in directly from the east, representing the main thrust of the front. Together, these two armies contained over 170,000 men and more than 350 tanks and self-propelled guns, and they could also call upon the support of the 1st Guards Tank Corps and the 25th Rifle Corps. Standing in reserve, once again, was a complete army, the 3rd Guards Tank Army (General P. S. Rybalko), containing a full 731 tanks and self-propelled guns. Supporting the thrust of 63rd and 3rd Armies, and maintaining the operational link with the Western Front, was the 61st Army (General P. A. Belov). Coming down on Orel from the northeast, it had the support of the 20th Tank Corps. All told, Bryansk Front committed 433,616 men to the operation.[45]

Facing this impressive battle array of 655,000 men was the German 2nd Panzer Army. Like so much of the Wehrmacht, it was by this point of the war an operational basket case hiding behind an impressive-sounding name. Although it contained three corps—moving right to left, the LV Corps (General Erich Jaschke), the LIII (General Heinrich Clössner), and the XXXV (General Lothar Rendulic)—it had precious few Panzers.[46] It had a single Panzer division (the 5th) in reserve, possessing a total of 93 tanks; Clössner's LIII Corps had another supposedly mobile division, the 25th *Panzergrenadier*, but it had no tanks at all; the 8th Panzer Division was on the way, with another 100 tanks, but it would not be arriving until July 12. Meanwhile, the 2nd Panzer Army's total of 14 front-line infantry divisions had to hold a front no less than 170 miles long. Like all the other German formations on the Eastern Front, it had surrendered its mobile units to Army Group South for the 1942 offensive—units that were now lost forever. The officers were professional and the men had not lost faith, but the matériel was sorely lacking. The 2nd Panzer Army was, in other words, a typical German field army, capable of tenacious defense but little else, and "far too weak to halt the massive forces arrayed against them."[47]

To make matters worse, just days before the Soviet offensive at Orel, the Gestapo paid a visit to the 2nd Panzer Army commander, General Rudolf Schmidt, and placed him under arrest. It seemed that his comments about the Nazi regime had been a bit too frank of late.[48] Schmidt's disappearance from the front at this crucial moment meant that General Walther Model (9th Army) took over simultaneous command of 2nd Panzer Army as well, becoming an ad hoc army group commander. It was the latest in what had by now become a German tradition in this war: the field commander under a cloud before a major offensive. These included the so-called Mechelen incident in 1940,[49] then the dismissal of General Georg Stumme of the XXXX Panzer

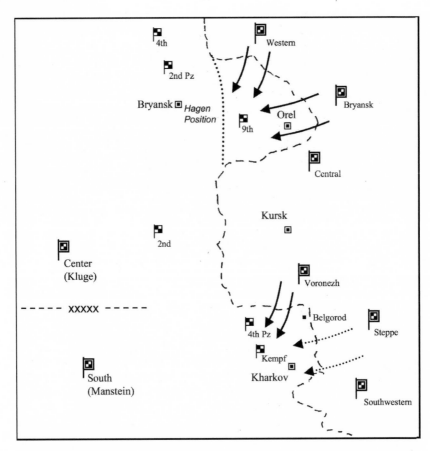

Soviet Counterstrokes at Kursk: Kutuzov and Rumiantsev (July–August 1943)

Corps just before Operation Blue in 1942, along with his chief of staff, Colonel Franz.[50] Schmidt was merely the latest. Perhaps they were all signs of a deeper malady: Hitler's uncertainty in the operational realm. Although none of these last-second command shifts appears to have hurt German operations, they certainly could not have helped.

Kutuzov began on July 12, the same day that the II S.S. Panzer Corps and the 5th Guards Tank Army were mixing it up at Prokhorovka. At 3:00 A.M., the front erupted from Zhizdra on the northwestern shoulder of the Orel salient to Novosil at the eastern point. Reconnaissance forces went first, seizing German combat outposts, followed by the kind of massive bombardment that was becoming a Soviet calling card, as well as raids by long-range bombers against German targets deep inside the salient.[51] At 6:05, the main assault units from both the Bryansk and Western fronts rolled into action. Given the balance of forces, the wildly stretched nature of 2nd Panzer Army's front-line divisions, and the fixing of German attention to the south of the Orel salient, toward Kursk, the offensive penetrated just about everywhere. One German source speaks of "a wide break-in within the first 48 hours, up to ten kilometers deep, against a weakly manned front,"[52] and this is an accurate assessment. What the Wehrmacht had been unable to achieve at all in its 10-day offensive toward Kursk, the Soviets had achieved with ease in two.

The greatest success came in the sector of the 11th Guards Army, where the Soviets were able to concentrate six Guards rifle divisions against a tiny, 10-mile stretch of the German line held by the 211th and 293rd Divisions of the LIII Corps (General Clössner). General Bagramian inserted his second-echelon rifle divisions by the afternoon and was already preparing to commit the 1st and 5th Tank Corps. For his part, Model brought up the 5th Panzer Division and threw it against the onrushing enemy. Its piecemeal counterattacks were able to stop the Soviets just short of a complete breakthrough, but only just. The next day, Bagramian renewed the attack, this time supported by 50th Army on his right, and made even more rapid progress. It was clear now that 5th Panzer Division was insufficient to shore up the situation.[53]

The Soviet assault on Orel from the east, out of Novosil, ran into tougher sledding from the start. Here a combination of factors worked in the Wehrmacht's favor. The German XXXV Corps commander, General Rendulic, was in the same dire straits as all of them: four depleted infantry divisions to cover an 80-mile front. His own radio intercepts, solid aerial reconnaissance, and perhaps a simple gut feeling allowed him to guess right about the intended Soviet breakthrough point, however, at the junction of the 56th and 262nd Infantry Divisions.[54] Rendulic didn't have much of a corps by this point, but he decided to concentrate overwhelmingly in that one sector, 26 of his 48 heavy antitank guns, for example, four extra infantry battalions, and more than 70 guns. He was only able to do this by stripping the rest of his front. As a result, Bryansk Front's opening attacks by 3rd and 63rd Armies turned into what one modern authority calls a "near disaster."[55] The six rifle divisions of the first echelon ran into a wall of fire, and the supporting tanks came to grief against the minefields and antitank guns. Rendulic's gunners managed to destroy 60 Soviet tanks, mainly heavy KV-1s, on that first day alone. Although German losses in the initial assault were heavier than they could afford, at least their line had held.

By now, however, the danger posed by Operation Kutuzov had become clear to Model, to Field Marshal Kluge (commander of Army Group Center), and to the high command. As it had proved many times already, the Wehrmacht rarely had difficulty with its reaction time. It was a strong suit for this maneuver-oriented army, and reinforcements were soon on their way to shore up what was clearly a crumbling position. Model pulled much of 9th Army out of the line in the south and shifted them to 2nd Panzer Army in the north: XXXXI Panzer Corps (General Joseph Harpe, with the 2nd, 8th, and 9th Panzer Divisions, as well as the *Grossdeutschland Panzergrenadier* Division), XXIII Corps (General Johannes Friessner), and *Gruppe Esebeck*.[56] It represented a major part of the Citadel offensive, and its transfer to the northern half of the Orel salient meant that the Kursk offensive was now finished. In fact, it is today fairly certain that Model had been aware of the Soviet buildup against Orel, and had deliberately withheld some of his divisions from getting too deeply involved in the drive on Kursk. That would help explain the complete and rapid halt of his assault formations by the third day of the Citadel assault, and would also help to explain the rapidity of the redeployment to the north.

Model also rearranged command relationships within the salient, a necessary step because of his own temporary status as army group commander. He trusted General Harpe, and he now created a new multi-corps *Gruppe Harpe*: XXXXI Panzer Corps, LIII Corps, and XXIII Corps, an ad hoc army, and about one-third of the total troops under Model's command.[57] Harpe's mission was to blunt the Soviet drive across the northern face of the salient, identified by Model as the Soviet *Schwerpunkt* and thus given priority as reinforcing divisions came up to the front. In the east, Rendulic was managing to hold his own, but he would have to do so only with the meager forces available. Crisis followed crisis in Rendulic's sector, and the Soviet insertion of the 3rd Guards Tank Army (General Rybalko) on July 19 brought the tension here even higher. Freed from its commitment to Operation Citadel, it added tremendous weight—another 600 tanks—to the Soviet assault. There were no more German reinforcements to be had, and Rendulic's own forward units were down to a fraction of their strength. German Stuka attacks and elements of the Panzer divisions on loan from *Gruppe Harpe* managed, once again, to keep the line intact, although it was a tough couple of days.

By now, a week into Operation Kutuzov, the Soviets had landed a great blow, had traded casualties with an enemy force that could not afford them, and had overrun major portions of the original German front line. There had been no true operational-level breakthrough. Perhaps it had been too ambitious to expect one. After all, as 9th Army's rear, and thus the strategic and logistical base for Operation Citadel, the Orel salient contained an immense number of German formations, and Model had been able to turn them around rapidly and hustle enough of them north to prevent a catastrophe. Still, the offensive had destroyed the German defensive position around Orel. What had been a nice, sharp bend of the salient pointing toward Novosil, Rendulic's sector of the line, now resembled a broken nose. The assault by Bryansk Front had punched it in badly. In the northwest, too, the assault by 11th Guards Army, along with its supporting tank corps, had ripped a jagged gash into what had formerly been a smooth, straight line. The German front line was compromised, more and more Soviet forces were on their way, and the German replacement and reinforcement well had run completely dry. Even an amateur could take a quick glimpse at a map, read a handful of field reports, and conclude the obvious: the Orel salient was doomed.

One of those amateurs was Hitler. Temperamentally averse to any withdrawal, distrusting his generals and their overly complex schemes, and a trench soldier by experience, Hitler usually had one response to a general who wanted to retreat: the *Haltbefehl*—the stand-fast order. It had saved them all in the winter of 1941–1942, he thought, and he had imposed it then against the orders of virtually every one of his higher commanders. Now they were telling him again to retreat: Model, Kluge, and his chief of staff, General Kurt Zeitzler. The Orel salient, the Donbas, the bridgehead in the Kuban, the Crimea—a long list of outposts were eating up Germany's limited supply of divisions, they told him. "Naturally," he had spit at Zeitzler during one of those marathon Führer conferences at Rastenburg. "It's always the same. Retreat and retreat. We'll soon be back on the German border and the Russian gets his country back without losing a man."[58] Nor did he want to hear any of their utterly sensible recommendations to build a defensive position in the rear, along the Dnepr River, a fortified line to which the shattered formations could repair and reform in the event of a defeat.

The most pressing emergency was Orel, and this time Hitler changed his mind. Model was enough of an independent spirit to disagree with Hitler, argue with him, and occasionally shout at him. Combined with his obvious loyalty, even enthusiasm, for the regime, he was able to get away with things that other generals could not. He had presented a plan to build a backstop, a fortified line across the base of the Orel salient along the Desna River, screening the next major city in line, Bryansk. Once it was ready, his armies, the 9th and 2nd Panzer, would evacuate Orel and the salient around it and repair to the newly dug position, christened the Hagen position (*Hagenstellung*).[59] Although Hitler predictably rejected it, Model went ahead anyway with surveys and the preliminary work—activities that went on uninterrupted for weeks and gained momentum. As the situation at Orel went from bad to worse, with forces from the Soviet Central Front joining in from the southern face of the salient, even Hitler had to bow to the inevitable. First, on July 22 came permission for Model to fight an "elastic defense,"[60] quite out of character for Hitler. Then on July 25 came an abrupt order from the Führer: Model and both of his armies were to retire at once to the Hagen position.

Once again, we can see the dynamic of the multifront war at work and recognize how difficult it is to analyze any single front in World War II apart from the others. Soviet attacks toward Orel were grinding up the Wehrmacht, and logic called for a retreat. Hitler had ignored the logic often enough in his career, however. At Stalingrad, he had forced an army of over 200,000 men to sit until it died. What had happened this time, however, was a bolt of lighting out of the west: the overthrow and arrest of Benito Mussolini and the creation of a new government in Italy under Marshal Pietro Badoglio. The new men in Rome promised fidelity to the Axis and swore that the war would go on, but Hitler did not believe it, nor did anyone in the German high command. Hitler knew that Italy was going to be trouble, and he needed divisions to counter it—to cow the Italians into behaving, and to dissuade the Allies from trying to take advantage of the unsettled situation in Italy. Perhaps it was even to still the voices of doubt in his own mind; the fall of Mussolini could not have been a pleasant image. In the forefront of his thoughts was the II S.S. Panzer Corps, a political army around which the Fascists in Italy could rally; he had already cut the orders for its transfer to the west. Beyond these considerations, evacuation of the Orel Salient and a retreat to the much shorter Hagen position, essentially the chord at the base of a semicircle, would free up a number of divisions now tied down holding the bulge. It would be a "shortening of the front" (*Frontverkürzung*). Model already knew that, of course; his staff studies indicated a total savings of 19 divisions.[61] It was the same argument that he and so many others had been using on Hitler in varying circumstances for a year. Now, Marshal Badoglio had apparently convinced the Führer where all the German generals had failed.

Operation *Herbstreise* ("Autumn Voyage") now began, the evacuation of the Orel salient. Retreat operations do not get a great deal of respect in the literature, but they are highly complex undertakings. There is an old, perhaps apocryphal tale of the elder Helmuth von Moltke receiving some accolade for his generalship during the Franco-Prussian War and being told that he would rank with the greatest captains of all time, such as Frederick the Great, Turenne, and Napoleon. "No," the great Prussian commander is said to have responded, "for I have never conducted a retreat."[62] For Model and the men of the 9th and 2nd Panzer Armies, this retreat came with strings attached that made it especially difficult: the orders for the evacuation had come on the fly, the Soviets were breathing down their necks from all points of the compass, and their destination—the Hagen line—was nowhere near complete. Who knew if it would even hold? Moreover, the retreat was taking place on the heels of a great offensive battle. The Germans had stockpiled mountains of equipment, ammunition, and fuel just behind their front line, ready to feed things forward as Operation Citadel picked up speed. An army planning on a sustained advance suddenly had to turn around and go back. The Orel salient was 60 miles deep, and Operation *Herbstreise* intended it to be empty within three weeks. The staff had to map out a series of intermediate lines, decide which tactical units were going to leapfrog which other units on the way out, and avoid what one staff officer called the "dreadful mess" (*heilloses Durcheinander*) of one friendly force crossing the path of another.[63] They had to preposition supplies along the retreat path, improve the principal roads, and plan for alternate routes in case Soviet action blocked the main roads. The task list was nearly endless. It is almost predictable that in the midst of such a difficult operation, one that even if handled well threatened to fall apart of its own weight, it rained non-stop, generating a whole new level of mud-drenched chaos.

Despite all the problems, Model triumphed. The operation began on July 31. The units held their cohesion, even when necessity had them shuffled between and among commanders. The rains made it difficult to get around, but they probably also had something to do with an ebbing of Soviet offensive pressure. Model had to shift his scanty and exhausted reserve divisions hither and yon, plugging this hole, throwing back that penetration. Partisans within the salient were a steady problem, as was the difficulty of evacuating the 20,000 wounded in the zone of the 2nd Panzer Army alone. Moreover, Model had made things immeasurably worse on all levels by carrying out a scorched-earth policy, destroying the rye harvest in the district and forcing the entire civilian population—some 250,000 unfortunate victims—into a hasty evacuation under inhuman conditions.[64]

By August 15, the first German units reached the Hagen line, a bit ahead of schedule. The Soviets apparently did not recognize it as the final German position, and they launched a series of high-cost attacks on it. The fighting never really stopped, although the focus was soon to shift to other sectors of the front. In other words, an operation to blast into the salient from multiple directions and liquidate the German forces there had transformed itself into a frontal assault, a bloody slugfest. This, incidentally, is almost exactly what would have happened to the Germans at some point even if they had succeeded in flattening out the Kursk salient.

On August 5, the Soviet Army reoccupied Orel. The cost to both sides had been shocking. Consider these numbers. During Operation Citadel (July 1–10), the 9th and 2nd Panzer Armies combined had taken 21,248 casualties. The fight to defend the Orel salient from July 11 to 31, however, had cost them another 62,305, for a casualty total of nearly 85,000 men that month. The retreat had not been without cost either. Let us add another 20,000 casualties—a reasonable estimate—and the German casualties in fighting for this single position, one they eventually decided to evacuate, topped 100,000 men. As for the Soviets, the qualities of mass and aggression and multiechelon deep battle that it had displayed in Operation Kutuzov, qualities that usually earn the praise of historians as characteristics of a special type of operational art, had also triumphed. They had managed to win back the salient and reconquer a great city, at a cost sometimes estimated at 429,000 casualties, and perhaps much higher.[65]

The time for any heroicizing of German and Soviet operations should be long past. These two armies were guaranteed to generate massive casualties. Some of the reasons are obvious. The front was huge, the number of divisions engaged immense, the rival dictators ruthless. Beyond those basic factors, however, lies the reality of two intertwined ways of war. On the German side, you had an army fighting *Bewegungskrieg*, the war of movement. In the attack, its commanders were ruthless and aggressive, and even in the defense, it used a near-constant series of combined arms counterattacks. It knew no other way to fight. Moreover, even with all their disagreements with Hitler and their contempt for his dilettantish conduct of operations, the officer corps shared one thing with him: a determination to fight on until the end. Only a small number of them ever broke that bond.

As for the Soviet army, its own theories about the conduct of operations always seemed on the verge of taking precedence over reality. Operational art, especially in its breakthrough phase, was a fascinating and logical response to the problem of sustaining battlefield momentum. It made so much sense: smash through an enemy position with a first echelon, and then keep smashing along the same axis, feeding in a second echelon and perhaps even a third. When it worked—against a weakened or surprised enemy defensive line, for example—it could inspire awe. The infantry manning the Romanian 3rd and 4th Army fronts outside of Stalingrad in late 1942 barely had a chance, and Soviet attacks had broken into their operational depth effortlessly. What happened, however, if that first echelon failed to crack through? A second one was behind it, waiting, and the commander's response was almost always the same: insert the second echelon to complete the breakthrough that the first had begun. "Inserting the second echelon," however, is military boilerplate for a much more mundane and clumsy reality. It means launching a frontal assault against an enemy position that was by now fully alert and had already defeated a first attack. Hence we have the German observation of a Soviet tendency toward "senseless, wild hammering" in battle, homing in on the same breakthrough point over and over again, long after any possibilities for success had vanished.[66]

What had eventually taken place at Orel, however, seemed to have little to do with *Bewegungskrieg* or operational art or any other intellectual construct. The two great salient battles of 1943 had managed to confound both sides. At Orel in particular, the Wehrmacht's desire to maneuver had come to grief against the difficulty of extricating itself from a full-blown Soviet attack. All of those postwar claims by the German generals that they could have triumphed in the east, if only Hitler had allowed them to maneuver, need to take Orel into account. Here Hitler allowed a retreat to shorten the line, doing just what historians always accuse him of failing to do. The result? Over 100,000 German casualties. Apparently maneuver had its own problems. Likewise, the Soviet desire to go deep met only disappointment at Orel. Lining up virtually all of your strength against a single point on the enemy's line might be intellectually satisfying, but it is no guarantee of success, and if your opponent guesses your intention, as General Rendulic apparently did, you are going to have big problems. By the rain-soaked ending of the Orel campaign, with the exhausted German infantry manning the Hagen position and the Soviets still trying to crack it, there was little that was artistic about the operations on either side.

The Citadel–Kutuzov operational sequence had come to an end. By now, both opponents were drowning in blood, and the campaigning season had barely gotten underway.

Planning for the Southern Front: Manstein's War

If 1943 had seen merely the Kursk and Orel operations, it might be tempting to call it a draw, or perhaps award the advantage to the Soviets. In fact, the rest of the year would show how hopeless the Wehrmacht's position on the Eastern Front had become. Operation Citadel represented a single throw of the dice for the Germans. There were no other options and no other offensive operations. For the Soviet Army, however, Operation Kutuzov was merely the beginning of a seemingly endless series of offensives that would last for the rest of the year, pick up again in 1944, and then extend to the end of the war. The leading Western authority on the Soviet Union in World War II, David M. Glantz, has analyzed no fewer than eight separate Soviet operations planned for 1943[67]:

1. The defense of the Kursk salient, successfully completed by July 12.
2. Operation Kutuzov against the Orel salient, launched on July 13 and successfully completed by August 15 with the salient cleared and the German defenders now ensconced in the Hagen position.
3. Operation Rumiantsev, to be launched by the Voronezh and Steppe fronts toward Belgorod and the group of German forces around Kharkov.
4. Operation Suvorov, a thrust in the north by the Kalinin and Western fronts against the German forces in front of Smolensk and Roslavl.
5. An operation in the Donbas by the Southwestern and Southern fronts to smash through the German line along the Mius.
6. The Chernigov–Poltava operation, to be conducted by the Central, Voronezh, and Steppe fronts, a continuation of Operation Rumiantsev intended to drive the Germans back to the Dnepr.
7. The Bryansk operation, an assault by the Bryansk Front against the German forces at Bryansk, a follow-up to operations Kutuzov and Suvorov; and
8. The Novorosisk–Taman and Melitopol operations, offensives by the Southern and North Caucasus Fronts.

In other words, the Soviet operational scheme for the rest of 1943 had the army on the offensive everywhere. Once the Southern and North

Caucasus fronts had joined in, this would be an offensive across the entire length of the southern front, "from Velikiye Luki to the Black Sea," as one Soviet staff officer put it.[68]

If there is a kernel of genius in Soviet war making at this point, this was it: the fully realized vision of consecutive operations. All of these campaigns would be hard fought against a Wehrmacht that could still defend itself skillfully. All of them would fall short of complete strategic breakthroughs into open space. All would turn, at some point, into grinding struggles of attrition. Yet the very Soviet ability to run them, one after the other, presented the Wehrmacht with an insurmountable problem. The German command structure could only react to so many emergencies before it failed to react altogether. The limited number of reserve divisions could only plug so many holes, and the Wehrmacht ran out of divisions before the Soviet army ran out of offensives.

It is possible to criticize this schedule of operations. Because the Soviet army ran them sequentially rather than simultaneously, they offered a skilled German commander like Manstein the ability to do what he did best: parry threats through maneuver, shuffle his reserves from one spot to the next, and hit overextended Soviet spearheads with sharp and well-timed counterblows. There was debate within the Soviet high command over this point, with Marshal Zhukov arguing for a smaller number of offensives in more critical sectors, with larger forces seeking the envelopment and destruction of the defending German armies. Stalin argued for "numerous frontal blows delivered across a broad front," and his arguments held sway.[69] Zhukov, the trained professional, wanted to fight deep battle according to the doctrinal manuals; Stalin, less adventurous but recognizing that he held the operational advantages and seeing no need to court undue risk, adopted a more orthodox approach, one "that forced the enemy to divide his resources and throw them from one sector to another, trying to shut off a front where here and there there were gigantic breaches made by Soviet forces through his defenses."[70] Such a sequential broad front approach allowed a number of advantages: the maximum possible preparation time for each offensive, the careful stockpiling of supplies and ammunition, and a reduced number of slipups in a highly bureaucratized and centralized authoritarian system where lower-level initiative was unlikely to make up for overly rigid planning. The conclusion has to be that in this case, Stalin was probably right to insist on the conservative approach.

German strategy in this period is more difficult to evaluate, given that Manstein was doing little but reacting to one grave threat after another. Army Group South now had four armies on line: from left to right, the 4th Panzer Army (General Hermann Hoth) and *Armee-Abteilung Kempf* deployed south of Kursk around Belgorod and Kharkov, with the 4th Panzer Army facing generally north and *Kempf* facing generally east; the 1st Panzer Army (General Eberhard von Mackensen) holding the middle stretches of the Donets River around Izyum and facing generally to the north; and a reconstituted 6th Army (formerly *Armee-Abteilung Hollidt*, under General Karl-Adolf Hollidt) far out on the operational balcony, holding the line of the Mius, facing due east.[71] All of them were threadbare—the 4th Panzer and *Kempf* Armies by virtue of having been in on the mutual mauling at Kursk, and the 1st Panzer and 6th Armies by virtue of having handed over their armor to make the Kursk offensive possible. On paper, it looked somewhat like a line: four armies abreast, infantry divisions deployed forward, Panzer divisions held in reserve to react to any Soviet breakthroughs. In reality, it was something else: undersupplied, weak across the board but particularly weak in infantry, and holding a stairstep front that extended to the east by bounds from Belgorod in the north to Taganrog in the south. As a result, it was far longer than it ought to have been and was liable to be penetrated at virtually any point the Soviets chose.

Despite all those disadvantages, Manstein still saw operational possibilities. He belonged to an officer corps that was trained to see them, and more than anyone else in the Wehrmacht, he exemplified that tradition. In his memoirs, Manstein devoted what is by a considerable margin the longest chapter to this defensive struggle (*Abwehrkampf*) in the east. Manstein, a gifted writer, skillfully laid out his case. The numerical superiority enjoyed by the Soviets at this point was not going to be easy to overcome:

> On July 17th, 1943, the 29 infantry and 13 Panzer divisions of the army group faced 109 Soviet rifle divisions, nine rifle brigades, 10 tank corps, seven mechanized corps, and seven cavalry corps, to which we must add 20 independent tank brigades, 16 tank regiments, and eight antitank brigades. By September 7th, another 55 rifle divisions, two tank and two mechanized, corps, eight tank brigades, and 12 tank regiments appeared before us, transferred mainly from the sectors of Army Group Center and North. All told, the balance of forces was something like 7–1 in favor of the Soviet enemy.[72]

Comparing tank production yielded numbers that were just as depressing. "As much as Hitler's energy had resulted in astonishing war production," he noted, German factories could churn out only 500 tanks per month. The Soviets, by contrast, could treble or even quadruple that figure.

As for the Wehrmacht itself, Manstein noted that the hard fighting had left deep wounds, increasing the attrition of its manpower and making deep inroads into the heart of the force, "the experienced front-line fighters and officers."[73] From the onset of Citadel to the end of August, Manstein noted, the German tradition of aggressive conduct and leading from the front had turned Army Group South into a tomb for the officer corps. No fewer than seven division commanders had fallen in battle during that relatively brief period, along with 38 regimental commanders, and what still appears today as the incredible figure of 252 battalion commanders.

Facing these superior numbers, Manstein argues, the Army Group was going to be lucky even to "maintain itself in the field." It was nothing less than "a battle against a hydra."[74] Even so, Manstein was certain that he had two advantages that could help to overcome the deficit. First, there was "the qualitative advantage of the German soldier."[75] Today, this seems a foolish and perhaps even dangerous belief, but generations—no, centuries—of Prussian and German commanders had hewn to it as an article of faith. The military history of Germany was filled with tales of outnumbered forces triumphing against the odds: Frederick the Great at Hohenfriedeberg and Rossbach and Leuthen, Blücher at Möckern (the northern sector of the battle of Leipzig in 1813), Friedrich Karl, the Red Prince, at the battle of Königgrätz in 1866. Manstein knew all this history, as did all of his colleagues. If German armies had waited to be numerically superior to the foe before attacking, they would have waited in vain. The fabric of this way of war involved refusing to compute the numbers, forgetting about the odds, and trusting to fate. In that sense, Manstein was no different from the generations of officers who had preceded him.

His identification with the past went even deeper, however. If there was one tradition that the German officer corps had preserved carefully over the centuries, it was the necessity to disagree, defy, and even disobey. Every one of them knew the famous stories. At the battle of Mollwitz in 1740, Frederick the Great's first battle, Count Schwerin had actually ordered him to leave the battlefield when it seemed that the young monarch's life was at risk. During the Franco-Prussian war, General Steinmetz had ignored his printed orders, preferring to march toward the sound of the guns at the battle of Spichern in 1870. During the opening phase of the Tannenberg campaign in 1914, General Hermann von François had rejected orders that had him sitting passively waiting for a Russian attack. He, too, had marched to the sound of the guns and launched an attack on a vastly larger Russian force at Stallupönen. None of these hard chargers had ever received a reprimand; some even got promoted. For a resource-poor state, these obstreperous commanders often created or exploited operational opportunities that might otherwise have been lost if the commanders had waited for orders.

The classic example of this unruly but flexible system of command had always been the story of Friedrich Wilhelm von Seydlitz, Frederick the Great's cavalry commander, during the hard-fought battle of Zorndorf against these same Russians in 1758. At a crucial moment in the battle, when vigorous Russian attacks had destroyed Frederick's plans for the day and it seemed that all was lost, the king ordered his cavalry into action on his threatened left flank. When Seydlitz seemed dilatory in responding, another order arrived, replete with threats if the general did not respond immediately. Seydlitz had not been ignoring his king. Rather, he had been busy reconnoitering the best path forward for his men. He paused from his work and told the royal messenger, "Tell the king that after the battle my head is at his disposal, but meantime I hope he will permit me to exercise it in his service."[76] Within the hour, he was leading a charge against the Russian right, an action that saved the day at Zorndorf.

Given the weight of that history, we should not be surprised to learn that Manstein was a difficult subordinate. He had proven it during 1940, in the battle over the operational plan for the campaign against France. He had proven it in the opening phase of Operation Barbarossa in 1941, when he had chafed at restrictions placed on his LVI Panzer Corps during the drive through the Baltic states; he had repeatedly peppered the high command with demands for more forces and support during Crimean campaign of 1941–1942; and he spent much of the winter campaign of 1942–1943 threatening a complete collapse of his front if he did not receive more men, more tanks, more divisions.

So it was now in this difficult campaign. On the occasion of a fairly minor disagreement about the correct placement of the armored reserves in August, Manstein wrote to General Zeitzler,

If my misgivings about the coming development of the situation continue to be ignored, my intentions as commander—which seek only to solve difficulties that are not of my own making—continue to be frustrated, then I can only conclude that the Führer lacks the necessary trust in my leadership of the Army Group. In no way do

I think myself infallible. Every man makes mistakes, even commanders like Frederick the Great and Napoleon. I might point out that 11th Army won the Crimean campaign under very difficult circumstances and that Army Group South, placed in an almost hopeless situation at the end of last year, mastered that one too.

If the Führer believes that he has a commander or an army group headquarters that has better nerves than we showed last winter, that shows more initiative than we did in the Crimea, on the Donets, or at Kharkov, that improvises better than we did in the Crimea or in the last winter campaign, or who has the ability to predict the inevitable course of events better than we can, then I am ready to give up my post.

It is the final line of this letter of complaint, however, that links it most firmly to the long chain of Prussian–German military history: "As long as I am at this post," he wrote, "I must have the possibility of using my own head."[77] Perhaps it was an attempt to channel the fiery spirit of Seydlitz, looking for inspiration in the words of a spiritual forebear who had died 170 years ago that very month. With an uncertain future and a present that was unraveling by the day, Manstein and all the rest of them were fleeing into their own history.

To Kharkov

The fight for the Ukraine should have been Manstein's war. He finally had the Russians exactly where he always claimed to want them. They were on the move, out in the open, and vulnerable to one of his famous counterstrokes. Yet for all his undeniable operational skill, the fall of 1943 would be another season of disaster for Army Group South.

The action opened in the far south. On July 17, with the fighting only just dying down at Kursk, the Soviets opened an offensive against the German 6th Army along the Mius.[78] In any other war, this powerful offensive would have qualified as the main event of the campaigning season. In this one, it sometimes gets lost altogether. Launching the offensive were the forces of the Southern Front (General F. I. Tolbukhin), moving right to left the 51st, 5th Shock, 28th, and 44th Armies, with a fifth formation, the 2nd Guards Army, forming the second echelon. The central armies, the 5th Shock and 28th, would attack on a narrow front, just 12 miles. Once they had smashed the German front, the 2nd Guards would move through the hole. The German 6th Army was greatly outnumbered, but it sat in good terrain behind a river, a position that it had been able to fortify for five months. It had three corps on line, from right to left the XXIX, XVII, and *Korps Mieth* (once again an undersupported ad hoc formation named for its commander, General Friedrich Mieth), along with a single mobile division (the 16th *Panzergrenadier*) behind the front as army reserve.[79]

In what was becoming a familiar sequence of events, the initial Soviet attack blasted through the German line in the designated attack sector, crossing the Mius in the center of the line just north of Kuibyshev. The Germans, fighting from prepared positions for a change, resisted stubbornly, made skillful use of the terrain, and launched hasty counterattacks with small motorized *Kampfgruppen*. The result was something less than a full operational breakthrough for the Soviet attackers. Nevertheless, Tolbukhin now decided to insert his second-echelon 2nd Guards Army, some would say a bit too precipitately, sending it over the Mius into what was by now a crowded bridgehead some 12 miles wide by 10 deep.

The Germans reacted rapidly. Manstein knew the danger of allowing the Soviets to occupy any sort of position across a major river. First came the fortification of the position, then the buildup of forces, and eventually a breakout, either as a diversionary operation for an offensive somewhere else on the front, or as the main effort itself. Soon armored reinforcements were on their way to the Mius from all over Army Group South, including II S.S. Panzer Corps (transferred from 1st Panzer Army along the Donets) and the XXIV Panzer Corps (the last formation in Army Group South's mobile reserve). The commander of the 6th Army, General Hollidt, was eventually able to seal off the penetration and even beat it back by the end of July. There are reports of Tolbukhin being downcast, feeling that his offensive had failed. In fact, by drawing the Panzers to the Mius, he had played his role to perfection. Looking back, even Manstein would later describe his own decision to transfer so much armor to the Mius as "disastrous."[80]

The Soviets were now three for three. They had defended Kursk, smashed the Orel salient, and diverted most of the German operational reserve to the Mius. The state was set for their most dramatic victory of all. Their next offensive, Operation Rumiantsev, aimed at the destruction of German forces deployed to the south of the Kursk salient, the 4th Panzer Army on the left and *Armee-Abteilung Kempf* on the right.[81] Once again it was able to take advantage of the fact that the

Germans were sitting in an exposed salient, a bulge formed where the front ran north and then bent nearly 90 degrees to the west. The forces involved in the assault were the Voronezh Front (General N. F. Vatutin) facing south and the Steppe Front (General I. S. Konev) facing west, with five armies involved in the initial blow. From right to left, they were the 6th Guards and 5th Guards Armies (Voronezh Front), and the 53rd, 69th, and 7th Guards Armies (Steppe Front). Supporting Vatutin's initial blow from the north was a second echelon of armored forces: the 1st Guards Tank Army (behind the 6th Guards Army) and the 5th Guards Tank Army (behind the 5th Guards Army). Once the shock groups had broken through the German defenses, the tank armies were to pass though the opening and head for Bogodukhov, dominating the approaches to the city of Kharkov from the west and northwest. From here, they would carry out an encirclement of the city in cooperation with Konev's forces coming in from the east. Moreover, three more armies stood off to the right of Vatutin's shock group (the 38th, 40th, and 27th Armies, right to left), with orders to join in as the offensive gained momentum. Another army stood on the left, also ready to jump in: the 57th, part of the Southwestern Front (General R. I. Malinovsky), and deployed almost exactly to the east of Kharkov. Two air armies, the 2nd and 5th, would provide air support.

All told, the assault would involve no fewer than nine Soviet armies, two tank armies, and two air armies arrayed in a semicircle around the Belgorod salient—well over a million men. It was a massive a blow, but a simple concept. It was, in the words of the best recent history of the campaign, "vintage Zhukov."[82] However, Operation Rumiantsev requires more than the mere counting of cannon. The Soviets experienced difficulties aplenty in the planning phase. The formations involved in the offensive had been configured for positional defense. They now had to rush into an offensive with little transition or preparation time. Most of the planning seems to have been done via oral discussion. No written orders for Rumiantsev would appear until two days into the operation.[83] Moreover, many of these formations had suffered terribly in the Kursk fighting, the 5th Guards Tank Army above all. Virtually all the units were understrength and exhausted, and replacements were only just beginning to arrive. All these things took time, and an offensive originally envisioned for late July did not begin until August 3.

There was little that Hoth, Kempf, or Manstein could do to match this concentration of force. The defenders were the same two armies that had just launched the southern prong of the Kursk attack. Both the 4th Panzer Army on the left and *Armee-Abteilung Kempf* on the right were weak shadows of their former selves. They had spent the last two weeks evacuating the small penetration they had made toward Prokhorovka and slowly withdrawing to their original start line. Once again, we cannot say they were particularly ready to defend themselves. They were not occupying any sort of prepared position. They too were exhausted, the logistics were on the verge of collapse, and their replacement deficit, particularly in infantry, made the Soviet problems look tame.

Thus it should come as no surprise that the opening attacks of Operation Rumiantsev succeeded almost everywhere. Heralded by a massive three-hour artillery barrage, the ground attack began at 7:55 A.M. By 10:00 A.M., Soviet assault groups had overrun the first German defensive line, and by 1:00 P.M., the forward elements of the 1st and 5th Guards Tank Armies—the second echelon—were already passing through the gaps. Once again, Zhukov was concentrating his armies on narrow frontages; the 1st Guards Tank Army, for example, was operating on a front of just three kilometers, and the 5th Guards Tank Army only five.[84] The front line city of Belgorod fell on August 5, day three of the operation—and the same day, incidentally, that the Soviets reoccupied Orel.

The assault came as a shock to Manstein and his staff alike. They realized they'd been had, and orders now went out hastily recalling all those Panzer divisions from the far south: S.S. *Panzergrenadier* Divisions *Totenkopf* and *Das Reich*, along with the 3rd Panzer Division, went to Hoth; the 5th S.S. *Panzergrenadier* Division *Wiking* to Kempf. They would arrive quickly, but still too late to fix what was already an operational disaster. The principal Soviet success came in the center, on the operational border between the 4th Panzer Army and the *Armee-Abteilung*. As the second-echelon tank armies began hurtling to the south, they split the seam between the two German armies, and with Soviet pressure driving 4th Panzer Army generally southwest and Kempf generally southeast, the gap was growing larger by the hour. By nightfall on August 7, five days into the offensive, it stood at 30 miles—a great deal of operational space for a Soviet tank army.[85]

Two armies with open flanks and a highly mobile enemy between them already flushed with victory was a potential catastrophe. Yet at this moment, the lead elements of the German Panzer divisions began to arrive. The result was a gigantic clash of armor around Bogodukhov and Akhtyrka, a swirling melee that checked the Soviets for a time and left both sides bruised and bleeding. Both German armies were able to break contact and reestablish the thinnest of defensive lines by the end of August, but the margin had been narrow, and no one studying this campaign should equate German survival with victory.

On August 22, Soviet forces reentered Kharkov, the fourth-largest city in the country. It was the signal for what by now had become a habit for the Wehrmacht: the firing of a general. This time the victim was General Kempf, whose *Armee-Abteilung* had been responsible for the defense of the city. We can't argue that he had done anything particularly wrong in the defense, and his withdrawal from Kharkov had been necessary in order to avoid encirclement. His dismissal was a ritual sacrifice more than anything else. His replacement was Manstein's former chief of staff, General Otto Wöhler, and with Kempf gone, the former *Armee-Abteilung* now received a new designation as 8th Army.[86]

There is a deeper significance to the fall of Kharkov, however. The Soviets had lost the city to the Wehrmacht in 1941. They had attempted and failed to retake it in May 1942 as part of one of their earliest planned counteroffensives. They retook it in early 1943 as part of their great winter counteroffensive that had started at Stalingrad. They had lost it again to Manstein's own counterstroke in March 1943. Now they had won it back, this time permanently.

There is today in military intellectual circles a great deal of discussion of Clausewitz's concept of the culmination point. It is the notion that no offensive goes on forever. Its level of force begins to ebb at some point, as the attackers begin to feel the pinch of longer supply lines, heavy losses, and simple exhaustion. The defenders now hold the advantages: they have fallen back on their supply lines, replacements reach the front more easily, and they are under the firm control of their commanders. It is time for the "shining sword of revenge," in Clausewitz's famous phrase.

This culmination point can be many things. It can be an event, a moment in time, or a state of mind. It can also be a place. On this sector of the sprawling Eastern Front, it is obvious just where the culmination point stood from 1941 to 1943, the operational limit for both of these armies, a spot that was just a bit too far for either one of them to sustain momentum and logistics. That culmination point was the city of Kharkov.

Conclusion: To the Dnepr

The Wehrmacht was now in deep trouble in the south. It was sitting on a rolling, open plain between the Donets and Dnepr rivers. Attacking was out of the question, given the wounds it had sustained and the increasingly lopsided balance of forces. It had already proven beyond a shadow of a doubt that it was no longer capable of defending itself against a determined Soviet offensive, and trying to do so where it currently stood would have amounted to suicide. Its supreme commander, Adolf Hitler, had a limited operational repertoire in which the no-retreat order usually held pride of place. The Wehrmacht, in other words, could not advance, stand still, or retreat. Once again, for a week or so, the army was sailing through a perfect storm of command gridlock.

A front that had been leaking for over a year was now falling apart altogether. The Soviets were on the move everywhere; virtually every front from the Baltic to the Black seas was grinding forward. In mid-August, with German armor concentrated in the Kharkov sector, the combined forces of Southern Front (Tolbukhin) and Southwestern Front (Malinovsky) launched another great offensive against the German front on the Mius. Unlike the previous month's attempt, the attackers cracked the defensive line with ease this time, and well they should have: there were by now no German Panzer divisions in reserve to rush to the threatened sector, while they were able to call on the concentrated artillery fire of no fewer than 5,000 guns.[87] The situation maps were a blizzard of red arrows heading west. Army Group South stood on the brink of dissolution.

Something had to give, however, and playing contrary to the stereotype in the German military memoirs, Hitler was the one who caved first. The last week of August and the first week of September saw a constant series of command meetings. Hitler flew out to Vinnitsa on August 27. Kluge flew to East Prussia a couple of days later. Manstein and Kluge flew to East Prussia on September 3, followed by another visit by the Führer to the east, this time to Manstein's Army Group South headquarters at Zaporozhye on September 8. Frankly, no one conducted himself with any dignity in the course of the discussions. Manstein played a card that by now should have been familiar to Hitler. He made impossible demands for reinforcements, at first 10 divisions, later upped to 12—in other words, a new field army. Without them, he could not hold the current positions as Hitler was demanding.[88] Instead, he would have no choice but to retreat.

Perhaps he was surprised when, at the Zaporozhye meeting, Hitler agreed. He finally handed the field marshal the freedom he had been demanding, the right to conduct mobile operations—in this case, a general retreat of Army Group South. He also, at long last, agreed to end one of the most absurd operational situations in the entire war, the so-called Kuban bridgehead, still held by the nearly forgotten 17th Army (General Richard Ruoff) and representing the last gasp of the Wehrmacht's ill-conceived Caucasus campaign of 1942.[89] The only major field formation still remaining in Army Group A (Field Marshal Ewald von Kleist), the 17th Army had been sitting out on its remote perch ever since, in nearly tropical conditions, holding its positions amid the jungles and bayous. If the bridgehead had ever held any operational potential—as a springboard for a renewed offensive into the Caucasus, for example—that time was long since past. Ruoff and his men now crossed over Kerch Strait and headed back to the Crimea.

As for Army Group South, it was headed back to the Dnepr. As was his wont in his memoirs, Manstein described the retreat as a kind of *Heldenepos*—a heroic epic against the odds. In fact, it was something much more mundane: a beaten army trudging back step by step. With its logistics largely still a matter of horse-drawn wagons, often *panjes* stolen from the local populace, the Wehrmacht did not blitz its way back to the Dnepr. The Soviets were nipping at its heels the entire time, and there was a great deal of gritty fighting of the rear-guard variety. Occasionally the attackers would run into a German Panzer division inserted into the line to deal with some local emergency; then both sides would maul each other again. But there were far too many miles of front and far too few Panzer divisions to make much of a difference. There was tactical action aplenty, but on the operational level, this was a retreat, plain and simple, through what one Wehrmacht officer called "a bunch of towns with unpronounceable names."[90]

However, there were some interesting operational problems. A decreasingly mobile army group spread out over a 440-mile breadth of front had to converge onto just six crossing sites over one of the world's great rivers. From north to south, the Wehrmacht could get over the Dnepr River at Kiev, Kanev, Cherkassy, Kremenchug, Dnepropetrovsk, and Zaporozhye. Allowing a Soviet mechanized formation to slip around a flank or through a seam and reach one of them before the Germans did would have been a disaster.[91]

There was also the issue of the 6th Army. It wasn't going back to the Dnepr at all. Like all the Soviet rivers—the Donets, the Don, and the Volga—the Dnepr forms a massive bend along its course, jutting out to the east with its point approximately at Dnepropetrovsk. Holding such a huge salient would be wasteful of units and equipment, and at any rate, the Wehrmacht no longer had them to spare. As a result, the 6th Army would go back to a much shorter prepared line from Zaporozhye running due south to Melitopol and thence to the shores of the Sea of Azov. Here it would bar the way to the lower Dnepr, protect the Perekop isthmus, and prevent Soviet armies from cutting off the Crimea. As it would be remaining in front of the Dnepr, 6th Army now moved from Army Group South to Army Group A, joining 17th Army which was even now arriving in the Crimea.

Finally, in giving approval for the retreat, Hitler had also insisted that Army Group South maintain a series of bridgeheads on the left (eastern) bank of the Dnepr, at Kiev, Cherkassy, Zaporozhye, and Dnepropetrovsk. The plan was to hold most of the bridgeheads only long enough to get the main body over the river, at which point the defenders would evacuate them. Others, like the one at Zaparozhye, were to remain in existence. Normally a prudent measure if there was to be any hope of a renewed friendly offensive in this sector, the order did nothing by this point but put more good men at risk.

In the end, the entire notion of holding the Melitopol–Dnepr line may strike us as quaint. The various Soviet fronts—from right to left, Central, Voronezh, Steppe, Southwestern, and Southern—reached the river at about the same time as the Germans, and virtually all of them managed to cross it. Some of them did so under fire, wherever sufficient German forces stood on the higher western bank. Too few of them did not. Some of it was luck, as Soviet formations hit seams between the German armies or simply caught an exhausted opponent napping. Some of it was intentional, however, as the Soviet front deployed mobile groups to race ahead of the main forces, ad hoc formations that were able to take advantage of the unsettled situation on the German side of the river.

There was no epic here. For the Wehrmacht, disaster followed disaster. By the end of September, Soviet armies had reached the Dnepr and had soon hurtled across it. Our usual image of Soviet mass needs revision for this phase of operations. One reliable source puts it in different terms:

At the beginning of the last week in September more and more Soviet armies, driving over 150 miles to the west, drew up at the river Dnepr. . . . Within a week, as Soviet troops improvised rafts or used little boats hidden by partisans, or hacked timber to build the first bridges, twenty-three bridgeheads, ranging in depth from a thousand yards to twenty miles, dotted the western banks of the mighty Dnepr.[92]

Within weeks, they were across the river at Bukrin south of Kiev, and at Cherkassy, Kremenchug, and Dnepropetrovsk, eventually linking up to form a huge position on the western bank. Calling it a bridgehead, the usual designation, is a considerable understatement: it was as big as some European countries. The Soviets were across the river, and across it in force; the Germans lost the Dnepr line before they had ever really manned it. Difficulties arose from time to time, as they will in any operation this size. A three-brigade airborne drop to expand the Bukrin bridgehead on September 26 went badly wrong. We can round up the usual suspects for a 1943 airborne operation: insufficient transport aircraft, lack of fuel, bad weather. The real problem was excessive complexity.

In October, the Soviet Southern Front once again blasted through the German 6th Army's line between Zaporozhye and Melitopol. Driving west at top speed, it reached the lower reaches of the Dnepr and also occupied Perekop on its left flank. The German 17th Army was now cut off in the Crimea. It had just barely managed to escape a potential tomb in the Kuban, and it now faced a second consecutive death sentence. In November, the Voronezh Front (now renamed 1st Ukrainian Front) launched its drive toward Kiev. Having failed to break out of Bukrin bridgehead to the south of Kiev, Vatutin shifted the weight of his attack to the Lyutezh bridgehead north of the city. It was a tricky operation in close proximity to the enemy. As one brigade commander wrote,

> It was a difficult mission. Over 300 tanks and self-propelled guns, hundreds of artillery pieces, armored personnel carriers, and motor vehicles had to be moved quickly and secretly from the Veliky Bukrin bridgehead, then for nearly 125 miles along the front line, and, finally, across the Desna and again across the Dnepr to another bridgehead.[93]

From here, on November 3, the Soviet attack developed smoothly. "Speed and resolution in breaking through the enemy defense—this is what will ensure our success," Vatutin told his commanders, and it proved to be the recipe for victory at Kiev. It helps when the enemy is utterly fought out, and you can lead off your attack with a 2,000-gun barrage along a four-mile front. By November 5, Soviet forces had fought into Kiev, and the next day, the Soviet command announced the liberation of "the mother of Russian cities." A Soviet attempt to continue the drive to the west failed, as German XXXXVIII Panzer Corps under General Hermann Balck launched a series of well-timed counterattacks that inflicted heavy casualties on the Soviet attackers at Zhitomir, Brussilov, and Fastov. Balck's chief of staff, General Mellenthin, later claimed that "from the tactical aspect the conduct of operations was the most brilliant in my experience. General Balck handled his corps with masterly skill."[94] That seems true enough, but by this time, it hardly mattered.

The verdict was in. The Soviets had smashed the Wehrmacht in the Ukraine. The Germans could not stand. They had no response to the storm breaking down on them. With the change in designation of the Soviet fronts in the sector from their descriptive names (Voronezh, Steppe, Southwestern, and Southern) to the almost anonymous 1st Ukrainian, 2nd Ukrainian, 3rd Ukrainian, and 4th Ukrainian, it might have seemed even more frightening. The Germans might defend themselves vigorously in this or that sector, or make a late counterattack, but viewed from the operational level, there was no doubt that they were heading home.

As we contemplate this military catastrophe—one of the greatest defeats in all of military history—let us conclude with one more passage from Manstein's expertly written memoir, *Verlorene Siege*. It is late August 1943, and as usual, the field marshal is railing against Hitler, complaining about the lack of reinforcements, the lack of understanding, and the lack of action from the high command:

> Field Marshal von Kluge visited the Führer's headquarters on August 28th, with the result that we heard nothing more about withdrawals from his front. Northern Army Group, too, now alleged that it was unable to spare a single division. As far as the other operational theaters were concerned, Hitler first wanted to await developments, to see, for example, whether the British would now land in Apulia or the Balkans or tie down their forces down in Sardinia—a contingency that was just as improbable as it was unimportant.[95]

Today, Manstein no longer resides in the pantheon of Western heroes. We are much more likely to note his close identification with the National Socialist regime, his loyal service—despite the occasional professional disagreement—to the Führer, his history of abetting the regime's war crimes, at the very least, and perhaps much more than that.

Let us leave all those profound questions in abeyance for the moment. Instead, let us note the characteristics of Manstein, this undeniably gifted operational commander, that link him inexorably to the chain of his own tradition. It is almost commonplace today to argue that the German way of war was a blinkered perception of modern conflict, a military culture that privileged the operational view above more important questions of strategy: logistics, intelligence, industrial production, and especially politics.

As we read his memoirs, it is clear that Manstein never attempted to hide his priorities. He really did believe that holding this or that position along the coast of the Sea of Azov, at Taganrog, let us say, or Mariupol or Berdiansk or Melitopol, was more important to Germany's overall war effort than maintaining the Axis. It is easy to scoff at Italy today, but in this war, Italy made a difference, and a big one. Germany could either face the rest of the world alone, or face it as part of a coalition. Manstein thought it meaningless, and in that sense, he was the exemplar of an increasingly dangerous German military tradition.

Even more noticeable is Manstein's repeated assertions in *Verlorene Siege* that he was fighting for a "stalemate peace" (*Remis-Frieden*) in the east. Given what we know about Stalin's own intentions and the recent declaration of the Western powers at the beginning of 1943 that they were fighting for the unconditional surrender of the Axis powers, his declaration seems hard to take seriously. Manstein was not an ordinary soldier, as he declares in his memoirs. He was an army group commander, working at a level just below the German high command. The postwar memoirs of equivalent Western commanders—Patton, Bradley, Montgomery—display plenty of awareness of the overall strategic situation in which they had to operate. Manstein and his colleagues deliberately refused to cast their sights that high, however. He maintained to the end that he was merely fighting a delaying action, a *hinhaltender Widerstand*. He never explained just what he was expecting or what hope he could possibly have had for the future, even as the deaths mounted into the millions. In that sense, he and all his colleagues were fighting a lost war, one without strategy or hope.[96]

Perhaps, every now and then, war really does offer us a definite lesson, one that we can teach to future generations of officers and scholars alike. Let us call it Manstein's First Law: it's only a delaying action if you actually have something to look forward to.

7

Kesselring's War: Italy, 1943

A Day at Rastenburg: September 8, 1943

Some wartime staffs function better than others. Some work at a high pitch of efficiency. All walk into their share of walls from time to time. Others become completely dysfunctional. For this last category, let us travel to the Wolfsschanze, Adolf Hitler's military headquarters at Rastenburg, in the cool forests of sylvan East Prussia. Today, the town is called Kętrzyn and sits in northeastern Poland.

The chief of the operations department sighed. What a day.[1]

No . . . what a week!

Things were falling apart in the east. The Russian—*der Russe*—was on the march, and every single German army on the front was in trouble. It was time to retreat, and time for mobile operations—*Bewegliche Kriegführung*, they were now calling it. You couldn't call it a retreat—that didn't fly with Hitler. The *Haltbefehl* was all he knew. *Halten um jeden Preis!* Stand fast! Hold on! Fight to the last men! These were empty words now, mere *Schlagworte*, "slogans."

Then there was Italy. The Allied invasion would take place any day now. They could all feel it. And then what? Would the Italians fight? Reports out of the country were sketchy, but the picture was disturbing.

He sighed. It had been a bad week, and now it was time for some tough decisions, about Russia, Italy, the war—and his own career. He had written some depressing letters to his wife of late. He felt bad when he did that, but he had to talk to someone.

While everything was falling apart, what were they all doing? Heusinger looked down at the scribbles in his *Tagebuch*, but he already knew the answer. "Flying," he thought to himself, that's what they were all doing. In the last week alone, Manstein had flown to Rastenburg to consult with the Führer, and the moment he departed, Kluge had arrived. Then, when that was done, the Führer had flown out to the front: on September 3 to Vinnitsa, and then a few days later to Zaporozhye.

The trouble was, while Hitler was gone from Rastenburg, nothing got done.

And an even bigger trouble, Heusinger laughed bitterly: when Hitler returned, nothing got done either.

He recalled the day's events. With trouble rising up like a flood all around them, Heusinger had sat, bored, through a five-hour demonstration of new weapons and equipment at Rastenburg. Hitler loved these sessions, of course, spouting off specifications and throw weights and production figures. He had almost swooned over a self-propelled gun mounted on an old Czech tank chassis,[2] then some newly designed gas masks—something that Hitler could talk about from personal experience: he made a lot of references to the Western Front in 1917. Finally, a scale model of a new 100-ton tank had been unveiled,[3] and there was a long discussion about that one. By the end, Heusinger could barely stifle a yawn, and neither could a lot of other people in the room. Time weighed heavily at Rastenburg.

It was either late in the evening or early in the morning when Keitel burst in; Heusinger couldn't quite remember. There had been an Anglo-American landing at Salerno and an Italian armistice with the Western powers. It was the end of the Axis. It was as if Keitel had set off a bomb in the room: absolute chaos erupted, with everyone shouting at once and Hitler screaming, his face contorted with rage, threatening to have Badoglio and the king of Italy arrested, or even shot. "I told you all, but no one would believe me," he yelled. "I told you all!"[4]

Years later, Heusinger would remember it like it was yesterday. It had been a typical staff meeting by that point in the war: five hours of sheer boredom, then five minutes of insanity. Looking back, he couldn't help but wonder: Couldn't they have done something better with those lost five hours?

Despite the usual stereotypes and clichés, Adolf Hitler didn't lose World War II all by himself—unless starting the war in the first place was Germany's crucial error. His erratic leadership didn't help, but at his side every step of the way was a group of highly trained staff officers, standing around, wasting time, and stifling yawns.

Invasion: Nine More Days that Shook the World

The Allies followed up their successful Sicilian campaign with landings in Italy proper.[5] Once again, there was no great enthusiasm within the U.S. high command for these plans, but this campaign was virtually inevitable for all the same reasons that had brought Allied armies to North Africa and from there to Sicily in the first place: they weren't going to be fighting the Germans anywhere else that winter. Planners could also point to the modern Italian air complex at Foggia in the southern portion of the country. Flying from Foggia, Allied bombers would be much closer to the Romanian oil fields at Ploesti on which so much of the German war effort depended. Finally, the Allies were already deeply involved in surrender negotiations with the new Badoglio government. A precisely timed Italian surrender, or perhaps even a decision to switch sides, might allow the landings to proceed without much fighting and let the Allied armies make great gains quite rapidly.

For the German high command, September must have seemed like July redux. We have already examined that disastrous nine-day period from July 5 to July 13, a brief span of time in which Germany's accumulated and potential problems all seemed to burst into flower simultaneously. The first days of September would be even worse, as yet another avalanche of complex and puzzling events tumbled down on German military planners all at once. Like that first nine-day crisis, this second one demonstrated once again how deeply intertwined the various fronts of this global war were.

Early September was a period of particularly high tension. Hitler had no trust whatsoever in the new Italian government of Marshal Pietro Badoglio, nor in the marshal's repeated protestations that Italy would remain a faithful ally of the Reich. The Germans had been sending forces into Italy all through August and had some 16 divisions in the country by the end of the month, divided between Field Marshal Erwin Rommel's Army Group B in northern Italy and Field Marshal Albert Kesselring's High Command South (*Oberbefehlshaber-Süd*) further down the peninsula.[6] Ostensibly there to protect Germany's ally against an Allied invasion, this massive military presence was already beginning to resemble an army of occupation.

With that in mind, let us examine another microhistory, a blink of an eye in this long and bloody war. For the Germans, early September was a combination of things known, things unknown, and things suspected.

❧·❧

Monday, September 1. There has apparently been a breakthrough in surrender talks between the Allies and Italy, which have been ongoing for two weeks at Cassibile in Sicily.[7] The Badoglio government telegraphs the Allies that it agrees to the terms of an armistice. The Germans are aware that treachery is afoot, but not the extent or exact nature of it.[8]

Tuesday, September 2. The chief Italian negotiator, General Giuseppe Castellano, flies back to Cassibile to meet with his opposite number, General Walter Bedell Smith, General Dwight D. Eisenhower's chief of staff.

Wednesday, September 3. Field Marshal Erich von Manstein and Field Marshal Günther Kluge, commanding Army Group South and Center, respectively, fly to Rastenburg to discuss the catastrophic situation on the Eastern Front and to press Hitler for a decision: either send reinforcements to the east, or permit the two of them to revert to mobile operations—that is, carry out a retreat. Hitler is hesitant. He seems to realize that the situation in the east has become untenable, but he cannot free any divisions at this precise moment. He has been warning for weeks that something big is about to happen in the Mediterranean.

The same day. Something big happens in the Mediterranean. Allied forces invade Italy. The British 8th Army, under the command of General Montgomery, launches Operation Baytown, a short hop over the Strait of Messina from Sicily to the province of Calabria in the toe of the Italian boot.

The same day. Smith and Castellano sign an armistice taking Italy out of the war. Plans call for it to be announced publicly on September 8, the day before the planned Allied landing at Salerno, just south of Naples. Paratroopers of the U.S. 82nd Airborne Division prepare to execute Operation Giant II, an airborne landing outside of Rome, intending to link up with Italian troops and liberate the capital at the moment that Italy surrenders.[9]

Friday, September 5. By now certain that Italy intends to surrender, Hitler has instructions issued to Field Marshal Kesselring to ready his units in Italy for any emergency that may arise. Rommel's units similarly prepare for action in the north. Both prepare to execute Operation Axis (*Achse*), the military measures to be taken in case of Italian surrender. German aerial reconnaissance reports a large movement of Allied landing craft along the North African coast.

Sunday, September 7. Hitler draws up an ultimatum to Marshal Badoglio, demanding that Italy cease all anti-German activities. He plans to serve it on the Italians on September 9. German aerial reconnaissance spots a large Allied flotilla moving out of Bizerte in Tunisia. Its precise destination is unknown, but it is clearly more than a support fleet for the British 8th Army in Calabria. The Allies are about to carry out a major landing somewhere else.

Monday, September 8. Badoglio gets cold feet. He decides to repudiate the original agreement with the Allies because of "the disposition and strength of the German forces in the Rome area."[10] He fears a violent German takeover of all of Italy.

The same day. The Führer flies to the east to confer with Manstein at Army Group South headquarters at Zaporozhye. After much back and forth between the two, Hitler agrees to a retreat by Army Group South to the Dnepr River, along with an evacuation of the Kuban bridgehead.

The same day. With Allied troop transports already sailing toward the beaches at Salerno in southern Italy, Eisenhower cannot wait any longer. He and Badoglio were due to announce the surrender simultaneously by radio, but he has heard nothing from the marshal. At 6:30 P.M., as scheduled, Eisenhower goes on Radio Algiers to announce that "the Italian government has surrendered its armed forces unconditionally." He calls on the people of Italy to "help eject the German aggressor from Italian soil."[11] Waiting 10 minutes, and still hearing nothing from Badoglio, Eisenhower orders the text of the marshal's proclamation to be broadcast in English.

The same day, an hour later. After a day of to-ing and fro-ing and bitter arguments within the Italian government, Badoglio goes on Radio Rome at 7:45 P.M., an hour late, to announce that Italy has surrendered as a result of the "impossibility of continuing the unequal struggle against the overwhelming power of the enemy."[12] That done, the Italian government flees Rome. Kesselring issues the code word, *Achse*, and Operation Axis begins.

The same day. General Maxwell Taylor, the 82nd Airborne Division's artillery commander, undertakes a clandestine mission to Rome. Not liking what he sees of Italian military preparations, he decides to cancel Giant II, only hours before the start of the operation. Indeed, the planes are already on the runway.

Tuesday, September 9. Hitler returns to Rastenburg. British troops carry out Operation Slapstick, a seaborne landing in Apulia on the Italian heel seizing the major port of Taranto.

The same day. U.S. 5th Army, under the command of General Mark W. Clark, lands at Salerno on the western coast of Italy, just south of Naples. Operation Avalanche has begun.

Once again, one is left stunned by the complexity of this war. Its multiple uncertainties should give any historian pause in being too critical of wartime decision making. Many things that are completely obvious to us today were utterly obscure at the moment they were taking place. A historian with access to the archival record of all the wartime participants—able to reconstruct in minute detail what each side was thinking at any given moment—enjoys a kind of omniscience that is not only false, but arguably injurious to our understanding of a historical event. What all the actors have at the time are questions: Should Kluge receive more divisions? Should Manstein? Where would those divisions come from? What exactly was the attitude of the Italians? Where exactly was that big Allied flotilla out of Bizerte headed?

With the complexities increased by the interrelated nature of the fronts, World War II again proves the wisdom of the great Prussian general, Helmuth von Moltke, who once famously described strategy as "a system of expedients" (*ein System von Aushilfen*). In his 1871 essay "On Strategy" ("*Über Strategie*"), he put it this way:

> Only the laymen perceives in the unfolding of a campaign the consistent execution of an original idea, one that the commander has worked out in all details beforehand and to which he has adhered firmly to the end.[13]

You did your best, in other words, making a lot of it up as you went along. As the situation changed, your plan had to change as well. It was one of the foundation stones of the Prussian, and later the German, way of war: command flexibility.[14]

Virtually every day of this war brought an event that threw the planners for a loop. There were individual periods, like the July or September nexus, where each hour seemed to bring a new crisis, an individual event of enormous import like the surrender of Italy or Operation Avalanche, one that has since generated a mountain of its own scholarly literature. Some days it was enough to take your breath away—or make your hair fall out. The best planners reacted by coming up with a workable plan B; the lesser ones went to pieces. Most simply muddled through, but no one ever mastered the art of fighting World War II.

Operation Axis

Moltke also said something else that became famous. Writing in his *History of the 1870 War* (*Geschichte des Krieges 1870*), he claimed that

> It is an illusion to believe that one can work out a plan of campaign far in advance and then carry it through to the end. The first collision with the enemy's main body, and the outcome of that clash, creates a new situation (*Lage*).[15]

Usually shortened in military discourse to "no plan survives contact with the enemy," it has become one of the most quoted aphorisms in the canon. The condensed version usually leaves off the important qualifier about "the first collision with the enemy's main body" (*der erste Zusammenstoss mit der feindlichen Hauptmacht*), but it works nonetheless as a general truism, warning the commander that the enemy will have something to say about how things go.

The only problem with this famous quote is that it is not true. Sometimes—rarely, to be sure, but sometimes—your plans go off exactly as you draw them up, or even succeed beyond your wildest dreams. The Wehrmacht had already had a few such moments in this war: Case Yellow in 1940, for example,[16] or Operation 25, the campaign in Yugoslavia in 1941.[17] Another wildly successful undertaking was Operation Axis. In any operation, so much depends on the attitude of the enemy. Some fight tooth and nail, some put up a good appearance, and some disappear altogether. In response to Operation Axis, the Italian army chose the third option.

Operation Axis deserves more scholarly attention than it has gotten. The operation was of immense scope and vast complexity and could have gone wrong at virtually any point. Even a casual glance at the operational plan would seem to uncover any number of places where it could have collapsed. Beyond that, it was something completely new. Military history knows no operation quite like it: a murderous and bloody assault on an erstwhile ally in which the casualties would run into the tens of thousands. Perhaps only the Wehrmacht, one of the most ruthless military organizations of all time, one that executed tens of thousands of its own soldiers in the course of the war, could have run it as effectively.

The Germans had two army groups in Italy. Army Group B (under Rommel) was in upper Italy, with its headquarters at Garda. Despite its designation as an army group, Rommel's command was essentially the size of a small army, with eight divisions grouped into four corps: Corps Witthöft (44th and 71st Infantry Divisions); LXXXVII Corps (76th and 94th Infantry Divisions); II S.S. Panzer Corps (S.S. *Panzergrenadier* Division *Leibstandarte* Adolf Hitler and 24th Panzer Division); and LI Mountain Corps (65th and 305th Infantry Divisions, still in the process of arriving in September). Overseeing this relatively modest array, Rommel's mission was to disarm no fewer than three Italian armies. They included the 8th Army, headquartered in Padua (XXIII, XXIV, and XXXV Corps); the 5th Army, headquartered in Viterbo (II and XVI Corps); and the 4th Army, headquartered in Sospel in southern France (I, XII, and XV Corps). The task of disarming the 4th Army would also involve units from the German 19th Army, currently occupying the region as part of Army Group D.[18]

The second main grouping of German forces in Italy was Kesselring's *OB-Süd*. He too had eight divisions, grouped into three corps: XI Parachute Corps (*Fliegerkorps*) in the vicinity of Rome (2nd *Fallschirmjägerdivision* and 3rd *Panzergrenadier* Division); XIV Panzer Corps (1st Parachute Panzer Division Hermann Göring, 15th *Panzergrenadier* Division, and 16th Panzer Division), in the region of Naples; and LXXVI Panzer Corps (26th Panzer Division, 29th *Panzergrenadier* Division, and the 1st *Fallschirmjäger* Division) in the far south. Once again, the mission was daunting: to disarm the Italian forces around Rome and points south. The sector around Rome itself was Kesselring's biggest worry because it included the heaviest formations in the Italian army: the *Corpo d'Armata motocorazzato* (literally a "motorized army corps," but usually described in German sources, quite rightly, as a "Panzer corps"). It included the *Centauro* and *Ariete* armored divisions, the motorized infantry division *Piave*, as well as the *Granatiere de Sardegna* ("Sardinian Grenadiers") infantry division; the XVII Corps (motorized infantry division *Piacenza*, infantry divisions *Re* and *Lupi di Toscana*, and the 220th and 221st Coastal Divisions); and the *Corpo d'Armata de Roma* (the "Rome Army Corps"), including the infantry division *Sassari*, the light infantry division *Podgora*, and an armored infantry regiment. Further to the south lay the Italian 7th Army (headquartered in Potenza), including the IX, XIX, and XXXI Corps.[19] Kesselring was also responsible for disarming Italian forces on the islands of Corsica, Sardinia, and Elba. He had the *Reichsführer-S.S.* Brigade on Corsica, as well as the 90th *Panzergrenadier* Division on Sardinia.[20] But here, too, German forces were vastly outnumbered, with two Italian corps on Sardinia (the XIII and XXX) and one on Corsica (the VII). As for Elba, it had only a single Italian coastal regiment in occupation, along with garrison troops—some 6,000 men in all. The German contingent on this beautiful little island numbered a mere 80 men, however, and they couldn't have been feeling very comfortable.[21]

We could say the same for the entire Wehrmacht in Italy. There is no German documentation to show that anyone was particularly confident that Operation Axis would go smoothly. On the contrary, the entire operation took place in a state of the highest consternation on the German side, especially with the Allies about to descend somewhere on the Italian coast. Kesselring, Rommel, and the rest thought that they could handle the Italians, and probably give a decent accounting against the Allies. No one was excited about trying to do both at the same time.

There was one last element of uncertainty. Although everyone agreed that the mission was to "disarm" the Italians, *Entwaffnung* was an undefined term at best. In the course of the operation, which commenced on the evening of September 8, *Entwaffnung* came to mean almost anything, from surrounding Italian barracks with tanks and issuing a bold *pronunciamento* demanding the surrender of the unit, to protracted negotiations between the German and Italian commanders, to German appeals to their old comrades and brothers in arms from North Africa. Kesselring used all of those stratagems in order to induce the Italian formations guarding Rome—the *Centauro* and *Ariete* armored divisions and the motorized infantry division *Piave*—to lay down their weapons on September 9, a crucial factor in keeping open the German lines of communication to the formations stranded in southern Italy.[22]

It didn't always go so peacefully, however. The first attempt by the 3rd *Panzergrenadier* Division to rush the capital came up against tough resistance at Manziana and Monterosi, and there would be fighting up and down the peninsula and in the islands: Naples, Barletta, Monterotondo, and Corsica.[23] This was low-intensity stuff, but a few spots witnessed full-scale pitched battles. The most notable was the Greek island of Cephalonia, where German mountain troops (*Gebirgsjäger*) under General Hubert Lanz had to overcome tough Italian resistance from the *Acqui* Division. The fighting here lasted until September 21, with *Acqui* surrendering and the Germans shooting thousands of Italian prisoners who fell into their hands.[24]

The Wehrmacht carried out the entire operation with maximum speed and maximum brutality—its standard calling cards. When first drawn up, Operation Axis had been a fairly sober theoretical exercise dealing with the problems that might arise as a result of an Italian surrender. Now, however, Hitler had declared the surrender to be an act of treachery, with his ire directed personally at Badoglio and the Italian king, Victor Emmanuel III.[25] What had begun as an objective operational study now morphed into what one source calls "a murderous act of revenge, marked by resentment and accentuated by racism."[26] Kesselring may appear to us as "Smiling Albert" in all those photographs and *Wochenschau* newsreels, but a smile can mask many emotions. He supposedly told an associate at the time that he "only had hatred left for the Italians,"[27] and he described the Italian capitulation as "the most dastardly treachery" and "a truce with the enemy behind our backs." Although he wasn't averse to appealing to the Italians to continue the fight against the Allies or disarming them if they refused, that is where his spirit of charity ended: "No quarter can be given to turncoats," he ordered, and urged his men to "mow down" anyone who resisted German power in Italy. Hitler rarely smiled in photographs, and no one should be surprised that his anger exceeded even that of Kesselring. As far as the Führer was concerned, the entire "clique of traitors" around Badoglio deserved to be shot.[28]

It is difficult in reading accounts of Operation Axis in action to avoid the conclusion that the Wehrmacht carried it out with an unseemly enthusiasm. If the German army were a person, we might be tempted to psychoanalyze him. Perhaps this was a case of transference, the shifting of anger from the enemy it could not really hurt to a helpless partner within easy reach. The numbers are not easy to come by, but the Germans killed somewhere between 7,000 and 12,000 Italian officers and men in the course of Operation Axis, many of them shot after they had surrendered. Moreover, the operation resulted in over 600,000 "military internees" (*Militärinternierte*), a term chosen deliberately so that their German captors could evade the rules of the Geneva Convention on the treatment of prisoners of war. Most became slaves in the armaments factories serving the Reich.[29]

Finally, the loot was prodigious. The Italian fleet got away, making for Malta and the Balearic Islands, but the Germans captured the equipment of the *Regio Esercito* and *Regia Aeronautica* nearly in toto: 977 tanks, armored cars, and assault guns; 5,568 guns; 8,736 mortars; 1,173 antitank guns; and much more.[30] Italian equipment wasn't up to the standards of the other powers, but it was good enough for a weapons-strapped Wehrmacht. Just as with previous generations of "booty weapons" (*Beutewaffen*) from Czechoslovakia in 1939 and France in 1940, Italian weaponry would play a crucial role in equipping second-line German formations and garrison troops.

The operation was a signal triumph, perhaps even the "the last victory of the German Wehrmacht," as some wags called it.[31] The question must still arise, however: Why was it so easy? The numbers were imposing enough. By the summer of 1943, there were 3,488,000 Italians in uniform in Italy, southern France, or the Balkans, facing about 600,000 Germans. After a few short days of Operation Axis, the attackers had disarmed about a million men. The other two and a half million had disappeared, seemingly without a trace. It was an unprecedented event in modern military history.

In attempting to explain the collapse, historians have customarily assigned blame to Marshal Badoglio and the king. Neither one had informed the armed forces in advance of the surrender negotiations. Secrecy was absolutely essential if the Germans were not to find out. Having delivered his belated radio announcement, Badoglio fled Rome, taking the king with him and heading for the safety of Allied lines in the south. They made good their escape, resurfacing in Brindisi a few days later.[32] It was arguably correct for the king to try and flee, as a way of maintaining some sort of political continuity, but the disappearance of the high command was a catastrophe. We cannot overestimate the surprise to the rank and file. The last time Badoglio had been on the radio was in July, just after deposing Mussolini. Back then, he had announced, "The war goes on and Italy remains faithful to its word" (*La guerra continua e l'Italia resta fedele alla parola data*).[33] He had been silent ever since. Now he had reappeared suddenly to announce that it was all over. The disappearance of higher authority left the army in the worst possible position, blindsided and leaderless, without higher orders or strategy. It also had an adversary breathing down its neck, one who was fully prepared, heavily armed, and as ruthless as they come.

Perhaps, however, the mangled surrender of Italy was the result of systemic factors, deeper reasons that go beyond personality, beyond Badoglio's double-dealing and the king's waffling. Negotiating the surrender of a wartime power was a highly complex undertaking for everyone concerned. It had to balance Italian sensibilities, Allied strategic imperatives, and the presence of the Wehrmacht all at once. The notion of treating it as a closely held affair, in essence a plot by a small cabal of Allied and Italian officers, was naive in the extreme. So was the belief that both the military forces and public opinion of a modern Western state could simply turn around on a dime in wartime. These are all factors to weigh in the balance when evaluating the Italian surrender and the lightning success of Operation Axis, and not all of them were Badoglio's fault.

In theory, surrender should be the easiest thing in the world. What happened in Italy is yet another illustration of the vast gulf separating war in theory from war in reality. Let us leave the final words on Operation Axis to the pertinent eighth volume of the German official history, *Germany and the Second World War* (*Das Deutsche Reich und der Zweite Weltkrieg*). Like all of this imposing work, the section on Operation Axis is magisterial, sober in tone, and certainly not given to overstatement or breathlessness. This is one of those times that it slips out of character, however. The attempt to work out a smooth Italian exit from the Axis and a seamless switching of sides was a worthy one, the official history argues. It collapsed, however, "in a jungle of illusion, fraud, deception, misunderstanding, incompetence, cowardice, dilettantism, and indecision."[34] That just about covers it.

Preparatory Moves: Baytown and Slapstick

The Allied invasion of Italy emerged out of a complex and protracted planning process. A little bit of choice can be a dangerous thing, and too many options can be paralyzing. With their unlimited control of the air and sea, the Allies could consider multiple scenarios, various numbers of landings, and multiple beaches. Operational schemes came and went: Musket, a landing by General Clark's entire 5th Army at Taranto; Brimstone, which had Clark hitting the beaches in Sardinia; Goblet, a landing by British V Corps at Crotone in northern Calabria; and many others.[35] None was any more or less daring than the others. All aimed prudently at southern Italy, within the range of Allied air cover flying out of Sicily. None was particularly inspired; nor was anyone particularly enthusiastic about them. The final plan for the invasion of Italy, the Baytown–Slapstick–Avalanche sequence, exploited Allied amphibious mobility, but it also bore all the hallmarks of being designed by a committee. Moreover, everyone on the committee knew that a cross-Channel invasion was on the drawing board for 1944, and that this entire theater was about to become a sideshow. Landing craft, the sine qua non of a littoral campaign, were already in short supply, necessitating sequential, as opposed to simultaneous, landings, to name just one problem.

Montgomery's 8th Army kicked things off with Operation Baytown, landing in Calabria on the very toe of the Italian boot. Until the last moment, Montgomery was telling anyone who would listen that he considered the entire operation unnecessary. He was distressed by Baytown's lack of focus: "I have been ordered to invade the mainland of the continent of Europe on the 30th August," he wrote at the time. "In the absence of information to the contrary, I must assume that some resistance will be offered by the enemy. I have been given no object for the operation. Is my object to secure the Straits for the Navy and to act as a diversion for Avalanche? If not, please define what it is."[36] Montgomery often appears in U.S. histories of the war as an insufferable blowhard, and some of his anger might come from a wounded sense of amour propre, because he was now clearly leading the secondary assault, but his questions seem reasonable enough. He knew he was landing too far away from Clark's scheduled assault at Salerno, about 150 miles away as the crow flies, but more like 300 miles of bad, twisting road in southern Italy. The two operations could in no way be complementary, he thought, which proved to be true. He also had no faith at all in the Italian surrender plans. He told Field Marshal Alexander on September 5 that "when the Germans found out what was going on, they would stamp on the Italians," which also proved to be a solid assessment.[37]

After a few days' delay, while he gathered enough landing craft, Montgomery sent his army across the Strait at 3:45 A.M. on September 3. His operational calling card had always been the cautious approach, the "infinite capacity for taking pains," as he once put it,[38] and Baytown was no different. He laid on a typical banquet of fire support: naval bombardment from destroyers lying just offshore, the Desert Air Force flying offensive patrols overhead, and a monstrous 630-gun artillery barrage paving the way for the ground troops. The two principal formations of the XIII Corps (General Miles Dempsey), the 5th Division on the left and the 1st Canadian Division on the right, now came ashore just north of Reggio Calabria.

In this case, the meticulous preparation proved to be wholly unnecessary. The initial landings struck air. German defenders were present in Calabria, elements of the 29th *Panzergrenadier* Division under General Walter Fries, but they had already begun a planned withdrawal a few days before the landing, and managed to escape the effects of the bombardment.[39] Likewise, Italian troops were in the sector, belonging to the 7th Army, but they offered no resistance, and the dozens of coastal artillery batteries in the sector—which could have smashed the landing—remained completely silent. It might be just as well; they had not been fired, quite literally, in years. German accounts have the Italian crews abandoning their guns and milling around the inland towns in the days before the invasion, and they also speak of intact wire communications "from Reggio to Messina"[40]—that is to say, ongoing contacts between Italian troops on the mainland and the Allies on Sicily. Allied air attacks targeted the Germans while avoiding Italian sites altogether. Fries's mission was not to oppose the landings, but merely to carry out demolitions and delay the British advance. His men destroyed roads, culverts, and bridges as they went, turning an already road-poor region into a primitive wasteland.[41]

As a result, Baytown soon degenerated into a series of short, time-consuming amphibious hooks up both sides of the Calabrian peninsula. It took six days for Montgomery to reach his first major objective, the Catanzaro isthmus, where there is a perceptible narrowing of the peninsula. Although an operational map shows two divisions moving abreast, with the 5th Division up the western coast of Calabria and the 1st Canadian up the eastern, the reality is that a single battalion group from each division actually moved overland, while the rest had to be shipped around the coast.[42] An amphibious landing by the 231st Brigade at Pizzo Calabro on September 8 encountered stiff resistance, and in general all of the 8th Army's operations moved far too deliberately to cut off or encircle anyone. It is equally difficult to conjure up a way that they could have moved more rapidly, however. Not until September 15 did Montgomery's formations finally break out of their potential prison in Calabria, with the 5th Infantry Division reaching Sapri on the Gulf of Policastro and the 1st Canadian Division entering Trebisacce on the eastern coast.[43]

As Montgomery struggled up out of the toe of the Italian boot, British forces carried out Operation Slapstick, a landing in the province of Apulia on the heel. Big operational targets beckoned here, especially the ports of Taranto, Brindisi, and Bari. All three could serve as convenient ports of supply for British 8th Army as it advanced up the eastern side of the Italian peninsula. Slapstick was something of an improvisation. The sequence of operations chosen by Allied operational planners left just one major formation uncommitted, the British 1st Airborne Division, but there were no available air transport assets to stage an airborne landing. Once the Italian surrender removed the Italian fleet as a strategic consideration, the British hurriedly—literally overnight—scraped together a plan to carry the division to Taranto on the ships of the 12th British Cruiser Squadron. This landing also met no opposition—quite the contrary. It was one of the few Allied operations to benefit from active Italian cooperation, and the 1st Airborne Division seized control of the port without fighting.

The German defenders were, ironically enough, the *German* 1st Airborne (*Fallschirmjäger*) Division. The divisional commander, General Richard Heidrich, already had orders from the high command of the Wehrmacht (OKW) calling for a "quick and vigorous withdrawal of land and air forces from southern Italy."[44] He skillfully withdrew from Apulia, with his rear guards making the British pay for each mile of ground and his engineers carrying out a comprehensive program of demolitions that slowed down the British even when they faced no tactical opposition. The only rough spot in the Slapstick landing was the disaster that befell the fast minesweeper *Abdiel*, which struck a mine and went down with its entire crew, as well as its load of paratroopers.[45]

Even so, Slapstick was a success, a rapid and improvised strike that deserves more attention than it usually receives. At a minimal cost in casualties, the British 1st Airborne Division was now in the operational picture. Soon it was advancing out of Apulia, seizing the major ports of Brindisi and Bari by September 14, while the German 1st Airborne retired slowly before it, burning, wrecking, and demolishing as it went.

Avalanche: Planning

The same day as Slapstick, the U.S. 5th Army was scheduled to land near Salerno, 150 miles up the western coast of Italy and 40 miles south of Naples. General Clark had two corps in the initial landing: the British X Corps on his left under General R. L. McCreery, including the British 46th and 56th Infantry Divisions; and U.S. VI Corps on his right under Major General Ernest J. Dawley, containing the U.S. 36th "Texas" Infantry Division in the initial landing, with the 45th Infantry Division in the floating reserve. McCreery's X Corps would bear the main burden of the assault because it had to land, establish itself ashore, and then wheel to the northwest and advance on the great city of Naples. To support that mission, the corps received a large complement of light troops: three battalions of U.S. Army rangers and two more of British commandos. The light troops would hold the extreme left, with the rangers landing at Maiori and seizing the Chiunzi Pass on the way to Naples, while the commandos landed at Vietri sul Mare, then wheeled southeast to take the town of Salerno itself. U.S. VI Corps was there mainly to protect the flank of the British wheel. Dawley's men would land at Paestum and advance up to the high ground overlooking the beaches from the east and south.[46]

A balanced line, two corps abreast, two divisions each: this was war by an old and traditional book. Nevertheless, the landing was destined for trouble from the start, the result of two problems that everyone in the Allied camp recognized but could find no way to solve. First of all, the chosen plain at Salerno was bisected by the Sele River, as well as its principal tributary, the Calore. The two rivers would create a gap that would separate the two assault corps at the moment of their landing. Although neither the Sele not the Calore was anyone's idea of a great river, their banks were steep, and the breadth required for the deployment of the two corps on either side of the rivers actually created a gap of nearly 10 miles. If the Germans were able to recognize the gap and exploit it with a thrust from their Panzers, they could slice the Allied bridgehead into two segments and then destroy them piecemeal. Closing the Sele gap before the enemy could take advantage of it had to be a priority for the landing force.

The second problem was the topography. Salerno was a typical European beach. One German commander described it as "a small flat plain surrounded by a crescent of steeply rising hills and mountain ranges."[47] The landing sector, in other words, formed an easily observed bowl. High ground surrounded it on all sides, putting the Allied landing forces under constant German observation. They would be easy targets for German artillery fire from the moment they left their assault craft, and unless they pushed inland rapidly and seized the high ground, they were going to stay that way. It was not an appealing operational prospectus.

It is interesting to note the pre-Avalanche discussions on the problem. Here is the pertinent volume in the U.S. Army official history discussing the "serious disadvantages" of a large-scale landing at Salerno:

> The Sele river, which empties into the gulf about 16 miles south of Salerno and divides the plain into two distinct sectors, would split the Avalanche invasion forces. The steep vertical banks of the Sele, and its principal tributary, the Calore, would hamper maneuver and require the assault troops early in the landing phase to bring ashore enough bridging to span the streams and provide communication between the two invasion forces. Mountains enclosing the Sele plain would limit the depth of the initial beachhead and expose the troops to enemy observation, fire, and attack from higher ground.

"But since there was no solution to the problem," the history concludes, "the planners simply refused to dwell on it."[48]

No trained staff officer or field commander on either side would need more than a glance at the map in order to identify the problem areas. Napoleon called it the *coup d'oeil*, the "glance of the eye" that was able to spot the key terrain on a potential battlefield. The Germans spoke of the commander's ability to recognize the *Schwerpunkt*, the point of main effort. Whichever term we use, General Clark recognized the terrain problems of the Salerno beach. So did Montgomery. So did Patton, currently enduring his Sicilian exile after the infamous slapping incidents. As the reserve commander of 5th Army, in case Clark were incapacitated or killed, Patton was briefed on the operation by the army's chief of staff on September 2. "I told him that just as sure as God lives," Patton wrote in his diary that night, "the Germans will attack down that river."[49]

The Sele gap was thus not a mistake of the Allied planners, something that a smarter commander would have avoided. Rather, it emerged from the matrix of Allied strategic planning. A challenge to the reader: put yourself into the shoes of Allied planners in 1943. You have committed to a major landing in Italy, one that requires strong air support from land-based planes in Sicily and one that needs to seize a major port south of Rome as its supply base. Add that up, and what do you get? You get a landing around Naples. Now that you've committed to Naples, find a beach broad enough to land two army corps abreast—two Western army corps, that is, fully mechanized, with all their men and equipment and accoutrement—and room for stockpiles of ammunition, fuel, and food.

Add that up, and what do you get? You get a landing in the Bay of Salerno. And once you've figured that out, and examine the sector more carefully, what do you do? You land on the stretch of beach between Salerno and Paestum. You get a beach with a meandering river right down the middle of it. You get Operation Avalanche. It is an almost classic case of the systemic factors that make war more difficult than it appears to be. Once the operation is firmly on the schedule, problems simply fall by the wayside. The planners simply refuse to dwell on them.

The news would have come as cold comfort to the poor troops tasked with the Salerno landing. Avalanche went in on September 9 in the highly confused atmosphere of the Italian surrender and the first day of Operation Axis. The peninsula was a swirl of chaos as German and Italian formations parleyed, glowered, and shot at one another. Allied commanders from Eisenhower on down had little idea of what was taking place, and one can only wonder at the impact on morale of the decision to broadcast the announcement of the armistice with Italy to the troops on board the invasion fleet. It only seemed to bewilder them, and their commanders at all levels had to make it clear that whatever the men might be thinking, the invasion of Italy had not been canceled.[50]

Avalanche: Operations

Operation Avalanche was a milestone, the first big U.S.-directed operation of the war, a test to see whether the young American army and its commanders were up to the challenge of planning and spearheading a complex amphibious operation. The results were not encouraging, and even the U.S. commander, General Clark, would later describe it as a "near disaster."

The landings went in at 3:30 A.M. Launched against what was hoped to be light Italian fire, they instead ran into fierce German opposition from the start. A huge body of literature lays all the problems at Clark's feet, and the indictment usually leads off with his decision to dispense with the preliminary bombardment in order to achieve surprise. German defensive fire on the beaches was heavy, U.S. assault troops had to navigate a storm of bullets and shell fire as they approached the beach, and losses were heavy. Clark actually claimed that the Germans rigged up a loudspeaker and shouted, "Come on in and give yourselves up. We have you covered." The story is almost certainly apocryphal, but it does say something about the intensity of the defensive fire.[51]

Just for the record, however, omitting the opening bombardment was not something that Clark himself had invented. In mid-1943, Anglo-American planning circles were giving a great deal of thought to the problems of large-scale amphibious warfare. They had already staged two opposed landings, and they all knew that the big one, the cross-Channel invasion, was going to be taking place in 1944. A number of ideas were floating in the air about how best to achieve surprise and carry out a successful landing with the least loss of life. A rapid strike without much in the way of preliminary shellfire was one of those ideas.[52] Like a lot of theoretical notions, this one failed to pan out. It joined a long list of other failed doctrines—from Italy's "binary division" to U.S. daylight strategic bombing by unescorted B-17s or General Lesley McNair's enthusiasm for the tank destroyer. Although all of them were wrong turns, perhaps, on the eventual path to victory in World War II, that is not to say that they were ridiculous.

The real problem at Salerno after the first few hours was not the lack of bombardment. Rather, it was a simple matter of force levels. There were only three Allied divisions in the initial landing (the 46th and 56th British and the 36th U.S), as compared to the seven that had landed in Operation Husky. Defending the beaches at Salerno was a full-strength German Panzer division (the 16th, destroyed at Stalingrad and now rebuilt under the command of General Rudolf Sieckenius), further reinforced by antitank and antiaircraft guns. Stationing his division near Eboli and Battipaglia on the high ground overlooking the Salerno plain, Sieckenius faced a tough task. He had to guard no less than 25 miles of beach with a single division, but also needed to retain some capability for a mobile counterstrike. To take care of the first mission, he dug eight strongpoints (*Stützpunkte*) along his front between Salerno and Agropoli—deep trenches, machine gun positions, and wire, each manned by a single infantry platoon. Although we can hardly say they constituted a line, they would delay whatever happened to land in front of them. At the same time, however, he formed four mobile *Kampf-gruppen*, each consisting of a battalion of infantry supported by tanks and artillery. He deployed three of them within a mile or two of the beach, while retaining a fourth in division reserve, well inland.[53] The artillery was emplaced on high ground, so it could look down on any landing force hitting the beach.

The 16th Panzer Division was overstretched at Salerno. Neverthe-less, Sieckenius's deployment of the division managed to balance posi-tional defense, maneuver potential, and firepower, and it demonstrated the flexibility of a Panzer division under the leadership of a veteran commander. The division spent the first day of the landing launching small counterattacks, spearheaded by groups of five to seven tanks, sometimes with their supporting infantry, but more often alone. At no time did the 16th Panzer threaten "to throw the invaders into the sea," in the classic formulation.[54] It did manage to unhinge the Allied land-ing schedule and limit the depth of the initial beachhead, however.

On the negative side for the Germans, the Panzers proved once again to be no match for Allied firepower. As always, it came from a variety of sources. The characteristic Allied calling card of naval gunfire put in an appearance, in this case the 6-inch guns of the cruisers U.S.S. *Philadelphia* and U.S.S. *Savannah*, and Allied aircraft flying from Sicily and from the decks of five British aircraft carriers prowled the skies over the beachhead relentlessly.[55] The badly outnumbered Luftwaffe did put in an occasional appearance over the battlefield in the course of the first day, but the German soldiers and tank crews on the ground could be forgiven for not noticing. As one analyst puts it, "the only effective tactic for the German was to slip in at high speed, fire rock-ets and drop the bombs at all likely targets, and run away at high speed."[56] Both General Clark and the U.S. official history were critical of the German defenders for not using "their armor in mass very early in the day" and for employing "piecemeal efforts" on the beach.[57] The criticisms are correct, as far as they go. It is difficult to attack successfully while dispersed. High levels of defensive firepower have a way of doing that, however, enforcing dispersion as a means of survival, whatever the commander's intent may be. The Wehrmacht had already learned on the beaches of Sicily to take U.S. firepower seriously. As it was, the 16th Panzer Division lost two thirds of its armor in the course of the day. By nightfall, Sieckenius had only 35 tanks still operational and decided to order his division into a defensive position well inland (from Bellizzi through Persano to Capaccio), where he could monitor the Allied buildup but stay out of the range of the Allied guns.[58]

German analysts usually view Salerno as a four-phase battle.[59] The first had been 16th Panzer Division's fight on the beaches on September 9, a successful delaying action purchased at the cost of a great deal of the division's armor. The second phase, September 10–11, was a consolidation and reinforcement phase for both sides. The Allies sought to broaden and deepen their beachhead, pushing out against stiff German opposition, landing portions of the 45th Division out of the floating reserve along with small elements of British 7th Armoured Division. To the Germans, the size of the landing at Salerno—involving nearly 600 warships in all, along with several thousand aircraft—had made it clear that this was no diversionary effort, but a *Grosslandung*, an operation in the grand style.[60] Almost immediately, elements of two more German divisions were rushing to the landing site to join the 16th Panzer. These were old friends whom the Allies had fought in Sicily, the 1st Parachute Panzer Division Hermann Göring and the 15th *Panzergrenadier* Division, with all three divisions making up the XIV Panzer Corps.[61] Its old commander, the redoubtable Hans Hube, was on a four-week furlough at the time of the U.S. landing, and taking his place would be another formidable personality, General Hermann Balck. Soon another corps joined the fray, the LXXVI Panzer Corps, under General Traugott Herr, coming up from Calabria and Apulia with two more divisions, the 26th Panzer and the 29th *Panzergrenadier*. Together, the XIV and LXXVI Panzer Corps made up the German 10th Army, under General Heinrich Vietinghoff. Finally, now that the Germans had sorted out the touchy situation at Rome, the 3rd *Panzergrenadier* Division had become available, and it too was barreling down the road toward Salerno. At Salerno, in sum, the Wehrmacht's local surge capacity managed to outstrip the Allies in the two crucial days of September 10 and 11. Soon, three Allied divisions were fighting elements of six German ones. No one should be surprised that it turned into a tough fight, however we may wish to assess Mark Clark's generalship.

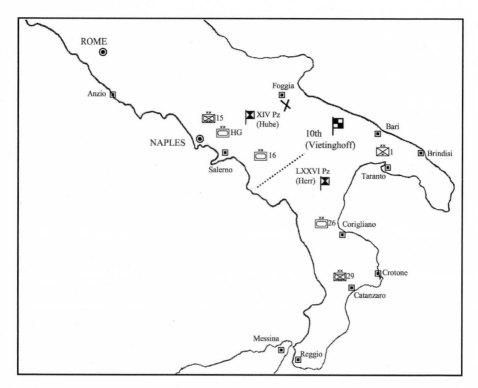

Trouble for the Allies: German Forces in Southern Italy (September 1943)

Like the entire Wehrmacht by this point in the war, the combat power here was less than it appeared to be. All the divisions were understrength, and three had been through the recent mauling in Sicily and were still deep in the rebuilding process. The Hermann Göring Division could call on just 25 serviceable tanks, for example, and had not yet rebuilt its *Panzergrenadier* regiment. Vietinghoff took two battalions of infantry away from the 1st Airborne Division and attached them to the Göring Division—a stopgap that did nothing for unit cohesion. The other formations were having their own problems. The 15th *Panzergrenadier* had only seven tanks, and the 26th Panzer Division should have an asterisk next to its name in the record books: it had no tanks at all. Nevertheless, the Germans at Salerno were still a force to be reckoned with, and much of that was due to the corps commanders. Both Herr and Hube were recent veterans of the hyperintense fighting on the Eastern Front in 1942. As commander of the 16th Panzer Division

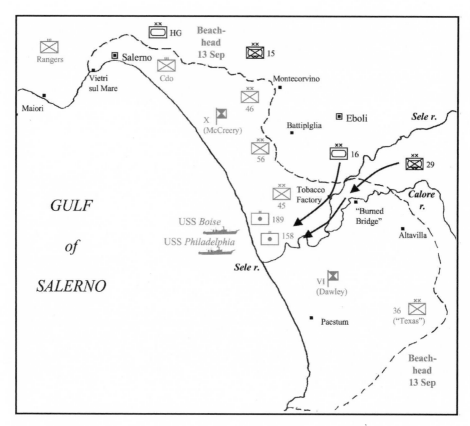

Big Trouble: Salerno (September 13, 1943)

during Operation Blue, Hube had spearheaded the drive from the Don to the Volga, and he had successfully defended a narrow corridor from heavy Soviet tank assaults coming at him from all directions.[62] Herr had commanded the 13th Panzer Division during the Caucasus campaign and had been in on the final drive toward the key gateway city of Ordzhonikidze.[63] Balck had led the 11th Panzer Division during its hectic defensive stand along the Chir River in the aftermath of Stalingrad and later took over the XXXXVIII Panzer Corps.[64] Beyond that, all three were hard-charging commanders who led from the front. Herr and Hube, in particular, had paid a heavy price for it in the course of their careers: Hube had lost an arm in World War I, and Herr had suffered a head injury during the fight for Ordzhonikidze.

As the other divisions arrived to join the 16th Panzer, phase three of the Salerno battle began. This was without a doubt the most dangerous moment for the Americans in the entire war thus far. They were sitting in a bad situation, an infantry division and a half perched on a flat plain, a bit unsteady, with their backs to the sea in a frail and bifurcated bridgehead. In front of them was a situation that the Germans could not have drawn up any better in a sand-table *Kriegsspiel*: a solid line of two Panzer corps abreast, XIV Panzer on the right and LXXVI Panzer on the left, arrayed in classic *konzentrisch* fashion around the bridgehead, with two tough and ruthless commanders just waiting for the "go" signal. The Germans spent September 12 sending out reconnaissance probes, edging forward out of Altavilla and Battipaglia, and finally realizing the true vulnerability of the Sele gap. Vietinghoff was apparently dumbfounded that the Allies had "split themselves into two sections."[65] There was no doubt in his mind, or in the minds of Herr or Balck or Kesselring himself, that they all stood on the verge of a great victory at Salerno.

The next day, September 13, Vietinghoff lowered the boom. Three divisions—the 16th Panzer, 29th *Panzergrenadier*, and 26th Panzer—now launched themselves into a full-blown counteroffensive against the Salerno bridgehead, targeting the seam between British X Corps and U.S. VI Corps. The focus of the fighting quickly became the so-called tobacco factory, a solid group of five brick buildings overlooking the Sele River.[66] The U.S. defenders were badly strung out. The 36th Division was holding an incredible 35 miles of front, its "line" was little more than a series of disconnected outposts in most places, and the Germans were able to penetrate it almost anywhere they chose. The *Schwerpunkt* of the attack was the Sele–Calore corridor. Here, elements of the 16th Panzer Division hit the 2nd Battalion, 143rd Infantry Regiment hard on both flanks and essentially scattered it, inflicting 500 casualties and taking hundreds of prisoners. The 45th Division, while still not completely landed, was meanwhile attempting a tricky sidestep to the left to make contact with the British X Corps. With one division vastly overstretched and the other making a difficult lateral move under enemy fire, it was inevitable that the force of the German attack would crack the American position wide open. By 5:15 P.M., the Panzers had broken into the clear, heading for the sea. All that now stood in their way was the U.S. gun line, howitzers of the 189th and 158th Field Artillery Battalions, along with a handful of recently landed tank destroyers of the 636th Tank Destroyer Battalion.

The bridgehead hung in the balance at this point, and it might well have fallen were it not for a single humble feature of the terrain: a burned bridge over the Calore River. It halted what had been a full-bore drive of 29th *Panzergrenadier* Division, and there are at least a few witnesses who claimed to have seen German commanders dismounting from their tanks and consulting their maps at this point.[67] There are other ways over the Calore, but the pause lasted just long enough to give U.S. gunners time to open up and pour on destructive fire. However unsteady U.S. infantry and armor was in this phase of the war—and Salerno indicates that there were still big problems—there had never been anything wrong with the guns. Their fire halted the German drive, and just in time, too. A few hundred yards behind the batteries and tank destroyers was Clark's 5th Army command post, defended by a hastily formed line of what the U.S. official history calls "miscellaneous headquarter troops—cooks, clerks, and drivers."[68]

Nevertheless, it had been a hard day of fighting, and the issue was still in doubt. As night fell, some of the Panzers were only a mile and a half from the sea. To German army commander Vietinghoff, it seemed that the attacks had successfully crumpled the bridgehead, and that the Allies were about to reembark.[69] "The battle of Salerno appears to be over," reads the 10th Army "war diary" (*Kriegstagebuch*) for September 13. Vietinghoff was even more explicit in a message to Kesselring:

> After a defensive battle lasting four days, enemy resistance is collapsing. Tenth Army pursuing on a wide front. Heavy fighting still in process near Salerno and Altavilla. Maneuver in process to cut off the retreating enemy from Paestum.[70]

His enthusiasm wasn't completely contagious, however. His corps commanders Balck and Herr had been under Allied fire that day, a lot of it, and they were not quite so sure they had the enemy on the run.

Just a few thousand yards away from the Germans, however, the commander of the "retreating enemy," General Clark, was spending a worried night. He had called the VI Corps commander, General Dawley, his division commanders (Major General Fred Walker for the 36th Division and Major General Troy Middleton for the 45th), and his staff to his command post for consultation and discussion about what to do next. "It was obvious," he later wrote, "that we had barely escaped disaster."[71] It had been a hard day for everyone in the bridgehead. While the British had put up a stout resistance, attacks by the Hermann Göring and 15th *Panzergrenadier* Divisions had punched their way into Vietri sul Mare and threatened to split the main force from the rangers fighting to the west at Monte de Chiunzi, and there were no reserves to be had. That was nothing, however, compared to the plight of VI Corps. Here is Clark's assessment:

> [We] were most urgently in need of reorganization before we could withstand another attack. Elements of the 142nd and 143rd RCTs (regimental combat teams) had been thrown back from Altavilla; Company K, 143rd, was cut off; the 1st Battalion of the 142nd had lost all but sixty of its men; the 2nd Battalion, 143rd, had been beaten up in the Sele–Calore corridor and lost 508 officers and men; and the 157th's 1st Battalion had been badly bruised west of Persano, where the Germans had seized the key tobacco factory buildings on high ground.[72]

He knew he was holding little more than a "clawhold" on the continent. That night he gave serious thought to evacuating the bridgehead and to making preparations for demolition of supplies. Operation Sealion, it would have been called. Many have accused him of having a case of the jitters, and his memoirs are unnecessarily defensive about his actions on the beach. "I knew that if I was involved in a theoretical problem at the War College, I would at this point get hell from some instructor if I failed to issue orders to be prepared for possible destruction of those supplies." He was absolutely correct, and although he is probably dissembling when he says he never even discussed the possibilities with his staff, his judgment was correct in the end. "This wasn't a theoretical problem, and I couldn't see how I'd do anything but damage morale if I issued such orders at Salerno. . . . I decided, the only way they're going to get us off this beach is to push us, step by step, into the water." He also briefly considered reembarking VI Corps and shifting it to the British beaches north of the Sele River, a maneuver that would have gone by the name of Operation Seatrain. It would have erased the Sele gap problem, but only by creating dozens of other ones, such as how to load down the landing craft with men and supplies without beaching them, and how to do so under direct enemy fire. In the end, he decided to drop that plan too.[73]

He did make a number of decisions, however, that showed that he was at the very least still struggling to stay on top of an emergency situation. Even before the German Panzers had launched their attack on the morning of the 13th, he had already ordered an emergency drop directly onto the beachhead by the 2nd Battalion, 504th Parachute Infantry Regiment (82nd Airborne Division), the same sort of instant reinforcement Patton had used in much less dire circumstances in

Sicily. They would arrive late that night, just before midnight. He also ordered a second airborne drop, this one behind German lines at Avellino in the British sector by the 2nd Battalion of the 509th Parachute Infantry Regiment. Its mission was to disrupt German communications and block any more German reinforcements from reaching the beachhead.

Finally, it was probably that night that he decided to relieve the commander of the VI Corps, Dawley, although he thought it best to wait until the immediate crisis had eased. During the height of the fighting on September 13, Clark had gotten a telephone call from Dawley. It was the very moment of the breakthrough, and German troops were fanning out into VI Corps's rear areas. "What are you doing about it?" Clark had asked. "Nothing," Dawley answered. "I have no reserves. All I've got is a prayer."[74] Dawley would stay in command until September 20, but that was enough time for Eisenhower to visit the bridgehead. By now it was clear that the storm had subsided and that the Allies had survived their ordeal. Eisenhower still wasn't pleased, however; during a briefing from Dawley, the supreme commander whirled on him and hissed, "For God's Sake, Mike! How did you manage to get your troops so fucked up?"[75] Beyond questions of Dawley's personal fitness lies a simple observation. There had only been four U.S. corps commanders in this theater: generals Lloyd Fredendall, George Patton, Omar Bradley, and now Dawley. Eisenhower had fired two of them and had a third currently cooling his heels in Sicily. Apparently "the conduct of battle," what the Germans call *Kampfführung*,[76] was a more difficult job in this army than we like to admit.

No one could know it, but the tide of this battle had already turned. By September 14, the Allies in the Salerno bridgehead were already deep in the process of assembling a true avalanche of men and firepower that would all but destroy their attackers in the course of the next few days. Reinforcements were on the way. The third regiment of the 45th Division (the 180th) arrived during the day, and the 3rd Division was on the way up from Sicily. The British 7th Armoured Division also began to land in X Corps sector. Along with the two drops already mentioned, Clark ordered another airborne drop directly onto the bridgehead, this one involving the 505th Parachute Infantry Regiment. If the Germans had won the battle of the surge on September 10 and 11, the Allies had won a decisive victory by the 14th.[77]

More than the reinforcements, it was firepower that proved to be the margin of victory for the Allies at Salerno. The day before, Eisenhower had requested the use of strategic bombers at Salerno. These huge multiengine craft, designed to smash entire German cities, now arrived to play a tactical role over this relatively tiny battlefield. Over 500 bombers (187 B-25s, 166 B-26s, and 170 B-17 "Flying Fortresses") spent the day plastering the narrow Battipaglia–Eboli–Ponte Sele corridor, the assembly point for any renewed German assault. Joining in the mayhem were the 15-inch guns of two British battleships, H.M.S. *Warspite* and H.M.S. *Valiant*, which the commander in chief of the Mediterranean fleet, Admiral Andrew Cunningham, had ordered north from Malta. Joining them from the United States were the U.S.S. *Philadelphia* and the U.S.S. *Boise*. Roaming just off the mouth of the Sele, *Philadelphia* fired over a thousand 6-inch rounds at point-blank ranges, and *Boise* would come close to that number.[78] Further, more and more artillery was landing, until it seemed that the beachhead could hold no more. During the fighting on the 13th alone, for example, U.S. artillery fired 3,650 rounds in just four hours of action, and the totals over the next few days would dwarf that one.

While still in the mountains, the Germans were fairly safe from this hurricane of fire. Once they tried to maneuver down onto the plain, however, they ran into a wall of steel and never really got untracked. Their first attack on September 14, for example, involved elements of the 16th Panzer and 29th *Panzergrenadier* Divisions. Beginning at 8:00 A.M., it was a probe, eight tanks and a battalion of infantry. Within minutes, U.S. fire had destroyed seven tanks and immobilized the eighth. In the course of the day, German positions in the corridor, at Altavilla, and Eboli, and Battipaglia, were essentially flattened, and so were the towns themselves. General Walker advanced through Altavilla after the battle, and even he was shocked at the fate of the old town. "Not a single building was intact," he said. "The town will have to be rebuilt. It cannot be repaired."[79]

If there was one shared memory on the German side of the battle of Salerno, it was the Allied naval bombardment. Every memoir mentions it. It not only laid on the high explosive, but also it gave the soldier on land the queasy feeling of being part of an unequal struggle. "Especially unpleasant," wrote an officer of the Hermann Göring Division, in a classic understatement.[80] General Balck, commanding XIV Panzer Corps, complained in his memoirs of "the heavy naval artillery, to which we had no answer" (*dem wir nichts entgegensetzen konnten*).[81]

German losses in all this were terrific, and by September 14, pressure against the beachhead began to slacken perceptibly. After a day of regrouping, Vietinghoff ordered one last German attack on September 16, with two battalions of the newly arrived 26th Panzer Division linking up with the Hermann Göring Division to hit the British in Salerno. They had barely gotten underway when British fire of all kinds—artillery, naval, tanks—stopped them in their tracks. They had made two hundred yards in exchange for massive casualties: bad math for the Wehrmacht.

It is precisely this characteristic—incessant waves of enemy fire making maneuver impossible—that most impressed Wehrmacht officers who had to fight the Western armies. They might occasionally sniff that U.S. soldiers were soft or loved their lives too deeply or lacked aggressiveness. General Sieckenius of the 16th Panzer Division noted a lack of imagination and a tendency to reject "daring thrusts."[82] As Rommel had learned at El Alamein, however, it wasn't easy to face an army that had an unlimited supply of ammunition, that could afford around-the-clock bombing, and that could use naval vessels to shoot up tanks. In many ways, Italy was second-rate war making—a nonstrategic theater, limited opportunities for maneuver, no sense of the back being to the wall, two forces fighting over someone else's home.[83] Both sides knew it. In 1943, all the great battles were taking place deep inside the Soviet Union. The fighting in Italy would be no less fierce, however, and the levels of firepower were ungodly. No less an authority than the OKW, the high command of the German Wehrmacht, had no problem equating the two fronts. The battle for Italy was no sideshow, it wrote, but a "great struggle" (*Grosskampf*) that in many respects surpassed even the "harshness of the battles in the east."[84]

That storm of Allied fire at Salerno, and especially the nearly limitless power of American industry that stood behind it, had been yet another learning moment for the Wehrmacht. It had gone to school in 1942 at El Alamein against the British, and then another, even harder school at Stalingrad against the Soviet army. Now, at Salerno, it had come up against yet another army—clumsy, lacking finesse and elegance, but apparently in love with high explosives—that it could not vanquish. It was yet another way of war for which it could not formulate an effective response.

In the course of this battle, the Wehrmacht had gone through its entire impressive set of moves: rapid response, lightning maneuver, concentric attack. It had been an unsettling experience for U.S. Army commanders at all levels. Perhaps it had reawakened nightmares of a previous encounter at Kasserine, but Salerno was much worse: an army fighting with the sea at its back. To Vietinghoff, Balck, and Herr, it must have seemed like a master schooling a novice in some arcane martial art, until the novice remembered to fire.

The U.S. Army at Salerno

Superior Allied firepower had triumphed at Salerno. But what can we say of the U.S. Army beyond a demonstrated ability to blow things up? In most military histories, "superior firepower" is a coded insult to an army's quality. Certainly U.S. war making had displayed a range of problems at Salerno. The planning at all levels had been slipshod, a result of inexperience more than anything. Nothing that it had gone through in North Africa or Sicily had prepared it for what it ran into in Operation Avalanche. It had to come up to speed overnight, but that wasn't easy when it was operating in a theater that never really had the full attention of its commanders. It was well known that no one, especially the U.S. Army chief of staff, General George Marshall, really wanted to be there. Making things worse by the time of the Salerno landing, a theater that had started as plan B was receding further in importance. The real brains in the U.S. Army were now planning the Overlord landing. As a result, Salerno threw inexperienced U.S. manpower against the veterans of the Wehrmacht. The defenders were hardly supermen, but they had fought the Soviets in a variety of times and places, and they were used to suppressing the urge to flee.

Certainly, the U.S. Army had been inept at times in 1943. The infantry formations tended to panic under tank attack, just like inexperienced infantry the world over. The coordination of the arms was uniformly poor. It won battles, but only after the infantry had gotten out of the way, usually by being overrun and creating a clear field of fire for the guns. In this period of its evolution, it had to rely on extraordinary measures like strategic bombing and naval gunfire to save it from its tactical failures. Then again, it could afford to do so, so no one should really view this as a problem.

Was bad generalship an issue at Salerno? Perhaps. Clark's presents us with a classic historical question, and judging him is a tough call. It has not been easy to find many historians saying good things about him.[85] The indictment is a lengthy one. He was a blatant careerist and a glory hog whose ambition exceeded all bounds, even in a career (generalship within the U.S. Army) that is practically defined by overweening ambition. He was a man who cared more about public relations and cultivating a heroic image than he did about actual war fighting. He was a general who only let photographers shoot his good side (his left, for the record).[86] He was cocky to the point of arrogance, dubbed by some cynical subordinates "Marcus Aurelius Clarkus."[87] He was peremptory with his subordinates. He was inexperienced, and he jumped up over more experienced and deserving officers. He was a hard-core Anglophobe, distrusting his British allies while commanding a campaign in which inter-Allied cooperation was essential. It goes on and on, and the arguments deserve careful consideration.

At the same time, the historian cannot resist the temptation to exclaim, "Really?" Was Clark actually more of an egotistical glory hound than General Patton? Was he really more interested in cultivating his own image than Field Marshal Rommel? No one loved war photographers more than the Desert Fox. Was he really promoted too rapidly? Compared to Eisenhower? In February 1941, Eisenhower had been a lieutenant colonel. Two short years later, he was a four-star general, perhaps the world's record for rapid promotion. Just by way of comparison, Clark had been a lieutenant colonel in July 1941 and a three-star general by November 1942. The point that is easy to miss here is this: in an army expanding as rapidly as this one was, going from zero to flat out in just two years, just about every officer was going to be promoted early.[88]

When it comes down to it, few of these personal accusations against Clark hold water. They are a form of ad hominem argument, directed against the man rather than being grounded in the facts of the matter. In any organization as large as the U.S. Army, certain individuals are bound to be more popular than others. In any field of endeavor, anyone promoted as rapidly as Clark had been was going to have his detractors. It happens in civilian as well as military life.

Salerno certainly tested Clark. He appeared at times to be overwhelmed, and he has paid for his indiscretions with a great deal of bad press. But we should point out that he spent the night of September 13 doing what he had to do: taking stock and taking a sober view of things. He also spent two full and difficult days—September 13 and 14—rotating between his command post and tours of the front, where he braved heavy enemy fire to rally the troops. Each reader will have to make a personal decision on his worth as a commander; historians seem wedded to a one-sided view. Perhaps Clark's real problem was this: it was his fate to command an army in the Mediterranean, a theater that had already proved to be a graveyard of American military reputations, rather than Western Europe a year later, where all the commanders miraculously wound up looking pretty good.

Finally, Salerno showed an army that still tended to overplan, to overthink things, and to conduct operations that may have briefed well but were overwrought and had a tendency to turn into disaster. It often seems as if the main purpose of the U.S. Army's operations in 1943 was to establish the bona fides of the airborne arm, whether the operations made sense or not. The landing at Avellino on September 14 was yet another example of a half-baked parachute drop. The reasons why should be eminently familiar by now: overly hasty preparation that allowed some of the commanders a mere two hours to study the map; inexplicable navigational errors; ineffective radar; high winds; high altitude. Like all the previous drops, this one scattered badly, with some men landing 25 miles away from their intended drop zones. Only 15 of the 40 transport planes dropped their men within five miles of Avellino. Once they were on the ground, the paratroopers found that the rough terrain made it difficult to reassemble the force. For the next few days, these highly trained personnel, representing a significant U.S. military investment, spent most of their energy trying to evade German patrols. Although some of the battalion was able to trickle back through German lines to safety, the Avellino drop had no operational impact whatsoever.[89] In the end, it didn't really matter—perhaps the greatest operational indictment of them all.

Conclusion: After Salerno

Knowing now that he could not destroy the Allied bridgehead, and with Montgomery's 8th Army finally coming up out of Calabria, Vietinghoff began to disengage his forces. Phase four of the battle, the German withdrawal from Salerno, now began. It had been a bewildering couple of weeks for the Wehrmacht's commanders. The Allies had survived a crisis at Salerno, but the Germans had survived an entire series of them: handling the defection of Italy, disarming three million Italian soldiers, and defending against no fewer than three Allied amphibious landings. Now it was time to take stock.

The primary question for the German leadership was where to hold the line in Italy. A command dispute that had been simmering ever since the fall of Sicily now came to a head. German forces in Italy were under two separate commands, Rommel's Army Group B (headquartered at Garda in northern Italy) and Kesselring's OB-Süd command, headquartered at Frascati, just south of Rome. The bifurcated command had worked about as well as might be expected—that is to say, badly. From his perch up north, Rommel recommended abandoning all of central and southern Italy and concentrating German forces in the north. Holding the southern marches of a long, narrow peninsula against an enemy with absolute control of the sea made no sense to him.

Any Allied landing high up on the boot threatened to cut off German forces stationed in the south. The Wehrmacht had already lost one army group at Tunis, and Rommel warned against losing another one. It would be better to defend high up in the boot, at Pisa or perhaps even further north. The only thing worth defending in Italy, he thought, was the Po River valley, Italy's main population and resource center. Some officers on his staff wanted to retreat to the Alps and build a defensive line there that would be all but invulnerable.

Rival commander Kesselring argued just the opposite. The Allies wouldn't go deep in their initial landings, he was certain. Air power was too important to their success, and they would never land outside their own umbrella. Although it is common to attribute his point of view to his relentless optimism, he also had good arguments on his side. The best place to defend Italy was at its "waist" (*Taille*) south of Rome, where the peninsula was at its narrowest and would need a smaller commitment of German divisions.[90] His own staff had done studies calculating a requirement of just nine divisions in the line and two in reserve, a much smaller force than Rommel would need to hold in the north.

It was an intriguing strategic debate, with pros and cons on both sides, seasoned by a great deal of personal animosity between Rommel and Kesselring, snippy comments, and moments of wounded vanity. Hitler blew this way and that, as always, "schwankte lange hin und her," in the words of Kesselring's capable chief of staff, General Siegfried Westphal.[91] To be fair, the Führer had reasons to hesitate. This was late August, and the almost intolerable tensions of the moment—with the defeat at Kursk and the Soviet hammer blows against Orel and Belgorod—had put Italy on the back burner for the moment. The virtual collapse of the Wehrmacht's line in the east, however, didn't bode well for assuming a bold forward position in Italy. Consequently, he first inclined toward Rommel's more conservative proposal. As his relationship with the field commanders in the east continued to deteriorate, however, Kesselring's recommendation must have sounded like music to his ears. Finally, he had a commander who wanted to stand and fight, who wasn't obsessed with "operating," and who wasn't pestering him for permission to retreat.

The easing of the crisis in Italy, along with the relatively conservative Allied landing at Salerno, had proven Kesselring right, much to the field marshal's relief. Hitler now came around. Kesselring's stock began to go up, and in November, he finally received his own field command, Army Group C, giving him operational control of all German forces in Italy. Under his unified command, the Wehrmacht would make its stand well south of Rome. It was an aggressive, in-your-face declaration of intent, given the context of a strategic defensive in a relatively minor theater.

Kesselring's decision to fight in the south set the parameters for the long, bloody campaign to follow. Using Salerno as its "pivot" (*Angelpunkt*), German 10th Army now swung back from Salerno and occupied the first of a seemingly endless series of defensive lines stretching across the Italian boot from the Tyrrhenian Sea in the west to the Adriatic Sea in the east: "security lines" (*Sicherungslinien*), then "resistance lines" (*Widerstandslinien*), and finally full-blown, heavily fortified defensive "positions" (*Stellungen*).[92] Step by step, the 10th Army retreated to the north, first occupying Security Lines 1, 2, and 3, then resistance lines Zero and Viktor, and ultimately the Bernhard and Gustav positions. Several of these would become famous in the west: the Viktor line had its western anchor along the Volturno River and meandered across the peninsula to Termoli on the Adriatic, and thus became immortal in U.S. military histories as the Volturno line. The Bernhard position used the Garigliano River as its main barrier in the west and became the Garigliano line. The *Gustav-Stellung* became the most famous of all, bending back to the Rapido River and passing through the Apennines just in front of a town—and a forbidding monastery—called Cassino.

The Allies spent the rest of the war trying to punch through these lines, advancing inch by inch up the Italian boot against tenacious German defenders. It was hard, bloody fighting, essentially one frontal assault after another. The Italian peninsula has a rocky spine, the Apennine mountains, and literally hundreds of rivers, gullies, and gorges radiate out to both coasts, each one of them forming a perfect defensive line. The Germans would make a stand on one position, prepare another to the rear, then retreat when Allied pressure had compromised their line. Terrain and climate ruled here. The small breadth of the front strangled opportunities for maneuver, the mountains and rainy weather served as force multipliers for the defense, and the inadequate road network made concentration or *Schwerpunkt* building practically impossible. Italy was a defensive tactician's dream, and a nightmare for the attacker.

On the operational level, by contrast, the theater was "Warfare 101." Two allied armies were moving abreast, Clark's 5th Army in the west and Montgomery's 8th in the east. The German 10th Army stretched across the peninsula in front of them, anchored firmly on each coast and passing through the high Apennines. The array rarely changed:

XIV Panzer Corps along the Tyrrhenian coast, LXXVI Panzer Corps in the center, and the XI Airborne Corps (*Fliegerkorps*) holding the Adriatic flank. The theater was small enough to allow the aficionado to memorize the designation of each division on both sides. It was an operational problem without a solution, especially with the Allies starving their armies in Italy to feed the demands of planning for Operation Overlord. As a result, the 1943 fighting was destined to wind up as a static war of position (*Stellungskrieg*).

Kesselring would earn a reputation as a defensive genius for managing to hold onto Italy until the end of the war. A typical modern evaluation in the English-language literature describes him in glowing terms as a "decisive commander":

> Kesselring established himself as a master of the defensive who was able time and again to thwart Allied aims in the Mediterranean with significantly smaller forces. . . . His imprint of the battle for Tunisia had been minimal, but this changed dramatically when the fighting shifted to Italy. The prolonged German defense of Italy was a product of Kesselring's genius for defensive operations. Throughout that campaign it was Kesselring who dictated German strategy by the firm exercise of command and by his ability to shrewdly maneuver his forces against the Allies.[93]

Another labels him a "master of defensive warfare," a commander with "an instinctive feel for battle," a general "able to inflict maximum damage on the enemy before withdrawing to fight another day."[94] Still others claim that he was "as good a general as emerged from the German army in the Second World War."[95]

Every single one of these claims is dubious, however. Let us start with the operational simplicity. Defending the Italian boot against an opponent grinding his way up from the south was probably the easiest item in the entire operational playbook of World War II. "Able time and again to thwart the Allies in the Mediterranean"? Hardly. His supreme command had resulted in disaster in Tunis and the quick abandonment of Sicily. "Instinctive feel for battle"? At Salerno, this Napoleonic (and arguably antique) notion had come up against 15-inch naval shell fire and carpet bombing by B-17s. "Ability to shrewdly maneuver his forces"? He brought a great deal of experience—ten years' worth—of Luftwaffe command on the operational level, but this was a campaign virtually without maneuver. Kesselring was able to shift around battalions and regiments to fit the demands of an updated form of trench warfare, certainly. But a master of maneuver? Hardly. Finally, the notion that he inflicted "maximum damage on the enemy" and then shrewdly withdrew his forces to fight again is utterly false. Counting the totals from the entire length of the Italian campaign, the Allies would suffer 312,000 casualties, splitting that total among a vast array of separate national contingents: Americans, British, Commonwealth (Canadians, New Zealanders, South Africans, Indians), a French expeditionary corps, a Polish corps of two divisions, a Jewish brigade of volunteers from Palestine, a Greek brigade, and even a formation from Brazil, the 1st Infantry Division. These were high losses for a nondecisive theater, and no one should ever downplay them. The German casualty figure, however, serves to place them in perspective. Kesselring presided over the loss of no fewer than 415,615 men, all of them, it should be said, German.[96] Even as a limited campaign of delay and attrition, the German defense of Italy was an utter failure.

Italy was a campaign that no one had really wanted. The Werhmacht had better things to do with its spare forces. A commitment of 11 divisions, while seemingly quite modest, adds up to a full field army. It was something that the collapsing Eastern Front could have used desperately. The Anglo-American armies had come to Italy to overthrow Mussolini, to destroy the Axis, and to stay busy while they readied Operation Overlord. The high command of the U.S. army, in particular, had no wish to get bogged town in positional fighting in Italy. With the Allies now in Italy in force, however, and the Wehrmacht making a pugnacious stand well below Rome, both sides had to face the fact: they had a campaign on their hands. War often forces both sides to do things they don't want, but never was that more true than in Italy in 1943. It was the unloved campaign.

Check that. There was one powerful figure who actually did want to fight in Italy, who reveled in it, and who kept the faith to the end: Kesselring himself. In the end, his boast that he could defend Italy created this horrible campaign. No reasonable person denies an army's right to defend itself. Kesselring's decision, however, needs to be viewed within the long-term history of German war making. Since the age of Frederick the Great in the eighteenth century, Prussian commanders had attempted to fight wars that were "short and lively" (*kurtz und vives*). Their state was one of the smallest in Europe, the fifth of the five great powers, lacking defensible boundaries, and easily outproduced and outmuscled by the enemy power that surrounded it: France, Austria, Russia, and the Netherlands. As a result, from an early period,

Prussia realized that it had to fight short, sharp wars that ended in a rapid victory, rather than slugging matches where superior resources and manpower eventually told.

Entire generations of Prussian officers had internalized these notions, and so did their later German descendants. Their solution to their strategic problem was something they called *Bewegungskrieg*, the war of movement, a risky and aggressive posture that maneuvered major units of the army in such a way as to surround and destroy the enemy's main body as rapidly as possible. If it failed, the result was a stalemated war, a *Stellungskrieg*, or war of position, in which the hostile armies bashed one another frontally in a war of attrition. Traditionally, Prussian and German commanders had viewed positional fighting as a degenerate form of warfare, something that only happened when the default method had inexplicably failed. It was also a temporary form, one that the commander tolerated only until the moment came to restart the offensive

Until 1943, that is. Field Marshal Kesselring may well be one of the most important German commanders of all time, but not for the reasons usually adduced. The Fredericks and the Moltkes, the Red Princes and the Schlieffens, the Guderians and the Rommels and the Mansteins all have a deserved place in the histories. All of them sought to employ maximum aggression and aptitude for high-speed maneuver to win massive battles of encirclement and annihilation, the *Kesselschlacht* and the *Vernichtungsschlacht*. Rossbach and Leuthen, Königgrätz and Sedan, the Ardennes in 1940 and Gazala in 1942—all of these battles relied on an officer corps willing to risk everything in aggressive maneuver, and all of them were great victories against the odds.

Kesselring, by contrast, marched to a different drummer. German commanders had fought positional battles before, most notably the generation of officers in the trench years of World War I. There had been no choice then, and in 1918 General Erich von Ludendorff had reverted to the mobile offensive. Kesselring, however, was the first German army commander of all time who willfully and eagerly chose to fight a *Stellungskrieg* that he knew he would never abandon. Historians may never know the exact reasons why. He may have misunderstood the strategic situation, believing that Germany still had a legitimate chance to win that war. He may have been deluding himself, using blind faith in the Führer as an excuse to fight on. He may have simply been a careerist, concerned only with currying Hitler's favor. In the manner of these things, he was probably all three. At any rate, he had committed an outnumbered and outproduced German field army to a *Stellungskrieg* against superior opposition. It was a campaign he had no chance of winning—the last thing the Wehrmacht needed at this point of the war.

Kesselring handled the campaign skillfully, giving a bravura performance. Let us suggest a further test of his greatness, however. Let us transfer the field marshal from the friendly confines of Italy to the wide-open spaces of the Eastern Front. Let us task him with holding the Donets or the Dnepr or the Desna against massive Soviet tank armies hurtling at him from multiple directions. Give him a single understrength Panzer division, or less, as a strategic reserve, and then have the Führer command him to hold at all costs. Then it would be far easier to judge what sort of defensive genius he really was.

Conclusion: Fighting a Lost War

Timing is everything, as they say.

That is precisely the reason why the year 1943 fails to get a lot of attention from historians of World War II. Crammed in between the drama of 1942 and 1944, it is the "forgotten year" (*das vergessene Kriegs-jahre*), and will probably never receive the attention that it deserves.[1] The former year, of course, saw Wehrmacht field armies destroyed at El Alamein and Stalingrad. The latter was the year of the great D-day landing in Normandy, which for Americans at least remains the main event of the war. For aficionados of the Eastern Front, 1944 will always be the year of Operation Bagration, the massive Soviet offensive in Byelorussia, "the worst defeat in German military history."[2] It smashed not merely a field army, but all of Army Group Center, and it remains one of the greatest victories in the history of land warfare.

The year 1943, by contrast, saw few events that one might consider decisive. Despite the high drama and the monstrous losses, all of the decisions had already happened. The Western Allies spent the year slogging their way around the Mediterranean: Tunisia, Sicily, Italy. The Eastern Front saw the failed German offensive at Kursk (Operation Citadel). Once virtually unknown in the West, it became the subject of a great deal of interest in the postwar era, being elevated to the status of the greatest tank battle of all time. Today, historians have been cutting Kursk down to size, reducing it from an all-out attempt at a strategic breakthrough on the 1941–1942 model to a spoiling operation designed to smash a buildup of Soviet strength on the central front and retain the initiative in the east.

Certainly, it was a bad year for the Germans across the board. At sea, the Allies finally seemed to have gotten the German U-boat menace under control. "Black May" was the crucial month, in which improved Allied convoy tactics sent no fewer than 41 submarines to the bottom, about 25 percent of Germany's total number of operational boats. In the air, the German people got a grisly foretaste of what was to come when the combined allied air forces launched Operation Gomorrah in July, a solid week of raids against Hamburg. The resulting firestorm burned down the great city and killed 47,000 people, and this at a time when strategic bombing was still in its relative infancy. Hamburg was the first to go, but not the last.

Those were bad, but German strategy had historically never revolved around air or sea power. This "grab for world power" (*Griff nach der Weltmacht*)[3] was in the hands of the army from day one. Undefeated from 1939 to 1941, and then nearly destroyed in the Soviet Union in 1941–1942, it had by 1943 moved solidly into the loser's column. Its calling card continued to be *Kampfkraft*, "fighting power," a combination of aggressive field commanders, sound doctrine, and highly motivated soldiers, and it could still give headaches to its enemies.[4] The Western allies learned some hard lessons at Kasserine, during the first days of the Allied invasion of Sicily, and in the first hours of Operation Avalanche at Salerno. Likewise, in the east, the Wehrmacht showed flashes of the old fire during Field Marshal Erich von Manstein's counterstroke at Kharkov in early 1943. Even when the army failed, as at Kursk, it continued to show signs of life. The wreckage of General Pavel Rotmistrov's 5th Guards Tank Army at Prokhorovka would testify sufficiently to that.

No one awards style points in war, however, and all the Wehrmacht had to show for its efforts in 1943 was one defeat after the other. Tunisia, Sicily, Italy, Kursk, Orel, Belgorod, Kharkov, the Dnepr: it was a record of futility, with millions of casualties and a mountain of equipment lost. The course of the fighting would see it increasingly isolated. First, it lost its allied armies in the East—the Hungarians, Romanians, and Italians—all of whom were beginning to see the reality of the situation even if the German high command was not. Even worse, defeats in Tunisia, Sicily, and Italy destroyed the Axis alliance and drove Italy out of the war. Bereft of allies, its tiny navy smashed, and its once feared air force increasingly outclassed, the "land army" (*Landheer*) now faced a world of enemies alone.[5]

But let us think a bit harder about how the year 1943 might have looked to the German army itself, from Hitler on down to the field commanders. They knew that they had weathered a storm—a big one. The year had opened with German armies running for their lives: the 1st Panzer out of the Caucasus and Rommel's *Panzerarmee* from El Alamein. A third force (6th Army) couldn't run; it was already entombed at Stalingrad. They had lost the 6th Army, of course, but the other two armies mastered their respective crises. By the end of the winter 1942–1943, the Germans had reestablished a respectable front and even retaken Kharkov—hard to believe when you look at a situation map from a few months earlier. The massive post-Kursk Soviet counteroffensives had inflicted a great deal of pain and forced the Germans into retreat again, this time back across the Dnepr. The Soviets dealt out a fierce pounding to the Wehrmacht in all these battles, and the Germans found it impossible to hold the line of the great river. Nonetheless, the Soviet bridgeheads over the Dnepr witnessed fierce fighting until the end of the year, with the Panzer divisions of Army Group South launching one desperate counterattack after another: against the Soviet bridgehead at Chernobyl from October 3 to 8, at Krivoi Rog from October 23 to 28, and especially against the perimeter of the Kiev bridgehead from November to December. Although they came nowhere close to pushing the Soviets back across the Dnepr, all these counterstrokes managed to take back some ground lost earlier, and to inflict immense casualties on the now-overstretched Soviet forces. Likewise, in Army Group Center, a December counterattack (Operation Nikolaus), cobbled together from a pair of Panzer divisions, actually managed to restore a continuous front west of the Dnepr along the border between the 9th and 2nd Armies, closing an operational gap between the two armies that had been open for months.[6]

Although the long-term prognosis was bad, the Wehrmacht was dishing out its fair share of pain to the Red Army. In driving the Germans back across the Dnepr, for example, the Soviets had paid a monstrous price, suffering no fewer than 701,474 casualties. When we include the bridgehead battles in that total, including the German counterattacks, the figure rises to 1,687,164, over 400,000 of whom were killed. Even Soviet resources were not limitless, something we tend to forget, and by-mid December 1943, the Red Army ceased its offensives for a moment, the Germans restored their front, and the situation appeared to have stabilized. The Soviets had lunged forward in classic style, fighting a truly deep battle for the first time, but it still had many miles to go on the road from the Dnepr to Berlin.

Likewise, the Western Allies had had their successes in the Mediterranean during 1943, above all in Tunisia, where an Axis army (consisting to a large extent of Italians) had marched into captivity in May. The invasion of Sicily in July had ended in unsatisfying fashion, however, with a skillful German delaying action rescuing the entire Axis force on the island. The Allies began the Italian campaign in panic mode at Salerno in September, and while they eventually settled down, they had experienced nothing but frustration since then. By December, the Allies were still hung up in front of the main German defensive position 80 miles south of Rome, the Gustav line. Fronted by a swift river (the appropriately named Rapido), anchored on the monastery of Monte Cassino, then running to the Sangro River on the Adriatic, it was difficult to attack frontally and virtually impossible to flank. The stalemate set the stage for one of the most controversial Allied operations of the war, Operation Shingle, the amphibious landing at Anzio by U.S. VI Corps (General John P. Lucas) in January 1944. It miscarried badly, with heavy casualties and yet another stabilized front. For the next three months, VI Corps sat in a very shallow bridgehead under German observation and constant fire. Lucas became increasingly distant and irritable, and Clark would eventually relieve him. He would be the third U.S. corps commander to feel the ax, out of a total of only six.[7] By the end of the year, the Western Allies were well and truly mired in Italy, and like the Soviets, they, too, were a long way from where they wanted to be.

One Wehrmacht, two superior enemies; one grinding in slowly from the east, another seemingly trapped in a hard slog up the Italian boot. Once again, the math couldn't have been worse. But was it just possible that there were some in the German military—not just Hitler, but men among the staff and field commanders—who looked around at the end of this horrible year, took a deep breath, and began to hope that with a tweak here and there, a little more willpower, and perhaps a bit of luck, they might actually survive their ordeal?[8]

Fighting a Lost War

Today, historians have recreated in meticulous detail the forlorn nature of any such hope. Historically and objectively speaking, World War II, the war that Hitler and the high command had planned, prosecuted, and directed, was lost. The Wehrmacht's best chance of winning this war had come and gone, perhaps in 1941, perhaps in 1940 or even 1939. Perhaps the best chance of winning a general war never existed at all, except in Hitler's mind. That is certainly the opinion of many experts today, primarily the dean of German operational military historians, Karl-Heinz Frieser. He points out that Hitler had started a war in 1939 for which he had no plausible strategy: a power without a navy trying conclusions with a coalition possessing strong naval forces and controlling the resources of their various world empires.[9] Frieser was speaking of Britain and France, but even after France went out, Germany was unable to subdue Britain, and Hitler's increasing sense of desperation at that failing probably had a lot to do with the invasion of the

Soviet Union in June 1941 and the declaration of war on the United States in December of that year. The entire project, in other words, might well have been doomed from the start.

Of course, "doom" is not a historical concept, and we should beware of using the term too frivolously. The muse of history is fickle, often playful, and directs the course of events this way and that. Even today, the unfolding of World War II has the power to shock the observer. The Wehrmacht had enough tactical and operational superiority at the outset, enough *Kampfkraft*, to make up for a whole host of strategic failings. It proved it in Poland, Norway, France, and the Low Countries, the Balkans, and in the opening phases of Operation Barbarossa. It was a series of campaigns that brought Germany a world empire, even if it was one of the shortest-lived of all time.

The odds have a way of catching up, however. The campaign into the Soviet Union won a series of the greatest operational victories of all time, inflicted millions of casualties, and took many more millions of prisoners, but came to grief in front of Moscow. First the Wehrmacht creaked to a halt from high losses, logistical failures, and the winter freeze, then the Soviets smashed it with a vast counteroffensive in front of the capital. An attempt to restart the forward momentum in 1942, Operation Blue, likewise failed. First the Wehrmacht came to a halt in Stalingrad and the Caucasus, and then received a thrashing. This time, Soviet armies under the control of General G. K. Zhukov achieved their decisive victory, encircling an entire German field army in Stalingrad. An analogous situation developed in North Africa, where Rommel's *Panzerarmee Afrika* first came to a halt at El Alamein, then faced an onslaught from the British 8th Army that it was unable to resist.

By any reasonable reckoning, the worm had now turned. After 1941, or 1942 at the latest, conjuring up a German victory becomes increasingly difficult. The two-front war was not just a problem to be solved though rational means; it was a conundrum, an unsquarable circle. No matter how Hitler and Zeitzler juggled the numbers, they didn't add up. Thus, Hitler could declare in "Directive 51" (*Führerweisung 51*) that an invasion from the West constituted a more serious danger to the Reich than a collapse on the Eastern Front. "The danger in the east remains," the Führer had written, "but a greater danger is evident in the west: a landing by the Anglo-Saxon powers!"[10] Strong words, and yet within months, as the Western Allies delayed their landing and fierce Soviet attacks over the Dnepr and all across the front continued unabated, he had no choice but to send substantial Panzer formations to the east, including the entire II S.S. Panzer Corps (consisting by now of the 9th and 10th S.S. Panzer Divisions).

The strategic edifice was creaking in the air, on the sea, and especially on land. Yet the Wehrmacht fought on, and the officer corps did not waver. Despite all their alleged disagreements with their Führer, disputes that formed the basis for an entire body of postwar memoirs, the commanders remained loyal. They served his ends, they fought his war, and they eagerly accepted his assignments when another officer was found wanting.

The real *Problematik* of World War II only becomes evident in 1943: the war was lost, a lot of smart minds in the officer corps recognized it, and yet Hitler had no trouble finding commanders who would continue to serve him loyally. He had spent the war hiring and firing, much like Stalin or Churchill or any CEO, and in the course of 1943, he finally identified and assembled the team he wanted. He already had General Kurt Zeitzler, the chief of the General Staff, a competent staff officer and a convinced National Socialist. In the field, Hitler believed that the time for large-scale operations, "operations in the classic style,"[11] had come and gone. By early 1944, the generals who wanted to "operate"—the replacement term for *Bewegungskrieg*—were gone: Manstein, Kluge, and Kleist on the army group level, General Hermann Hoth of 4th Panzer Army. In their places were firm-jawed commanders like General Ferdinand Schörner (appointed to the command of Army Group South Ukraine, the successor formation of Army Group A, in October 1943) and Field Marshal Walther Model (appointed to the command of Army Group North Ukraine, the successor of Army Group South, in March 1944). The point is not that Hitler was appointing bunglers or political hacks. Model and Schörner were "keine Günstlinge oder Troupiers," as the best German scholar studying the officer corps puts it.[12] They were competent and professional in the field. What really recommended them to Hitler, however, was that each was a "stander" (*Steher*), a man who would stay put and stand fast where and when Hitler told him to.[13] They weren't operators, and they weren't General Staff officers who sat around staring at their maps all day. They were men of will and determination who considered retreat a personal insult and were willing to fight to the last German soldier in a hopeless war. Schörner, for example, was willing to shoot hundreds, perhaps thousands, of his own soldiers in order to keep the others in line and to prevent the collapse of discipline on his front.[14] And in Italy, Hitler had, to his delight, found perhaps the purest *Steher* of them all: Field Marshal Albert von Kesselring.

An army defending itself to the death and bravely resisting the attacks of a superior enemy usually earns our respect. Likewise, every culture in the world holds a special place of reverence for the general leading armies in defense of the homeland. Not this army, however, and not these commanders. We need to write the history of war year 1943 with a complete absence of romance. The Wehrmacht was not defending the fatherland. It was fighting to hold far-flung conquests it had made in a brutal war of aggression—the very definition of ill-gotten gains. Every day that it stayed in the field, every day that Schörner held another series of rigged courts-martial against "deserters," every day that Model or Kesselring stood fast, meant the condemnation of thousands of unfortunates to death: civilians caught in the immediate crossfire, inhabitants of occupied countries like the Netherlands whom their German masters were deliberately starving to death, slave laborers being worked to death in the Reich's armament factories, and those whom Hitler and his insane racialist ideology had identified as existential enemies of the German people: the Jews.

Though they would later attempt to disassociate themselves from it, the German officer corps was the indispensable cog in this war machine. The war would go on as long as the officers wanted it to, and not a day longer. Although they were not all Nazis, and Hitler had not captivated all of them in a personal sense, his sensibilities and his policies—antisocialism, anti-Bolshevism, and anti-Semitism—had produced at least a "partial identification" (*Teilidentität*) with his regime. His early successes had impressed them all: rearmament and restoration of German sovereignty; a series of bloodless border conquests, and then a refight of World War I against Britain and France. Next came an existential struggle against the Soviet Union in which the Wehrmacht obliterated all the customary legal, ethical, and moral boundaries of modern war. Enough of them supported Hitler's crusade against Bolshevism to suppress whatever scruples they might have felt about his call for an "annihilation struggle" (*Vernichtungskampf*) in the east. Finally, there was a global struggle against every great power that Hitler could find, and he found a lot of them. Gradually, as things went bad, some began to mutter, and a small number of them decided to kill him.

For the most part, however, they were with him every step of the way. Certainly those who fought paid a price for their misguided devotion. Picture this officer corps at war: General Paul Hausser with his one eye; General Hans Hube with his single arm; General Walther Nehring putting together a rickety defense in front of Tunis while constantly having to change the bandage on his festering arm; General

Traugott Herr commanding in Italy while still trying to shake off the effects of a recent head wound; General Wolfgang Fischer, commander of the 10th Panzer Division in Tunisia, paying the ultimate price for driving into a poorly marked minefield in Tunisia. They fought for Hitler, they suffered, and they died in droves.

Now they were lost, fighting a war that all reason must surely have told them they could not win. The fact that they were all accepting bribes from the regime (euphemized as "donations" from a grateful Führer) was a partial reason why. But how much of their decision to fight on was due to reason? They had all learned in an old, traditional school of war. It was a vision of conflict as a test of will, in which the smaller, weaker competitor could triumph over the stronger through grit, guts, and a spirit of aggression. The pageant of Prussian officers of the past showed them the way. Did reason tell them they could not win? They could look back to Blücher, who once criticized a commander by saying that he should have "thought less and fought more."[15] Did the cause appear lost? They could hear the words of the Red Prince, Friedrich Karl, telling them, "You've never lost a battle if you don't have the feeling you're beaten—and I didn't have that feeling."[16] Were they outnumbered on all fronts? Hadn't the great chief of the General Staff, Count Alfred von Schlieffen, once aphorized his entire art of war into a pithy "from inferiority to victory"?[17] And hadn't Frederick the Great once shook his fist at fate, declaring that he would attack his enemies and continue to attack them, "even if they stood on the top of the Zobtenberg, if they stood on the steeples of Breslau"? Had he not "conducted a war of five million against 80 million,"[18] the same thing they were now doing? The traditional way of war, operational-level *Bewegungskrieg*, had failed, but perhaps another old Prussian virtue, *Beharrlichkeit* ("tenacity" or "steadfastness"), could rescue something from the ruins, or drag things out until some miracle occurred.[19] In this sense, World War II was not really Hitler's war at all. This one belonged to the officers, the operator and the *Steher* alike.

Fighting a lost war, the old Prussian–German officer corps was gambling on its own history. After all, this was a caste that had managed to survive the rise of absolute monarchy with its influence intact. It had managed to survive, and eventually to subdue, the French Revolution and Napoleon. It had survived the rise of modern industrial capitalism and mass politics, arguably with its power increased. It had even survived defeat in World War I and the revolution of 1918, surely its greatest institutional triumph of all. Perhaps, many officers felt at the time, they would survive even Hitler and this latest catastrophe.

In this judgment, as in so many others they had made in 1943, they were wrong. The officer corps was going down, and so was the Junker caste from which it had emerged centuries before. Toward the end of the war, many of them sat in British prisons, unaware that their captors were taping their conversations. In a moment of despair, one of them had suddenly realized the gravity of it all, the wrong turn they had all taken. "We used to be colonels and generals," General Robert Sattler blurted out, "but after the war we're going to be shoe-shine boys and bellhops."[20] Sattler's complaint might be the best epitaph of all for 1943. Although the war was lost, the officers remained loyal to the regime and to the fight. In the process, they signed a death warrant, not only for millions of soldiers and civilians, but for their own caste as well. The campaigns of 1943 marked the beginning of the end for one of the longest-running acts on the European political stage.

There would be no turning back now. They had all embarked on a great and terrible adventure, and they would see it through. The Prussians had coined a word for it a long time ago, as a way to memorialize a unit that had ridden off on a suicide mission: the *Totenritt*, the "death ride." It was an order, even a senseless one, that you carried out without hesitation, "whatever it takes."[21] It required personal bravery, of course, but also a cold eye and a kind of recklessness that had brought German arms some of their greatest victories in the past. At its best, the German way of war had balanced the man of thought with the man of action. It gave equal time to "the genius of Gneisenau and the aggression of Blücher."[22] It recognized the importance of an intellectual like Seeckt and a muddy-boots operator like the Red Prince. As its strategic position collapsed in 1943, however, with a world of enemies howling for blood and a corps of officers in the hostile camp eager for a piece of it, it jettisoned its intellectual tradition altogether. A high point for this new German military irrationality might be General Alfred Jodl's speech to the Gauleiters on November 7, 1943, in which he declared that defeat was unthinkable. "Germany will win," he declared, "because we have to win. Otherwise world history will have lost its meaning."[23]

Any rational person in their place would have sued for peace in 1943. The handwriting was on the wall, what the Germans call the *Menetekel*. They had all been "weighed in the balance, and found wanting."[24] The officer corps was well past caring, however. Marching to the sound of the guns, as it had for centuries, its blood was up, and all it had left was a "one-sided actionism."[25] It is surely no coincidence that the journal that had served as a forum for ideas within the officer corps since the

Napoleonic period, the *Militär-Wochenblatt*, had ceased publishing alto-gether by 1943.[26] It no longer had a raison d'être. In a conversation with Admiral Karl Dönitz in August of that fateful year, Hitler had given them the only wisdom they needed: "We just have to gather all our faith and all our strength and act," he had proclaimed to the *Grossadmiral*.[27] The officers had responded. On the eve of the Allied invasion of Sicily, General Paul Conrath, the commander of the Hermann Göring Para-chute Panzer Division, had bragged to Field Marshal Albert Kesselring, "An immediate, reckless rush at the enemy—that's my strength."[28] To ride the *Totenritt*, you had to substitute faith—blind faith—for rational thought. Indeed, you had to stop thinking altogether.

Notes

Preface

1. For "Armee eingeschlossen . . . ," see the dispatch from General Friedrich Paulus, commander of the 6th Army, reprinted in Manfred Kehrig, *Stalingrad: Analyse und Dokumentation einer Schlacht* (Stuttgart: Deutsche Verlags-Anstalt, 1974), 559–560.

2. For a more complete evocation of this argument, see Robert M. Citino, *The German Way of War: From the Thirty Years' War to the Third Reich* (Lawrence: University Press of Kansas, 2005).

3. "Unsere Kriege kurtz und *vives* seyn müssen, massen es uns nicht konveniret die Sachen in die Länge zu ziehen, weil ein langwieriger Krieg ohnvermerkt Unsere admirable Disciplin fallen machen, und das Land depeupliren, Unsere Resources aber erschöpfen würde." Hugo von Freytag-Loringhoven, *Feldherrngrösse: Von Denken und Haldeln bevorragender Heerführer* (Berlin: E. S. Mittler, 1922), 56.

4. See, among numerous examples from the German literature, Major Bigge, "Ueber Selbstthätigkeit der Unterführer im Kriege," *Beihefte zum Militär-Wochenblatt* 1894 (Berlin: E. S. Mittler, 1894), 17–55, from the text of a lecture given to the Military Society in Berlin on November 29, 1893. See also General Wilhelm von Blume, "Selbstthätigkeit der Führer im Kriege," *Beihefte zum Militär-Wochenblatt* (Berlin: E. S. Mittler, 1896), 479–534. For a twentieth-century example, see Erich Weniger, "Die Selbständigkeit der Unterführer und ihre Grenzen," *Militärwissenschaftliche Rundschau* 9, no. 2 (1944): 101–115.

5. For the 1866 war, the authoritative works are Geoffrey Wawro, *The Austro-Prussian War: Austria's War with Prussia and Italy in 1866* (Cambridge: Cambridge University Press, 1996), and Dennis E. Showalter, *The Wars of German Unification* (London: Arnold, 2004), although Gordon Craig, *The Battle of Königgrätz: Prussia's Victory over Austria, 1866* (Philadelphia: Lippincott, 1964), may still be read with profit. For the western campaign, see the older German literature: Major General Oscar von Lettow-Vorbeck, *Geschichte des Krieges von 1866 in Deutschland*, vol. 1, *Gastein-Langensalza* (Berlin: E. S. Mittler, 1896); and for an account by one of Prussia's most brilliant writers, see Theodor Fontane, *Der deutsche Krieg von 1866*, vol. 2, *Der Feldzug in West- und Mitteldeutschland* (Berlin: R. v. Decker, 1871).

6. For Steinmetz's impact on the battle of Spichern, see Citino, *German Way of War*, 176–179.

7. The authoritative source on the battle of Tannenberg is Dennis E. Showalter, *Tannenberg: Clash of Empires* (Washington, D.C.: Brassey's, 2004). See also Citino, *German Way of War*, 224–230.

8. For a brilliant exploration of the Red Prince's character, one that locates his genius precisely in his "boldness" (*Kühnheit*), see Hans Delbrück, "Prinz Friedrich Karl," in *Historische und Politische Aufsätze* (Berlin: Georg Stilke, 1907), 302–316.

9. Wolfgang Foerster, "Prinz Friedrich Karl," *Militärwissenschaftliche Rundschau* 8, no. 2 (1943): 90.

10. For a comprehensive version of this argument, see Robert M. Citino, *Death of the Wehrmacht: The German Campaigns of 1942* (Lawrence: University Press of Kansas, 2007).

11. For the final drive on Ordzhonikidze, see Earl F. Ziemke and Magna E. Bauer, *Moscow to Stalingrad: Decision in the East* (Washington, D.C.: Center of Military History, 1987), 453–454, along with Citino, *Death of the Wehrmacht*, 239–243.

12. Hitler sent both Halder and List packing as part of the great "leadership crisis" at the Führer's Vinnitsa headquarters in the southern Soviet Union in September 1942. For details, see the German official history, *Das Deutsche Reich und der Zweite Weltkrieg* (hereinafter *DRZWk*), vol. 6, *Die Ausweitung zum Weltkrieg und der Wechsel der Initiative, 1941–1943* (Stuttgart: Deutsche Verlags-Anstalt, 1990), hereafter *DRZWk*, part 6, "Der Krieg gegen Die Sowjetunion, 1942–43," by Bernd Wegner. See especially the sections on "Hitlers 'zweiter Feldzug': Militärische Konzeption und strategtische Grundlagen" (761–815) and "Der Beginn der Sommeroffensive" (868–898), and "September in Vinnica: Der Huohepunkt der Krise," 951–961. Heim lost his command of the XXXXVIII Panzer Corps for failing to move vigorously enough against the Soviet breakthough along the northern Don in Operation Uranus. See Hans Doerr, *Der Feldzug nach Stalingrad: Versuch eines operativen Uberblickes* (Darmstadt: E. S. Mittler, 1955), 63–66, Richard L. DiNardo, *Germany and the Axis Powers: From Coalition to Collapse* (Lawrence: University Press of Kansas, 2005), 150–153, Kehrig, *Stalingrad*, 132–133; and Citino, *Death of the Wehrmacht*, 294–296.

13. See *DRZWk*, part 6, Wegner, "Der Krieg gegen Die Sowjetunion, 1942–43," 6:954: "oft genug nicht nur unkonventioneller, sondern auch unprofessioneller und fehlerhafter operativer Entschlüsse Hitlers."

14. For the details of the "Dual Campaign," see Citino, *Death of the Wehrmacht*, 254–258.

15. The term "ways of war," with its corollary of separate and unique national military cultures, appeared first in the seminal work of Russell F. Weigley, *The American Way of War: A History of United States Military Strategy and Policy* (New York: Macmillan, 1973), but has become much more prominent of late in military historical discourse. See, among others, Citino, *German Way of War*; Isabel V. Hull, *Absolute Destruction: Military Culture and the Practices of War in Imperial Germany* (Ithaca, N.Y.: Cornell University Press, 2005); Brian

McAllister Linn, *The Echo of Battle: The Army's Way of War* (Cambridge, Mass.: Harvard University Press, 2007), and Peter A. Lorge, *The Asian Military Revolution: From Gunpowder to the Bomb* (Cambridge: Cambridge University Press, 2008). For a useful introduction to the topic, see "Comparative Ways of War: A Roundtable," *Historically Speaking* 11, no. 5 (November 2010): 20–26, including contributions by Citino, "The German Way of War Revisited"; Linn, "The American Way of War Debate: An Overview"; Lorge, "The Many Ways of Chinese Warfare"; and James Jay Carafano, "Wending through the Way of War."

16. The two poles of Holocaust historiography might best be represented by Christopher R. Browning, *Ordinary Men: Reserve Police Battalion 101 and the Final Solution in Poland* (New York: HarperCollins, 1992), for the functionalists, and Lucy S. Dawidowicz, *The War against the Jews, 1933–1945* (New York: Holt, Rinehart and Winston, 1975), or Daniel Jonah Goldhagen, *Hitler's Willing Executioners: Ordinary Germans and the Holocaust* (New York: Alfred A. Knopf, 1996), for the intentionalists.

17. See, among other references for this quote, Adolf Heusinger, *Befehl im Widerstreit: Schicksalsstunden der deutschen Armee 1923–1945* (Tübingen: Rainer Wunderlich Verlag Hermann Leins, 1950), 235. Heusinger was chief of the Operations Section (*Operationsabteilung*) of the German General Staff during much of the war, would serve briefly as chief of the General Staff in June 1944 when General Kurt Zeitzler became ill, and after the war would become the first inspector general of the armed forces of the Federal Republic of Germany, the Bundeswehr.

18. The scene is apocryphal. For the original source, see Paul Schmidt, *Statist auf diplomatischer Bühne, 1923–45: Erlebnisse des Chefdolmetschers im Auswärtigen Amt mit den Staatsmännern Europas* (Bonn: Athenäum-Verlag, 1949), 464.

19. For a partial list of sources, see the following works by active U.S. military officers: David A. Shunk, "Field Marshal von Manstein's Counteroffensive of Army Group South, February–March, 1943: The Last Operational Level Victory of the Panzer Forces on the Eastern Front" (M.A. thesis, U.S. Army Command and General Staff College, Fort Leavenworth, Kans., 1986); Lawrence L. Izzo, "An Analysis of Manstein's Winter Campaign on the Russian Front, 1942–43: A Perspective of the Operational Level of War and its Implications" (student paper, U.S. Army Command and General Staff College, Fort Leavenworth, Kans., 1986); Russell J. Goehring, "Sequencing Operations: The Critical Path of Operational Art" (monograph, U.S. Army Command and General Staff College, Fort Leavenworth, Kans., 1987); Richard J. Rowe Jr., "Counterattack: A Study of Operational Priority" (monograph, U.S. Army Command and General Staff College, Fort Leavenworth, Kans., 1987); Albert Bryant Jr., "Agility: A Key to the Operational Art" (monograph, U.S. Army Command and General Staff College, Fort Leavenworth, Kans., 1988); and Herbert L. Frandsen, "Counterblitz: Conditions to a Successful Counteroffensive" (monograph, U.S. Army Command and General Staff College, Fort Leavenworth, Kans., 1990).

20. For a succinct and authoritative introduction to the Kursk historiography, see the dean of German operational historians, Karl-Heinz Frieser, "Schlagen aus der Nachhand—Schlagen aus der Vorhand: Die Schlachten von Ch'arkov und Kursk 1943," in *Gezeitenwechsel im Zweiten Weltkrieg? Die Schlachten von Ch'arkov und Kursk im Frühjahr und Sommer 1943 in operativer Anlage, Verlauf und politischer Bedeutung,* ed. Roland G. Foerster (Berlin: E. S. Mittler, 1996), 101–135.

21. See Carlo D'Este, *Bitter Victory: The Battle for Sicily, 1943* (New York: Harper Collins, 1988).

22. Since the publication of Gerhard L.Weinberg's magisterial *A World at Arms: A Global History of World War II,* first published in 1994 and now in a second edition (Cambridge: Cambridge University Press, 2005), with its emphasis on the "inter-relationships between the various theaters and the choices faced by those in positions of leadership" (xxiv–xxv), tracing these connections has become the sine qua non of World War II scholarship. For two more recent one-volume histories of the conflict that also emphasize the global and interconnected nature of the event, see Evan Mawdsley, *World War II: A New History* (Cambridge: Cambridge University Press, 2009), and Thomas W. Zeiler, *Annihilation: A Global Military History of World War II* (Oxford: Oxford University Press, 2011).

23. See Michael Stürmer, *The German Empire: A Short History* (New York: Modern Library, 2000), 12–13.

24. For a survey of recent trends in scholarly military history, see Robert M. Citino, "Military Histories Old and New: A Reintroduction," *American Historical Review* 112, no. 4 (October 2007): 1070–1090.

Chapter 1. The Last Victory?

1. For the German breakdown in Stalingrad, see the German official history, *Das Deutsche Reich und der Zweite Weltkrieg* (hereinafter *DRZWk*), vol. 6, *Der Globale Krieg: Die Ausweitung zum Weltkrieg und der Wechsel der Initiative, 1941–1943* (Stuttgart: Deutsche Verlags-Anstalt, 1990), especially part 6, "Der Krieg gegen die Sowjetunion, 1942–43," by Bernd Wegner, 6:995.

2. For Montgomery's diary entry, see Niall Barr, *The Pendulum of War: The Three Battles of El Alamein* (New York: Overlook Press, 2005), 369. Montgomery had just received a jolt: a visit to his tactical headquarters by General Harold Alexander, commander in chief of the Middle East; General Richard McCreery, the major general of armored forces at Alexander's headquarters; and the minister resident in the Middle East, Richard Casey.

3. Erwin Rommel, *Krieg Ohne Hass: Herausgegeben von Frau Lucie-Maria Rommel und Generalleutnant Fritz Bayerlein, ehemaliger Chef des Stabes der Panzerarmee Afrika* (Heidenheim: Verlag Heidenheimer Zeitung, 1950), 267.

4. Ibid., 268.

5. *DRZWk*, part 6, Wegner, "Der Krieg gegen die Sowjetunion," 6:994. Stalingrad, Jodl declared, was "praktisch erobert."

6. *DRZWk*, part 5, Reinhard Stumpf, "Der Krieg im Mittelmeerraum 1942/43: Die Operationen in Nordafrika und im mittleren Mittelmeer," 6:721: "wichtig, dass sich die Achse (. . .) in Tunis festsetzte."

7. The entire text is reprinted in Walther von Seydlitz, *Stalingrad: Konflikt und Konsequenz: Erinnerungen* (Oldenburg: Stalling, 1977), 167.

8. Hitler on the American people: "Because the emigration process in Europe was a selection process of the most capable, but because in all European peoples this competence lay primarily in the Nordic admixture, the American union actually extracted from people who were very diverse in principle the (racially) Nordic elements dispersed among them." See Gerhard L. Weinberg, ed., *Hitler's Second Book: The Unpublished Sequel to "Mein Kampf" by Adolf Hitler* (New York: Enigma Books, 2003), 117. While doing archival work in 1958, Weinberg came across a manuscript written in 1928 by none other than Adolf Hitler, a work dealing with National Socialist foreign policy that had, for various reasons, remained unpublished. By 1961, Weinberg had it in print in the original German and intended to follow up with a carefully translated, annotated English edition. Another hastily prepared English edition soon appeared in print, however, derailing that plan. The new translation was amateurish, and the book appropriated many of Weinberg's own notes without his permission; he describes it here as a "pirated edition." One reviewer called it a "burlesque imitation" of the original, and anyone with a copy of it will agree. The 2003 edition is vastly superior to the 1961 English version in every way. The new translation, by Krista Smith, skillfully conveys both the meaning of the original German and all the stylistic lapses for which Hitler's writing is known, and the introductory material and the explanatory notes are invaluable and complete. For the now-obsolete version, see *Hitler's Secret Book* (New York: Grove Press, 1961).

9. The title of the memoirs of Dwight D. Eisenhower, *Crusade in Europe* (Garden City, N.Y.: Doubleday, 1948).

10. Rick Atkinson, *An Army at Dawn: The War in North Africa, 1942–1943* (New York: Henry Holt, 2002), 8. Volume 1 of the Liberation Trilogy, *Army at Dawn* shows how blurred the line can become between popular and scholarly history when writing on military affairs. As in all his works, Atkinson grounds the narrative in firm research in both the archives and the secondary literature; this is a scholarly work in the best sense of the term. At the same time, he is a far better writer than most historians, and he spends more time weaving a compelling narrative than is typical in the world of high scholarship. The result is a tour de force, and a true rarity: a book that can actually appeal to a scholar seeking hard information and a member of the educated public looking for a good read. It won a Pulitzer Prize for all the right reasons.

11. For a reprint of the original photograph, see David E. Scherman, ed., *Life Goes to War: A Picture History of World War II* (New York: Pocket Books, 1977),

36–37. "The armed services," runs the caption, "were delighted with such lay-outs in *Life*, whose editors, exposed to continual reports from its overseas cor-respondents of Axis military resurgence, were genuinely alarmed at America's unreadiness. *Life* hoped its saber rattling would prod its readers and Congress into acknowledging a rapidly expanding German fighting force." See, on the same pages, images of U.S. troops training with a wooden dummy bearing a sign that identifies it as a "60 mm mortar," and one of the first Boeing B-17 prototypes (the YB-17) stuck nose down in a field after a crash.

12. The interwar period has generated an enormous literature, seen by schol-ars and military professionals alike as a laboratory of change in doctrine, train-ing, and weaponry, in which some succeeded (the Germans), others failed (the French), and still others squandered rich opportunities (the British). For an overview, see two essential works: Williamson Murray and Allan R. Millett, eds., *Military Innovation in the Interwar Period* (Cambridge: Cambridge Univer-sity Press, 1996), and Harold R. Winton and David R. Mets, *The Challenge of Change: Military Institutions and New Realities, 1918–1941* (Lincoln: University of Nebraska Press, 2000). The list of monographs dealing with the era is immense. See, among others, Robert M. Citino, *The Evolution of Blitzkrieg Tactics: Ger-many Defends Itself against Poland, 1918–1933* (Westport, Conn.: Greenwood, 1987), and, by the same author, *The Path to Blitzkrieg: Doctrine and Training in the German Army, 1920–1939* (Boulder, Colo.: Lynne Rienner, 1999); James S. Corum, *The Roots of Blitzkrieg: Hans von Seeckt and German Military Reform* (Lawrence: University Press of Kansas, 1992); Eugenia C. Kiesling, *Arming against Hitler: France and the Limits of Military Planning* (Lawrence: University Press of Kansas, 1996); David E. Johnson, *Fast Tanks and Heavy Bombers: Inno-vation in the U.S. Army, 1917–1945* (Ithaca, N.Y.: Cornell University Press, 1998); William O. Odom, *After the Trenches: The Transformation of U.S. Army Doctrine, 1918–1939* (College Station: Texas A&M University Press, 1999); and Harold R. Winton, *To Change an Army: General Sir John Burnett-Stuart and British Armored Doctrine, 1927–1938* (Lawrence: University Press of Kansas, 1988).

13. See the body of work by Heinz Guderian, *Achtung—Panzer! The Devel-opment of Armoured Forces, Their Tactics and Operational Potential* (London: Arms and Armour, 1992); "Bewegliche Truppenkörper: Ein kriegsgeschichtliche Studie," part 1, "Die Schlittenfahrt des Grossen Kurfürsten im Winterfeldzug, 1678–79," *Militär-Wochenblatt* 112, no. 18, November 11, 1927; "Die Panzertrup-pen und ihr Zusammenwirken mit den anderen Waffen," *Militärwissenschaftliche Rundschau* 1, no. 5 (1936); "Schnelle Truppen einst und jetzt," *Militärwis-senschaftliche Rundschau* 4, no. 2 (1939); and finally, his memoir, *Panzer Leader* (New York: Ballantine, 1957). For the development of the Panzer division, see also Richard Ogorkiewicz, *Armoured Warfare: A History of Armoured Forces and their Vehicles* (New York: Arco, 1970), 73. For a fine, well-researched, and heav-ily negative biography of the German Panzer commander, see Russell A. Hart, *Guderian: Panzer Pioneer or Myth Maker?* (Washington, D.C.: Potomac Books, 2006).

14. For the AEF in World War I, see Mark Ethan Grotelueschen, *The AEF*

Way of War: The American Army and Combat in World War I (Cambridge: Cambridge University Press, 2007), a study both of the inadequacy of prewar U.S. doctrine and the inability of U.S. infantry divisions to learn on the fly. For the Tank Corps, the work of choice is still Dale E. Wilson, *Treat 'em Rough! The Birth of American Armor, 1917–1920* (Novato, Calif.: Presidio, 1989).

15. For the complexities of the National Defense Act of 1920, which constructed "a multi-tiered system based on voluntary participation and diverse degrees of readiness," see Allan R. Millett and Peter Maslowski, *For the Common Defense: A Military History of the United States of America* (New York: Free Press, 1984), 366–367.

16. David E. Johnson, "From Frontier Constabulary to Modern Army: The U.S. Army between the World Wars," in Winton and Mets, *Challenge of Change*, 180–181.

17. The best biography of Billy Mitchell remains Alfred F. Hurley, *Billy Mitchell: Crusader for Air Power* (Bloomington: Indiana University Press, 1975).

18. See the discussion in Russell F. Weigley, *Eisenhower's Lieutenants: The Campaign of France and Germany, 1944–1945* (Bloomington: Indiana University Press, 1981), especially the chapter entitled "The American Army," 1–7, a near-perfect distillation of the fundamental points of Weigley's scholarship.

19. For "open warfare," see Grotelueschen, *AEF Way of War*, 8, 32–35, 48–49. General John J. Pershing himself claimed that "the essential difference between open and trench warfare . . . is characterized by the presence or absence of the rolling barrage ahead of the infantry" (49).

20. Johnson, "Frontier Constabulary," 167.

21. There is an immense literature on the inadequacies of the M-4 Sherman tank. See, above all, Belton Y. Cooper, *Death Traps: The Survival of an American Armored Division in World War II* (Novato, Calif.: Presidio, 2000). Cooper served with the 3rd Armored Division's Maintenance Battalion and saw action from Normandy to Germany in 1944–1945. In that time, the division lost 648 Shermans and had another 700 tanks damaged and put back into service. Weigley, *Eisenhower's Liuetenants*, 20–22, contains a typically thorough and fair assessment.

22. For a biographical sketch of General McNair, see Robert M. Citino, *Armored Forces: History and Sourcebook* (Westport, Conn.: Greenwood, 1994), 256–257. For the entire vexed question of "active antitank defense," see the critical but fair analysis included in Christopher R. Gabel, *Seek, Strike, and Destroy: U.S. Army Antitank Destroyer Doctrine in World War II* (Fort Leavenworth, Kans.: Command and General Staff College, 1985). See also the highly critical commentary in Roman Johann Jarymowycz, *Tank Tactics: From Normandy to Lorraine* (Boulder, Colo.: Lynne Rienner, 2001), 92, where the author calls the tank destroyer "McNair's pocket battleship solution—an armored fighting vehicle that could run away from trouble."

23. For the troubled origins and travails of "daylight prevision bombing," see Donald L. Miller, *Masters of the Air: America's Bomber Boys Who Fought the Air War against Nazi Germany* (New York: Simon & Schuster, 2006). Miller

argues that the real problem with the U.S. air doctrine of "precision daylight bombing" was that the entire idea was dreamed up by a handful of USAAF officers sitting around in a room, quite literally. There was no objective evidence whatsoever that it would work, no experimentation, no trial and error. The same thing can be said for the notion that the B-17 had no need for a long-range escort fighter and that it could defend itself against German fighters. As Miller shows convincingly, no one had ever tested these propositions in the prewar era. In place of evidence, there were slogans, repeated until they became mantras. "The bomber will always get through" was one, and so was the Norden bombsight's alleged ability to "drop a bomb in a pickle barrel at 20,000 feet." See especially his critique of the Air Corps tactical school at Maxwell, Alabama (38–41). See also Robert M. Citino, "Wild Blue Yonder," *Front and Center*, October 25, 2009, http://www.historynet.com/wild-blue-yonder.htm.

24. There is a substantial literature on the rise of the U.S. armored force and its tangled relationship to the demise of the cavalry branch. See, among others, George F. Hofmann and Donn A. Starry, eds., *Camp Colt to Desert Storm: The History of the U.S. Armored Forces* (Lexington: University Press of Kentucky, 1999); George F. Hofmann, *Through Mobility We Conquer: The Mechanization of U.S. Cavalry* (Lexington: University Press of Kentucky, 2006); Matthew Darlington Morton, *Men on Iron Ponies: The Death and Rebirth of the Modern U.S. Cavalry* (DeKalb: Northern Illinois University Press), 2009; and especially the recent work by Robert S. Cameron, *Mobility, Shock, and Firepower: The Emergence of the U.S. Army's Armor Branch, 1917–1945* (Washington, D.C.: Center of Military History, 2008), which analyzes the ways that "technology, doctrine training, leadership, and organization" interacted "within a context shaped by political considerations, the Army's corporate nature, and a view of warfare in flux to create a uniquely American way of armored warfare" (xix).

25. Johnson, "Frontier Constabulary," 191–192. See also Cameron, *Mobility, Shock, and Firepower*, for the development of a "new doctrinal base" for the armored division emphasizing missions "deep in the hostile rear" (270–273).

26. Atkinson, *Army at Dawn*, 10.

27. The only dedicated monograph on the maneuvers, an excellent work in every way (including maps), is Christopher R. Gabel, *The U.S. Army GHQ Maneuvers of 1941* (Washington, D.C.: Center of Military History, 1992). See also the pertinent chapters in Carlo D'Este, *Patton: A Genius for War* (New York: Harper, 1995), 392–407, and Cameron, *Mobility, Shock, and Firepower*, 325–359.

28. For a colorful account of Patton's exploits in Louisiana, see D'Este, *Genius for War*, 395–397. Gabel, *U.S. Army GHQ Maneuvers*, is apparently less convinced of the veracity of the Patton legend. See his more sober account on 96–111, which notes, among other things, that both commanders, generals Lear and Krueger, "recognized the possibilities of an end run through Texas" (106), as well as Gabel's judgment that Patton's drive through Nacogdoches "actually owed more to J. E. B. Stuart than to Heinz Guderian" (188).

29. D'Este, *Patton*, 396.

30. For the Carolina maneuvers, Gabel, *U.S. Army GHQ Maneuvers*, is authoritative. See especially "Phase I: The Battle of the Pee Dee River" (132–154) and "Phase II: The Battle of Camden" (155–169). For the Drum capture story, see D'Este, *Patton*, 399.

31. For the army's analysis of the maneuvers, see Gabel, *U.S. Army GHQ Maneuvers*, 170–194. See also Mark Perry, *Partners in Command: George Marshall and Dwight Eisenhower in War and Peace* (New York: Penguin, 2007), 8.

32. Russell F. Weigley, *The American Way of War: A History of United States Military Strategy and Policy* (Bloomington: Indiana University Press, 1973).

33. For "strategy of attrition," see Weigley, *American Way of War*, 3–17; for "strategy of annihilation," see 128–152. For the link between the two: "At the beginning, when American military resources were still slight, America made a promising beginning in the nurture of strategists of attrition; but the wealth of the country and its adoption of unlimited aims in war cut short that development, until the strategy of annihilation became characteristically the American way in war" (xxii).

34. Grant "would fight all the time, every day, keeping the enemy army always within his own army's grip, allowing the enemy no opportunity for deceptive maneuver, but always pounding away until his own superior resources permitted the Federal armies to survive while the enemy army at last disintegrated." Ibid., 143.

35. See Waldemar Erfurth, "Das Zusammenwirken getrennter Heeresteile," parts 1–4, *Militärwissenschaftliche Rundschau* 4, no. 1 (1939): 14–41; 4, no. 2 (1939): 156–178; 4, no. 3 (1939): 290–314; and 4, no. 4 (1939): 472–499.

36. General of Artillery Max Ludwig, "Die Operation auf der innerer und der äusserer Linie im Lichte unserer Zeit," *Militär-Wochenblatt* 126, no. 1 (July 4, 1941): 7–10.

37. For the debate over the Bolero–Sledgehammer–Roundup sequence, see Richard W. Steele, *The First Offensive, 1942: Roosevelt, Marshall, and the Making of American Strategy* (Bloomington: Indiana University Press, 1973).

38. The phrase is contained in the famous Marshall Memorandum, presented to British planners in April 1942. See Steele, *First Offensive*, 100–114, along with Perry, *Partners in Command*, 73–77, and Andrew Roberts, *Masters and Commanders: How Four Titans Won the War in the West, 1941–1945* (New York: Harper, 2008), 137–166. For the pertinent volume in the U.S. Army's official history, *The U.S. Army in World War II* (known colloquially as the Green Book series), see Ray S. Cline, *The War Department: Washington Command Post: The Operations Division* (Washington, D.C.: Center of Military History, 1990).

39. For Major Wedemeyer's achievement, see Charles E. Kirkpatrick, *An Unknown Future and a Doubtful Present: Writing the Victory Plan of 1941* (Washington, D.C.: Center of Military History, 1992), which emphasizes the general nature of the plan as a blueprint for "an efficient and effective military organization" and not the "relative successes and failures of the plan in its various details" (124)—a judicious conclusion. See also Perry, *Partners in Command*,

250–251. Recent research is calling into question the importance of Wedemeyer's plan, in favor of "Plan Dog," drawn up by Admiral Harold R. Stark (chief of naval operations) and the "Consolidated Balance Sheet," compiled by civilian economist Stacy May. See James Lacey, "World War II's Real Victory Program," *Journal of Military History* 75, no. 3 (July 2011): 811–834.

40. See the tables in Kirkpatrick, *Unknown Future*, 100–102.

41. The best single volume on Midway continues to be Jonathan Parshall and Anthony Tully, *Shattered Sword: The Untold Story of the Battle of Midway* (Washington, D.C.: Potomac Books, 2005). See also Dallas Woodbury Isom, *Midway Inquest: Why the Japanese Lost the Battle of Midway* (Bloomington: Indiana University Press, 2007), which focuses on the central question of the battle: why the Japanese could not launch another air strike before the U.S. dive bombers arrived.

42. For Guadalcanal, see Richard B. Frank, *Guadalcanal: The Definitive Account of the Landmark Battle* (New York: Penguin, 1992), and Stanley Coleman Jersey, *Hell's Islands: The Untold Story of Guadalcanal* (College Station: Texas A&M University Press, 2008). For the difficult naval struggle in the waters around the island, see James D. Hornfischer, *Neptune's Inferno: The U.S. Navy at Guadalcanal* (New York: Bantam: 2011).

43. See Thomas B. Buell, *Master of Sea Power: A Biography of Fleet Admiral Ernest J. King* (Annapolis, Md.: Naval Institute Press, 1995).

44. For the classic formulation, see B. H. Liddell Hart, *The British Way in Warfare* (London: Faber and Faber, 1932). David French, *The British Way in Warfare, 1688–2000* (London: Unwin Hyman, 1990), both updated and took issue with much of what Liddell Hart had to say. See also Keith Neilson and Greg Kennedy, eds., *The British Way in Warfare: Power and the International System, 1856–1956: Essays in Honour of David French* (Farnham, U.K.: Ashgate, 2010).

45. Steele, *First Offensive*, 34–45.

46. For World War II as a battle of shipping and control of the "world ocean," see Evan Mawdsley, *World War II: A New History* (Cambridge: Cambridge University Press, 2009), 248–293.

47. Quoted, for example, in Charles B. MacDonald, *The Mighty Endeavor: The American War in Europe* (New York: Da Capo, 1992), 78.

48. Quoted in Atkinson, *Army at Dawn*, 14.

49. Quoted in MacDonald, *Mighty Endeavor*, 80.

50. For details on Operation Blue, see Robert M. Citino, *Death of the Wehrmacht* (Lawrence: University Press of Kansas, 2007), 152–182, as well as Earl F. Ziemke and Magna E. Bauer, *Moscow to Stalingrad: Decision in the East* (Washington, D.C.: Center of Military History, 1987), 283–308, 333–348, and Earl F. Ziemke, *Stalingrad to Berlin: The German Defeat in the East* (Washington, D.C.: Center of Military History, 1987), 3–36.

51. Douglas Porch, *The Path to Victory: The Mediterranean Theater in World War II* (New York: Farrar, Straus and Giroux, 2004), xi.

52. For Operation Torch, the entry of the U.S. Army into World War II, see the pertinent volume in the Green Book series, George F. Howe, *North-*

west Africa: Seizing the Initiative in the West (Washington, D.C.: Center of Military History, 1957), and the equivalent volume in the British official history, I. S. O. Playfair and C. J. C. Molony, *The Mediterranean and the Middle East*, vol. 4, *The Destruction of the Axis Forces in Africa* (London: H.M.S.O., 1966), 109–164. Like all the Green Books, Howe's volume displays deep research, deft writing, and an authoritative tone. On the negative side, all of the Green Books try to be all things to all people, often shifting at random among the tactical, operational, and strategic levels of war. As a result, they occasionally serve to bewilder a researcher looking for a clear operational-level analysis. Playfair and Molony, by contrast, manage a much tighter focus, including full treatment of air and naval operations. See also Atkinson, *Army at Dawn*, 21–32; Porch, *Path to Victory*, 342–345; MacDonald, *Mighty Endeavor*, 68–114; Carlo D'Este, *World War II in the Mediterranean, 1942–1945* (Chapel Hill, N.C.: Algonquin Books, 1990), 1–21; Matthew Jones, *Britain, the United States, and the Mediterranean War, 1942–44* (New York: St. Martin's Press, 1996), 1–35; Martin Kitchen, *Rommel's Desert War: Waging World War II in North Africa, 1941–1943* (Cambridge: Cambridge University Press, 2009), 353–379; the authoritative military account by Kenneth Macksey, *Crucible of Power: The Fight for Tunisia, 1942–1943* (London: Hutchinson, 1969), 1–74; and the useful synopsis in Charles A. Anderson, *Algeria–French Morocco* (Washington, D.C.: Center of Military History, n.d.).

53. See Howe, *Northwest Africa:* for the Western Task Force, 39–46; for the Central Task Force, 46–50; and for the Eastern Task Force, 50–54.

54. Eisenhower, *Crusade in Europe*, 80.

55. For a good introduction to the atmosphere of French intrigue and uncertainty forming the backdrop to Torch, see MacDonald, *Mighty Endeavor*, 82–100.

56. Clark actually lost his pants in the escape attempt. For details of the bold—perhaps overbold—"secret mission to Africa," see the primary source: Mark W. Clark, *Calculated Risk* (New York: Enigma Books, 2007), the general's memoirs originally published in 1950, which make the duncelike caricature with which historians have invested Clark increasingly difficult to sustain, 58–76. See also Eisenhower's letter to Clark, November 12, 1942, labeled "Secret," in which Eisenhower tells Clark that "the newspapers have stressed *loss of pants*" (italics in the original), in *The Papers of Dwight David Eisenhower: The War Years: II*, ed. Alfred D. Chandler Jr. (Baltimore, Md.: Johns Hopkins Press, 1970), 749–750.

57. For the Oran landing, see the standard accounts in Howe, *Northwest Africa*, 192–228, Playfair and Molony, *Destruction of the Axis Forces in Africa*, 146–150, Atkinson, *Army at Dawn*, 69–81, and the useful account for all three of the beaches in Anderson, *Algeria–French Morocco*.

58. For the landing at Algiers, see Howe, *Northwest Africa*, 229–252, Playfair and Molony, *Destruction of the Axis Forces in Africa*, 140–146, and Atkinson, *Army at Dawn*, 91–103.

59. For the American landings on the Atlantic coast in Morocco, see especially Howe, *Northwest Africa*, 96–181. As befitting the largest all-American

landing in North Africa, it is by far the most detailed account in the U.S. Army official history. See also Playfair and Molony, *Destruction of the Axis Forces in Africa*, 150–153 and Atkinson, *Army at Dawn*, 103–115.

60. Eisenhower to George Smith Patton Jr., November 19, 1942, in Eisenhower, *Papers*, 684–685.

61. For the spread of tanks at Fedala, see Atkinson, *Army at Dawn*, 136. At Mehdia, only seven of the 45 tanks reached shore (Atkinson, *Army at Dawn*, 145). See also Howe, *Northwest Africa*, 130–131, where the situation at Fedala appears in far less dire terms.

62. See Hal Vaughan, *FDR's 12 Apostles: The Spies Who Paved the Way for the Invasion of French North Africa* (Guilford, Conn.: Lyons Press, 2006), for "the beginning of a long string of espionage, sabotage, and psychological warfare that the United States would carry out in World War II" (xiii).

63. An unforgettable scene well related as only Atkinson can. See *Army at Dawn*, 91–96. For the primary source, see Robert Daniel Murphy, *Diplomat among Warriors* (New York: Doubleday, 1964), 131.

64. Atkinson, *Army at Dawn*, 136.

65. The relatively minor scale of the fighting in Tunisia—less than a full division per side—has generated an enormous literature, while battles many times the size taking place in the Soviet Union have elicited only minor interest among Western historians. For the best of this often triumphal literature, see Howe, *Northwest Africa*, 275–344; Playfair and Molony, *Destruction of the Axis Forces in Africa*, 165–191; Porch, *Path to Victory*, 353–369; Atkinson, *Army at Dawn*, 161–263; Charles A. Anderson, *Tunisia* (Washington, D.C.: Center of Military History, n.d.); and B. H. Liddell Hart's typically cogent account in *History of the Second World War* (Old Saybrook, Conn.: Konecky & Konecky, 1970), 334–342. Interestingly enough, in a series that is often drenched in operational detail, the German official history touches lightly on the particulars of this microscopic campaign. See *DRZWk*, part 5, Stumpf, "Der Krieg im Mittelmeerraum," 6:715–725.

66. Hitler's particular obsession over Norway—long attributed to Churchill only—would last for a while. See Heinrich Rodemer, "Invasion in Südeuropa . . . oder in Norwegen?" *Die Wehrmacht* 7, no. 12 (June 9, 1943): 4–5, 19. See also *DRZWk*, part 5, Stumpf, "Der Krieg im Mittelmeerraum," 6:711.

67. It was not until just before the invasion, perhaps the day before, that Kesselring came around to the notion that the Allies intended to land in North Africa. For the "war of nerves" in the preinvasion weeks and Kesselring's assessment of the strategic situation, see Albert Kesselring, *Soldat bis zum letzten Tag* (Bonn: Athenäum, 1953), 185–187. For the English translation, see *Kesselring: A Soldier's Record* (New York: Morrow, 1954), 161–163.

68. For the general atmosphere of uncertainty, as well as Mussolini's prescience, see the memoirs of General Walter Warlimont of the OKW, *Im Hauptquartier der deutschen Wehrmacht, 1939–1945: Grundlagen, Formen, Gestalten* (Frankfurt am Main: Bernard & Graefe, 1962), 282–285: "Nordafrika deutenden Warnungen Mussolinis und schliesslich sogar noch angesichts der auf-

marschierenden Armada am 7. November abends viele andere Ziele eines Landungsangriffs im Mittelmeer für möglich halten wollte, nur nicht den in jeder Hinsicht nächstliegenden Raum von Franz. Nordafrika" (282). See also Siegfried Westphal, *Heer in Fesseln: Aus den Papieren des Stabschefs von Rommel, Kesselring und Rundstedt* (Bonn: Athenäum-Verlag, 1950), 188–189.

69. *DRZWk*, part 5, Stumpf, "Der Krieg im Mittelmeerraum," 6:720–721.

70. Playfair and Molony, *Destruction of the Axis Forces in Africa*, 171–172.

71. For Operation Anton, see *DRZWk*, part 5, Stumpf, "Der Krieg im Mittelmeerraum," 6:740–745, as well as Warlimont, *Im Hauptquartier der deutschen Wehrmacht*, 284.

72. Quoted in *DRZWk*, part 5, Stumpf, "Der Krieg im Mittelmeerraum," 6:713 ("Nordafrika muss als Vorfeld von Europa unbedingt gehalten werden"), and Atkinson, *Army at Dawn*, 164.

73. The campaign historian of the race for Tunis, as it has become known, must be humble: attempting to draw a definitive account will always fail, wrecking upon the shoals of multiple conflicting accounts, the difficulty of reconciling the various Allied columns and German *Kampfgruppen* involved, and—not least—the microscopic size of the forces engaged (about a single division on each side) spread out over such a vast expanse of terrain. The fact that it was the first campaign of the U.S. Army in the ETO has led dozens of scholars to try to do it, but none may be counted as definitive, and all contradict one another on various points. The present account draws heavily on three manuscripts written by General Walther K. Nehring and part of the U.S. Army's Foreign Military Studies series: "The First Phase of the Engagements in Tunisia, up to the Assumption of the Command by the Newly Activated Fifth Panzer Army headquarters on 9 Dec 1942," manuscript D-086; "The Development of the Situation in North Africa (1 Jan–28 Feb 1943)," manuscript D-120; and "The First Phase of the Battle in Tunisia," manuscript D-147, a continuation of D-086. All three are available in the U.S. Army Heritage and Education Center in Carlisle, Pennsylvania. Nehring was not only the prototypical hard-nosed man of action, he was also a military intellectual of some note. See his prewar work on antitank weapons and tactics, *Panzerabwehr* (Berlin: E. S. Mittler und Sohn, 1936), as well as his postwar history of the German tank arm, *Die Geschichte der deutschen Panzerwaffe, 1916 bis 1945* (Berlin: Propyläen Verlag, 1969). For Tunis, see also the edited reprint of the D-147 in Vance von Borries, "The Battle for Tunisia," *Strategy and Tactics*, no. 140 (February 1991): 5–20. From the Allied side, the account here will follow the after-action report written by General K. A. N. Anderson, the commander of the British 1st Army, "Operations in North West Africa from 8th November 1942 to 13th May 1943," *Supplement to the London Gazette*, November 6, 1946.

74. "Soweit als möglich nach Westen zu erweitern." *DRZWk*, part 5, Stumpf, "Der Krieg im Mittelmeerraum," 6:721.

75. Nehring, "The First Phase of the Engagements," 7. See also *DRZWk*, part 5, Stumpf, "Der Krieg im Mittelmeerraum," 6:721.

76. Nehring, "The First Phase of the Engagements," 9.

77. Howe, *Northwest Africa*, 391; Playfair and Moloney, *Destruction of the Axis Forces in Africa*, 171–172.

78. Howe, *Northwest Africa*, 295.

79. See, among many examples, "Tätigkeitsbericht der Division von Manteuffel: Abteilung Ic für die Zeit vom 1.1.43–31.3.43," 1–7, http://www.wwii-photos-maps.com/germandivisions/divisionbroichmannteuffel/17-2-43%20-%20 31-3-43%20%20Roll%202278/slides/0021.html.

80. Playfair and Molony, *Destruction of the Axis Forces in Africa*, 172–173.

81. Anderson, "Operations in North West Africa," 5463.

82. *DRZWk*, part 5, Stumpf, "Der Krieg im Mittelmeerraum," 6:719: "Damit begann ein sehr interessantes Täuschungsmanöver mit der Bezeichnung von Kommandobehörden, das bald von den Deutschen übernommen wurde und anzeigt, welche Rolle die Propaganda beim Endkampf um Afrika spielte. Die britische 1. Armee befand sich noch längere Zeit im Aufbau und verfügte bis zum 15. Dezember über keinen und auch später nur über einen einzigen Korpsstab (V. Korps, Generalleutnant Allfrey)."

83. See Robert M. Citino, "Clausewitz Was Right: The Race for Tunis," *Front and Center*, February 18, 2010, http://www.historynet.com/clausewitz-was-right-the-race-to-tunis.htm.

84. Atkinson, *Army at Dawn*, 176.

85. Lynne Olson, *Citizens of London: The Americans Who Stood with Britain in Its Darkest, Finest Hour* (New York: Random House, 2010), detailing the activities of John Gilbert Winant, the U.S. ambassador to London; radio correspondent Edward R. Murrow; and industrialist W. Averell Harriman. The Murrow quote is found on 195.

86. Clark, *Calculated Risk*, 107, and Porch, *Path to Victory*, 367.

87. Clark, *Calculated Risk*, 109.

88. For the Marshall warning to Eisenhower, see Michael Korda, *Ike: An American Hero* (New York: Harper, 2007), 349.

89. Anderson, "Operations in North West Africa," 5453.

90. Playfair and Molony, *Destruction of the Axis Forces in Africa*, 157.

91. Anderson, "Operations in North West Africa," 5450.

92. *DRZWk*, part 5, Stumpf, "Der Krieg im Mittelmeerraum," 6:727.

93. For the best study of *Kampfkraft*, one that has not gone unchallenged in the scholarly literature, see Martin Van Creveld, *Fighting Power: German and U.S. Army Performance, 1939–1945* (Westport, Conn.: Greenwood Press, 1982).

94. Macksey, *Crucible of Power*, 93.

95. Atkinson, *Army at Dawn*, 212–213; Howe, *Northwest Africa*, 283–284.

96. Anderson, "Operations in North West Africa," 5455.

97. Again, any time a well-drawn scene is required, see Atkinson, *Army at Dawn*, 189–191.

98. Kesselring, *Soldat bis zum letzten Tag*, 194: "Nehring rief mich in begreiflicher Aufregung an und zog aus diesem Vorgang die schwärzesten Konsequenzen. Ich konnte seine weitgehenden Befürchtungen nicht teilen, suchte ihn zu beruhigen und meldete meinen Besuch für den folgenden Tag an"

("Nehring rang me up in the a state of understandable excitement and drew the blackest conclusions from the raid. Unable as I was to share his worst fears, I asked him to be calm and said I would arrive the following day").

99. For the most comprehensive study of the Tiger tank in action against inferior Western armor, see Christopher W. Wilbeck, "Swinging the Sledgehammer: The Combat Effectiveness of German Heavy Tank Battalions in World War II" (M.A. thesis, U.S. Army Command and General Staff College, Fort Leavenworth, Kans., 2002).

100. This account of the "battle of the Tebourba Gap" relies heavily on Nehring's own account in "First Phase of the Battle in Tunisia," manuscript D-147.

101. MacDonald, *Mighty Endeavor*, 117–119. See also Thomas J. Mayock, "The North African Campaigns," in *The Army Air Forces in World War II*, vol. 2, *Europe: Torch to Pointblank, August 1942 to December 1943*, ed. Wesley Frank Craven and James Lea Cate (Chicago: University of Chicago Press, 1949): "The Eastern Air Command and the Twelfth (Air Force) could have demonstrated the JU87's obsolescence, as the Allied air in the Middle East had done, had they been able to get at it in strength. But, in late November, they were operating from just three forward fields: Bône, 120 miles from the lines, and Youks and Souk-el-Arba, 150 and 70 miles back, respectively—the last two frequently muddied. Nor could additional fields be easily located and prepared, for the Allies possessed mostly the hill country of Tunisia" (89).

102. Carl von Clausewitz, *On War*, ed. and trans. Michael Howard and Peter Paret (Princeton, N.J.: Princeton University Press, 1984), 566–573. Clausewitz discussed the *Kulminationspunkt* in book 7 ("The Attack"), chap. 22 ("The Culminating Point of Victory").

103. Howe, *Northwest Africa*, 305, 309.

104. Playfair and Molony, *Destruction of the Axis Forces in Africa*, 187–188, contains a rather bloodless account. For the drama, see Atkinson, *Army at Dawn*, 241–246, and Anderson, *Tunisia*, 12.

105. Eisenhower, *Crusade in Europe*, 123–124.

106. The authoritative account is Gabel, *Seek, Strike, and Destroy*.

107. See the interview with then–Lieutenant Colonel John K. Waters, part of the Senior Officers Oral History Program, Project 80-4 (1980), 617–619. A copy is on file at the U.S. Army Heritage and Education Center.

108. *DRZWk*, part 5, Stumpf, "Der Krieg im Mittelmeerraum," 6:722.

109. Atkinson, *Army at Dawn*, 18, 41.

Chapter 2. Manstein, the Battle of Kharkov, and the Limits of Command

1. The phrase belongs to General Hans-Georg Reinhardt. See Johannes Hürter, *Hitlers Heerführer: Die deutschen Oberbefehlshaber im Krieg gegen die Sowjetunion, 1941/42* (Munich: R. Oldenbourg, 2006), 616. Hürter's book is com-

prehensive, exhaustively researched, and elegantly argued, and today stands unsurpassed as an analysis of the Wehrmacht's higher field commanders on the army and army group level.

2. "Drei Jahre Krieg—drei Jahre Sieg," *Die Wehrmacht* 6, no. 18 (September 2, 1942): 4–5.

3. Erich von Manstein, *Verlorene Siege* (Bonn: Athenäum, 1955), 440. For the English translation, see *Lost Victories* (Novato, Calif.: Presidio, 1982), 410. For those who read German, the original volume of memoirs is much to be preferred, as entire sections not deemed of interest to an English-speaking audience are missing in the translated edition.

4. Hans Delbrück, "Prinz Friedrich Karl," in *Historische und Politische Aufsätze* (Berlin: Georg Stilke, 1907): "Die Kühnheit, welche eben dadurch die Schlacht gewinnt, dass sie es wagt, auch einmal eine zu verlieren" (308).

5. Carl von Clausewitz, *On War*, ed. and trans. Michael Howard and Peter Paret (Princeton, N.J.: Princeton University Press, 1976), book 2, chap. 2 (136).

6. The best analysis of the battle of Rossbach and the two armies who fought it is Dennis E. Showalter, *The Wars of Frederick the Great* (London: Longman, 1996), 177–192. See also Robert M. Citino, *The German Way of War: From the Thirty Years' War to the Third Reich* (Lawrence: University Press of Kansas, 2005), 72–82.

7. For Chancellorsville, there is still no rival to Stephen W. Sears, *Chancellorsville* (Boston: Houghton Mifflin, 1996).

8. For the Königgrätz campaign, the two required volumes are Geoffrey Wawro, *The Austro-Prussian War: Austria's War with Prussia and Italy in 1866* (Cambridge: Cambridge University Press, 1996), and Dennis E. Showalter, *The Wars of German Unification* (London: Arnold, 2004), 161–200. See also Citino, *German Way of War*, 160–173.

9. The literature on Napoleon is beyond voluminous. David G. Chandler, *The Campaigns of Napoleon* (New York: Macmillan, 1966), is still the appropriate starting point, and Owen Connelly, *Blundering to Glory: Napoleon's Military Campaigns* (Lanham, Md.: Rowman & Littlefield, 2006), can still be read with profit for its myth busting.

10. The one indispensable book on the 1813 campaign is Michael V. Leggiere, *Napoleon and Berlin: The Franco-Prussian War in North Germany* (Norman: University of Oklahoma Press, 2002). See also Citino, *German Way of War*, 132–141.

11. For a discussion of the role of military history today within the broader field, see Robert M. Citino, "Military Histories Old and New: A Reintroduction," *American Historical Review* 112, no. 4 (October 2007): 1070–1090.

12. See Manstein, *Verlorene Siege*. For his typically negative assessments of colleagues General Walther von Brauchitsch, chief of the OKH, and General Franz Halder, chief of the General Staff, see 71–72 and 76.

13. Quoted in Dana V. Sadarananda, *Beyond Stalingrad: Manstein and the Operations of Army Group Don* (Mechanicsburg, Pa.: Stackpole, 2009), 10.

14. Field Marshal Lord Carver, "Manstein," in *Hitler's Generals: Authorita-*

tive Portraits of the Men Who Waged Hitler's War, ed. Correlli Barnett (New York: Quill, 1989), 221.

15. Theodor Busse, "Der Winterfeldzug 1942/1943 in Südrussland," in *Nie ausser Dienst: Zum achtzigsten Geburtstag von Generfeldmarschall Erich von Manstein* (Cologne: Markus Verlagsgesellschaft, 1967), 45–63. It is a Festschrift of sorts, with contributions from Ulrich de Maizière, "Zum Geleit," 7–8; Walther von Schultzendorff, "Der Mensch und der Soldat Erich von Manstein," 9–34; Adolf Heusinger, "Der 'unbequeme' operative Kopf," 35–43; Andreas Hillgruber, "In der Sicht des kritischen Historikers," 65–83; and Walther Wenck, "Nie ausser Dienst," 85–95.

16. F. W. von Mellenthin, *German Generals of World War II as I Saw Them* (Norman: University of Oklahoma Press, 1977), 19, 29.

17. General Ulrich de Maizière, "Zum Geleit," in *Nie ausser Dienst*, 7.

18. B. N. Liddell Hart, *The German Generals Talk* (New York: Quill, 1979), 63. See also Liddell Hart's more generous and expansive encomium in his foreword to the English edition of von Manstein's *Lost Victories*: "The general verdict among the German generals I interrogated in 1945 was that Field Marshal von Manstein had proved the ablest commander in their Army, and the man they had most desired to become its Commander-in-Chief. It is very clear that he had a superb sense of operational possibilities and an equal mastery in the conduct of operations, together with a greater grasp of the potentialities of mechanized forces than any of the other commanders who had not been trained in the tank arm. In sum, he had military genius" (13).

19. Hubert Essame, "Field Marshal Erich von Manstein," *Army Quarterly and Defence Journal* 104, no. 1 (1973): 40–43, a tribute written on the occasion of the field marshal's death.

20. Sadarananda, *Beyond Stalingrad*, xi.

21. For a representative sample of an anti-Manstein critique, see Marcel Stein, *Field Marshal von Manstein, a Portrait: The Janus Head* (Solihull, U.K.: Helion, 2007).

22. See Mungo Melvin, *Manstein: Hitler's Greatest General* (London: Weidenfeld & Nicolson, 2010), combining deep research and sensible conclusions, not to mention the operational acumen of a general in the British army.

23. See Manstein, *Verlorene Siege*, 398, where he speaks of the possibility of a "Remislösung." See also Andreas Hillgruber, "In der Sicht des kritischen Historikers," in *Nie ausser Dienst*, 78–79.

24. See Robert M. Citino, *Death of the Wehrmacht: The German Campaigns of 1942* (Lawrence: University Press of Kansas, 2007), 69–81.

25. Manstein, *Verlorene Siege*, 290–302. Manstein's eldest son, Gero, was killed in the fighting in this sector. He was serving at the time as a junior officer in the 51st Panzer Grenadier Regiment, 18th Infantry Division.

26. For the course of Operation Blue, see Citino, *Death of the Wehrmacht*, 165–180.

27. The dispatch is included in Manfred Kehrig, *Stalingrad: Analyse und Dokumentation einer Schlacht* (Stuttgart: Deutsche Verlags-Anstalt, 1974),

559–560. For a helpful overview of the entire operational sequence, see Hans-Adolf Jacobsen and Hans Dollinger, eds., *Der Zweite Weltkrieg in Bildern und Dokumenten*, vol. 5, *Kriegswende, 1942/1943* (Munich: Verlag Kurt Desch, 1968), 90–137.

28. The best book on military relations between the Wehrmacht and its minor allies is Richard L. DiNardo, *Germany and the Axis Powers: From Coalition to Collapse* (Lawrence: University Press of Kansas, 2005). Peter Gosztony, *Hitlers fremde Heere: Das Schicksal der nichtdeutschen Armeen im Ostfeldzug* (Düsseldorf: Econ Verlag, 1976), remains useful for operational details.

29. Horst Scheibert, *Zwischen Don und Donez* (Neckargemünd: Kurt Vowinckel Verlag, 1961), 25–29.

30. Ibid., 69. Scheibert was a company commander in the 6th Panzer Division.

31. Ibid., 26.

32. Ibid., 23.

33. For the tense armored battles along the Chir, see F. W. von Mellenthin, *Panzer Battles: A Study of the Employment of Armor in the Second World War* (New York: Ballantine, 1956), 211–222.

34. "Eine traurige Bilanz!" Scheibert, *Zwischen Don und Donez*, 30.

35. Carl Wagener, *Heeresgruppe Süd: Der Kampf im Süden der Ostfront, 1941–1945* (Bad Nauheim: Podzun, 1967), 193, makes the point that Paulus's instructions "den Ausbruch vorbereiten" ("to prepare the breakout") presented him with a scarcely soluble problem, in view of his low mobility. The best operational analysis of Winter Storm remains Horst Scheibert, *Entsatzversuch Stalingrad: Dokumentation einer Panzerschlacht in Wort und Bild: Das LVII. Panzerkorps im Dezember 1942* (Neckargmünd: Kurt Vowinckel Verlag, 1956).

36. For Manstein's portrayal of Stalingrad as *Tragödie*, see *Verlorene Siege*, 319–396. See 319 for the Spartan funereal inscription.

37. Wagener, *Heeresgruppe Süd*, 188.

38. The indispensable work on all the Soviet winter offensives of 1942–1943 (Little Saturn, the Ostrogozhk–Rossosh operation, Operation Gallop, and Operation Star) is David M. Glantz, *From the Don to the Dnepr: Soviet Offensive Operations, December 1942–August 1943* (London: Frank Cass, 1991). David M. Glantz and Jonathan House, *When Titans Clashed: How the Red Army Stopped Hitler* (Lawrence: University Press of Kansas, 1995), continues to be useful as an operational précis.

39. Scheibert, *Zwischen Don und Donez*, 36, 43.

40. For a crisp description of Badanov's ride, see Glantz and House, *When Titans Clashed*, 139–141.

41. The primary source on Manstein's winter counteroffensive of 1943 is chap. 13 of *Verlorene Siege*, "Der Winterfuldzug 1942/42 in Sudrüssland," 397–472, although like the entire book, it needs to be read with caution. See also Friedrich Schulz, "Der Rückschlag im Süden der Ostfront 1942/43," Manuscript T-15 in the Foreign Military Studies series. The original is available in the U.S. Army Military History Institute/Army Heritage and Education Cen-

ter in Carlisle, Pennsylvania. The author was a German general who ended the war as commander of Army Group South. The report is comprehensive—with its seven appendices, on matters as diverse as "The Conduct of Battle by XXXXIX Mountain Corps in the Caucasus Sector" (appendix 3) and "The Italian Expeditionary Army" (appendix 6), it comprises 343 pages, plus maps. The entire report is also available in English translation as "Reverses on the Southern Wing." There are two indispensable English-language works: Sadarananda, *Beyond Stalingrad*, and Glantz, *From the Don to the Dnepr*. Even more important is the first book based on the archival records of Army Group Don/South: Eberhard Schwarz, *Die Stabilisierung der Ostfront nach Stalingrad: Mansteins Gegenschlag zwischen Donez und Dnjepr im Frühjahr 1943* (Göttingen: Muster-Schmidt Verlag, 1985). Wagener, *Heeresgruppe Süd*, devotes a chapter to the "rettender Gegenangriff," 211–220; he commanded XXXX Panzer Corps during the fighting. See also Wagener, "Der Gegenangriff des XXXX. Panzerkorps gegen den Durchbruch der Panzergruppe Popow im Donezbecken Februar 1943," *Wehrwissenschaftliche Rundschau* 7 (1957): 21–36. One of the first Soviet historians to analyze the campaign was Colonel V. P. Morozov, writing during the period of the Khrushchev thaw. See "Warum der Angriff im Frühjahr im Donezbecken nicht zu Ende geführt wurde," *Wehrwissenschaftliche Rundschau* 14 (1964): 414–430, 493–500. See also his monograph *Westlich von Voronezh: Kurzer militärhistorischer Abriss der Angriffsoperationen der sowjetischen Truppen in der Zeit von Januar bis Februar 1943* ([East] Berlin: Verlag des Ministeriums für Nationale Verteidigung, 1959). See also Busse, "Der Winterfeldzug 1942/1943 in Südrussland," and two works by the dean of modern German operational historians, Karl-Heinz Frieser: "Schlagen aus der Nachhand—Schlagen aus der Vorhand: Die Schlachten von Char'kov und Kursk 1943," in *Gezeitenwechsel im Zweiten Weltkrieg? Die Schlachten von Char'kov und Kursk im Frühjahr und Sommer 1943 in operativer Anlage, Verlauf und politischer Bedeutung*, edited by Roland G. Foerster (Berlin: E. S. Mittler, 1996), and "Mansteins Gegenschlag am Donez: Operative Analyse des Gegenangriffs der Heeresgruppe Süd im February/März 1943," *Militärgeschichte* 9 (1999): 12–18 (with Friedhelm Klein). Finally, for a period source from the glossy German magazine *Die Wehrmacht*, see the article by Kriegsberichter Hermann Pirich, "Das geschah zwischen Charkow und Dnjepro," *Die Wehrmacht* 7, no. 9 (April 28, 1943): 21–22. Pirich's article was reprinted—in what appears to be a loose translation from the German—by the U.S. Army Command and General Staff College as "The Struggle for Kharkov and the Dnieper, February–March 1943," in *Military Review* 23, no. 9 (December 1943): 86–89.

42. Franz von Adonyi-Naredy, *Ungarns Armee im Zweiten Weltkrieg: Deutschlands letzter Verbündeter* (Neckargemünd: Kurt Vowinckel Verlag, 1971), 84.

43. For a narrative of the offensive, as well as the pertinent archival sources, see David M. Glantz, "The Red Army's Donbas Offensive (February–March 1942) Revisited: A Documentary Essay," *Journal of Slavic Military Studies* 18, no. 3 (2005): 369–503. The title is evidently a misprint. It should read "February–March 1943."

44. Schwarz, *Stabilisierung der Ostfront*, has the 2nd Army "fighting for its life" ("Die 2. Armee kämpft um ihr Überleben"), 83.

45. Glantz, "Red Army's Donbas Offensive," 369–370.

46. Wagener, *Heeresgruppe Süd*, 215.

47. For Zeitzler's promotion of National Socialism within the army, see Geoffrey P. Megargee, *Inside Hitler's High Command* (Lawrence: University Press of Kansas, 2000), 181–183.

48. See the pertinent chapter in Wagener, *Heeresgruppe Süd*, 201–209. For the Soviet point of view, Andrei Grechko, *Battle for the Caucasus* (Moscow: Progress Publishers, 1971), is still useful. Grechko was an army commander in the Caucasus.

49. Wagener, *Heeresgruppe Süd*, 207.

50. Grechko, *Battle for the Caucasus*, 259.

51. The standard English translation is Carl von Clausewitz, *On War*, ed. and trans. Michael Howard and Peter Paret (Princeton, N.J.: Princeton University Press, 1984), with introductory essays by Paret, Howard, and Bernard Brodie. See book 7, chap. 4, "The Diminishing Force of the Attack," 527; chap. 5, "The Culminating Point of the Attack," 28; and chap. 22, "The Culminating Point of Victory," 566–573.

52. Glantz, *From the Don to the Dnepr*, 146.

53. See Schwarz, *Stabilisierung der Ostfront*, 118–121. Manstein, for one, took notice, remarking, "If a general of the army had ordered the withdrawal," rather than an S.S. commander, "Hitler would have hauled him in front of a court martial" (*Verlorene Siege*, 453).

54. For the *Rochade*, see Manstein, *Verlorene Siege*, 405. The term is translated, badly, as "leap-frogging" in the English translation (*Lost Victories*, 374). In similar clumsy fashion, Moltke's famous dictum, "Strategy is a system of expedients" ("Die Strategie ist ein System der Aushilfen"), becomes "Strategy is a system of stop-gaps" (367). Manstein actually introduces the term "backhand blow" a bit later in his memoirs, with reference to planning for the Kursk offensive (477), but it is clear that he was using the same concept in planning the winter counteroffensive.

55. For the Rastenburg meeting, see Manstein, *Verlorene Siege*, 437–444.

56. Glantz is typically perceptive on this point: "Ironically, in a sense, he (Manstein) was assisted by the stubbornness of Hitler who demanded that all territory be held." *From the Don to the Dnepr*, 148.

57. Manstein, *Verlorene Siege*, 405.

58. For evidence of how Hitler could string out a conversation to avoid having to follow his advisor's recommendations, see Helmut Heiber, ed., *Hitlers Lagebesprechungen: Die Protokollfragmente siner militärischen Konferenzen, 1942–1945* (Stuttgart: Deutsche Verlags-Anstalt, 1962). He was expert at throwing out questions to derail strategic discussion: "How many tanks precisely does 17th Panzer have? (81), "How much gasoline does a 3-ton truck use?" (95), and "Why don't we organize special flamethrower detachments?" (453; "That

is a fearsome weapon," Hitler comments). For the English translation of this important primary source, see Helmut Heiber and David M. Glantz, eds., *Hitler and His Generals: Military Conferences, 1942–1945* (New York: Enigma, 2003). The introduction by Gerhard L. Weinberg is essential reading.

59. Nor was Manstein alone in this underestimation of Soviet military leadership. See the quote from General Hermann Hoth, "The Russians have learnt a lot since 1941. They are no longer peasants with simple minds. They have learnt the art of war from us." Melvin, *Manstein*, 347.

60. Frieser and Klein, "Mansteins Gegenschlag am Donez," 12.

61. Wagener, "Gegenangriff der XXXX. Panzerkorps," 27.

62. Even in the age of "new wars" and COIN, Soviet "operational art" continues to exert an almost magnetic pull on the educational establishments of the U.S. Army, especially the Command and General Staff College (CGSC) and the School of Advanced Military Studies (SAMS), both at Fort Leavenworth, Kansas. For a representative sampling of essays circulated within the U.S. military, see Michael D. Krause and R. Cody Phillips, eds., *Historical Perspectives of the Operational Art* (Washington, D.C.: Center of Military History, 2007).

63. The true strength of Glantz's work on the Soviet military is its complete lack of romanticism and its sober refusal to substitute a new enthusiasm for Soviet war making for one that has now been discredited, the German. For his criticism of the blind optimism of the Soviet High Command, see "Red Army's Donbas Offensive," 503, as well as *From the Don to the Dnepr*, 145.

64. See Morozov, "Warum der Angriff im Frühjahr im Donezbecken nicht zu Ende geführt wurde," 429.

65. See the discussion in Schwarz, *Stabilisierung der Ostfront*, 196–197.

66. Frieser and Klein, "Mansteins Gegenschlag am Donez," 17.

67. The definition of war in paragraph 1 of the German manual *Truppenführung*.

68. Frieser and Klein, "Mansteins Gegenschlag am Donez," 16.

69. For a discussion of the difficulty of the *retour offensive*, Clausewitz's "blitzende Schwert der Vergeltung," see Wagener, "Gegenangriff der XXXX. Panzerkorps," 21.

70. See, among literally hundreds of references, Sadarananda, *Beyond Stalingrad*, 146: "Manstein's counterstroke had regained the initiative for the German side and brought German forces back to the approximate line they held in the summer of 1942." For a German account by two wartime field commanders, see Alfred Philippi and Ferdinand Heim, *Der Feldzug gegen Sowjetrussland, 1941 bis 1945: Ein operative Überblick* (Stuttgart: W. Kohlhammer, 1962). Alfred Philippi composed part 1 of the work "Die Planung und der Verlauf des Feldzuges der Jahre 1941–1942," while Heim was responsible for part 2, "Stalingrad und der Verlauf des Feldzuges der Jahre 1943–1945." Heim writes that Manstein's counteroffensive "hatte die vier Monate zuvor bei Stalingrad ins Rollen gekommene sowjetische Lawine nach Überwindung unerhörter

Krisen und dazu mit einem Minimum an Kräften in der gleichen Linie zum Stehen gebracht, aus der die Deutschen im Sommer zuvor in Richtung Kaukasus und Wolga angetreten waren" (207).

71. Johann Adolf Graf von Kielmansegg, "Bemerkungen eines Zeitzeugen zu den Schlachten von Char'kov und Kursk aus der Sicht des damaligen Generalstabsoffiziers Ia in der Operationsabteilung der generalstabs des Heeres," in *Gezeitenwechsel im Zweiten Weltkrieg? Die Schlachten von Char'kov und Kursk im Frühjahr und Sommer 1943 in operativer Anlage, Verlauf und politischer Bedeutung,* ed. Roland G. Foerster (Berlin: E. S. Mittler, 1996), 142.

72. See the note of exultation in "Wieder in Charkow," *Die Wehrmacht* 7, no. 7 (March 31, 1943): 10–11.

73. See "Die Wende des Winterkrieges," *Die Wehrmacht* 7, no. 8 (April 14, 1943): 4–5.

74. The title of the chapter on Kharkov in Melvin, *Manstein,* 308–346.

Chapter 3. The Limits of Fighting Power

1. See Robert M. Citino, "Tough Call in Tunisia: Eisenhower's Winter Line," *Front and Center,* February 25, 2010, http://www.historynet.com/tough-call-in-tunisia-eisenhowers-winter-line.htm.

2. General Lloyd R. Fredendall's father had been the sheriff of Laramie, Wyoming. See Douglas Porch, *The Path to Victory: The Mediterranean Front in World War II* (New York: Farrar, Straus and Giroux, 2004), 383. Rick Atkinson, *An Army at Dawn: The War in North Africa, 1942–1943* (New York: Henry Holt, 2002, 273, calls Fredendall *père* the "scourge of cattle rustlers" in the Wyoming Territory. Robert H. Berlin, *U.S. Army World War II Corps Commanders: A Composite Biography* (Fort Leavenworth, Kans.: U.S. Army Command and General Staff College, 1989), notes that 24 of the army's 34 wartime corps commanders attended West Point, and that 23 of them graduated. "The twenty-fourth, Lloyd R. Fredendall, was dismissed in both 1902 and 1903 for failing mathematics" (4–5).

3. For discussion of the French formations fighting in Tunisia, see the article by their commander, General Alphonse Juin, "La Campagne de Tunisie," *Miroir de l'Histoire* 8, no. 87 (1957): 312–324, and Marcel Spivak and Armand Leoni, *Les Forces Françaises dans la Lutte contre l'Axe en Afrique,* vol. 2 (Vincennes: Ministère de la Défense, 1985), 205–215.

4. See the pertinent Green Book, George F. Howe, *Northwest Africa: Seizing the Initiative in the West* (Washington, D.C.: Center of Military History, 1957), 374–376.

5. For Eilbote, see Kenneth Macksey, *Crucible of Power: The Fight for Tunisia, 1942–1943* (London: Hutchinson, 1969), 124–132, and the volume in the British official history, I. S. O. Playfair and C. J. C. Molony, *The Mediterranean and the Middle East,* vol. 4, *The Destruction of the Axis Forces in Africa* (London: H.M.S.O., 1966), 277–284.

6. Jack Coggins, *The Campaign for North Africa* (Garden City, N.Y.: Doubleday, 1980), 118–120, a volume also useful for the author's carefully drawn maps; Carlo D'Este, *World War II in the Mediterranean, 1942–1945* (Chapel Hill, N.C.: Algonquin Books, 1990), 13–16, and Atkinson, *Army at Dawn*, 270–280.

7. For the success at Sened Station and the debacle on the road to Maknassy, see Howe, *Seizing the Initiative*, 387–388, 392–393, Atkinson, *Army at Dawn*, 306–307, 312–317, and Charles A. Anderson, *Tunisia* (Washington, D.C.: Center of Military History, n.d.), 16–17.

8. The primary source for the great retreat is Erwin Rommel, *Krieg Ohne Hass: Herausgegeben von Frau Lucie-Maria Rommel und Generalleutnant Fritz Bayerlein, ehemaliger Chef des Stabes der Panzerarmee Afrika* (Heidenheim: Verlag Heidenheimer Zeitung, 1950), 287–343. For the English translation, see the analogous sections in *The Rommel Papers*, ed. B. H. Liddell Hart (New York: Da Capo, 1953), 337–396. Liddell Hart has chosen to insert portions of Rommel's correspondence with his wife, Lu—sometimes to good effect, other times to the reader's distraction. The German official history is also quite useful. See *Das Deutsche Reich und der Zweite Weltkrieg* (hereinafter *DRZWk*), vol. 6, *Der Globale Krieg: Die Ausweitung zum Weltkrieg und der Wechsel der Initiative, 1941–1943* (Stuttgart: Deutsche Verlags-Anstalt, 1990), especially part 5, Reinhard Stumpf, "Der Krieg im Mittelmeerraum 1942/43: Die Operationen in Nordafrika und im mittleren Mittelmeer," 6:725–739. George Forty, *The Armies of Rommel* (London: Arms and Armour, 1997), 152–166, offers a great deal of useful data on weapons, doctrine, and orders of battle. For useful operational detail, see also the works by Rommel's chiefs of staff, first Siegfried Westphal and then Alfred Gause. For Westphal, see *Heer in Fesseln: Aus den Papieren des Stabschefs von Rommel, Kesselring und Rundstedt* (Bonn: Athenäum-Verlag, 1950), 186–188; the same work in English translation is *The German Army in the West* (London: Cassell, 1951), 118–121; *Erinnerungen* (Mainz: Von Hase & Koehler, 1975), 176–187; and "Notes on the Campaign in North Africa, 1941–1943," *Journal of the Royal United Service Institution* 105, no. 617 (1960): 70–81. Both Franz Kurowski, *General der Kavallerie Siegfried Westphal, Generalstabschef dreier Feldmarschälle Rommel, Kesselring und von Rundstedt* (Würzburg: Flechsig, 2007), 67–87, and Geoffrey P. Megargee, "Siegfried Westphal," in *Chief of Staff: The Principal Officers Behind History's Great Commanders*, vol. 2, *World War II to Korea and Vietnam*, ed. David T. Zabecki (Annapolis, Md.: Naval Institute Press, 2008), 37–49, place Westphal in his historical context. Megargee offers a sharp and critical eye when discussing the German staff and field commanders. For Alfred Gause, see "Der Feldzug in Nordafrika im Jahre 1942," *Wehrwissenschaftliche Rundschau* 12, no. 11 (November 1962): 652–680, and "Der Feldzug in Nordafrika im Jahre 1943," *Wehrwissenschaftliche Rundschau* 12, no. 12 (December 1962): 720–728. Incidentally, Gause places the distance of the retreat at 1,800 miles (3,000 kilometers) (676). For analysis from the British side, begin with the primary source, Bernard Law Montgomery, *Memoirs of Field-Marshal the Viscount Montgomery of Alamein* (London: Collins, 1958), 140–169, and then move on to Playfair and Molony, *Destruction of the Axis Forces in Africa*, 215–238,

Robin Neillands, *Eighth Army: The Triumphant Desert Army that Held the Axis at Bay from North Africa to the Alps, 1939–45* (New York: Overlook, 2004), 173–189, and C. L. Verney, *The Desert Rats: The 7th Armoured Divisions in World War II* (Mechanicsburg, Pa.: Stackpole Books, 2002), 127–161. Finally, see the typically fine illustrated volume from Janusz Piekalkiewicz, *Der Wüstenkrieg in Afrika, 1940–1943* (Munich: Südwest Verlag, 1985), especially 225–238. Piekalkiewicz has written a series of these books. They have won a reading audience on both sides of the Atlantic and are nearly indispensable to any analysis of German operations in the war. For other representative samples of his oeuvre, see *Krieg auf dem Balkan* (Munich: Südwest Verlag, 1984), and *Stalingrad: Anatomie einer Schlacht* (Munich: Südwest Verlag, 1977).

9. A welcome change from the tendency to gloss over the retreat is the chapter in the Bruce Allen Watson, *Exit Rommel: The Tunisian Campaign, 1942–43* (Mechanicsburg, Pa.: Stackpole, 2007), "Rommel's Road to Tunisia: The Great Withdrawal" (26–45).

10. Westphal, *Heer in Fesseln*, has Rommel "broken inside" (*innerlich zerbrochen*). For the English version, see Westphal, *German Army in the West*, 121 ("inwardly broken"). See also Westphal, *Erinnerungen*, 186, in which the author calls Rommel "a broken man" (*ein gebrochener Mann*).

11. For the verbatim text of the Hitler's *Haltbefehl*, see Westphal, *Erinnerungen*, 176, and Rommel, *Krieg Ohne Hass*, 268. In *Rommel Papers*, 321, editor Liddell Hart claims that the text as given in Rommel is "a shortened version of the order" and provides a "full version" (unfortunately, in English).

12. For discussion of the *Haltbefehl* and Rommel's reaction to it, see Robert M. Citino, *Death of the Wehrmacht: The German Campaigns of 1942* (Lawrence: University Press of Kansas, 2007), 286–288.

13. For the end at El Alamein, see the fine operational account in *DRZWk*, part 5, Stumpf, "Der Krieg im Mittelmeerraum," 6:706–709.

14. A representative sample of the historian's indictment of Montgomery may be found in B. H. Liddell Hart, *History of the Second World War* (Old Saybrook, Conn.: Konecky & Konecky, 1970), 305–306, in which the British pundit zeroes in on the "old faults of caution, hesitation, slow motion, and narrow maneuver," the half-hearted attempts to cut off Rommel that were "again too narrow and too slow," the "unwillingness to push on in the dark," and, finally, Montgomery's tendency to concentrate "too closely on the battle to keep in mind the essential requirements of its decisive exploitation."

15. Rommel, *Krieg Ohne Hass*, 385.

16. The best proof of the difficulty of actually achieving a *Kesselschlacht* in the desert was Rommel's great offensive in May 1942 at Gazala (Operation Theseus). See Citino, *Death of the Wehrmacht*, 116–151, and the lively account in Samuel W. Mitcham Jr., *Rommel's Greatest Victory: The Desert Fox and the Fall of Tobruk, 1942* (Novato, Calif.: Presidio, 1998). Rommel's initial maneuver onto the rear of the British 8th Army essentially encircled his enemy. Two days later, however, he himself was encircled in "the Cauldron," the rear of a still-

cohesive British defensive position south of Gazala. In neither case did a true battle of encirclement ensue, however much each side was able to destroy the other's matériel.

17. For the operational planning process and prebattle briefings for Lightfoot and Supercharge, see the tendentious but still relatively accurate presentation in Montgomery, *Memoirs*, 118–139.

18. For the details of this chaotic operational sequence, see *DRZWk*, part 5, Stumpf, "Der Krieg im Mittelmeerraum," 6:726 ("Die aus den Aufklärungsabteilungen 33 und 580 Gruppe Voss verschleierte das Absetzen bis zum Morgen").

19. Rommel, *Krieg Ohne Hass*, 294, refers to Ramcke's escape as an "outstanding achievement" ("Der Marsch der Fallschirmjäger war eine hervorragende Leistung"). Westphal, *Erinnerungen*, 180, has Rommel less impressed. According to the field marshal, writes Westphal, Ramcke had "merely done his duty" ("Der in strengen Massstäben denkende Rommel hielt das, was Ramcke getan hatte, für selbstverständliche Pflicht").

20. Rommel, *Krieg Ohne Hass*, 295–296, admits that the *Panzerarmee* was still in a state of panic at the moment. See also Watson, *Exit Rommel*, 32.

21. For a battle that ended in the destruction of an entire field army, Beda Fomm has certainly been underserved in the Western literature. Both Liddell Hart, *History of the Second World War*, 116–118, and Williamson Murray and Allan R. Millett, *A War to be Won: Fighting the Second World War* (Cambridge, Mass.: Harvard University Press, 2000), 90–101, contain brief operational sketches.

22. Operation Crusader has generated a vast, mainly British, literature. The best starting point is Correlli Barnett, *The Desert Generals* (Bloomington: Indiana University Press, 1982).

23. Rommel's second offensive, his helter-skelter drive from El Agheila to Gazala, usually receives but a few lines in the literature. The best operational account is in *DRZWk*, part 5, Stumpf, "Der Krieg im Mittelmeerraum," 6:569–588, "Die Wiedereroberung der Cyrenaika."

24. See Watson, *Exit Rommel*, 34–45, and *DRZWk*, part 5, Stumpf, "Der Krieg im Mittelmeerraum," 6:728.

25. *DRZWk*, part 5, Stumpf, "Der Krieg im Mittelmeerraum," 6:728.

26. Ibid. The German is "möglichst grossen Sprung."

27. Rommel, *Krieg Ohne Hass*, 304–305, "Auf dem Wege von Tobruk nach Mersa el Brega verloren wir kaum einen Mann." See also Forty, *Armies of Rommel*, 162–164.

28. *DRZWk*, part 5, Stumpf, "Der Krieg im Mittelmeerraum," 6:729.

29. Rommel, *Krieg Ohne Hass*, 305–306.

30. See Rommel's discussion of the problem in *Rommel Papers*, 357–358 ("This apart, the situation was very similar to the one we had faced in the winter of 1941–42"). These passages do not appear to be present in *Krieg Ohne Hass*. See also Major General Alfred Toppe, "Desert Warfare: German Experiences in

World War II," manuscript P-129, available in both the German original and English translation at the U.S. Army Heritage and Education Center (USAHEC) in Carlisle, Pennsylvania.

31. It says much about the relatively understudied nature of this phase of the desert war that the best operational account of Montgomery's attack at Mersa el Brega is still Playfair and Molony, *Destruction of the Axis Forces in Africa*, 217–227, now 45 years old.

32. Rommel, *Krieg Ohne Hass*, 319, called Montgomery's assault at Mersa el Brega "a blow into the void" ("ein Stoss ins Leere.")

33. For this characteristic German form of defense, one that formed the core of the pre-1935 Reichswehr training regimen, see Günther Blumentritt, "Hinhaltender Kampf," B-704, available in both the German original and English translation at USAHEC.

34. For the Duce's message to the troops ("Resistance to the utmost, I repeat resistance to the utmost with all troops of the German–Italian Panzerarmee in the Buerat position"), see Rommel, *Krieg Ohne Hass*, 325–326, Gause, "Der Feldzug in Nordafrika im Jahre 1942," 679, and Playfair and Molony, *Destruction of the Axis Forces in Africa*, 229.

35. *DRZWk*, part 5, Stumpf, "Der Krieg im Mittelmeerraum," 6:733: "angesichts die kümmerlichen Reste der Panzerarmee vielleicht zu systematichen."

36. Playfair and Molony, *Destruction of the Axis Forces in Africa*, 228. For the battle of the Buerat-*Stellung*, see Rommel, *Krieg Ohne Hass*, 330–336.

37. Playfair and Molony, *Destruction of the Axis Forces in Africa*, 231. For the use of the Valentine in the theater, see Bryan Perrett, *The Valentine in North Africa, 1942–43* (London: Ian Allan, 1972).

38. See Neillands, *Eighth Army*, 187–189, and Playfair and Molony, *Destruction of the Axis Forces in Africa*, 233–234.

39. For a short précis of 7th Armoured Division's action at Buerat, see Verney, *Desert Rats*, 145–148.

40. Playfair and Molony, *Destruction of the Axis Forces in Africa*, 236.

41. Gause, "Der Feldzug in Nordafrika im Jahre 1942," 721.

42. Playfair and Molony, *Destruction of the Axis Forces in Africa*, 238. "Traveled far," however, is something of an understatement. The army had traveled well over 1,000 miles in desert conditions.

43. *DRZWk*, part 5, Stumpf, "Der Krieg im Mittelmeerraum," 6:738: "Grosse logistische und bürokratische Apparate, wie sie bei westalliierten Kommandobehörden üblich waren, hatten mancherlei Vorteile, beschleunigten aber die Entschlussfassung nicht." Stumpf goes on to contrast Allied *Befehlstaktik* (a system of command and control based on the giving and receiving of orders) with the German system of *Auftragstaktik* (one based on missions, with the means and methods of achieving the mission up to the lower-ranking commander).

44. See Montgomery, *Memoirs*, 352, in which he labels "the infinite capacity for taking pains and preparing for every possible contingency" as "the foun-

dation of all success in war," and then, taking infinite pains, repeats the point on 353–354.

45. The battle of Kasserine Pass has had its fair share of attention in the literature—far more than is typical for what amounted, in the end, to little more than a corps-sized encounter. The size becomes irrelevant, however, when we consider other factors: the last offensive gasp of the Axis forces in Africa; Field Marshal Rommel's last throw of the dice in the kind of high-speed Panzer drive that had served to cement his reputation over the last two years; and especially the high drama of the U.S. Army's first encounter with the Wehrmacht. For the voice of the manager—calm, orderly, and detail-oriented—start with Dwight D. Eisenhower, *Crusade in Europe* (Garden City, N.Y.: Doubleday, 1948), 141–148. For the war fighter and operator seeking the knockout blow, see Rommel, *Krieg Ohne Hass*, 347–362, which should be read in tandem with Albert Kesselring, *Soldat bis zum letzten Tag* (Bonn: Athenäum, 1953), 202–206, as well as Franz Kurowski, *Generalfeldmarschall Albert Kesselring: Oberbefehlshaber an allen Fronten* (Berg am See: Kurt Vowinckel-Verlag, 1985), 176–196. Next, turn to the official histories on both sides. The four full chapters in Howe, *Seizing the Initiative*, have enough operational detail to satisfy even the purist, but as always in the Green Books, there are moments when the narrative fails to cohere. From the German side, we turn now to *DRZWk*, vol. 8, *Die Ostfront: Der Krieg im Osten und an den Nebenfronten*, part 6, "Der Krieg an den Nebenfronten," especially Gerhard Schreiber, "Das Ende des nordafrikanischen Feldzugs und der Krieg in Italian 1943 bis 1945," 1100–1162. Schreiber is a fine historian, known for his work on German relations with Italy, but he devotes barely two pages (1105–1106) to the military encounter at Kasserine, and indeed covers the entire vast war from Kasserine to the Po river valley in just 60 pages. The operational detail is minimal throughout, certainly when compared to other entries in the *DRZWk* series, and must be considered a disappointment. Perhaps it is a sign of battle fatigue for this magnificent scholarly series, or merely a reminder of how much of a peripheral front Tunisia remains to German analysts even today. At any rate, the battle of the official histories ends, in this case, in a knockout for the Americans.

We may detect another sign of Tunisia's second-rate status in perusing the pages of the *Militär-Wochenblatt*, the semiofficial journal of the German Wehrmacht. The feature *Grossdeutschlands Freiheitskrieg* continued to headline the journal, as it had since the start of the war. A survey of military events on all fronts since the last issue and a marvelous source for the corporate thought of the officer corps regarding the fighting, it contains little reportage on North Africa from Torch to Tunisia, and it provides almost none of the relevant operational details—this after dwelling in living color on details of Rommel's drive into Egypt the previous summer. See "Die britisch-amerikanische Überfall auf Französisch-Nordafrika," *Grossdeutschlands Freiheitskrieg*, part 171, *Militär-Wochenblatt* 127, no. 21 (November 20, 1942): 557–560; "Die Feindmächte in Nordafrika," *Grossdeutschlands Freiheitskrieg*, part 172, *Militär-Wochenblatt* 127, no. 22 (November 27, 1942): 584–587; "Yankeeterror in Nordafrika," *Gross-*

deutschlands Freiheitskrieg, part 173, *Militär-Wochenblatt* 127, no. 23 (December 4, 1942): 616; "In Tunesien grössere Kämpfe im Gange," *Grossdeutschlands Freiheitskrieg,* part 174, *Militär-Wochenblatt* 127, no. 24 (December 11, 1942), which, however, describes these "great battles" in a single paragraph (640–641); and "Kämpfe in Tunisien," *Grossdeutschlands Freiheitskrieg,* part 175, *Militär-Wochenblatt* 127, no. 25 (December 18, 1942): 670–671, again describing events on the Tunisian front (including General Nehring's counterstroke at Tebourba) in a single paragraph. Finally, Tunisia is all but missing in action in both of the standard German-language histories of the General Staff, Walter Görlitz, *Der deutsche Generalstab: Geschichte und Gestalt, 1657–1945* (Frankfurt am Main: Verlag der Frankfurter Hefte, 1950), and Waldemar Erfurth, *Die Geschichte des deutschen Generalstabes von 1918 bis 1945* (Berlin: Musterschmidt, 1957).

For the professional literature, begin with Gause, "Der Feldzug in Nordafrika im Jahre 1943," 721, who also disposes of Kasserine Pass in a single paragraph. For other examples of the professional literature, see Kurt E. Wolff, "Tank Battle in Tunisia," a reprint of a German article originally published in *Das Reich,* in *Military Review* 23, no. 6 (September 1943): 61–63; George F. Howe, "Faid—Kasserine: The German View," *Military Affairs* 13, no. 4 (Winter 1949): 216–222, a useful abridgment of one of his Green Book chapters; "Interior Lines in Tunisia," a reprint of a British analysis published in *Military Review* 23, no. 5 (August 1943): 30; and Herman W. W. Lange, "Rommel at Thala," *Military Review* 41, no. 9 (September 1961): 72–84. A fine work from the U.S. military community is Mark T. Calhoun, "Defeat at Kasserine: American Armor Doctrine, Training, and Battle Command in Northwest Africa, World War II" (M.A. thesis, U.S. Army Command and General Staff College, Fort Leavenworth, Kans., 2003). Calhoun rightly identifies the problems of the U.S. Army in Tunisia as "inferior equipment and illogical doctrine" (81). And finally, for the story from the inside by a fine U.S. Army officer who saw his command destroyed and was taken prisoner by the Germans, see the interview with John K. Waters, part of the Senior Officers Oral History Program, Project 80-4 (1980), 617–619. A copy is on file at USAHEC.

The monographic literature in English is copious. Pride of place goes to Macksey, *Crucible of Power,* 140–178, Watson, *Exit Rommel,* Martin Blumenson, *Kasserine Pass: Rommel's Bloody, Climactic Battle for Tunisia* (New York: Cooper Square Press, 2000), and Atkinson, *Army at Dawn.* The author's writing in chapter 9 ("Kasserine") alone, 338–392, is worth the Pulitzer Prize. Other works to be read with profit include the sturdy operational account in Liddell Hart, *History of the Second World War,* 402–410; D'Este, *World War II in the Mediterranean,* 13–21; Porch, *Path to Victory,* 384–390; and Orr Kelly, *Meeting the Fox: The Allied Invasion of Africa, from Operation Torch to Kasserine Pass to Victory in Tunisia* (New York: John Wiley & Sons, 2002), 227–258.

46. For Kasserine planning, see Watson, *Exit Rommel,* 73–74, and Martin Kitchen, *Rommel's Desert War: Waging World War II in North Africa* (Cambridge: Cambridge University Press, 2009), 427–433.

47. See Albert Kesselring, *Kesselring: A Soldier's Record* (New York: William

Morrow, 1954), 179–181, with his reference to the "Eigenwilligkeit der beiden Oberbefehlshaber" (translated, on 181, as "pigheadedness" of the two commanders).

48. For the immolation of Alger's battalion, see Atkinson, *Army at Dawn*, 350–352, and Howe, *Seizing the Initiative*, 421–422.

49. Blumenson, *Kasserine Pass*, 144–145.

50. Interview with John K. Waters, 583–609.

51. Watson, *Exit Rommel*, 79–80.

52. Howe, *Seizing the Initiative*, 437: "Thirty-four planes which could not be flown any more were demolished."

53. Atkinson, *Army at Dawn*, 349. The toll: 75 casualties, all 12 tank destroyers, and "sixteen other vehicles."

54. Rommel, *Krieg Ohne Hass*, 351–355.

55. See, for example, the *exzentrisch* maneuvers toward the end of Operation Typhoon, in Robert M. Citino, *The German Way of War: From the Thirty Years' War to the Third Reich* (Lawrence: University Press of Kansas, 2005), 297–299, and a reprise of the phenomenon during the summer offensive of 1942, Operation Blue, in Citino, *Death of the Wehrmacht*, 224–227.

56. For the confused state of U.S. defenses in the pass, see Howe, *Seizing the Initiative*, 447–448, and Atkinson, *Army at Dawn*, 371–373.

57. Howe, *Seizing the Initiative*, 447: "I want you to go to Kasserine right away and pull a Stonewall Jackson. Take over up there." See also Blumenson, *Kasserine Pass*, 231.

58. For the battle in the pass, with good order of battle information for the Germans, see Watson, *Exit Rommel*, 91–93.

59. Quoted in Atkinson, *Army at Dawn*, 375.

60. See Dwight D. Eisenhower, *At Ease: Stories I Tell to My Friends* (Garden City, N.Y.: Doubleday, 1967), 360. The entire episode is revealing for the dissonance of command relationships within the complexities of modern war.

61. Howe, *Seizing the Initiative*, 466. See also Lange, "Rommel at Thala."

62. For the superior quality of U.S. artillery, especially in terms of fire control and massing of fires, see Boyd Dastrup, *The Field Artillery: History and Sourcebook* (Westport, Conn.: Greenwood Press, 1994), 60–61.

63. For opinion on Rommel within the German officer corps, see Alfred Jodl's postwar testimony in front of the International Military Tribunal at Nuremberg mocking the campaigns of the Desert Fox as "Rommel's little shooting expedition in North Africa." Quoted in Ralf Georg Reuth's critical biography, *Rommel: The End of a Legend* (London: Haus, 2005), 188.

64. Rommel, *Krieg Ohne Hass*, 357. See also his praise for the American army's "stubborn defense of the Kasserine Pass" (*die zähe Verteidigung des Kasserinepasses durch die Amerikaner*), 362.

65. For Fredendall's amazing use of the language—"amazing" not being used here in the good sense—see Howe, *Seizing the Initiative*, 378. Here is the exact wording of Fredendall's order to General Paul Robinett, delivered during a phone conversation on January 19, 1943: "Move your command, i.e., the walk-

ing boys, pop guns, Baker's outfit and the outfit which is the reverse of Baker's outfit and the big fellows to M, which is due north of where you are now, as soon as possible. Have your boss report to the French gentleman whose name begins with J at a place which begins with D which is five grid squares to the left of M."

66. Quoted in Atkinson, *Army at Dawn*, 400. He also added that Fredendall was a "common, low son-of-a-bitch."

67. *DRZWk*, part 5, Stumpf, "Der Krieg im Mittelmeerraum," 6:739: "Das Ende der im eigentlichen Sinne operativen Kriegführung der Achse in Nordafrika."

68. For Operation Capri, its muddled planning and uninspired execution, see Rommel, *Krieg Ohne Hass*, 364–367. The field marshal blamed the catastrophic course of the battle main on the delay in launching it ("Tatsächlich kam der Angriff um etwa acht Tage zu spät," 367).

69. Quoted in Atkinson, *Army at Dawn*, 410.

70. For the collapse of Axis logistics in Tunisia, the monograph by Alan J. Levine, *The War against Rommel's Supply Lines, 1942–1943* (Westport, Conn.: Praeger, 1999), especially 115–181, is still the most useful source.

71. For the creation of 18th Army Group, see Howe, *Seizing the Initiative*, 485–500. Particularly helpful is the chart opposite 486, "Allied Command Relationships in the Mediterranean, March 1943." Alexander was not happy after his first trip to the front to visit his new command, reporting to the prime minister and the chief of the Imperial General Staff on February 27, 1943, "I am frankly shocked at whole situation as I found it. . . . hate to disappoint you but final victory in North Africa is not just around the corner." Playfair and Molony, *Destruction of the Axis Forces in Africa*, 304.

72. Quoted in Porch, *Path to Victory*, 395.

73. Quoted in Atkinson, *Army at Dawn*, 401. For other choice pieces of Pattonian rhetorical bombast upon taking over II Corps, see Ladislas Farago, *Patton: Ordeal and Triumph* (Yardley, Pa.: Westholme, 2005), 242–247, and Carlo D'Este, *Patton: A Genius for War* (New York: Harper, 1996), 456–470.

74. For Operation Wop, see Howe, *Seizing the Initiative*, 545–547.

75. For Operation Pugilist Gallop, see Montgomery, *Memoirs*, 159–163. Playfair and Molony, *Destruction of the Axis Forces in Africa*, 331–355, offers the most complete account of the operational details. Liddell Hart, *History of the Second World War*, 416–422, with its criticism of Montgomery's failure to achieve a "decisive victory," has become the received wisdom on the battle (421). Neillands, *Eighth Army*, 191–207, contributes oral testimony from many of Montgomery's soldiers throughout the text. For a discussion of the flanking maneuvers so common in the desert, see "Desert 'Hooks'—Outflanking Movements in Desert Warfare," *Military Review* 24, no. 11 (February 1945): 115–119.

76. Atkinson, *Army at Dawn*, 420.

77. For the primary source on "this secret move to the Bizerte sector," involving 110,000 men and 30,000 vehicles, see Omar N. Bradley, *A Soldier's Story* (New York: Modern Library, 1999), 56–70.

78. See the article by British Colonel F. Stephens, commander of the 1st Battalion of the Rifle Brigade, "Collapse in Tunisia," *Military Review* 25, no. 1 (April 1945): 79–82; and the memoirs of Colonel Hans von Luck, *Panzer Commander* (Westport, Conn.: Praeger, 1989), 120–139. The article by Luck, "The End in North Africa," *Military History Quarterly* 1, no. 4 (1989): 118–127, is an abridgment of the pertinent chapter of his memoirs.

79. The German official history does so explicitly, labeling Tunis "ein zweites Stalingrad" (*DRZWk*, part 6, Schreiber, "Das Ende des nordafrikanischen Feldzugs," 8:1109). See also Kitchen, *Rommel's Desert War*, 422–458.

80. In early March, Arnim estimated total Axis strength in Tunisia as 350,000 men, of whom a third—120,000 men—were fighting troops. See Howe, *Seizing the Initiative*, 510.

81. Most historians place the number of Axis POWs at Tunis somewhere in the quarter-million range, but the variations can be significant, from 275,000 in Howe, *Seizing the Initiative*, 510, to Bradley, *A Soldier's Story* ("the total prisoner count for the Allied armies exceeded a quarter-million, more than half of whom were Germans," 99), to *DRZWk*, part 6, Schreiber, "Das Ende des nordafrikanischen Feldzugs" ("zwischen 267,000 und 275,000 überwiegend kampferprobte Italiener und Deutsche," 8:1109), to Blumenson, *Kasserine Pass* ("the defeat exceeded the disaster at Stalingrad," 313). Kitchen, *Rommel's Desert War*, 456, has "130,000 men from the Army Group" going into captivity, although it is unclear whether they are Germans or Italians. Playfair and Molony, *Destruction of the Axis Forces in Africa*, 460, gives a figure of 238,243. British journalist David Rame (the pseudonym of A. D. Divine), *Road to Tunis* (New York: Macmillan, 1944), 292, has the Axis losing no fewer than 975,000 men, although he is apparently speaking of the entire North African campaign. Anderson, *Tunisia*, 27, gives "nearly 200,000 battle casualties (an entire field army), 275,000 prisoners of war." Charles B. MacDonald, *The Mighty Endeavor: The American War in Europe* (New York: Da Capo, 1992), 139, goes further than a lost field army: "In all of the fighting in North Africa, the Axis had lost 340,000 men, an entire army group." German sources are no more authoritative. General Walter Warlimont of the OKW, *Im Hauptquartier der deutschen Wehrmacht, 1939–1945: Grundlagen, Formen, Gestalten* (Frankfurt am Main: Bernard & Graefe, 1962), 329, describes the surrender as a "catastrophe" (*Katastrophe*), and says that "two German–Italian armies around 300,000 men strong" went into captivity at Tunis. For the English translation of Warlimont's memoirs, see *Inside Hitler's Headquarters, 1939–45* (Novato, Calif.: Presidio, 1964), 313. Liddell Hart, *History of the Second World War*, 431, is skeptical of such figures, pointing out that the ration strength of the Army Group Africa in late April was 170,000–180,000, "so it is hard to see how the number of prisoners taken could have exceeded this strength by nearly 50 per cent." Similarly, see the after-action report written by General K. A. N. Anderson, the commander of the British 1st Army, "Operations in North West Africa from 8th November 1942 to 13th May 1943," *Supplement to the London Gazette*, November 6, 1946, 5464, in which he gives the estimated strength of Axis forces in Africa on April

1 as 196,700. See also the fine discussion of the casualty and prisoner count and the significance of Axis losses in Porch, *Path to Victory*, 412–414.

82. Using terms first coined by historian Brian McAllister Linn, *The Echo of Battle: The Army's Way of War* (Cambridge, Mass.: Harvard University Press, 2007), 1–9, the U.S. Army in Tunisia was a force led largely by "managers," certainly, but one with a fair leavening of "heroes" as well. Moreover, the force's preference for technological solutions to its battlefield problems might also place it into the realm of the "guardians."

83. The best dissection of the German high command, especially good on the energy- and time-consuming wrangle between the OKH and OKW, is Geoffrey P. Megargee, *Inside Hitler's High Command* (Lawrence: University Press of Kansas, 2000). For the expansion of the OKW, see 205–206.

84. For the impact of the Tunis fiasco on Jodl, see the critical biography by Bodo Scheurig, *Alfred Jodl: Gehorsam und Verhängnis* (Berlin: Propyläen, 1991), 253: "Der Verlust Nordafrikas deprimierte ihn. Es war—nominell—sein Stalingrad." See also the chapter by Walter Görlitz, "Keitel, Jodl, and Warlimont," in *Hitler's Generals*, ed. Correlli Barnett (New York: Quill, 1989), 138–171. The memoirs by the oft-maligned Field Marshal Wilhelm Keitel, *Mein Leben: Pflichterfüllung bis zum Untergang: Hitlers Generalfeldmarschall und Chef des Oberkommandos der Wehrmacht in Selbstzeugnissen* (Berlin: Edition Q, 1998), while not creating any particular sympathy for the author, at least explain the day-to-day context of Keitel's behavior and make it more understandable. The English translation is *In the Service of the Reich* (New York: Stein and Day, 1979). For the scholar studying 1943, Keitel's memoirs cut off all too sharply with Stalingrad. He was in the midst of writing the volume when he was executed by hanging on October 16, 1946.

85. See Westphal, *Heer in Fesseln*, 203–204: "Glauben Sie mir, es ist eine böse Sache, Krieg zu führen und selbst in der Nähe. Wenn aber vollends der Krieg in einem anderen Erdteil geführt werden soll, dann, mein Herr, ist es das Meisterstück menschlichen Geistes, alles Nötige zu besorgen." For the difficulties of the Axis in determining how and why the war in North Africa should be prosecuted, see Ralf Georg Reuth, *Entscheidigung im Mittelmeer: Die südliche Peripherie Europas in der deutschen Strategie des Zweiten Weltkrieges, 1940–1942* (Koblenz: Bernard & Graefe, 1985). See also the introduction by Andreas Hillgruber (7–8). Michael Howard, *The Mediterranean Strategy in the Second World War* (New York: Praeger, 1968), makes the case that the Anglo-American Allies were better able to place the theater in its proper relationship to wartime strategy, and they did so precisely because of, rather than in spite of, their disagreements (70–71). For the dynamic of the Anglo-American relationship and its impact on operations, see Andrew Buchanan, "A Friend Indeed? From Tobruk to El Alamein: The American Contribution to Victory in the Desert," *Diplomacy and Statecraft* 15, no. 2 (June 2004): 279–301.

Chapter 4. The Battle of Kursk

1. The three vignettes presented here are drawn from Adolf Heusinger, *Befehl im Widerstreit: Schicksalsstunden der deutschen Armee, 1923–1945* (Tübingen: Rainer Wunderlich, 1950). Heusinger was chief of the Operations Section (*Operationsabteilung*) of the General Staff from 1940 to 1944, and later the first inspector general of the postwar German Bundeswehr.

2. Ibid., "Ende Mai 1945: Lagevortrag im Führerhauptquartier bei Rastenburg," 250–254.

3. "Friedrich der Grosse hat selbst nach Kunersdorf nicht versagt. Und damals hatte er so gut wie nichts mehr." Ibid., 251. For the disaster at Kunersdorf (August 12, 1759), see Dennis E. Showalter, *The Wars of Frederick the Great* (New York: Longman, 1996), 242–250.

4. Heusinger, *Befehl im Widerstreit*, "Mitte Juni 1943: Am Abend einer Besprechung Hitlers mit dem Oberbefehlshabern der Heeresgruppen and Armeen sowie deren Chefs im Hauptquartier des Oberkommandos des Heeres im Mauerwald bei Angerburg: Der Chef der Operationsabteilung im Oberkommando des Heeres im Gespräch mit den Chefs der Heeresgruppen im Osten," 255–258.

5. "Aber so viel ist klar: das Mittelmeer ist zu unserem Unglück immer der Kriegsschauplatz der halben Massnahmen geblieben." Ibid., 255.

6. For the successful *Büffelbewegung*, see Earl F. Ziemke, *Stalingrad to Berlin: The German Defeat in the East* (Washington, D.C.: Center of Military History, 1987), 115–117.

7. "Bis zum 10. Juni war ich dafür. Jetzt erscheint mir das Wagnis zu gross." Heusinger, *Befehl im Widerstreit*, 256.

8. Ibid., "4. Juli 1943: Vorabend des Angriffs gegen den Kursker Bogen. Eine Panzerabteilung in der Ausgangsstellung," 259–260.

9. "Vier Seiten! Je länger der Krieg, desto länger die Reden!" Ibid., 259.

10. For the tormented career path of General Walther von Seydlitz, see his own account, *Stalingrad: Konflikt und Konsequenz: Erinnerungen* (Oldenburg: Stalling, 1977), as well as Hans Martens, *General v. Seydlitz, 1942–1945: Analyse eines Konfliktes* (Berlin: v. Kloeden, 1971).

11. "Und heute nacht trifft noch eine Pionierkompanie ein, wegen der russischen Stellungen. Verdammt spät!" Heusinger, *Befehl im Widerstreit*, 260.

12. See Robert M. Citino, "Downsizing: Historians and the Battle of Kursk," *Front and Center*, June 16, 2010, http://www.historynet.com/downsizing-historians-and-the-battle-of-kursk.htm.

13. The battle of Kursk has generated an enormous literature, although it is of uneven quality and has been badly shaken by a recent wave of long-overdue revisionism. A good place to start would be the reference work Rolf-Dieter Müller and Gerd R. Ueberschär, *Hitler's War in the East, 1941–1945: A Critical Assessment* (Providence, R.I.: Berghahn Books, 1997), 180–182. From here, move on to the primary sources, especially the literature found in the German mem-

oirs and the U.S. Army's Foreign Military Studies series, although the wise researcher will use all of it with caution and careful fact-checking. Erich von Manstein, *Verlorene Siege* (Bonn: Athenäum Verlag, 1955), 473–507, is a cleverly presented account of the author's struggle for (and then against) the operational plan for an offensive at Kursk. The version of events found in the English translation, *Lost Victories* (Novato, Calif.: Presidio, 1982), 443–449, is a completely different one and wholly inadequate, comprising a mere seven pages, and is yet another reason why no one who reads German should ever use the English version alone for scholarly purposes. It appears to be a précis of the full chapter found in *Verlorene Siege*. A slightly different translation of the shorter piece is also to be found in Erich von Manstein, "Operation Citadel: A Study in Command Decision," *Marine Corps Gazette* 40, no. 8 (August 1956): 44–47. Read Manstein's account in conjunction with Heinz Guderian, *Erinnerungen eines Soldaten* (Heidelberg: Kurt Vowinckel, 1951), 253–284; the English translation is *Panzer Leader* (New York: Ballantine, 1957), 215–251. The accounts by these two important commanders contradict each other at many points. F. W. von Mellenthin, *Panzer Battles: A Study of the Employment of Armor in the Second World War* (New York: Ballantine, 1956), 258–283, an account by the chief of staff of the XXXXVIII Panzer Corps during Citadel, only further muddies the waters; even basic questions, such as which officers were present at the famous Munich conference planning session in May 1943, receive different answers. Other primary-source literature includes Theodor Busse, "Der Angriff Zitadelle im Osten 1943," Manuscript T (for "Thema")-26, by the chief of staff for Army Group South. Both the German original and English translation may be found in the U.S. Army Heritage and Education Center in Carlisle, Pennsylvania. See the ancillary reports on each of the armies, also included in T-26: Erhard Raus, "Der Angriff Zitadelle im Osten 1943: Abschnitt der Armee-Abteilung Kempf," by the commander of the XI Corps; Friedrich Fangohr, "Zitadelle: Der Angriff der 4. Panzer-Armee im July 1943," by the chief of staff of the 4th Panzer Army; Peter von der Groeben, "Die Schlacht der 2. Panzer-Armee und 9. Armee im Orel-Bogen vom 5. Juli bis 18. August 1943," by the operations officer of 2nd Panzer Army; and Hans Seidemann, "Der Angriff Zitadelle im Osten 1943: Die Beteiligung durch die Luftwaffe," by the commander of the VIII Flieger Corps. The English-speaking world owes a debt of gratitude to scholar Stephen H. Newton, who has compiled, translated, and analyzed all of these reports in *Kursk: The German View: Eyewitness Reports of Operation Citadel by the German Commanders* (New York: Da Capo, 2002). The original English translations were often hurried and unprofessional. Newton is a skilled translator, and his detailed operational knowledge allows him to give the most precise translations we are ever likely to get. His volume is indispensable and deserves the widest possible readership. Carl Wagener, *Heeresgruppe Süd: Der Kampf im Süden der Ostfront, 1941–1945* (Bad Nauheim: Podzun, 1967), 231–244, is a solid account by the commander of the XXXX Panzer Corps and speaks authoritatively on the operational problems. A final published primary source that is rarely read in the

West but that includes a great deal of insight into the genesis of Operation Citadel is Walter Bussmann, "Kursk—Orel—Dnjepr: Erlebnisse und Erfahrungen im Stab des XXXXVI Panzerkorps während des 'Unternehmens Zitadelle,'" *Vierteljahrshefte für Zeitgeschichte* 41, no. 4 (October 1993): 503–518, by an officer on the staff of the XXXXVI Panzer Corps during the battle.

Crucial secondary literature from the German side starts with Ernst Klink, *Das Gesetz des Handelns: Die Operation Zitadelle, 1943* (Stuttgart: Deutsche Verlags-Anstalt, 1966), whose depth of research and judicious conclusions allow this text to wear its increasing age quite well; the appendices (*Anlagen*) substitute for at least a day of archival research. Read Klink in conjunction with the pertinent portions of the German official history, *Das Deutsche Reich und der Zweite Weltkrieg* (hereafter *DRZWk*), vol. 8, *Die Ostfront, 1943/44: Der Krieg im Osten and an den Nebenfronten* (Munich: Deutsche Verlags-Anstalt, 2007), part 1, Bernd Wegner, "Von Stalingrad nach Kursk," 1–79; part 2, Karl-Heinz Frieser, "Die Schlacht im Kursker Bogen," 81–208; and part 3, Bernd Wegner, "Die Aporie des Krieges," 209–274. Together, these three sections add up to a major scholarly monograph on Kursk and its origins, course, and aftermath, written by two of the deans of operational military history in Germany. "Official history," with all its negative connotations, this is not. A third absolutely indispensable volume for the way in which Kursk scholarship has been changing is Roland G. Foerster, ed., *Gezeitenwechsel im Zweiten Weltkrieg? Die Schlachten von Ch'arkov und Kursk im Frühjahr und Sommer 1943 in operativer Anlage, Verlauf und politischer Bedeutung* (Berlin: E. S. Mittler, 1996), the edited papers of the 35th International Military History Day, a 1993 scholarly conference in Ingolstadt sponsored by the Federal German Militärgeschichtliches Forschungsamt (Military History Research Office). See, among other pieces, Günter Roth, "Vorwort," 9–18; Roland G. Foerster, "Einführung," 19–25; David M. Glantz, "Prelude to Kursk; Soviet Strategic Operations, February–March 1943," 29–56; Nikolaj Rumanicev, "Die Schlachten bei Kursk: Vorgeschichte, Verlauf und Ausgang," 57–67; Boris V. Sokolov, "The Battle for Kursk, Orel, and Char'kov: Strategic Intentions and Results: A Critical View of the Soviet Historiography," 69–88; Karl-Heinz Frieser, "Schlagen aus der Nachhand— Schlagen aus der Vorhand: Die Schlachten von Ch'arkov und Kursk 1943," 101–135; Johann Adolf Graf von Kielmansegg, "Bemerkungen eines Zeitzeugen zu den Schlachten von Char'kov und Kursk aus der Sicht des damaligen Generalstabsoffiziers Ia in der Operationsabteilung der Generalstabs des Heeres," 137–148; Gerhard L. Weinberg, "Zur Frage eines Sonderfriedens im Osten," 173–183; and Bernd Wegner, "Das Ende der Strategie: Deutschlands politische und militärische Lage nach Stalingrad," 211–227.

Other important German-language literature includes the three-part article General Gotthard Heinrici, expanded (*ergänzt*) by Friedrich Wilhelm Hauck, "Zitadelle: Der Angriff auf den russischen Stellungsvorsprung bei Kursk," *Wehrwissenschaftliche Rundschau* 15, no. 8 (August 1965): 463–486; no. 9 (September 1965): 529–544; and no. 10 (October 1965): 582–604. With notes and maps, this text begins to approach the length of a scholarly monograph. Alfred

Philippi and Ferdinand Heim, *Der Feldzug gegen Sowjetrussland, 1941 bis 1945* (Stuttgart: W. Kohlhammer Verlag, 1962), especially part 2, Ferdinand Heim, "Stalingrad und der Verlauf des Feldzuges der Jahre, 1943–1945," is good at conveying just how much of an operational fizzle Citadel really was. See "Der Angriff und sein bäldiges Ende," 211–212. Heim was the commander of the XXXXVIII Panzer Corps given the hopeless task of stopping the Soviet drive from the north along the Don in Operation Uranus, and Hitler actually had him arrested and placed in solitary confinement, to await death for cowardice and dereliction of duty, a sentence that was later commuted. Two articles by Roman Töppel remain useful, especially in demythologizing Kursk: "Legendenbildung in der Geschichtsschreibung: Die Schlacht bei Kursk," *Militärgeschichtliche Zeitschrift* 61, no. 2 (2002): 369–401, and "Kursk: Mythen und Wirklichkeit einer Schlacht," *Vierteljahrhefte für Zeitgeschichte* 57, no. 3 (2009): 349–385. Two articles written for the battle's sixtieth anniversary contain useful operational details: Siegbert Kreuter, "Die Schlacht um Kursk: Das Unternehmen Zitadelle vom 5.–15.7.1943," *Österreichische Militärische Zeitschrift* 41, no. 6 (2003): 583–586, and Dieter Brand, "Vor 60 Jahren: Prochorovka: Aspekte der Operation Zitadelle; Juli 1943 im Abschnitt der Heeresgruppe Süd," *Österreichische Militärische Zeitschrift* 41, no. 5 (2003): 587–597.

Literature in English is copious and runs the gamut from high scholarship to the more popular variety. Without a doubt, the leading scholarly work in English is David M. Glantz and Jonathan M. House, *The Battle of Kursk* (Lawrence: University Press of Kansas, 1999). On all counts—depth of operational detail, research, organization, engagement with the scholarly controversies—it is a towering achievement unlikely to be superseded for a long, long while. Mungo Melvin, *Manstein: Hitler's Greatest General* (London: Weidenfeld & Nicolson, 2010), 347–381, is critical of the field marshal and concludes that "Manstein's memoir surely would have been all the better had he, just the once, acknowledged that he had been outfought at Kursk by a superior enemy" (381).

Ziemke, *Stalingrad to Berlin*, chap. 7, "Operation Zitadelle," still forms the standard scholarly narrative, the one that it is necessary to refute, and despite its age, it should not be cast away. Timothy P. Mulligan, "Spies, Ciphers and 'Zitadelle': Intelligence and the Battle of Kursk," *Journal of Contemporary History* 22, no. 2 (April 1987): 235–260, and David Thomas, "Foreign Armies East and German Military Intelligence in Russia, 1941–45," *Journal of Contemporary History* 22, no. 2 (April 1987): 261–301, read together, effectively recreate the battle for intelligence in and around Kursk, like the operation itself, as a decisive victory for the Soviet military. Other works of note are Robin Cross, *Citadel: The Battle of Kursk* (New York: Sarpedon, 1993), one of the first works to question the myth of Prokhorovka as the greatest tank battle in history, and Niklas Zetterberg and Anders Frankson, *Kursk, 1943: A Statistical Analysis* (London: Frank Cass, 2000), one of the first to bring hard numbers to bear on the question. Benjamin R. Simms, "Analysis of the Battle of Kursk," *Armor*, March–April 2003, 7–12, offers useful insight regarding the principles of war from the U.S. military community, although the literature from this quarter alone would fill a separate book. Popular literature like Geoffrey Jukes, *Kursk: The Clash of Armor, July 1943* (New York: Ballantine, 1969), Martin Caidin, *The Tigers Are Burning* (New York: Hawthorn, 1974), and the pertinent passages in Matthew Cooper, *The German Army, 1933–1945* (Chelsea, Mich.: Scarborough House, 1991), 441–459, will continue to be read, and although all are out of date and out of step with much of the research, they still have much to recommend them in terms of narrative and scope. Cooper in particular is still very good on operational-level analysis and orders of battle.

There is today a fairly hefty presence of Soviet works translated into English. Begin with Georgi K. Zhukov, *Marshal Zhukov's Greatest Battles* (New York: Cooper Square, 2002), with the introduction by David M. Glantz; Marshal Pavel Rotmistrov, "The Tank Battle at Kursk," in *Battles Hitler Lost: First-Person Accounts of World War II by Russian Generals on the Eastern Front* (New York: Richardson & Steirman, 1986), 86–99; and, for a ground-level view, Nikolai Litvin, *800 Days on the Eastern Front: A Russian Soldier Remembers World War II* (Lawrence: University Press of Kansas, 2007), 10–43.

Three final works deserve mention. Walter S. Dunn Jr., *Kursk: Hitler's Gamble, 1943* (Westport, Conn.: Praeger, 1997), reminds us that a great deal of fine military history emerges from outside the traditional academy. As in everything he writes, Dunn displays meticulous scholarship here. M. K. Barbier, *Kursk: The Greatest Tank Battle, 1943* (St. Paul, Minn.: MBI, 2002) is a true rarity: a profusely illustrated volume that contains serious and erudite scholarship. Dennis E. Showalter, *Hitler's Panzers: The Lightning Attacks that Revolutionized Warfare* (New York: Berkley Caliber, 2009), 253–273, combines sophisticated analysis of both the Wehrmacht and the Red Army—its "density, redundancy, management, movement" (273)—with writing so vivid that it makes you feel as if you were there. Showalter has been doing it so long and so successfully that we sometimes forget how gifted he is.

14. For Prokhorovka, see Robert M. Citino, "The Greatest Tank Battle of All Time," *Front and Center*, June 6, 2010, http://www.historynet.com/the-greatest-tank-battle-of-all-time.htm. See also Rotmistrov, "Tank Battle at Kursk," 95.

15. For the origins and operations of the Waffen-S.S., begin with Gerald Reitlinger, *The S.S.: Alibi of a Nation, 1922–1945* (Englewood Cliffs, N.J.: Prentice-Hall, 1981), a reprint of the original work from 1956; George H. Stein, *The Waffen S.S.: Hitler's Elite Guard at War, 1939–1945* (Ithaca, N.Y.: Cornell University Press, 1966); and Charles W. Sydnor Jr., *Soldiers of Destruction: The S.S. Death's Head Division, 1933–1945* (Princeton, N.J.: Princeton University Press, 1977). The chapter on the Waffen-S.S. in Heinz Höhne, *Order of the Death's Head* (New York, Ballantine, 1971), 493–545, is still a useful summary. For individual commanders, Roland Smelser and Enrico Syring, eds., *Die S.S.: Elite unter den Totenkopf: 30 Lebensläufe* (Paderborn: Ferdinand Schöningh, 2000), is the work of choice. See especially the entries by Christopher Clark, "Josef 'Sepp' Dietrich," 119–133, and Enrico Syring, "Paul Hausser: 'Türöffner' und Kommandeur 'seiner' Waffen-S.S.," 190–207. Karl H. Theile, *Beyond "Mon-*

sters" and "Clowns": The Combat S.S.: De-Mythologizing Five Decades of German Elite Formation (New York: University Press of America, 1997), provides a useful operational précis for each of the Waffen-S.S. divisions; Karl Cerff, *Die Waffen-S.S. im Werhmachtbericht* (Osnabrück: Munin-Verlag, 1971), is just what it says it is: unvarnished selections touching on the S.S. from the OKW *Wehrmachtsberichte*. The author undercuts his own attempt to write the book "keines Kommentars" by dedicating it "der Männern der Waffen-S.S., die als Soldaten wie andere auch ihre Pflicht getan haben" (9). There also exists an enormous literature intended mainly for military history buffs. Much of it flirts with admiration for the Waffen-S.S., and some of it goes a lot farther than that. See, for example, Will Fey, *Armor Battles of the Waffen-S.S., 1943–45* (Mechanicsburg, Pa.: Stackpole, 2003); Patrick Agte, *Michael Wittmann and the Waffen S.S. Tiger Commanders of the Leibstandarte in World War II*, 2 vols. (Mechanicsburg, Pa.: Stackpole, 2006); Michael Reynolds, *Men of Steel: I S.S. Panzer Corps: The Ardennes and Eastern Front, 1944–45* (Barnsley, United Kingdom: Pen & Sword, 2009); and, by the same author, *Sons of the Reich: II S.S. Panzer Corps: Normandy, the Ardennes, and on the Eastern Front* (Barnsley, United Kingdom: Pen & Sword, 2009). Other useful works in the genre include Bruce Quarrie, *Hitler's Teutonic Knights: S.S. Panzers in Action* (Wellingborough: Patrick Stephens, 1986), Gordon Williamson, *Loyalty Is My Honor: Personal Accounts from the Waffen-S.S.* (London: MBI, 1999), and Michael Sharpe and Brian L. Davis, *Waffen-S.S. Elite Forces-1* (Edison, N.J.: Chartwell, 2007).

16. The phrase is ubiquitous. See, for example, a few relevant examples from the Italian scholarly literature: Augusto Arias, "Operazione Citadel: Canto del Cigno dei Corazzati Tedeschi in Oriente," *Rivista Militare* 23, no. 7 (1967): 808–829, and Renato Verna, "Fronte Russo 1943: il Canto del Cigno della 'Panzerwaffe': la Battaglia di Kursk (5–16 Luglio)," part 1, *Rivista Militare* 24, no. 4 (1968): 437–454, and part 2, *Rivista Militare* 24, no. 5 (1968): 536–549.

17. Listing all of David M. Glantz's books (along with those he has written in tandem with Jonathan House) would turn into a kind of endless footnote. For the Glanztian oeuvre—deep research, minute detail, and laconic writing— see the following representative samples, all of which are authoritative: David M. Glantz, *From the Don to the Dnepr: Soviet Offensive Operations, December 1942–August 1943* (London: Frank Cass, 1991); David M. Glantz and Jonathan House, *When Titans Clashed: How the Red Army Stopped Hitler* (Lawrence: University Press of Kansas, 1995); David M. Glantz, *Zhukov's Greatest Defeat: The Red Army's Epic Disaster in Operation Mars, 1942* (Lawrence: University Press of Kansas, 1999); David M. Glantz with Jonathan House, *To the Gates of Stalingrad: Soviet German Combat Operations, April–August 1942* (Lawrence: University Press of Kansas, 2009), and David M. Glantz with Jonathan House, *Armageddon in Stalingrad: September–November 1942* (Lawrence: University Press of Kansas, 2009). For Citadel, see Glantz and House, *Battle of Kursk*. Suffice it to say that this is not an exhaustive list.

18. So said the Germans at the time and in the years after the war. See, for example, Busse, "Der Angriff Zitadelle": "Gleichzeitig bot der Frontbogen

westlich Kursk ein räumlich begrenztes Operationsziel, das dem Mass der verfügbaren eigenen Kräfte entsprach. Mit Abschneid des Bogens war das Ziel erreicht und gleichzeitig eine kräftesparende Frontverkürzung gewonnen" (9–10). For counterexamples to this tendency to demythologize Kursk, see two examples from the Russian military community: Colonel O. B. Rakhmanin, "On International Aspects of the Kursk Salient Battle (6th Anniversary)," *Military Thought* 12, no. 3 (2003): 119–130; and Colonel P. I. Lisitskiy and Lieutenant General S. A. Bogdanov, "Upgrading Military Art during the Second Period of the Great Patriotic War," *Military Thought* 14, no. 1 (2005): 191–200. Rakhmanin, in particular, is full of fire, condemning "so-called evidence piled up by so-called historians in an effort to demonstrate that the great battle was of a limited local importance" (122).

19. Frieser, "Schlagen aus der Nachhand," 118–121. See also *DRZWk*, part 2, Frieser, "Die Schlacht im Kursker Bogen," 8:119–131, in which the author speaks of "der Mythos von Prochorovka."

20. See Zetterberg and Frankson, *Kursk, 1943*, 105–110. According to the authors, "the German losses in destroyed tanks were very small compared to the losses suffered by the Red Army" (108).

21. See Robert M. Citino, "Creating Kursk: General Rotmistrov's Portrait," *Front and Center*, June 23, 2010, http://www.historynet.com/creating-kursk-general-rotmostrov's-portrait.htm.

22. Frieser, "Schlagen aus der Nachhand," 121–122. See also the account of losses in *DRZWk*, part 2, Frieser, "Die Schlacht im Kursker Bogen," 8:131–132.

23. Nor did Rotmistrov even succeed at his basic task. See Glantz and House, *Battle of Kursk*, 195, who conclude that "Rotmistrov had diverted but not halted the German advance on 12 July."

24. *DRZWk*, part 2, Frieser, "Die Schlacht im Kursker Bogen," points out that the divisions Leibstandarte and Reich possessed 186 tanks on July 11, the day before Prokhorovka, but 190 tanks on July 13, the day after (8:130).

25. Frieser, "Schlagen aus der Nachhand," 125.

26. The title given to the German translation of Jukes's book on Kursk: *Die Schlacht der 6000 Panzer: Kursk und Orel, 1943* (Rastatt: Moewig, 1982).

27. Frieser, "Schlagen aus der Nachhand," 123–124.

28. Mellenthin, *Panzer Battles*, 264.

29. The phrase comes from the German field service regulation, *Truppenführung*, adopted in 1933 and still in force throughout World War II: "The conduct of war is an art, a free and creative activity that rests on scientific principles." For discussion of the document and its impact on German doctrine, see Robert M. Citino, *The Path to Blitzkrieg: Doctrine and Training in the German Army, 1920–1939* (Boulder, Colo.: Lynne Rienner, 1999), 223–229. For a fresh translation of *Truppenführung* into English, see Bruce Condell and David T. Zabecki, *On the German Art of War: Truppenführung* (Boulder, Colo.: Lynne Rienner, 2001). Here the translation is "War is an art, a free and creative activity founded on scientific principles" (17).

30. For the primary source of this swaggering sense of German military

superiority even after Stalingrad, see Manstein, *Verlorene Siege*: "Die Faktoren zur Geltung zu bringen, die noch immer unsere Überlegenheit gegenüber dem Gegner darstellen: die bessere und wendigere Truppenführung und den höheren Kampfwert, sowie die grössere Beweglichkeit (wenigstens im Sommer) unserer Truppen," 476. See the discussion in Marcel Stein, *Generalfeldmarschall Erich von Manstein: Kritische Betrachtung des Soldaten und Menschen* (Mainz: v. Hase & Koehler, 2000), 153.

31. Mellenthin, *Panzer Battles*, 264.

32. For Soviet preparations at Kursk, see Glantz and House, *Battle of Kursk*, 65–67; Mark Healy, *Kursk, 1943* (Westport, Conn.: Praeger, 2004), a reprint of the 1993 original from Osprey Publishing, 30–31; and Janusz Piekalkiewicz, *Operation Citadel: Kursk and Orel: The Greatest Tank Battle of the Second World War* (Novato, Calif.: Presidio, 1987), 70–87.

33. Manstein remained confident, "durch Offensiven mit weitgesteckten Zielen zu beweglicher Operationsführung, in der wir dem Feind nun einmal überlegen waren," *Verlorene Siege*, 481; for Hitler's smaller aims in 1943 ("Wir können in diesem Jahr keine grossen Operationen machen"), see *DRZWk*, part 1, Wegner, "Von Stalingrad nach Kursk," 8:61. For the context of Hitler's words, see the "Lagebesprechung vom 18.2.1943," reprinted verbatim in Eberhard Schwarz, *Die Stabilisierung der Ostfront nach Stalingrad: Mansteins Gegenschlag zwischen Donez und Dnjepr im Frühjahr, 1943* (Göttingen: Muster-Schmidt, 1986), Anlage C 1, 255.

34. For Operational Order No. 5 (*Operationsbefehl* Nr. 5), see Klink, *Gesetz des Handelns*, Anlage I, 1, 277–278.

35. "Die Bildung einer starken Panzer-Armee." Ibid., 277.

36. "Stoss nach Norden aus der Gegend von Charkow im Zusammenwirken mit einer Angriffsgruppe aus dem Gebiet der 2. Pz.Armee." Ibid.

37. "Bis Mitte April." Ibid.

38. For the *Büffelbewegung*, see Stephen H. Newton, *Hitler's Commander: Field Marshal Walther Model—Hitler's Favorite General* (New York: Da Capo, 2006), 211–217.

39. For the pre-Citadel travails of Army Group Center, see von der Groeben, "Die Schlacht der 2. Panzer-Armee und 9. Armee im Orel-Bogen," T-26, 4–8, and the smooth translation by Newton, *Kursk: The German View*, 102–103.

40. "Die Truppe, seit Monaten Tag und Nacht im Kampf ohne jede Ruhe, ist sehr beansprucht. . . . Eine Reihe von Berichten von Truppenkommandeuren, die als 'Draufgänger' bekannt sind, lässt klar erkennen, dass die Truppe teilweise apathisch ist und nur unter stärkstem Druck der Führung das Ziel—den Donez—erreicht hat." In Schwarz, *Stabilisierung der Ostfront*, Anlage F, "Stellungnahme des Oberbefehlshabers der 4. Panzerarmee an einer Anfrage des Oberbefehlshabers der Heeresgruppe Süd, 21.3.1943 (Auszug aus dem Kriegstagebuch des Panzer AOK 4)," 285.

41. For a critical but fair assessment of Zeitzler, nicknamed the *Kugelblitz*

("ball of lighting"), including the verbal message he delivered to all General Staff officers upon assuming the post of chief, urging "faith in our Führer, faith in our victory, faith in our work," see Geoffrey P. Megargee, *Inside Hitler's High Command* (Lawrence: University Press of Kansas, 2000), 181–183.

42. For Operational Order No. 6 (*Operationsbefehl* Nr. 6), see Klink, *Gesetz des Handelns*, Anlage I, 6, 292–294.

43. "Ich habe mich entschlossen, sobald die Wetterlage es zulässt, als ersten der diesjährigen Angriffsschläge den Angriff 'Zitadelle' zu führen." Ibid., 292.

44. Bussmann, "Kursk—Orel—Dnjepr," 506. Bussmann kept the *Kriegstagebuch* for the XXXXVI Panzer Corps during the battle. For the advantages and disadvantages of the "KTB" as a historical source, see Walther Hubatsch, "Das Kriegstagebuch als Geschichtsquelle," *Wehrwissenschaftliche Rundschau* 15, no. 11 (1965): 615–623.

45. Klink, *Gesetz des Handelns*, 292.

46. Kielmansegg, "Bemerkungen eines Zeitzeugen zu den Schlachten von Char'kov und Kursk," 144.

47. See, for example, Christian Hartmann, *Halder: Generalstabschef Hitlers, 1938–1942* (Paderborn: Ferdinand Schöningh, 1991), 319, wherein Hartmann discusses the "psychological function" of such language, allowing German planners to ignore unpleasant realities.

48. Klink, *Gesetz des Handelns*, 292.

49. For Model's opposition to the assault at Kursk, see Newton, *Hitler's Commander*, 217–224.

50. For the Munich Conference, see the descriptions of Guderian, *Erinnerungen eines Soldaten*, 278–280; Manstein, *Verlorene Siege*, 488–492; Mellenthin, *Panzer Battles*, 261–263; and Glantz and House, *Battle of Kursk*, 1–3.

51. The terms *polycracy* and *polycratic* appear in the writings of leftist German historians of the Bielefeld school to describe the political culture of both the *Kaiserreich* and the Third Reich, which they characterize as chaotic systems with weak dictatorships and competing organs of power. See, for example, the works of Hans-Ulrich Wehler, Hans Mommsen, and Martin Broszat.

52. See Stein, *Generalfeldmarschall Erich von Manstein*, 154, for his characterization of the "Krieg der Generale."

53. The term comes from Ian Kershaw, *Hitler*, 2 vols. (New York: Norton, 1998–2000), especially vol. 1, *1889–1936: Hubris*, 527–589. "In the Darwinist jungle of the Third Reich, the way to power and advancement was through anticipating the 'Führer will,' and, without waiting for directives, taking initiatives to promote what were presumed to be Hitler's aims and wishes" (530). For a discussion of the impact on German military history, see Robert M. Citino, *The German Way of War: From the Thirty Years' War to the Third Reich* (Lawrence: University Press of Kansas, 2005), 277–278.

54. "Die Lage an der Ostfront sachlich schilderte." Guderian, *Erinnerungen eines Soldaten*, 279.

55. "Eine tiefe, sehr sorgfältig organisierte Abwehr," in ibid. Contrary to

Guderian's account, General Model was not present. He had already presented his objections to the offensive in writing. See *DRZWk*, part 1, Wegner, "Von Stalingrad nach Kursk," 8:75n90.

56. "Ungewöhnlich stark an Artillerie und Panzerabwehr." Guderian, *Erinnerungen eines Soldaten*, 279.

57. "Manstein hatte—wie öfters Auge in Auge mit Hitler—keinen guten Tag." Ibid.

58. Manstein, *Verlorene Siege*, 491: "So verlockend die weitere Verstärkung unserer Panzerkräfte auch sei. . . . "

59. Ibid. The German phrase is "das Herz über das Hindernis werfen müsse." Manstein goes on to admit that it was "Ein Vergleich, der, wie mir alsbald klar wurde, Hitler, welcher Pferde und Reiter nicht schätzte, allerdings nicht ansprechen konnte."

60. Töppel, "Kursk: Mythen und Wirklichkeit einer Schlacht," 351–352.

61. Glantz and House, *Battle of Kursk*, 2.

62. "In den Luftbildern seien auch sämtliche verfallenen Gräben aus früheren Kampfhandlungen enthalten." Manstein, *Verlorene Siege*, 490.

63. "Der Angriff zwecklos wäre." Guderian, *Erinnerungen eines Soldaten*, 279.

64. Ibid.

65. "Eine Verschiebung von 'Zitadelle' keinen Vorteil biete." Manstein, *Verlorene Siege*, 491.

66. Guderian, *Erinnerungen eines Soldaten*, 281. There seems little reason to doubt the veracity of this tale. Although neither one of Guderian's major witnesses (Hitler or Keitel) lived long enough to verify it in writing, both General Wolfgang Thomale and Karl Saur from the Armaments Ministry were also there and never contradicted it. Hitler's phrase was, "Mir ist bei dem Gedanken an diesen Angriff auch immer ganz mulmig im Bauch." Guderian's response: "Dann haben Sie das richtige Gefühl für die Lage. Lassen Sie die Finger davon!"

67. Frieser, "Schlagen aus der Nachhand," 110–113.

68. Manstein, *Verlorene Siege*, 476–484.

69. Ibid., 477–479.

70. "Ich kriege immer einen Horror," Hitler said at the time, "wenn ich so etwas höre, dass man sich irgendwo absetzen muss, um dann 'operieren' zu können." Philippi and Heim, *Der Feldzug gegen Sowjetrussland*, 228. See Manstein, *Verlorene Siege*, 489–490, regarding General Model: "Wie Hitler denken mochte, war er (Model) ein Oberbefehlshaber 'der nicht operierte, sondern stand.'" For a postwar work placing the clash between "operating" and "standing fast" at the center of its analysis, see Frido von Senger und Etterlin, *Der Gegenschlag: Kampfbeispiele und Führungsgrundsätze der beweglichen Abwehr* (Neckargemünd: Kurt Vowinckel Verlag, 1959).

71. Numerous sources offer reliable opposing orders of battle for Citadel. The two best are *DRZWk*, part 2, Frieser, "Die Schlacht im Kursker Bogen," 8:87–103, with its numerous tables, and Glantz and House, *Battle of Kursk*, 51–75.

Wagener, *Heeresgruppe Süd*, 231–238, is also useful. On the question of mechanized formations, see Heinrici and Hauck, "Zitadelle," part 2, 531n41.

72. Von der Groeben, "Die Schlacht der 2. Panzer-Armee und 9. Armee im Orel-Bogen," T-26.

73. Fangohr, "Zitadelle," T-26.

74. "Zur offensiven Abdeckung." Busse, "Der Angriff Zitadelle," T-26, 17.

75. On this point, see Citino, *Death of the Wehrmacht: The German Campaigns of 1942* (Lawrence: University Press of Kansas, 2007), 70–71, 149.

76. According to Piekalkiewicz, *Operation Citadel*, 110–111, the Luftwaffe concentrated about two-thirds of its total strength on the eastern front for the Kursk offensive.

77. See the tables in Glantz and House, *Battle of Kursk*, 65, and Piekalkiewicz, *Operation Citadel*, 111.

78. Glantz and House, *Battle of Kursk*, 62.

79. Ibid., 62–63.

80. See the chart in ibid., 61.

81. Ibid., 63.

82. *DRZWk*, part 2, Frieser, "Die Schlacht im Kursker Bogen," speaks both of "die aussichtlose deutsche Ausgangslage" and a "Frontalangriff ohne Überraschungseffekt" (8:83, 84).

83. Mellenthin, *Panzer Battles*, 271.

84. Ziemke, *Stalingrad to Berlin*, 136–137.

85. The phrase is "rollenden Materialabnutzungsschlacht." *DRZWk*, part 2, Frieser, "Die Schlacht im Kursker Bogen," 8:110.

86. See Stephen H. Newton, "Hoth, von Manstein, and Prokhorovka: A Revision in Need of Revising," in *Kursk: The German View: Eyewitness Reports of Operation Citadel by the German Commanders*, ed. Stephen H. Newton, 357–369. Newton takes issue with Glantz and House, *Battle of Kursk*, 146, who maintain that "Hoth fundamentally and, in retrospect, fatally altered his plans."

87. Quoted in Glantz and House, *Battle of Kursk*, 168.

88. Ibid., 152. See the description of the start of the clash at Prokhorovka in *DRZWk*, part 2, Frieser, "Die Schlacht im Kursker Bogen," 8:124–125, in which the dean of German operational historians demolishes the myth that "two tank armies in closed phalanx simultaneously went over to the offensive."

89. Glantz and House, *Battle of Kursk*, 193.

90. See Manstein, *Verlorene Siege*, 502: "Jetzt den Kampf abzubrechen, würde voraussichtlich bedeuten, dass man den Sieg verschenkte!" See the demolition of the point in *DRZWk*, part 2, Frieser, "Die Schlacht im Kursker Bogen," 8:139–147, "Hitlers Haltbefehl: ein verschenkter Sieg?"

91. For Alvensleben, see Citino, *German Way of War*, 182–186. From the German professional literature, see Lieutenant Colonel Obkircher, "General Constantin von Alvensleben: Zu seinem 50. Todestag, 28 März," *Militar-Wochenblatt* 126, no. 39 (March 7, 1942): 1111–1115.

92. For the huge literature on the war in South Africa, see Fred R. van

Hartesveldt, *The Boer War: Historiography and Annotated Bibliography* (Westport, Conn.: Greenwood Press, 2000). The best general work is Bill Nasson, *The South African War, 1899–1902* (Oxford: Oxford University Press, 2000). See also the pertinent chapter in Robert M. Citino, *Quest for Decisive Victory: From Stalemate to Blitzkrieg in Europe, 1899–1940* (Lawrence: University Press of Kansas, 2002), 31–63. Useful in part are Thomas Pakenham, *The Boer War* (New York: Random House, 1979), which makes more claims to originality than it can sustain; Byron Farwell, *The Great Anglo-Boer War* (New York: Norton, 1976), which has all the advantages and disadvantages of popular history; Michael Barthorp, *The Anglo-Boer Wars: The British and the Afrikaners, 1815–1902* (New York: Blandford Press, 1987), which marries crisp writing to wonderful photographs and has the advantage of covering the entire nineteenth century, albeit sketchily; and Edgar Holt, *The Boer War* (London: Putnam, 1958). William McElwee, *The Art of War: Waterloo to Mons* (Bloomington: Indiana University Press, 1974), places the war in the context of pre-1914 doctrinal and technological change. The best account of operations in the war, and still an impressive achievement, is W. Baring Pemberton, *Battles of the Boer War* (London: Batsford, 1964). In general, all these works focus on the British role in the fighting, British doctrine, and British problems in using the new technology of war, to the general detriment of the Afrikaner view. There is a large literature in Afrikaans, of course, but the language barrier makes it unavailable to most Western scholars. The situation remains unchanged, as it has for decades: there is still a need for a synthesis, a general history of the war incorporating both English and Afrikaans sources.

93. For the Russo-Japanese War, see the scholarly works by Bruce Menning, *Bayonets before Bullets: The Imperial Russian Army, 1861–1914* (Bloomington: Indiana University Press, 1992), which includes a solid history of the war (152–199) in the context of an analysis of doctrine, training, and organization in the Russian army throughout the period; Richard W. Harrison, *The Russian Way of War: Operational Art, 1904–1940* (Lawrence: University Press of Kansas, 2001), 7–23, which looks carefully at operations; and the pertinent chapter in Citino, *Quest for Decisive Victory*, 101–141. Beyond these three, the war has not been well served by English-language historians. The two major works devoted solely to it are R. M. Connaughton, *The War of the Rising Sun and Tumbling Bear: A Military History of the Russo-Japanese War* (London: Routledge, 1988), and Reginald Hargreaves, *Red Sun Rising: The Siege of Port Arthur* (Philadelphia: Lippincott, 1962). Connaughton's work has the virtue of breadth, but it references little recent research and contains a barely minimal scholarly apparatus. McElwee, *Art of War*, 241–255, offers an insightful discussion, centered around doctrine and technology. See also the pertinent sections in J. F. C. Fuller, *A Military History of the Western World*, vol. 3, *From the American Civil War to the End of World War II* (New York: Da Capo, 1956), 141–181. Beyond these few works, one must consult the observers' reports, which are often quite informative. See, for example, the U.S. Army's *Reports of Military Observers Attached to the Armies in Manchuria during the Russo-Japanese War* (Washington, D.C.: Gov-

ernment Printing Office, 1906), and its *Epitome of the Russo-Japanese War* (Washington, D.C.: Government Printing Office, 1907), as well as the British series *The Russo-Japanese War: Reports from British Officers Attached to the Japanese Forces in the Field*, 3 vols. (London: General Staff, 1907). *The War in the Far East by the Military Correspondent of the "Times"* (New York: Dutton, 1905) is useful, as is Major-General W. D. Bird, *Lectures on the Strategy of the Russo-Japanese War* (London: Hugh Rees, 1911). Finally, Tadayoshi Sakurai, *Human Bullets: A Soldier's Story of the Russo-Japanese War* (Lincoln: University of Nebraska Press, 1999), is indispensable for the experience of the Japanese foot soldier.

94. The standard monograph on the Balkan wars is currently Edward J. Erickson, *Defeat in Detail: The Ottoman Army in the Balkans, 1912–1913* (Westport, Conn.: Praeger, 2003). See also the pertinent chapter in Citino, *Quest for Decisive Victory*, 101–141. Beyond those works, inquiry into the Balkan wars must still base itself on primary sources and period accounts. Lieutenant Hermenegild Wagner, *With the Victorious Bulgarians* (Boston: Houghton Mifflin, 1913), is a useful analysis of the Bulgarian war effort by the German correspondent of the *Reichspost*, although rival correspondents often attacked his veracity. The other side of the hill receives attention in Ellis Ashmead-Bartlett, *With the Turks in Thrace* (New York: George H. Doran, 1913), an account by the special correspondent of the London *Daily Telegraph*. Philip Gibbs and Bernard Grant cover both sides in *The Balkan War: Adventures of War with Cross and Crescent* (Boston: Small, Maynard, and Company, 1913). *The Balkan War Drama* (London: Andrew Melrose, 1913) is an anonymous account, mainly of Serbian operations, by "A Special Correspondent." N. E. Noel-Buxton, *With the Bulgarian Staff* (New York: Macmillan, 1913), is a general account written by a member of the British Parliament. Jean Pélissier, *Dix mois de guerre dans les Balkans, Octobre 1912–Août 1913* (Paris: Perrin, 1914), is a collection of articles by a French journalist first published in *La Dépêche*. Three extremely useful works are Lieutenant-Colonel Boucabeille, *La Guerre Turco-Balkanique, 1912–1913: Thrace—Macédoine—Albanie—Epire* (Paris: Librairie Chapelot, 1914); A. Kutschbach, *Die Serben im Balkankrieg 1912–1913 und im Kriege gegen die Bulgaren* (Stuttgart: Frank'sche Verlagshandlung, 1913); and the German translation of the memoirs of Turkish III Corps commander Mahmud Mukhtar Pasha, *Meine Führung im Balkankriege, 1912* (Berlin: E. S. Mittler and Son, 1913).

95. Contrary to popular belief, the development did not surprise the commanders. For doctrinal questions arising in Germany out of the new pre-1914 dominance of firepower, see "Kampf und Gefecht," *Militär-Wochenblatt* 84, no. 27 (March 25, 1899): 694–698, and Captain Langemak, "Kriechen oder Springen? Ein Beitrag zu unserer Gefechtsausbildung," *Militär-Wochenblatt* 84, no. 28 (March 7, 1905): 653–660.

96. For the development of *Stosstrupptaktik*, the leading work is Ralf Raths, *Vom Massensturm zur Stosstrupptaktik: Die deutsche Landkriegtaktik im Spiegel von Dienstvorschriften und Publizistik, 1906 bis 1918* (Freiburg, i.Br.: Rombach, 2009),

which has argued forcefully for the prewar roots of doctrinal change in wartime. Bruce I. Gudmundsson, *Stormtroop Tactics: Innovation in the German Army, 1914–1918* (Westport, Conn.: Praeger, 1989), is still useful, as is Timothy S. Lupfer, *The Dynamics of Doctrine: The Changes in German Tactical Doctrine during the First World War* (Fort Leavenworth, Kans.: U.S. Army Command and General Staff College, 1981).

97. Frieser, "Schlagen aus der Nachhand," 107.

Chapter 5. Smashing the Axis

1. The decision cycle, a loop of observation–orientation–decision–action (often referred to in the U.S. military as the Boyd cycle), became popular within U.S. military circles in the 1980s. See, for example, Robert R. Leonhard, *The Art of Maneuver: Maneuver-Warfare Theory and AirLand Battle* (Novato, Calif.: Presidio, 1991), 51, 87–88, 277. Colonel John Boyd developed an oral briefing on the topic, entitled "Patterns of Conflict," backed up by hundreds of slides. He never did consign it to print, however. See Richard M. Swain, *"Lucky War": Third Army in Desert Storm* (Fort Leavenworth, Kans.: U.S. Army Command and General Staff College Press, 1997), 97n3.

2. This vignette is taken from Dwight D. Eisenhower, *Crusade in Europe* (Garden City, N.Y.: Doubleday, 1948), 174.

3. See Eisenhower's letter to General George Marshall, July 17, 1943, labeled "Secret," in which Eisenhower describes "the sight of hundreds of vessels, with landing craft everywhere, operating along the shoreline from Licata on the eastward." It was, he wrote, "unforgettable." *The Papers of Dwight David Eisenhower, The War Years: II*, ed. Alfred D. Chandler Jr. (Baltimore, Md.: Johns Hopkins Press, 1970), 1258–1259.

4. The vignette is taken from the memoirs of the German liaison officer to the Italian 6th Army on Sicily, General Frido von Senger und Etterlin, *Krieg in Europa* (Cologne: Kiepenhauer & Witsch, 1960), 185. "Ich sah am 12.7. wenige Kilometer weiter östlich an der Küste stehend dasselbe Schauspiel wie General Eisenhower, und kann daher dessen Worte an den Chef des USA-Generalstabs zu den meinen machen." For the English translation, see *Neither Fear nor Hope: The Wartime Career of General Frido von Senger und Etterlin, Defender of Cassino* (Novato, Calif.: Presidio, 1989), 150.

5. Senger speaks of "total superiority"—"diese ganze Überlegenheit eines von See her angreifenden Gegners," and argues that, "muss man mit eigenen Augen beobachtet haben." Senger und Etterlin, *Krieg in Europa*, 185. The English translation in *Neither Fear nor Hope*, 150, is "ubiquitous superiority."

6. Laurence Rees, *World War II behind Closed Doors: Stalin, the Nazis and the West* (New York: Pantheon, 2008), makes the thoughtful point that "for Stalin, the ability to reject or accept an invitation to a summit with Roosevelt was one of the easiest levers of power he had in the relationship" (212).

7. There are innumerable accounts of the Casablanca conference. For a

beautifully drawn word portrait, see Rick Atkinson, *An Army at Dawn: The War in North Africa, 1942–1943* (New York: Henry Holt, 2002), 265–300. Both the British and U.S. official histories offer useful material, analysis, and leads for future research. See I. S. O. Playfair and C. J. C. Molony, *The Mediterranean and the Middle East*, vol. 4, *The Destruction of the Axis Forces in Africa* (London: H.M.S.O., 1966), 261–266; George F. Howe, *Northwest Africa: Seizing the Initiative in the West* (Washington, D.C.: Center of Military History, 1957), 349–355; Maurice Matloff and Edwin M. Snell, *Strategic Planning for Coalition Warfare, 1941–1942* (Washington, D.C.: Center of Military History, 1953), 376–382; Arthur B. Ferguson, "Origins of the Combined Bomber Offensive," in *The Army Air Forces in World War II*, vol. 2, *Europe: Torch to Pointblank, August 1942 to December 1943*, ed. Wesley Frank Craven and James Lea Cate (Chicago: University of Chicago Press, 1949), 274–307; and Samuel Eliot Morison, *History of United States Naval Operation in World War II*, vol. 9, *Sicily—Salerno—Anzio, January 1943–June 1944* (Boston: Little, Brown, 1954), 5–13. For fine scholarly syntheses, see Douglas Porch, *The Path to Victory: The Mediterranean Theater in World War II* (New York: Farrar, Straus and Giroux, 2004), 366–369, 415–419, and Matthew Jones, *Britain, the United States, and the Mediterranean War, 1942–44* (New York: St. Martin's Press, 1996), 35–49. For an emphasis on the operational questions decided on Casablanca, see Carlo D'Este, *Warlord: A Life of Winston Churchill at War, 1874–1945* (New York: Harper, 2008), 611–619; Mark Perry, *Partners in Command: George Marshall and Dwight Eisenhower in War and Peace* (New York: Penguin, 2007), 146–151; and Andrew Roberts, *Masters and Commanders: How Four Titans Won the War in the West, 1941–1945* (New York: Harper, 2008), 316–345.

8. Nor did the Casablanca directive (CCS 166/1/D) work out any sort of formal system of command for the combined bomber offensive (CBO). It was up "to the appropriate British and United States Air Force Commanders, to govern the operation of the British and United States Bomber Commands in the United Kingdom." Ferguson, "Origins of the Combined Bomber Offensive," 306–307. "Very probably," Ferguson argues with some understatement, "the omission was intentional." For the CBO in action, especially during its first troubled year, see Donald L. Miller, *Masters of the Air: America's Bomber Boys Who Fought the Air War against Nazi Germany* (New York: Simon & Schuster, 2007), 160–184. Among the copious literature on the Allied bombing of Germany, see also Alfred C. Mierzejewski, *The Collapse of the German War Economy, 1944–1945: Allied Air Power and the German National Railway* (Chapel Hill: University of North Carolina Press, 1988), which identifies Allied attacks on the railroad system and especially the major German marshaling yards as the crucial factor in disrupting the German economy, although he places the decisive point quite late in the war: early 1945. For the wartime role of strategic bombing in general, the indispensable work is still Gian P. Gentile, *How Effective Is Strategic Bombing? Lessons Learned from World War II to Kosovo* (New York: New York University Press, 2001).

9. See the pertinent volume in the Green Book series, Albert N. Garland

and Howard McGaw Smyth, *Sicily and the Surrender of Italy* (Washington, D.C.: Center of Military History, 1965), 4–5: "Handy of OPD saw the continuation of operations in the Mediterranean beyond North Africa as logistically unfeasible and strategically unsound." For Handy's verdict on the Casablanca conference, see Roberts, *Masters and Commanders*, 337. Speaking of U.S. planners, Handy felt that "the British on the planning level just snowed them under. . . . If a question comes up and you have a paper ready to present on it, you have a big edge on the other guy who hasn't."

10. "We believe," the British chiefs of staff wrote at the time, "that this policy will afford earlier and greater relief, both direct and indirect, to Russia than if we were to concentrate on 'Bolero' to the exclusion of all other operations. . . . To make a fruitless assault before the time is ripe would be disastrous to ourselves, of no assistance to Russia and devastating to the morale of occupied Europe." Quoted in Arthur Bryant, *The Turn of the Tide: A History of the War Years Based on the Diaries of Field-Marshal Lord Alanbrooke, Chief of the Imperial General Staff* (Garden City, N.Y.: Doubleday, 1957), 440. For Brooke's own commentary, see 432.

11. Quoted in Garland and Smyth, *Sicily and the Surrender of Italy*, 7.

12. Bryant, *Turn of the Tide*, 452–453. For one of hundreds of sources describing Eisenhower's travails at Casablanca and the choosing of the Husky command team, see the recent biography of Eisenhower by Michael Korda, *Ike: An American Hero* (New York: Harper, 2007), 359–363: "Not until the Americans had a chance to reflect on the arrangement did it dawn on them, too late, that they had been snookered" (361).

13. For the "unconditional surrender" announcement, see Atkinson, *Army at Dawn*, who characterizes Roosevelt's claim that the notion "just popped into my mind" as "ludicrous" (294). The principal scholarly works remain Anne Armstrong, *Unconditional Surrender: The Impact of the Casablanca Policy upon World War II* (New Brunswick, N.J.: Rutgers University Press, 1961); Raymond Gish O'Connor, *Diplomacy for Victory: FDR and Unconditional Surrender* (New York: Norton 1971); and Robert Dallek, *Franklin D. Roosevelt and American Foreign Policy, 1932–1945* (Oxford: Oxford University Press, 1995), a new edition of the seminal work first published in 1979.

14. For what became the received wisdom on the German attitude toward *bedingungenlos Kapitulation*, see Walter Görlitz, *Der deutsche Generalstab: Geschichte und Gestalt, 1657–1945* (Frankfurt am Main: Verlag der Frankfurter Hefte, 1950), 609: "Die bedingungslose Übergabe bildete im Grunde genommen den tödlichen Schlag für all die alten Hoffnungen der 'Schattenregierung' wie der Generalstabsopposition, dass die alliierten Mächte mit einer 'anständigen' deutschen Regierung verhandeln würden." This line found echoes in the west as well. See, for example, J. F. C. Fuller, *The Conduct of War, 1789–1961: A Study of the Impact of the French, Industrial, and Russian Revolutions on War and Its Conduct* (New York: Da Capo, 1992), 279. It has not gone uncontested, however. Gerhard L. Weinberg, *A World at Arms: A Global History of World War II*, 2nd ed. (Cambridge: Cambridge University Press, 2005), 438–439 and 1044n94,

maintains—on the basis of research done within the German scholarly community—that the unconditional surrender announcement actually "had little resonance there" (1044). Even some in the German resistance believed that "unconditional surrender" was a positive development. See Hans B. Gisevius, *To the Bitter End* (Boston: Houghton Mifflin, 1947), 467: "At first many oppositionists thought that 'unconditional surrender' might be the only terms in which to talk to the German generals. It was necessary, many believed, to show our generals a clenched fist, so that they would at last understand that their plight too was growing serious." For an argument that castigates the U.S. failure to nurture and cooperate with the German resistance, see Agostino von Hassell and Sigrid MacRae, *Alliance of Enemies: The Untold Story of the Secret American and German Collaboration to End World War II* (New York: Thomas Dunne, 2006).

15. The best account of the tortuous Allied planning process for Operation Husky, including the decision to go ahead with the invasion in winds that were estimated as a force 5 gale—a precursor to Overlord—is the primary source, Eisenhower, *Crusade in Europe*, 159–172. Equally indispensable is Bernard Law Montgomery, *Memoirs of Field-Marshal the Viscount Montgomery of Alamein* (London: Collins, 1958), especially 170–184, and Bryant, *Turn of the Tide*, 543–546. The Green Book chapter by Garland and Smyth, *Sicily and the Surrender of Italy*, 52–68, 88–111, still impresses with its depth of detail, and the pertinent chapter in the British official history, C. J. C. Molony, *The Mediterranean and Middle East*, vol. 5, *The Campaign in Sicily, 1943, and the Campaign in Italy, 3rd September 1943 to 31st March 1944* (London: H.M.S.O., 1973), 1–34, more than meets the high standard for scholarship, documentation, and analysis set earlier in the series by I. S. O. Playfair. Andrew J. Birtle, *Sicily* (Washington, D.C.: Center of Military History, n.d.), is a useful précis, part of the U.S. Army Campaigns of World War II series. Within the literature, see also Rick Atkinson, *The Day of Battle: The War in Sicily and Italy, 1943–1944* (New York: Henry Holt, 2007), 1–72, vol. 2 of the Liberation Trilogy and a worthy companion to his fine *Army at Dawn*; and Carlo D'Este, *Bitter Victory: The Battle for Sicily, 1943* (New York: Harper Perennial, 1988), 17–126. D'Este is Atkinson's only real rival for military history that is simultaneously rewarding in a scholarly sense and well-crafted literature, and *Bitter Victory* is also the only volume in the literature devoted to Husky alone. See also the pertinent sections from the Sicily chapter in Hanson Baldwin, *Battles Lost and Won: Great Campaigns of World War II* (New York: Harper & Row, 1966), 187–196; Porch, *The Path to Victory*, 415–421; Charles B. MacDonald, *The Mighty Endeavor: The American War in Europe* (New York: Da Capo, 1992), 150–154. Perhaps the most sharply argued work on Sicily are the pertinent portions of Adrian R. Lewis, *Omaha Beach: A Flawed Victory* (Chapel Hill: University of North Carolina Press, 2001), 79–83.

16. For the first eight plans and the origins of the Easter plan, see Montgomery, *Memoirs*, 173–175.

17. "If the German garrison at the time of attack should be substantially

greater than two fully manned and equipped divisions, then the assault as we were planning it was too weak." Eisenhower, *Crusade in Europe*, 163.

18. For the airmen's demands that airfields had to have primacy, see Garland and Smyth, *Sicily and the Surrender of Italy*, 58–59.

19. For Husky's various iterations, see the map in D'Este, *Bitter Victory*, 80–81. For problems with the echelon attack, its "complication, dispersion, and successive rather than simultaneous assaults," see Eisenhower, *Crusade in Europe*, 163.

20. For these highly complex debates over darkness, moonlight, and the proposed date of the offensive, see Garland and Smyth, *Sicily and the Surrender of Italy*, 10–11, as well as Morison, *Sicily—Salerno—Anzio*, 20–22.

21. For Montgomery's objections to the earlier operational plans, see Montgomery, *Memoirs*, 175–177; for his bravura May 2 briefing (the one that led off with his immortal phrase, "I know well that I am regarded by many people as being a tiresome person. I think this is very probably true") and that led to the adoption of the Easter plan, see 177–182. Among the sea of literature on Montgomery, Alex Graeme-Evans, "Field Marshal Bernard Montgomery: A Critical Assessment," *Flinders Journal of History and Politics* 4 (1974): 124–142, stands out for its bite and reasoned analysis.

22. The DUKW was an "ingenious vehicle, able to swim and roll," and "capable of carrying 25 troops and their equipment, or 5,000 pounds of general cargo, or twelve loaded litters." Garland and Smyth, *Sicily and the Surrender of Italy*, 104.

23. The fullness of Patton's response is characteristic: "No, goddammit, I've been in the Army thirty years and when my superior gives me an order I say, 'Yes, Sir!,' and then do my Goddamndest to carry it out." Quoted in Morison, *Sicily—Salerno—Anzio*, 20n15. Morison's commentary: "Very different from the British Army, where 'Monty's' objections broke up the initial plan." See also Carlo D'Este, *Patton: A Genius for War* (New York: Harper Perennial, 1995), 494.

24. Quoted in D'Este, *Bitter Victory*, 153.

25. "Übersicht über die Lage beim Ausscheiden Italiens aus dem Krieg," Walter Warlimont, *Im Hauptquartier der deutschen Wehrmacht, 1939–1945: Grundlagen, Formen, Gestalten* (Frankfurt am Main: Bernard & Graefe, 1962), 334.

26. Hitler offered five German divisions; the Duce responded that three should suffice, one each for Sicily, Sardinia, and the mainland. See the German official history, *Das Deutsche Reich und der Zweite Weltkrieg* (hereinafter *DRZWk*), vol. 8, *Die Ostfront, 1943/44: Der Krieg im Osten und an den Nebenfronten*, part 6, "Der Krieg an den Nebenfronten," especially Gerhard Schreiber, "Das Ende des nordafrikanischen Feldzugs und der Krieg in Italian 1943 bis 1945," 1110, and Siegfried Westphal, *Heer in Fesseln: Aus den Papieren des Stabchefs von Rommel, Kesselring und Rundstedt* (Bonn: Athenäum-Verlag, 1950), 218.

27. Warlimont, *Im Hauptquartier der deutschen Wehrmacht*, 346–347.

28. See "Besprechung des Führers mit Sonderführer v. Neurath am 20. Mai 1943," in *Hitlers Lagebesprechungen: Die Protokollfragmente seiner militärischen Konferenzen, 1942–1945*, ed. Helmut Heiber (Stuttgart: Deutsche Verlags-Anstalt, 1962), 222.

29. The leading work on the deterioration and collapse of the Axis is Josef Schröder, *Italiens Kriegsaustritt, 1943: Die deutschen Gegenmassnahmen im italienischen Raum: Fall "Alarich" und "Achse"* (Göttingen: Musterschmidt-Verlag, 1969), which argues that "Das politische Bündnis zwischen Deutschland und Italien, das zu einem militärischen Bündnis ohne Vorbehalt ausgeweitet worden war, hatte schon lange vor dem Fall von Tunis seine grenzen erreicht" (11).

30. The Balkans, Hitler thought, might well be "more dangerous than the Italian problem" ("fast noch gefährlicher sei als das Problem Italien"), because "even if worst came to worst we could always seal off Italy somewhere" ("wir ja im schlimmsten Falle immer noch irgendwo abriegeln können"). See Warlimont, *Im Hauptquartier der deutschen Wehrmacht*, 335.

31. For the bewildering divergence of opinion within the German command, itself a function of the immense size of the theater and the absolute Allied superiority at sea, see "Report to the Führer at Headquarters, Wolfsschanze, May 14th 1943 at 1730," the record of the meeting between Admiral Karl Dönitz and Hitler, in *Fuehrer Conferences on Naval Affairs, 1939–1945*, ed. Jak P. Mallmann Showell (London: Chatham, 1990), 327–330.

32. Senger und Etterlin, *Krieg in Europa*, 153–156.

33. "Bei einem feindlichen Grossangriff die masse der auf Sizilien stationierten Truppen auf das Festland zu überführen." Ibid., 154.

34. Keitel "hielt offenbar eine erfolgreiche Abwehr für ebenso aussichtlos wie General Warlimont." Ibid.

35. Kesselring tended "zu einer Unterschätzung der Chancen, die ein zu Wasser und in der Luft überlegener Gegner gerade bei Landungen haben musste." Ibid., 154–155.

36. "Diese Divergenz war bedauerlich." Ibid., 156.

37. For the primary source on this amazing episode, see Ewen Montagu, *The Man Who Never Was* (New York: J. P. Lippincott, 1954). The best recent monograph is Denis Smyth, *Deathly Deception: The Real Story of Operation Mincemeat* (Oxford: Oxford University Press, 2010). For a review, see Robert M. Citino, "Turn Me On, Dead Man: Mincemeat Goes to War," *Front and Center*, August 10, 2010, http://www.historynet.com/turn-me-on-dead-man-mincemeat-goes-to-war.htm. For Smyth's retort, see Denis Smyth, "Mincemeat: An Author Has His Say," *Front and Center*, August 16, 2010, http://www.historynet.com/mincemeat-an-author-has-his-say.htm.

38. The Mincemeat planners went to incredible lengths to give their dead body a backstory. What was he doing on this flight? Why was he carrying these important papers? He had to have a convincing life back in Britain, and it is here that we enter the theater of the absurd. The planners gave "Major Martin" letters from his father, warning notes from his bank manager complain-

ing about his tendency to overdraft, and expired leave passes, all suitably weathered. They even gave him a sex life, an attractive young fiancée named Pam, with photograph and love letters. Smyth, *Deathly Deception*, 135–136.

39. For Operation Animals, see ibid., 261–265.

40. For the term *Tunis-Stau*, see Warlimont, *Im Hauptquartier der deutschen Wehrmacht*, 335.

41. For German defenses and order of battle on Sicily, see the pertinent reports in the Foreign Military Studies series, especially T (for "Thema")-2, an omnibus including the following reports: Walter Fries, "Der Kampf um Sizilien" and "Der Kampf der 29. Panzer-Grenadier-Division auf Sizilien"; Bogislaw von Bonin, "Betrachtungen über den italienischen Feldzug 1943/1944," part 1, "Kampf um Sizilien, 10.7.–16.8.43"; Helmut Bergengruen, "Der Kampf der Panzer Division 'Hermann Goering' auf Sizilien"; and Wilhelm Schmalz, "Der Kampf um Sizilien im Abschnitt der Brigade Schmalz." Fries was the commander of the 29th *Panzergrenadier* Division, Bergengruen the chief of staff for Panzer Division Hermann Goering, and Bonin the chief of staff of the XIV Panzer Corps. See also the reports by Eberhard Rodt, "15th Panzer Grenadier Division in Sicily," C-077, and Paul Conrath, "Der Kampf um Sizilien," C-087. Rodt commanded the 15th *Panzergrenadier* Division, and Conrath commanded the Hermann Goering Panzer Division. All of these reports are available in both German and English at the U.S. Army Heritage and Education Center in Carlisle, Pennsylvania.

42. "Trosse, Kolonnen und rückwärtige Dienste." Conrath, "Der Kampf um Sizilien," 2.

43. "Intensive Einflussnahme auf die Ausbildung." Ibid., 3.

44. Ibid., 3. There is dispute on this particular point. See Fries, "Der Kampf um Sizilien," 6, which describes the division as "well equipped and completely battleworthy" ("gut ausgerüstet und voll kampfkräftig bezeichnet werden").

45. Both the British and American airborne drops on Sicily are capably analyzed in William B. Breuer, *Drop Zone Sicily: Allied Airborne Strike, July 1943* (Novato, Calif.: Presidio, 1983). For a laconic reading of the Ponte Grande disaster, see the volume in the British official history, *The Second World War, 1939–1945: Army*, T. B. H. Otway, *Airborne Forces* (London: Imperial War Museum, 1990), 117–124. See also W. G. F. Jackson, *The Battle for Italy* (New York: Harper & Row, 1967), 49–50, one of the best operational accounts of the Sicilian and Italian campaigns and a book that deserves a reprint.

46. Jackson, *Battle for Italy*, 49, gives a figure of eight officers and 65 men.

47. Otway, *Airborne Forces*, 122.

48. For the U.S. landings, and the airborne component of Husky in general, see the exciting account by James M. Gavin, at the time the youthful commander of the 505th Parachute Infantry Regiment, *On to Berlin: Battles of an Airborne Commander, 1943–1946* (New York: Viking, 1978), 14–50. For deeper insight into Gavin's wartime experience, see Barbara Gavin Fauntleroy, *The General and His Daughter: The Wartime Letters of General James M. Gavin to His Daughter Barbara* (New York: Fordham University Press, 2007), 14–53. Also

useful is T. B. Ketterson, ed., *82d Airborne Division in Sicily and Italy*, R-11960, a booklet edited by the division historian of the 82nd Airborne, http://cgsc .contentdm.oclc.org/cdm4/item_viewer.php?CISOROOT=/p4013coll8&CISO PTR=103&CISOBOX=1&REC=10.

49. Gavin, *On to Berlin*, 24. "There was still some doubt as to whether we were in Sicily, Italy, or the Balkans."

50. "Die übrigen Landungen aus der Luft . . . haben sich auf die deutsche Kampfführung nicht ausgewewirkt." Bergengruen, "Der Kampf der Panzer Division 'Hermann Goering' auf Sizilien," 5.

51. For a detailed discussion of the new landing ships, see Samuel Eliot Morison, *History of United States Naval Operation in World War II*, vol. 2, *Operations in North African Waters, October 1942–June 1943*, 266–271.

52. For a fascinating discussion of this very point, see James Jay Carafano, *G.I. Ingenuity: Improvisation, Technology, and Winning World War II* (Westport, Conn.: Praeger Security International, 2006).

53. See the map "The Invasion of Sicily: Plan for Landings, 10 July 1943," map 90 in Vincent J. Esposito, ed., *The West Point Atlas of American Wars*, vol. 2, *1900–1953* (New York: Praeger, 1959).

54. *DRZWk*, part 6, Schreiber, "Das Ende des nordafrikanischen Feldzugs und der Krieg in Italian," 8:1113.

55. "Die Enttäuschungen lösten einander ab. . . . Feigheit oder Verrat?" Albert Kesselring, *Soldat bis zum letzten Tag* (Bonn: Athenäum, 1953), 222. For the English translation (quoted here), see Albert Kesselring, *Kesselring: A Soldier's Record* (New York: William Morrow, 1954), 196.

56. For the disastrous last-second shift of the German divisions on Sicily, see Rodt, "15th Panzer Grenadier Division in Sicily," 8–9.

57. "Die Dinge spielten sich hinter den Kulissen ab" and "eine Entscheidung nicht aus sachlichen, sondern aus persönlichen Gründen." Senger und Etterlin, *Krieg in Europa*, 163.

58. For the German counterattack on day one, see Conrath, "Der Kampf um Sizilien," 8–10, and Bergengruen, "Der Kampf der Panzer Division 'Hermann Goering' auf Sizilien," 1–4. Bergengruen needs to be used with caution, as his dates are obviously incorrect. Garland and Smyth, *Sicily and the Surrender of Italy*, 147–162, are—as should be expected—useful for the U.S. side, less so for the German.

59. "Zum konzentrischen Angriff aud den südostw. Gela gelandeten Feind." Bergengruen, "Der Kampf der Panzer Division 'Hermann Goering' auf Sizilien," 2.

60. Conrath, "Der Kampf um Sizilien," 4–6. See also Bergengruen, "Der Kampf der Panzer Division 'Hermann Goering' auf Sizilien," 1: "Was seitens der Italiener geschehen würde, was bis zur letzten Minute geheim geblieben. Die vorgesetzten Dienststellen (ital. Korps u. Armee) schwiegen sich aus."

61. The attacks were going in over "a bad third-class road" ("Eine schmale Strasse III. Ordnung"). Bergengruen, "Der Kampf der Panzer Division 'Hermann Goering' auf Sizilien," 2.

62. Conrath, "Der Kampf um Sizilien," 8–9.
63. Garland and Smyth, *Sicily and the Surrender of Italy*, 154.
64. Bergengruen, "Der Kampf der Panzer Division 'Hermann Goering' auf Sizilien," 3.
65. Conrath, "Der Kampf um Sizilien," 8–9.
66. "Tiger haben in den Olivenhainen wenig Schussfeld und viel Materialschäden." Bergengruen, "Der Kampf der Panzer Division 'Hermann Goering' auf Sizilien," 3.
67. Garland and Smyth, *Sicily and the Surrender of Italy*, 154–155.
68. "Fehler und Versagen der beiden Kampfgruppen. . . . lagen (um es noch einmal herauszustellen): in der Unerfahrenheit der Truppe, in den mangelhaften Ausbildung, in dem fehlenden Zusammenwirken der verbundenen Waffen und in der mangelnden Eignung der Regimentskommandeure des Panzer- und des Grenadier-Regiments." Conrath, "Der Kampf um Sizilien," 8–9; "Die jungen Soldaten der Division tapfer gekämpft." Ibid., 9.
69. For the activities of the 45th Infantry Division on Sicily, see the document "45th Infantry Division in the Sicilian Campaign as Compiled from G-3 Journal for Period July 10, 1943–Aug 22, 1943," http://cgsc.contentdm.oclc .org/cdm/compoundobject/collection/p4013coll8/id/113.
70. The late 1980s witnessed a slew of articles in U.S. professional military journal on the Wehrmacht, its qualities, and what contemporary military forces might learn from it. See, among others, Roger A. Beaumont, "On the Wehrmacht Mystique," *Military Review* 66, no. 7 (July 1986): 44–56; Antulio Echevarria II, "Auftragstaktik: In Its Proper Perspective," *Military Review* 66, no. 10 (October 1986): 50–56; Daniel J. Hughes, "Abuses of German Military History," *Military Review* 66, no. 12 (December 1986): 66–76; Martin van Creveld, "On Learning from the Wehrmacht and Other Things," *Military Review* 68, no. 1 (January 1988): 62–71; and Roger A. Beaumont, "'Wehrmacht Mystique' Revisited," *Military Review* 70, no. 2 (February 1990): 64–75. Although much of the literature—steeped as it is in concepts of operational art and Air-Land battle—is badly dated, the Hughes article remains essential reading.
71. "General Conrath hatte zu wenig Erfahrung im Kampf moderner gemischter Waffen." Quoted in Conrath, "Der Kampf um Sizilien," 10.
72. This action receives excellent treatment in Atkinson, *Day of Battle*, 81–83, as well as Garland and Smyth, *Sicily and the Surrender of Italy*, 150–153. For analysis of the naval side, see Morison, *Sicily—Salerno—Anzio*, 102–105.
73. Garland and Smyth, *Sicily and the Surrender of Italy*, 161.
74. "Der Kampf um Sizilien war von den Alliierten bereits am 10.7. gewonnen." Conrath, "Der Kampf um Sizilien," 9.
75. Garland and Smyth, *Sicily and the Surrender of Italy*, 164; Conrath, "Der Kampf um Sizilien," 7.
76. Garland and Smyth, *Sicily and the Surrender of Italy*, 163.
77. "In the light of the present situation, this order appeared incomprehensible and illogical, and we did not follow it" ("Dieser Befehl erschien in der

gegebenen Lage unverständlich und unsinnig und wurde nicht befolgt"). Bergengruen, "Der Kampf der Panzer Division 'Hermann Goering' auf Sizilien," 4.

78. Still the best operational account of the German counterattack on D+1 is D'Este, *Bitter Victory*, 290–309. See also Atkinson, *Day of Battle*, 91–105, Garland and Smyth, *Sicily and the Surrender of Italy*, 164–174, and Fries, "Der Kampf um Sizilien," 18. The account in James Scott Wheeler, *The Big Red One: America's Legendary 1st Infantry Division from World War I to Desert Storm* (Lawrence: University Press of Kansas, 2007), 228–236, emphasizes the role of the divisional artillery in halting the German attack.

79. Quoted in Carlo D'Este, *Patton*, 507. See also Martin Blumenson and Kevin M. Hymel, *Patton: Legendary World War II Commander* (Dulles, Va.: Potomac Books, 2008), 55.

80. The "victory report" is referenced in Garland and Smyth, *Sicily and the Surrender of Italy*, 170, but does not appear in either Conrath, "Der Kampf um Sizilien," or Bergengruen, "Der Kampf der Panzer Division 'Hermann Goering' auf Sizilien"—the divisional commander and his Ia, respectively.

81. Atkinson, *Day of Battle*, 103.

82. D'Este, *Bitter Victory*, 300.

83. Quoted in Atkinson, *Day of Battle*, 103–104.

84. For the friendly-fire disaster over the beachhead, see Breuer, *Drop Zone Sicily*, 136–155. See also Gavin, *On to Berlin*, 42.

85. As related in Atkinson, *Day of Battle*, 109.

86. For Kesselring's initial optimistic judgment, as well as his rapid disillusionment, see Kesselring, *Soldat bis zum letzten Tag*, 222–224. The German divisional commanders, Rodt and Conrath, apparently agreed: "Auch die Führer der beiden deutschen Divisionen spielten mit diesem Gedanken, der der deutschen auf Angriff abgestellten Führungstraditionen entsprach." Senger und Etterlin, *Krieg in Europa*, 166.

87. "Seinen ersten in die Augen springenden Abwehrerfolg als Oberbefehlshaber erhoffte." Senger und Etterlin, *Krieg in Europa*, 182.

88. For a caustic analysis and judgment on Kesselring's decision to reinforce Sicily, see *DRZWk*, part 6, Schreiber, "Das Ende des nordafrikanischen Feldzugs und der Krieg in Italian," 8:1113: "Am Ende wollte Kesselring doch lieber neue Truppen auf die Insel bringen lassen, gewissermassen um Zeitgewinn *herbeizusterben*" (italics in original).

89. For the order of battle of the *Kampfgruppe*, see Schmalz, "Der Kampf um Sizilien im Abschnitt der Brigade Schmalz," 5.

90. D'Este, *Patton*, 515; Atkinson, *Day of Battle*, 124.

91. Omar N. Bradley, *A Soldier's Story* (New York: Modern Library, 1999), 135. Bradley continued, "I had counted heavily on that road. Now if we've got to shift over, it'll slow up our entire advance." See also Atkinson, *Day of Battle*, 124.

92. Garland and Smyth, *Sicily and the Surrender of Italy*, 244–257, is still the

place to start for Patton's "western sweep" and "pounce on Palermo." See also Atkinson's description of "an army unreined" in *Day of Battle*, 129–135, and D'Este's account of "the Palermo venture" in *Bitter Victory*, 412–427.

93. Atkinson, *Day of Battle*, 133. Patton's mobility wasn't only mechanized. U.S. infantry carried out some prodigious marches in the course of the western sweep. Especially noteworthy here is the 3rd Infantry Division under General Lucian K. Truscott Jr., whose troops became famous for a high-speed march known as the Truscott trot. See Stephen D. Coats, "The 'Truscott Trot': Training for Operation Husky, 1943," in *Combined Arms in Battle since 1939*, ed. Roger J. Spiller (Fort Leavenworth, Kans.: U.S. Army Command and General Staff College, 1992), 277–282.

94. See "U.S. 7th Army: General Order No. 18," reprinted in George S. Patton Jr., *War as I Knew It* (New York: Bantam, 1981), 61–62.

95. Dennis E. Showalter, *Hitler's Panzers: The Lightning Attacks that Revolutionized Warfare* (New York: Berkley Caliber, 2009), 194. Hube's reputation—and tough-guy nickname—was occasionally the subject of sarcastic remarks from Hitler. See, for example, the entry "Mittaglage vom 1. Februar 1943 in der Wolfsschanze," in Heiber, *Hitlers Lagebesprechungen*, 125: "Und darunter: 'Hube—der Mann!'"

96. For Troina, see Bradley, *Soldier's Story*, 144–157. For Allen and Roosevelt's dismissal, see 154–157: "By now Allen had become too much of an individualist to submerge himself without friction in the group undertakings of war" (155).

97. For the British (and Canadian) drive in the east, see "J.K.," "The Campaign in Sicily," *Journal of the Royal United Service Institution* 101 (February–November 1956): 221–229, and William J. McAndrew, "Fire or Movement? Canadian Tactical Doctrine, Sicily—1943," *Military Affairs* 51, no. 3 (July 1987): 140–145.

98. The best German account of *Lehrgang* is Bonin, "Betrachtungen über den italienischen Feldzug," 24–33. For a lessons-learned approach from within the U.S. military community, see Barton V. Barnhart, "The Great Escape: An Analysis of Allied Actions Leading to the Axis Evacuation of Sicily in World War II" (M.A. thesis, U.S. Army Command and General Staff College, Fort Leavenworth, Kans., 2003).

Chapter 6. Manstein's War

1. The last sentence of F. Scott Fitzgerald, *The Great Gatsby* (New York: Scribner, 1925), 180.

2. For the battle of Kolin, see Frederick's own testimony in Gustav Berthold Volz, ed., *Ausgewählte Werke Friedrichs des Grossen*, vol. 1, *Historische und militärische Schriften, Briefe* (Berlin: Reimar Hobbing, 1900), especially "Kolin," 118–121. See also Jay Luvaas, ed., *Frederick the Great on the Art of War* (New York: Free Press, 1966), 216–233. Dennis E. Showalter, *The Wars of Fred-*

erick the Great (London: Longman, 1996), 158–167, paints a portrait of a closely fought battle that ended with the king "a long way from home, with an army battered to a pulp and his conduct of the battle being widely and sharply criticized by his senior officers" (167).

3. The Mansteins were one of the old noble families of Brandenburg-Prussia ("preussischer Uradel") who had served the dynasty since the time of the Great Elector. See Walther von Schultzendorff, "Der Mensch und der Soldat Erich von Manstein," in *Nie ausser Dienst: Zum achtzigsten Geburtstag von Generalfeldmarschall Erich von Manstein* (Cologne: Markus Verlagsgesellschaft, 1967), 10. At Kolin, General C. H. von Manstein "commanded the task force following Moritz's in the line of march." Showalter, *Wars of Frederick the Great*, 161–162.

4. The leading published account of the meeting remains Erich von Manstein, *Verlorene Siege* (Bonn: Athenäum Verlag, 1955), 501–503. For adept analysis of the Rastenburg meeting and its aftermath, well grounded in the archival sources, see the German official history, *Das Deutsche Reich und der Zweite Weltkrieg* (hereinafter *DRZWk*), vol. 8, *Die Ostfront, 1943/44* (Munich: Deutsche Verlags-Anstalt, 2007), part 2, Karl-Heinz Frieser, "Die Schlacht im Kursker Bogen," 140–143.

5. "Die Italiener kämpften überhaupt nicht," Hitler told them. "Der Verlust der Insel sei wahrscheinlich." Manstein, *Verlorene Siege*, 502.

6. See Robert M. Citino, "Nine Days that Shook the World: The Death of the Kursk Offensive," *Front and Center*, March 23, 2011, http://www.history net.com/nine-days-that-shook-the-world-the-death-of-the-kursk-offesive .htm.

7. "Die 'Zitadelle' war mehr als eine verlorene Schlacht." Walter Warlimont, *Im Hauptquartier der deutschen Wehrmacht, 1939–1945: Grundlagen, Formen, Gestalten* (Frankfurt am Main: Bernard & Graefe, 1962), 348.

8. For the best analysis of Hoth's generalship at Kursk, see Stephen H. Newton, ed., *Kursk: The German View: Eyewitness Reports of Operation Citadel by the German Commanders* (New York: Da Capo, 2002), especially the chapter entitled, "Hoth, von Manstein, and Prokhorovka: A Revision in Need of Revising," 357–369.

9. Warlimont, *Im Hauptquartier der deutschen Wehrmacht*, 350–351, notes the "completely unrealistic expectations" ("gänzlich irrealen Vorstellungen"), as when Hitler declared that "the enemy could be thrown back into the sea" ("den gelandeten Feind in das Meer zurückwerfen zu können").

10. "So wurden 12. und 18. Pz. Div. an die bedrohten Stellen nordostw. Bolchoff und nördlich Uljanowo geworfwen." Peter von der Groeben, "Die Schlacht der 2. Panzer-Armee und 9. Armee im Orel-Bogen vom 5. Juli bis 18. August 1943," 16. This account is by the operations officer of 2nd Panzer Army. It is contained within the omnibus report by Theodor Busse, "Der Angriff Zitadelle im Osten 1943," part of the Foreign Military Studies series, Manuscript T (for "Thema")-26, by the chief of staff for Army Group South. Both the German original and English translation of these reports may be found in

the U.S. Army Heritage and Education Center in Carlisle, Pennsylvania. See also Newton, *Kursk*, 109.

11. "Der Insel auch 'mit den . . . deutschen Kräften . . . allein . . . nicht zu halten' sein würde." Warlimont, *Im Hauptquartier der deutschen Wehrmacht*, 350.

12. "Diese Zahl mag man heute nicht glauben!" Johann Adolf Graf von Kielmansegg, "Bemerkungen eines Zeitzeugen zu den Schlachten von Char'kov und Kursk aus der Sicht des damaligen Generalstabsoffiziers Ia in der Operationsabteilung der Generalstabs des Heeres," in *Gezeitenwechsel im Zweiten Weltkrieg? Die Schlachten von Ch'arkow und Kursk im Frühjahr und Sommer 1943 in operativer Anlage, Verlauf und politischer Bedeutung*, ed. Roland G. Foerster (Berlin: E. S. Mittler, 1996), 138.

13. "Da muss man eine Null an die 17 hängen, und dann reicht es immer noch nicht." Ibid.

14. Historians have only recently come to emphasize the linkages between the global war's various theaters, and that emphasis has become a feature in the best one-volume histories of the conflict in particular. See above all Gerhard L. Weinberg's magnum opus, *A World at Arms: A Global History of World War II*, 2nd ed. (Cambridge: Cambridge University Press, 2005), but also Evan Mawdsley, *World War II: A New History* (Cambridge: Cambridge University Press, 2009), and Thomas W. Zeiler, *Annihilation: A Global Military History of World War II* (Oxford: Oxford University Press, 2011). If a common theme unites them, it is the notion of global war. Although Weinberg does not shrink from stressing Hitler's role in starting the war—he was an intentionalist on this point even before historians had coined the term—and although he gives primacy to the European conflict, he also offers wide-ranging analysis on the global linkages between war in Europe, Africa, and Asia. Tellingly, the opening vignette in the preface to *A World at Arms* deals not with the German invasion of Poland. Instead, it describes the battle of Kohima in 1944, where the British and Indians won a decisive victory over a Japanese army invading India, and it offers satirical commentary on the views of the Indian Nationalist Subhas Chandra Bose (xiii).

15. "Auch mir fällt vieles schwer, das können Sie mir glauben. . . . " Adolf Heusinger, *Befehl im Widerstreit: Schicksalsstunden der deutschen Armee, 1923–1945* (Tübingen: Rainer Wunderlich, 1950), 210–211.

16. "Einseitigkeit" (one-sidedness) was perhaps the highest term of opprobrium in the German military vocabulary. See Robert M. Citino, "'Die Gedanken sind frei': The Intellectual Culture of the Interwar German Army," *Army Doctrine and Training Bulletin* (Canada) 4, no. 3 (Fall 2001): 53–54, published simultaneously in French translation as "'Die Gedanken sind frei': Culture Intellectuelle de l'Armée Allemande de l'Entre-Deux-Guerres."

17. There is some truth here. The Soviet army outnumbered the Wehrmacht many times over by this point in the war. See *DRZWk*, part 2, Frieser, "Die Schlacht im Kursker Bogen," 8:149, who begins his analysis of "the causes of the German failure" with a discussion of "the law of numbers" ("Gesetz der Zahl").

18. "Dem russischen Soldaten fühlte sich der deutsche immer noch überlegen. . . . Aber die Quantität triumphierte über die Qualität." Carl Wagener, *Heeresgruppe Süd: Der Kampf im Süden der Ostfront, 1941–1945* (Bad Nauheim: Podzun, 1967), 248.

19. F. W. Mellenthin, *Panzer Battles: A Study of the Employment of Armor on the Second World War* (New York: Ballantine, 1956), 349–350.

20. For the ideological origins of "the Other," see Edward Said, *Orientalism* (New York: Vintage, 1979), 1–3, 5.

21. Heinz Guderian, *Erinnerungen eines Soldaten* (Heidelberg: Kurt Vowinckel, 1951), translated into English as *Panzer Leader* (New York: Ballantine, 1957). For Mellenthin, see note 19 above.

22. Hans von Luck, *Panzer Commander* (Westport, Conn.: Praeger, 1989).

23. Heinz Werner Schmidt, *With Rommel in the Desert* (New York: Bantam, 1977). Manstein, *Verlorene Siege*, translated into English as *Lost Victories* (Novato, Calif.: Presidio, 1982).

24. Frido von Senger und Etterlin, *Krieg in Europa* (Cologne: Kiepenhauer & Witsch, 1960), translated into English as *Neither Fear nor Hope: The Wartime Career of General Frido von Senger und Etterlin, Defender of Cassino* (Novato, Calif.: Presidio, 1989).

25. Historians have as yet come nowhere near to exploring this immense collection of documents; to do so would take a lifetime of research. For an overview, see *Guide to Foreign Military Studies, 1945–54: Catalog and Index* (Karlsruhe: Historical Division, Headquarters, U.S. Army Europe, 1954), which runs 253 pages, along with "Supplement to Guide to Foreign Military Studies 1945–54: Catalog and Index" (Karlsruhe: Historical Division, Headquarters, U.S. Army Europe, 1959).

26. For a typical disclaimer, see the opening of Busse, "Der Angriff Zitadelle im Osten 1943," 3: "Lagenkarten oder Akten standen für die Bearbeitung nicht zur Verfügung. Alle Bearbeiter konnten sich nur auf die Erinnerung und einige wenige persönliche Aufzeichnungen stützen."

27. Personal animus, even highly justified, also may have played a role in shifting all blame to Hitler. Alfred Philippi and Ferdinand Heim, *Der Feldzug gegen Sowjetrussland, 1941 bis 1945* (Stuttgart: W. Kohlhammer Verlag, 1962), is a reasoned analysis of operations in the east, but the informed reader will want to know that Heim had been arrested and imprisoned on Hitler's orders during the war.

28. Mellenthin, *Panzer Battles*, 350.

29. Ibid., 354.

30. Ibid., 350.

31. The best scholarly work on the German officer corps, with a special focus on the commanders of the *Ostheer* (the army of the east) is Johannes Hürter, *Hitlers Heerführer: Die deutschen Oberbefehlshaber in Krieg gegen die Sowjetunion, 1941/42* (Munich: R. Oldenbourg, 2006). Hürter describes both the professional and moral deterioration of the army and army group commanders in the first two years of the war in the east, the breakdown of their inter-

nal unity vis-à-vis the Führer, and their descent into both criminality and incompetence. For another strong voice within the German scholarly community, see David Stahel, *Operation Barbarossa and Germany's Defeat in the East* (Cambridge: Cambridge University Press, 2009). In the English-language literature, no scholar comes close to Geoffrey P. Megargee in demolishing notions of a German genius for war. See his *Inside Hitler's High Command* (Lawrence: University Press of Kansas, 2000) and *War of Annihilation: Combat and Genocide on the Eastern Front, 1941* (Lanham, Md.: Rowman & Littlefield, 2006).

32. For two examples among many in the professional literature of the U.S. military, in the era in which "operational art" had become a kind of totem, see Clayton R. Newell and Michael D. Krause, eds., *On Operational Art* (Washington, D.C.: Center of Military History, 1994), and Michael D. Krause and R. Cody Phillips, eds., *Historical Perspectives of the Operational Art* (Washington, D.C.: Center of Military History, 2007). The former volume, written at the height of operational art fever, is excruciatingly theoretical. See the chapters by James J. Schneider, "Theoretical Implications of Operational Art," 17–30; Glenn K. Otis, "The Ground Commander's View—I," 31–46; Crosbie Saint, "The Ground Commander's View—II," 47–64; and William A. Stofft, "Leadership at the Operational Level of War," 189–196. Richard M. Swain, "Reading about Operational Art," 197–210, brings the reader back down to earth by discussing actual literature, a marker of Swain's entire scholarly oeuvre. Hans Henning von Sandrart, "Operational Art in a Continental Theater," 119–132, offers a contemporary view from the perspective of the Federal German *Bundeswehr*.

33. For the scholarly *Kulminationspunkt* of Tukhachevsky worship, see Shimon Naveh, *In Pursuit of Excellence: The Evolution of Operational Theory* (London: Frank Cass, 1997). The author's reliance on systems theory for his operational analysis makes the book nearly unreadable. For a less opaque presentation on Tukhachevksy, see Roman Johann Jarymowycz, "Jedi Knights in the Kremlin: The Soviet Military in the 1930s and the Genesis of Deep Battle," in *Military Planning and the Origins of the Second World War in Europe*, ed. B. J. C. McKercher and Roch Legault (Westport, Conn.: Praeger, 2001), 122–124. See also Mary R. Habeck, *Storm of Steel: The Development of Armor Doctrine in Germany and the Soviet Union, 1919–1939* (Ithaca, N.Y.: Cornell University Press, 2003); Sally Webb Stoecker, *Forging Stalin's Army: Marshal Tukhachevsky and the Politics of Military Innovation* (Boulder, Colo.: Westview Press, 1998); and Frederick Carleton Turner, "The Genesis of the Soviet 'Deep Operation': The Stalin-Era Doctrine for Large-Scale Offensive Maneuver Warfare" (Ph.D. diss., Duke University, 1988). A useful corrective to the tendency of scholars to focus on one man is found in Richard W. Harrison, *The Russian Way of War: Operational Art, 1904–1940* (Lawrence: University Press of Kansas, 2001), 169–217, which analyzes the contributions of numerous other Soviet contributors to deep battle, especially G. S. Isserson. Harrison is a formidable scholar, and next to David M. Glantz is the leading scholar of the Soviet mil-

itary in the United States. His *Architect of Soviet Victory in World War II: The Life and Theories of G. S. Isserson* (Jefferson, N.C.: McFarland, 2010) answered the scholarly world's need for a biography of this crucial figure.

34. A point well made by Bruce Menning, "The Deep Strike in Russian and Soviet Military History," *Journal of Soviet Military Studies* 1, no. 1 (April 1988): 9–28.

35. For "consecutive operations," see, for example, Frederick Kagan, "Army Doctrine and Modern War: Notes toward a New Edition of FM 100-5," *Parameters* 27, no. 1 (Spring 1997): 134–151.

36. Quoted in Jacob W. Kipp, "The Origins of Soviet Operational Art, 1917–1936," in Krause and Phillips, *Historical Perspectives of the Operational Art*, 237.

37. For a discussion of Tuchachevsky's operational vision, see Paddy Griffith, *Forward into Battle: Fighting Tactics from Waterloo to the Near Future* (Novato, Calif.: Presidio, 1990), 131, and Robert M. Citino, *Death of the Wehrmacht: The German Campaigns of 1942* (Lawrence: University Press of Kansas, 2007), 289–290.

38. See, for example, Major M. Braun, "Gedanken über Kampfwagen- und Fliegerverwendung bei den russischen Herbstmanövern 1936," *Militär-Wochenblatt* 121, no. 28 (January 22, 1937): 1589–1592. See also the report by the U.S. military attaché in Moscow, Lieutenant Colonel Philip R. Faymonville, on the 1935 Soviet maneuvers in Kiev, which featured an airborne landing by 500 men and an attack on the paratroopers by a "strong detachment of fast tanks." David M. Glantz, "Observing the Soviets: U.S. Army Attachés in Eastern Europe During the 1930s," *Journal of Military History* 55, no. 2 (April 1991): 153–183, especially 163–165.

39. See David M. Glantz, "Soviet Operational Art since 1936: The Triumph of Maneuver War," in Krause and Phillips, *Historical Perspectives of the Operational Art*, 247–248.

40. For discussion of the "Not a Step Back" order, see Citino, *Death of the Wehrmacht*, 173–174.

41. "Political officers confined themselves to matters of morale and propaganda, and even Stalin began to trust his subordinates as professional experts." David M. Glantz and Jonathan House, *When Titans Clashed: How the Red Army Stopped Hitler* (Lawrence: University Press of Kansas, 1995), 288.

42. "Es war im Russlandfeldzug zur Regel geworden, dass die deutsche Seite die Entscheidung im Sommer suchte, die russische im Winter." Wagener, *Heeresgruppe Süd*, 201.

43. The successful Soviet operation known as Kutuzov has received little attention from English-language historians compared to what they have lavished on the failed German Operation Citadel. Books on the German offensive toward Kursk number in the double digits, while Kutuzov has not a single dedicated scholarly monograph. It is easy to list the excuses: lack of Russian-language skills in the American scholarly community, tendency to identify with the Germans, difficulty in accessing the Russian sources and archives. The adop-

tion in the West of the German view on the war in the Soviet Union has led most monographs on Kursk to finish on July 13, when Hitler decided to call off the offensive. See, for example, Martin Caidin, *The Tigers Are Burning* (New York: Hawthorn, 1974), Walter S. Dunn Jr., *Kursk: Hitler's Gamble, 1943* (Westport, Conn.: Praeger, 1997), Mark Healy, *Kursk, 1943* (1993; reprint, Westport, Conn.: Praeger, 2004), and Lloyd Clark, *The Battle of the Tanks: Kursk, 1943* (New York: Atlantic Monthly, 2011). Even the usually reliable Earl F. Ziemke, *Stalingrad to Berlin: The German Defeat in the East* (Washington, D.C.: Center of Military History, 1987), rushes through Kutuzov in a few pages (see 136–142). The scholar seeking sources will have to start with individual secondary works on the German–Soviet war or on the battle of Kursk, the best of which offer a chapter or two on the Soviet offensives toward Orel and Belgorod–Kharkov. See, for example, the seminal works by S. M. Shtemenko, *The Soviet General Staff at War, 1941–1945* (Moscow: Progress Publishers, 1981); John Erickson, *The Road to Berlin: Continuing the History of Stalin's War with Germany* (Boulder, Colo.: Westview, 1983), which offers a chapter on "Breaking the Equilibrium: Kursk and Its Aftermath" (87–135); David M. Glantz and Jonathan House, *The Battle of Kursk* (Lawrence: University Press of Kansas, 1999), 225–240; and David M. Glantz, "Soviet Military Strategy during the Second Period of War (November 1942–December 1943): A Reappraisal," *Journal of Military History* 60, no. 1 (January 1996): 115–150. Geoffrey Jukes, *Kursk: The Clash of Armor, July 1943* (New York: Ballantine, 1969), offers good coverage of Kutuzov, as does M. K. Barbier, *Kursk: The Greatest Tank Battle, 1943* (St. Paul, Minn.: MBI, 2002). For the tangled historiography of the battle, see Boris V. Sokolov, "The Battle for Kursk, Orel, and Char'kov: Strategic Intentions and Results: A Critical View of the Soviet Historiography," in Foerster, *Gezeitenwechsel im Zweiten Weltkrieg?*, 69–88. From the German side, the required source is Groeben, "Die Schlacht der 2. Panzer-Armee und 9. Armee im Orel-Bogen vom 5. Juli bis 18. August 1943." For the English translation of this report, see Newton, *Kursk*, 97–119.

44. Glantz and House, *Battle of Kursk*, 230.

45. Ibid. Exactitude in numbers of this magnitude is elusive. See *DRZWk*, part 2, Frieser, "Die Schlacht im Kursker Bogen," 8:174, who gives a number of 561,111 men for "the Bryansk Front and the left wing of the Western Front."

46. "Auch die Bezeichnung 2. 'Panzerarmee' war inzwischen zur Farce geraten, da diese Armee (abgesehen von späteren Unterstellungen) keinen einzigen Kampfpanzer mehr besass." *DRZWk*, part 2, Frieser, "Die Schlacht im Kursker Bogen," 8:174.

47. Glantz and House, *Battle of Kursk*, 232.

48. Upon the arrest of his brother for treasonous activities (*Landesverrat*), the Gestapo discovered several incriminating letters from General Schmidt, "which criticized the Führer very sharply" ("die sehr scharf gegen den Führer gerichtet waren"). See Hürter, *Hitlers Heerführer*, 602–603.

49. For the Mechelen incident, see Jean Vanwelkenhuyzen, "Die Krise vom Januar 1940," *Wehrwissenschaftliche Rundschau* 5, no. 2 (February 1955): 66–90.

50. For the Stumme incident, which saw the commander of both the 23rd

Panzer Division (General Hans von Boineburg-Lengsfeld) and the XXXX Panzer Corps (General Georg Stumme) dismissed on the very eve of Operation Blue in 1942, see Citino, *Death of the Wehrmacht*, 164–165.

51. For Soviet artillery density in the offensive, see *DRZWk*, part 2, Frieser, "Die Schlacht im Kursker Bogen," 8:175, who gives a figure of 200 artillery pieces ("Geschütze und Granatwerfer") per kilometer, as compared to less than two tubes per kilometer for the German defenders.

52. Groeben, "Die Schlacht der 2. Panzer-Armee und 9. Armee im Orel-Bogen vom 5. Juli bis 18. August 1943," 15; Newton, *Kursk*, 108.

53. Glantz and House, *Battle of Kursk*, 234.

54. See the primary source: Lothar Rendulic, "Die Schlacht von Orel, Juli 1943: Wahl und Bildung des Schwerpunktes," *Österreichische Militärische Zeitschrift* 1, no. 3 (1963): 130–138.

55. Glantz and House, *Battle of Kursk*, 234.

56. For Model's deft generalship during the Orel battle, see Stephen H. Newton, *Hitler's Commander: Field Marshal Walther Model—Hitler's Favorite General* (New York: Da Capo, 2006), 255–262, as well as *DRZWk*, part 2, Frieser, "Die Schlacht im Kursker Bogen," 8:186: "An dieser Stelle erscheint es notwendig, jenem Klischeebild vom 'Nazigeneral' Model, der bedenkenlos Hitlers Befehle umgesetzt habe, entgegenzutreten." On Model generally, see also Marcel Stein, *Generalfeldmarschall Walter Model: Legende und Wirklichkeit* (Bissendorf: Biblio, 2001).

57. Newton, *Hitler's Commander*, 258–259.

58. "Natürlich. Immer räumen und räumen! Dann sind wir bald an der Reichsgrenze angelangt. Und der Russe gewinnt sein Land zurück, ohne einen Mann einzubüssen." Heusinger, *Befehl im Widerstreit*, 266.

59. For the retreat to the *Hagenstellung*, see *DRZWk*, part 2, Frieser, "Die Schlacht im Kursker Bogen," 8:186–187.

60. Ziemke, *Stalingrad to Berlin*, 139.

61. The total included five Panzer, three *Panzergrenadier*, and 11 infantry divisions. *DRZWk*, part 2, Frieser, "Die Schlacht im Kursker Bogen," 8:188.

62. Mellenthin, *Panzer Battles*, 291.

63. Walter Bussmann, "Kursk—Orel—Dnjepr: Erlebnisse und Erfahrungen im Stab des XXXXVI Panzerkoprs während des 'Unternehmens Zitadelle,'" *Vierteljahrshefte für Zeitgeschichte* 41, no. 4 (October 1993): 515.

64. Glantz and House, *Battle of Kursk*, 240.

65. For casualties on both sides, see *DRZWk*, part 2, Frieser, "Die Schlacht im Kursker Bogen," 8:188. Reflecting the trend in current post-Soviet historiography, Sokolov, "Battle for Kursk, Orel, and Char'kov," 82, gives a figure of 860,000 Soviet casualties for Operation Kutuzov, or about twice the number officially admitted.

66. The observation comes from Field Marshal Walther Model, commander of the 9th Army, after the fighting in the Rzhev salient. Quoted in David M. Glantz, *Zhukov's Greatest Defeat: The Red Army's Epic Disaster in Operation Mars, 1942* (Lawrence: University Press of Kansas, 1999), 301.

67. Glantz, "Soviet Military Strategy," 143–145. For the unfolding sequence of operations, see Erickson, *Road to Berlin*, 113–135.

68. Marshal A. M. Vasilevsky, the chief of the General Staff, quoted in Glantz, "Soviet Military Strategy," 145n34.

69. Glantz, "Soviet Military Strategy," 145.

70. The words are Vasilevsky's, quoted in ibid.

71. For a general view of the situation on the southern front after Kursk, see Wagener, *Heeresgruppe Süd*, 245–254.

72. "Schliesslich sollte das Kräfteverhältnis etwa 7:1 für die Sowjets betragen." Manstein, *Verlorene Siege*, 509.

73. "Die erfahrenen Frontkämpfer und Offiziere." Ibid.

74. "Wir standen in der Tat einer Hydra gegenüber, der für jeden abgeschlagenen Kopf zwei neue zu wachsen schienen." Ibid., 509, 514.

75. "Die Überlegenheit des deutschen Soldaten." Ibid., 510.

76. For the Seydlitz episode, see Robert M. Citino, *The German Way of War: From the Thirty Years' War to the Third Reich* (Lawrence: University Press of Kansas, 2005), 100. Christopher Duffy, *Frederick the Great: A Military Life* (London: Routledge and Kegan Paul, 1985), 167, notes that the story first appeared only in 1797, long after Seydlitz's death.

77. "Solange ich jedoch an dieser Stelle stehe, muss ich auch die Möglichkeit haben, von meinem Kopf Gebrauch zu machen." Manstein, *Verlorene Siege*, 516–517.

78. For the offensive on the Mius, see Erickson, *Road to Berlin*, 115–116.

79. For the German defenses, see the translated German report by Martin Francke, "Sixth Army Defends the Mius River Line," in Newton, *Kursk*, 305–349. Francke was the staff officer who kept the 6th Army's *Kriegstagebuch*.

80. So says the English translation of Manstein, *Lost Victories*, 452; Manstein's own German in *Verlorene Siege*, 516, offers us *verhängnisvoll*.

81. Operation Rumiantsev, like Kutuzov, is nearly missing in the English-language historiography. All the same sources listed in note 43 above are pertinent here as well. In this case, however, there is something nearly akin to a dedicated monograph: the chapter in David M. Glantz, *From the Don to the Dnepr: Soviet Offensive Operations, December 1942–August 1943* (London: Frank Cass, 1991), 215–365, "Operation 'Polkovodets Rumyantsev': The Belgorod-Khar'kov Operation, August 1943." Glantz, as always, offers a typically judicious and detailed account, based heavily on Soviet archival sources, and it remains the starting point for any historical inquiry into Rumiantsev. See also Glantz and House, *Battle of Kursk*, 241–254; *DRZWk*, part 2, Frieser, "Die Schlacht im Kursker Bogen," 8:190–200, and Shtemenko, *Soviet General Staff at War*, 235–255.

82. Glantz and House, *Battle of Kursk*, 241.

83. Shtemenko, *Soviet General Staff at War*, 243–244.

84. Glantz and House, *Battle of Kursk*, 246.

85. "Zwischen diesen beiden deutschen Grossverbänden riss bis zum Abend

der 7. August eine mehr als 50 Kilometer breite Lücke auf." *DRZWk*, part 2, Frieser, "Die Schlacht im Kursker Bogen," 8:193.

86. A change in command supported by Manstein (*Verlorene Siege*, 519). See the discussion in *DRZWk*, part 2, Frieser, "Die Schlacht im Kursker Bogen," 8:197–198.

87. Erickson, *Road to Berlin*, 124.

88. "Beweglicher Operationsführung." Manstein, *Verlorene Siege*, 526.

89. The Kuban campaign, which saw a virtually isolated Wehrmacht fighting in lagoon and jungle, is virtually absent from the historiography. There are two useful monographs: Wolfgang Pickert, *Vom Kuban-Brückenkopf bis Sewastopol: Flakartillerie im Verband der 17. Army* (Heidelberg: Scharnhorst Buchkameradschaft, 1955), and Friedrich Forstmeier, *Die Räumung des Kuban-Brückenkopfes im Herbst 1943* (Darmstadt: Wehr und Wissen Verlagsgesellschaft, 1964). As the title indicates, the former is concerned mainly with the role of antiaircraft assets, while the latter analyzes the entire campaign in some detail. The campaign also featured prominently in German wartime propaganda on the home front, with images of the troops in far-flung exotic locales apparently holding their own against the Soviets. See Gert Habedanck, "Im Kuban Brückenkopf," *Die Wehrmacht* 7, no. 9 (April 28, 1943): 10–11; Gert Habedanck, "Stutzpunkt Florescu im Kuban Brückenkopf," *Die Wehrmacht* 7, no. 10 (May 12, 1943): 6–7; Gert Habedanck, "In den Dschungeln bei Noworossijsk," *Die Wehrmacht* 7, no. 11 (May 26, 1943): 4–5, 14; "Rumänen: Kameraden am Kuban," *Die Wehrmacht* 7, no. 11 (May 26, 1943): 22; "Niemandsland Noworossijsk-Süd," *Die Wehrmacht* 7, no. 12 (June 9, 1943): 10; "Flak am Kuban," *Die Wehrmacht* 7, no. 13 (June 13, 1943): 6; von Koerber, "Schweigestützpunkt in den Lagunen," part 1, *Die Wehrmacht* 7, no. 18 (September 1, 1943): 10–11; and von Koerber, "Schweigestützpunkt in den Lagunen," part 2, *Die Wehrmacht* 7, no. 21 (October 13, 1943): 10–11.

90. "Irgendeines Dorfes mit unaussprechlichem Namen." Wagener, *Heeresgruppe Süd*, 245.

91. For the operational details of the retreat to the Dnepr, see Rolf Hinze, *Crucible of Combat: Germany's Defensive Battles in the Ukraine, 1943–44* (Solihull: Helion, 2009), 26–146.

92. Erickson, *Road to Berlin*, 127.

93. Ivan Yakubovsky, "The Liberation of Kiev," in *Battles Hitler Lost: First-Person Accounts of World War II by Russian Generals on the Eastern Front* (New York: Richardson & Steirman, 1986), 101.

94. Mellenthin, *Panzer Battles*, 318.

95. "Hinsichtlich der anderen Kriegsschauplätze wollte Hitler zunächst die Weiterentwicklung der Lage abwarten, d.h. ob die Engländer nun in Apulien order auf dem Balkan landen, oder—was ebenso unwahrscheinlich wie unwichtig war—ihre Kräfte auf Sardinien festlegan würden." Manstein, *Verlorene Siege*, 523.

96. For an argument along these lines, see Bernd Wegner, "Das Ende der

Strategie: Deutschlands politische und militärische Lage nach Stalingrad," in Foerster, *Gezeitenwechsel im Zweiten Weltkrieg?*, 211–227.

Chapter 7. Kesselring's War

1. This vignette draws on Adolf Heusinger, *Befehl im Widerstreit: Schicksalsstunden der deutschen Armee, 1923–1945* (Tübingen: Rainer Wunderlich, 1950), "Anfang September 1943: Hitler mit zahlreichen Ingenieuren und Kostrukteuren, Offizieren, Parteifunktionären bei einer Vorführung neuer Panzer, Panzerabwehrgeschütze, Geschütze und anderer Waffen im Führerhauptquartier bei Rastenburg," 272–275.

2. "Ein Sturmgeschütz auf den Unterbau des veralteten Tschechenpanzers." Ibid., 273.

3. "Das Holzmodell eines 100-Tonnen Panzers." Ibid., 275.

4. "Was habe ich den Herren nicht schon längst gesagt? Aber sie wollten es ja nicht glauben. Man muss den König und Badoglio unverzüglich verhaftet. So eine Schweinerei!" Ibid.

5. The same historiographical dynamic we observed in the Sicilian campaign is at work when studying operations in Italy: Anglo-American historians have dwelled on it to the point of obsession, trodding a by now well-worn narrative path, while the Germans seem to have barely noticed it. The official histories bear out this point. The Green Book series devotes two complete volumes to the subject, Albert N. Garland and Howard McGaw Smyth, *Sicily and the Surrender of Italy* (Washington, D.C.: Center of Military History, 1965), and Martin Blumenson, *Salerno to Cassino* (Washington, D.C.: Center of Military History, 1969). There is a great deal of overlap between the two volumes, and the decision to include the surrender of Italy in the Sicily volume rather than the Salerno one is questionable, drawing an artificial and unsatisfying distinction between phenomena that really need to be studied as a whole. Given the incredible complexity of the sequence of events, however, there is probably no good solution to the problem, short of publishing a 1,000-page volume. The U.S. Navy's official history is also indispensable: Samuel Eliot Morison, *History of United States Naval Operation in World War II*, vol. 9, *Sicily—Salerno—Anzio, January 1943–June 1944* (Boston: Little, Brown, 1954). The official British point of view is almost as well represented in C. J. C. Molony, *The Mediterranean and Middle East*, vol. 5, *The Campaign in Sicily, 1943, and the Campaign in Italy, 3rd September 1943 to 31st March 1944* (London: H.M.S.O., 1973). The German official history, as already noted in the discussion of the Sicilian campaign, devotes a relatively brief amount of space to the fighting in Italy. See *Das Deutsche Reich und der Zweite Weltkrieg* (hereinafter *DRZWk*), vol. 8, *Die Ostfront, 1943/44: Der Krieg im Osten und an den Nebenfronten*, part 6, "Der Krieg an den Nebenfronten," especially Gerhard Schreiber, "Das Ende des nordafrikanischen Feldzugs und der Krieg in Italian 1943 bis 1945," 1100–1162, handling all the campaigns from Tunis to the end of the war, politics and all,

in a mere 62 pages. For a series that has established such high standards for itself, the poverty of treatment here is disappointing. In investigating the German viewpoint of this controversial campaign, a good place to start is with the testimony in the Foreign Military Studies series, available in both German and English at the U.S. Army Heritage and Education Center in Carlisle, Pennsylvania. Like all contemporaneous archival records, it needs to be read with care. See Siegfried Westphal et al., "Der Feldzug in Italien, Apr 1943–Mai 1944," manuscript T-1a, especially the crucial chapter 6 by General Heinrich von Vietinghoff, "Die Kämpfe der 10. Armee in Süd- und Mittelitalien under besonderer Berücksichtigung der Schlachten bei Salerno, am Volturno, Garigliano, am Sango und um Cassino." Vietinghoff was commander of the 10th Army, the formation that opposed the Allied landing. Inserted in the chapter as an *Anlage* (appendix), but apparently unnumbered and not listed in the exhaustive catalog and index, is Wilhelm Schmalz, "Der Kampf der Panzerdivision 'Hermann Göring' bei Salerno vom 9.–17.9.1943." Also useful is Vietinghoff's précis of the larger chapter, "Beurteiling der Lage durch die Höchsten Dienststellen im August 1943: Einsatz des AOK 10," manuscript MS-117. See also Max Ulrich, "15th Panzer Grenadier Division, 3 September 1943," manuscript D-021, and Karl Graf von Klinkowstroem, "Der Abfall Italiens und die Kämpfe um Rom: Gesehen com Stabe der OB-Süd," manuscript D-301.

Published primary sources abound, and the scholar will need at the very least to read the memoirs of the main participants. For the Americans, these include Dwight D. Eisenhower, *Crusade in Europe* (Garden City, N.Y.: Doubleday, 1948), 201–219, and Mark W. Clark, *Calculated Risk* (New York: Enigma Books, 2007), a reprint of the general's memoirs that appeared first in 1950. For the British, see Bernard Law Montgomery, *Memoirs of Field-Marshal the Viscount Montgomery of Alamein* (London: Collins, 1958), and Arthur Bryant, *Triumph in the West, 1943–1946: Based on Diaries and Autobiographical Notes of Field Marshal the Viscount Alanbrooke* (London: Collins, 1959). For the Germans, begin with Albert Kesselring, *Soldat bis zum letzten Tag* (Bonn: Athenäum, 1953), translated into English as *Kesselring: A Soldier's Record* (New York: William Morrow, 1954); Siegfried Westphal, *Heer in Fesseln: Aus den Papieren des Stabchefs von Rommel, Kesselring und Rundstedt* (Bonn: Athenäum-Verlag, 1950), translated into English as *The German Army in the West* (London: Cassell, 1951), and, by the same author, *Erinnerungen* (Mainz: Von Hase & Koehler, 1975); and Frido von Senger und Etterlin, *Krieg in Europa* (Köln: Kiepenhauer & Witsch, 1960), translated into English as *Neither Fear nor Hope: The Wartime Career of General Frido von Senger und Etterlin, Defender of Cassino* (Novato, Calif.: Presidio, 1989). See also Walter Warlimont, *Im Hauptquartier der deutschen Wehrmacht, 1939–1945: Grundlagen, Formen, Gestalten* (Frankfurt am Main: Bernard & Graefe, 1962); Italy was an OKW theater, and Warlimont writes about it with authority. For the English translation, see *Inside Hitler's Headquarters, 1939–45* (Novato, Calif.: Presidio, 1962). Helmut Heiber, ed., *Hitlers Lagebesprechungen: Die Protokollfragmente siner militärischen Konferenzen, 1942–1945* (Stuttgart: Deutsche Verlags-Anstalt, 1962), is also essential for the completely dysfunctional state of the German high command in these days. It too is available in English. See Helmut Heiber and David M. Glantz, eds., *Hitler and His Generals: Military Conferences, 1942–1945* (New York: Enigma, 2003). Finally, although it is a secondary source, Josef Schröder, *Italiens Kriegsaustritt, 1943: Die deutschen Gegenmassnahmen im italienischen Raum: Fall "Alarich" und "Achse"* (Göttingen: Musterschmidt-Verlag, 1969), is essential for German plans and operations, both for its incisive analysis and its exhaustive treatment of the German documentary and archival records.

The secondary literature in English is massive, especially if one includes biographies of the principal participants. Begin with Rick Atkinson, *The Day of Battle: The War in Sicily and Italy, 1943–1944* (New York: Henry Holt, 2007), Carlo D'Este, *Fatal Decision: Anzio and the Battle for Rome* (New York: Harper Perennial, 1992), Douglas Porch, *The Path to Victory: The Mediterranean Theater in World War II* (New York: Farrar, Straus and Giroux, 2004), and the pertinent sections in Charles B. MacDonald, *The Mighty Endeavor: The American War in Europe* (New York: Da Capo, 1992), 190–247. All these works feature meticulous analysis and often inspired writing. See also D'Este's *World War II in the Mediterranean, 1942–1945* (Chapel Hill, N.C.: Algonquin Books, 1990), as well as Martin Blumenson's essential biography, *Mark Clark* (London: Jonathan Cape, 1984), a work that serves at least as a partial rehabilitation of this oft-maligned figure. The most useful short summary of the campaign's opening is *Salerno: American Operations from the Beaches to the Volturno, 9 September–6 October 1943* (Washington: Center of Military History, 1990), a reprint of a pamphlet originally published by the War Department's Historical Division in 1944. A vast number of works deal with individual units and formations. There is a large body of literature from Texas, for example, a state that contributed the 36th Infantry Division to the campaign. See Clifford H. Peek Jr., *Five Years—Five Countries—Five Campaigns: An Account of the One-Hundred-Forty-First Infantry in World War II* (Munich: 141st Infantry Regiment Association, 1945), Robert L. Wagner, *The Texas Army: A History of the 36th Division in the Italian Campaign* (Austin, Tex.: n.p., 1972), and Martin Blumenson, "The 36th Infantry Division in World War II," in *The Texas Military Experience: From the Texas Revolution to World War II*, ed. Joseph G. Dawson III (College Station: Texas A&M University Press, 1995), 128–136. For the other U.S. division that landed at Salerno, see Flint Whitlock, *The Rock of Anzio: From Sicily to Dachau: A History of the 45th Infantry Division* (Boulder, Colo.: Westview, 1998).

For the British perspective, see Eric Linklater, *The Campaign in Italy* (London: H.M.S.O., 1951), W. G. F. Jackson, *The Battle for Italy* (New York: Harper & Row, 1967), John Strawson, *The Italian Campaign* (New York: Carroll & Graf, 1988), and Bernard Ireland, *The War in the Mediterranean, 1940–1943* (Barnsley: Leo Cooper, 1993). Jackson was a British officer on the staff of General Alexander, and his account of operations is perhaps the most lucid and balanced one available. See also Hugh Pond, *Salerno* (London: William Kimber, 1961), and Des Hickey and Gus Smith, *Operation Avalanche: The Salerno Landings, 1943*

(New York: McGraw-Hill, 1984): Matthew Jones, *Britain, the United States, and the Mediterranean War, 1942–44* (New York: St. Martin's Press, 1996), is a useful analysis of both operations and high strategy within the Mediterranean fight generally. Both Christopher Buckley, *Road to Rome* (London: Hodder and Stoughton, 1945), and Richard Tregaskis, *Invasion Diary* (Lincoln: University of Nebraska Press, 2004), offer the perspective of journalists attached to the British and U.S. armies, respectively. Tregaskis's account is a harrowing one, including a detailed account of the head wound he received in the fighting. For further discussion on this point, see Robert M. Citino, "Dick Tregaskis's Diaries," *Front and Center*, January 24, 2010, http://www.historynet.com/dick-tregaskis's-diaries.htm.

6. The best evocation of the tense situation in Italy is Siegfried Westphal, who writes of the "labile Sommer 1943," the "unstable" summer, in *Heer in Fesseln*, 214–226.

7. For the "parleys at Cassibile," see Garland and Smyth, *Sicily and the Surrender of Italy*, 474–479.

8. For the origins of German planning in case of an Italian surrender, see Schröder, *Italiens Kriegsaustritt*, 176–195.

9. For Giant I and II, the proposed U.S. airborne operations into Italy, see the useful discussion in James M. Gavin, *On to Berlin: Battles of an Airborne Commander, 1943–1946* (New York: Viking, 1978), 51–63.

10. Reprinted in Garland and Smyth, *Sicily and the Surrender of Italy*, 502.

11. For Eisenhower's contempt toward Badoglio's "fear and trembling," see *Crusade in Europe*, 186. The text of Eisenhower's announcement can be found in Garland and Smyth, *Sicily and the Surrender of Italy*, 508.

12. Ibid., 509. For Badoglio's justification to Hitler of the Italian surrender, see Schröder, *Italiens Kriegsaustritt*, 281–282.

13. "Nur der Laie glaubt, in dem Verlauf eines Feldzuges die konsequente Durchführung eines im voraus gefassten, in allen Einzelheiten überlegten und bis ans Ende festgehaltenen ursprünglichen Gedankens zu erblicken." See Ernst Kabisch, "Systemlose Strategie," *Militär-Wochenblatt* 125, no. 26 (December 27, 1940): 1235. For Helmuth von Moltke's writings, see *Moltke on the Art of War: Selected Writings*, ed. Daniel J. Hughes (Novato, Calif.: Presidio, 1993). This particular passage is found on 45, 92.

14. For the origins of this flexible command system, often described as *Auftragstaktik*, see Antulio J. Echevarria II, *After Clausewitz: German Military Thinkers before the Great War* (Lawrence: University Press of Kansas, 2000), 32–42, 94–103.

15. "Es ist eine Täuschung, wenn man glaubt, einen Feldzugsplan auf weit hinaus feststellen und bis zu Ende durchführen zu können. Der erste Zusammenstoss mit der feindlichen Hauptmacht schafft je nach seinem Ausfall eine neue Lage." Kabisch, "Systemlose Strategie," 1235.

16. The one indispensable book on 1940, a rare thing to say for a campaign that has generated such a large literature, is Karl-Heinz Frieser, *The Blitzkrieg*

Legend: The 1940 Campaign in the West (Annapolis: Naval Institute Press, 2005), a welcome English-language translation of the original work, *Blitzkrieg-Legende: Der Westfeldzug 1940* (Oldenbourg: Wissenschaftliche Verlag, 1995).

17. For the German campaign in Yugoslavia, practically ignored by historians, see George E. Blau, *The German Campaign in the Balkans (Spring 1941)*, pamphlet 20-260 (Washington, D.C.: Department of the Army, 1953), Janusz Piekalkiewicz, *Krieg auf dem Balkan* (Munich: Südwest Verlag, 1984), and John F. Antal, "Operation 25: The Wehrmacht's Conquest of Yugoslavia," in *Maneuver Warfare: An Anthology*, ed. Richard D. Hooker Jr. (Novato, Calif.: Presidio, 1993), 391–404.

18. For the Italo-German deployments in Italy, allied at the time but soon to become hostile, see *DRZWk*, part 6, Schreiber, "Das Ende des nordafrikanischen Feldzugs und der Krieg in Italian," 8:1119. See also the map "Verteilung der italienischen Divisionen, Stand: 1.3.1943," in Schröder, *Italiens Kriegsaustritt*, facing 136.

19. *DRZWk*, part 6, Schreiber, "Das Ende des nordafrikanischen Feldzugs und der Krieg in Italian," 8:1119–1120.

20. Senger und Etterlin, *Krieg in Europa*, 196–199, stresses the hopelessness of the situation on the islands: "Die Weisung, derartig isolierte Inseln zu verteidigen, schien mir ein neues Musterbeispiel dafür, wie die Bedeutung von Wasser und Luft für moderne Operationen verkannt wurde" (197).

21. *DRZWk*, part 6, Schreiber, "Das Ende des nordafrikanischen Feldzugs und der Krieg in Italian," 8:1120.

22. The best account of the fighting around Rome, based on the German archival sources, is Schröder, *Italiens Kriegsaustritt*, 287–293.

23. *DRZWk*, part 6, Schreiber, "Das Ende des nordafrikanischen Feldzugs und der Krieg in Italian," 8:1120.

24. See Kerstin von Lingen, *Kesselring's Last Battle: War Crimes Trials and Cold War Politics, 1945–1960* (Lawrence: University Press of Kansas, 2009), 32–33. *DRZWk*, part 6, Schreiber, "Das Ende des nordafrikanischen Feldzugs und der Krieg in Italian," 8:1124, speaks of the "heroic resistance" ("heroischen Widerstand") of the Italians on Cephalonia.

25. Heusinger, *Befehl im Widerstreit*, 275.

26. "Einem von Ressentiments geprägten sowie rassistisch akzenturieren, mörderischen Racheakt." *DRZWk*, part 6, Schreiber, "Das Ende des nordafrikanischen Feldzugs und der Krieg in Italian," 8:1123.

27. Von Lingen, *Kesselring's Last Battle*, 32.

28. Ibid., 32–33.

29. *DRZWk*, part 6, Schreiber, "Das Ende des nordafrikanischen Feldzugs und der Krieg in Italian," 8:1123–1124, as well as von Lingen, *Kesselring's Last Battle*, 33–34. On the question of the internees, see also Gerhard Schreiber, *Die italienischen Militärinternierten im deutschen Machtbereich, 1943–1945: Verraten–Verachtet–Vergessen* (Munich: Oldenbourg-Verlag, 1990).

30. *DRZWk*, part 6, Schreiber, "Das Ende des nordafrikanischen Feldzugs und der Krieg in Italian," 8:1124.

31. "Die erfolgreiche Durchführung von Fall 'Achse' lässt sich sarkastisch als letzter Sieg der deutschen Wehrmacht bezeichnen." Ibid.

32. Schröder, *Italiens Kriegsaustritt*, 291, labels the flight of the king, Badoglio, and the other ministers as the chief reason ("der Hauptgrund") for the failure of the Italian army to offer any resistance to the Germans.

33. The best scholarly account of the "forty-five days of Marshal Badoglio" remains F. W. Deakin, *The Brutal Friendship: Mussolini, Hitler and the Fall of Italian Fascism* (New York: Harper & Row, 1962), 487–548.

34. "Einem Dschungel der Täuschung, des Betrugs, der Irreführung, der Missverständnisse, der Inkompetenz, der Feigheit, des Dilettantismus und der Entscheidigungsschwäche." *DRZWk*, part 6, Schreiber, "Das Ende des nordafrikanischen Feldzugs und der Krieg in Italian," 8:1122. For the messy end to Italy's war, see also Elena Agarossi, *A Nation Collapses: The Italian Surrender of September 1943* (Cambridge: Cambridge University Press, 2006).

35. See Blumenson, *Salerno to Cassino*, 8–15, especially the map on 12.

36. See his signal to Alexander, dated August 19, 1943, in Montgomery, *Memoirs*, 191–192, as well as D'Este, *Fatal Decision*, 34–35.

37. "They might possibly do useful guerrilla work, sabotage, and generally ensure complete non-cooperation on the part of the local population. But I did not see them fighting the Germans." Montgomery, *Memoirs*, 195.

38. See ibid., "Some Thoughts on High Command in War," 347–354.

39. The successful German retreat from Calabria in the face of what the Germans saw as a "primitive diversionary maneuver" ("primitives Ablenkungsmanöver") is ably covered in Schröder, *Italiens Kriegsaustritt*, 269–274.

40. Ulrich, "15th Panzer Grenadier Division," 3.

41. For the 29th *Panzergrenadier*'s orders, see Vietinghoff, "Die Kämpfe der 10. Armee in Süd- und Mittelitalien," 18. For rear-guard skirmishes and demolitions that were being reported to the German public as full-scale battles, see "Strassenkampf unter der Sonne Italiens," *Die Wehrmacht* 7, no. 22 (October 27, 1943): 11.

42. In fact, Vietinghoff went so far as to say that the Canadian advance up the east coast "exerted no influence at all on German movements" ("Das Vorgehen der 1. kanadischen Div. an der Ostküste hat keinen Einfluss auf die deutschen Bewegungen ausgeübt"). Ibid., 20.

43. See the map "Lageentwicklung in Italien vom 3. Bis 20. September 1943" in *DRZWk*, part 6, Schreiber, "Das Ende des nordafrikanischen Feldzugs und der Krieg in Italian," 8:1140.

44. "Durch schnelle und wendige Führung die Verbände der 10. Armee und der Luftwaffe aus Süditalien herauszubringen." Ibid., 1127–1128.

45. For Operation Slapstick, see Molony, *Campaign in Sicily, 1943*, 242–243, who gives a casualty figure of "48 naval officers and men and 120 of 6th Parachute Battalion." See also Jackson, *Battle for Italy*, 117–119. For German defenses in Apulia, see Vietinghoff, "Die Kämpfe der 10. Armee in Süd- und Mittelitalien," 40–41.

46. The best sources for the planning of Operation Avalanche, the "first

breach" of German defenses on the European continent, are Jackson, *Battle for Italy*, 81–96, Clark, *Calculated Risk*, 145–151, Blumenson, *Salerno to Cassino*, 16–42, and Molony, *Campaign in Sicily, 1943*, 230–236.

47. "Die nicht sehr grosse flache Ebene wurde im Halbkreis von steil ansteigenden Hügeln and Bergketten." Vietinghoff, "Die Kämpfe der 10. Armee in Süd- und Mittelitalien," 26.

48. The U.S. Army Green Books are of varying quality as history, criticism, and literature, but Blumenson's work ranks near the top of the list in all three categories. See *Salerno to Cassino*, 26.

49. Quoted in Carlo D'Este, *Patton: A Genius for War* (New York: Harper, 1996), 554.

50. "I never again expect to witness such scenes of pure joy," one man would later recall. "We would dock in Naples harbor unopposed, with an olive branch in one hand and an opera ticket in the other." See MacDonald, *Mighty Endeavor*, 206–207.

51. Confusion remains as to exactly what Clark was talking about. For the original claim, see Clark, *Calculated Risk*, 156. The commander of the VIX Panzer Corps agrees that German defenders were equipped with loudspeakers and that they did demand the surrender of U.S. troops as they landed, although he disputes the gangsterish wording. See Hermann Balck, *Ordnung im Chaos: Erinnerungen, 1893–1948* (Osnabrück: Biblio Verlag, 1981), 455: "Ohne mein Wissen hatte man im Küstenabschnitt in jedem Stützpunkt Lautsprecher aufgestellt, die die Amerikaner zur Übergabe auffordern sollten. Das taten sie selbstverständlich nicht, was auch kein vernünftiger Mensch erwarten konnte." MacDonald, *Mighty Endeavor*, 209, attributes the "long-persistent myth" to Allied beach control parties who were directing traffic with loudspeakers. See also Blumenson, *Salerno to Cassino*, 83n16.

52. For more on this point, see the tightly argued chapter "Joint and Combined Amphibious Doctrine" in Adrian R. Lewis, *Omaha Beach: A Flawed Victory* (Chapel Hill: University of North Carolina Press, 2001), 57–90, especially 83–86.

53. For the deployment of the 16th Panzer Division, especially the "kleinen, im Dünensand gegrabenen Stützpunkten," see Vietinghoff, "Die Kämpfe der 10. Armee in Süd- und Mittelitalien," 26–27. See also *DRZWk*, part 6, Schreiber, "Das Ende des nordafrikanischen Feldzugs und der Krieg in Italian," 8:1129.

54. Or to "throw them back onto their ships," in the German formulation. See Vietinghoff, "Die Kämpfe der 10. Armee in Süd- und Mittelitalien," 22 ("so schnell wie möglich durch Gegenangriffe wieder auf seine Schiffe zu zwingen").

55. Morison, *Sicily—Salerno—Anzio*, 266–267.

56. See James S. Corum, *Wolfram von Richtofen: Master of the German Air War* (Lawrence: University Press of Kansas, 2008), 344.

57. See, for example, Clark, *Calculated Risk*, 168, as well as Blumenson, *Salerno to Cassino*, 86.

58. The commander of the 10th Army described himself as "not unsatisfied" (*nicht unzufrieden*) with the course of the first day's fighting because the 16th Panzer Division, fighting alone, had held the line against the land, sea, and air forces of the Allies. Vietinghoff, "Die Kämpfe der 10. Armee in Süd- und Mittelitalien," 29. See also *DRZWk*, part 6, Schreiber, "Das Ende des nordafrikanischen Feldzugs und der Krieg in Italian," 8:1129.

59. *DRZWk*, part 6, Schreiber, "Das Ende des nordafrikanischen Feldzugs und der Krieg in Italian," 8:1130–1131.

60. Vietinghoff, "Die Kämpfe der 10. Armee in Süd- und Mittelitalien," 21.

61. See Schmalz, "Der Kampf der Panzerdivision 'Hermann Göring' bei Salerno." For VIX Panzer Corps, see Balck, *Ordnung im Chaos*, 449–463.

62. For Hube along the Volga, see Robert M. Citino, *Death of the Wehrmacht: The German Campaigns of 1942* (Lawrence: University Press of Kansas, 2007), 247–248.

63. For the Nalchik-Ordzhonikidze campaign, see the primary source from Eberhard von Mackensen, *Vom Bug zum Kaukasus: Das III Panzerkorps im Feldzug gegen Sowjetrussland, 1941–42* (Neckargemünd: Kurt Vowinckel, 1967), 102–111. Useful secondary accounts include Wilhelm Tieke, *The Caucasus and the Oil: The German–Soviet War in the Caucasus, 1942–43* (Winnipeg: J. J. Fedorowicz, 1995), 221–237; and Joel S. A. Hayward, *Stopped at Stalingrad: The Luftwaffe and Hitler's Defeat in the East* (Lawrence: University Press of Kansas, 1998), 174–176.

64. For Balck's battles along the Chir, see the classic account by his chief of staff, F. W. Mellenthin, *Panzer Battles: A Study of the Employment of Armor on the Second World War* (New York: Ballantine, 1956), 211–222.

65. From the 10th Army war diary (*Kriegstagebuch*), quoted in Blumenson, *Salerno to Cassino*, 112.

66. For the fighting around the tobacco factory (*Tabakfabrik*), see the definitive account in Atkinson, *Day of Battle*, 222–227.

67. For the role of the burned bridge, see Vietinghoff, "Die Kämpfe der 10. Armee in Süd- und Mittelitalien," 33–34.

68. For a detailed account of the crisis point of the battle, see Blumenson, *Salerno to Cassino*, 112–117.

69. For reports that the Americans were withdrawing, see Vietinghoff, "Die Kämpfe der 10. Armee in Süd- und Mittelitalien," 34: "Die Truppe meldete: 'Feind baut ab.'"

70. "Nach 4-tägiger Abwehrschlacht Feindwiderstand im Zusammenbrechen. 10. Armee in zügiger Verfolgung auf breiter Front. Im Raum Salerno-Altavilla noch harte Kämpfe. Überholende Verfolgung auf Paestum im Gange." Schröder, *Italiens Kriegsaustritt*, 298–299. Vietinghoff sent the message to Kesselring, and the ever optimistic field marshal sent it to Hitler's headquarters. Ibid., 299n60. For more good analysis of the situation in the German camp, based on the *Kriegstagebuch* of the 10th Army, see also Blumenson, *Salerno to Cassino*, 116–117. After the war, Vietninghoff was much more circumspect in his claims for the fighting. See "Die Kämpfe der 10. Armee in Süd-

und Mittelitalien," 34, "Die bis zum Abend beim AOK einlaufenden Meldungen klangen siegesgewiss; das AOK urteilte ruhiger. . . . Aber erst die nächsten Tage konnten entscheiden, ob der Gegner nach diesem Misserfolg das Landunternehmen bei Salerno aufgeben . . . ")

71. Clark, *Calculated Risk*, 166. The principal bone of contention regarding Clark's chapter on Salerno is whether he seriously considered evacuating the bridgehead. He says not. A number of witnesses and participants say at least preliminary preparations were underway. See, to give just one example, Molony, *Campaign in Sicily, 1943*, 307.

72. Clark, *Calculated Risk*, 166. For a detailed account of the travails of the 142nd and 143rd RCTs, see Wagner, *Texas Army*, 19–56.

73. Clark, *Calculated Risk*, 163.

74. Ibid., 164.

75. Atkinson, *Day of Battle*, 234, but see also the appended note (645).

76. See, for discussion of this concept, Franz Halder, "Stellungnahme zu Wagener, 'Gedanken über Kampfführung im Osten,'" manuscript P-082, on file at the U.S. Army Heritage and Education Center.

77. For the buildup, see Jackson, *Battle for Italy*, 116–117.

78. Morison, *Sicily—Salerno—Anzio*, 286–294.

79. Blumenson, *Salerno to Cassino*, 146.

80. Schmalz, "Der Kampf der Panzerdivision 'Hermann Göring' bei Salerno," 5. The phrase is "besonders unangenehm."

81. Balck, *Ordnung im Chaos*, 455.

82. Blumenson, *Salerno to Cassino*, 144.

83. "Kriegführung in der zweiten Riehe." *DRZWk*, part 6, Schreiber, "Das Ende des nordafrikanischen Feldzugs und der Krieg in Italian," 8:1152.

84. "Härte der Ostschlachten." Ibid., 1145.

85. See Robert M. Citino, "The American Eagle: Mark W. Clark," *Front and Center*, April 2, 2010, http://www.historynet.com/the-american-eagle-mark-w-clark.htm, and "The American Eagle? Mark W. Clark," *Front and Center*, April 8, 2010, http://www.historynet.com/the-american-eagle-mark-w-clark-2.htm.

86. Porch, *Path to Victory*, 488–489.

87. Blumenson, *Mark Clark*, 282.

88. See, for example, Peter J. Schifferle, *America's School for War: Fort Leavenworth, Officer Education, and Victory in World War II* (Lawrence: University Press of Kansas, 2010), who makes the point that "all prewar projections, and even the initial projections made after 1940, grossly underestimated the need for large headquarters to form, train, deploy, and sustain ground forces, grossly underestimated the needs of service forces, and nearly completely failed to understand the needs of the burgeoning army air forces for senior officer and staffs" (167–168).

89. For the German view of this latest bungled airborne operation, see Vietinghoff, "Die Kämpfe der 10. Armee in Süd- und Mittelitalien," 35.

90. The only scholarly work to deal with the crucial decision of where to

hold the line in the Italian peninsula is Ralph S. Mavrogordato, *Command Decisions: Hitler's Decision on the Defense of Italy* (Washington, D.C.: Center of Military History, 1990).

91. Westphal, *Heer in Fesseln*, 238.

92. *DRZWk*, part 6, Schreiber, "Das Ende des nordafrikanischen Feldzugs und der Krieg in Italian," 8:1131–1132. For a representative sampling of German accounts of the fighting as it was occurring, see Günter Greiner, "Die Letzten am Feind: Absetzung an der Volturno-Front," *Die Wehrmacht* 7, no. 24 (November 24, 1943): 7; Bernd E. H. Overhues, "Auf den Höhen über Pozzilli: Ein Kampfbericht aus den Westhängen der Abruzzen," *Die Wehrmacht* 7, no. 25 (December 8, 1943): 4–6, 17; and Günter Greiner, "Wasser—ein Verbündeter: Pioniere an den westlichen Süditalienfront," *Die Wehrmacht* 7, no. 25 (December 8, 1943): 7.

93. D'Este, *Fatal Decision*, 87–88.

94. Porch, *Path to Victory*, 423.

95. Dominick Graham and Shelford Bidwell, *Tug of War: The Battle for Italy* (London: Hodder & Stoughton, 1986), 38. Also quoted in D'Este, *Fatal Decision*, 87.

96. *DRZWk*, part 6, Schreiber, "Das Ende des nordafrikanischen Feldzugs und der Krieg in Italian," 8:1161.

Conclusion: Fighting a Lost War

1. For the "forgotten year," see the German official history, *Das Deutsche Reich und der Zweite Weltkrieg* (hereinafter *DRZWk*), vol. 8, *Die Ostfront, 1943/44: Der Krieg im Osten und an den Nebenfronten* (Munich: Deutsche Verlags-Anstalt, 2007), part 4, "Der Rückschlag des Pendels: das Zurückweichen der Ostfront von Sommer 1943 bis Sommer 1944," especially the "Prolog," apparently written by Karl-Heinz Frieser, 277. The "Kriegsjahre" being spoken of here is not 1943 as such, but the period from Kursk to the Soviet offensive resulting in the destruction of Army Group Center (Operation Bagration).

2. "Die schwerste Niederlage in der deutschen Militärgeschichte," *DRZWk*, part 5, "Der Zusammenbruch im Osten: Die Rückzugskämpfe seit Sommer 1944," Karl-Heinz Frieser, "Der Zusammenbruch der Heeresgruppe Mitte im Sommer 1944," 8:592–593.

3. The title of Fritz Fischer's seminal revisionist work on the origins of World War I, *Griff nach der Weltmacht: Die Kriegszielpolitik des kaiserlichen Deutschland, 1914/18* (Düsseldorf: Droste Verlag, 1961).

4. See Martin van Creveld, *Fighting Power: German and U.S. Army Performance, 1939–1945* (Westport, Conn.: Greenwood Press, 1982), translated into German as *Kampfkraft: Militärische Organisation und militärische Leistung, 1939–1945* (Freiburg: Verlag Rombach, 1989).

5. A point made repeatedly, for example, by the commander of the German 10th Army in Italy. See General Heinrich von Vietinghoff, "Die Kämpfe

der 10. Armee in Süd- und Mittelitalien under besonderer Berücksichtigung der Schlachten bei Salerno, am Volturno, Garigliano, am Sango und um Cassino," chapter 6 of Siegfried Westphal et al., "Der Feldzug in Italien, Apr 1943–Mai 1944" manuscript T-1a, available in the U.S. Army Heritage and Education Center in Carlisle, Pennsylvania: "In einen unsicheren, vielleicht feindlichen Land standen nunmehr die wenigen deutschen Divn. allein and weit auseinandergezogen, von Luftwaffe und Marine kaum zu unterstützen, einer unmittelbaren Grossaktion aller drei Wehrmachtsteile der Alliierten gegenüber" (21).

6. For a useful counterargument to the notion that the post-Kursk Wehrmacht had lost the initiative and launched no more offensives in the last two years of the war, see Gregory Liedtke, *"Furor Teutonicus:* German Offensives and Counter-Attacks on the Eastern Front, August 1943 to March 1945," *Journal of Slavic Military Studies* 21, no. 3 (July 2008): 563–587.

7. Lucas, according to his commander, was "tired physically and mentally from the long responsibilities of command in battle." Mark W. Clark, *Calculated Risk* (New York: Enigma Books, 2007), 244.

8. See Robert M. Citino, "1943: Operation Restored Hope?" *Front and Center*, March 24, 2010, http://www.historynet.com/1943-operation-restored-hope.htm.

9. For the contours of this argument, see Karl-Heinz Frieser, *The Blitzkrieg Legend: The 1940 Campaign in the West* (Annapolis, Md.: Naval Institute Press, 2005), 12–16.

10. "Weisung Nr. 51" is reprinted in Walther Hubatsch, ed., *Hitlers Weisungen für die Kriegführung, 1939–1945: Dokumente des Oberkommandos der Wehrmacht* (Frankfurt: Bernard & Graefe, 1962), 233–238. For the English translation, see *Hitler's War Directives, 1939–1945,* ed. H. R. Trevor-Roper (London: Sidgwick and Jackson, 1964), 149–153.

11. "Die Zeit der Operationen grösseren Stiles." *DRZWk,* part 7, Bernd Wegner, "Deutschland am Abgrund," 8:1170–1171.

12. Johannes Hürter, *Hitlers Heerführer: Die deutschen Oberbefehlshaber in Krieg gegen die Sowjetunion 1941/42* (Munich: R. Oldenbourg, 2006), 348, 609.

13. Crucial to the increased Nazification of the army was the appointment of Hitler's adjutant, Rudolf Schmundt, to the position of chief of the personnel office (*Chef des Heerespersonalamtes*) in late 1942. See Dermot Bradley and Richard Schulze-Kossens, eds., *Tätigkeitsbericht des Chefs des Heerespersonalamtes General der Infanterie Rudolf Schmundt, 1.10.1942–29.20.1944* (Osnabrück: Biblio Verlag, 1984), which shows Schmundt emphasizing both youth ("in gewissem Unfange das Offizierkorps zu verjüngen ist," 35) and National Socialist ardor ("In der Truppenführung sollen nur Generale verwendung finden, die Zuversicht ausstrahlen und den Kampf für unsere Weltanschauung innerlich bejahen," 111–112).

14. See Gerhard Weinberg, *A World at Arms* (Cambridge: Cambridge University Press, 2005), who describes Schörner as a man of "extreme National

Socialist views" (455), a man who displayed "ruthless fanaticism" (670), who shot "German soldiers after rigged courts martial" (573), whose art of war consisted of "holding fast by having lots of Germans shot" (801), and who at the end of the war "deserted his men to try to evade capture as a civilian" (824).

15. "Weniger kalkuliert und mehr geschlagen." Quoted in Eberhard Kessel, "Blucher: Zum 200. Geburtstag am 16. Dezember," *Militärwissenschaftliche Rundschau* 7, no. 4 (1942): 305.

16. Lieutenant Wolfgang Foerster, "Prinz Friedrich Karl," *Militärwissenschaftliche Rundschau* 8, no. 2 (1943): 90–91.

17. "Aus der Unterlegenheit zum Sieg." *DRZWk*, part 8, Karl-Heinz Frieser, "Zusammenfassung," 8:1218.

18. See "Neuzeitliche Lehren aus der Kriegführung Friedrichs des Grossen," *Militär-Wochenblatt* 115, no. 29 (February 4, 1931): 1113.

19. See Helmut Beck-Broichsitter, "Über die Beharrlichkeit im Angriff," *Militärwissenschaftliche Rundschau* 9, no. 1 (1944): 57–64. Beck-Broichsitter was a *Ritterkreuzträger* and one of the Wehrmacht's most highly decorated fighters. For tenacity's partner, see Hugo von Freytag-Loringhoven, "Optimismus im Kriege," *Militärwissenschaftliche Rundschau* 9, no. 2 (1943): 84–96, a reprint of a piece published originally in 1911.

20. "Armes Deutschland! Früher waren wir Oberste und Generale, aber nach dem Kriege werden wir Stiefelputzer und Gepäckträger sein. Wir werden doch keine Pension kriegen." Sönke Neitzel, ed., *Abgehört: Deutsche Generäle in britischer Kriegsgefangenschaft, 1942–1945* (Berlin: Propyläen, 2005), 121. The English translation in *Tapping Hitler's Generals: Transcripts of Secret Conversations, 1942–45* (St. Paul, Minn.: Frontline Books, 2007), is rendered as "boot-blacks and porters" (89).

21. Geoffrey Wawro, *The Franco-Prussian War: The German Conquest of France, 1870–1871* (Cambridge: Cambridge University Press, 2003), 168.

22. "Das Genie Gneisenaus und die Kampflust Blüchers." Waldemar Erfurth, "Die Zusammenwirken getrennter Heeresteile," part 1, *Militärwissenschaftliche Rundschau* 4, no. 1 (1939): 28–41.

23. "Deutschland wird siegen, weil wir siegen müssen, denn sonst hätte die Weltgeschichte ihren Sinn verloren." See Hans-Adolf Jacobsen and Hans Dollinger, eds., *Der Zweite Weltkrieg in Bildern und Dokumenten*, vol. 6, *Sturm auf die "Festung Europa," 1943* (Munich: Verlag Kurt Desch, 1968), 9–10. See also the comment by his biographer: "Unvorstellbar, dass Moltke oder Schlieffen je einer ähnlichen Sprache erlegen wären." Bodo Scheurig, *Alfred Jodl: Gehorsam und Verhängnis* (Berlin: Propyläen, 1991), 264.

24. The origin of "Menetekel" is in the Bible's Daniel 5:25–28, in which King Belshazzar sees the "writing on the wall," consisting of the words "mene, mene, tekel, u-Pharsin"—a dire prophecy indeed. Among the dozens of uses of the word in German military histories of World War II, see Hellmuth Günther Dahms, *Der Zweite Weltkrieg* (Frankfurt: Ullstein, 1966), 126: "Während Josef Goebbels die Casablanca-Formel zum Menetekel für alle Lauen und Zagenden

erhob, erstrebte Adolf Hitler einen aufsehenerregenden militärischen Erfolg, der Deutschland und seine Bundesgenossen wieder mit Zuversicht erfüllen würde."

25. Isabel V. Hull, *Absolute Destruction: Military Culture and the Practices of War in Imperial Germany* (Ithaca, N.Y.: Cornell University Press, 2005), 170.

26. Its absence was noted within U.S. military circles. See the short article "In Memoriam: Militär-Wochenblatt," in *Military Review* 23, no. 6 (September 1943): 60.

27. "Conversations with the Fuehrer at the Fuehrer's Headquarters between August 9 and 11, 1943," in *Fuehrer Conferences on Naval Affairs, 1939–1945*, ed. Jak P. Mallmann Showell (London: Chatham, 1990), 360.

28. "Herr Feldmarschall, das sofortige Drauflosmarschieren ist meine Stärke." Albert Kesselring, *Soldat bis zum letzten Tag* (Bonn: Athenäum, 1953), 221. The English translation of Kesselring's memoirs has it, "If you mean to go for them, Field-Marshal, then I'm your man." Albert Kesselring, *Kesselring: A Soldier's Record* (New York: William Morrow, 1954), 194.

Bibliography

"45th Infantry Division in the Sicilian Campaign as Compiled from G-3 Journal for Period July 10, 1943–Aug 22, 1943." U.S. Army Combined Arms Research Library (CARL) Digital Library. http://cgsc.contentdm.oclc.org/cdm4/document.php?CISOROOT=/p4013coll8&CISOPTR=113&REC=13.

Adonyi-Naredy, Franz von. *Ungarns Armee im Zweiten Weltkrieg: Deutschlands letzter Verbündeter.* Neckargemünd: Kurt Vowinckel Verlag, 1971.

Agarossi, Elena. *A Nation Collapses: The Italian Surrender of September 1943.* Cambridge: Cambridge University Press, 2006.

Agte, Patrick. *Michael Wittmann and the Waffen S.S. Tiger Commanders of the Leibstandarte in World War II.* 2 vols. Mechanicsburg, Pa.: Stackpole, 2006.

Anderson, Charles A. *Algeria–French Morocco.* Washington, D.C.: Center of Military History, n.d.

———. *Tunisia.* Washington, D.C.: Center of Military History, n.d.

Anderson, K. A. N. "Operations in North West Africa from 8th November 1942 to 13th May 1943." *Supplement to the London Gazette*, November 6, 1946.

Antal, John F. "Operation 25: The Wehrmacht's Conquest of Yugoslavia." In *Maneuver Warfare: An Anthology*, edited by Richard D. Hooker Jr., 391–404. Novato, Calif.: Presidio, 1993.

Arias, Augusto. "Operazione Citadel: Canto del Cigno dei Corazzati Tedeschi in Oriente." *Rivista Militare* 23, no. 7 (1967): 808–829.

Armstrong, Anne. *Unconditional Surrender: The Impact of the Casablanca Policy upon World War II.* New Brunswick, N.J.: Rutgers University Press, 1961.

Ashmead-Bartlett, Ellis. *With the Turks in Thrace.* New York: George H. Doran, 1913.

Atkinson, Rick. *An Army at Dawn: The War in North Africa, 1942–1943.* New York: Henry Holt, 2002.

———. *The Day of Battle: The War in Sicily and Italy, 1943–1944.* New York: Henry Holt, 2007.

Balck, Hermann. *Ordnung im Chaos: Erinnerungen, 1893–1948.* Osnabrück: Biblio Verlag, 1981.

Baldwin, Hanson. *Battles Lost and Won: Great Campaigns of World War II.* New York: Harper & Row, 1966.

The Balkan War Drama. London: Andrew Melrose, 1913.

Barbier, M. K. *Kursk: The Greatest Tank Battle, 1943.* St. Paul, Minn.: MBI, 2002.

Barnett, Correlli, ed. *Hitler's Generals: Authoritative Portraits of the Men Who Waged Hitler's War*. New York: Quill, 1989.

————, ed. *The Desert Generals*. Bloomington: Indiana University Press, 1982.

Barnhart, Barton V. "The Great Escape: An Analysis of Allied Actions Leading to the Axis Evacuation of Sicily in World War II." M.A. thesis, U.S. Army Command and General Staff College, Fort Leavenworth, Kans., 2003.

Barr, Niall. *The Pendulum of War: The Three Battles of El Alamein*. New York: Overlook Press, 2005.

Barthorp, Michael. *The Anglo-Boer Wars: The British and the Afrikaners, 1815–1902*. New York: Blandford Press, 1987.

Beaumont, Roger A. "On the Wehrmacht Mystique." *Military Review* 66, no. 7 (July 1986): 44–56.

————. "'Wehrmacht Mystique' Revisited." *Military Review* 70, no. 2 (February 1990): 64–75.

Beck-Broichsitter, Helmut. "Über die Beharrlichkeit im Angriff." *Militärwissenschaftliche Rundschau* 9, no. 1 (1944): 57–64.

Bergengruen, Helmut. "Der Kampf der Panzer Division 'Hemann Goering' auf Sizilien." Manuscript T-2, U.S. Army Heritage and Education Center, Carlisle, Pa.

Berlin, Robert H. *U.S. Army World War II Corps Commanders: A Composite Biography*. Fort Leavenworth, Kans.: U.S. Army Command and General Staff College, 1989.

Bigge, Major. "Ueber Selbstthätigkeit der Unterführer im Kriege." *Beihefte zum Militär-Wochenblatt* 1894. Berlin: E. S. Mittler, 1894.

Bird, W. D. *Lectures on the Strategy of the Russo-Japanese War*. London: Hugh Rees, 1911.

Birtle, Andrew J. *Sicily*. Washington, D.C.: Center of Military History, n.d.

Blau, George E. *The German Campaign in the Balkans (Spring 1941)*. Pamphlet 20-260. Washington, D.C.: Department of the Army, 1953.

Blume, Wilhelm von. "Selbstthätigkeit der Führer im Kriege." *Beihefte zum Militär-Wochenblatt*. Berlin: E. S. Mittler, 1896.

Blumenson, Martin. "The 36th Infantry Division in World War II." In *The Texas Military Experience: From the Texas Revolution to World War II*, edited by Joseph G. Dawson III, 128–136. College Station: Texas A&M University Press, 1995.

————. *Kasserine Pass: Rommel's Bloody, Climactic Battle for Tunisia*. New York: Cooper Square Press, 2000.

————. *Mark Clark*. London: Jonathan Cape, 1984.

————. *Salerno to Cassino*. Washington, D.C.: Center of Military History, 1969.

Blumenson, Martin, and Kevin M. Hymel. *Patton: Legendary World War II Commander*. Dulles, Va.: Potomac Books, 2008.

Blumentritt, Günther. "Hinhaltender Kampf." Manuscript B-704, U.S. Army Heritage and Education Center, Carlisle, Pa.

Bonin, Bogislaw von. "Betrachtungen über den italienischen Feldzug, 1943/

1944." Part 1, "Kampf um Sizilien, 10.7.–16.8.43." Manuscript T-2, U.S. Army Heritage and Education Center, Carlisle, Pa.

Borries, Vance von. "The Battle for Tunisia." *Strategy and Tactics*, no. 14, (February 1991): 5–20.

Boucabeille, Lieutenant Colonel. *La Guerre Turco-Balkanique, 1912–1913: Thrace—Macédoine—Albanie—Epire.* Paris: Librairie Chapelot, 1914.

Bradley, Dermot, and Richard Schulze-Kossens, eds. *Tätigkeitsbericht des Chefs des Heerespersonalamtes General der Infanterie Rudolf Schmundt, 1.10.1942–29.20.1944.* Osnabrück: Biblio Verlag, 1984.

Bradley, Omar N. *A Soldier's Story.* New York: Modern Library, 1999.

Brand, Dieter. "Vor 60 Jahren: Prochorovka: Aspekte der Operation Zitadelle; Juli 1943 im Abschnitt der Heeresgruppe Süd." *Österreichische Militärische Zeitschrift* 41, no. 5 (2003): 587–597.

Braun, M. "Gedanken über Kampfwagen- und Fliegerverwendung bei den russischen Herbstmanövern 1936." *Militär-Wochenblatt* 121, no. 28 (January 22, 1937): 1589–1592.

Breuer, William B. *Drop Zone Sicily: Allied Airborne Strike, July 1943.* Novato, Calif.: Presidio, 1983.

Browning, Christopher R. *Ordinary Men: Reserve Police Battalion 101 and the Final Solution in Poland.* New York: HarperCollins, 1992.

Bryant, Albert, Jr. "Agility: A Key to the Operational Art." Monograph. U.S. Army Command and General Staff College, Fort Leavenworth, Kans., 1988.

Bryant, Arthur. *The Turn of the Tide: A History of the War Years Based on the Diaries of Field-Marshal Lord Alanbrooke, Chief of the Imperial General Staff.* Garden City, N.Y.: Doubleday, 1957.

———. *Triumph in the West, 1943–1946: Based on Diaries and Autobiographical Notes of Field Marshal the Viscount Alanbrooke.* London: Collins, 1959.

Buchanan, Andrew. "A Friend Indeed? From Tobruk to El Alamein: The American Contribution to Victory in the Desert." *Diplomacy and Statecraft* 15, no. 2 (June 2004): 279–301.

Buckley, Christopher. *Road to Rome.* London: Hodder and Stoughton, 1945.

Buell, Thomas B. *Master of Sea Power: A Biography of Fleet Admiral Ernest J. King.* Annapolis, Md.: Naval Institute Press, 1995.

Busse, Theodor. "Der Angriff Zitadelle im Osten 1943." Manuscript T-26, U.S. Army Heritage and Education Center, Carlisle, Pa.

———. "Der Winterfeldzug 1942/1943 in Südrussland." In *Nie ausser Dienst: Zum achtzigsten Geburtstag von Generalfeldmarschall Erich von Manstein,* 45–63. Cologne: Markus Verlagsgesellschaft, 1967.

Bussmann, Walter. "Kursk—Orel—Dnjepr: Erlebnisse und Erfahrungen im Stab des XXXXVI Panzerkorps während des 'Unternehmens Zitadelle.'" *Vierteljahrshefte für Zeitgeschichte* 41, no. 4 (October 1993): 503–518.

Caidin, Martin. *The Tigers Are Burning.* New York: Hawthorn, 1974.

Calhoun, Mark T. "Defeat at Kasserine: American Armor Doctrine, Training, and Battle Command in Northwest Africa, World War II." M.A. thesis,

U.S. Army Command and General Staff College, Fort Leavenworth, Kans., 2003.

Cameron, Robert S. *Mobility, Shock, and Firepower: The Emergence of the U.S. Army's Armor Branch, 1917–1945.* Washington, D.C.: Center of Military History, 2008.

Carafano, James Jay. *G.I. Ingenuity: Improvisation, Technology, and Winning World War II.* Westport, Conn.: Praeger Security International, 2006.

———. "Wending through the Way of War" in "Comparative Ways of War: A Roundtable," *Historically Speaking* 11, no. 5 (November 2010): 25–26.

Carver, Field Marshal Lord. "Manstein." In *Hitler's Generals: Authoritative Portraits of the Men Who Waged Hitler's War,* edited by Correlli Barnett, 221. New York: Quill, 1989.

Cerff, Karl. *Die Waffen-S.S. im Wehrmachtbericht.* Osnabrück: Munin-Verlag, 1971.

Chandler, David G. *The Campaigns of Napoleon.* New York: Macmillan, 1966.

Citino, Robert M. "'Die Gedanken sind frei': The Intellectual Culture of the Interwar German Army." *Army Doctrine and Training Bulletin* (Canada) 4, no. 3 (Fall 2001): 53–54.

———. "Military Histories Old and New: A Reintroduction." *American Historical Review* 112, no. 4 (October 2007): 1070–1090.

———. "The German Way of War Revisited." In "Comparative Ways of War: A Roundtable." *Historically Speaking* 11, no. 5 (November 2010): 20–21.

———. *Armored Forces: History and Sourcebook.* Westport, Conn.: Greenwood, 1994.

———. *Death of the Wehrmacht: The German Campaigns of 1942.* Lawrence: University Press of Kansas, 2007.

———. *Quest for Decisive Victory: From Stalemate to Blitzkrieg in Europe, 1899–1940.* Lawrence: University Press of Kansas, 2002.

———. *The Evolution of Blitzkrieg Tactics: German Defends Itself against Poland, 1918–1933.* Westport, Conn.: Greenwood, 1987.

———. *The German Way of War: From the Thirty Years' War to the Third Reich.* Lawrence: University Press of Kansas, 2005.

———. *The Path to Blitzkrieg: Doctrine and Training in the German Army, 1920–1939.* Boulder, Colo.: Lynne Rienner, 1999.

———. "'Die Gedanken sind frei': Culture Intellectuelle de l'Armée Allemande de l'Entre-Deux-Guerres." *Le Bulletin de Doctrine et d'Instruction de l'Armée de Terre* (Canada) 4, no. 3 (Autumn 2001): 51–59.

Clark, Christopher. "Josef 'Sepp' Dietrich." In *Die S.S.: Elite unter den Totenkopf: 30 Lebensläufe,* edited by Ronald Smelser and Enrico Syring, 119–133. Paderborn: Ferdinand Schöningh, 2000.

Clark, Lloyd. *The Battle of the Tanks: Kursk, 1943.* New York: Atlantic Monthly, 2011.

Clark, Mark W. *Calculated Risk.* New York: Enigma Books, 2007.

Clausewitz, Carl von. *On War.* Edited and translated by Michael Howard and Peter Paret. Princeton, N.J.: Princeton University Press, 1984.

Cline, Ray S. *The War Department: Washington Command Post: The Operations Division*. Washington, D.C.: Center of Military History, 1990.

Coats, Stephen D. "The 'Truscott Trot': Training for Operation Husky, 1943." In *Combined Arms in Battle Since 1939*, edited by Roger J. Spiller, 277–282. Fort Leavenworth, Kans.: U.S. Army Command and General Staff College, 1992.

Coggins, Jack. *The Campaign for North Africa*. Garden City, N.Y.: Doubleday, 1980.

"Comparative Ways of War: A Roundtable." *Historically Speaking* 11, no. 5 (November 2010): 20–26.

Condell, Bruce, and David T. Zabecki. *On the German Art of War: Truppenführung*. Boulder, Colo.: Lynne Rienner, 2001.

Connaughton, R. M. *The War of the Rising Sun and Tumbling Bear: A Military History of the Russo-Japanese War*. London: Routledge, 1988.

Connelly, Owen. *Blundering to Glory: Napoleon's Military Campaigns*. Lanham, Md.: Rowman & Littlefield, 2006.

Conrath, Paul. "Der Kampf um Sizilien." Manuscript C-087, U.S. Army Heritage and Education Center, Carlisle, Pa.

Cooper, Belton Y. *Death Traps: The Survival of an American Armored Division in World War II*. Novato, Calif.: Presidio, 2000.

Cooper, Matthew. *The German Army. 1933–1945*. Chelsea, Mich.: Scarborough House, 1991.

Corum, James S. *The Roots of Blitzkrieg: Hans von Seeckt and German Military Reform*. Lawrence: University Press of Kansas, 1992.

———. *Wolfram von Richtofen: Master of the German Air War*. Lawrence: University Press of Kansas, 2008.

Craig, Gordon. *The Battle of Königgrätz: Prussia's Victory over Austria, 1866*. Philadelphia: Lippincott, 1964.

Craven, Wesley Frank, and James Lea Cate, eds. *The Army Air Forces in World War II*. Vol. 2, *Europe: Torch to Pointblank, August 1942 to December 1943*. Chicago: University of Chicago Press, 1949.

Cross, Robin. *Citadel: The Battle of Kursk*. New York: Sarpedon, 1993.

D'Este, Carlo. *Bitter Victory: The Battle for Sicily, 1943*. New York: Harper Perennial, 1988.

———. *Fatal Decision: Anzio and the Battle for Rome*. New York: Harper Perennial, 1992.

———. *Patton: A Genius for War*. New York: Harper, 1995.

———. *Warlord: A Life of Winston Churchill at War, 1874–1945*. New York: Harper, 2008.

———. *World War II in the Mediterranean, 1942–1945*. Chapel Hill, N.C.: Algonquin Books, 1990.

Dahms, Hellmuth Günther. *Der Zweite Weltkrieg*. Frankfurt: Ullstein, 1966.

Dallek, Robert. *Franklin D. Roosevelt and American Foreign Policy, 1932–1945*. Oxford: Oxford University Press, 1995.

Dastrup, Boyd. *The Field Artillery: History and Sourcebook*. Westport, Conn.: Greenwood Press, 1994.

Dawidowicz, Lucy S. *The War against the Jews, 1933–1945.* New York: Holt, Rinehart and Winston, 1975.

Dawson, Joseph G., ed., *The Texas Military Experience: From the Texas Revolution to World War II.* College Station: Texas A&M University Press, 1995.

Deakin, F. W. *The Brutal Friendship: Mussolini, Hitler and the Fall of Italian Fascism.* New York: Harper & Row, 1962.

Delbrück, Hans. *Historische und Politische Aufsätze.* Berlin: Georg Stilke, 1907.

———. "Prinz Friedrich Karl." In *Historische und Politische Aufsätze,* 302–316. Berlin: Georg Stilke, 1907.

"Desert 'Hooks'—Outflanking Movements in Desert Warfare." *Military Review* 24, no. 11 (February 1945): 115–119.

Das Deutsche Reich und der Zweite Weltkrieg. Vol. 6, *Der Globale Krieg: Die Ausweitung zum Weltkrieg und der Wechsel der Initiative, 1941–1943.* Stuttgart: Deutsche Verlags-Anstalt, 1990.

Das Deutsche Reich und der Zweite Weltkrieg. Vol. 8, *Die Ostfront, 1943/44: Der Krieg im Osten and an den Nebenfronten.* Munich: Deutsche Verlags-Anstalt, 2007.

DiNardo, Richard L. *Germany and the Axis Powers: From Coalition to Collapse.* Lawrence: University Press of Kansas, 2005.

Doerr, Hans. *Der Feldzug nach Stalingrad: Versuch eines operativen Uberblickes.* Darmstadt: E. S. Mittler, 1955.

"Drei Jahre Krieg—drei Jahre Sieg." *Die Wehrmacht* 6, no. 18 (September 2, 1942): 4–5.

Duffy, Christopher. *Frederick the Great: A Military Life.* London: Routledge and Kegan Paul, 1985.

Dunn, Walter S., Jr. *Kursk: Hitler's Gamble, 1943.* Westport, Conn.: Praeger, 1997.

Echevarria, Antulio, II. "Auftragstaktik: In Its Proper Perspective." *Military Review* 66, no. 10 (October 1986): 50–56.

———. *After Clausewitz: German Military Thinkers before the Great War.* Lawrence: University Press of Kansas, 2000.

Eisenhower, Dwight D. *At Ease: Stories I Tell to My Friends.* Garden City, N.Y.: Doubleday, 1967.

———. *Crusade in Europe.* Garden City, N.Y.: Doubleday, 1948.

———. *The Papers of Dwight David Eisenhower, The War Years: II.* Edited by Alfred D. Chandler Jr. Baltimore, Md.: Johns Hopkins Press, 1970.

Epitome of the Russo-Japanese War. Washington, D.C.: Government Printing Office, 1907.

Erfurth, Waldemar. "Das Zusammenwirken getrennter Heeresteile." Parts 1 through 4. *Militärwissenschaftliche Rundschau* 4, nos. 1–4 (1939).

———. *Die Geschichte des deutschen Generalstabes von 1918 bis 1945.* Berlin: Musterschmidt, 1957.

Erickson, Edward J. *Defeat in Detail: The Ottoman Army in the Balkans, 1912–1913.* Westport, Conn.: Praeger, 2003.

Erickson, John. *The Road to Berlin: Continuing the History of Stalin's War with Germany*. Boulder, Colo.: Westview, 1983.

Esposito, Vincent J., ed., *The West Point Atlas of American Wars*, vol. 2, *1900–1953*. New York: Praeger, 1959.

Essame, Hubert. "Field Marshal Erich von Manstein," *Army Quarterly and Defence Journal* 104, no. 1 (1973): 40–43.

Fangohr, Friedrich. "Zitadelle: Der Angriff der 4. Panzer-Armee im July 1943." Manuscript T-26, U.S. Army Heritage and Education Center, Carlisle, Pa.

Farago, Ladislas. *Patton: Ordeal and Triumph*. Yardley, Pa.: Westholme, 2005.

Farwell, Farwell. *The Great Anglo-Boer War*. New York: Norton, 1976.

Fauntleroy, Barbara Gavin. *The General and His Daughter: The Wartime Letters of General James M. Gavin to His Daughter Barbara*. New York: Fordham University Press, 2007.

Ferguson, Arthur B. "Origins of the Combined Bomber Offensive." In *The Army Air Forces in World War II*. Vol. 2, *Europe: Torch to Pointblank, August 1942 to December 1943*, edited by Wesley Frank Craven and James Lea Cate, 274–307. Chicago: University of Chicago Press, 1949.

Fey, Will. *Armor Battles of the Waffen-S.S. 1943–45*. Mechanicsburg, Pa.: Stackpole, 2003.

Fischer, Fritz. *Griff nach der Weltmacht: Die Kriegszielpolitik des kaiserlichen Deutschland, 1914/18*. Düsseldorf: Droste Verlag, 1961.

Fitzgerald, F. Scott. *The Great Gatsby*. New York: Scribner, 1925.

"Flak am Kuban." *Die Wehrmacht* 7, no. 13 (June 13, 1943): 6.

Foerster, Roland G. "Einführung." In Foerster, *Gezeitenwechsel im Zweiten Weltkrieg?*, 19–25.

———, ed. *Gezeitenwechsel im Zweiten Weltkrieg? Die Schlachten von Ch'arkov und Kursk im Frühjahr und Sommer 1943 in operativer Anlage, Verlauf und politischer Bedeutung*. Berlin: E. S. Mittler, 1996.

Foerster, Wolfgang. "Prinz Friedrich Karl." *Militärwissenschaftliche Rundschau* 8, no. 2 (1943): 90–91.

Fontane, Theodor. *Der deutsche Krieg von 1866*. Vol. 2, *Der Feldzug in West- und Mitteldeutschland*. Berlin. R. v. Decker, 1871.

Forstmeier, Friedrich. *Die Räumung des Kuban-Brückenkopfes im Herbst 1943*. Darmstadt: Wehr und Wissen Verlagsgesellschaft, 1964.

Forty, George. *The Armies of Rommel*. London: Arms and Armour, 1997.

Frandsen, Herbert L. "Counterblitz: Conditions to a Successful Counteroffensive." Monograph. U.S. Army Command and General Staff College, Fort Leavenworth, Kans., 1990.

Frank, Richard B. *Guadalcanal: The Definitive Account of the Landmark Battle*. New York: Penguin, 1992.

French, David. *The British Way in Warfare, 1688–2000*. London: Unwin Hyman, 1990.

Freytag-Loringhoven, Hugo von. *Feldherrngrösse: Von Denken und Handeln hevorragender Heerführer*. Berlin: E. S. Mittler, 1922.

————. "Optimismus im Kriege." *Militärwissenschaftliche Rundschau* 9, no. 2 (1943): 84–96.

Fries, Walter. "Der Kampf der 29. Panzer-Grenadier-Division auf Sizilien." Manuscript T-2, U.S. Army Heritage and Education Center, Carlisle, Pa.

————. "Der Kampf um Sizilien." Manuscript T-2, U.S. Army Heritage and Education Center, Carlisle, Pa.

Frieser, Karl-Heinz. "Der Rückschlag des Pendels: Das Zurückweichen der Ostfront von Sommer 1943 bis Sommer 1944." *Das Deutsche Reich und der Zweite Weltkrieg.* Vol. 8, *Die Ostfront, 1943/44: Der Krieg im Osten and an den Nebenfronten.* Munich: Deutsche Verlags-Anstalt, 2007.

————. "Der Zusammenbruch im Osten: Die Rückzugskämpfe seit Sommer 1944." *Das Deutsche Reich und der Zweite Weltkrieg.* Vol. 8, *Die, Ostfront 1943/44: Der Krieg im Osten and an den Nebenfronten.* Munich: Deutsche Verlags-Anstalt, 2007.

————. "Die Schlacht im Kursker Bogen." In *Das Deutsche Reich und der Zweite Weltkrieg,* vol. 8, *Die Ostfront, 1943/44: Der Krieg im Osten and an den Nebenfronten,* 81–208. Munich: Deutsche Verlags-Anstalt, 2007.

————. "Schlagen aus der Nachhand—Schlagen aus der Vorhand: Die Schlachten von Ch'arkow und Kursk 1943." In Foerster, *Gezeitenwechsel im Zweiten Weltkrieg?,* 101–135.

————. *Blitzkrieg-Legende: Der Westfeldzug 1940.* Oldenbourg: Wissenschaftliche Verlag, 1995.

————. *The Blitzkrieg Legend: The 1940 Campaign in the West.* Annapolis: Naval Institute Press, 2005.

Frieser, Karl-Heinz, with Friedhelm Klein. "Mansteins Gegenschlag am Donez: Operative Analyse des Gegenangriffs der Heeresgruppe Süd im Februar/März 1943." *Militärgeschichte* 9 (1999): 12–18.

Fuller, J. F. C. *A Military History of the Western World.* Vol. 3, *From the American Civil War to the End of World War II.* New York: Da Capo, 1956.

————. *The Conduct of War, 1789–1961: A Study of the Impact of the French, Industrial, and Russian Revolutions on War and Its Conduct.* New York: Da Capo, 1992.

Gabel, Christopher R. *Seek, Strike, and Destroy: U.S. Army Tank Destroyer Doctrine in World War II.* Fort Leavenworth, Kans.: U.S. Army Command and General Staff College, 1985.

————. *The U.S. Army GHQ Maneuvers of 1941.* Washington, D.C.: Center of Military History, 1992.

Garland, Albert N., and Howard McGaw Smyth. *Sicily and the Surrender of Italy.* Washington, D.C.: Center of Military History, 1965.

Gause, Alfred. "Der Feldzug in Nordafrika im Jahre 1942." *Wehrwissenschaftliche Rundschau* 12, no. 11 (November 1962): 652–680.

————. "Der Feldzug in Nordafrika im Jahre 1943." *Wehrwissenschaftliche Rundschau* 12, no. 12 (December 1962): 720–728.

Gavin, James M. *On to Berlin: Battles of an Airborne Commander, 1943–1946.* New York: Viking, 1978.

Gentile, Gian P. *How Effective is Strategic Bombing? Lessons Learned from World War II to Kosovo*. New York: New York University Press, 2001.

Gibbs, Philip, and Bernard Grant. *The Balkan War: Adventures of War with Cross and Crescent*. Boston: Small, Maynard, and Company, 1913.

Gisevius, Hans B. *To the Bitter End*. Boston: Houghton Mifflin, 1947.

Glantz, David M. "Observing the Soviets: U.S. Army Attachés in Eastern Europe during the 1930s." *Journal of Military History* 55, no. 2 (April 1991): 153–183.

———. "Prelude to Kursk: Soviet Strategic Operations, February-March 1943." In Foerster, *Gezeitenwechsel im Zweiten Weltkrieg?*, 29–56.

———. "Soviet Military Strategy during the Second Period of War (November 1942–December 1943): A Reappraisal." *Journal of Military History* 60, no. 1 (January 1996): 115–150.

———. "Soviet Operational Art since 1936: The Triumph of Maneuver War." In *Historical Perspectives of the Operational Art*, edited by Michael D. Krause and R. Cody Phillips, 247–248. Washington, D.C.: Center of Military History, 2007.

———. "The Red Army's Donbas Offensive (February–March 1942) Revisited: A Documentary Essay." *Journal of Slavic Military Studies* 18, no. 3 (2005): 369–503.

———. *From the Don to the Dnepr: Soviet Offensive Operations, December 1942–August 1943*. London: Frank Cass, 1991.

———. *Zhukov's Greatest Defeat: The Red Army's Epic Disaster in Operation Mars, 1942*. Lawrence: University Press of Kansas, 1999.

Glantz, David M., and Jonathan House. *When Titans Clashed: How the Red Army Stopped Hitler*. Lawrence: University Press of Kansas, 1995.

———. *The Battle of Kursk*. Lawrence: University Press of Kansas, 1999.

Glantz, David M., with Jonathan House. *Armageddon in Stalingrad: September–November 1942*. Lawrence: University Press of Kansas, 2009.

———. *To the Gates of Stalingrad: Soviet German Combat Operations, April–August 1942*. Lawrence: University Press of Kansas, 2009.

Goehring, Russell J. "Sequencing Operations: The Critical Path of Operational Art." Monograph. U.S. Army Command and General Staff College, Fort Leavenworth, Kans., 1987.

Goldhagen, Daniel Jonah. *Hitler's Willing Executioners: Ordinary Germans and the Holocaust*. New York: Alfred A. Knopf, 1996.

Görlitz, Walter. "Keitel, Jodl, and Warlimont." In *Hitler's Generals*, edited by Correlli Barnett, 138–171. New York: Quill, 1989.

———. *Der deutsche Generalstab: Geschichte und Gestalt, 1657–1945*. Frankfurt am Main: Verlag der Frankfurter Hefte, 1950.

Gosztony, Peter. *Hitlers fremde Heere: Das Schicksal der nichtdeutschen Armeen im Ostfeldzug*. Düsseldorf: Econ Verlag, 1976.

Graeme-Evans, Alex. "Field Marshal Bernard Montgomery: A Critical Assessment." *Flinders Journal of History and Politics* 4 (1974): 124–142.

Graham, Dominick, and Shelford Bidwell. *Tug of War: The Battle for Italy*. London: Hodder & Stoughton, 1986.

Grechko, Andrei. *Battle for the Caucasus.* Moscow: Progress Publishers, 1971.

Greiner, Günter. "Die Letzten am Feind: Absetzung an der Volturno-Front." *Die Wehrmacht* 7, no. 24 (November 24, 1943): 7.

———. "Wasser—ein Verbündeter: Pioniere an den westlichen Süditalien-front." *Die Wehrmacht* 7, no. 25 (December 8, 1943): 7.

Griffith, Paddy. *Forward into Battle: Fighting Tactics from Waterloo to the Near Future.* Novato, Calif.: Presidio, 1990.

Groeben, Peter von der. "Die Schlacht der 2. Panzer-Armee und 9. Armee im Orel-Bogen vom 5. Juli bis 18. August 1943." Manuscript T-26, U.S. Army Heritage and Education Center, Carlisle, Pa.

Grossdeutschlands Freiheitskrieg. Part 171. "Die britisch-amerikanische Überfall auf Französisch-Nordafrika." *Militär-Wochenblatt* 127, no. 21 (November 20, 1942): 557–560.

Grossdeutschlands Freiheitskrieg. Part 172. "Die Feindmächte in Nordafrika." *Militär-Wochenblatt* 127, no. 22 (November 27, 1942): 584–587.

Grossdeutschlands Freiheitskrieg. Part 173. "Yankeeterror in Nordafrika." *Militär-Wochenblatt* 127, no. 23 (December 4, 1942): 616.

Grossdeutschlands Freiheitskrieg. Part 174. "In Tunesien grössere Kämpfe im Gange." *Militär-Wochenblatt* 127, no. 24 (December 11, 1942): 639–643.

Grossdeutschlands Freiheitskrieg. Part 175. "Kämpfe in Tunisien." *Militär-Wochenblatt* 127, no. 25 (December 18, 1942): 669–673.

Grotelueschen, Mark Ethan. *The AEF Way of War: The American Army and Combat in World War I.* Cambridge: Cambridge University Press, 2007.

Guderian, Heinz. "Bewegliche Truppenkörper: Ein kriegsgeschichtliche Studie," part 1, "Die Schlittenfahrt des Grossen Kurfürsten im Winterfuldzug 1678–79." *Militär-Wochenblatt* 112, no. 18 (November 11, 1927): 649–652.

———. "Die Panzertruppen und ihr Zusammenwirken mit den anderen Waffen." *Militärwissenschaftliche Rundschau* 1, no. 5 (1936): 607–626.

———. "Schnelle Truppen einst und jetzt." *Militärwissenschaftliche Rundschau* 4, no. 2 (1939): 229–243.

———. *Achtung—Panzer! The Development of Armoured Forces, Their Tactics and Operational Potential.* London: Arms and Armour, 1992.

———. *Erinnerungen eines Soldaten.* Heidelberg: Kurt Vowinckel, 1951.

———. *Panzer Leader.* New York: Ballantine, 1957.

Gudmundsson, Bruce I. *Stormtroop Tactics: Innovation in the German Army, 1914–1918.* Westport, Conn.: Praeger, 1989.

Guide to Foreign Military Studies 1945–54: Catalog and Index. Karlsruhe: Historical Division, Headquarters, U.S. Army Europe, 1954.

Habeck, Mary R. *Storm of Steel: The Development of Armor Doctrine in Germany and the Soviet Union, 1919–1939.* Ithaca, N.Y.: Cornell University Press, 2003.

Habedanck, Gert. "Im Kuban Brückenkopf." *Die Wehrmacht* 7, no. 9 (April 28, 1943): 10–11.

———. "In den Dschungeln bei Noworossijsk." *Die Wehrmacht* 7, no. 11 (May 26, 1943): 4–5, 14.

―――. "Stutzpunkt Florescu im Kuban Brückenkopf," *Die Wehrmacht* 7, no. 10 (May 12, 1943): 6–7.

Halder, Franz. "Stellungnahme zu Wagener, 'Gedanken über Kampfführung im Osten.'" Manuscript P-082, U.S. Army Heritage and Education Center, Carlisle, Pa.

Hargreaves, Reginald. *Red Sun Rising: The Siege of Port Arthur*. Philadelphia: Lippincott, 1962.

Harrison, Richard W. *Architect of Soviet Victory in World War II: The Life and Theories of G. S. Isserson*. Jefferson, N.C.: McFarland, 2010.

―――. *The Russian Way of War: Operational Art, 1904–1940*. Lawrence: University Press of Kansas, 2001.

Hart, Russell A. *Guderian: Panzer Pioneer or Myth Maker?* Washington, D.C.: Potomac Books, 2006.

Hartmann, Christian. *Halder: Generalstabschef Hitlers, 1938–1942*. Paderborn: Ferdinand Schöningh, 1991.

Hassell, Agostino von, and Sigrid MacRae. *Alliance of Enemies: The Untold Story of the Secret American and German Collaboration to End World War II*. New York: Thomas Dunne, 2006.

Hayward, Joel S. A. *Stopped at Stalingrad: The Luftwaffe and Hitler's Defeat in the East*. Lawrence: University Press of Kansas, 1998.

Healy, Mark. *Kursk, 1943*. 1993; reprint, Westport, Conn.: Praeger, 2004.

Heiber, Helmut, ed. *Hitlers Lagebesprechungen: Die Protokollfragmente siner militärischen Konferenzen, 1942–1945*. Stuttgart: Deutsche Verlags-Anstalt, 1962.

Heiber, Helmut, and David M. Glantz, eds. *Hitler and his Generals: Military Conferences, 1942–1945*. New York: Enigma, 2003.

Heim, Ferdinand. "Stalingrad und der Verlauf des Feldzuges der Jahre 1943–1945." In *Der Feldzug gegen Sowjetrussland, 1941 bis 1945: Ein operative Überblick*, by Alfred Philippi and Ferdinand Heim, 201–293. Stuttgart: W. Kohlhammer, 1962.

Heinrici, Gotthard, and Friedrich Wilhelm Hauck. "Zitadelle: Der Angriff auf den russischen Stellungsvorsprung bei Kursk." *Wehrwissenschaftliche Rundschau* 15, nos. 8–10 (August–September 1965).

Heusinger, Adolf. "Der 'unbequeme' operative Kopf." In *Nie ausser Dienst: Zum achtzigsten Geburtstag von Generalfeldmarschall Erich von Manstein*, 35–43. Cologne: Markus Verlagsgesellschaft, 1967.

―――. *Befehl im Widerstreit: Schicksalsstunden der deutschen Armee 1923–1945*. Tübingen: Rainer Wunderlich Verlag Hermann Leins, 1950.

Hickey, Des, and Gus Smith. *Operation Avalanche: The Salerno Landings, 1943*. New York: McGraw-Hill, 1984.

Hillgruber, Andreas. "In der Sicht des kritischen Historikers." In *Nie ausser Dienst: Zum achtzigsten Geburtstag von Generalfeldmarschall Erich von Manstein*, 65–83. Cologne: Markus Verlagsgesellschaft, 1967.

Hinze, Rolf. *Crucible of Combat: Germany's Defensive Battles in the Ukraine, 1943–44*. Solihull: Helion, 2009.

Hitler's Secret Book. New York: Grove Press, 1961.

Hofmann, George F. *Through Mobility We Conquer: The Mechanization of U.S. Cavalry.* Lexington: University Press of Kentucky, 2006.

Hofmann, George F., and Donn A. Starry, eds. *Camp Colt to Desert Storm: The History of the U.S. Armored Forces.* Lexington: University Press of Kentucky, 1999.

Höhne, Heinz. *Order of the Death's Head.* New York: Ballantine, 1971.

Holt, Edgar. *The Boer War.* London: Putnam, 1958.

Hornfischer, James D. *Neptune's Inferno: The U.S. Navy at Guadalcanal.* New York: Bantam: 2011.

Howard, Michael. *The Mediterranean Strategy in the Second World War.* New York: Praeger, 1968.

Howe, George F. "Faid—Kasserine: The German View." *Military Affairs* 13, no. 4 (Winter 1949): 216–222.

———. *Northwest Africa: Seizing the Initiative in the West.* Washington, D.C.: Center of Military History, 1957.

Hubatsch, Walther. "Das Kriegstagebuch als Geschichtsquelle." *Wehrwissenschaftliche Rundschau* 15, no. 11 (1965): 615–623.

———, ed. *Hitlers Weisungen für die Kriegführung 1939–1945: Dokumente des Oberkommandos der Wehrmacht.* Frankfurt: Bernard & Graefe, 1962.

Hughes, Daniel J. "Abuses of German Military History." *Military Review* 66, no. 12 (December 1986): 66–76.

———, ed. *Moltke on the Art of War: Selected Writings.* By Helmuth von Moltke. Novato, Calif.: Presidio, 1993.

Hull, Isabel V. *Absolute Destruction: Military Culture and the Practices of War in Imperial Germany.* Ithaca, N.Y.: Cornell University Press, 2005.

Hurley, Alfred F. *Billy Mitchell: Crusader for Air Power.* Bloomington: Indiana University Press, 1975.

Hürter, Johannes. *Hitlers Heerführer: Die deutschen Oberbefehlshaber im Krieg gegen die Sowjetunion, 1941/42.* Munich: R. Oldenbourg, 2006.

"In Memoriam: Militär-Wochenblatt." *Military Review* 23, no. 6 (September 1943): 60.

"Interior Lines in Tunisia." *Military Review* 23, no. 5 (August 1943): 30.

Ireland, Bernard. *The War in the Mediterranean, 1940–1943.* Barnsley: Leo Cooper, 1993.

Isom, Dallas Woodbury. *Midway Inquest: Why the Japansese Lost the Battle of Midway.* Bloomington: Indiana University Press, 2007.

Izzo, Lawrence L. "An Analysis of Manstein's Winter Campaign on the Russian Front, 1942–43: A Perspective of the Operational Level of War and its Implications." Student paper. U.S. Army Command and General Staff College, Fort Leavenworth, Kans., 1986.

"J.K." "The Campaign in Sicily." *Journal of the Royal United Service Institution* 101 (February–November 1956): 221–229.

Jackson, W. G. F. *The Battle for Italy.* New York: Harper & Row, 1967.

Jacobsen, Hans-Adolf, and Hans Dollinger, eds. *Der Zweite Weltkrieg in Bildern und Dokumenten*. Vol. *5, Kriegswende, 1942/1943*. Munich: Verlag Kurt Desch, 1968.

———. *Der Zweite Weltkrieg in Bildern und Dokumenten*. Vol. 6, *Sturm auf die "Festung Europa" 1943*. Munich: Verlag Kurt Desch, 1968.

Jarymowycz, Roman Johann. "Jedi Knights in the Kremlin: The Soviet Military in the 1930s and the Genesis of Deep Battle." In *Military Planning and the Origins of the Second World War in Europe*, edited by B. J. C. McKercher and Roch Legault, 122–124. Westport, Conn.: Praeger, 2001.

———. *Tank Tactics: From Normandy to Lorraine*. Boulder, Colo.: Lynne Rienner, 2001.

Jersey, Stanley Coleman. *Hell's Islands: The Untold Story of Guadalcanal*. College Station: Texas A&M University Press, 2008.

Johnson, David E. "From Frontier Constabulary to Modern Army: The U.S. Army between the World Wars." Harold R. Winton and David R. Mets. *The Challenge of Change: Military Institutions and New Realities, 1918–1941*. Lincoln: University of Nebraska Press, 2000.

———. *Fast Tanks and Heavy Bombers: Innovation in the U.S. Army, 1917–1945*. Ithaca, N.Y.: Cornell University Press, 1998.

Jones, Matthew. *Britain, the United States, and the Mediterranean War, 1942–44*. New York: St. Martin's Press, 1996.

Juin, Alphonse. "La Campagne de Tunisie." *Miroir de l'Histoire* 8, no. 87 (1957): 312–324.

Jukes, Geoffrey. *Die Schlacht der 6000 Panzer: Kursk und Orel, 1943*. Rastatt: Moewig, 1982.

———. *Kursk: The Clash of Armor, July 1943*. New York: Ballantine, 1969.

Kabisch, Ernst. "Systemlose Strategie." *Militär-Wochenblatt* 125, no. 26 (December 27, 1940): 1235.

Kagan, Frederick. "Army Doctrine and Modern War: Notes toward a New Edition of FM 100-5." *Parameters* 27, no. 1 (Spring 1997): 134–151.

"Kampf und Gefecht." *Militär-Wochenblatt* 84, no. 2 (March 25, 1899): 694–698.

Kehrig, Manfred. *Stalingrad: Analyse und Dokumentation einer Schlacht*. Stuttgart: Deutsche Verlags-Anstalt, 1974.

Keitel, Wilhelm. *In the Service of the Reich*. New York: Stein and Day, 1979.

———. *Mein Leben: Pflichterfüllung bis zum Untergang: Hitlers Generalfeldmarschall und Chef des Oberkommandos der Wehrmacht in Selbstzeugnissen*. Berlin: Edition Q, 1998.

Kelly, Orr. *Meeting the Fox: The Allied Invasion of Africa, from Operation Torch to Kasserine Pass to Victory in Tunisia*. New York: John Wiley & Sons, 2002.

Kershaw, Ian. *Hitler*. 2 vols. New York: Norton, 1998–2000.

Kessel, Eberhard. "Blucher: Zum 200. Geburtstag am 16. Dezember." *Militärwissenschaftliche Rundschau* 7, no. 4 (1942): 305.

Kesselring, Albert. *Kesselring: A Soldier's Record*. New York: William Morrow, 1954.

———. *Soldat bis zum letzten Tag*. Bonn. Athenäum, 1953.

Ketterson, T. B., ed. *82d Airborne Division in Sicily and Italy*. Manuscript R-11960, U.S. Army Combined Arms Research Library (CARL) Digital Library. http://cgsc.contentdm.oclc.org/cdm4/item_viewer.php?CISO ROOT=/p4013coll8&CISOPTR=103&CISOBOX=1&REC=10.

Kielmansegg, Johann Adolf Graf von. "Bemerkungen eines Zeitzeugen zu den Schlachten von Char'kov und Kursk aus der Sicht des damaligen Generalstabsoffiziers Ia in der Operationsabteilung der Generalstabs des Heeres." In Foerster, *Gezeitenwechsel im Zweiten Weltkrieg?*, 137–148.

Kiesling, Eugenia C. *Arming against Hitler: France and the Limits of Military Planning*. Lawrence: University Press of Kansas, 1996.

Kipp, Jacob W. "The Origins of Soviet Operational Art, 1917–1936." In *Historical Perspectives of the Operational Art*, edited by Michael D. Krause and R. Cody Phillips, 213–246. Washington, D.C.: Center of Military History, 2007.

Kirkpatrick, Charles E. *An Unknown Future and a Doubtful Present: Writing the Victory Plan of 1941*. Washington, D.C.: Center of Military History, 1992.

Kitchen, Martin. *Rommel's Desert War: Waging World War II in North Africa, 1941–1943*. Cambridge: Cambridge University Press, 2009.

Klink, Ernst. *Das Gesetz des Handelns: Die Operation Zitadelle, 1943*. Stuttgart: Deutsche Verlags-Anstalt, 1966.

Klinkowstroem, Karl Graf von. "Der Abfall Italiens und die Kämpfe um Rom: Gesehen com Stabe der OB-Süd." Manuscript D-301, U.S. Army Heritage and Education Center, Carlisle, Pa.

Korda, Michael. *Ike: An American Hero*. New York: Harper, 2007.

Krause, Michael D., and R. Cody Phillips, eds. *Historical Perspectives of the Operational Art*. Washington, D.C.: Center of Military History, 2007.

Kreuter, Siegbert. "Die Schlacht um Kursk: Das Unternehmen Zitadelle vom 5.-15.7.1943." *Österreichische Militärische Zeitschrift* 41, no. 6 (2003): 583–586.

Kurowski, Franz. *General der Kavallerie Siegfried Westphal, Generalstabschef dreier Feldmarschälle Rommel, Kesselring und von Rundstedt*. Würzburg: Flechsig, 2007.

———. *Generalfeldmarschall Albert Kesselring: Oberbefehlshaber an allen Fronten*. Berg am See: Kurt Vowinckel-Verlag, 1985.

Kutschbach, A. *Die Serben im Balkankrieg 1912–1913 und im Kriege gegen die Bulgaren*. Stuttgart: Frank'sche Verlagshandlung, 1913.

Lacey, James. "World War II's Real Victory Program." *Journal of Military History* 75, no. 3 (July 2011): 811–834.

Lange, Herman W. W. "Rommel at Thala." *Military Review* 41, no. 9 (September 1961): 72–84.

Langemak, Captain. "Kriechen oder Springen? Ein Beitrag zu unserer Gefechtsausbildung." *Militär-Wochenblatt* 84, no. 28 (March 7, 1905): 653–660.

Leggiere, Michael V. *Napoleon and Berlin: The Franco-Prussian War in North Germany*. Norman: University of Oklahoma Press, 2002.

Leonhard, Robert R. *The Art of Maneuver: Maneuver-Warfare Theory and Air-Land Battle*. Novato, Calif.: Presidio, 1991.

Lettow-Vorbeck, Oscar von. *Geschichte des Krieges von 1866 in Deutschland.* Vol. 1, *Gastein-Langensalza.* Berlin: E. S. Mittler, 1896.

Levine, Alan J. *The War against Rommel's Supply Lines, 1942–1943.* Westport, Conn.: Praeger, 1999.

Lewis, Adrian R. *Omaha Beach: A Flawed Victory.* Chapel Hill: University of North Carolina Press, 2001.

Liddell Hart, B. H. *The British Way in Warfare.* London: Faber and Faber, 1932.

———. *The German Generals Talk.* New York: Quill, 1979.

———. *History of the Second World War.* Old Saybrook, Conn.: Konecky & Konecky, 1970.

Liedtke, Gregory. "*Furor Teutonicus*: German Offensives and Counter-Attacks on the Eastern Front, August 1943 to March 1945." *Journal of Slavic Military Studies* 21, no. 3 (July 2008): 563–587.

Lingen, Kerstin von. *Kesselring's Last Battle: War Crimes Trials and Cold War Politics, 1945–1960.* Lawrence: University Press of Kansas, 2009.

Linklater, Eric. *The Campaign in Italy.* London: H.M.S.O., 1951.

Linn, Brian McAllister. "The American Way of War Debate: An Overview." In "Comparative Ways of War: A Roundtable." *Historically Speaking* 11, no. 5 (November 2010): 22–23.

———. *The Echo of Battle: The Army's Way of War.* Cambridge, Mass.: Harvard University Press, 2007.

Lisitskiy, P. I., and S. A. Bogdanov. "Upgrading Military Art during the Second Period of the Great Patriotic War." *Military Thought* 14, no. 1 (2005): 191–200.

Litvin, Nikolai. *800 Days on the Eastern Front: A Russian Soldier Remembers World War II.* Lawrence: University Press of Kansas, 2007.

Lorge, Peter A. "The Many Ways of Chinese Warfare." In "Comparative Ways of War: A Roundtable." *Historically Speaking* 11, no. 5 (November 2010): 24–25.

———. *The Asian Military Revolution: From Gunpowder to the Bomb.* Cambridge: Cambridge University Press, 2008.

Luck, Hans von. "The End in North Africa." *Military History Quarterly* 1, no. 4 (1989): 118–127.

———. *Panzer Commander.* Westport, Conn.: Praeger, 1989.

Ludwig, Max. "Die Operation auf der innerer und der äudsserer Linie im Lichte unserer Zeit." *Militär-Wochenblatt* 126, no. 1 (July 4, 1941): 7–10.

Lupfer, Timothy S. *The Dynamics of Doctrine: The Changes in German Tactical Doctrine during the First World War.* Fort Leavenworth, Kans.: U.S. Army Command and General Staff College, 1981.

Luvaas, Jay, ed. *Frederick the Great on the Art of War.* New York: Free Press, 1966.

MacDonald, Charles B. *The Mighty Endeavor: The American War in Europe.* New York: Da Capo, 1992.

Mackensen, Eberhard von. *Vom Bug zum Kaukasus: Das III Panzerkorps im Feldzug gegen Sowjetrussland 1941–42.* Neckargemünd: Kurt Vowinckel, 1967.

Macksey, Kenneth. *Crucible of Power: The Fight for Tunisia, 1942–1943*. London: Hutchinson, 1969.

Maizière, Ulrich de. "Zum Geleit." In *Nie ausser Dienst: Zum achtzigsten Geburtstag von Generalfeldmarschall Erich von Manstein*, 7. Cologne: Markus Verlagsgesellschaft, 1967.

Mallmann Showell, Jak P., ed. *Fuehrer Conferences on Naval Affairs, 1939–1945*. London: Chatham, 1990.

Manstein, Erich von. "Operation Citadel: A Study in Command Decision." *Marine Corps Gazette* 40, no. 8 (August 1956): 44–47.

———. *Lost Victories*. Novato, Calif.: Presidio, 1982.

———. *Verlorene Siege*. Bonn: Athenäum, 1955.

Martens, Hans. *General v. Seydlitz, 1942–1945: Analyse eines Konfliktes*. Berlin: v. Kloeden, 1971.

Matloff, Maurice, and Edwin M. Snell. *Strategic Planning for Coalition Warfare, 1941–1942*. Washington, D.C.: Center of Military History, 1953.

Mavrogordato, Ralph S. *Command Decisions: Hitler's Decision on the Defense of Italy*. Washington, D.C.: Center of Military History, 1990.

Mawdsley, Evan. *World War II: A New History*. Cambridge: Cambridge University Press, 2009.

Mayock, Thomas J. "The North African Campaigns." In *The Army Air Forces in World War II*. Vol. 2, *Europe: Torch to Pointblank, August 1942 to December 1943*, edited by Wesley Frank Craven and James Lea Cate. Chicago: University of Chicago Press, 1949.

McAndrew, William J. "Fire or Movement? Canadian Tactical Doctrine, Sicily—1943." *Military Affairs* 51, no. 3 (July 1987): 140–145.

McElwee, William. *The Art of War: Waterloo to Mons*. Bloomington: Indiana University Press, 1974.

Megargee, Geoffrey P. "Siegfried Westphal." In *Chief of Staff: The Principal Officers Behind History's Great Commanders*. Vol. 2, *World War II to Korea and Vietnam*, edited by David T. Zabecki, 37–49. Annapolis, Md.: Naval Institute Press, 2008.

———. *Inside Hitler's High Command*. Lawrence: University Press of Kansas, 2000.

———. *War of Annihilation: Combat and Genocide on the Eastern Front, 1941*. Lanham, Md.: Rowman & Littlefield, 2006.

Mellenthin, F. W. von. *German Generals of World War II as I Saw Them*. Norman: University of Oklahoma Press, 1977.

———. *Panzer Battles: A Study of the Employment of Armor in the Second World War*. New York: Ballantine, 1956.

Melvin, Mungo. *Manstein: Hitler's Greatest General*. London: Weidenfeld & Nicolson, 2010.

Menning, Bruce. "The Deep Strike in Russian and Soviet Military History." *Journal of Soviet Military Studies* 1, no. 1 (April 1988): 9–28.

———. *Bayonets before Bullets: The Imperial Russian Army, 1861–1914*. Bloomington: Indiana University Press, 1992.

Mierzejewski, Alfred C. *The Collapse of the German War Economy, 1944–1945: Allied Air Power and the German National Railway.* Chapel Hill, N.C.: University of North Carolina Press, 1988.

Miller, Donald L. *Masters of the Air: America's Bomber Boys Who Fought the Air War against Nazi Germany.* New York: Simon & Schuster, 2006.

Millett, Allan R., and Peter Maslowski. *For the Common Defense: A Military History of the United States of America.* New York: Free Press, 1984.

Mitcham, Samuel W., Jr. *Rommel's Greatest Victory: The Desert Fox and the Fall of Tobruk, 1942.* Novato, Calif.: Presidio, 1998.

Molony, C. J. C. The *Mediterranean and Middle East.* Vol. 5, *The Campaign in Sicily, 1943, and the Campaign in Italy, 3rd September 1943 to 31st March 1944.* London: H.M.S.O., 1973.

Montagu, Ewen. *The Man Who Never Was.* New York: J. P. Lippincott, 1954.

Montgomery, Bernard Law. *Memoirs of Field-Marshal the Viscount Montgomery of Alamein.* London: Collins, 1958.

Morison, Samuel Eliot. *History of United States Naval Operation in World War II.* Vol. 2, *Operations in North African Waters, October 1942–June 1943.* Boston: Little, Brown, 1947.

———. *History of United States Naval Operation in World War II.* Vol. 9, *Sicily—Salerno—Anzio, January 1943–June 1944.* Boston: Little, Brown, 1954.

Morozov, V. P. "Warum der Angriff im Frühjahr im Donezbecken nicht zu Ende geführt wurde." *Wehrwissenschaftliche Rundschau* 14 (1964): 414–430, 493–500.

———. *Westlich von Voronezh: Kurzer militärhistorischer Abriss der Angriffsoperationen der sowjetischen Truppen in der Zeit von Januar bis Februar 1943.* (East) Berlin: Verlag des Ministeriums für Nationale Verteidigung, 1959.

Morton, Matthew Darlington. *Men on Iron Ponies: The Death and Rebirth of the Modern U.S. Cavalry.* DeKalb: Northern Illinois University Press, 2009.

Mukhtar Pasha, Mahmud. *Meine Führung im Balkankriege, 1912.* Berlin: E. S. Mittler and Son, 1913.

Müller, Rolf-Dieter, and Gerd R. Ueberschär. *Hitler's War in the East, 1941–1945: A Critical Assessment.* Providence, R.I.: Berghahn Books, 1997.

Mulligan, Timoth P. "Spies, Ciphers and 'Zitadelle': Intelligence and the Battle of Kursk." *Journal of Contemporary History* 22, no. 2 (April 1987): 235–260.

Murphy, Robert Daniel. *Diplomat among Warriors.* New York: Doubleday, 1964.

Murray, Williamson, and Allan R. Millett. *A War to be Won: Fighting the Second World War.* Cambridge, Mass.: Harvard University Press, 2000.

———, eds. *Military Innovation in the Interwar Period.* Cambridge: Cambridge University Press, 1996.

Nasson, Bill. *The South African War, 1899–1902.* Oxford: Oxford University Press, 2000.

Naveh, Shimon. *In Pursuit of Excellence: The Evolution of Operational Theory.* London: Frank Cass, 1997.

Nehring, Walther K. *Die Geschichte der deutschen Panzerwaffe, 1916 bis 1945.* Berlin: Propyläen Verlag, 1969.

———. *Panzerabwehr*. Berlin: E. S. Mittler und Sohn, 1936.

———. "The Development of the Situation in North Africa (1 Jan–28 Feb 1943)." Manuscript D-120, U.S. Army Heritage and Education Center, Carlisle, Pa.

———. "The First Phase of the Battle in Tunisia." Manuscript D-147, U.S. Army Heritage and Education Center, Carlisle, Pa.

———. "The First Phase of the Engagements in Tunisia, up to the Assumption of the Command by the Newly Activated Fifth Panzer Army Headquarters on 9 Dec 1942." Manuscript D-086, U.S. Army Heritage and Education Center, Carlisle, Pa.

Neillands, Robin. *Eighth Army: The Triumphant Desert Army that Held the Axis at Bay from North Africa to the Alps, 1939–45*. New York: Overlook, 2004.

Neilson, Keith, and Greg Kennedy, eds. *The British Way in Warfare: Power and the International System, 1856–1956: Essays in Honour of David French*. Farnham, U.K.: Ashgate, 2010.

Neitzel, Sönke, ed. *Abgehört: Deutsche Generäle in britischer Kriegsgefangenschaft 1942–1945*. Berlin: Propyläen, 2005.

———. *Tapping Hitler's Generals: Transcripts of Secret Conversations, 1942–45*. St. Paul, Minn.: Frontline Books, 2007.

"Neuzeitliche Lehren aus der Kriegführung Friedrichs des Grossen." *Militär-Wochenblatt* 115, no. 29 (February 4, 1931): 1113.

Newell, Clayton R., and Michael D. Krause, eds. *On Operational Art*. Washington, D.C.: Center of Military History, 1994.

Newton, Stephen H. "Hoth, von Manstein, and Prokhorovka: A Revision in Need of Revising." In *Kursk: The German View: Eyewitness Reports of Operation Citadel by the German Commanders*, edited by Stephen H. Newton, 357–369. New York: Da Capo, 2002.

———. *Hitler's Commander: Field Marshal Walther Model—Hitler's Favorite General*. New York: Da Capo, 2006.

———, ed. *Kursk: The German View: Eyewitness Reports of Operation Citadel by the German Commanders*. New York: Da Capo, 2002.

Nie ausser Dienst: Zum achtzigsten Geburtstag von Generalfeldmarschall Erich von Manstein. Cologne: Markus Verlagsgesellschaft, 1967.

"Niemandsland Noworossijsk-Süd." *Die Wehrmacht* 7, no. 12 (June 9, 1943): 10.

Noel-Buxton, N. E. *With the Bulgarian Staff*. New York: Macmillan, 1913.

Obkircher, Lieutenant Colonel. "General Constantin von Alvensleben: Zu seinem 50. Todestag, 28 März." *Militar-Wochenblatt* 126, no. 39 (March 7, 1942): 1111–1115.

O'Connor, Raymond Gish. *Diplomacy for Victory: FDR and Unconditional Surrender*. New York: Norton 1971.

Odom, William O. *After the Trenches: The Transformation of U.S. Army Doctrine, 1918–1939*. College Station: Texas A&M University Press, 1999.

Ogorkiewicz, Richard. *Armoured Warfare: A History of Armoured Forces and Their Vehicles*. New York: Arco, 1970.

Olson, Lynne. *Citizens of London: The Americans Who Stood with Britain in Its Darkest, Finest Hour*. New York: Random House, 2010.

Otis, Glenn K. "The Ground Commander's View—I." In Newell and Krause, *On Operational Art*, 31–46.

Otway, T. B. H. *Airborne Forces*. London: Imperial War Museum, 1990.

Overhues, Bernd E. H. "Auf den Höhen über Pozzilli: Ein Kampfbericht aus den Westhängen der Abruzzen." *Die Wehrmacht* 7, no. 25 (December 8, 1943): 4–6, 17.

Pakenham, Thomas. *The Boer War*. New York: Random House, 1979.

Parshall, Jonathan, and Anthony Tully. *Shattered Sword: The Untold Story of the Battle of Midway*. Washington, D.C.: Potomac Books, 2005.

Patton, George S., Jr. *War as I Knew It*. New York: Bantam, 1981.

Peek, Clifford H., Jr. *Five Years—Five Countries—Five Campaigns: An Account of the One-Hundred-Forty-First Infantry in World War II*. Munich: 141st Infantry Regiment Association, 1945.

Pélissier, Jean. *Dix mois de guerre dans les Balkans, Octobre 1912–Août 1913*. Paris: Perrin, 1914.

Pemberton, W. Baring. *Battles of the Boer War*. London: Batsford, 1964.

Perrett, Bryan. *The Valentine in North Africa, 1942–43*. London: Ian Allan, 1972.

Perry, Mark. *Partners in Command: George Marshall and Dwight Eisenhower in War and Peace*. New York: Penguin, 2007.

Philippi, Alfred. "Die Planung und der Verlauf des Feldzuges der Jahre 1941–1942." In *Der Feldzug gegen Sowjetrussland, 1941 bis 1945: Ein operative Überblick*, by Alfred Philippi and Ferdinand Heim, 10–200. Stuttgart: W. Kohlhammer, 1962.

Philippi, Alfred, and Ferdinand Heim. *Der Feldzug gegen Sowjetrussland, 1941 bis 1945: Ein operative Überblick*. Stuttgart: W. Kohlhammer, 1962.

Pickert, Wolfgang. *Vom Kuban-Brückenkopf bis Sewastopol: Flakartillerie im Verband der 17. Army*. Heidelberg: Scharnhorst Buchkameradschaft, 1955.

Piekalkiewicz, Janusz. *Der Wüstenkrieg in Afrika, 1940–1943*. Munich: Südwest Verlag, 1985.

———. *Krieg auf dem Balkan*. Munich: Südwest Verlag, 1984.

———. *Operation Citadel: Kursk and Orel: The Greatest Tank Battle of the Second World War*. Novato, Calif.: Presidio, 1987.

———. *Stalingrad: Anatomie einer Schlacht*. Munich: Südwest Verlag, 1977.

Pirich, Hermann. "Das geschah zwischen Charkow und Dnjepro." *Die Wehrmacht* 7, no. 9 (April 28, 1943): 21–22.

———. "The Struggle for Kharkov and the Dnieper, February–March 1943." Translated by the U.S. Army Command and General Staff College. *Military Review* 23, no. 9 (December 1943): 86–89.

Playfair, I. S. O., and C. J. C. Molony. *The Mediterranean and the Middle East*. Vol. 4, *The Destruction of the Axis Forces in Africa*. London: H.M.S.O., 1966.

Pond, Hugh. *Salerno*. London: William Kimber, 1961.

Porch, Douglas. *The Path to Victory: The Mediterranean Theater in World War II.* New York: Farrar, Straus and Giroux, 2004.

Quarrie, Bruce. *Hitler's Teutonic Knights: S.S. Panzers in Action.* Wellingborough, United Kingdom: Patrick Stephens, 1986.

Rakhmanin, O. B. "On International Aspects of the Kursk Salient Battle (6th Anniversary)." *Military Thought* 12, no. 3 (2003): 119–130.

Rame, David (pseudonym of A. D. Divine). *Road to Tunis.* New York: Macmillan, 1944.

Raths, Ralf. *Vom Massensturm zur Stosstrupptaktik: Die deutsche Landkriegtaktik im Spiegel von Dienstvorschriften und Publizistik, 1906 bis 1918.* (Freiburg, i.Br.: Rombach, 2009.

Raus, Erhard. "Der Angriff Zitadelle im Osten 1943: Abschnitt der Armee-Abteilung Kempf." Manuscript T-26, U.S. Army Heritage and Education Center, Carlisle, Pa.

Rees, Laurence. *World War II behind Closed Doors: Stalin, the Nazis and the West.* New York: Pantheon, 2008.

Reitlinger, Gerald. *The S.S.: Alibi of a Nation, 1922–1945.* 1956; reprint, Englewood Cliffs, N.J.: Prentice-Hall, 1981.

Rendulic, Lothar. "Die Schlacht von Orel, Juli 1943: Wahl und Bildung es Schwerpunktes." *Österreichische Militärische Zeitschrift* 1, no. 3 (1963): 130–138.

Reports of Military Observers Attached to the Armies in Manchuria during the Russo-Japanese War. Washington, D.C.: Government Printing Office, 1906.

Reuth, Ralf Georg. *Entscheidung im Mittelmeer: Die südliche Peripherie Europas in der deutschen Strategie des Zweiten Weltkrieges, 1940–1942.* Koblenz: Bernard & Graefe, 1985.

———. *Rommel: The End of a Legend.* London: Haus, 2005.

Reynolds, Michael. *Men of Steel: I S.S. Panzer Corps: The Ardennes and Eastern Front, 1944–45.* Barnsley, United Kingdom: Pen & Sword, 2009.

———. *Sons of the Reich: II S.S. Panzer Corps: Normandy, the Ardennes, and on the Eastern Front.* Barnsley, United Kingdom: Pen & Sword, 2009.

Roberts, Andrew. *Masters and Commanders: How Four Titans Won the War in the West, 1941–1945.* New York: Harper, 2008.

Rodemer, Heinrich. "Invasion in Südeuropa . . . oder in Norwegen?" *Die Wehrmacht* 7, no. 12 (June 9, 1943): 4–5, 19.

Rodt, Eberhard. "15th Panzer Grenadier Division in Sicily." Manuscript C-077. U.S. Army Heritage and Education Center, Carlisle, Pa.

Rommel, Erwin. *Krieg Ohne Hass: Herausgegeben von Frau Lucie-Maria Rommel und Generalleutnant Fritz Bayerlein, ehemaliger Chef des Stabes der Panzer-armee Afrika.* Heidenheim: Verlag Heidenheimer Zeitung, 1950.

———. *The Rommel Papers.* Edited by B. H. Liddell Hart. New York: Da Capo, 1953.

Roth, Günther. "Vorwort." In Foerster, *Gezeitenwechsel im Zweiten Weltkrieg?*, 9–18.

Rotmistrov, Pavel. "The Tank Battle at Kursk." In *Battles Hitler Lost: First-*

Person Accounts of World War II by Russian Generals on the Eastern Front, edited by Sergei Sokolov, 86–99. New York: Richardson & Steirman, 1986.

Rowe, Richard J., Jr. "Counterattack: A Study of Operational Priority." Monograph. U.S. Army Command and General Staff College, Fort Leavenworth, Kans., 1987.

"Rumänen: Kameraden am Kuban." *Die Wehrmacht* 7, no. 1 (May 26, 1943): 22.

Rumanicev, Nikolaj. "Die Schlachten bei Kursk: Vorgeschichte, Verlauf und Ausgang." In Foerster, *Gezeitenwechsel im Zweiten Weltkrieg?,* 57–67.

The Russo-Japanese War: Reports from British Officers Attached to the Japanese Forces in the Field. 3 vols. London: General Staff, 1907.

Sadarananda, Dana V. *Beyond Stalingrad: Manstein and the Operations of Army Group Don.* Mechanicsburg, Pa.: Stackpole, 2009.

Said, Edward. *Orientalism.* New York: Vintage, 1979.

Saint, Crosbie. "The Ground Commander's View—II." In Newell and Krause, *On Operational Art,* 47–64.

Sakurai, Tadayoshi. *Human Bullets: A Soldier's Story of the Russo-Japanese War.* Lincoln: University of Nebraska Press, 1999.

Salerno: American Operations from the Beaches to the Volturno, 9 September–6 October 1943. 1994; reprint, Washington: Center of Military History, 1990.

Sandrart, Hans Henning von. "Operational Art in a Continental Theater." In Newell and Krause, *On Operational Art,* 119–132.

Scheibert, Horst. *Entsatzversuch Stalingrad: Dokumentation einer Panzerschlacht in Wort und Bild: Das LVII. Panzerkorps im Dezember 1942.* Neckargmünd: Kurt Vowinckel Verlag, 1956.

———. *Zwischen Don und Donez.* Neckargemünd: Kurt Vowinckel Verlag, 1961.

Scherman, David E., ed. *Life Goes to War: A Picture History of World War II.* New York: Pocket Books, 1977.

Scheurig, Bodo. *Alfred Jodl: Gehorsam und Verhängnis.* Berlin: Propyläen, 1991.

Schifferle, Peter J. *America's School for War: Fort Leavenworth, Officer Ecucation, and Victory in World War II.* Lawrence: University Press of Kansas, 2010.

Schmalz, Wilhelm. "Der Kampf der Panzerdivision 'Hermann Göring' bei Salerno vom 9.–17.9.1943." In Siegfried Westphal et al., "Der Feldzug in Italien, Apr 1943–Mai 1944." Manuscript T-1a, U.S. Army Heritage and Education Center, Carlisle, Pa.

———. "Der Kampf um Sizilien im Abschnitt der Brigade Schmalz." Manuscript T-2, U.S. Army Heritage and Education Center, Carlisle, Pa.

Schmidt, Heinz Werner. *With Rommel in the Desert.* New York: Bantam, 1977.

Schmidt, Paul. *Statist auf diplomatischer Bühne, 1923–45: Erlebnisse des Chefdolmetschers im Auswärtigen Amt mit den Staatsmännern Europas.* Bonn: Athenäum-Verlag, 1949.

Schneider, James J. "Theoretical Implications of Operational Art." In Newell and Krause, *On Operational Art,* 17–30.

Schreiber, Gerhard. "Das Ende des nordafrikanischen Feldzugs und der Krieg in Italian 1943 bis 1945." In *Das Deutsche Reich und der Zweite Weltkrieg,* vol.

8, *Die Ostfront, 1943/44: Der Krieg im Osten and an den Nebenfronten*, 1100–1162. Munich: Deutsche Verlags-Anstalt, 2007.

———. *Die italienischen Militärinternierten im deutschen Machtbereich, 1943–1945: Verraten–Verachtet–Vergessen*. Munich: Oldenbourg-Verlag, 1990.

Schröder, Josef. *Italiens Kriegsaustritt, 1943: Die deutschen Gegenmassnahmen im italienischen Raum: Fall "Alarich" und "Achse."* Göttingen: Musterschmidt-Verlag, 1969.

Schultzendorff, Walther von. "Der Mensch und der Soldat Erich von Manstein." In *Nie ausser Dienst: Zum achtzigsten Geburtstag von Generalfeldmarschall Erich von Manstein*, 9–34. Cologne: Markus Verlagsgesellschaft, 1967.

Schulz, Friedrich. "Der Rückschlag im Süden der Ostfront 1942/43." Manuscript T-15, U.S. Army Heritage and Education Center, Carlisle, Pa.

———. "Reverses on the Southern Wing." Manuscript T-15, U.S. Army Heritage and Education Center, Carlisle, Pa.

Schwarz, Eberhard. *Die Stabilisierung der Ostfront nach Stalingrad: Mansteins Gegenschlag zwischen Donez und Dnjepr im Frühjahr 1943*. Göttingen: Muster-Schmidt Verlag, 1985.

Sears, Stephen W. *Chancellorsville*. Boston: Houghton Mifflin, 1996.

Seidemann, Hans. "Der Angriff Zitadelle im Osten 1943: Die Beteiligung durch die Luftwaffe." Manuscript T-26, U.S. Army Heritage and Education Center, Carlisle, Pa.

Senger und Etterlin, Frido von. *Der Gegenschlag: Kampfbeispiele und Führungsgrundsätze der beweglichen Abwehr*. Neckargemünd: Kurt Vowinckel Verlag, 1959.

———. *Krieg in Europa*. Cologne: Kiepenhauer & Witsch, 1960.

———. *Neither Fear nor Hope: The Wartime Career of General Frido von Senger und Etterlin, Defender of Cassino*. Novato, Calif.: Presidio, 1989.

Seydlitz, Walther von. *Stalingrad: Konflikt und Konsequenz: Erinnerungen*. Oldenburg: Stalling, 1977.

Sharpe, Michael, and Brian L. Davis. *Waffen-S.S. Elite Forces-1*. Edison, N.J.: Chartwell, 2007.

Showalter, Dennis E. *Hitler's Panzers: The Lightning Attacks that Revolutionized Warfare*. New York: Berkley Caliber, 2009.

———. *Tannenberg: Clash of Empires*. Washington, D.C.: Brassey's, 2004.

———. *The Wars of Frederick the Great*. London: Longman, 1996.

———. *The Wars of German Unification*. London: Arnold, 2004.

Shtemenko, S. M. *The Soviet General Staff at War, 1941–1945*. Moscow: Progress Publishers, 1981.

Shunk, David A. "Field Marshal von Manstein's Counteroffensive of Army Group South, February–March, 1943: The Last Operational Level Victory of the Panzer Forces on the Eastern Front." M.A. thesis, U.S. Army Command and General Staff College, Fort Leavenworth, Kans., 1986.

Simms, Benjamin R. "Analysis of the Battle of Kursk." *Armor*, March–April 2003, 7–12.

Smelser, Ronald, and Enrico Syring, eds. *Die S.S.: Elite unter den Totenkopf: 30 Lebensläufe*. Paderborn: Ferdinand Schöningh, 2000.

Smyth, Denis. *Deathly Deception: The Real Story of Operation Mincemeat*. Oxford: Oxford University Press, 2010.

Sokolov, Boris V. "The Battle for Kursk, Orel, and Char'kov: Strategic Intentions and Results: A Critical View of the Soviet Historiography." In Foerster, *Gezeitenwechsel im Zweiten Weltkrieg?*, 69–88.

Spiller, Roger J., ed. *Combined Arms in Battle since 1939*. Fort Leavenworth, Kans.: U.S. Army Command and General Staff College, 1992.

Spivak, Marcel, and Armand Leoni. *Les Forces Françaises dans la Lutte contre l'Axe en Afrique*. Vol. 2. Vincennes: Ministère de la Défense, 1985.

Stahel, David. *Operation Barbarossa and Germany's Defeat in the East*. Cambridge: Cambridge University Press, 2009.

Steele, Richard W. *The First Offensive, 1942: Roosevelt, Marshall, and the Making of American Strategy*. Bloomington: Indiana University Press, 1973.

Stein, George H. *The Waffen S.S.: Hitler's Elite Guard at War, 1939–1945*. Ithaca, N.Y.: Cornell University Press, 1966.

Stein, Marcel. *Generalfeldmarschall Erich von Manstein: Kritische Betrachtung des Soldaten und Menschen*. Mainz: v. Hase & Koehler, 2000.

———. *Generalfeldmarschall Walter Model: Legende und Wirklichkeit*. Bissendorf: Biblio, 2001.

———. *Field Marshal von Manstein, a Portrait: The Janus Head*. Solihull, U.K.: Helion, 2007.

Stephens, F. "Collapse in Tunisia." *Military Review* 25, no. 1 (April 1945): 79–82.

Stoecker, Sally Webb. *Forging Stalin's Army: Marshal Tukhachevsky and the Politics of Military Innovation*. Boulder, Colo.: Westview Press, 1998.

Stofft, William A. "Leadership at the Operational Level of War." In Newell and Krause, *On Operational Art*, 189–196.

"Strassenkampf unter der Sonne Italiens." *Die Wehrmacht* 7, no. 22 (October 27, 1943): 11.

Strawson, John. *The Italian Campaign*. New York: Carroll & Graf, 1988.

Stumpf, Reinhard. "Der Krieg im Mittelmeerraum 1942/43: Die Operationen in Nordafrika und im mittleren Mittelmeer." *Das Deutsche Reich und der Zweite Weltkrieg*. Vol. 6, *Der Globale Krieg: Die Ausweitung zum Weltkrieg und der Wechsel der Initiative, 1941–1943*. Stuttgart: Deutsche Verlags-Anstalt, 1990.

Stürmer, Michael. *The German Empire: A Short History*. New York: Modern Library, 2000.

"Supplement to Guide to Foreign Military Studies, 1945–54: Catalog and Index." Karlsruhe: Historical Division, Headquarters, U.S. Army Europe, 1959.

Swain, Richard M. *"Lucky War": Third Army in Desert Storm*. Fort Leavenworth, Kans.: U.S. Army Command and General Staff College, 1997.

———. "Reading about Operational Art." In Newell and Krause, *On Operational Art*, 197–210.

Sydnor, Charles, Jr. *Soldiers of Destruction: The S.S. Death's Head Division, 1933–1945*. Princeton, N.J.: Princeton University Press, 1977.

Syring, Enrico. "Paul Hausser: 'Türöffner' und Kommandeur 'seiner' Waffen-S.S." In *Die S.S.: Elite unter den Totenkopf: 30 Lebensläufe*, edited by Ronald Smelser and Enrico Syring, 190–207. Paderborn: Ferdinand Schöningh, 2000.

Theile, Karl H. *Beyond "Monsters" and "Clowns": The Combat S.S.: De-Mythologizing Five Decades of German Elite Formations*. New York: University Press of America, 1997.

Thomas, David. "Foreign Armies East and German Military Intelligence in Russia 1941–45." *Journal of Contemporary History* 22, no. 2 (April 1987): 261–301.

Tieke, Wilhelm. *The Caucasus and the Oil: The German–Soviet War in the Caucasus, 1942–43*. Winnipeg: J. J. Fedorowicz, 1995.

Toppe, Alfred. "Desert Warfare: German Experiences in World War II." Manuscript P-129, U.S. Army Heritage and Education Center, Carlisle, Pa.

Töppel, Roman. "Kursk: Mythen und Wirklichkeit einer Schlacht." *Vierteljahrhefte für Zeitgeschichte* 57, no. 3 (2009): 349–385.

———. "Legendenbildung in der Geschichtsschreibung: Die Schlacht bei Kursk." *Militärgeschichtliche Zeitschrift* 61, no. 2 (2002): 369–401.

Tregaskis, Richard. *Invasion Diary*. Lincoln: University of Nebraska Press, 2004.

Trevor-Roper, H. R., ed. *Hitler's War Directives, 1939–1945*. London: Sidgwick and Jackson, 1964.

Turner, Frederick Carleton. "The Genesis of the Soviet 'Deep Operation': The Stalin-Era Doctrine for Large-Scale Offensive Maneuver Warfare." Ph.D. diss., Duke University, 1988.

Ulrich, Max. "15th Panzer Grenadier Division, 3 September 1943." Manuscript D-201, U.S. Army Heritage and Education Center, Carlisle, Pa.

Van Creveld, Martin. "On Learning from the Wehrmacht and Other Things." *Military Review* 68, no. 1 (January 1988): 62–71.

———. *Fighting Power: German and U.S. Army Performance, 1939–1945*. Westport, Conn.: Greenwood Press, 1982.

———. *Kampfkraft: Militärische Organisation und militärische Leistung, 1939–1945*. Freiburg: Verlag Rombach, 1989.

van Hartesveldt, Fred R. *The Boer War: Historiography and Annotated Bibliography*. Westport, Conn.: Greenwood Press, 2000.

Vanwelkenhuyzen, Jean. "Die Krise vom Januar 1940." *Wehrwissenschaftliche Rundschau* 5, no. 2 (February 1955): 66–90.

Vaughan, Hal. *FDR's 12 Apostles: The Spies Who Paved the Way for the Invasion of French North Africa*. Guilford, Conn.: Lyons Press, 2006.

Verna, Renato. "Fronte Russo 1943: Il Canto del Cigno della 'Panzerwaffe': La Battaglia di Kursk (5–16 Luglio)." Parts 1 and 2. *Rivista Militare* 24, nos. 4–5 (1968).

Verney, C. L. *The Desert Rats: The 7th Armoured Divisions in World War II.* Mechanicsburg, Pa.: Stackpole Books, 2002.

Vietinghoff, Heinrich von. "Beurteiling der Lage durch die Höchsten Dienststellen im August 1943: Einsatz des AOK 10." Manscript MS-117, U.S. Army Heritage and Education Center, Carlisle, Pa.

———. "Die Kämpfe der 10. Armee in Süd- und Mittelitalien under besonderer Berücksichtigung der Schlachten bei Salerno, am Volturno, Garigliano, am Sango und um Cassino." In Siegfried Westphal et al., "Der Feldzug in Italien, Apr 1943–Mai 1944." Manuscript T-1a, U.S. Army Heritage and Education Center, Carlisle, Pa.

Volz, Gustav Berthold, ed. *Ausgewählte Werke Friedrichs des Grossen.* Vol. 1, *Historische und militärische Schriften, Briefe.* Berlin: Reimar Hobbing, 1900.

von Koerber. "Schweigestützpunkt in den Lagunen." Part 1. *Die Wehrmacht 7,* no. 18 (September 1, 1943): 10–11.

———. "Schweigestützpunkt in den Lagunen." Part 2, *Die Wehrmacht 7,* no. 21 (October 13, 1943): 10–11.

Wagener, Carl. "Der Gegenangriff des XXXX. Panzerkorps gegen den Durchbruch der Panzergruppe Popow im Donezbecken Februar 1943." *Wehrwissenschaftliche Rundschau 7* (1957): 21–36.

———. *Heeresgruppe Süd: Der Kampf im Süden der Ostfront, 1941–1945.* Bad Nauheim: Podzun, 1967.

Wagner, Hermenegild. *With the Victorious Bulgarians.* Boston: Houghton Mifflin, 1913.

Wagner, Robert L. *The Texas Army: A History of the 36th Division in the Italian Campaign.* Austin, Tex.: n.p., 1972.

The War in the Far East by the Military Correspondent of the "Times." New York: Dutton, 1905.

Warlimont, Walter. *Im Hauptquartier der deutschen Wehrmacht, 1939–1945: Grundlagen, Formen, Gestalten.* Frankfurt am Main: Bernard & Graefe, 1962.

———. *Inside Hitler's Headquarters, 1939–45.* Novato, Calif.: Presidio, 1964.

Waters, John K. Senior Officers Oral History Program, Project 80-4. U.S. Army Heritage and Education Center, Carlisle, Pa., 1980.

Watson, Bruce Allen. *Exit Rommel: The Tunisian Campaign, 1942–43.* Mechanicsburg, Pa.: Stackpole, 2007.

Wawro, Geoffrey. *The Austro-Prussian War: Austria's War with Prussia and Italy in 1866.* Cambridge: Cambridge University Press, 1996.

———. *The Franco-Prussian War: The German Conquest of France, 1870–1871.* Cambridge: Cambridge University Press, 2003.

Wegner, Bernd. "Die Aporie des Krieges." In *Das Deutsche Reich und der Zweite Weltkrieg,* vol. 8, *Die Ostfront, 1943/44: Der Krieg im Osten and an den Nebenfronten,* 209–274. Munich: Deutsche Verlags-Anstalt, 2007.

———. "Der Krieg gegen Die Sowjetunion, 1942–43." *Das Deutsche Reich und der Zweite Weltkrieg.* Vol. 6, *Die Ausweitung zum Weltkrieg und der Wechsel der Initiative, 1941–1943.* Stuttgart: Deutsche Verlags-Anstalt, 1990.

———. "Das Ende der Strategie: Deutschlands politische und militärische Lage nach Stalingrad." In Foerster, *Gezeitenwechsel im Zweiten Weltkrieg?*, 211–227.

———. "Von Stalingrad nach Kursk." In *Das Deutsche Reich und der Zweite Weltkrieg*, vol. 8, *Die Ostfront, 1943/44: Der Krieg im Osten and an den Nebenfronten*, 1–79. Munich: Deutsche Verlags-Anstalt, 2007.

Weigley, Russell F. *Eisenhower's Lieutenants: The Campaign of France and Germany, 1944–1945*. Bloomington: Indiana University Press, 1981.

———. *The American Way of War: A History of United States Military Strategy and Policy*. New York: Macmillan, 1973.

Weinberg, Gerhard L. "Zur Frage eines Sonderfriedens im Osten." In Foerster, *Gezeitenwechsel im Zweiten Weltkrieg?*, 173–183.

———. *A World at Arms: A Global History of World War II*. 2nd ed. Cambridge: Cambridge University Press, 2005.

———, ed. *Hitler's Second Book: The Unpublished Sequel to "Mein Kampf" by Adolf Hitler*. New York: Enigma Books, 2003.

Wenck, Walther. "Nie ausser Dienst." In *Nie ausser Dienst: Zum achtzigsten Geburtstag von Generalfeldmarschall Erich von Manstein*, 85–95. Cologne: Markus Verlagsgesellschaft, 1967.

"Die Wende des Winterkrieges." *Die Wehrmacht* 7, no. 8 (April 14, 1943): 4–5.

Weniger, Erich. "Die Selbständigkeit der Unterführer und ihre Grenzen." *Militärwissenschaftliche Rundschau* 9, no. 2 (1944): 101–115.

Westphal, Siegfried. *Erinnerungen*. Mainz: Von Hase & Koehler, 1975.

———. *The German Army in the West*. London: Cassell, 1951.

———. *Heer in Fesseln: Aus den Papieren des Stabschefs von Rommel, Kesselring und Rundstedt*. Bonn: Athenäum-Verlag, 1950.

———. "Notes on the Campaign in North Africa, 1941–1943." *Journal of the Royal United Service Institution* 105, no. 617 (1960): 70–81.

Westphal, Siegfried, et al. "Der Feldzug in Italien, Apr 1943–Mai 1944." Manuscript T-1a, U.S. Army Heritage and Education Center, Carlisle, Pa.

Wheeler, James Scott. *The Big Red One: America's Legendary 1st Infantry Division from World War I to Desert Storm*. Lawrence: University Press of Kansas, 2007.

Whitlock, Flint. *The Rock of Anzio: From Sicily to Dachau: A History of the 45th Infantry Division*. Boulder, Colo.: Westview, 1998.

"Wieder in Charkow." *Die Wehrmacht* 7, no. 7 (March 31, 1943): 10–11.

Wilbeck, Christopher W. "Swinging the Sledgehammer: The Combat Effectiveness of German Heavy Tank Battalions in World War II." M.A. thesis, U.S. Army Command and General Staff College, Fort Leavenworth, Kans., 2002.

Williamson, Gordon. *Loyalty is My Honor: Personal Accounts from the Waffen-S.S.* London: MBI, 1999.

Wilson, Dale E. *Treat 'em Rough! The Birth of American Armor, 1917–1920*. Novato, Calif.: Presidio, 1989.

Winton, Harold R. *To Change an Army: General Sir John Burnett-Stuart and*

British Armored Doctrine, 1927–1938. Lawrence: University Press of Kansas, 1988.

Winton, Harold R., and David R. Mets. *The Challenge of Change: Military Institutions and New Realities, 1918–1941*. Lincoln: University of Nebraska Press, 2000.

Wolff, Kurt E. "Tank Battle in Tunisia." *Military Review* 23, no. 6 (September 1943): 61–63.

Yakubovsky, Ivan. "The Liberation of Kiev." In *Battles Hitler Lost: First-Person Accounts of World War II by Russian Generals on the Eastern Front*, edited by Sergei Sokolov, 101. New York: Richardson & Steirman, 1986.

Zabecki, David T., ed. *Chief of Staff: The Principal Officers behind History's Great Commanders*. Vol. 2, *World War II to Korea and Vietnam*. Annapolis, Md.: Naval Institute Press, 2008.

Zeiler, Thomas W. *Annihilation: A Global Military History of World War II*. Oxford: Oxford University Press, 2011.

Zetterberg, Niklas, and Anders Frankson. *Kursk, 1943: A Statistical Analysis*. London: Frank Cass, 2000.

Zhukov, Georgi K. *Marshal Zhukov's Greatest Battles*. New York: Cooper Square, 2002.

Ziemke, Earl F. *Stalingrad to Berlin: The German Defeat in the East*. Washington, D.C.: Center of Military History, 1987.

Ziemke, Earl F., and Magna E. Bauer. *Moscow to Stalingrad: Decision in the East*. Washington, D.C.: Center of Military History, 1987.

Index